EA

# WARREN COUNTY, GEORGIA

## Lois Helmers

Warrenton ●

ISBN 978-0615927619

Published by
Badgley Publishing Company
Canal Winchester, Ohio
www.BadgleyPublishingCompany.com

# EARLY RECORDS OF WARREN COUNTY, GEORGIA

HISTORY OF WARREN COUNTY, GEORGIA .................... 1

DISTINGUISHED MEN OF WARREN COUNTY ................. 5

EARLY MARRIAGES ................................................. 13

ENGLISH CROWN LAND GRANTS IN
ST. PAUL PARISH.................................................37

THE FIRST MINUTE BOOK,
WARREN INFERIOR COURT...................................175

MINUTES OF INFERIOR COURT – 1807-1814 ................. 193

ADMINISTRATOR'S BOND BOOK A ................................. 213

DEED BOOK A ....................................................... 235

DEED BOOK B ....................................................... 307

WILL BOOK A ....................................................... 369

WILL BOOK B........................................................ 375

ABOUT THE AUTHOR ............................................... 395

INDEX ................................................................ 397

# HISTORY OF WARREN COUNTY, GEORGIA

Warren County, comprising 286 square miles was created December 19, 1793 from parts of Columbia, Richmond and Wilkes counties. It is located west of Augusta about 30 miles. Warren was the 20th county created in Georgia and is named after Joseph Warren, a colonial physician and Revolutionary War soldier. The area's first inhabitants were Creek Indians, who established the famous Upper Trading Path between Augusta and Creek settlements as far west as the Mississippi River.

**Joseph Warren**

Warrenton, the county seat, was incorporated in 1810. The original courthouse was built in 1809, burned down in 1853 and its replacement suffered the same fate in 1909.

The first recorded wool mill and one of the first iron foundries in Georgia were located on a spot named Shoals, on the Ogeechee River. They were established by Colonel William Bird, a veteran of the American Revolution, and his partner, Benjamin A. Hamp. In 1812 Thomas Cheely bought the property and erected a gristmill on it. The two mills were burned by Union General William T.

Sherman's troops in 1864. Cheely's house, built with slave labor in 1825, remains.

The town of Norwood developed around a gristmill owned by Radford Gunn, and the community was known as Gunn's Mill until 1888.

Railroad service came early to Warren County when the Georgia Railroad line was built just north of Warrenton in the 1830s. Early railroad depots were located close by in Camak, Norwood and Barnett. The link between Warrenton and Camak for many years was made by mule-car until rail service was finally established in 1873.

In 1642, Father Isaac Joques, a Jesuit missionary, was the first recorded white man to see Lake George which he called Lac du St. Sacrement.

From 1754-1763, the British and French battled for control of the frontier from Albany to Montreal in the French and Indian War. Sir William Johnson commanded the British forces, built the Military Road from Fort Edward to the site of Fort William Henry, and renamed the lake, Lake George.

The county was settled through land grants. Abraham Wing, John Thurman, the Jessup Brothers, and James Caldwell were among the early grant holders and land developers.

Headrights were granted by the Colonial and State Governments from 1754 to 1800 in Warren County:

1757 to 1774 - Joshua Atkinson, Ezekiel Abbett, Henry Abbett, William Alexander, James Anderson, Isaac Atwood, Abram Ayres, John Anderson, Rich Austin, Thomas Ayres, John Allen, F. Ashmon, Ed Ashton, Micajah Andrews, Nicholas Andrews.

1785 to 1788 - John Appling, David Allen, Gideon Allen, Samuel Allen, Isaac Atwood.

1793 - James Archer

The Royal Charter of June, 1732, given by King George II to the Trustees for Establishing the Colony of Georgia in America, defined the boundaries of the new colony as lying between the Savannah and Altamaha Rivers, extending as far north as those rivers flowed and thence from their sources in a straight line to the South Seas. The land in question was in possession of the Creek and Cherokee Nations, and when James Edward Oglethorpe, one of the Trustees and the leader of the colony, landed at Yamacraw Bluff on the Savannah River on February 12, 1733, he was well aware that some agreement with the Indians was necessary. His first treaty with the Creeks in 1733 assured him of a small area along the Savannah River, running north along it to a point opposite today's Rincon, passing through that town and today's Eden in a diagonal line to the Ogeechee, thence south and a little west in a straight line to the Altamaha River, or, as it has been described elsewhere, "the area between the Savannah and the Altamaha as high as the tides flowed." This was the small part of the original charter grant in which the colonists settled and here they laid out the City of Savannah.

The 1733 Treaty with the Creeks reserved two parcels of land for themselves. One was an area from Pipemaker's Bluff to Palachucolas Creek and the other was the Islands of Ossabow, Sapelo, and St. Catherine. It was not until 1757 at a congress held at Savannah that a treaty between the English and the Creeks gave to Georgia the three great Sea Islands and the small tract of land in reserve near Savannah. By this time, the colonists had settled considerably beyond the limits of the first treaty and came to look upon all this land as their own. Oglethorpe had early fortified St. Simons Island knowing well that it was outside of the treaty boundary as well as the charter limits.

The next year in 1758, without treaty or permissions from the Indians, an Act of the Assembly created seven parishes, i.e., St. Paul, St. George, St. Matthew, Christ Church, St. Philip, St. John and St. Andrew. By Royal Proclamation in 1763, the English Crown extended Georgia's southern boundary to the St. Mary's River, and by Act of Assembly again, the four new parishes of St. David, St. Patrick, St. Thomas and St. Mary were created from that extension in 1765.

The Creeks were uneasy about these expansions and in order to quiet them and to redefine the western boundary, a new treaty was made in 1763 at Augusta. The limits of the settlers went as far as the Little River to the north, down the Ogeechee to the southwest corner of the present boundary line of Bulloch County, southward crossing the upper reaches of the Canoochee River and ended at the St. Marys.

The last of the Royal Provincial treaties was in 1773 and this included what was called the Ceded Lands, a rich area acquired from the Creeks and Cherokees north of the Little River to the Broad and west almost to the Oconee River. Settlement in this area was barely begun when the first fires of the Revolution were seen in the Province and until that war was over, Georgia remained a relatively narrow strip along the Savannah to the Ogeechee River.

In 1752, after the relinquishment of the charter, Georgia became a Royal Province and under the English Crown and its Royal Governors, fee simple grants were made to the land which gave a clear title to the grantees. These Royal Grants, in the Georgia Surveyor General Department of the Office of the Secretary of State, begin in 1755. The three year gap between 1752 and 1755 is variously explained by historians, but in any case, the latter year is the first date for the grants.

# DISTINGUISHED MEN OF WARREN COUNTY

**Bird, Colonel William**, a graduate of the University of Pennsylvania; served under Washington in the Revolutionary War. Settled at "The Shoals" in Hancock County, Georgia, in 1796. Shoals is now in Warren County. Bird established the first woolen mill and iron foundry in Georgia. The community is also called Village Shoals and Shoals of Ogeechee. William and Catherine Bird raised a family of six daughters and four sons. The plantation acquired the name of "The Aviary," reputedly given to it because of the beauty and charm of the daughters. The old Bird home "The Aviary," was situated in a shaded location just above the dam on the eastern side.......Upon the summit of a hill in the rear is a graveyard. The old dwelling was destroyed by fire in 1894. Colonel Bird was noted for his eccentricity. Upon his death in 1813, his will bore out this impression. The document made his sons Wilson and John managers of the estate, and provided for Fitzgerald's education through medical college; but in one sentence he gave his holsters and pistols to William, with no further mention of him in the entire will. To his three unmarried daughters he left a share to be given them upon their majority or marriage. But to his wife he left only his riding chair, horse, and harness, and a servant for her use so she may visit occasionally as she does at present, provided that she remained at the Shoals; otherwise she would have to bear all of her own expenses out of her dower."

**Bushnel, David**, a notable resident (also known as David Bush), a Warrenton physician, teacher at Warrenton Academy, and father of the submarine. As an engineer in the Continental Army during the American Revolution, he invented a one-man submarine known as the "Turtle."

**David Bushnell and his Submarine "Turtle"**

**Candler, William**, William Candler was born, grew to manhood, and married in South River Settlement along the James River in Virginia. In 1755, at age nineteen, William joined the Quaker meeting at South River (present-day Lynchburg, Virginia.) Several years thereafter, he was elected clerk of the Quaker Meeting. He acquired modest tracts of land at South River including one sharing property lines with his future father-in-law, Joseph Anthony, and his father, Daniel. In 1760, William Candler contracted to carry supplies to soldiers stationed at Dunkard Bottom on the New River (present-day Radford, Virginia.) In 1761, he married Elizabeth Anthony. William Candler was the executor of his father's 1765 will filed in early 1766 in Bedford County, Virginia. Later in 1766, he asked the Quaker meeting officials to settle his business and give him a certificate of good standing for departure. A group of Quaker colonizers from Cane Creek, under the leadership of Joseph Maddock, moved to Georgia in about 1770 to take up a large grant given to them by Georgia Governor Wright. They named this colony Wrightsborough. A short time later, William Candler was appointed as Surveyor of this county, a major political appointment in colonial America. At first a major in the British militia, Candler resigned his commission and joined the fight for American Independence. His distinction as a Major, then later Colonel of the Georgia

~ 6 ~

"Refugees" of the American Revolution has been chronicled by his descendants.

**Fort, Tomlinson**, physician and legislator, was born on July 14, 1787, in Warren County, where his father, Arthur Fort, settled some time before the Revolution. He received his education at home, subsequently graduating at the Medical University of Pennsylvania, under the celebrated Dr. Rush, and began the practice of his profession at Milledgeville. In the War of 1812, he commanded a company and received a wound in the knee that made him a cripple for life. For twelve years he served in the state legislature; edited the old Federal Union for several years; was elected representative in Congress in 1826, and served one term; was for some time president of the Central Bank of Georgia, and for twelve years one of the trustees of the state university. In 1849 he published a work called "Fort's Medical Practice," in which he attacked many of the old errors of his profession, and which marked him as a progressive man. His valuable collection of books and papers was destroyed by the Federal army on its march to the sea. He died at Milledgeville on May 17, 1859.

**Dr. and Mrs. Tomlinson Fort**

**Gibson, William**, who died at his home in the city of Macon, in April, 1893, was one of the distinguished lawyers and jurists of Georgia, upon whose history he left a distinct and worthy impress. He was born in Warren County, Georgia, March 22, 1822, and that county was likewise the birthplace of his parents, Thomas and Mary Rose (Gardner) Gibson, showing that the respective families were founded in that section of Georgia in the pioneer era. His maternal grandfather, Sterling Gardner, was a soldier in the war of the Revolution, in which he served under General Nathaniel Greene in the southern campaign. William Gibson was colonel of the Forty-eighth Georgia volunteer infantry in the Confederate service of the Civil War and proved a gallant and efficient officer. He took part in the battles of Mechanicsville, June 27, 1862; Cold Harbor, Virginia, June 28, 1862, Malvern Hill, July 1, 1862, Second Manassas and Sharpsburg, Maryland, Sept. 1862, Chancellorsville, Virginia, May 1863, Gettysburg, Pennsylvania, July 1-3, 1863, being shot down on the field in the last mentioned engagement and captured by the Federal troops. He was held as a prisoner of war until April, 1864, when he was exchanged, and he resigned his commission and retired from the service in October of that year. Judge Gibson was a man of high intellectual ability and profound learning in the law, having been admitted to the bar of Georgia in 1839, at the age of seventeen. He was engaged in the practice of his profession in Warrenton, Warren County, until January, 1856, when he removed to Augusta, which continued to be his home until 1886, when he removed to Macon, where he passed the remainder of his life, secure in the esteem and admiration of all who knew him. In 1853 he was called to the bench of the superior court of the northern circuit, and from 1866 to 1870 he was judge of the superior court of the middle circuit. From 1870 to 1879 he was the honored judge of the Augusta circuit. He represented Richmond County in the state legislature from 1857 to 1863, and in 1865, he was president of the state senate. Judge Gibson was a staunch Democrat in his political allegiance, and was a zealous member of the Methodist Episcopal Church South. In March, 1843, he was united in marriage to Miss Martha Mitchell Rogers, daughter of Micajah Rogers, of Warren County, Georgia, and he is survived by four children, namely: Thomas H., Mary D., Martha Amanda, and George Micajah.

**Col. Wm. Gibson**

**Hatch, Albert S.**, cashier of the Merchants Bank, of Augusta, and secretary and treasurer of the Equitable Trust Company, of the same city, is a native Georgian, having been born at the family homestead, about two miles distant from the city of Augusta, in Richmond County, Oct. 20, 1866. He is a son of Albert and Sarah Elizabeth (Sherman) Hatch, the former of whom was born in the vicinity of Lake Champlain, Clinton County, New York, in 1818, and the latter in 1824 in Warren County, Georgia, where their marriage was solemnized in the year 1842. He was a harness-maker by trade, and was the founder of the harness and saddlery business of Day & Tannahill, of Augusta, the same being one of the largest concerns of the sort in the South. Albert Hatch died on Jan. 11, 1879, and his widow survived him by many years, her death occurring June 21, 1902.

**Hamilton, J. F.**, A community in Warren County is Mesena and Beall Springs. Mesena is an acronym consisting of the first letter of each daughter's name in the family of Hamilton. Beall Springs grew up around a mineral springs used by Native Americans long before the state acquired the land in 1773. The Beall family, as the first white settlers to own the land surrounding the springs, allowed the public to continue using the water. In the nineteenth century Beall Springs became a popular resort, complete with hotel and leisure-time activities.

**Houstoun, John**, John Houstoun was twice governor of Georgia, the first mayor of the city of Savannah, and an early supporter of independence from Britain. He commanded the Georgia militia in the invasion of Florida during the American Revolution (1775-83) and represented Georgia in the Continental Congress. Houston County, in central Georgia, is named in his honor.

The date and place of Houstoun's birth are not known. The best evidence indicates that he was born sometime between 1746 and 1748 in either Frederica or on the Houstoun plantation, Rosdue. Houstoun's father was Sir Patrick Houstoun, fifth baronet of Scotland, who was one of the earliest settlers of the colony of Georgia. His mother, Priscilla Dunbar, came from Scotland to Georgia in 1736. John Houstoun married Hannah Bryan, though the date of this union is unknown. They had no children.

**John Houstoun**

**Houstoun, Sir Patrick**, Sir Patrick Houstoun was an early settler in Georgia, the owner of the Rosdue and Retreat plantations. A Loyalist, he lost out after the War. But son William took the American side and was elected a delegate to the Continental Congress in New York. Another son John became the Governor of Georgia in 1784.

**Roney, Henry C.**, one of the leading members of the Augusta bar and formerly judge of the superior court of the Augusta circuit, was born on the homestead plantation, in Warren County, Georgia, December 31, 1845, a son of Thomas and Jane V. (Stanford) Roney, both of whom were likewise born in Warren County, the former being of Irish and the latter of English lineage. The father was a planter by vocation and was a man of marked mentality and strong character. He and his wife passed the closing years of their lives in McDuffie County, Georgia.

**Warren, Joseph** - Joseph Warren was born in Roxbury in 1741, son of Joseph and Mary (Stevens) Warren. He graduated from Harvard in 1759 and married Elizabeth Horton in 1764. He studied medicine with Dr. James Lloyd and practiced in Boston. As a Freemason, he joined St. Andrews Lodge, a newly organized group, which included many political agitators. A radical leader in activities leading to the Revolution, he delivered addresses commemorating the Boston Massacre in 1772 and 1775, and drafted the Suffolk Resolves. Elected to the Provincial Congress in 1774, he served as president pro tem and was chairman of the Provincial Committee of Safety. He was commissioned second major-general in 1775, but served as a volunteer in the battle at Bunker Hill in which he was killed in 1775.

# EARLY MARRIAGES

| Groom | Bride | Date |
|---|---|---|
| Nathan McG. Tilby | Sarah Jacobs | March 1, 1794 |
| Phillip Logan | Leah Littleton | March 29, 1794 |
| Presley Sanford | Polly Wynne | April 4, 1794 |
| Nathan Brewtib | Nancy Fontaine | May 18, 1794 |
| Benjamin Howard | Nancy Moore | June 7, 1794 |
| Thomas Luckett | Betsy Sims | June 22, 1794 |
| Nicholas Williams | Betsy Baker | June 22, 1794 |
| William Hart | Mary Bass | June 27, 1794 |
| James George | Mary Hardin | June 29, 1794 |
| Dempsey Hood | Charity Hill | August 5, 1794 |
| Barton Atchison | Prudence Hill | missing |
| Mark Hardin | Frances Newsom | missing |
| Ezekiel Alexander | M(missing) Neal | missing |
| Robert McTier | Polly Chandler | August 30, 1794 |
| John Hays | Betsy Meadows | September 9, 1794 |
| Philip Barnheart | Rachel Williams | September 10, 1794 |
| Malcolm Johnston | Ann Burnley | October 8, 1794 |
| William Elliott | Elizabeth Burns | November 10, 1794 |
| Hugh Rees | Elizabeth Newsom | November 19, 1794 |
| Isaac Bankston | Polly Goings | December 2, 1794 |
| Silson Thrower | Betsy Marsh | December 6, 1794 |
| Ambrose Peavy | Lavina Rowland | December 10, 1794 |
| Walter Newman | Argent Culpepper | December 16, 1794 |
| Joseph Carter | Frances Wynne | December 21, 1794 |
| Joseph Williamson | Agnes Williams | December 24, 1794 |
| William Breed | Frances Brantley | December 25, 1794 |
| William Matthews | Sibbia Green | December 26, 1794 |
| James Mitchell | Lucena Heath | December 31, 1794 |
| Littleberry Strange | Nancy Lawton | December 31, 1794 |
| Henry Bonner | Mary Vaughn | January 30, 1795 |
| John Addison Johnston | Nancy Clark | February 13, 1795 |
| Gideon George | Tabitha Burnley | March 4, 1795 |

| | | |
|---|---|---|
| Robert Black | Lavina Bruton | March 18, 1795 |
| Elias Blount | Phoebe Shaw | March 20, 1795 |
| Thomas Cary | Elizabeth Ellis | March 26, 1795 |
| Peter Ryan | Fanny Walker | March 31, 1795 |
| Richard Moore | Jean Jones | March 31, 1795 |
| Nathaniel Perritt | Nancy Hill | March 31, 1795 |
| John Thompson | Nancy Grimsley | March 31, 1795 |
| Dixon Perryman | Ann Vining | March 31, 1795 |
| William Sanders | Betsy Dennis | May 26, 1795 |
| Ephriam Peebles | Sarah Drake | June 2, 1795 |
| Joshua Moses | Sarah Mims | missing |
| James Branham | Sally Tommy | June 18, 1795 |
| John Brantley | Rebecca Hill | June 22, 1795 |
| William Newman | Hannah Simmons | July 29, 1795 |
| James Farlin | Abegail Harris | September 24, 1795 |
| James Chastain | Sarah Morgan | September 28, 1795 |
| James Bray | Betsy Neal | October 18, 1795 |
| Daniel Hutchinson | Nancy Burkhalter | October 25, 1795 |
| Samuel Newman | Anna Lovett | October 20, 1795 |
| Drury Thompson | Susannah Anglin | October 27, 1795 |
| Hillery Fowler | Mary O'Neal | November 1, 1795 |
| Thomas Cocks | Susannah Peavy | November 3, 1795 |
| John Cobb | Mary Hargrove | missing |
| James Elliott | Susannah Harris | missing |
| George Dawkins | Elinor Dawkins | 1796 |
| Jessee James | Phoebe Brewer | 1796 |
| Alexander McCarty | Patsy Franklin | February 15, 1796 |
| Richard Hutchinson | Charity Golden | March 4, 1796 |
| William Perry | Nancy Abbett | March 4, 1796 |
| Turner Persons | Sally Williams | March 4, 1796 |
| Christopher Preston | Millie Wadley | March 4, 1796 |
| John Rhodes | Phoebe Thompson | March 20, 1796 |
| Isaac Hart | Sarah Buffington | May 10, 1796 |
| Jonathan Nobles | Jean Dicken | May 24, 1796 |
| Benjamin Harding | Mourning Smith | June 6, 1796 |

| | | |
|---|---|---|
| Stephen Sayager | Pollie Middlebrooks | June 10, 1796 |
| David Golden | Elizabeth Harbuck | June 10, 1796 |
| Michael Harvey | Polly Clower | July 30, 1796 |
| John Saxon | Nancy Rogers | August 13, 1796 |
| John Greeson | Mary Ann Coughsan | August 20, 1796 |
| John Moore | Ann Moore | October 1, 1796 |
| John McCray | Charity Fugett | February 20, 1797 |
| James Bonner | Sally Hill | March 8, 1797 |
| Wood Moreland | Sally Heath | April 11, 1797 |
| George M. McClung | Anny Whatley | April 11, 1797 |
| William Ward | Milliford Whiting | missing |
| William Wilder | Elizabeth Hotnel | July 4, 1797 |
| William Watson | Abegail Torrence | July 6, 1797 |
| Walter Fitzsimmons | Keziah Butt | August 10, 1797 |
| Benjamin Crenshaw | Pollie Hight | August 14, 1797 |
| Michael Horn | Elizabeth Carter | August 28, 1797 |
| Benjamin Shepard | Cassandra Montray | October 4, 1797 |
| Jesse Duberry | Pollie Duberry | October 10, 1797 |
| Jesse Matthews | Pollie Peebles | October 20, 1797 |
| James Weeks | Pollie Cafter | November 21, 1797 |
| George Cotton | Sallie Cary | December 26, 1797 |
| David Mims | Betsy Brown | December 27, 1797 |
| Thomas Wilkins | Rebecca Ford | December 27, 1797 |
| Samuel Loughlin | Celia Zachary | December 29, 1797 |
| Elijah Horn | Polly Booth | January 2, 1798 |
| John Forrest | Amelia Beall | January 5, 1798 |
| Edward Short | Catherine Sims | January 20, 1798 |
| William Mims | Elizabeth Hilton | January 20, 1798 |
| William Hunt | Elizabeth Bass | January 28, 1798 |
| Rowland Green | Betsy Bass | January 30, 1798 |
| James Simmons | Polly Alexander | January 31, 1798 |
| Thomas Fontaine | Sally Threewitts | February 14, 1798 |
| William Lloyd | Pollie Coling | February 20, 1798 |
| William Heath | Sallie Bonner | February 21, 1798 |
| Alexander | Theresa Peebles | February 22, 1798 |

| | | |
|---|---|---|
| Flewellin | | |
| William Davis | Peggy Manning | February 27, 1798 |
| John McCoy | Mary Fontaine | April 15, 1798 |
| Willie Grissle | Sarah Hadley | April 27, 1798 |
| Samuel Fickling | Susannah Jones | May 12, 1798 |
| Littleberry Patillo | Mary Ann Simpson | May 26, 1798 |
| Jacob Dansby | Catherine Baker | May 27, 1798 |
| Thomas Mitchell | Mary Wall | missing |
| Edward Castleberry | Patsy Heath | missing |
| Rowland Dixon | Nancy Ross | missing |
| James Taylor | Nancy Moore | August 11, 1798 |
| John Kilgore | Nancy Bishop | September 22, 1798 |
| Joshua Runnolds | Sarah James | October 17, 1798 |
| Isaac Ball | Sally Wheeler | October 18, 1798 |
| Henry Williams | Elizabeth Goodwin | November blank, 1798 |
| James Cotton | Martha Perryman | November 9, 1798 |
| John Parker | Rachel Kelly | November 10, 1798 |
| Samuel Ledbetter | Martha Crittenden | November 30, 1798 |
| Solomon Brown | Betsy Mims | December 23, 1798 |
| John Sims | Rebecca Harris | December 26, 1798 |
| Luke Patrick | Sally Brewer | missing |
| William Williams | Elizabeth Crook | February 5, 1799 |
| Johnston Runnolds | Anna Nobles | March 13, 1799 |
| Matthew Davis | Sarah Logan | May 5, 1799 |
| Moses Gatling | Avy Rose | May 14, 1799 |
| Thomas Doles | Susannah Yarbrough | May 20, 1799 |
| Dr. Ignatius Sims | Henrietta Thompson | June 7, 1799 |
| Hilton Peavy | Nellie Peavy | June 13, 1799 |
| Ephriam Bishop | Betsy Moore | June 17, 1799 |
| Alexander Hunter | Lydia Wynne | June 26, 1799 |
| Robert Bonner | Elizabeth Heath | July 2, 1799 |
| John Oliver | Sarah Lowe | July 4, 1799 |
| John Keener | Mary McKindley | July 6, 1799 |
| Elisha Poore | Polly Lunsford | July 8, 1799 |
| Henry Avant | Sarah Vining | July 9, 1799 |
| Robert Bennett | Polly Glasgow | July 17, 1799 |

| | | |
|---|---|---|
| Nathan Jackson | Priscilla Sanders | July 18, 1799 |
| Charles Rayburn | Dora Williford | July 18, 1799 |
| Merrit Mitchell | Sally Hutchison | July 19, 1799 |
| Leonard Desieur | Polly Malone | missing |
| Elijah Conner | Polly Upton | August 14, 1799 |
| Frederick Glover | Nancy Jones | September 3, 1799 |
| James Hilburn | Nancy Jackson | September 17, 1799 |
| Stephen Todd | Sibella Williams | September 20, 1799 |
| Jones Kendrick | (blank) Lawrence | October 7, 1799 |
| John Griffin | Elizabeth Costly | October 15, 1799 |
| Jonathan Hagathy | Fairiby Cook | October 16, 1799 |
| Samuel Newman | Anna Lovett | October 27, 1799 |
| Peter Peavy | Vevinah Aarons | November 2, 1799 |
| James Davison | Mary Butler | November 15, 1799 |
| John Henry | Amy Bishop | November 15, 1799 |
| Lewis Wright | Patsy Heath | November 18, 1799 |
| Elisha Neal | Nancy Yarbrough | November 30, 1799 |
| Jonas Ray | Obedience Ellington | December 11, 1799 |
| Stafford Williams | Sarah Dismukes | December 16, 1799 |
| Robert Wynne Jr. | Jennie Perkins | December 17, 1799 |
| John Reed | Betsy Lowe | December 25, 1799 |
| Matthew Mims | Ursie Harville | December 27, 1799 |
| Daniel Crenshaw | Selethe Cook | December 27, 1799 |
| Lanier Humphreys | Susannah Spinks | January blank, 1800 |
| Fisher Gaskins | Rhoda Rowe | January 17, 1800 |
| Robert Bowman | Peggy Dove | January 21, 1800 |
| Aaron Smith | Elizabeth Abercrombie | January 21, 1800 |
| James Williams | Peggy Slatter | January 23, 1800 |
| John Thrasher | Sarah Bearden | January 25, 1800 |
| James Darnall | Polly Davis | February 5, 1800 |
| Thomas Maddox | Polly Neal | February 10, 1800 |
| Aaron Jones | Dicy Willoughby | February 12, 1800 |
| John Gibson | Fanny Flewellin | February 22, 1800 |
| William Jones | Bathsheba Abercrombie | February 22, 1800 |
| Austin Pruitt | Nancy Yarbrough | February 27, 1800 |

| | | |
|---|---|---|
| Azariah Butts | Elizabeth Doles | March 4, 1800 |
| Nathaniel Pruitt | Polly Perkins | March 16, 1800 |
| James Dunaway | Sarah Lee | March 30, 1800 |
| Asa Newsom | Nancy Newsom | April 6, 1800 |
| Joseph Miller | Alice Woolsey | April 7, 1800 |
| Charles Oliver | S. Templene | April 27, 1800 |
| Seth Woolsey | Honor Miller | May 5, 1800 |
| William Kellum | Deborah Stubbs | May 10, 1800 |
| Sherod Barden | Elizabeth Fickling | June 25, 1800 |
| Reubin Lockett | Sarah Hill | June 27, 1800 |
| Andrew Walker | Naomi Moore | July 10, 1800 |
| Moses Boynton | Tabitha Chapman | July 11, 1800 |
| Goodwin Mitchell | Elizabeth Cox | July 15, 1800 |
| William Taylor | Elizabeth Hutchison | August 5, 1800 |
| James Williams | Nancy Wilkinson | August 12, 1800 |
| Solomon Thompson | Frances Parker | August 18, 1800 |
| John Harrison | Elizabeth Newman | August 24, 1800 |
| Laban Chapman | Hannah Richardson | August 30, 1800 |
| William Willis | Mary Eades | October 18, 1800 |
| William Richardson | Peggy Aaron | October 28, 1800 |
| Pierce Crossly | Susannah McCowan | November 2, 1800 |
| Micajah Darden | Dicy Darden | November 10, 1800 |
| Elijah Anglin | Susannah Wheeler | November 19, 1800 |
| John Williams | Nancy Camp | November 24, 1800 |
| Joseph Hancock | Mary Brady | November 25, 1800 |
| William Jones | Ketrina Abercrombie | November 26, 1800 |
| William Simmons | Sarah Wright | December 3, 1800 |
| Furney Griffin | Elizabeth Norton | December 3, 1800 |
| Jacob Clowers | Sally Darden | December 7, 1800 |
| William Flournoy | Nancy Wallace | December 24, 1800 |
| Austin Baker | Maret Hern | December 24, 1800 |
| Charles Webb | Polly Hackett | December 25, 1800 |
| Isaac Daniel | Polly Johnston | December 25, 1800 |
| Isaac Revison | Sarah Cody | January 7, 1801 |
| Peter Mullins | Tabitha Wynne | January 8, 1801 |
| James Gibson | Rachel Waggoner | January 9, 1801 |

| | | |
|---|---|---|
| John Hollis | Frances Pembleton | January 12, 1801 |
| Pleasant Moorman | Nancy Beall | January 15, 1801 |
| Samuel Howell | Patsy McCrary | January 17, 1801 |
| Jeremiah Daniel | Patsy Edmondson | January 17, 1801 |
| William Jones | Susannah Parham | January 17, 1801 |
| Elijah Grenade | Zilpha Dove | January 21, 1801 |
| William Landrum | Agnes Smith | January 23, 1801 |
| Alexander Avera | Jane Curry | January 24, 1801 |
| Nathaniel Hutchinson | Rebecca Harbuck | February 1, 1801 |
| Willis Roberts | Apsilla Alexander | February 2, 1801 |
| John Gilpin | Clara Bond | February 9, 1801 |
| Ephriam Ivy | Celia Finch | February 9, 1801 |
| William Wade | Sally Simons | March 1801 |
| Thomas Lovett | Elizabeth Johnston | March 8, 1801 |
| Thomas Simmons | Rebecca Simmons | March 17, 1801 |
| Francis F. Raskin | Elizabeth Threewitts | March 24, 1801 |
| Cullen Alford | Pheriby Wooten | April 10, 1801 |
| Timothy Matthews | Patsy Flewellin | April 13, 1801 |
| John P. Jones | Mary Punkett | May 4, 1801 |
| Thomas Bowman | Deborah Wall | May 18, 1801 |
| William Hutchinson | Patsy Burkhalter | June 2, 1801 |
| Henry Hadley | Elizabeth Matthews | June 10, 1801 |
| Josephus Tucker | Susannah Tucker | June 11, 1801 |
| Charles Stewart | Elizabeth Moore | June 11, 1801 |
| Leroy Mims | Elizabeth Benton | June 16, 1801 |
| Anderson Ball | Phoebe Jenkins | June 20, 1801 |
| John Thomas | Phoebe Guyland | June 26, 1801 |
| Gardner Smith | Rebecca Nobles | July 1, 1801 |
| Hugh Logan | Nancy Tuning | July 5, 1801 |
| James Hardin | Nancy Morgan | July 9, 1801 |
| John Moore | Margaret Digby | July 11, 1801 |
| Henry Harris | Patsy Marshall | July 12, 1801 |
| Jeremiah Crane | Mary Weldon | August 12, 1801 |
| Jesse Dennis | Nancy McGraw | September 24, 1801 |
| Phillip Johnston | Mourning Howell | October 22, 1801 |
| Joshua Stephens | Polly Britt | October 24, 1801 |

| | | |
|---|---|---|
| John Keener | Mary McKindley | October 24, 1801 |
| William Brooks | Mary Simms | October 28, 1801 |
| John Breed | Lucy Dennis | November 5, 1801 |
| William Gardner | Sallie Neal | November 29, 1801 |
| James Wood | Caroline Matilda Buffin | December 28, 1801 |
| John Poor | Sallie Hobson | December 29, 1801 |
| Dinkins Ivey | Lydia Hogans | January 1, 1802 |
| Arthur Taylor | Sarah Williams | January 2, 1802 |
| David Whatley | Frances Poor | January 2, 1802 |
| Henry Walker | Fanny Parham | January 5, 1802 |
| Marritt Wheeler | Rebecca Kemp | January 7, 1802 |
| Henry Prince | Polly Pace | January 8, 1802 |
| Charles Dean | Ann O'Briant | January 9, 1802 |
| Andrew Hodges | Elizabeth Potter | January 22, 1802 |
| John Hill | Elizabeth Moore | February 13, 1802 |
| Benjamin Oliver | Nancy Ross | March 8, 1802 |
| John Wilson | Celia Howell | March 13, 1802 |
| Thomas Davis | Nancy Short | March 13, 1802 |
| James Howell | Rebecca Dunaway | March 17, 1802 |
| James Armstrong | Phoebe Simmons | April 17, 1802 |
| Isham Boman | Peggy Greesom | April 25, 1802 |
| Job Todd | Gracy Williford | April 29, 1802 |
| Henry Brewer | Nancy Doles | May 16, 1802 |
| John Cox | Rachel Stephens | May 19, 1802 |
| George Cooper | Linnie Parrish | June 2, 1802 |
| Hardy Newsom | Charity Wright | June 5, 1802 |
| Henry Moss | Sally Gardner | June 8, 1802 |
| Nicholas Highland | Lydia Hartsfield | June 10, 1802 |
| Francis Walker | Sallie Thorn | July 1, 1802 |
| Daniel Connell | Pollie Smith | July 2, 1802 |
| William Keener | Vashti Gibbs | July 10, 1802 |
| William Butler | Elizabeth Woodward | July 14, 1802 |
| John Sullivant | Sallie Pierce | July 27, 1802 |
| Silas Todd | Pollie Lindsey | July 28, 1802 |
| Baalam Brooks | Mary McGlamery | August 11, 1802 |
| William Tait | Sallie Howard | August 17, 1802 |
| John Fowler | Zilpha Howell | August 22, 1802 |

| | | |
|---|---|---|
| John Wynne | Elizabeth Harris | September 7, 1802 |
| Jacob Fair | Sally Hays | September 8, 1802 |
| John Robertson | Jennie Berry | October 4, 1802 |
| William Proctor | Peggy Brady | October 11, 1802 |
| David Morgan | Peggy W. Brady | October 17, 1802 |
| Shemei Drake | Nancy White | October 18, 1802 |
| Michael Rowe | Susannah Hathorne | October 19, 1802 |
| Joshua Mitchell | Patsy Williams | November 1, 1802 |
| Henry Hill | Beady Walker | December 11, 1802 |
| David Castleberry | Sarah Howard | December 14, 1802 |
| Claiborne Ogletree | Betsy Gibson | December 15, 1802 |
| Bailey Hays | Mary Stubbs | December 15, 1802 |
| Tolliver Cox | Frances Davison | December 20, 1802 |
| Allen Davis | Rebecca Cahoon | December 21, 1802 |
| John Smith | Patsy Staton | December 25, 1802 |
| Thomas Flake | missing | January 10, 1803 |
| Samuel Davis | Polly Verdin | January 14, 1803 |
| James Wade | Charity Cooper | February 6, 1803 |
| Benjamin Humphreys | Sally Dickens | February 15, 1803 |
| Doctor Lockett | Mary Hill | February 20, 1803 |
| John Patterson | Sally Lockett | February 20, 1803 |
| Robert McCrary | Treacy Rogers | February 21, 1803 |
| Charles H. Deveraux | Polly Bruton | February 22, 1803 |
| Thomas T. Walker | Phoebe Medlock | March 19, 1803 |
| James Smith | Nancy Williams | March 24, 1803 |
| Abel James | Sarah Miller | March 28, 1803 |
| George Parham | Betsy Hill | March 29, 1803 |
| Hartwell Heath | Nancy Parham | March 29, 1803 |
| James Hogwood | Polly Harvill | March 30, 1803 |
| David Williams | Peggy Nixon | April 1, 1803 |
| William Slatter | Mary Crawford | April 3, 1803 |
| Leaven McGee | Mary Dunn | April 9, 1803 |
| Hyram Perry | Nancy Flake | April 11, 1803 |
| Moses Gatlin | Chloe Rowe | April 16, 1803 |
| Samuel Harris | Betsy Wells | April 16, 1803 |
| Isaac Williams | Rhoda Jones | April 24, 1803 |

| | | |
|---|---|---|
| Edward Harper | Hannah Yarbrough | May 21, 1803 |
| Moses Fillingin | Nancy Fillingin | May 25, 1803 |
| Robert Night | Elizabeth Bird | June 9, 1803 |
| Moses Williams | Mary Hardy | June 10, 1803 |
| Jeremiah Perry | Elizabeth Walker | June 27, 1803 |
| Robert Parker | Hannah Hutchins | July 7, 1803 |
| James Neves | Concord Hambleton | July 19, 1803 |
| Mordecai Malone | Penny Edmondson | July 27, 1803 |
| Bray Warren | Hetty Mitchell | August 2, 1803 |
| James Burt | Rebecca Burt | August 6, 1803 |
| Robert Daniel | Holland Rowe | August 20, 1803 |
| David Dove | Elizabeth Finch | August 21, 1803 |
| Henry Atchison | Winnie Hill | August 30, 1803 |
| William Chambliss | Martha Robertson | September 19, 1803 |
| Isaac Barbarie | Nancy Smith | September 21, 1803 |
| George Fickling | Ephathan Barden | September 27, 1803 |
| Daniel James | Elizabeth Gibson | October 8, 1803 |
| James Minton | Sarah Pool | October 15, 1803 |
| James Crissap | Sarah McCoy | October 18, 1803 |
| Howell Hight | Penny Wall | November 3, 1803 |
| James Threewitts | Sally Fontaine | November 8, 1803 |
| Levin Stanford | Nelly McGee | November 20, 1803 |
| James Bailey | Sarah Johnson | December 6, 1803 |
| Jesse Miller | Patsy Dennis | December 15, 1803 |
| Richard Fletcher | Cathy Hardin | December 31, 1803 |
| David Sallis | Letty Nichols | January 6, 1804 |
| Samuel Harrold | Susannah Harrall | January 13, 1804 |
| Jonathan Fuller | Jincy Hodges | January 23, 1804 |
| John Hardy | Sucky Mullins | January 24, 1804 |
| William Ansley | Ann Ray | February 6, 1804 |
| Arnold Atchinson | Patsy Gibson | February 11, 1804 |
| Edward Jenkins | Eliza Sheffield | February 14, 1804 |
| William Murray | Mary Rayburn | February 14, 1804 |
| James Heath | Elizabeth Heath | February 26, 1804 |
| William D. Wright | Nancy Heath | March 6, 1804 |
| William Bird | Mary Matthews | March 8, 1804 |
| William Ewell | Judith Higginbotham | March 14, 1804 |
| Henry Cocroff | Peggy Sandford | March 26, 1804 |

| | | |
|---|---|---|
| Joseph Hill | Nancy Finch | April 24, 1804 |
| Benjamin Walker | Patsy Butler | May 8, 1804 |
| Amos Wheeler | Charlotte Tindall | May 14, 1804 |
| Elias Beall | Polly Neal | May 19, 1804 |
| David Jones | Lydia Rowe | May 24, 1804 |
| Thomas Lowe | Elizabeth Rowe | June 13, 1804 |
| Nathan Davis | Catherine Rogers | July 26, 1804 |
| Josiah Draper | Sophia Stanford | August 2, 1804 |
| John Russell | Elizabeth Murphy | August 15, 1804 |
| William White | Sarah Hogans | August 16, 1804 |
| James Cody | Elizabeth Adams | August 17, 1804 |
| John Burge | Winnie Thurman | August 18, 1804 |
| John Rowland | Nancy Wilson | August 27, 1804 |
| John Anglin | Nancy Edmondson | September 15, 1804 |
| Benjamin Carpenter | Polly Jackson | September 15, 1804 |
| John Atchison | Rebecca Jenkins | September 27, 1804 |
| John Sheffield | Susannah Hight | September 27, 1804 |
| Thomas Redless | Nancy Smith | September 29, 1804 |
| Washington Hardaway | Sally Cody | October 1, 1804 |
| John Hardaway | Patsy Rowe | October 1, 1804 |
| Ishmael Broom | Nancy Myhand | October 16, 1804 |
| John Wade | Jerusha Taylor | October 31, 1804 |
| Whitfield Tucker | Eliza Darden | December 3, 1804 |
| Whitfield Tucker | Eliza Darden | December 3, 1804 |
| Thomas Hinton | Patsy Duckworth | December 11, 1804 |
| Dennis Brooks | Elvy Stanford | December 12, 1804 |
| James Ansley | Elizabeth Jones | December 18, 1804 |
| Thomas Harriss | Jincy Wynne | December 19, 1804 |
| Henry Harris | Concord Carter | December 22, 1804 |
| Aaron Grier Jr. | Polly Grier | December 22, 1804 |
| Ephriam McGee | Elizabeth McGlamery | December 24, 1804 |
| Samuel Moses | M. Dennis | December 24, 1804 |
| Robert Taylor | Mary Chambers | December 27, 1804 |
| Joab Brooks | Delilah Langford | December 27, 1804 |
| William Hoof | Tabitha Burson | December 28, 1804 |

| | | |
|---|---|---|
| Thomas Terry | Polly Faulks | January 7, 1805 |
| Dudley Peebles | Susannah Peebles | January 7, 1805 |
| William Ward | Susannah Wynne | January 7, 1805 |
| Hugh Blair | Polly Lee | January 14, 1805 |
| Samuel Barksdale | Lucy Bunkley | January 16, 1805 |
| Orren Parker | Nancy Hutchins | January 21, 1805 |
| James Handley | Sally Henry | January 23, 1805 |
| William Bunkley | Betty Slatter | January 26, 1805 |
| Richard Lovett | Sally Johnston | February 4, 1805 |
| Jonah Brook | Sally Wall | February 5, 1805 |
| Ambrose Murphy | Sarah Horn | February 12, 1805 |
| Matthew Harris | Mrs. Susannah Jones | February 12, 1805 |
| John Benton | Lavina Morris | February 13, 1805 |
| Barnard Fickling | Rebecca Moore | March 6, 1805 |
| Joseph Leonard | Millie Howell | March 6, 1805 |
| James Wheeler | Cassy Kinsey | March 16, 1805 |
| Joel Lasseter | Mary Beasley | March 21, 1805 |
| William Hoof | Sallie Breed | March 25, 1805 |
| Thomas Williams | Polly Ivy | March 26, 1805 |
| Adam Broom | Mary S. Wheeler | March 30, 1805 |
| John Wilson | Martha Dismukes | April 2, 1805 |
| David Chapman | Milly Chapman | April 10, 1805 |
| Nicholas Booty | Sallie Locke | April 15, 1805 |
| Neil Ferguson | Tabitha Chapman | April 29, 1805 |
| Richard Hopkins | Hannah Smith | May 5, 1805 |
| John Crokett | Pheriba Payne | May 8, 1805 |
| Joseph Hill | Elizabeth Heath | May 23, 1805 |
| John Moore | Elizabeth Davis | May 24, 1805 |
| William B. Allison | Alla Hutchins | May 28, 1805 |
| Micajah Perry | Polly Banks | May 31, 1805 |
| Nathan Harris | Rhoda Champion | June 1, 1805 |
| James Turner | Elizabeth Morris | June 1, 1805 |
| Vincent Wheeler | Nelly Nixon | June 3, 1805 |
| Daniel Eades | Charity Watson | June 3, 1805 |
| Jeremiah Holden | Jenny Gunn | June 17, 1805 |
| Isham Reese | Polly Rogers | June 8, 1805 |
| Thomas Jones | Sarah Mitchell | June 22, 1805 |
| John K. Revers | Sally Burkhalter | June 22, 1805 |

| | | |
|---|---|---|
| Benjamin Matthews | Polly Jones | July 4, 1805 |
| Moses Williams | Edy Barrow | July 4, 1805 |
| Thomas Jones | Kizzy Bazemore | July 4, 1805 |
| John Blount | Sally Pruitt | July 8, 1805 |
| Ambrose Abley | Elizabeth Parham | July 8, 1805 |
| John Quinn | Mary Tapper | July 11, 1805 |
| Littleberry Bagwell | Winnie Castleberry | July 11, 1805 |
| Jones Burkhalter | Kissy Basemore | July 12, 1805 |
| Reubin Nantz | Rosanna Sanders | July 13, 1805 |
| John Johnston | Elizabeth McNabb | July 16, 1805 |
| Robert Oliver | Patience Pitts | July 16, 1805 |
| Phillip Brooks | Nancy Sherley | July 25, 1805 |
| John Womack | Sarah Lewis | August 12, 1805 |
| David Benagin | Nancy Zachary | August 13, 1805 |
| Phillip Brantley | Rebecca Harbuck | September 5, 1805 |
| Ebenezer Bird | Betsy Bryson | September 10, 1805 |
| Willie Dorman | Frances Crawford | September 11, 1805 |
| Churchwell Gibson | Mary Brantley | September 11, 1805 |
| Daniel Culpepper | Jemima Wright | September 24, 1805 |
| Byrd Pruitt | Rebecca Turner | October 7, 1805 |
| Ambrose Shillings | Polly Fields | October 26, 1805 |
| John Lynn | Lavina Ivy | October 28, 1805 |
| Richard Murphy | Effie McDuffie | October 30, 1805 |
| Winfrey Lary | Phoebe Richards | November 2, 1805 |
| Joshua Williams | Peggy Filligin | November 6, 1805 |
| James Buckelaw | Elizabeth James | November 7, 1805 |
| John Matthews | Mary Smith | November 12, 1805 |
| Zachary Hobson | Leamander Grenade | November 18, 1805 |
| Spencer Seals | Elizabeth Burnley | November 25, 1805 |
| John McDaniel | Charlotte Nichols | November 27, 1805 |
| Henry T. Anthony | Pollie Lovell | November 30, 1805 |
| Jonathan Dunaway | Elizabeth Dennis | December 7, 1805 |
| James Cooke | Rebecca Potts | December 13, 1805 |
| Benjamin Napier | Pollie Williford | December 13, 1805 |
| Samuel M. Smith | Elizabeth M. Hill | December 15, 1805 |
| William McNash | Pollie Hatcher | December 17, 1805 |

| | | |
|---|---|---|
| George Dashiels | Nellie Stanford | missing |
| Harden Chambers | Vicy Kinney | missing |
| William Davidson | Sarah Geaslin | December 26, 1805 |
| Adam Livingston | Patsy Womack | December 28, 1805 |
| Ambrose Chapman | Elizabeth Stone | January 13, 1806 |
| David Holeman | Patsy Gibson | January 17, 1806 |
| Murphy Champion | Kinsy Newsom | January 18, 1806 |
| Burrell Maybrunk | Marion Newsom | January 18, 1806 |
| William Darden | Pollie Dewberry | January 20, 1806 |
| Joseph Grenade | Catherine Johnson | January 27, 1806 |
| Bishai Breed | Nancy Barber | February 2, 1806 |
| John Ward | Nancy Jones | February 2, 1806 |
| Benjamin M (torn) | Polly Hill | February 3, 1806 |
| Aaron Livingston | Jean Allen | February 5, 1806 |
| William Brown | Polly Owen | February 21, 1806 |
| Ebenezer Bird | Patsey Byrom | February 25, 1806 |
| William Jackson | Candace B(torn) | March 22, 1806 |
| William Green | Elizabeth Darden | March 25, 1806 |
| Anson Highfield | Fanny Burge Heath | March 28, 1806 |
| John Boy (torn) | Lydia Welle (torn) | April 2, 1806 |
| Amos Parsons | Patsy Gardner | April 8, 1806 |
| William Snelling | Elizabeth Pickard | April 15, 1806 |
| Thomas Jones | Pollie Matthews | May 2, 1806 |
| Nathan Sherley | Mary Brooks | May 13, 1806 |
| David Jones | Mary Mendenhall | May 14, 1806 |
| Thomas Jones | Polly Matthews | May 21, 1806 |
| Cleveras Andrews | Elizabeth Jones | May 26, 1806 |
| Nathan Culpepper | Fannie Gardiner | May 27, 1806 |
| Alexander Perryman | Jane W. Vining | June 4, 1806 |
| Solomon Castleberry | Rebeckah Lovett | June 14, 1806 |
| Amos Waggoner | Betsy Millirons | June 15, 1806 |
| Samuel Hyde | Caty Gibson | June 18, 1806 |
| Thomas Hall | Patsy Finch | June 25, 1806 |
| Andrew R. Stephens | Margaret Grier | July 7, 1806 |
| Simon Herrold | Jenny Rushing | July 10, 1806 |

| | | |
|---|---|---|
| Joshua Windham | Elizabeth Jones | July 11, 1806 |
| David Rhodes | Mary Hustice | July 11, 1806 |
| Josua Draper | Elizabeth Morgan | August 10, 1806 |
| John Beville | Franky Boynton | September 4, 1806 |
| William Shaw | Hannah Hodgerson | September 8, 1806 |
| Silas Buckholts | Sarah Roberts | September 19, 1806 |
| William Cooper | Elizabeth Slatter | September 29, 1806 |
| Charles Stewart | Henrietta Hargraves | October 1, 1806 |
| John Littleton | Elizabeth Kinsey | October 2, 1806 |
| Walter Beall | Rebecca Neal | October 22, 1806 |
| Jonathan Newman | Carrie Lovett | October 26, 1806 |
| Henry Conaway | Nancy Turner | November 9, 1806 |
| James Hutchens | Susannah Castleberry | November 13, 1806 |
| William Jones | Patience Davis | November 16, 1806 |
| Elijah Horn | Margaret Nugent | November 21, 1806 |
| John Ross | Polly Matthews | December, 1806 |
| John Digby | Belinda Slade | December 1, 1806 |
| Samuel Johnston | Rosamond Spinks | December 3, 1806 |
| Benjamin Matthews | Rebekah Pierson | December 6, 1806 |
| Archibald Little | Mary Butrel | December 15, 1806 |
| John Chaffing | Clotilda Darden | December 15, 1806 |
| William Paulk | Henrietta Buckholts | December 24, 1806 |
| Moses Butt | Eliza Brown | December 30, 1806 |
| Henry Wilson | Mary Stanford | January 15, 1807 |
| John Roberson | Sally Harris | January 20, 1807 |
| Moses Ivey | Elizabeth George | January 26, 1807 |
| Theophilus Hill | Rebeccah Gibson | January 28, 1807 |
| Thomas Huston | Lucy Boynton | January 31, 1807 |
| Nathaniel Brooks | Drusilla Morris | February 7, 1807 |
| Robert Culpepper | Pheriba Wright | February 8, 1807 |
| Joshua Howell | Jennie Darden | February 9, 1807 |
| Benjamin Chapman | Patsy Shaw | February 25, 1807 |
| David Bailey | Milly Johnston | March 5, 1807 |
| Joel Kinsey | Tabitha Johnston | March 5, 1807 |
| Robert M. | Emily M. Bird | March 24, 1807 |

| | | |
|---|---|---|
| Cunningham | | |
| Robert Sheffield | Anne Hight | March 24, 1807 |
| William Torrence | Mary Scott | April 5, 1807 |
| Benjamin Weatherby | Mildred Bonner | April 7, 1807 |
| Asa Chapman | Synthia Lockett | April 7, 1807 |
| John Moneyham | Elizabeth Millirons | April 12, 1807 |
| Abram Hill | Catherine Gibson | June 9, 1807 |
| William Few | Hannah Andrews | June 13, 1807 |
| William Gibson | Polly Duckworth | June 17, 1807 |
| John Howard | Sarah Jones | June 30, 1807 |
| Rie Newsom | Dicy Newsom | July 13, 1807 |
| John Davidson | Linsey Smith | July 16, 1807 |
| Terrence Ivey | Polly George | July 21, 1807 |
| David Jones | Elizabeth Shamling | August 4, 1807 |
| Isaac Pate | Rachel Gibson | August 6, 1807 |
| James Lynn | Nancy Harbuck | August 13, 1807 |
| William Barrow | Rebeckah Heath | August 13, 1807 |
| James Ricketson | Jane Simpson | August 24, 1807 |
| Robert Tait | Sally Oliver | August 25, 1807 |
| Allen Carter | Sally Edmonds | September 3, 1807 |
| Thomas Draper | Rebekah Grenade | September 5, 1807 |
| Joseph Baker | Rachel Wade | September 11, 1807 |
| Myrick Hunneycutt | Polly Linch | September 11, 1807 |
| Elisha Smallwood | Nancy Davis | September 15, 1807 |
| Thomas Grimes | Polly Bunkley | September 24, 1807 |
| William Mullens | Fanny Williams | September 30, 1807 |
| James McCormick | Catherine Oliver | October 5, 1807 |
| Samuel Jones | Elizabeth Neal | October 5, 1807 |
| James Jenkins | Sally Flake | October 8, 1807 |
| Joel Smith | Sarah Banks | October 10, 1807 |
| Jacob Harbuck | Sally Rickerson | October 15, 1807 |
| John Morris | Sally Carter | November 4, 1807 |
| Henry Loyless | Lavinah Carter | November 5, 1807 |
| James Johnston | Polly Jarrett | November 6, 1807 |
| Hardy Pitts | Drusilla Neal | November 18, 1807 |
| Thomas Gibson | Patsy Neal | November 18, 1807 |

| James Crowder | Hannah Burnley | November 19, 1807 |
|---|---|---|
| James Vaughn | Elizabeth Darden | November 23, 1807 |
| William Myhand | Nancy Lock | November 23, 1807 |
| David Adams | Polly Johnston | November 27, 1807 |
| John Myrick | Verlinda Harris | November 29, 1807 |
| Price Willis | Nancy Coleman | December 18, 1807 |
| John C. Turner | Sally Fluwellen | December 23, 1807 |
| Nelson Gunn | Jane Reynolds | December 24, 1807 |
| Daniel Dennis | Nancy Breed | December 29, 1807 |
| John Killabrew | Patsy Lindsey | December 29, 1807 |
| Joseph White | Winnie Wheeler | January 4, 1808 |
| Wrigley Lokey | (blank) McGee | January 7, 1808 |
| James Lesly | Eliza Bird | January 13, 1808 |
| John Hutcheson | Fanny Smith | January 16, 1808 |
| Abner Bailey | Elizabeth Parker | January 19, 1808 |
| Lewis Wright | Nancy Hill | January 21, 1808 |
| John Kellam | Nancy Rigby | January 23, 1808 |
| John Lewis | Patsy Waggoner | January 27, 1808 |
| Peter Clower | Loveny Mitchell | January 28, 1808 |
| John Walker | Polly Moore | February 3, 1808 |
| John Brooks | Nancy Nunn | February 16, 1808 |
| David Lynn | Lucy Kinsey | February 18, 1808 |
| Elijah Gosea | Hixy Avent | February 19, 1808 |
| Young Seymore | Teletha Cohoon | February 25, 1808 |
| James Cobb | Ann Jones | February 25, 1808 |
| John Bonner | Catherine Haynes | February 25, 1808 |
| John McCrary | Amelia Beall | February 27, 1808 |
| Samuel McCrery | Jinney Beall | March 8, 1808 |
| William Wynne | Lucy Harris | March 12, 1808 |
| William Wynne | Lucy Harris | March 13, 1808 |
| George Cotton | Rebeccah Pennington | March 17, 1808 |
| Samuel Geesling | Mary Smith | April 2, 1808 |
| Elijah Jones | Margaret Beall | April 9, 1808 |
| John Bunkley | Mariah Barksdale | April 9, 1808 |
| Dickinson Culpepper | Franky Wynne | April 10, 1808 |
| John Sanders | Lucinda Malone | April 12, 1808 |

| | | |
|---|---|---|
| William Harbuck | Hannah Merritt | April 14, 1808 |
| Thomas Battle | Polly Baker | April 17, 1808 |
| Henry Harbuck | Hester Greeson | April 21, 1808 |
| Solomon Draper | Lucy Dennis | April 27, 1808 |
| Henry Carlton | Nancy Moore | April 27, 1808 |
| Moses Jackson | Rebeckah Strother | May 17, 1808 |
| John Butts | Tempy Green | May 18, 1808 |
| William Shoder | Polly King | May 28, 1808 |
| William Taylor | Sally Rose | June 2, 1808 |
| William Ball | Elizabeth Gray | June 6, 1808 |
| Josiah Sallis | Patience Jones | June 6, 1808 |
| Isom Wheeler | Eddea Smith | June 12, 1808 |
| Daniel Thomas | Lavinah Smith | June 19, 1808 |
| Lemuel Wynne | Lucy Fretwell | June 23, 1808 |
| Henry Brown | Aley Burnley | June 23, 1808 |
| Sims Kelly | Polly Kemp | June 28, 1808 |
| Wright Mims | Eliza Kendall | June 29, 1808 |
| John Green | Nancy Daniel | June 29, 1808 |
| Thomas Deason | Cynthia Averil | July 2, 1808 |
| William Dunaway | Lavinah Brewer | July 28, 1808 |
| John Woods | Patsy Culpepper | August 2, 1808 |
| Benjamin Bryant | Polly Brazil | August 7, 1808 |
| John Matthews | Polly Rogers | August 7, 1808 |
| Bala Hardin | Betsy Cox | August 9, 1808 |
| Hardy Green | Elizabeth Jones | August 9, 1808 |
| Dennis L. Ryan | Mary Haynes | August 30, 1808 |
| Samuel Pearson | Patience Jones | September 2, 1808 |
| Windor Hillman | Gracy McMath | September 10, 1808 |
| David Herrington | Elizabeth Holaday | September 12, 1808 |
| Littleberry Little | Rebecca Newsom | September 15, 1808 |
| Jeremiah Pool | Milly Hancock | September 24, 1808 |
| John Wirgley | Elizabeth Kelly | September 27, 1808 |
| William Henry | Nancy Drake | October 2, 1808 |
| Ensil Farr | Catherine Smith | October 4, 1808 |
| Gideon Beddingfield | Henrietta Ball | October 9, 1808 |
| Benjamin Hardin | Patsy Cox | October 9, 1808 |
| Michael Rogers | Elender McFarlin | October 22, 1808 |

| | | |
|---|---|---|
| James Ledbetter | Sally Camp | November 12, 1808 |
| John Wright | Temperance Ogletree | November 13, 1808 |
| James Butt | Patsy Jones | November 19, 1808 |
| William Luckett | Jane Sims | December 1, 1808 |
| Robert Ellis | Martha Grenade | December 3, 1808 |
| Jesse Davidson | Peggy King | December 4, 1808 |
| Watkins Davis | Sarah Matthews | December 6, 1808 |
| Benjamin G. Gancy | Caroline Bird | December 8, 1808 |
| Daniel Burgin | Polly McGee | December 13, 1808 |
| Clody Camp | Mary Harwell | December 19, 1808 |
| John Runnolds | Patsy Harold | December 21, 1808 |
| John King | Mary Jackson | December 27, 1808 |
| Richard Barrow | Betsey Jones | December 29, 1808 |
| Robert Fleming | Polly Watson | December 29, 1808 |
| Lovett Smith | Eliza Fort | December 29, 1808 |
| Dunwoodie Dozier | Eliza Chapman | December 31, 1808 |
| John Tharp | Elizabeth Hatcher | January 2, 1809 |
| Silas Pace | Margaret Sill | January 5, 1809 |
| John Vining | Polly Hubert | January 5, 1809 |
| John Gibson | Elizabeth Dozier | January 7, 1809 |
| Aaron Johnston | Jessie Freeman | January 13, 1809 |
| Willis Randle | Millie Moore | January 17, 1809 |
| Highland Livingston | Sarah Cardal | January 22, 1809 |
| Allen Andrews | Dicy Allen | January 23, 1809 |
| Lewis Harrell | Crisa Farr | January 26, 1809 |
| John Rushing | Suckey Gardner | January 30, 1809 |
| James J. Dale | Hester Duckworth | February 9, 1809 |
| Solomon Warner | missing | February 9, 1809 |
| Amos Johnston | Sally Bishop | February 11, 1809 |
| Henry Adams | Rebecca Sanders | February 13, 1809 |
| Leonard Pratt | Elizabeth Brooks | February 14, 1809 |
| Stephen Granberry | Eliza Spurling | February 18, 1809 |
| Willis Hobbs | Polly Pool | February 20, 1809 |
| William Mitchell | Rebecca Newsom | February 23, 1809 |
| Joshua Rowe | Elizabeth Rigby | February 23, 1809 |
| Renay Eades | Elizabeth Harden | March 2, 1809 |

| | | |
|---|---|---|
| Amos Newsom | Nancy Adams | March 3, 1809 |
| John Smith | Elizabeth Camp | March 13, 1809 |
| Parot Rouse | Mary Mash | March 15, 1809 |
| Granville Moody | Anne Harris | March 23, 1809 |
| James Armstrong | Rachel Coleman | April 12, 1809 |
| William Holland | Elizabeth Fluellin | April 15, 1809 |
| William Reese | Lettice McCrery | May 20, 1809 |
| Hardy Pace | Succy Turner | May 20, 1809 |
| Richmond Dennis | Frances Jones | May 31, 1809 |
| Daniel Rowland | Eliza Harville | June 1, 1809 |
| Joseph Johnston | Polly Darden | June 6, 1809 |
| John Green | Nancy Daniel | June 28, 1809 |
| Jeptha Brantley | Lucy Persons | July 12, 1809 |
| Robert Chapman | Polly Stone | July 17, 1809 |
| Samuel Ansley | Mary Tillman | July 21, 1809 |
| Willoughby S. Hill | Nancy A. Tharp | August 2, 1809 |
| John Matthews | Polly Rogers | August 4, 1809 |
| John Chambers | Obedience Ledbetter | August 7, 1809 |
| Middleton Usry | Polly Newsom | September 2, 1809 |
| Elbert Bishop | Eleanor Stanford | September 5, 1809 |
| Lemuel Roats | Lavina Flinn | September 11, 1809 |
| David Herrington | Elizabeth Holaday | September 13, 1809 |
| Crawford Newsom | Elizabeth Newsom | September 14, 1809 |
| Jacob Willis | Sally Rogers | September 17, 1809 |
| John Harrison | Elizabeth Smith | September 22, 1809 |
| Anthony Jones | Sarah Barrow | September 24, 1809 |
| Henry Chambless | Rachel Dannelly | October 6, 1809 |
| Daniel Kinsey | Levicy Davidson | October 9, 1809 |
| Gideon Beddingfield | Henrietta Bull | October 9, 1809 |
| William Pile | Hannah Cloud | October 12, 1809 |
| Benjamin Matthews | Sally Wilmouth | October 12, 1809 |
| Bird Gilbert | Sally Spinks | October 19, 1809 |
| William Teddley | Polly Perry | October 29, 1809 |
| James Jackson | Sally Beall | November 2, 1809 |
| William Byrom II | Isabella Akins | November 15, 1809 |
| Drury Pate | Sarah Johnston | November 17, 1809 |

| John James | Polly Parish | November 23, 1809 |
|---|---|---|
| Michael Deason | Polly Deason | November 26, 1809 |
| James Sallis | Rebeckah Ivy | December 12, 1809 |
| James Gafford | Elizabeth Dickens | January 2, 1810 |
| Francis Benton | Susannah Holland | January 6, 1810 |
| William McNeill | Peggy Bailey | January 25, 1810 |
| James Rogers | Sophia Cooksey | January 25, 1810 |
| William Warner | Patsy Neal | February 6, 1810 |
| Jesse Williams | Milberry Wheless | February 12, 1810 |
| Jacob Johnston | Patsy Smith | February 18, 1810 |
| Willis Hobbs | Polly Pool | February 22, 1810 |
| Elisha Gardner | Elizabeth Rushin | March 4, 1810 |
| Edmond Johnston | Sally Crenshaw | March 17, 1810 |
| Harris McKinney | Jincy Ivey | May 17, 1810 |
| James Standford | Polly McGee | March 18, 1810 |
| Perry Powell | Nancy Lyon | March 22, 1810 |
| Edwin Baker | Nancy Baker | May 13, 1810 |
| James Littleton | Lydia Tydwell | May 17, 1810 |
| William Blount | Mrs. Elizabeth Wright | May 17, 1810 |
| Stephen Grizzle | Elizabeth Harrison | May 27, 1810 |
| George W. Hardwick | Mary Fontaine | June 27, 1810 |
| Jared Wright | Dicy Cobb | August 1, 1810 |
| Irby Dewberry | Temperance Heath | August 1, 1810 |
| Abner Norris | Peggy Davis | August 4, 1810 |
| William Doster | Margaret Edge | August 6, 1810 |
| Stephen W. Bromley | Petheny Garrett | August 7, 1810 |
| Willis Terry | Jinsy Edwards | August 26, 1810 |
| Thomas Lockhart | Tempy Rogers | September 4, 1810 |
| William Greeson | Sucky Hill | September 5, 1810 |
| Lewis Krinze | Gatsy M. Wingate | September 15, 1810 |
| John Hutchins | Sally Irby | September 28, 1810 |
| William Newsom | Frances Hardaway | October 1, 1810 |
| John Daniel | Elizabeth Hutchins | October 2, 1810 |
| James Hicks | Polly Hutchins | October 2, 1810 |
| William Northen | Rebecca Weatherby | October 3, 1810 |

| | | |
|---|---|---|
| John Parham | Catherine Dansby | October 7, 1810 |
| Warren Barrow | Polly Heath | October 17, 1810 |
| Thomas Ivy | Peggy Gibson | October 18, 1810 |
| Timothy Reading | Fannie Hardaway | November 12, 1810 |
| Abner Abbett | Susannah Averett | November 15, 1810 |
| Allen Duckworth | Theresa Rees | December 4, 1810 |
| James Lockett | Sally Darden | December 13, 1810 |
| John Matthews | Sally Moore | December 18, 1810 |
| Michael Moore Esq. | Nancy Smith | January 3, 1811 |
| James Gray Jr. | Betsey Hadley | January 10, 1811 |
| Caswell Ball | Betsy Parham | January 10, 1811 |
| Aaron Jackson | Elizabeth Fleming | January 15, 1811 |
| Fisher Gaskins | Polly Lacy | January 17, 1811 |
| William McMath | Polly Amos | January 23, 1811 |
| Hardy Hopson | Patsey Turner | January 24, 1811 |
| Hampton Parish | Sally Smith | January 31, 1811 |
| Presley Spinks | Martha Jones | January 31, 1811 |
| William Gunn | Pleasant Stephens | February 3, 1811 |
| James Bonner | Nancy Bonner | February 19, 1811 |
| Archelaus Wilson | Sarah Wilson | March 7, 1811 |
| Joseph Rhodes | Sally Rhodes | April 8, 1811 |
| Joseph Wright | Polly Walker | April 11, 1811 |
| Henry McNease | Polly McNease | May 5, 1811 |
| John Turner | Nancy Parham | May 16, 1811 |
| John Hygh | Elizabeth Harris | May 27, 1811 |
| Robert Hill | Sarah Hill | July 11, 1811 |
| Thomas Avera | Tabitha Davis | September 11, 1811 |
| Moses McKinney | Harriet Burgholder | September 21, 1811 |
| Elijah Dickens | Susannah Jackson | October 15, 1811 |
| John Coffield | Harriet Jackson | October 15, 1811 |
| John Lock | Rosy Morris | November 5, 1811 |
| Allen Dykes | Polly Bledsoe | November 7, 1811 |
| Wiley Hight | Nancy Brantley | December 19, 1811 |
| Samuel Yarbrough | Mrs. Nancy Manning | January 4, 1812 |
| Joseph Mil'n. Semmes | Mary Torrence, widow | January 16, 1812 |
| James Gray | Susannah Cody | January 20, 1812 |

| James Peek | Peggy Swain | January 25, 1812 |
| Fielding Hill | Isabella Gibson | January 30, 1812 |
| Britton Carroll | Winnifred Benton | February 6, 1812 |
| Bolland Lacy | Phalby Peevy | February 25, 1812 |
| Moses Ivy | Sarah Banks | March 10, 1812 |
| John Smythe | Elizabeth Peevy | May 4, 1812 |
| Richard Stonestreet | Mary Dicken | May 10, 1812 |
| Thomas Myhand | Susannah Benton, widow | June 25, 1812 |
| William Abbett | Penelope Newsom | August 9, 1812 |
| John Henderson | Polly King | August 24, 1812 |
| John White | Rachel Carter | November 24, 1812 |
| James Harbuck | Martha Harris | December 24, 1812 |
| Robert Armstrong | Priscilla Dennis | December 31, 1812 |
| John Davidson | Elizabeth May | January 18, 1813 |
| John McEwen | Lucy Morris | January 28, 1813 |
| Elijah Boynton | Elizabeth Jackson | February 18, 1813 |
| James Armstrong | Lavina Harbuck | February 21, 1813 |
| Churchwell Rosy | Sally Parrish | March 4, 1813 |
| Thomas Fisher | Epsy Burkhalter | May 23, 1813 |
| William Denmark | Mary Cochrum | May 30, 1813 |
| Ishmael McDaniel | Sallie Harvill | June 2, 1813 |
| John Gibson | Clarissa Britt, widow | June 8, 1813 |
| Thomas Shambless | Nelly McNiece | June 23, 1813 |
| William Harrell | Milly Barrow | June 24, 1813 |
| Dolphin Davis | Jemima Kendall | July 15, 1813 |
| Abraham Grierson | Susannah Sheffield | August 3, 1813 |
| Nicholas Andrews | Marcella Ransom | August 18, 1813 |
| Nathan Maffett | Elizabeth Blount | September 2, 1813 |
| Orian Davis | Polly Parker | September 23, 1813 |
| Henry B. Thompson | Louisa Sophia Cratin | October 26, 1813 |
| James McCarty | Drusilla Ghesling | December 2, 1813 |
| Charles Moore | Elizabeth Ellington | December 22, 1813 |
| Thomas Tieson | Drusilla Mays | December 21, 1813 |
| James M. Bates | Elizabeth Ghesling | December 21, 1813 |
| John Smith | Nancy Anderson | December 30, 1813 |

# English Crown Land Grants in St. Paul Parish

Alexander, William
150 acres, District of Augusta
Granted September 30, 1757 Grant Book A, page 489
Bounded on all sides by vacant land.

Allen, John
400 acres, St. Paul Parish
Granted May 4, 1773 Grant Book I, page 966
Bounded on the south by David Russell, northwest by land surveyed for some person unknown.

Alleson, William
100 acres, Wrightsboro Township, St. Paul Parish
Surveyed August 31, 1769 Plat Book C, page 3
No grant recorded.

Alston, Philip
150 acres, St. Paul Parish
Granted August 5, 1766 Grant Book E, page 325
Bounded on the east and northeast by Philip Alston and the Savannah River, northwest by Daniel Wallicon and Philip Alston.

Anderson, Charles
400 acres, St. Paul Parish
Granted October 4, 1768 Grant Book G, page 192
Bounded on all sides by vacant land.

Anderson, David
100 acres, St. Paul Parish
Granted February 2, 1768 Grant Book G, page 17
Bounded on the southeast by Owen Day, northeast by Augusta Township, and northwest by Isaac Atwood, southwest by part of tract ordered to Owen Sullivan.

Anderson, James
Town Lot #19, Second row, Augusta, containing 1 acre.
Granted July 2, 1765 Grant Book E, page 192

Anderson, John
500 acres, St. Paul Parish
Granted May 5, 1770 Grant Book I, page 14
Bounded on the north and west by the Little River.

Andrews, Micajah
100 acres, St. Paul Parish
Granted November 1, 1774 Grant Book M, page 618
Bounded on the northeast by Thomas Garnet, northwest by Alexander Scot, and on the southeast by Edward Cartledge.

Ansley, Benjamin
100 acres, Wrightsboro Township, St. Paul Parish
Granted November 1, 1774 Grant Book M, page 619
Bounded on the southeast by James Cone and William Lynn.

Ansley, Benjamin
100 acres, St. Paul Parish
Granted November 1, 1774 Grant Book M, page 620
Bounded on the west by Candler, southwest by Thomas Ansley and Tanner, north by Oliver.

Ansley, Thomas
Granted November 6, 1770 Grant Book I, page 195
Town Lot #28, Wrightsboro, St. Paul Parish; 200 acres, Township of Wrightsboro, St. Paul Parish, bounded on the west by John Murray, partly southeast by William Fannier, on all other sides by vacant land.

Ansley, Thomas
100 acres, Wrightsboro Township, St. Paul Parish
Granted July 7, 1772 Grant Book I, page 689
Bounded on the south by Cowper land.

Ashfield, Henry
Town Lot #70, Wrightsboro, St. Paul Parish; 350 acres, Wrightsboro
Township, St. Paul Parish, bounded on the southwest by Joseph Maddock.
Granted July 3, 1770 Grant Book I, page 114

Ashmore, Frederick
100 acres, Wrightsboro Township, St. Paul Parish
Granted June 7, 1774 Grant Book I, page 1059
Bounded on the east by William Wallace.

Ashmore, Frederick
250 acres, St. Paul Parish
Granted February 7, 1775

Ashmore, James
150 acres, St. Paul Parish
Survey date not given
Granted June 7, 1774 Grant Book M, page 972 Plat Book C, page
445 Grant Book I, page 1077

Ashton, Edward
200 acres, St. Paul Parish
Granted September 6, 1774 Grant Book M, page 277
Bounded on the northwest by Woodtucker.

Atkinson, Joshua
200 acres, District of Augusta
Granted June 7, 1757 Grant Book A, page 405

Atwood, Isaac
Town Lot #8, Augusta, containing 1 acre.
Granted August 5, 1766 Grant Book E, page 326
Bounded on the north by the Bay of Augusta, south by a street,
east by James Jarers' lot, and west by James Jackson's lot.

Atwood, Isaac
500 acres, St. Paul Parish
Granted April 7, 1767 Grant Book F, page 152
Bounded by the back line of the Township of Augusta and the lots
thereof known by #37, #38, and #39; and on every other side by
vacant land. Tract was originally allotted and laid out to Cornelius
Doherty who transferred his right and title therein and thereto unto
the said Isaac Atwood.

Austin, Richard
Granted July 3, 1770 Grant Book I, page 115

Town Lot #3, Wrightsboro, St. Paul Parish; 100 acres, Wrightsboro Township, St. Paul Parish, bounded on the north by Little River and Joshua Sanders land, said (south-?) by Brevard Herds, on all other sides by vacant land.

Ayres, Abraham
150 acres, St. Paul Parish
Granted January 2, 1770 Grant Book G, page 488
Bounded on the southeast by Great Kioka Creek, and northeast by Joshua Bradley.

Ayres, Abraham
150 acres, St. Paul Parish
Granted June 7, 1774 Grant Book I, page 698

Ayres, Thomas
500 acres, St. Paul Parish
Granted February 5, 1771 Grant Book I, page 245
Bounded on the northeast by Leonard Claiborne, partly on the northwest by Thomas McDowell and Richard Castleberry, partly on the southeast by William Castleberry, and on all other sides by vacant land.

Ayres, William
100 acres, St. Paul Parish
Granted August 2, 1774

Bacon, John
150 acres, St. Paul Parish
Granted July 7, 1772 Grant Book M, page 152 Grant Book I, page 673.

Bacon, John
250 acres, St. Paul Parish
Granted February 7, 1775 Grant Book M, page 983
Bounded on the northwest by John Crawford.

Bailey, George
1000 acres, St. Paul Parish
Granted November 1, 1774 Grant Book M, page 627
Bounded on the southeast by said George Bailey.

Baldwin, David
200 acres, Wrightsboro Township, St. Paul Parish
Granted March 5, 1771 Grant Book I, page 261
Bounded on the east by land ordered William Hixxon, partly

on the northwest by land ordered John Stewart, Jr., and on all other sides by vacant land.

Barfield, Solomon
100 acres, Wrightsboro Township, St. Paul Parish
Granted November 1, 1774 Grant Book M, page 630
Bounded on the east by John Howard, north by the said John Howard, west by Aaron Singefield, and south by the old Indian line and path.

Barnard, Edward
500 acres, District of Augusta
Granted February 5, 1757 Grant Book A, page 417
Bounded on the southeast by the Savannah River, northeast by Nathaniel Bassett, northwest by John Pettygrew, and southwest by Thomas Bassett.

Barnard, Edward
450 acres, District of Augusta, St. Paul Parish
Surveyed December 10, 1756 Plat Book M, page 12
Granted February 7, 1764 Grant Book D, page 384
Bounded on the east by the Savannah River, north by Thomas Smith, and south by Township lots of Augusta.

Barnard, Edward
160 acres, St. Paul Parish
Surveyed March 4, 1760 Plat Book M, page 78
Granted March 5, 1765 Grant Book E, page 116
Bounded on the east by the Savannah River; southwest by James Frazer, deceased; north by Richard Spencer, deceased.

Barnard, Edward
100 acres, St. Paul Parish
Granted October 29, 1765

Barnard, Edward
Town Lot #33, Augusta
Granted May 3, 1768

Barnard, Edward
650 acres, St. Paul Parish
Granted February 6, 1770 Grant Book E, page 278 Grant
Book F, page 438 Grant Book G, page 513
Tract surrounds a tract of Nicholas Caskell on three sides and is
bounded on the east and southeast by Robert Hatcher, south by
Sherwood Bugg.

Barnard, Edward
350 acres, St. Paul Parish
Granted October 1, 1771 Grant Book I, page 424
Bounded on the southwest by Leonard Claiborne, southeast by
William Burgamy, northeast partly by Edmund Bugg and partly by
vacant land, northwest by land surveyed for Weakly.

Barnard, Edward
500 acres, St. Paul Parish
Granted February 7, 1775 Grant Book M, page 980
Bounded on the northeast by Robert Morrow, northwest by Robert
Middleton and Samuel Janson, southwest by the old Indian line
and path, southeast by Thomas Young.

Barnard, Edward
500 acres, St. Paul Parish
Granted February 7, 1775 Grant Book M, page 981
Bounded on the northeast by Charles Jordan.

Barnard, Edward
200 acres, St. Paul Parish
Granted February 7, 1775 Grant Book M, page 982
Bounded on the north by David Peacy, William Candler, and
vacant land; west by Elizabeth Dicott.

Barnard, Timothy
200 acres, St. Paul Parish
Granted January 3, 1775 Grant Book M, page 847

Bounded on the southeast by Oliver Mathis and Isaac Lewis, southwest by Stephen Day.

Barnes, George
150 acres, St. Paul Parish
Granted November 1, 1774 Grant Book M, page 629

Barnett, Nathan
200 acres, St. Paul Parish
Granted April 2, 1771 Grant Book I, page 279

Barnett, William
50 acres, St. Paul Parish
Granted July 7, 1772 Grant Book I, page 696
Bounded on the west by said grantee.

Barnett, William
33 acres, St. Paul Parish
Surveyed October 26, 1758 Plat Book C, page 27
No grant recorded.
Tract is an island at Woods Cutoff in the Savannah River. Original warrant says tract located in the Savannah River near a place called Point Comfort.

Barnett, William
200 acres, St. Paul Parish
Granted April 2, 1771 Grant Book I, page 280

Barry, George
500 acres, St. Paul Parish
Granted November 1, 1774 Grant Book M, page 622

Barry, George
500 acres, St. Paul Parish
Granted November 1, 1774 Grant Book M, page 623

Bassett, Thomas
500 acres, District of Augusta, St. Paul Parish
Original survey date unknown but resurveyed on July 16, 1785
Plat Book M, page 1
Granted May 1, 1762 Grant Book D, page 96

Bounded on the northeast and southeast by the Savannah River and Rocky Creek. "Robert Walton of said county (Richmond) bought a reserve of 500 acres of land formerly surveyed for and granted to Thomas Bassett, in the district of Augusta and Parish of St. Paul, which was confiscated and sold as the property of James Seamore to the said Robert Walton. . ." (see Plat Book M, page 1.)

Bassett, Thomas
530 acres, St. Paul Parish
Surveyed July 17, 1766 Plat Book M, page 77
Granted June 7, 1768 Grant Book G, page 117
Tract was originally allotted to Thomas Bassett, Sr., deceased, the late father of Thomas Bassett.   Bounded on the east by the Savannah River, south by Mr. Macartan and Mr. Campbell, north by Joseph and Sarah Day, west by vacant land.

Beall, Jacob
300 acres, St. Paul Parish
Granted April 13, 1761 Grant Book C, page 113
Bounded on the south by John Stewart, and east by the Savannah River.

Beall, Jacob
100 acres, St. Paul Parish
Granted July 7, 1772 Grant Book I, page 690
Bounded on the east by John Phillips, and west by Hezekiah Wade.

Beavin, Benjamin
150 acres, St. Paul Parish
Granted November 7, 1769 Grant Book G, page 454

Beck, George
Town Lot #59, Wrightsboro, St. Paul Parish; 150 acres, Wrightsboro
Township, St. Paul Parish.
Granted July 3, 1770 Grant Book I, page 116

Begbie, Francis
500 acres, St. Paul Parish
Granted December 6, 1774 Grant Book M, page 778

~ 44 ~

Bounded on the north by John Germany, Richard Meadoweys, and Great Kioka Creek; southwest by John Pitman and vacant land.

Begbie, Francis
500 acres, St. Paul Parish
Granted January 3, 1775 Grant Book M, page 857
Bounded on the southwest by Robinson, and northwest by the Little River.

Beidell, Absalom
250 acres, Wrightsboro, St. Paul Parish
Granted December 6, 1774 Grant Book M, page 777
Bounded on the northwest by Robert McClung and vacant land, and southwest by Joseph Hollingsworth.

Bell, Henry
150 acres, St. Paul Parish
Surveyed September 17, 1761 Plat Book C, page 27
Granted January 4, 1763 Grant Book D, page 272
Bounded on the south by John Stewart, west by Nehemiah Wade. Original warrant says, "150 acres in the River Swamp between McBean's Swamp and Spirit Creek near lands granted John Fitch and Jacob Bell."

Bennett, John
100 acres, St. Paul Parish
Granted July 7, 1772 Grant Book I, page 658
Bounded on the west by John Perkins.

Bennett, John
150 acres, St. Paul Parish
Granted August 2, 1774 Grant Book M, page 160
Bounded on the southeast by William Jackson, northeast by Edmund Bugg, and on the northwest by Edward Barnard.

Bentz, Charles
100 acres, St. Paul Parish
Granted August 2, 1774 Grant Book M, page 153
Bounded on the northeast by John Shaw.

Bereston, Aaron
200 acres, St. Paul
Granted May 1, 1759 Grant Book B, page 140
Bounded on the east by the Savannah River and Williams Creek, northwest by Hugh Middleton.

Biggot, Elisha
100 acres, Wrightsboro Township, St. Paul Parish
Granted June 7, 1774 Grant Book I, page 1093
Bounded on the northeast by John Slatter.

Bird, Richard
100 acres, St. Paul Parish
Surveyed June 26, 1769 Plat Book C, page 27
No grant recorded.

Bishop, James
100 acres, Wrightsboro Township, St. Paul Parish
Granted June 7, 1774 Grant Book I, page 1066

Bishop, James
250 acres, Wrightsboro Township, St. Paul Parish
Granted December 6, 1774 Grant Book M, page 775
Bounded on the north by Isaac Dennis, John Dennis, and Little River; west by Ralph Kilgore; southwest by Daniel Miles.

Blake, William
200 acres, St. Paul Parish
Surveyed October 24, 1769 Plat Book C, page 28
Granted March 6, 1770 Grant Book G, page 535

Blanchard, Rheuben
150 acres, St. Paul Parish
Granted January 3, 1775 Grant Book M, page 852
Bounded on the west and south by John Seventz.

Boggs, Joseph
100 acres, Wrightsboro Township, St. Paul Parish
Granted January 19, 1773 Grant Book I, page 843
Bounded on the east by Thomas Andsley, and south by John Smith.

Bolton, Robert
550 acres, St. Paul Parish
Granted February 7, 1775 Grant Book M, page 973
Bounded on the south by John Rae and Benjamin Jones, west by
George Galphin, and east by Bugg and unknown land.

Booth, Abraham
100 acres, St. Paul Parish
Granted August 2, 1768 Grant Book G, page 149
Bounded on the north and west by the Little River.

Booth, Abraham
150 acres, St. Paul Parish
Granted August 2, 1774 Grant Book M, page 159

Booth, William
300 acres, District of Augusta
Granted March 28, 1758 Grant Book A, page 658
Bounded on the east by the Savannah River, and on the south by
Williams Creek.

Bostick, Chesley
Town Lot #36, a corner lot, Augusta
Granted September 2, 1766 Grant Book E, page 351
Bounded on the east by Ilia Street, west by Lot #37, north by a
back street, and south by the town common.

Bostick, Chesley
Town Lot #6, on the bay, Augusta
Granted December 6, 1774 Grant Book L, page 200

Bostick, Chesley
1000 acres, St. Paul Parish
Granted December 6, 1774 Grant Book M, page 773-B
Bounded on the south by Isaac Low, said Chesley Bostick, and
vacant land; and partly on the north by Jolly.

Bostick, Chessly
100 acres, St. Paul Parish
Surveyed November 9, 1765 Grant Book C, page 27
No grant recorded.

Bounded on the east by the Savannah River, south by John Phillip, west by John Fitch, and on the north by John Fitch.

Bostick, John
250 acres, St. Paul Parish
Granted January 1, 1765 Grant Book E, page 87
Bounded on the north by the Savannah River, and on the west by Sarah Clark.

Bourquin, Henry
500 acres, St. Paul Parish
Granted December 6, 1774 Grant Book M, page 773
Bounded on the southeast by John Carson and Samuel Wenslet, southwest by John Jamieson.

Bourquin, Henry Lewis
500 acres, St. Paul Parish
Granted November 1, 1774 Grant Book M, page 625
Bounded on the southwest by Daniel McNiear, Nathaniel Woods, and land laid out; north by John Parker, Daniel Richardson, James McFarland, James Grierson, and vacant land.

Bowie, James
100 acres, Wrightsboro Township, St. Paul Parish
Granted September 6, 1774 Grant Book M, page 282

Boyd, John
200 acres, St. Paul Parish
Granted June 7, 1774 Grant Book I, page 1019
Bounded on the southeast partly by James Frierson and partly by vacant land, southwest by Isaac Lewis, on all other sides by vacant land.

Boyd, John
400 acres, St. Paul Parish
Granted January 3, 1775 Grant Book M, page 850
Bounded on the northwest by Robert Germany, and on the southeast by Isaac Lewis and John Boyd.

Bradley, Joshua
250 acres, St. Paul Parish

Granted October 3, 1769 Grant Book G, page 421
Bounded on the southwest by Abraham Ayres.

Bradley, Joshua
100 acres, St. Paul Parish
Granted July 5, 1774 Grant Book M, page 12
Bounded on the south by said Joshua Bradley, northeast by land laid out for Ebenezer Smith.

Brewer, James
300 acres, St. Paul Parish
Granted November 7, 1769 Grant Book G, page 471
Bounded on the east by John Cleckler and William Taylor, south by Herran.

Bricon, John
150 acres, St. Paul Parish
Granted September 6, 1774 Grant Book M, page 287
Bounded on the southwest by James Emett.

Brown, Coleman
150 acres, St. Paul Parish
Granted August 2, 1774 Grant Book M, page 164

Brown, James
396 acres, St. Paul Parish
Granted February 5, 1760 Grant Book B, page 318
Bounded on the northeast and south by the Savannah River.

Brown, James
Town Lot #1, First Row, Augusta
Granted February 5, 1760 Grant Book B, page 319

Brown, James
150 acres, St. Paul Parish
Granted October 4, 1774 Grant Book M, page 423
Bounded on the east by Weakley and on the northwest by James Oliver.

Brown, John
250 acres, St. Paul Parish

Granted January 19, 1773 Grant Book I, page 844
Bounded on the north by John Crawford.

Brown, Joseph
300 acres, St. Paul Parish
Granted March 2, 1773 Grant Book I, page 912
Bounded on the southwest by John Carson.

Bryan, John
100 acres, Wrightsboro Township, St. Paul Parish
Granted August 4, 1772 Grant Book I, page 707

Bryan, William
200 acres, St. Paul Parish
Granted December 6, 1774 Grant Book M, page 776
Bounded on the northwest by Colonel James Jackson, southeast by
Isaac Low. Page 21 is a blank page. This occurred because one
page was misnumbered in the original manuscript. No grants are
left out.

Bugg, Edmund
200 acres, St. Paul Parish
Granted December 4, 1770 Grant Book I, page 214
Bounded on the northeast and partly on the southeast by William
Chandler and on all other sides by vacant land.

Bugg, Edmund
38 acres, St. Paul Parish
Granted April 4, 1775 Grant Book M, page 1095
Bounded on the west by Sherwood Bugg, east by Edmund Bugg,
and on the south by the Savannah River.

Bugg, John
200 acres, St. Paul Parish
Surveyed May, 1769 Plat Book M, page 54
Granted October 3, 1769 Grant Book G, page 422
Bounded on the northwest by Jacob Castleberry.

Bugg, Sherwood
50 acres, St. Paul Parish
Granted July 5, 1768 Grant Book H, page 8

Bounded on the south by the Savannah River, west by Rocky Creek, and northeast by Robert Hatcher.

Bugg, Sherwood
400 acres, St. Paul Parish
Granted January 2, 1770 Grant Book G, page 489
Bounded on the south by north fork of Great Kioka Creek.

Bugg, Sherwood
300 acres, St. Paul Parish
Granted July 5, 1774 Grant Book M, page 6
Bounded on the northwest by John Upton, John Howard, and Benjamin Few; northeast by Thomas Kershaw and said Sherwood Bugg; northwest by said Sherwood Bugg; southwest by vacant land.

Bugg, Sherwood
300 acres, St. Paul Parish
Granted January 2, 1770 Grant Book G, page 490
Bounded on the southwest by north fork of Kioka Creek.

Bulloch, Archibald
400 acres, St. Paul Parish
Granted March 7, 1775 Grant Book M, page 1067
Bounded on the northeast by Hugh Middleton, Robert Middleton, and George Galphin; southeast by Alexander Scot and vacant land.

Bulloch, Archibald
200 acres, St. Paul Parish
Granted March 7, 1775 Grant Book M, page 1068
Bounded on the west by Little River and Booth, north by Stephen Herd and Little River, southwest by John Howard.

Bulloch, Archibald
600 acres, St. Paul Parish
Granted March 7, 1775 Grant Book M, page 1069
Bounded on the north by James Coats, Jacob Cassel, and Jacob Watson; south by John Watson, Governor Wright, and Job Smith; west by Isaac Jackson and Jacob Watson; east by Joseph Boggs.

Burgamy, William
500 acres, St. Paul Parish
Granted November 7, 1769 Grant Book G, page 455

Burgamy, William
200 acres, St. Paul Parish
Surveyed September 3, 1769 Plat Book M, page 33
Granted August 2, 1774 Grant Book M, page 165
Bounded on the northwest by William Jackson.

Burkes, John
200 acres, Wrightsboro Township, St. Paul Parish
Granted July 7, 1772 Grant Book I, page 688
Bounded on the south by John Bryan, and northeast by Holland Middleton.

Burnes, John
200 acres, St. Paul Parish
Granted May 7, 1765 Grant Book E, page 145
Bounded on the northwest by the Savannah River.

Burnet, Daniel
100 acres, St. Paul Parish
Granted October 4, 1774 Grant Book M, page 421
Bounded on the north, east and west by the Little River.

Burnet, John
150 acres, St. Paul Parish
Granted November 1, 1774 Grant Book M, page 624
Bounded on the southwest by Wallace.

Burns, Andrew
50 acres, Wrightsboro, St. Paul Parish
Granted January 3, 1775 Grant Book M, page 854
Bounded on the north by John Thompson, and southeast by James Jackson and Williams Creek.

Burton, Joseph
300 acres, St. Paul Parish
Granted February 5, 1760 Grant Book D, page 373
Bounded on the east by the Savannah River.

Butler, Patrick
150 acres, St. Paul Parish
Granted July 2, 1771 Grant Book I, page 359
Bounded on the east by land ordered Patrick Hollayan, and on all other sides by vacant land.

Caldwell, Alexander
100 acres, St. Paul Parish
Granted June 7, 1774 Grant Book I, page 1074

Callihan, David
100 acres, St. Paul Parish
Granted February 2, 1768 Grant Book G, page 21
Bounded on the southeast by Butler's Creek, north by Richard Wammock, east by land granted Williamson.

Campbell, John
200 acres, St. Paul Parish
Granted January 19, 1773 Grant Book I, page 845
Bounded on the east by Thomas Toney.

Campbell, Martin and McCartan, Francis
50 acres, District of Augusta, St. Paul Parish
Surveyed September 18, 1759 Plat Book C, page 230
Granted October 2, 1759 Grant Book B, page 202
Plat shows tract to be Lot #9, Augusta. Bounded on the northeast by the Savannah River, east by John Fitch, and west by John Pettygrew.

Campbell, Martin and McCartan, Francis
Town Lot #4, Augusta, St. Paul Parish
Granted August 2, 1768 Grant Book F, page 441

Campbell, Martin and McCartan, Francis
500 acres, St. Paul Parish
Granted July 1, 1760 Grant Book I, page 615
Bounded on the north by Thomas Bassett, east by the Savannah River, and south by Nathaniel Bassett.

Candler, William
100 acres, St. Paul Parish

Granted January 3, 1775 Grant Book M, page 864

Candler, William
200 acres, St. Paul Parish
Granted July 3, 1770 Grant Book I, page 44
Bounded on the southwest and northwest by Edmund Bugg.

Candler, William
50 acres, St. Paul Parish
Granted August 7, 1770 Grant Book I, page 68
Bounded on the northwest by Peter Parris.

Candler, William
500 acres, St. Paul Parish
Granted July 7, 1772 Grant Book I, page 684
Bounded on the northwest by Thomas Lynn and James Morrow, east by James Coan, southeast by William McFarland.

Candler, William
200 acres, St. Paul Parish
Granted August 2, 1774 Grant Book M, page 176
Bounded on the northwest by Daniel Pavey, and on the northeast by William Shields.

Candler, William
200 acres, St. Paul Parish
Granted November 1, 1774 Grant Book M, page 636
Bounded on the southwest by Robert Graves.

Carson, John
Town Lot #95, Wrightsboro, St. Paul Parish; 450 acres, Wrightsboro Township, St. Paul Parish.
Granted July 3, 1770 Grant Book I, page 118

Carson, John
150 acres, Wrightsboro Township, St. Paul Parish
Granted July 7, 1772 Grant Book I, page 697
Bounded on the west by Holland Middleton.

Cartledge, Edmund
300 acres, St. Paul Parish

Granted January 5, 1773 Grant Book I, page 826
Bounded on the southeast partly by said grantee, northeast by John Hagin, and on all other sides by vacant land.

Cartledge, Edmund
150 acres, St. Paul Parish
Granted October 1, 1771

Cartledge, Edmund
200 acres, St. Paul Parish
Granted January 5, 1773
Grant Book I, page 429
Grant Book I, page 827
Bounded on the southeast partly by George Limbacker and partly by Elias Valraven, and on all other sides by vacant land.

Castell, Jacob
200 acres, Wrightsboro Township, St. Paul Parish
Granted June 7, 1774 Grant Book I, page 1050

Castle, Jacob
100 acres, Wrightsboro, St. Paul Parish
Granted February 7, 1775 Grant Book M, page 986

Castleberry, Paul
350 acres, St. Paul Parish
Granted October 3, 1769 Grant Book G, page 425
Bounded on the northwest by Richard Castleberry.

Castleberry, Richard
250 acres, St. Paul Parish
Granted October 3, 1769 Grant Book G, page 423
Bounded on the southwest by Leonard Claiborne, northwest by Thomas Ayres, and on the southeast by Paul Castleberry.

Castleberry, William
150 acres, St. Paul Parish
Surveyed November 19, 1772 Plat Book C, page 38
Granted August 2, 1774 Grant Book M, page 167
Bounded on the southeast by William Castleberry.

Castleberry, William
250 acres, St. Paul Parish
Granted October 3, 1769 Grant Book G, page 424
Bounded on the east by Leonard Claiborne.

Castleberry, William
100 acres, St. Paul Parish
Granted July 4, 1769 Grant Book G, page 354

Chadwick, Thomas
100 acres, St. Paul Parish
Granted October 4, 1774 Grant Book M, page 424

Chandler, William
250 acres, St. Paul Parish
Granted August 1, 1769 Grant Book G, page 383
Bounded on the southwest by William Joiner, southeast by William Bugg, and on the northwest by Leonard Claiborne.

Chevalier, Charles Francis
250 acres, St. Paul Parish
Granted November 1, 1774 Grant Book M, page 643
Bounded on the north by William Jones and Thomas Fuller.

Chew, Samuel
200 acres, St. Paul Parish
Surveyed April 6, 1768 Plat Book C, page 37
No grant recorded.
Bounded on the north by the Savannah River, and southeast by Soap Creek. Original warrant says tract located about 40 miles above Augusta, at a place called Soap Creek.

Chew, Samuel
50 acres, St. Paul Parish
Granted July 7, 1761 Grant Book C, page 371
Bounded on the north by the Savannah River.

Chitwin, Joseph
400 acres, St. Paul Parish
Surveyed April 16, 1759 Plat Book C, page 37
No grant recorded.

Bounded on the northeast by the Savannah River, northwest by lands laid out to Patrick Clark.

Christian, John
100 acres, St. Paul Parish
Granted May 3, 1768 Grant Book G, page 96
Bounded on the west by Henry Bellto, north by Daniel Walahom, and northeast by John Lamar. Tract was originally ordered to be surveyed for Richard Southerton.

Claiborne, Leonard
850 acres, St. Paul Parish
Granted September 5, 1769 Grant Book G, page 407
Bounded on the southwest by Doctor Walsh, northeast by William Castleberry and vacant land, southeast by Richard Castleberry and Thomas Ayres.

Claiborne, Leonard Jr.
700 acres, St. Paul Parish
Granted September 1, 1767 Grant Book F, page 340

Claiborne, Leonard Jr.
150 acres, St. Paul Parish
Granted September 1, 1767 Grant Book F, page 341
Tract located at the falls of Great Kiokee Creek.

Clark, Barbara
200 acres, St. Paul Parish
Granted January 3, 1775 Grant Book M, page 863

Clark, Daniel and McGillivray, Lachlan
500 acres, District of Augusta
Granted September 8, 1756 Grant Book A, page 200
Bounded on the northeast by the Savannah River, southeast by Edward Barnard, and northwest by Rae and Barksdale.

Clark, Daniel and McGillivray, Lachlan
Town Lot #17, Augusta
Granted September 8, 1756 Grant Book A, page 201

Clark, John
Town Lot #16, Augusta
Granted February 7, 1764 Grant Book D, page 378

Clark, John
Lot #29, Augusta, containing 50 acres
Granted February 7, 1764 Grant Book D, page 379
Bounded on the east by the Town Common, southwest by John Fitch, northwest by Lot #30, and southeast by Lot #28.

Clark, John
Lot #4, Augusta, containing 50 acres
Granted February 7, 1764 Grant Book D, page 380
Bounded on the north by the Savannah River, east by Gilbert Fyffe, south by William Clark, and on the west by John Douglas.

Clark, John
300 acres, St. Paul Parish
Granted February 7, 1764 Grant Book D, page 381
Bounded on the northeast by the Savannah River, northwest by Matthew Allen, and on the southeast by Thomas Mooney.

Clark, William
Farm Lot #15, St. Paul Parish, containing 50 acres
Granted October 4, 1763 Grant Book D, page 341
Bounded on the northeast by lot of the widow Fife and Day, northwest by lot of David Douglas, southwest by Lot #21, southeast by Captain Williams.

Clark, William
Town Lot #27, Third Row, Augusta
Granted October 4, 1763 Grant Book D, page 342

Clarke, Patrick
200 acres, 70 miles north of Augusta
Surveyed February 15, 1754 Plat Book C, page 41
No grant recorded.
Tract is located in what became the Ceded Lands and was surveyed in two tracts, 150 acres on the north side of the Broad River, and 50 acres opposite on the south side. Tract was formerly possessed by Mr. Gregory Hains.

Clement, William
300 acres, District of Augusta
Granted September 30, 1757 Grant Book A, page 651
Bounded on the north by the Savannah River, and west by John Kennedy.

Clemm, William
200 acres, St. Paul Parish
Granted September 6, 1763 Grant Book D, page 329
Bounded on the north by the Savannah River.

Clemm, William
150 acres, St. Paul Parish
Granted October 2, 1764 Grant Book E, page 39
Bounded on the north by Daniel Deruzeau, and east by said William Clemm.

Clickler, John
100 acres, St. Paul Parish
Granted December 6, 1768 Grant Book G, page 226
Bounded on the east by Thomas Red, and northwest by William Taylor.

Clickler, John
450 acres, St. Paul Parish
Granted May 2, 1769 Grant Book G, page 314
Tract located on a branch of Uchee Creek.

Closman, Frederick
Town Lot #28, Augusta
Granted September 7, 1762 Grant Book D, page 214

Cloud, Joel
Town Lot #9, Wrightsboro, St. Paul Parish; 100 acres, St. Paul Parish, bounded on the west by land granted to Cloud, north by land surveyed for Samuel Hart.
Granted July 3, 1770 Grant Book I, page 119

Cloud, Joel
100 acres, Wrightsboro Township, St. Paul Parish
Granted April 7, 1772 Grant Book I, page 547

Bounded on the southeast by said grantee, and northeast by Samuel Hart.

Coan, James
200 acres, St. Paul Parish
Granted January 2, 1770 Grant Book G, page 495

Coats, Henry
200 acres, St. Paul Parish
Granted August 2, 1774 Grant Book M, page 169
Bounded on the northwest by Craft Hencott, southwest by Saunders Walen, and southeast by James Keff and vacant land.

Coats, James
200 acres, Wrightsboro Township, St. Paul Parish
Granted June 7, 1774 Grant Book I, page 1089
Bounded partly on the north and partly on the east by John Perkins and Joseph Boggs, partly on the south and partly on the west by Jacob Casten, on all other sides (parts) by vacant land.

Coats, Nathaniel
200 acres, St. Paul Parish
Granted August 2, 1774 Grant Book M, page 171
Bounded on the east by Leonard Claiborne and William McMunan.

Cobb, James Jr.
100 acres, St. Paul Parish
Granted July 5, 1774 Grant Book M, page 21
Bounded on the southwest by Samuel Wells.

Cobb, Joseph
150 acres, St. Paul Parish
Granted July 5, 1774 Grant Book M, page 22
Bounded on the east by William Jackson, west by William Burgamy.

Cobbs, James
50 acres, St. Paul Parish
Granted August 2, 1774 Grant Book H, page 119
Bounded on the west by Sherwood Bugg.

Cobbs, James
200 acres, Wrightsboro Township, St. Paul Parish
Granted December 6, 1774 Grant Book M, page 782
Bounded on the southwest by James Cobbs and on the northeast by William Lamar.

Cobbs, James
100 acres, St. Paul Parish
Granted December 6, 1774 Grant Book M, page 783
Bounded on the southwest by Barfield, and northeast by James Cobbs.

Cobbs, John
300 acres, St. Paul Parish
Granted November 1, 1774 Grant Book M, page 641
Bounded on the southwest, northwest, northeast, and southeast by Howard and Few; northeast by John Bennett; northwest by land ordered Benjamin Upton.

Cochrane, Cornelius
Town Lot #78, Wrightsboro, St. Paul Parish; 300 acres, Wrightsboro Township, St. Paul Parish, bounded on the northeast by Peter Perkins.
Granted July 3, 1770 Grant Book I, page 117

Coleman, Daniel
400 acres, St. Paul Parish
Granted June 7, 1774 Grant Book I, page 1020
Bounded on the northeast by B. Wells, Daniel Coleman, and

James Brown; southwest by land said to be Mitchell's and land of Robert Story.

Collins, Andrew
100 acres, St. Paul Parish
Surveyed August 13, 1759 Plat Book C, page 37
No grant recorded.
Bounded on the northeast by the Savannah River, and southeast by Bennett's improvement. Original warrant says, "100 acres adjoining Bennett's Improvement on the Savannah River."

Colman, Daniel
200 acres, St. Paul Parish
Granted August 2, 1774 Grant Book M, page 173
Tract located at the forks of the Great Kioka Creek.

Combes, William
50 acres, St. Paul Parish
Surveyed December 18, 1764 Plat Book M, page 11
Granted July 7, 1767 Grant Book F, page 288
Bounded on the north by Sarah Wisely. Tract surveyed as Coombs
and granted as Combes. William Combes was a disbanded soldier.

Cooke, Robert; Jackson, James; McIntosh, Alexander
800 acres, St. Paul Parish
Surveyed October 29, 1766 Plat Book C, page 88
Granted March 3, 1767 Grant Book F, page 116

Cooper, Isaac
200 acres, Wrightsboro Township, St. Paul Parish
Granted June 7, 1774 Grant Book I, page 1021
Bounded on the southeast by Bubbey (or Buffey.)

Coppe, Jonathan (The Reverend)
Town Lot #16, Augusta, containing 1 acre
Surveyed January 20, 1756. Not recorded in Plat Books; see
original warrant (dated August 17, 1755) in Colonial Detached Plat
File.
No grant recorded.
Original warrant says lot known by the number 16 in the Second
Row, containing one acre of land.

Cornell, George
200 acres, St. Paul Parish
Granted October 1, 1765 Grant Book E, page 246

Cornell, George
125 acres, St. Paul Parish
Granted March 1, 1768 Grant Book G, page 43
Bounded on the south by the Savannah River, southwest by Mr.
McGillivray, and Mr. Spencer, northwest by Benjamin
Williamson, and on the northeast by Christopher Fulbright.

Cosey, David
200 acres, St. Paul Parish
Surveyed December 9, 1771 Plat Book M, page 18
Granted April 6, 1773 Grant Book I, page 936

Cowen, George
100 acres, St. Paul Parish
Granted July 5, 1774 Grant Book M, page 20

Craus, Leonard
100 acres, St. Paul Parish
Granted September 5, 1758 Grant Book B, page 48
Bounded on the southeast by John Cornberger, northwest by
George Fowl, and on the northeast by Theobald Kiefer.

Crawford, Charles
250 acres, St. Paul Parish
Granted October 6, 1772 Grant Book I, page 768
Bounded on the east by Moses Deaser.

Crawford, Charles
200 acres, St. Paul Parish
Granted June 7, 1774 Grant Book I, page 1053
Bounded on the northeast by John McDonald.

Crawford, Charles
150 acres, St. Paul Parish
Granted January 3, 1775 Grant Book M, page 861
Bounded on the northwest by Ramsey, north by Peter Colbreath,
and east by Peter and Benjamin Youngblood.

Crawford, John
200 acres, St. Paul Parish
Granted February 2, 1773 Grant Book I, page 900
Bounded on the north by Grier's land.

Crawford, John
200 acres, St. Paul Parish
Granted November 1, 1774 Grant Book M, page 642
Bounded on the northwest by said John Crawford and Thomas
Green.

Crittenden, Elizabeth
550 acres, St. Paul Parish
Granted September 6, 1774 Grant Book M, page 297
Bounded on the east by the Savannah River, west by Charles Parks
and Arthur Owensbee, south by Arthur Owensbee.

Crittenden, William
100 acres, St. Paul Parish
Granted September 6, 1774 Grant Book M, page 298
Bounded on the southwest by Charles Anderson, and northeast by
William Satterwhite.

Crittenden, William
300 acres, St. Paul Parish
Granted April 4, 1775 Grant Book M, page 1098
Bounded on the southwest by Benjamin Wells, northeast by vacant
land, northwest by William Phelps, and southeast by Frederick
Ashmore. Crook, Robert; McKintosh, Alexander; Jackson, James,
seven lots in Augusta as follows: #27 (a vacant lot) and six lots,
#13, #14, #19, #20, #26, and #36. The latter six lots were
purchased by Crook, McKintosh, and Jackson from the original
proprietors. Total of 350 acres (50 acres per lot.) Original
proprietors not named.

Crosswell, Mary (widow)
Town Lot #26, a corner lot, in the third row, Augusta, containing 1
acre. Surveyed January 20, 1756
Not recorded in Plat Books. See original warrant (dated October
17, 1755) in Colonial Detached Plat File.
No grant recorded.

Cureton, Richard
100 acres, St. Paul Parish
Granted December 6, 1774
Grant Book M, page 780

Cutbreth, Peter
250 acres, St. Paul Parish
Granted August 2, 1774 Grant Book M, page 168

Bounded on the northwest by said Peter Cutbreth and surveyed land for some person unknown, southwest by Peter Youngblood, on all other sides by vacant land.

Daniel, William
300 acres, Wrightsboro Township, St. Paul Parish
Granted March 7, 1775 Grant Book M, page 1070
Bounded on the east by George Beck's and vacant land.

Danielly, John
100 acres, St. Paul Parish
Granted July 5, 1774 Grant Book M, page 24

Dasher, Martin
150 acres, St. Paul Parish
Granted October 29, 1765 Grant Book E, page 318
Bounded on the northeast by Ogeechee River, northwest by Micajah Plummer, southeast by Thomas Davis, and on the southwest by John Lane.

Davis, John
150 acres, Wrightsboro Township, St. Paul Parish
Granted June 7, 1774 Grant Book I, page 1084
Bounded on the northwest by Thomas Watson.

Davis, John
100 acres, Wrightsboro Township, St. Paul Parish
Granted November 1, 1774 Grant Book M, page 649
Bounded on the northeast by James Hill.

Davis, Theophilus
100 acres, St. Paul Parish
Granted October 4, 1774 Grant Book M, page 429
Bounded on the southwest by Thomas Morris.

Day, Josiah and Day, Mary
500 acres, St. Paul Parish
Surveyed March 10, 1758 and December 20, 1762. Recorded in Plat Book M, page 10 and Plat Book C, page 53.
Granted January 4, 1763 Grant Book D, page 271

Bounded on the east by the Savannah River; north by Brown, Martin Campbell, McBean, and Joseph Oaks; south by Thomas Bassett. Tract originally surveyed for Owen Day, father of Josiah and Mary Day (see Plat Book C, page 53 and Plat Book M, page 10.) Granted to Josiah and Mary Day.

Day, Owen (father of Josiah and Mary Day)
500 acres, St. Paul Parish
Surveyed March 10, 1758 and December 20, 1762. Recorded in Plat Book M, page 10 and Plat Book C, page 53.
Granted January 4, 1763 Grant Book D, page 271
Bounded on the east by the Savannah River; north by Brown, Martin Campbell, McBean, and Joseph Oaks; south by Thomas Bassett. Tract originally surveyed for Owen Day, father of Josiah and Mary Day (see Plat Book C, page 53 and Plat Book M, page 10.) Granted to Josiah and Mary Day.

Day, Stephen
50 acres, St. Paul Parish
Granted April 7, 1772 Grant Book H, page 75

Day, Stephen
Town Lot #61, Wrightsboro, St. Paul Parish; 200 acres, Wrightsboro
Township, St. Paul Parish.
Granted July 3, 1770 Grant Book I, page 120

Day, Stephen
150 acres, St. Paul Parish
Granted August 2, 1774 Grant Book M, page 179
Bounded on the northeast by said Stephen Day and vacant land.

DeArey, Joseph
200 acres, St. Paul Parish
Granted November 1, 1774 Grant Book M, page 647
Bounded on the southeast and southwest by John Wells, and northwest by William Johnston.

Denison, Patrick
150 acres, Wrightsboro Township, St. Paul Parish
Granted July 7, 1772 Grant Book I, page 674

Dennis, Abraham
Town Lot #29, Wrightsboro, St. Paul Parish; 300 acres, Wrightsboro Township, St. Paul Parish, bounded on the west by land granted Henry Ashfield and vacant land, east by land granted Cornelius Cochrane and vacant land, on all other sides by vacant land.
Granted July 3, 1770 Grant Book I, page 122

Dennis, Isaac
100 acres, Wrightsboro Township, St. Paul Parish
Granted September 6, 1774 Grant Book M, page 304
Bounded on the north by John Dennis, Benjamin Jackson and Little River; east by Benjamin Jackson and vacant land; south by vacant land; west by John Dennis and vacant land.

Dennis, Jacob
Town Lot #19, Wrightsboro, St. Paul Parish; 100 acres, Wrightsboro Township, St. Paul Parish, bounded on the northwest by Little River, east by land granted the said Jacob Dennis, south by land granted James McFarland.
Granted July 3, 1770 Grant Book I, page 123

Dennis, Jacob
100 acres, Wrightsboro Township, St. Paul Parish
Granted April 7, 1772 Grant Book I, page 548

Dennis, John
Town Lot #16, Wrightsboro, St. Paul Parish; 150 acres, St. Paul Parish, bounded on the west by Little River and land surveyed for Ralph Kilgore, east by land surveyed for said Dennis.
Granted July 3, 1770 Grant Book I, page 124

Dennis, John
200 acres, St. Paul Parish
Granted May 4, 1773 Grant Book I, page 971
Bounded on the north by the Little River, west by said grantee.

Dennis, John
150 acres, Wrightsboro Township, St. Paul Parish
Granted June 7, 1774 Grant Book I, page 1012

Bounded partly on the east and partly on the west by James McFarland, north by Jacob Dennis, and on all other sides by vacant land.

Dickie, George
200 acres, St. Paul Parish
Surveyed September 27, 1774 Plat Book C, page 54
No grant recorded.
Original warrant says tract located on a branch of Euchee Creek in St. Paul Parish including his improvement.

Didcott, Elizabeth
600 acres, St. Paul Parish
Surveyed August 10, 1774 Plat Book M, page 31
Granted November 1, 1774 Grant Book M, page 648
Bounded on the east by John Bennett, John Perkins, and vacant land; west by land surveyed for Stubbs and vacant land; south by John Slatter, William Candler, and Dial Parey.

Dobbins, John
250 acres, St. Paul Parish
Surveyed November 27, 1766 Plat Book M, page 6
Granted March 3, 1767 Grant Book F, page 102

Dobbins, John
200 acres, St. Paul Parish
Granted March 3, 1767 Grant Book F, page 101

Dodds, John
100 acres, St. Paul Parish
Granted August 7, 1770 Grant Book I, page 69
Bounded on the northeast by the Savannah River, and on the northwest by Samuel Getson and Robert Hatcher.

Dolittle, Joseph
150 acres, St. Paul Parish
Granted January 3, 1775 Grant Book M, page 869
Bounded on the northeast by unknown, northwest by Kioka Creek and Daniel Colman, southwest by vacant land.

Donelly, John
200 acres, St. Paul Parish
Granted September 5, 1769 Grant Book G, page 408

Donnolly, James and Donnolly, Catherine
550 acres, Wrightsboro Township, St. Paul Parish
Surveyed September 19, 1774 Plat Book C, page 53
No grant recorded.
Bounded on the north by Zachariah Phillips, Benjamin Few, and vacant land; south by Samuel Alexander; west by William Mitchell and Williams Creek (see original plat in Colonial Detached Plat File.)

Douglas, David
Town Lot #2, Augusta; 54 acres, Township of Augusta, bounded on the northeast by the Savannah River, northwest by John Finlay, southwest by Samuel Dean, southeast by John Douglas.
Granted December 16, 1756 Grant Book A, page 243

Douglas, John
Lot #3, Township of Augusta, St. Paul Parish containing 50 acres
Granted October 6, 1767 Grant Book F, page 378
Bounded on the northeast by the Savannah River, southeast by Lot #4 belonging to John Clarke, northwest by Lot #2 belonging to David Douglas, southwest by Lot #14 belonging to Robert Crooke.

Dover, John
Town Lot #74, Wrightsboro; 300 acres, Wrightsboro Township, St. Paul Parish.
Granted July 3, 1770 Grant Book I, page 616

Downs, Henry
350 acres, St. Paul Parish (including a 12 acre island)
Granted September 6, 1768 Grant Book G, page 173
Bounded on the northeast by the Savannah River.

Duckworth, Jeremiah
300 acres, St. Paul Parish
Granted January 19, 1773 Grant Book I, page 851

Duff, Dennis
100 acres, St. Paul Parish
Granted October 4, 1774 Grant Book M, page 430
Bounded on the west by William Wheat, north by Little River, and on the east by Mr. Herds.

Dunkin, John
300 acres, Wrightsboro Township, St. Paul Parish
Granted June 7, 1774 Grant Book

Dunn, Benjamin
Town Lot #75, Wrightsboro; 150 acres, Wrightsboro Township, St. Paul Parish.
Granted July 3, 1770 Grant Book I, page 121

Dunn, John
100 acres, Wrightsboro Township, St. Paul Parish
Granted October 6, 1772 Grant Book I, page 762

Dunn, Robert
350 acres, St. Paul Parish
Granted December 6, 1774 Grant Book M, page 784
Bounded on the southeast by Abenton Phelps.

Durozeaux, Daniel
500 acres, St. Paul Parish
Granted May 7, 1765 Grant Book E, page 146
Bounded on the east by the Savannah River, north by William Clemm, and on the south by James Paris.

Eatton, Mary
250 acres, St. Paul Parish
Granted July 5, 1774 Grant Book M, page 26

Eckles, Edward
Town Lot #96, Wrightsboro; 200 acres, Wrightsboro Township, St. Paul Parish.
Granted July 3, 1770 Grant Book I, page 127

Eckles, Edward
100 acres, Wrightsboro Township, St. Paul Parish

Granted September 6, 1774 Grant Book M, page 308
Bounded on the northeast by Mordecai Moore, northwest and southwest by Edward Eckles.

Eerherd, Gabriel
300 acres, St. Paul Parish
Granted July 5, 1774 Grant Book M, page 27
Bounded on the northeast by Charles Lucas.

Elam, William
Town Lot #25, Wrightsboro; 250 acres, Wrightsboro Township, St. Paul Parish.
Granted July 3, 1770 Grant Book I, page 125

Elam, William
100 acres, St. Paul Parish
Granted July 5, 1774 Grant Book M, page 31
Bounded on the southwest by said William Elam, northeast by John Bryan, and on all other sides by vacant land.

Elliott, Peter
100 acres, District of Augusta
Granted March 28, 1758 Grant Book A, page 588
Tract located on the south side of a branch of Briar Creek.

Elly, Jacob
200 acres, St. Paul Parish
Granted December 6, 1774 Grant Book M, page 787
Bounded on the southeast by James McFarland, northeast by Robert Lockridge, northwest by Little River and land of Jacob Dennis, southwest by John Dennis.

Elly, Michael
300 acres, St. Paul Parish
Granted March 7, 1775 Grant Book M, page 1073
Bounded on the north by Little River, southwest by land surveyed for persons unknown.

Emanuel, John
100 acres, District of Augusta
Granted June 7, 1757 Grant Book A, page 561

Emet, James
100 acres, St. Paul Parish
Granted August 2, 1774 Grant Book M, page 182
Bounded on the northeast by John Bradley.

Emitt, James
Town Lot #26, Wrightsboro; 200 acres, Wrightsboro Township, St. Paul Parish.
Granted July 3, 1770 Grant Book I, page 126
The 200 acre tract is bounded on the southeast by William Farmer, on all other sides by vacant land.

Faming, Joachim Noel
200 acres, St. Paul Parish
Granted May 4, 1773 Grant Book I, page 972
Bounded on the northeast by James Jervice.

Fanner, William
100 acres, St. Paul Parish
Granted October 4, 1774 Grant Book M, page 436
Bounded on the southwest by David Coosey and Theophilus Davis, east by Theophilus Davis.

Farley, Joseph
500 acres, St. Paul Parish
Granted November 1, 1774 Grant Book M, page 658
Bounded on the southwest by John Crawford and Thomas Grove, southeast by George Dickey, northwest by Thomas Johnson and vacant land.

Farmer, William
Town Lot #21, Wrightsboro, St. Paul Parish; 550 acres, Wrightsboro Township, St. Paul Parish, bounded on the southwest and partly on the southeast by Jonathan Sell, northwest by land of William, on all other sides by vacant land.
Granted July 3, 1770 Grant Book I, page 128

Farrel, John
Granted January 19, 1773 Grant Book I, page 850
Bounded on the northeast by the Savannah River, and on the southeast by James Laimonet.

Fenn, Zachariah
1000 acres, partly in St. George and partly in St. Paul Parishes
Granted April 7, 1772 Grant Book I, page 550
Bounded on the north and east by John Rae and land of said
Zachariah Fenn, southeast by land ordered Philip Alston, west by
land surveyed for said Zachariah Fenn.

Few, Benjamin and Howard, John
1000 acres, Wrightsboro Township, St. Paul Parish
Granted October 4, 1774 Grant Book M, page 558
Bounded on the northwest by Sherwood Bugg, Edmund Bugg,
John Burner, John Cobb, Frederick Francis, and William Candler;
southwest by William Jackson; by Daniel McCarty and Richard
Upton.

Few, Ignatius
100 acres, St. Paul Parish
Granted June 7, 1774 Grant Book I, page 1085
Bounded on the northeast partly by vacant land and partly by
William Few, and on all other sides by vacant land.

Few, William
350 acres, St. Paul Parish
Granted October 3, 1769 Grant Book G, page 430
Bounded on the northwest by Brown.

Finley, William
Lot #28, Township of Augusta, containing 50 acres
No survey or grant recorded, only the following endorsement,
recorded in Plat Book C, pages 174-175. Originally surveyed for
Nicholas Murphy on October 2, 1749 and signed over by Nicholas
Murphy to William Finley (date not shown) and signed over by
William Finley to Richard and Frances Warren on November 30,
1750.

Fitch, Ann (widow of John Fitch, deceased)
179 acres, St. Paul Parish
Granted September 6, 1768 Grant Book G, page 175
Bounded on the west and north by land ordered John Fitch
(Ann Fitch's deceased husband,) east by the Savannah River,

and south by John Phillips.

Fitch, Ann (widow)
500 acres, St. Paul Parish
Surveyed September 30, 1769 Plat Book C, page 63
Granted January 2, 1770 Grant Book G, page 499
Bounded on the southeast by John Tinckler. Original plat (on file in the Colonial Detached Plat File) shows tract bounded by John Tinkler, Spring Branch, and Black Run.

Fitch, Ann
Granted January 7, 1772 Grant Book I, page 493
Bounded on the west by John Morse, east by grantee.

Fitch, John
300 acres, District of Augusta
Granted September 8, 1756 Grant Book A, page 214
Bounded on the north and northeast by the Savannah River, and northwest by a large lagoon and Spirit Creek.

Fitch, John
300 acres, District of Augusta
Granted September 30, 1757 Grant Book A, page 560
Bounded on the north by a great lake which joins other lands of said John Fitch.

Fitch, John
50 acres, District of Augusta
Granted July 4, 1758 Grant Book B, page 41
Bounded on the south by Cornelius Doherty, east by Edward Barnard, north by land late of George Cadagan, deceased.

Flemen, David
100 acres, Wrightsboro Township, St. Paul Parish
Granted October 4, 1774 Grant Book M, page 440

Ford, Thomas
550 acres, St. Paul Parish
Granted March 2, 1773 Grant Book I, page 914

Forrester, Stephen
150 acres, St. Paul Parish
Granted July 5, 1774 Grant Book M, page 34
Bounded on the east by John Rock and William Davis, and south and west by Stephen Forrester.

Fort, Eli
100 acres, St. Paul Parish
Granted January 19, 1773 Grant Book I, page 849
Bounded on the northeast partly by William Tinkler, and on all other sides by vacant land.

Fox, James
150 acres, St. Paul Parish
Granted October 4, 1774 Grant Book M, page 435
Bounded on the southwest by LeKay Hammond, northeast by land surveyed for Wood Tucker, on all other sides by vacant land.

Francis, Frederick
150 acres, St. Paul Parish
Granted October 2, 1770 Grant Book I, page 171
Bounded partly on the northwest by Peter Jarvis, partly on the northeast and partly on the southwest by William Candler,
 and on all other sides by vacant land.

Fulbright, Christian
360 acres, St. Paul Parish
Granted October 2, 1759 Grant Book B, page 260
Bounded on the northwest by vacant land and on all other sides by the Savannah River.

Fuller, John
400 acres, St. Paul Parish
Granted July 5, 1774 Grant Book M, page 32
Bounded on the southeast by John Youngblood..

Fuller, Joshua
100 acres, St. Paul Parish
Granted February 7, 1775 Grant Book M, page 992
Bounded on the southeast by Stephen Day, and on the southwest by Fuller.

Fuller, Thomas
150 acres, St. Paul Parish
Granted June 7, 1774 Grant Book I, page 1061
Bounded on the west partly by John Howard and on all other sides by vacant land.

Fyffe, John
Lot #5, Township of Augusta, St. Paul Parish, containing 50 acres
Granted September 4, 1764 Grant Book E, page 36
Bounded on the north by the Savannah River and west by Patrick Clark.

Galphin, Barbara
200 acres, St. Paul Parish
Surveyed November 1, 1775 Plat Book C, page 70
No grant recorded.
Bounded on the southeast by John Rae, southwest by James Gray, northwest by Laughlin McGillivray, and on the northeast by the Savannah River.

Galphin, George
400 acres, District of Augusta
Granted December 9, 1756 Grant Book A, page 274
Bounded on all sides by the Savannah River and a lagoon called the Spanish Cutoff.

Galphin, George
200 acres, St. Paul Parish
Granted May 1, 1759 Grant Book B, page 139
Bounded on the north by said Galphin's land, west by Alexander Shaws, and on the east by the Savannah River.

Galphin, George
Town Lot #4, Town of Augusta
Granted July 7, 1761 Grant Book C, page 318

Galphin, George
Town Lot #10, Town of Augusta
Granted July 7, 1761 Grant Book C, page 319

Galphin, George
499 acres, Township of Augusta, St. Paul Parish
Granted July 7, 1761 Grant Book C, page 321
Bounded on the northeast by the Savannah River, southeast by lands laid out for the Trustees, northwest by land formerly allotted to Nicholas Fisher. Tract was formerly granted to Thomas Andrews.

Galphin, George
499 acres, Township of Augusta, St. Paul Parish
Granted July 7, 1761 Grant Book C, page 323
Bounded on the northeast by the Savannah River, southeast by Thomas Andrews, southwest and northwest by land vacant. Tract was formerly allotted to Nicholas Fisher.

Galphin, George
100 acres, St. Paul Parish
Granted October 4, 1763 Grant Book D, page 339

Galphin, George
200 acres, St. Paul Parish
Granted October 4, 1763 Grant Book D, page 340
Bounded on the east by the Savannah River.

Galphin, George
200 acres, St. Paul Parish
Surveyed October 18, 1766 Plat Book M, page 3
Granted January 6, 1767 Grant Book F, page 20
Grant shows tract bounded on the south by lands purchased by the said George Galphin of John Lemar; northwest by said grantee purchased of Alexander Shaw. Plat shows tract bounded on the north by land granted to John Lamer and purchased by George Galphin; southeast by land granted to Alexander Shaw and purchased by George Galphin; southwest by Joel Walker and vacant land.

Galphin, George
100 acres, partly in St. George and partly in St. Paul Parishes
Granted February 5, 1771 Grant Book I, page 251

Bounded on the northeast partly by said grantee, southeast by Thomas Galphin, and on all other sides by vacant land.

Galphin, George
200 acres, St. Paul Parish
Granted November 5, 1771 Grant Book I, page 456
Bounded on the southeast partly by Benjamin Bevins and on all other sides by vacant land.

Galphin, George
500 acres, partly in St. George and partly in St. Paul Parishes
Granted July 7, 1772 Grant Book I, page 655
Bounded on the east by Quinton Pooler.

Galphin, George
500 acres, St. Paul Parish
Granted February 7, 1775 Grant Book M, page 993
Bounded on the northeast by vacant land and southeast by John Scott.

Galphin, George
300 acres, St. Paul Parish
Granted February 7, 1775 Grant Book M, page 994
Bounded on the southeast by Thomas Jackson, Sir James Wright, and Thomas Watson; northwest by Joseph Mooney; northeast by Isaac Jackson and vacant land; southwest by Peter Perkins, Cornelius Cochran, and vacant land.

Galphin, George
200 acres, St. Paul Parish
Granted April 4, 1775 Grant Book M, page 1100
Bounded on the southeast by Joshua Bradley and vacant land; northwest by Abraham Ayres and vacant land; southwest by John Burnett, Abraham Ayres, and vacant land.

Galphin, George; Rae, John; McGillivray, Lachlan (surviving partners of Brown, Rae, and Company.)
500 acres, St. Paul Parish
Granted April 5, 1764 Grant Book D, page 399
Part of the 500 acres is on an island called New Savannah

Island and the other part on the mainland, bounded on the north and south by vacant land and on every other side by the Savannah River.

Garnet, Thomas
100 acres, St. Paul Parish
Granted May 5, 1772 Grant Book I, page 588
Bounded on the southeast by Little Kioka and on the northeast by Benjamin Bevins.

Gelphin, William
100 acres, St. Paul Parish
Granted February 7, 1775 Grant Book M, page 1001
Bounded on the northwest by the Little Kioka Creek.

Germany, John
200 acres, St. Paul Parish
Granted July 7, 1761 Grant Book C, page 367
Bounded on the east by the Savannah River.

Germany, John
100 acres, St. Paul Parish
Granted February 3, 1767 Grant Book F, page 61
Bounded on the northeast by the Savannah River and southeast by said John Germany.

Germany, John
150 acres, St. Paul Parish
Granted April 7, 1772 Grant Book I, page 553

Germany, John
100 acres, St. Paul Parish
Granted February 3, 1767 Grant Book F, page 62
Bounded on the northeast by the Savannah River and southeast by said John Germany.

Germany, Robert
200 acres, at the head of Michaels Creek, St. Paul Parish
Granted July 7, 1761 Grant Book C, page 369

Germany, Robert
416 acres, St. Paul Parish (including part of Uchee Island)
Granted November 4, 1766 Grant Book E, page 390
Bounded on the northeast by part of the Uchee Island granted to
John Rae, Jr. and the Savannah River; northeast by John Rae, Jr.

Germany, Samuel
150 acres, St. Paul Parish
Granted October 1, 1765 Grant Book E, page 247
Bounded on the northeast by the Savannah River, and northwest
by John Germany.

Germany, Samuel
200 acres, St. Paul Parish
Granted June 7, 1774 Grant Book I, page 1048
Bounded on the southwest by land supposed to be laid out, but to
what person is unknown.

Gerrard, Devereaux
200 acres, St. Paul Parish
Granted June 5, 1770 Grant Book I, page 22
Bounded on the east by Joel Walker, north by John Stewart, and on
the northwest by John Phillips.

Getson, Samuel
100 acres, St. Paul Parish
Granted August 7, 1770 Grant Book I, page 71
Bounded on the southwest by Samuel Lyon, partly on the
northwest and partly on the southeast by Robert Hatcher, and on
all other sides by vacant land.

Gilliland, Thomas
150 acres, St. Paul Parish
Granted October 2, 1759 Grant Book B, page 259
Bounded on the north by the Savannah River, and west by Kioka
Creek and Thomas Lloyd.

Gilliland, Thomas
200 acres, St. Paul Parish
Granted October 3, 1769 Grant Book G, page 432

Glover, John
200 acres, St. Paul Parish
Granted August 2, 1774 Grant Book M, page 188
Bounded on the northeast by the Savannah River, and northwest by McNeal.

Golden, Henry
200 acres, St. Paul Parish
Granted August 2, 1774 Grant Book M, page 190
Bounded on the northwest by Levi Sheftall and George Galphin; southeast by Micajah Andrews, Thomas Garner, and Benjamin Bevins; northeast by William Milbank and Edmund Cartridge.

Goodgame, John
100 acres, St. Paul Parish
Granted July 5, 1774 Grant Book M, page 44
Bounded on the southeast by McBean's Swamp opposite to land surveyed for Francis Lewis.

Goodgion, William
600 acres, St. Paul Parish
Granted March 7, 1775 Grant Book M, page 1074
Bounded on the north by Thomas Gillans, William Wheat, and Dennis Duff; west by William Linn and vacant land; east by Amos and Thomas Stapler and John Herd.

Graham, James
500 acres, St. Paul Parish
Granted January 3, 1775 Grant Book M, page 875
Bounded on the southeast by Richard Meadows, and northeast by James Reid.

Graham, James
500 acres, St. Paul Parish
Granted February 7, 1775 Grant Book M, page 1002
Bounded on the south by Jeremiah Ducks; east by Joseph Walker, Micajah Andrews, and vacant land; west by Daniel Coalman.

Graham, John
1500 acres, Wrightsboro Township, St. Paul Parish (on Little River)

Granted October 4, 1774 Grant Book M, page 442
Bounded on the northwest by Herd and Germany, Richard Austin, Joshua Saunders, Colonel James Grierson, John Stuart, Jr., David Baldwin, and vacant land; southeast by Colonel James Grierson and Mordecai Moore; northwest by vacant land; northeast by Ephraim Owen and Colonel James Grierson.

Graham, John
1000 acres, Wrightsboro Township, St. Paul Parish
Granted October 4, 1774 Grant Book M, page 443
Bounded on the southeast by Hunter and vacant land, southwest by John Dover and vacant land, northwest by vacant land, northeast by James Emett and vacant land.

Graham, John
1000 acres, St. Paul Parish
Granted October 4, 1774 Grant Book M, page 444
Bounded on the northeast by Samuel Waller and vacant land; southwest by David Threats, Euchee Creek, and vacant land; southeast by Charles Crawford, John Davis, Henry Jones, and vacant land.

Graham, John
600 acres, Wrightsboro Township, St. Paul Parish
Granted January 3, 1775 Grant Book M, page 881
Bounded on the southeast by John Graham and John Dover; southwest by vacant land, northwest by Peter Hart, Howell, and vacant land; northeast by Joel Cloud.

Graves, James
200 acres, St. Paul Parish
Granted April 3, 1770 Grant Book G, page 577
Bounded on the north and southwest by the Little River.

Graves, Robert
250 acres, St. Paul Parish
Granted October 4, 1774 Grant Book M, page 447

Gray, Isaac
100 acres, Wrightsboro Township, St. Paul Parish
Granted September 6, 1774 Grant Book M, page 311

Bounded on the north by Little River and west by Robert Lockridge.

Gray, James
Town Lot #17, in Second row, Augusta, containing 1 acre
Granted June 5, 1759 Grant Book D, page 63
Original warrant says, "a Lot in the Town of Augusta known by the number 17 containing 1 acre in the second row from the river in the said town."

Gray, James
Lot #41, Township of Augusta, containing 50 acres; one lot adjoining thereto on the head of the Township line, containing 50 acres.
Two lots total 100 acres, Township of Augusta, St. Paul Parish.
Granted January 3, 1764 Grant Book D, page 370
Bounded on the east by Sarah Wisely and Benjamin Horn, north by Thomas Giggs.

Gray, James
46 acres, St. Paul Parish
Granted December 4, 1764 Grant Book E, page 85
Bounded on the northeast by the Savannah River, southeast by James Paris, west by Edward Barnard, and south by Lot #18.

Gray, James
Lot #6, Township of Augusta, containing 50 acres
Granted September 3, 1765 Grant Book E, page 220
Bounded on the north by the Savannah River, east by Lachlan McBean, west by Lot #5, and on the south by Lot #15.

Gray, James
200 acres, St. Paul Parish
Surveyed September 20, 1774 Plat Book C, page 71
No grant recorded.
Bounded on the northeast by the Savannah River, and southeast by John Rae.

Greathouse, Jacob
100 acres, Wrightsboro Township, St. Paul Parish
Granted January 3, 1775 Grant Book M, page 876

Bounded on all sides by vacant land.

Green, Isaac
100 acres, Wrightsboro Township, St. Paul Parish
Granted September 6, 1774 Grant Book M, page 310
Bounded on the southeast by Hunter, northwest by John Dover, and on all other sides by vacant land.

Green, John Jr.
300 acres, St. Paul Parish
Surveyed September 15, 1769 Plat Book M, page 25
Granted April 2, 1771 Grant Book I, page 283
Bounded on the southeast partly by William McMurran and on all other sides by vacant land.

Greer, Thomas
250 acres, St. Paul Parish
Granted October 6, 1772 Grant Book I, page 750

Greirson, James
1000 acres, St. Paul Parish
Granted July 7, 1767 Grant Book F, page 296
Bounded on the northeast by the Little River.

Grierson, James
300 acres, St. Paul Parish
Granted February 7, 1775

Grierson, James
200 acres, St. Paul Parish
Granted February 7, 1775
Grant Book M, page 998
Grant Book M, page 999
Bounded on the north by said James Grierson, and southwest by John Bacon.

Grierson, James and Pettygrew, Jane
Township Lot #10, Township of Augusta, St. Paul Parish, containing 50 acres.
Granted December 1, 1767 Grant Book F, page 422

Bounded on the northeast by the Savannah River, west by James Paris, and on every other side by lots of Macarton and Campbell.

Griffin, Michael
300 acres, St. Paul Parish
Granted July 5, 1774 Grant Book M, page 42
Bounded on the east by Mr. Weldon's land, north by Samuel Germany, west by vacant land, and on the south by Isaac Weldon.

Groves, James
100 acres, St. Paul Parish
Granted April 7, 1772 Grant Book I, page 554

Grubbs, John
250 acres, St. Paul Parish
Granted October 4, 1774 Grant Book M, page 446

Grubs, Benjamin
200 acres, St. Paul Parish
Granted February 7, 1775 Grant Book M, page 996
Bounded on the north by James Ross and Charles Crawford, west by James Ross.

Hagens, Thomas
100 acres, St. Paul Parish
Granted December 5, 1769 Grant Book G, page 474
Bounded on the east by Cartilledge, and north and west by the Savannah River and the Great Kioka Creek.

Hall, Nathaniel and Inglis, Alexander
300 acres, St. Paul Parish
Granted July 7, 1772 Grant Book I, page 669
Bounded at the time of survey on the east by Thomas Bassett and Richard Van Munch, partly on the west and partly on the south by Mr. Barnard's mill land, and on all other sides by vacant land.

Hammond, LeRoy
250 acres, St. Paul Parish
Granted August 2, 1768 Grant Book G, page 153

Hammond, LeRoy
250 acres, including 3 small islands of 31 acres, St. Paul Parish
Surveyed September 18, 1766 Plat Book C, page 328
Granted May 5, 1767 Grant Book F, page 232
Bounded on the northeast by the Savannah River, southeast by Darby Kennedy, northwest by land surveyed for Thomas Read, southwest by vacant land. Originally surveyed for William Shields thence ordered to LeRoy Hammond on February 3, 1767. Surveyed as 450 acres for William Shields, thence divided and 250 acres granted to LeRoy Hammond (see Plat Book C, page 328.) It is not known to whom the remaining 200 acres were granted.

Hammond, LeRoy
50 acres, St. Paul Parish
Granted January 3, 1775 Grant Book M, page 885
Bounded on the northwest by Robert Hatcher.

Hampton, Nathan
300 acres, St. Paul Parish
Granted August 2, 1774 Grant Book M, page 203
Bounded on the east by John Scott.

Haniel, Craft
200 acres, St. Paul Parish
Granted June 7, 1774 Grant Book I, page 1064
Bounded on the southwest partly by William McMurran, northwest by John Green, and on all other sides by vacant land.

Harlan, Ezekiel
100 acres, St. Paul Parish
Surveyed April 16, 1758 Plat Book C, page 77
Granted December 7, 1762 Grant Book D, page 246
Bounded on the east by the Savannah River and Pistol Creek, west by Gideon Chevers.

Harris, Arthur
250 acres, St. Paul Parish
Surveyed November 24, 1759 Plat Book C, pages 81 and 369
No grant recorded.

Tract located on the Savannah River and Butlers Creek. Bounded on the east by the Savannah River and north by Thomas Bassett. Tract ordered to Arthur Harris and recertified to David Tobler on January 16, 1765 (see Plat Book C, page 369.) Surveyed for Arthur Harris.

Harris, Benjamin
200 acres, St. Paul Parish
Granted January 19, 1773 Grant Book I, page 857

Harris, James
100 acres, St. Paul Parish
Granted August 2, 1774 Grant Book M, page 207
Bounded on the northwest by Joel Walker and Deviux Gerrard.

Harris, Nathan
100 acres, St. Paul Parish
Granted July 7, 1772

Harris, Nathan
150 acres, St. Paul Parish
Granted August 2, 1774
Grant Book I, page 666
Grant Book M, page 202
Bounded on the northwest by Mr. Reese's old lines, and southwest by Dionysus Wright.

Hart, James
Town Lot #76, Wrightsboro, St. Paul Parish; 250 acres, Wrightsboro Township, St. Paul Parish.
Granted July 3, 1770

Hart, Peter
Grant Book I, page 129
Town Lot #1, Wrightsboro, St. Paul Parish; 100 acres in Wrightsboro settlements, St. Paul Parish, bounded on the northeast by said Peter Hart.
Granted November 6, 1770 Grant Book I, page 196

Hart, Peter
100 acres, St. Paul Parish

Surveyed August 31, 1769 Plat Book M, page 56
Granted July 5, 1774 Grant Book M, page 49
Bounded on the southwest by said Peter Hart.

Hart, Samuel
Town Lot #52, Wrightsboro, St. Paul Parish; 100 acres in Wrightsboro settlements, St. Paul Parish, bounded on the southwest by Joel Cloud, partly on the northwest by said Samuel Hart, partly on the northeast and partly on the northwest by James Hart, on all other sides by vacant land.
Granted November 6, 1770 Grant Book I, page 197

Hart, Samuel
100 acres, Wrightsboro Township, St. Paul Parish
Granted April 7, 1772 Grant Book I, page 558
Bounded on the northeast by James Hart, southeast by said grantee, and on the southwest by Joel Cloud.

Hartshorne, John
100 acres, Wrightsboro Township, St. Paul Parish
Granted October 4, 1774 Grant Book M, page 560
Bounded on the northeast by John Wilson and on the southwest by Jonathan Sell and Sidwell.

Harwell, Ann (widow)
Town Lot #21, Augusta
Granted May 1, 1759 Grant Book B, page 81

Hatcher, Robert
380 acres, St. Paul Parish
Granted April 4, 1775 Grant Book M, page 1101
Bounded on the north by Little River and on the west by Stephen Herd.

Hatcher, Robert
380 acres, St. Paul Parish
Granted April 4, 1775 Grant Book M, page 1102
Bounded on the northwest by Little River and Timothy Barnard, southwest by John Robinson.

Heard, Barnard
200 acres, St. Paul Parish
Granted August 2, 1768 Grant Book G, page 156
Bounded on the north by the Little River.

Heard, John
100 acres, St. Paul Parish
Granted July 5, 1774 Grant Book M, page 56
Bounded on the north by the Little River.

Herd, John
100 acres, St. Paul Parish
Granted April 7, 1767 Grant Book F, page 187
Bounded on the north by the Little River.

Herd, John
300 acres, St. Paul Parish
Granted December 6, 1774 Grant Book M, page 796
Bounded on the southeast by Mr. Telfair, Mr. Rae, and vacant land; northwest by the Little River.

Herd, Stephen
150 acres, St. Paul Parish
Granted August 2, 1768 Grant Book G, page 155
Bounded on the north and east by the Little River.

Heron, James
200 acres, St. Paul Parish
Granted November 3, 1767 Grant Book F, page 404

Hickinbottom, Joseph
100 acres, St. Paul Parish
Granted July 5, 1774 Grant Book M, page 48
Bounded on the southeast by Hammond, southwest by Standley, and on the west by Joseph McCarty.

Hickinbottom, Thomas
100 acres, St. Paul Parish
Surveyed August 13, 1759
Granted December 7, 1762
Plat Book C, page 77

Grant Book D, page 247

Higginbotham, Thomas
200 acres, St. Paul Parish
Granted November 6, 1770 Grant Book I, page 183
Bounded on the southeast by said grantee.

Higginbotham, Judity
200 acres, St. Paul Parish
Granted July 5, 1774 Grant Book M, page 45
Bounded on the northeast by Thomas Higginbotham.

Higginbottom, Thomas
150 acres, St. Paul Parish
Granted August 2, 1768 Grant Book G, page 154

Hill, James
Town Lot #49, Wrightsboro, St. Paul Parish; 100 acres, Wrightsboro Township, St. Paul Parish, bounded on the northwest by land said to be Colsons and by land ordered John Wilson, southeast by
land ordered Ambrose Holliday.
Granted April 2, 1771 Grant Book I, page 301

Hill, James
100 acres, St. Paul Parish
Granted July 5, 1774 Grant Book M, page 51
Bounded on the northwest by said James Hill, and southwest by William Candler.

Hill, John
Town Lot #47, Wrightsboro, St. Paul Parish; 200 acres, Wrightsboro Township, St. Paul Parish, bounded on the south by the Indian line.
Granted April 2, 1771 Grant Book I, page 300

Hixson, William
Town Lot #30, Wrightsboro, St. Paul Parish; 400 acres, Wrightsboro
Township, St. Paul Parish, bounded on the east by land belonging to John Stewart and Holland Middleton.

Granted July 3, 1770 Grant Book I, page 132

Hodgin, John
Town Lot #85, Wrightsboro, St. Paul Parish; 300 acres, Wrightsboro Township, St. Paul Parish, bounded on the southwest by the Indian land, northwest by Deborah Stubbs.
Granted July 3, 1770 Grant Book I, page 131

Hogan, Daniel
100 acres, St. Paul Parish
Granted September 6, 1774 Grant Book M, page 330
Bounded on the north by David Anderson.

Holiday, William
100 acres, St. Paul Parish
Granted March 2, 1773 Grant Book I, page 916

Holliday, Ambrose
Town Lot #88, Wrightsboro, St. Paul Parish; 100 acres, Wrightsboro
Township, St. Paul Parish.
Granted July 3, 1770 Grant Book I, page 617

Holliday, William
150 acres, St. Paul Parish
Granted April 6, 1773 Grant Book I, page 949

Holliday, William
100 acres, St. Paul Parish
Granted June 7, 1774 Grant Book I, page 1022
Bounded on the southwest by William Holliday.

Hollingsworth, Joseph
Town Lot #57, Wrightsboro, St. Paul Parish; 100 acres, Wrightsboro
Township, St. Paul Parish.
Granted July 3, 1770 Grant Book I, page 930

Holloway, John
Lot #21, Township of Augusta, St. Paul Parish, containing 50 acres
Granted April 7, 1767 Grant Book F, page 188

Bounded on the northeast by Lot #15, belonging to William Clark; east by land of Lachlan McBean; southwest by Lot #25; west by Lot #20, belonging to Crook and Jackson.

Holmes, David
200 acres, partly in St. George and partly in St. Paul Parishes.
Granted August 4, 1772 Grant Book I, page 706
Bounded on the south corner by Isaac Wood.

Hood, Abraham
Town Lot #23, in Third row, Augusta
Granted December 7, 1762 Grant Book D, page 240

Horn, Absolem
200 acres, St. Paul Parish
Granted September 6, 1774 Grant Book M, page 329
Bounded on the southwest by James Neal, and northwest by Thomas Jones.

Horn, Benjamin
Two lots (no numbers given), Township of Augusta, containing 50 acres each, for a total of 100 acres.
Surveyed April 6, 1758 Plat Book C, page 77
No grant recorded.
Bounded on the southwest by Edward Barnard, and northwest by Tinley, and northeast by John Fitch.

Horn, Jacob
300 acres, St. Paul Parish
Granted September 6, 1774 Grant Book M, page 328
Bounded on the southwest by William Barnett.

Horn, Jesse
100 acres, St. Paul Parish
Granted January 19, 1773 Grant Book I, page 856

Hosiach, Alexander
100 acres, St. Paul Parish
Granted June 2, 1772 Grant Book I, page 623
Bounded on the south by Christian Limbacker, southwest by John Hichee, and on the northeast by John Rae.

Hosaick, Alexander
200 acres, St. Paul Parish
Granted September 6, 1774 Grant Book M, page 324
Bounded on the northeast by John Boyd.

Houstoun, James
500 acres, St. Paul Parish
Granted February 7, 1775 Grant Book M, page 1006
Bounded on the northwest by Holland Middleton, and southwest by Charles Parks.

Houstoun, John
600 acres, St. Paul Parish
Granted October 4, 1774 Grant Book M, page 453
Bounded on the southwest and southeast by Edward Barnard, northeast by Andrew Jones, north by William Anderson and Ephraim Owin.

Houstoun, Sir Patrick
500 acres, St. Paul Parish
Granted October 4, 1774 Grant Book M, page 452
Bounded on the southwest by Alexander Scott, and west by John Scott.

Houstoun, Sir Patrick
500 acres, Wrightsboro Township, St. Paul Parish
Granted October 4, 1774 Grant Book M, page 451
Bounded on the south by Absolem Beidell, Jacob Greathouse, and vacant land; northwest by John Sidwell and Jonathan Sail; north by Robert McCluny; on all other sides by vacant land.

Howard, Benjamin
100 acres, Wrightsboro Township, St. Paul Parish
Granted January 19, 1773 Grant Book I, page 858
Bounded on the northwest by Upton's Creek, and on the southwest by Henry Sale.

Howard, John
Town Lot #45, Wrightsboro, St. Paul Parish; 250 acres, Wrightsboro Township, St. Paul Parish, bounded on the southeast

by Ralph Kilgore, south by John Whitsett, west by John Slatter, north by Little River.
Granted July 3, 1770 Grant Book I, page 130

Howard, John
550 acres, St. Paul Parish
Granted September 6, 1774 Grant Book M, page 327
Bounded on the northeast by David Threats and Peter Cutbreath; northwest by Peter Youngblood, Benjamin Youngblood, and John Crawford; southwest by Jacob Horn and Jesse Horn.

Howard, John and Few, Benjamin
1000 acres, Wrightsboro Township, St. Paul Parish
Granted October 4, 1774 Grant Book M, page 558
Bounded on the northwest by Sherwood Bugg, Edmund Bugg, John Burnet, John Cobb, Frederick Francis, and William Candler; southwest by William Jackson; southeast by vacant land; (blank) by Daniel McCarty and Richard Upton.

Howard, Rice
200 acres, St. Paul Parish
Surveyed May 9, 1769
Granted October 4, 1774
Plat Book C, pages 370 and 429
Grant Book M, page 561
Tract originally surveyed for Hugh Tennen, thence ordered to Richard Howard on December 3, 1771 (see Plat Book C, page 370.) Surveyed for Hugh Tennen and granted to Rice Howard (Richard Howard shown on plat). Bounded on the northeast and southeast by Walter Jackson and northwest by Ralph Kilgore. (See next entry below.)

Howard, Richard
200 acres, St. Paul Parish
Surveyed May 9, 1769
Granted October 4, 1774
Plat Book C, pages 370 and 429
Grant Book M, page 561
Tract originally surveyed for Hugh Tennen, thence ordered to Richard Howard on December 3, 1771 (see Plat Book C, page

370.) Surveyed for Hugh Tennen and granted to Rice Howard (Richard Howard shown on plat.) Bounded on the northeast and southeast by Walter Jackson, northwest by Ralph Kilgore. (See next entry above.)

Howell, James
100 acres, St. Paul Parish
Granted December 6, 1774

Hubbard, Richard
250 acres, St. Paul Parish
Granted October 4, 1774
Grant Book M, page 816
Grant Book M, page 559

Hume, James
500 acres, Wrightsboro Township, St. Paul Parish
Granted November 1, 1774 Grant Book M, page 664
Bounded on the northeast by Little River and Hatton
 Middleton, northeast by John West and vacant land, on all
other sides by vacant land.

Hume, James
500 acres, St. Paul Parish
Granted November 1, 1774 Grant Book M, page 665
Bounded on the northeast by Mr. Swints and vacant land, and on the southeast by Samuel Germany.

Hume, James
400 acres, St. Paul Parish
Granted December 6, 1774 Grant Book M, page 799
Bounded on the southwest by Mr. Mossman and Alexander Coldwell, southeast by Brown and vacant land, northeast by William Candler, northwest by Thomas Stapler.

Hume, John
300 acres, St. Paul Parish
Granted October 4, 1774 Grant Book M, page 556

Hume, John
700 acres, St. Paul Parish

Granted October 4, 1774 Grant Book M, page 557
Bounded on the southwest by John Tinkler Shepherd.

Hunter, John
Town Lot #15, Wrightsboro, St. Paul Parish; 200 acres, St. Paul
Parish, being part of the land reserved for the people called
Quakers.
Granted November 6, 1770 Grant Book I, page 198.

Illy, Michael
300 acres, St. Paul Parish
Surveyed August 12, 1770 Plat Book C, page 89
Granted January 1, 1771 Grant Book I, page 239
Bounded on the southwest by William Taylor and Patrick O'Bryan,
northeast by land surveyed for Hozick.

Illy, Michael
300 acres, St. Paul Parish
Granted October 4, 1774 Grant Book M, page 565

Inglis, Alexander
500 acres, St. Paul Parish
Granted November 1, 1774 Grant Book M, page 678
Bounded on the southwest by Mr. Bugg, and southeast by James
Story.

Inglis, Alexander and Hall, Nathaniel
300 acres, St. Paul Parish
Granted July 7, 1772 Grant Book I, page 669
Bounded at the time of survey on the east by Thomas Bassett and
Richard Van Munch, partly on the west and partly on the south by
Mr. Barnard's mill land, and on all other sides by vacant land.

Jackson, Absalom
Town Lot #17, Wrightsboro, St. Paul Parish; 200 acres,
Wrightsboro Township, St. Paul Parish, bounded on the northwest
by William Mitchell.
Surveyed June 26, 1769 Plat Book C, page 86
Granted July 3, 1770 Grant Book I, page 133

Jackson, Benjamin
Town Lot #51, Wrightsboro, St. Paul Parish; 250 acres, Wrightsboro Township, St. Paul Parish, bounded on the northwest by Little River.
Surveyed March 28, 1770 Plat Book C, page 89
Granted November 6, 1770 Grant Book I, page 199

Jackson, Benjamin
100 acres, St. Paul Parish
Surveyed August 31, 1769 Plat Book C, page 85
No grant recorded.
Bounded on the northwest by Williams Creek, southeast by James Jack, and northeast by Absalom Jackson and vacant land.

Jackson, Benjamin
100 acres, St. Paul Parish
Surveyed September 1, 1769
No grant recorded.
Plat Book C, page 87

Jackson, Benjamin
150 acres, St. Paul Parish
Surveyed May 2, 1769 Plat Book C, page 85
No grant recorded.
Bounded on the southeast by Williams Creek.

Jackson, Isaac
Town Lot #89, Wrightsboro, St. Paul Parish; 350 acres, Wrightsboro
Township, St. Paul Parish.
Surveyed April 6, 1769
Granted July 3, 1770
Plat Book C, page 86
Grant Book I, page 134

Jackson, James
150 acres, St. Paul Parish
Surveyed July 3, 1769 Plat Book C, page 88
Granted July 3, 1770 Grant Book I, page 52
Plat shows Uchee Creek running through center of tract.

Jackson, James
150 acres, St. Paul Parish
Surveyed July 3, 1769 Plat Book C, page 87
Granted July 3, 1770 Grant Book I, page 53
Bounded on the west by Euche Creek.

Jackson, James and McLean, Andrew
Town Lot #7, Augusta
Exact grant date unknown, but probably granted between
December 6, 1774 and February 2, 1775. Recorded in Grant Book
L, page 202.

Jackson, James
Town Lot #9, Augusta, St. Paul Parish, containing 1 acre.
Surveyed July 14, 1764 Plat Book C, page 88
Granted October 29, 1765 Grant Book E, page 286
Tract originally ordered to James Jackson who resigned lot to
Francis Macartan on October 22, 1765 (see Plat Book C, page 88.)
Plat shows tract bounded on the southeast by Isaac Atwood,
southwest by Main Street, northwest by George Galphin.
Surveyed for James Jackson and granted to Francis Macartan.

Jackson, James; Cooke, Robert; McIntosh, Alexander
800 acres, St. Paul Parish
Surveyed October 29, 1766 Plat Book C, page 88
Granted March 3, 1767 Grant Book F, page 116

Jackson, James; McKintosh, Alexander; Cooke, Robert
Seven lots in Augusta as follows: #27 (a vacant lot) and six
lots, #13, #14, #19, #20, #26, and #36. The latter six lots
were purchased by Crook, McKintosh, and Jackson from the
original proprietors. Total of 350 acres (50 acres per lot.) Original
proprietors not named.
Granted September 3, 1765 Grant Book E, page 227

Jackson, James and McLean, Andrew
50 acres, St. Paul Parish
Granted January 3, 1775 Grant Book M, page 891
Bounded on the southwest by Clark, northwest by David Douglas,
and southeast by Edward Barnard.

Jackson, Nathaniel
100 acres, St. Paul Parish
Granted February 7, 1775 Grant Book M, page 1008
Bounded on the northeast by Peter Perkins, and on all other sides by vacant land.

Jackson, Thomas
Town Lot #31, Wrightsboro, St. Paul Parish; 250 acres, Wrightsboro
Township, St. Paul Parish.
Surveyed April 5, 1769
Granted July 3, 1770

Jackson, Walter
Plat Book C, page 86
Grant Book I, page 135
Town Lot #86, Wrightsboro, St. Paul Parish; 100 acres, Wrightsboro Township, St. Paul Parish, bounded on the northwest and southeast by Hugh Tennen.
Surveyed May 28, 1769
Granted July 3, 1770

Jackson, William
450 acres, St. Paul Parish
Surveyed June 7, 1769
Granted October 3, 1769
Plat Book C, page 85
Grant Book I, page 620
Plat Book C, page 87
Grant Book G, page 436

Jamieson, John
600 acres, St. Paul Parish
Granted September 6, 1774 Grant Book M, page 335
Bounded on the southeast by Middleton.

Jarratt, Deverix
100 acres, St. Paul Parish
Granted September 6, 1774 Grant Book M, page 334
Bounded on the north by Deverix Jarratt.

Jarvis, James
300 acres, St. Paul Parish, known as the Cupboard
Surveyed April 10, 1758 Plat Book C, page 84
Granted May 21, 1762 Grant Book D, page 111
Original warrant says tract located at a place known as the
Cupboard near Augusta on the north side of Rocky Creek joining
lands granted Francis Wylly.

Jarvis, James
Town Lot #7, on the Bay of Augusta
Surveyed April 6, 1762 Plat Book C, page 88
Granted February 1, 1763 Grant Book D, page 284

Johnson, Lewis
513 acres, Wrightsboro Township, St. Paul Parish
Granted October 4, 1774 Grant Book M, page 563
Bounded on the northwest by John West, William Candler, Herd,
Germany, and Little River; northeast by John Graham, on all other
sides by vacant land.

Johnson, Richard
Town Lot #15, Second row, Augusta, St. Paul Parish
Granted March 5, 1765 Grant Book E, page 125

Johnson, William
Town Lot #31, Augusta
Surveyed June 10, 1763 Plat Book C, page 88
Granted September 6, 1774 Grant Book L, page 182
Being a corner lot between Black and Ellis Streets, and the
common of the town.

Johnson, William
350 acres, St. Paul Parish
Surveyed March 24, 1773 Plat Book C, page 90
Granted April 4, 1775 Grant Book M, page 1103
Bounded on the northwest by James Orrick.

Jones, Andrew
100 acres, St. Paul Parish
Surveyed December 1, 1772 Plat Book C, page 90
Granted September 6, 1774 Grant Book M, page 333

Jones, Benjamin
150 acres, St. Paul Parish
Surveyed March 13, 1773 Plat Book C, page 91
Granted July 5, 1774 Grant Book M, page 58
Bounded on the south by Peter Parrot.

Jones, Francis
200 acres, Wrightsboro Township, St. Paul Parish
Surveyed January 28, 1773 Plat Book C, page 90
Granted June 7, 1774 Grant Book I, page 1025
Bounded on the northeast by Richard Moore and Isaac Low, southwest by land supposed to belong to John Stubbs, partly on the southeast by Richard Moore, Jr., on all other sides by vacant land.

Jones, Francis
Town Lot #22, Wrightsboro, St. Paul Parish; 250 acres, Wrightsboro
Township, St. Paul Parish.
Surveyed July 8, 1769 Plat Book C, page 86
Granted July 3, 1770 Grant Book I, page 931

Jones, Henry
150 acres, St. Paul Parish
Granted November 1, 1774 Grant Book M, page 675
Bounded on the northwest by Moses Dias and vacant land, south by William Sims, and east by Sidwell.

Jones, Jacob
100 acres, St. Paul Parish
Surveyed April 12, 1773 Plat Book C, page 90
Granted December 6, 1774 Grant Book M, page 801
Bounded on the east by William Castleberry. Tract surveyed as Jas. Jones and granted as Jacob Jones.

Jones, John
200 acres, St. Paul Parish
Surveyed August 12, 1769 Plat Book C, page 89
Granted March 6, 1770 Grant Book G, page 553
Tract consists of certain slips of land in Wrightsboro
settlement between the tracts already granted Richard Jones,

John Jones (the grantee), John Stubbs, and others.

Jones, John
Town Lot #79, Wrightsboro, St. Paul Parish; 200 acres, Wrightsboro Township, St. Paul Parish.
Surveyed May 10, 1769
Granted July 3, 1770
Plat Book C, page 85
Grant Book I, page 927

Jones, John
200 acres, St. Paul Parish
Granted November 1, 1774 Grant Book M, page 676
Bounded on the southwest by Robert Walden, southeast by Thomas Gillard and William Wheat, west by Little River, northwest by William Grierson.

Jones, John
200 acres, Wrightsboro Township, St. Paul Parish
Surveyed January 18, 1770 Plat Book C, page 114
No grant recorded.
Bounded on the northwest by Jonathan Sallet, and northeast by Alexander Oliver.

Jones, Richard
150 acres, St. Paul Parish
Surveyed May 9, 1769
No grant recorded.

Jones, Robert
100 acres, St. Paul Parish
Surveyed December 5, 1772
Granted February 7, 1775

Jones, Thomas
200 acres, St. Paul Parish
Surveyed March 29, 1770
Granted April 7, 1772

Jones, Thomas
150 acres, St. Paul Parish

Surveyed March 13, 1773
Plat Book C, page 84
Plat Book C, page 90 Grant Book M, and page 1010
Plat Book C, page 89 Grant Book I, and page 561
Plat Book M, page 57
Bounded on the northeast by Daniel Coleman, and southeast by John Mitchel.

Jones, Thomas
100 acres, St. Paul Parish
Surveyed April 3, 1769
Granted March 7, 1775
Plat Book C, page 84
Grant Book M, page 1078

Jones, William
150 acres, St. Paul Parish
Surveyed August 12, 1766
Granted August 2, 1768

Jordan, Charles
400 acres, St. Paul Parish
Surveyed August 13, 1766
Granted November 6, 1770
Plat Book C, page 84 Grant Book G, and page 157
Plat Book C, page 87 Grant Book I, and page 184

Keff, James
100 acres, St. Paul Parish
Surveyed April 18, 1772 Plat Book C, page 117
Granted July 5, 1774 Grant Book M, page 60
Bounded on the southwest by William Candler.

Kelly, Spencer
100 acres, St. Paul Parish
Surveyed July 2, 1772 Plat Book C, page 117
Granted September 6, 1774 Grant Book M, page 336

Kender, Peter
150 acres, St. Paul Parish
Surveyed January 6, 1772 Plat Book C, page 117

Granted July 7, 1772 Grant Book I, page 676

Kennedy, John
200 acres, St. Paul Parish
Surveyed April 1764 Plat Book C, page 116
Granted September 4, 1764 Grant Book E, page 32
Bounded on the northeast by the Savannah River, northwest by land surveyed for Thomas Ross.

Kenshaw, Thomas
170 acres, St. Paul Parish
Granted August 2, 1774 Grant Book M, page 195
Bounded on the west by Sherwood Bugg and James Cobb; east by Robert Story, John Mitchell, and Thomas Jones; south by James G. Lasple.

Kilgore, Ralph
250 acres, District of Augusta
Granted December 16, 1756 Grant Book A, page 275
Bounded on the north by the Savannah River, and east by Kioka Creek.

Kilgore, Ralph
50 acres, St. Paul Parish
Surveyed April 3, 1756 Plat Book C, page 117
No grant recorded.
Bounded by Ralph Kilgore, Lachlan Macbran, the Great Kioka Creek, and the Savannah River. Tract located at the intersection of the two streams. Original warrant says tract located 14 miles above Augusta.

Kilgore, Ralph
100 acres, District of Augusta, St. Paul Parish
Granted March 28, 1758 Grant Book B, page 459

Kilgore, Ralph
350 acres, St. Paul Parish
Surveyed February 6, 1769 Plat Book C, page 116
No grant recorded.
Bounded on the northeast by the Little River.

Kilgore, William
100 acres, St. Paul Parish
Surveyed August 11, 1759 Plat Book C, page 116
Granted July 7, 1772 Grant Book I, page 672
Bounded on the northeast by the Savannah River. Original warrant says tract located about 30 miles above Augusta.

Kilgore, William
200 acres, St. Paul Parish
Granted April 4, 1775 Grant Book M, page 1104
Bounded on the south by Great Kioka Creek, and northeast by the Savannah River.

King, John
250 acres, St. Paul Parish
Surveyed November 27, 1766 Plat Book C, page 91
Granted April 7, 1767 Grant Book F, page 190
Plat shows Williams Creek running through center of tract.

Lamar, Zachariah
150 acres, St. Paul Parish
Surveyed February 14, 1769 Plat Book C, page 134
No grant recorded.
Bounded on the east by Kioka Creek.

LaMarr, William
200 acres, Wrightsboro Township, St. Paul Parish
Surveyed December 7, 1772 Plat Book C, page 136
Granted July 5, 1774 Grant Book M, page 61
Bounded on the northeast by Thomas Hart, and on all other sides by vacant land. Surveyed as Lemarr and granted as LaMarr.

Lamer, John
150 acres, St. Paul Parish
Surveyed November 1, 1759 Plat Book C, page 134 and
Plat Book M, page 2
Granted April 13, 1761 Grant Book C, page 59
Bounded on the east by the Savannah River, north by Nehemiah Wade, and on all other sides by vacant land. Plat Book C, page 134 shows name to be Lamar. Plat Book M, page 2 shows

name to be Lamer.  Granted as Lamer.

Lantor, Jacob
100 acres, St. Paul Parish
Surveyed May 27, 1769
Granted January 3, 1775
Plat Book C, page 131
Grant Book M, page 902

Larimore, Isaac
50 acres, St. Paul Parish
Surveyed December 12, 1772 Plat Book C, page 137
No grant recorded.
Bounded on the southwest by Duhart's Creek, northwest by Wamuck, and on the northeast by Jared Irwin.

Larrimore, James
100 acres, St. Paul Parish
Surveyed March 27, 1765 Plat Book C, page 132
Granted September 3, 1765 Grant Book E, page 234
Bounded on the north by the Savannah River, and east by John Clark.

Lee, John
400 acres, Wrightsboro Township, St. Paul Parish
Surveyed March 15, 1771 Plat Book C, page 135
Granted October 1, 1771 Grant Book I, page 432
Bounded on the northwest by John Jones and Edward Murphy, northeast by Alexander Oliver, and southeast by James Hill.  In addition, plat shows tract bounded on the southwest by John Wilson.

Lee, John
100 acres, Wrightsboro Township, St. Paul Parish
Granted December 6, 1774 Grant Book M, page 806
Bounded on the southwest by Joseph Maddock, southeast by Silas Pace, northwest by John Lee, and on the northeast by vacant land.

Lee, Thomas
Town Lot #30, Third row, Augusta
Surveyed October 12, 1762 Plat Book C, page 133

Granted October 29, 1765 Grant Book F, page 435

Lee, Thomas
100 acres, St. Paul Parish
Granted January 3, 1775 Grant Book M, page 897

Lee, Thomas
300 acres, St. Paul Parish
Surveyed July 13, 1761 Plat Book C, page 133
No grant recorded.
Bounded on the north by the Savannah River.

Lesslie, Joseph
100 acres, St. Paul Parish
Surveyed March 17, 1772 Plat Book C, page 136
Granted August 4, 1772 Grant Book I, page 702
Bounded on the northwest by Henry Downs, and southeast by John Dodson.

Lewis, David
200 acres, District of Augusta
Granted February 7, 1758 Grant Book A, page 570
Tract located on North Fork of Walnut Branch of Bryer Creek.

Lewis, David
Town Lot #37, Augusta
Granted December 5, 1769 Grant Book H, page 31

Lewis, David
100 acres, St. Paul Parish
Surveyed May 29, 1767 Plat Book C, page 133
Granted January 1, 1771 Grant Book I, page 240

Lewis, David
100 acres, District of Augusta
Surveyed October 29, 1757 Plat Book C, pages 166 and 436
No grant recorded.
Bounded on the southeast by Butler's Creek.

Lewis, Isaac
250 acres, St. Paul Parish

Surveyed May 26, 1772 Plat Book C, page 136
Granted June 7, 1774 Grant Book I, page 1049
Bounded on the southeast by James Grierson.

Lewis, John
100 acres, St. Paul Parish
Surveyed September 18, 1771 Plat Book C, page 135
Granted April 4, 1775 Grant Book M, page 1105
Bounded on the northeast by John Cluckler.

Lightenstone, John
150 acres, St. Paul Parish
Granted December 6, 1774 Grant Book M, page 803
Bounded on the southeast by Robert Cowen and vacant land, northeast by land lately run by William Candler, northwest by George Upton and Daniel McCarty.

Limbacker, Christian
150 acres, St. Paul Parish
Surveyed August 28, 1767 Plat Book C, page 133
Granted January 3, 1769 Grant Book G, page 255
Bounded on the west by Thomas Red, and east by George Galphin.

Limbacker, Christian
100 acres, St. Paul Parish
Surveyed November 16, 1768 Plat Book C, page 133
Granted June 6, 1769 Grant Book G, page 332
Bounded on the northeast by Elias Walraven.

Limbacker, George
400 acres, St. Paul Parish
Surveyed February 29, 1769 Plat Book C, page 134
Granted June 6, 1769 Grant Book G, page 331
Bounded on the southeast by William Kilgore, northwest by Elias Volraven and Christopher Limbacker, northeast by the Savannah River.

Linn, William
Town Lot #65, Wrightsboro, St. Paul Parish; 100 acres, Wrightsboro Township, St. Paul Parish, bounded on the south by land said to be Cones.

Granted July 3, 1770 Grant Book I, page 618

Lloyd, Thomas
100 acres, St. Paul Parish
Surveyed September 12, 1769 Plat Book C, page 132
No grant recorded.
Bounded on the northeast by the Savannah River, southeast by George Limbacker, and on the north by Thomas Lloyd.

Lloyd, Thomas
100 acres, St. Paul Parish
Surveyed April 11, 1763 Plat Book C, page 132
No grant recorded.
Bounded on the northeast by the Savannah River, northwest by Keg Creek, and on all other sides by vacant land.

Lockridge, Robert
Town Lot #20, Wrightsboro, St. Paul Parish; 100 acres, Wrightsboro Township, St. Paul Parish, bounded on the north by Little River.
Surveyed August 7, 1769 Plat Book C, page 131
Granted July 3, 1770 Grant Book I, page 137

Lockridge, Robert
100 acres, Wrightsboro Township, St. Paul Parish
Surveyed November 23, 1769 Plat Book C, page 135
No grant recorded.
Bounded on the north by Little River, and east by Robert Lockridge.

Loumore, Isaac
50 acres, St. Paul Parish
Granted August 2, 1774 Grant Book H, page 118
Bounded on the southwest by Duhart's Creek, northwest by Womack's Creek, and on the northeast by Jared Irwin.

Loumore, John
100 acres, St. Paul Parish
Granted November 1, 1774 Grant Book M, page 684
Bounded on the southeast by Charles Crawford, southwest by John McNeil, northwest by Peter Hendon, and on the

northeast by vacant land.

Low, Isaac
Town Lot #68, Wrightsboro, St. Paul Parish; 250 acres,
Wrightsboro Township, St. Paul Parish, bounded on the northeast
by Oliver Matthews.
Surveyed June 26, 1769 Plat Book C, page 131
Granted July 3, 1770 Grant Book I, page 136

Low, Isaac
250 acres, Wrightsboro Township, St. Paul Parish
Surveyed May 28, 1770 Plat Book C, page 134
Granted March 5, 1771 Grant Book I, page 269

Low, Isaac
50 acres, St. Paul Parish
Surveyed April 7, 1773 Plat Book C, page 137
No grant recorded.
Bounded on the east by Jacob McCarty.

Low, Isaac
500 acres, St. Paul Parish
Surveyed March 21, 1772 Plat Book C, page 135
No grant recorded.
Bounded on the northeast by Edward Barnard and vacant land.

Lowe, Beverly
200 acres, St. Paul Parish
Granted October 4, 1774 Grant Book M, page 568
Bounded on the southwest by Fanin.

Lowrance, Peter
200 acres, St. Paul Parish
Surveyed March 4, 1773 Plat Book C, page 137
Granted March 7, 1775 Grant Book M, page 1081
Bounded on the southwest by Francis Brown, and on the southeast
by William Phelps. Tract surveyed as Lourance and granted as
Lowrance.

Lucas, Charles
200 acres, St. Paul Parish

Surveyed June 30, 1772 Plat Book C, page 136
Granted July 5, 1774 Grant Book M, page 62

Lyford, William
600 acres, St. Paul Parish
Granted January 3, 1775 Grant Book M, page 901
Bounded on the northeast and southeast by Mr. Ross, William
Candler, and vacant land; southwest by Hugh Middleton; north by
Little River.

Lynn, Thomas
Town Lot #82, Wrightsboro, St. Paul Parish; 250 acres, St. Paul
Parish.
Surveyed April 21, 1769 Plat Book C, page 132
Granted July 3, 1770 Grant Book I, page 619
Bounded on all sides by vacant land.

Lynn, William
100 acres, St. Paul Parish
Surveyed September 2, 1769 Plat Book C, page 132
No grant recorded.
Bounded on the southwest by Cone.

Lyon, Samuel
229 acres, St. Paul Parish
Surveyed March 30, 1770 Plat Book C, page 131
Granted August 7, 1770 Grant Book I, page 75

Macartan, Francis
Town Lot #9, Augusta, St. Paul Parish, containing 1 acre
Surveyed July 14, 1764 Plat Book C, page 88
Granted October 29, 1765 Grant Book E, page 286
Tract originally ordered to James Jackson who resigned lot to
Macartan on October 22, 1765 (see Plat Book C, page 88.)
Surveyed for James Jackson and granted to Francis Macartan.
Bounded on the southeast by Isaac Atwood, southwest by Main
Street, and on the northwest by George Galphin.

Macartan, Francis and Campbell, Martin
Town Lot #26, Augusta
Granted March 3, 1767 Grant Book F, page 133

Macgillivray, Lachlan
100 acres, St. Paul Parish
Granted July 4, 1758 Grant Book B, page 28
Bounded on the east by Butler's Creek, and on the south by land of said Lachlan Macgillivray and Spencer.

Macgillivray, Lachlan
300 acres, St. Paul Parish
This grant could go with survey for Lachlan McGillivray on page 124, this book.
Granted July 4, 1758 Grant Book B, page 29
Bounded on the east by the Savannah River, and on the north by land of said Lachlan Macgillivray.

Macgillivray, Lachlan
400 acres, St. Paul Parish
This grant could go with survey for Lachlan McGillivray on page 124, this book.
Granted July 4, 1758 Grant Book B, page 30
Bounded on the east by the Savannah River, south by land of said Lachlan Macgillivray, and on the north by Bridge Creek.

Mackay, William
100 acres, St. Paul Parish
Surveyed May 5, 1770 Plat Book C, page 184
No grant recorded.
Bounded on the east by David Russell, and on the southwest by Great Ogeechee River.

Maddock, Joseph
Town Lot #66, Wrightsboro, St. Paul Parish; 300 acres, Wrightsboro Township, St. Paul Parish, bounded on the northeast by Henry Ashfield, southwest by John Oliver.
Surveyed June 27, 1769 Plat Book C, page 180
Granted July 3, 1770 Grant Book I, page 138

Maddock, Joseph
200 acres, Wrightsboro Township, St. Paul Parish
Surveyed July 23, 1769 Plat Book C, page 181
Granted April 2, 1771 Grant Book I, page 302

Bounded on the north by the cowpen land.

Maddock, Joseph
100 acres, Wrightsboro Township, St. Paul Parish
Surveyed December 2, 1772 Plat Book C, page 190
Granted June 7, 1774 Grant Book I, page 1013
Bounded on the northwest and partly on the northeast by John Lee, southwest by Ambrose Holliday, and on the southeast by Silas Pace.

Maddock, Joseph
200 acres, St. Paul Parish
Surveyed July 4, 1773 Plat Book C, page 189
Granted July 5, 1774 Grant Book M, page 70

Maddock, Joseph and Sell, Jonathan
500 acres, Wrightsboro Township, St. Paul Parish
Surveyed June 21, 1769 Plat Book C, pages 179 and 243
Granted July 3, 1770 Grant Book I, page 147
Tract is part of the land reserved for the said people called Quakers and intended for a cowpen (see Grant Book I, page 147.) Bounded partly on the south by said Joseph Maddock's land for a mill, and on all other sides by vacant land.

Maddock, Joseph and Vernon, Isaac
1100 acres, Wrightsboro Township, St. Paul Parish
Granted February 7, 1775 Grant Book M, page 1018
Bounded on the north by Joseph Maddock; west by John Oliver; south by George Birk, Isaac Vernon, and vacant land; east by Robert McClung and vacant land.

Maner, Mary
200 acres, St. Paul Parish
Surveyed January 20, 1772 Plat Book C, page 189
Granted May 4, 1773 Grant Book I, page 984
Bounded on the northeast by Edmund Cartledge.

Maneren, Robert
100 acres, St. Paul Parish
Surveyed July 11, 1772 Plat Book C, page 188
Granted January 19, 1773 Grant Book I, page 865

Marshall, John
300 acres, St. Paul Parish
Surveyed March 14, 1773 Plat Book C, page 186
Granted July 5, 1774 Grant Book M, page 69
Bounded on the southwest by said John Marshall and Frederick Ashmore, northeast by said John Marshall and Daniel Colman, southeast by said John Marshall and vacant land, northwest by Thomas Ford and vacant land.

Marshall, Mathew
54 acres, St. Paul Parish
Surveyed August 24, 1767 Plat Book C, page 178
No grant recorded.
Bounded on the northeast by the Savannah River, and on the northwest by Daniel Devereux.

Marshall, Matthew
200 acres, St. Paul Parish
Granted April 4, 1769 Grant Book G, page 302
Bounded on the south by Spirit Creek, northeast by the Savannah River, and on the northwest by Daniel Durozeaux.

Martin, Clement Sr.
250 acres, St. Paul Parish
Granted March 7, 1775 Grant Book M, page 1083
Bounded on the northeast by Samuel Alexander and James McFarland, northwest by Colonel James Jackson.

Mason, Ann (wife of Michael Mason)
500 acres, St. Paul Parish
Surveyed March 9, 1762 Plat Book C, page 184
Granted November 2, 1762 Grant Book D, page 229
Bounded on the southwest by Edward Barnard, southeast by the Savannah River, and on the northeast by Francis Macartan.

Mason, Ann
300 acres, St. Paul Parish
Surveyed February 23, 1762 Plat Book C, page 176
No grant recorded.
Bounded on the southwest by Thomas Cordery, and

on the northwest by Boggy Gut Creek.

Matthews, James
Lot #7, Augusta, St. Paul Parish, containing 50 acres
Surveyed December 15, 1737 Plat Book C, pages 174 and 381
No grant recorded.
Bounded on the northwest by land laid out for John Gray, southeast by the Common, northeast by the Savannah River.

Matthews, Oliver
Town Lot #6, Wrightsboro, St. Paul Parish; 250 acres, Wrightsboro
Township, St. Paul Parish, bounded on the south by Isaac Low.
Surveyed May 8, 1769 Plat Book C, page 181
Granted July 3, 1770 Grant Book I, page 928

Matthews, Thomas
250 acres, St. Paul Parish
Surveyed August 25, 1769 Plat Book C, page 183
No grant recorded.
Tract almost surrounds tract of Joseph Holingsworth. Bounded on the southwest by Isaac Vernon, and on the northwest by Robert McCling.

Matthews, John
200 acres, St. Paul Parish
Surveyed February 1, 1772 Plat Book C, page 190
Granted January 19, 1773 Grant Book I, page 871
Bounded on the north by John Harvey.

Maxwell, William
500 acres, St. Paul Parish
Granted January 3, 1775 Grant Book M, page 918
Bounded on the northwest by Dionysus Wright, William Hilliday, and vacant land; northeast by James Phillips.

McCartan, Francis and Campbell, Martin
Augusta Township Lots #17 and #23, containing 50 acres each,
a total of 100 acres.
Surveyed September 18, 1759 Plat Book C, page 230
Granted October 2, 1759 Grant Book B, page 201

Bounded on the northeast by said McCartan and Campbell, east by Samuel Vining and William Davis, north and west by John Pettygrew, south by Thomas Gigg.

McCartan, Francis and Campbell, Martin
50 acres, District (Township) of Augusta, St. Paul Parish
Surveyed September 18, 1759 Plat Book C, page 230
Granted October 2, 1759 Grant Book B, page 202
Plat shows tract to be Lot #9, Augusta. Bounded on the northeast by the Savannah River, east by John Fitch, and on the west by John Pettygrew.

McCartan, Francis and Campbell, Martin
Town Lot #4, Augusta
Granted August 2, 1768 Grant Book F, page 441

McCartan, Francis and Campbell, Martin
500 acres, St. Paul Parish
Granted July 1, 1760 Grant Book I, page 615
Bounded on the north by Thomas Bassett, east by the Savannah River, and on the south by Nathaniel Bassett.

McCarty, Daniel
200 acres, St. Paul Parish
Surveyed May 1, 1770 Plat Book C, page 185
Granted November 6, 1770 Grant Book I, page 187
Bounded on all sides by a tract of 500 acres of land ordered for John Walton.

McCarty, Daniel
100 acres, St. Paul Parish
Surveyed November 10, 1772 Plat Book C, page 189
Granted May 4, 1773 Grant Book I, page 981
Bounded on the northeast partly by R. Upton and on all other sides by vacant land.

McCarty, Jacob
200 acres, St. Paul Parish
Surveyed July 4, 1770 Plat Book C, page 185
Granted March 5, 1771 Grant Book I, page 271

Bounded on the northwest by Euchee Creek, southwest by Daniel McCarty, partly on the northeast by land ordered Isaac Low, on all other sides by vacant land.

McClen, Robert
Town Lot #64, Wrightsboro, St. Paul Parish; 300 acres, Wrightsboro Township, St. Paul Parish.
Granted July 3, 1770 Grant Book I, page 141

McClung, Robert
300 acres, St. Paul Parish
Surveyed June 8, 1769 Plat Book C, page 181
No grant recorded.

McDonald, John
100 acres, St. Paul Parish
Surveyed March 20, 1772 Plat Book C, page 188
No grant recorded.
Bounded on the northwest by Peter Candler.

McDowell, Thomas
250 acres, St. Paul Parish
Surveyed June 7, 1769 Plat Book C, page 180
Granted April 7, 1772 Grant Book I, page 570
Bounded on the northwest by Thomas Ayres.

McFarland, James
Town Lot #50, Wrightsboro, St. Paul Parish; 300 acres, Wrightsboro Township, St. Paul Parish, bounded on the east by land granted Isaac Dennis (plat shows Jacob Dennis on the east.) Plat shows tract bounded on the west by Little River.
Surveyed October 26, 1769 Plat Book C, page 180
Granted July 3, 1770 Grant Book I, page 145

McFarland, James
200 acres, Wrightsboro Township, St. Paul Parish
Surveyed April 29, 1771 Plat Book C, page 186
Granted September 3, 1771 Grant Book I, page 416
Bounded on the northeast by John Stubbs and John Jones, northwest by John Jones, southwest by Joseph Brown, and partly on the southeast by vacant land.

McFarland, William
100 acres, Wrightsboro Township, St. Paul Parish
Surveyed May 14, 1771 Plat Book C, page 187
Granted December 3, 1771 Grant Book I, Page 480

McFarland, William
150 acres, Wrightsboro Township, St. Paul Parish
Surveyed December 12, 1772 Plat Book C, page 190
Granted July 5, 1774 Grant Book M, page 67
Bounded on the southwest and partly on the west by
William McFarland and on all other sides by vacant land.

McGillivray, Lachlan
100 acres, St. Paul Parish
Granted December 3, 1760 Grant Book C, page 17
Tract located on Mill Creek near Augusta, bounded on the
southwest by Thomas Ross.

McGillivray, Lachlan
Town Lot #11, Second row, Augusta
Granted February 3, 1762 Grant Book D, page 44
Original warrant says lot is a corner lot on the main road.

McGillivray, Lachlan
Town Lot #40, Fourth row, Augusta
Granted January 3, 1764 Grant Book D, page 369

McGillivray, Lachlan
Town Lot #20, Augusta
Survey date not given Plat Book C, page 178
Granted March 6, 1764 Grant Book D, page 386
Plat shows lot to be a corner lot, bounded by Broad Street, the
Common, Runols Street, and Thomas Ford.

McGillivray, Lachlan
300 acres, St. Paul Parish
Surveyed November 1, 1775 Plat Book C, page 70
This plat could go with grant for Lachlan Macgillivray on page
114, this book. Tract is recorded in Plat Book C, page 70 with the
400 acre tract next below and the plat says tract of land includes
the 200 acres in dispute between James Gray and George Galphin.

Bounded on the southeast by Barbara Galphin's 200 acre tract, southwest by same tract of Barbara Galphin, northwest by 400 acre tract of said Lachlan McGillivray, and on the northeast by the Savannah River. See next entry below.

McGillivray, Lachlan
400 acres, St. Paul Parish
Surveyed November 1, 1775 Plat Book C, page 70
This plat could go with grant for Lachlan Macgillivray on page 114, this book.
Tract is recorded in Plat Book C, page 70 with the 300 acre tract next above and the plat says tract of land includes the 200 acres in dispute between James Gray and George Galphin. Bounded on the southeast by Barbara Galphin's 200 acre tract, 300 acre tract of said Lachlan McGillivray, and James Gray; northwest by the Savannah River, Bridge Creek, Mr. Galphin, and Alexander Shaw. See next entry above.

McGillivray, Lachlan and Clark, Daniel
500 acres, District of Augusta
Granted September 8, 1756 Grant Book A, page 200
Bounded on the northeast by the Savannah River, southeast by Edward Barnard, and on the northwest by Rae and Barksdale.

McGillivray, Lachlan and Clark, Daniel
Town Lot #17, Augusta
Granted September 8, 1756 Grant Book A, page 201

McGillivray, Lachlan; Rae, John; Galphin, George (surviving partners of Brown, Rae, and Company.)
500 acres, St. Paul Parish
Granted April 5, 1764 Grant Book D, page 399
Part of the tract is on an island called New Savannah Island and the other part is on the mainland, bounded on the north and south by vacant land, on every other side by the Savannah River.

McGillivray, Lachlan and Spencer, John
500 acres, District of Augusta
Granted February 7, 1758 Grant Book A, page 558
Bounded on the south by James Paris, east by the

Savannah River, and on the north by Butler's Creek.

McHenry, James
300 acres, District of Augusta
Granted May 1, 1759 Grant Book B, page 80

McHenry, James
Town Lot #22, Third row, Augusta
Surveyed November 12, 1756 Plat Book C, page 179
Granted May 1, 1759 Grant Book B, page 79

McIntosh, Alexander; Jackson, James; Cooke, Robert
800 acres, St. Paul Parish
Surveyed October 29, 1766 Plat Book C, page 88
Granted March 3, 1767 Grant Book F, page 116

McIntosh, William
200 acres, St. Paul Parish
Surveyed March 14, 1770 Plat Book C, page 180
Granted May 7, 1771 Grant Book I, page 312

McIntosh, William
200 acres, St. Paul Parish
Surveyed January 8, 1770 Plat Book C, page 191
No grant recorded.
Bounded on the south by Patrick O'Brien and vacant land.

McKay, James
1000 acres, Wrightsboro Township, St. Paul Parish
Granted November 1, 1774 Grant Book M, page 711
Bounded on the southwest by James Coats, Jacob Castle, John
Dunkin, William Miller, and vacant land; northwest by John More
and Richard Smith; northwest by Hixon Ross, the widow Stubbs,
and vacant land; southeast by John Perkins.

McKay, James
500 acres, St. Paul Parish
Granted November 1, 1774 Grant Book M, page 712
Bounded on the southwest by Craft Highwood, Henry Coats,
and James Hill; southeast by Benjamin Jones and vacant land,
northeast by Candler.

McKay, James
500 acres, St. Paul Parish
Granted December 6, 1774 Grant Book M, page 814
Bounded on the northwest by Joshua Sanders, and southwest by ceded lands.

McKay, James
500 acres, Wrightsboro Township, St. Paul Parish
Granted March 7, 1775 Grant Book M, page 1085
Bounded on all sides by vacant land.

McKay, Patrick
100 acres, St. Paul Parish
Surveyed May 8, 1770 Plat Book C, page 185
No grant recorded.
Bounded on the southeast by Glebe land, and north by William McKay.

McKinnen, Charles William
500 acres, St. Paul Parish
Original survey date unknown, but resurveyed June 14 and 15, 1831.
Recorded in Plat Book WWWW, page 9.
Granted February 7, 1775 Grant Book M, page 1030
Bounded on the north by James McFarland, east by John Graham, and east by John Dennis. Original plat (filed in Columbia County Loose Plat File) says tract found to contain 594 acres on resurvey. Tract went into Columbia County.

McKinnon, Charles William
Four tracts of 500 acres each, a total of 2000 acres, St. Paul Parish.
Granted February 7, 1775 Grant Book M, page 1031
Tract #1 bounded on all sides by vacant land. Tract #2, bounded on all sides by vacant land. Tract #3 bounded on the northeast by Hugh Middleton, southwest by Mr. Reid, southeast by John Germany. Tract #4 bounded on the southeast by John Jones, southwest by John Jones and vacant land.

McKintosh, Alexander; Crook, Robert; Jackson, James
Seven lots in Augusta as follows: #27 (a vacant lot) and

six lots, #13, #14, #19, #20, #26, and #36. The latter six lots were purchased by McKintosh, Crook, and Jackson from the original proprietors. Total of 350 acres (50 acres per lot.) Original proprietors not named.
Granted September 3, 1765 Grant Book E, page 227

McLean, Andrew
300 acres, St. Paul Parish
Granted January 3, 1775 Grant Book M, page 906

McLean, Andrew
500 acres, St. Paul Parish
Granted January 3, 1775 Grant Book M, page 904
Bounded on the southwest and northwest by Samuel Paine.

McLean, Andrew
400 acres, St. Paul Parish
Surveyed September 22, 1774 Plat Book M, page 7
Granted January 3, 1775 Grant Book M, page 905

McMurran, William
150 acres, St. Paul Parish
Surveyed February 19, 1767 Plat Book C, page 175
No grant recorded.
Bounded on the southwest by Cane Creek.

McMurrin, William
350 acres, St. Paul Parish
Surveyed November 21, 1769 Plat Book C, page 177
Granted March 6, 1770 Grant Book G, page 557
Bounded on the northwest by John Green.

McNeuir, Daniel
100 acres, St. Paul Parish
Surveyed July 4, 1772 Plat Book C, page 188
Granted January 19, 1773 Grant Book I, page 872

McNish, John
100 acres, St. Paul Parish
Surveyed May 5, 1759 Plat Book C, page 191
Bounded on the northwest by John Brunson.

McQueen, James
50 acres, St. Paul Parish
Surveyed October 24, 1772 Plat Book C, page 188
Bounded on the northwest by James McQueen.

Meadows, Richard
100 acres, St. Paul Parish
Surveyed March 25, 1765 Plat Book C, page 179
Granted May 7, 1765 Grant Book E, page 156
Plat shows tract bounded on the southeast by Great Kioka Creek.

Middleton, Holland
Town Lot #81, Wrightsboro, St. Paul Parish; 400 acres,
Wrightsboro Township, St. Paul Parish.
Surveyed August 17, 1769 Plat Book C, page 182
Granted July 3, 1770 Grant Book I, page 929

Middleton, Holland
150 acres, St. Paul Parish
Granted May 4, 1773 Grant Book I, page 985

Middleton, Holland Jr.
Town Lot #38, Wrightsboro, St. Paul Parish; 100 acres, St. Paul
Parish, bounded on the north and west by Little River.
Granted July 3, 1770 Grant Book I, page 144

Middleton, Holt
100 acres, St. Paul Parish
No grant recorded.
Bounded on three sides by the Little River.

Middleton, Holt
150 acres, St. Paul Parish
Surveyed May 23, 1769
No grant recorded.
Plat Book C, page 175

Middleton, Hugh
200 acres, St. Paul Parish
Surveyed February 14, 1769 Plat Book C, page 178
Granted November 7, 1769 Grant Book G, page 463

Bounded on the northwest by the Little River.

Middleton, Hugh
100 acres, St. Paul Parish
Surveyed September 16, 1758 Plat Book C, page 191
Granted January 3, 1775 Grant Book M, page 907
Bounded on the south by Aaron Bureston and on the east by the Savannah River.

Middleton, Robert
100 acres, St. Paul Parish
Surveyed April 23, 1773 Plat Book C, page 188
Granted August 2, 1774 Grant Book M, page 226
Bounded on the southwest by Jacob Welding.

Middleton, Robert
100 acres, St. Paul Parish
Surveyed March 12, 1770 Plat Book C, page 183
No grant recorded.
Bounded on the east by Robert Middleton.

Middleton, Robert
100 acres, St. Paul Parish
Surveyed September 9, 1769 Plat Book C, page 177
No grant recorded.

Miles, Daniel
100 acres, Wrightsboro Township, St. Paul Parish
Granted December 6, 1774 Grant Book M, page 809
Bounded on the northeast by James Bishop, west by Hugh Temrin, and on the southeast by vacant land.

Miles, William
Town Lot #71, Wrightsboro, St. Paul Parish; also all that tract of land containing 200 acres out of the reserve for Wrightsboro Township to include 100 acres ordered to the said William Miles by a former warrant situate and being in St. Paul Parish (see Grant Book I, page 200.) Tract bounded on the northwest by Joseph Memy.
Surveyed August 29, 1769 Plat Book C, page 179
Granted November 6, 1770 Grant Book I, page 200

Millbank, William
200 acres, St. Paul Parish
Surveyed September 11, 1772 Plat Book C, page 187
Granted January 3, 1775 Grant Book M, page 913
Bounded on the northeast by Edmund Cartledge, and northwest by B. Bevins.

Millen, David
200 acres, St. Paul Parish
Surveyed October 17, 1772 Plat Book C, page 186
Granted October 4, 1774 Grant Book M, page 579
Bounded on the north by the Savannah River.

Miller, John
150 acres, St. Paul Parish
Surveyed October 23, 1772 Plat Book C, page 187
Granted July 5, 1774 Grant Book M, page 72
Bounded on the southeast by Thomas Miller. Tract surveyed as 100 acres and granted as 150 acres.

Miller, Thomas
100 acres, St. Paul Parish
Surveyed October 23, 1772 Plat Book C, page 187
Granted July 5, 1774 Grant Book M, page 73
Bounded on the west by John Miller, and east by James McQueen.

Mitchell, John
150 acres, St. Paul Parish
Surveyed December 2, 1772 Plat Book C, page 190
Granted June 7, 1774 Grant Book I, page 1030
Bounded on the southeast by Robert Story and Daniel Coleman.

Mitchell, William
Town Lot #43, Wrightsboro, St. Paul Parish; 100 acres, Wrightsboro Township, St. Paul Parish, bounded on the southeast by Absalom Jackson, northwest by Williams Creek.
Surveyed May 12, 1769 Plat Book C, page 181
Granted July 3, 1770 Grant Book I, page 140

Moodie, Thomas
500 acres, St. Paul Parish

Surveyed August 18, 1774 Plat Book M, page 43
Granted November 1, 1774 Grant Book M, page 706
Bounded on the northeast by Nathan Hampton and Mr. Middleton, southwest by Michael Griffin and Mr. Weldon, northwest by Samuel Germany and vacant land.

Mooney, Joseph
Town Lot #27, Wrightsboro, St. Paul Parish; 550 acres, Wrightsboro Township, St. Paul Parish.
Surveyed July 5, 1769 Plat Book C, page 185
Granted July 3, 1770 Grant Book I, page 142

Moore, John
Town Lot #5, Wrightsboro, St. Paul Parish; 300 acres, Wrightsboro Township, St. Paul Parish, bounded on the north by land granted Richard Smith.
Surveyed July 27, 1769 Plat Book C, page 183
Granted July 3, 1770 Grant Book I, page 143

Moore, Mordecai
Town Lot #7, Wrightsboro, St. Paul Parish; 300 acres, Wrightsboro Township, St. Paul Parish.
Surveyed September 5, 1769 Plat Book C, page 177
Granted July 3, 1770 Grant Book I, page 146

Moore, Richard
Town Lot #42, Wrightsboro, St. Paul Parish; 200 acres, Wrightsboro Township, St. Paul Parish, bounded on the southwest partly by Isaac Low and partly by Richard Bird, on all other sides by vacant land.
Surveyed March 26, 1770 Plat Book C, page 177
Granted November 6, 1770 Grant Book I, page 201

Moore, Richard
Town Lot #46, Wrightsboro, St. Paul Parish; 100 acres, Wrightsboro
Township, St. Paul Parish.
Surveyed April 14, 1769 Plat Book C, page 184
Granted July 3, 1770 Grant Book I, page 356

Moore, Thomas
Town Lot #72, Wrightsboro, St. Paul Parish; 200 acres, St. Paul Parish.
Surveyed August 29, 1769 Plat Book C, page 176
Granted July 3, 1770 Grant Book I, page 355
The 200 acre tract is shown on the plat to be bounded on the southeast by Upton's Creek and on all other sides by vacant land.

Morgan, Thomas
Town Lot #39, Augusta, containing 1 acre
Granted March 2, 1773 Grant Book L, page 167
Lot located in the fourth row between lots #38 and #40.

Morris, Thomas
150 acres, St. Paul Parish
Surveyed December 9, 1771 Plat Book C, page 187
Granted April 7, 1772 Grant Book I, page 571

Morris, Thomas
200 acres, St. Paul Parish
Surveyed March 2, 1772 Plat Book C, page 188
Granted January 19, 1773 Grant Book I, page 867
Bounded on the northeast by the said grantee.

Morrow, George
300 acres, St. Paul Parish
Surveyed June 1, 1769 Plat Book C, page 178
No grant recorded.
Bounded on the northwest by James Morrow.

Morrow, James
350 acres, St. Paul Parish
Surveyed April 20, 1769 Plat Book C, page 182
No grant recorded.
Bounded on the southeast by George Morrow.

Morse, John
Town Lot #34, Augusta
Surveyed June 10, 1763 Plat Book C, page 179
Granted April 5, 1768 Grant Book F, page 437

Plat says lot in fourth row, fronting Back Street and joining the Common.

Morse, John
250 acres, St. Paul Parish
Granted February 7, 1775 Grant Book M, page 1016

Morse, John
97 acres, St. Paul Parish
Granted February 7, 1775 Grant Book M, page 1017
Bounded on the north by Phillips, east by Jacob Bill and Robert Jones, south by Jacob Bill and Phillips, west by Henderson and Fitch.

Morse, John
350 acres, St. Paul Parish
Surveyed September 29, 1766 Plat Book C, page 184
No grant recorded.
Bounded on the west by Spirit Creek and George Bailey, northeast by John Fitch.

Morton, Samuel
250 acres, St. Paul Parish
Surveyed May 19, 1773 Plat Book C, page 189
Granted July 5, 1774 Grant Book M, page 71
Bounded on the north by William Standley, William Wallace, and vacant land; east by Ebenezer Smith; south by John Hencrick and vacant land; west by James Ashmore, William Stanley and vacant land.

Morton, Samuel
200 acres, St. Paul Parish
Granted December 6, 1774 Grant Book M, page 807
Bounded on the southcast by Joshua Bradley and vacant land, southwest by Benjamin Harris and vacant land, northeast by Abraham Ayres.

Moser, Adam
100 acres, St. Paul Parish
Surveyed January 21, 1773 Plat Book C, page 190
Granted June 7, 1774 Grant Book I, page 1032

Bounded on the southwest by Peter Sallins and vacant land, partly on the northwest by land which appears to have been run, and on all other sides by vacant land.

Mossman, James
1000 acres, St. Paul Parish
Granted December 6, 1774 Grant Book M, page 811
Bounded on the southeast by Philip Perry, Samuel Waller, John Crawford, and Thomas Grier; southwest by William Ramsey, Rawls Perry, and Peter Culbreath.

Mossman, James
Granted December 6, 1774 Grant Book M, page 812
Bounded on the northeast by Thomas Stapler, Alexander Coldwell, Brown, and John Howard; southwest by John Danielly, William McFarland, and vacant land; west by William Linn and James Coan; northwest by Captain Goodgeon.

Mossman, James
500 acres, St. Paul Parish
Granted December 6, 1774 Grant Book M, page 813

Mullryne, John and Tattnall, Josiah
500 acres, St. Paul Parish
Granted February 7, 1775 Grant Book M, page 1022
Bounded on the east by John Tinkler, southwest by Andrew Jones, and on the northeast by Benjamin Williams.

Murphey, Edward
Town Lot #41, Wrightsboro, St. Paul Parish; 150 acres, Wrightsboro
Township, St. Paul Parish.
Surveyed April 15, 1769
Granted July 3, 1770
Plat Book C, page 183
Grant Book I, page 139

Murphy, Nicholas
Town Lot #25, Third row, Augusta
Granted December 3, 1760 Grant Book C, page 15

Murphy, Nicholas
Lot #28, Township of Augusta, containing 50 acres
No survey or grant recorded, only the following endorsement, recorded in Plat Book C, pages 174-175. Originally surveyed for Nicholas Murphy on October 2, 1749 and signed over by Nicholas Murphy to William Finley (date not shown) and signed over by William Finley to Richard and Frances Warren on November 30, 1750.

Murphy, Nicholas
250 acres, St. Paul Parish
Surveyed October 6, 1766 Plat Book C, page 182
No grant recorded.
Bounded on the southwest by William Bostick, northwest by Jacobson, northeast by Owen Sullivan, and on the southeast by Thomas Bassett.

Murry, John
100 acres, St. Paul Parish
Surveyed April 19, 1769 Plat Book C, page 176
No grant recorded.
Bounded on the northwest by Thomas Ansley.

Neal, James
200 acres, St. Paul Parish
Granted January 19, 1773 Grant Book I, page 875
Bounded partly on the south and partly on the east by Casselberry and on all other sides by vacant land.

Neal, Jonathan
150 acres, St. Paul Parish
Granted January 3, 1775 Grant Book M, page 920
Bounded on the southwest and southeast by Edward Barnard, and northwest by Robert Rae.

Nelson, James
100 acres, St. Paul Parish
Granted May 1, 1759 Grant Book B, page 84
Bounded on the east by the Savannah River.

Newberry, William
500 acres, District of Augusta
Granted February 5, 1757 Grant Book A, page 407
Bounded on the northeast by the Savannah River, and southeast by Witherington's Bluff.

Newton, James
100 acres, St. Paul Parish
Granted August 2, 1774 Grant Book M, page 236
Bounded on the northwest by Mr. Low, southeast by Mr. Hammond, southwest by Joseph Hickimbottom and Standley.

Newton, Samuel
100 acres, St. Paul Parish
Granted July 5, 1774 Grant Book M, page 78

Nicholson, Thomas
150 acres, St. Paul Parish
Granted August 2, 1774 Grant Book M, page 235
Bounded on the east by land formerly belonging to Edward Barnard, northwest by Rocky Creek.

Nordon, Thomas
150 acres, St. Paul Parish
Granted October 4, 1774

Oakes, Joseph
300 acres, St. Paul Parish
Granted December 4, 1759
Grant Book M, page 582
Grant Book B, page 333
Bounded on the north by Township of Augusta, east by McBean, and on every other side by land of Owen Day.

O'Bryan, Patrick
150 acres, St. Paul Parish
Granted June 5, 1770 Grant Book I, page 29
Bounded on the south by Thomas Read, and southwest by William Taylor.

Odam, Isaac
100 acres, St. Paul Parish
Granted February 4, 1772 Grant Book I, page 514
Bounded on the southwest by Christopher Clark.

Oliver, Alexander
Town Lot #60, Wrightsboro, St. Paul Parish; 100 acres, Wrightsboro Township, St. Paul Parish.
Granted July 3, 1770 Grant Book I, page 148

Oliver, Alexander
100 acres, St. Paul Parish
Granted July 5, 1774 Grant Book M, page 80
Bounded on the northwest by said Alexander Oliver and vacant land.

Oliver, James
Town Lot #36, Wrightsboro, St. Paul Parish;
100 acres, Wrightsboro
Township, St. Paul Parish.
Granted July 3, 1770 Grant Book I, page 151

Oliver, James
100 acres, St. Paul Parish
Granted August 2, 1774 Grant Book M, page 239
Bounded on the northwest by James Oliver and vacant land.

Oliver, John
Town Lot #11, Wrightsboro, St. Paul Parish; 350 acres, Wrightsboro Township, St. Paul Parish, bounded on the north by Joseph Maddock, south by Samuel Oliver.
Granted July 3, 1770 Grant Book I, page 150

Oliver, John
150 acres, Wrightsboro Township, St. Paul Parish
Granted August 2, 1774 Grant Book M, page 238
Bounded on the southwest by said John Oliver and on all other sides by vacant land.

Oliver, Samuel
Town Lot #91, Wrightsboro, St. Paul Parish; 250 acres,

Wrightsboro Township, St. Paul Parish, bounded on the north

by John Oliver, Granted July 3, 1770

Orick, James
100 acres, St. Paul Parish
Granted July 5, 1774
Outerbridge, White
Town Lot #35, Augusta
Granted July 4, 1758

Owen, Ephraim
Grant Book I, page 149
Grant Book M, page 81
Grant Book A, page 659
Town Lot #34, Wrightsboro, St. Paul Parish; 250 acres, Wrightsboro Township, St. Paul Parish, bounded on the north by Little River, east by land said to be Grisons, west by land granted John Anderson.
Granted July 3, 1770

Pace, Barnabas
100 acres, St. Paul Parish
Granted January 19, 1773
Grant Book I, page 152
Grant Book I, page 877
Bounded on the northwest by Peter Paris, south by Edmund Bugg, and on the north by Sherwood.

Pace, Knowls
100 acres, St. Paul Parish
Granted September 5, 1769 Grant Book G, page 413

Pace, Richard
22 acres, St. Paul Parish
Surveyed August 12, 1759 Plat Book C, page 417
Granted December 7, 1762 Grant Book D, page 241
Tract is an island in the Savannah River, bounded on every side by the said river and located about 32 miles above Augusta and about 1 mile below an island called Johnson's Island.

Pace, Silas
100 acres, Wrightsboro Township, St. Paul Parish
Granted November 1, 1774 Grant Book M, page 718
Bounded on the southwest by Joseph Maddock and on all other sides by vacant land.

Pace, Thomas
200 acres, St. Paul Parish
Granted May 2, 1769 Grant Book G, page 319

Paine, Samuel
100 acres, St. Paul Parish
Granted October 4, 1774 Grant Book M, page 509
Bounded on the northwest by Little River, northeast by Benjamin Rany, and on the southwest by Kilgore.

Paris, Peter
250 acres, St. Paul Parish
Granted February 5, 1771 Grant Book I, page 255
Bounded on the northeast by John Tinkler and land surveyed for Tucker, west by LeRoy Hammond.

Parker, John
200 acres, St. Paul Parish
Granted July 5, 1774 Grant Book M, page 89
Bounded on the southwest by Loveless Savage, and on the northeast by Richardson and Woodland.

Parks, Charles
450 acres, St. Paul Parish
Granted July 5, 1774 Grant Book M, page 83
Bounded on the east by Thomas Lloyd, and on the south by Thomas Lantor and Sheftall.

Parris, James
50 acres, Township of Augusta
Granted December 9, 1756 Grant Book A, page 252
Bounded on the north by the Savannah River, west by James Gray, and east by John Pettygrew.

Parris, James
100 acres, St. Paul Parish
Granted May 1, 1759 Grant Book B, page 121
Bounded on the south by the Savannah River, and north by said Parris' land.

Parris, James
350 acres, District of Augusta, St. Paul Parish
Granted March 5, 1756 Grant Book D, page 368
Bounded on the east by the Savannah River, and north by land of William Gray.

Parris, Peter
250 acres, St. Paul Parish
Granted January 2, 1770 Grant Book G, page 504
Bounded on the east by Sherwood Bugg.

Parsley, Nathaniel
100 acres, St. Paul Parish
Surveyed February 13, 1767 Plat Book C, page 364
Granted March 7, 1769 Grant Book G, page 286
Tract originally surveyed for William Taylor, thence ordered to Nathaniel Parsley on February 10, 1769 (see Plat Book C, page 364.) Granted to Nathaniel Parsley.

Parsley, Richard
100 acres, St. Paul Parish
Granted August 2, 1774 Grant Book M, page 242

Parvey (Pavey), Dial
200 acres, Wrightsboro Township, St. Paul Parish
Granted September 6, 1774 Grant Book M, page 368
Bounded on all sides by vacant land.

Paulk, Micajah
200 acres, St. Paul Parish
Granted July 5, 1774 Grant Book M, page 86

Payne, John
100 acres, St. Paul Parish
Granted December 3, 1760 Grant Book C, page 11

Bounded on the northwest by George Cadagan, deceased; east by Town of Augusta and Common; southeast by Patrick Clark; west by Edward Barnard and John Fitch.

Payne, Samuel
200 acres, St. Paul Parish
Granted July 3, 1770 Grant Book I, page 56
Bounded on the north by Little River, south by Keg Creek, and on the northeast by the Savannah River.

Payne, Samuel
100 acres, St. Paul Parish
Granted January 19, 1773 Grant Book I, page 879
Bounded on the north by the Little River.

Pencen, Thomas Roden
100 acres, St. Paul Parish
Granted July 5, 1774 Grant Book M, page 88
Bounded on all sides by vacant land.

Perkins, John
Town Lot #14, Wrightsboro, St. Paul Parish;
150 acres, Wrightsboro Township, St. Paul Parish.
Granted July 3, 1770 Grant Book I, page 153

Perkins, Peter
Town Lot #48, Wrightsboro, St. Paul Parish; 500 acres, Wrightsboro Township, St. Paul Parish, bounded on the southeast by Cornelius Cochrane.
Granted November 6, 1770 Grant Book I, page 202

Perrett, John
200 acres, St. Paul Parish
Surveyed November 10, 1774 Plat Book C, page 417
Granted April 4, 1775 Grant Book M, page 1111
Bounded on the northwest by Thomas Moore and vacant land, southwest by Mordecai Moore, and southeast by John Moore and vacant land.

Perry, Rawls
100 acres, St. Paul Parish

Granted January 19, 1773 Grant Book I, page 880
Bounded on the southwest by Moody Burt.

Petticrew, John
200 acres, District of Augusta
Granted April 5, 1757 Grant Book A, page 406
Bounded on the southeast by Edward Barnard, and southwest by Rocky Creek.

Pettygrew, Jane and Grierson, James
Township Lot #10, Township of Augusta, containing 50 acres
Granted December 1, 1767 Grant Book F, page 422
Bounded on the northeast by the Savannah River, west by James Paris, and on every other side by lots of Macarton and Campbell.

Pettygrew, John
Lots #17 and #18, Township of Augusta, 50 acres each, a total of 100 acres, located on the back of the lots of James Gray and James Parris and adjoining the lot of Edward Barnard to the west.
Surveyed December 10, 1757 Plat Book M, page 13
Granted June 5, 1759 Grant Book B, page 506

Phelps, Avington
150 acres, St. Paul Parish
Granted December 3, 1771 Grant Book I, page 481
Bounded on the east by land surveyed for Wells, south and partly west by land surveyed for Ebenezer Smith, on all other sides by vacant land.

Phelps, William
350 acres, St. Paul Parish
Granted July 5, 1774 Grant Book M, page 82
Bounded on the southwest by Benjamin Wells and James Brown.

Phillips, James
500 acres, St. Paul Parish
Granted December 6, 1774 Grant Book M, page 823
Bounded on the northwest by Rooks, William Satterwhite, and Dionysus Wright; southwest by William Maxwell; southeast by vacant land; northeast by Thomas Norden.

Phillips, Zachariah
100 acres, St. Paul Parish
Granted November 1, 1774 Grant Book M, page 717
Bounded on the north by Benjamin Few and Ignatius Few, northeast by John Thomson.

Phillips, John
150 acres, St. Paul Parish
Granted September 7, 1762 Grant Book D, page 193
Bounded on the east by the Savannah River, south by Jacob Bell, and west by John Fitch.

Phillips, Peter
100 acres, St. Paul Parish
Surveyed May 30, 1769 Plat Book C, page 417
No grant recorded.
Bounded on the north by the Little River.

Picket, James
200 acres, St. Paul Parish
Granted February 7, 1775 Grant Book M, page 1041
Bounded on the southeast by Stephen Day, and northwest by Samuel Newton.

Pooler, Quinton
100 acres, St. Paul Parish
Granted January 19, 1773 Grant Book I, page 878
Bounded on the northeast by the Savannah River and southeast by Thomas Read.

Pooler, Quinton
200 acres, St. Paul Parish
Granted July 5, 1774 Grant Book M, page 90

Powell, James Edward
1100 acres, St. Paul Parish
Surveyed August 17, 1774 Plat Book M, page 21
Granted October 4, 1774 Grant Book M, page 588
Bounded on the northwest by William Bennett, William Barnet, and Jacob Horn; northeast by John Howard, Jesse Horn, and

vacant land; southeast by Jacob Grubbs, John Bacon, and Colonel James Jackson; southwest by vacant land.

Qualls, Roger
200 acres, St. Paul Parish
Granted July 5, 1774 Grant Book M, page 91
Bounded on the northeast by the Savannah River, and on the northwest by Thomas Gilliland.

Qualls, Roger
150 acres, St. Paul Parish
Granted September 6, 1774 Grant Book M, page 370

Rae, James; Rae, Robert; Whitefield, George; Graham, Thomas
500 acres, St. Paul Parish
Granted January 1, 1771 Grant Book I, page 242

Rae, John
100 acres, St. Paul Parish
Granted April 2, 1765 Grant Book E, page 129
Bounded on the north by said John Rae, and east by John Pettegrew.

Rae, John
600 acres, St. Paul Parish
Granted October 29, 1765 Grant Book E, page 268
Bounded on the northeast by the Savannah River, southeast by William Turin and Company, and on the northwest by George Galphin.

Rae, John
200 acres, St. Paul Parish
Granted October 29, 1765 Grant Book E, page 269
Bounded on the northeast by the Savannah River, and on the southeast by George Galphin.

Rae, John
220 acres, St. Paul Parish
Surveyed June 22, 1765 Plat Book M, page 17
Granted October 29, 1765 Grant Book E, page 271

Tract located partly on Uchee Island and partly on the main land opposite island, about 12 miles above Augusta, which tract was originally allotted Isaac Barksdale, deceased.

Rae, John
200 acres, St. Paul Parish
Granted December 4, 1770 Grant Book I, page 229
Bounded on the northwest and southwest by land of said grantee, southeast by Zachariah Fenn, and on the northeast by the Savannah River.

Rae, John; Galphin, George; McGillivray, Lachlan (surviving partners of Brown, Rae, and Company.)
500 acres, St. Paul Parish
Granted April 3, 1764 Grant Book D, page 399
Part of the 500 acres is on an island called New Savannah Island and the other part on the mainland, bounded on the north and south by vacant land and on every other side by the Savannah River.

Rae, Robert; Whitefield, George; Rae, James; Graham, Thomas
500 acres, St. Paul Parish
Granted January 1, 1771 Grant Book I, page 242

Rahn, Jasper
100 acres, District of Augusta
Granted December 6, 1757 Grant Book A, page 519
Bounded on the south by Theobald Keiffer.

Rains, William
300 acres, St. Paul Parish
Surveyed August 12, 1759 Plat Book C, page 28
No grant recorded.
Original warrant says tract located on Rocky Creek about 8 miles of the south side of Brier Creek.

Ramsey, John
150 acres, St. Paul Parish
Granted January 3, 1775 Grant Book M, page 930
Bounded on the southwest by James Graves, and on the northwest by James McFarland.

Ramsey, Isaac
300 acres, St. Paul Parish
Granted September 6, 1774 Grant Book M, page 397

Ramsey, John
100 acres, St. Paul Parish
Granted January 19, 1773 Grant Book I, page 882
Bounded on the west by James McFarland.

Ramsey, Randall
600 acres, St. Paul Parish
Granted March 7, 1775 Grant Book M, page 1087
Bounded on the southeast by David Threats, and on the northwest
by James Graves and William Ramsey.

Ramsey, William
200 acres, St. Paul Parish
Granted September 6, 1774 Grant Book M, page 396
Bounded on the west by Randall Ramsey, and on the south and
east by Peter Cutbreath.

Randon, Peter
300 acres, St. Paul Parish
Granted November 1, 1774 Grant Book M, page 722
Bounded on the east by George Rosebergh, Captain William
Candler, and vacant land; north by said Peter Randon; west by
Nathan Narris and Dionysus Wright; south by William
Satterwwite.

Randon, Peter
500 acres, St. Paul Parish
Granted January 3, 1775 Grant Book M, page 929
Bounded on the northeast by land laid out for Mr. Herrons and
vacant land, and on the southwest by Daniel Riece and Peter
Randon.

Red, John
200 acres, St. Paul Parish
Granted April 4, 1775 Grant Book M, page 1112

Red, Thomas
Town Lot #2, on the bay, Augusta
Granted September 30, 1757 Grant Book A, page 547

Red, Thomas
500 acres, District of Augusta
Granted September 30, 1757 Grant Book A, page 548
Bounded on the northeast by the Savannah River, southeast by Thomas Goodale, and on the northeast by Township line of Augusta.

Red, Thomas
200 acres, District of Augusta, St. Paul Parish
Surveyed January 8, 1757 Plat Book M, page 14
Granted February 7, 1758 Grant Book B, page 442

Redman, William
150 acres, St. Paul Parish
Granted September 6, 1774 Grant Book M, page 402
Bounded on the northwest by Thomas Morris.

Rees, Daniel
150 acres, St. Paul Parish
Granted May 4, 1773 Grant Book I, page 993

Renn, Presley
150 acres, St. Paul Parish
Granted August 2, 1774 Grant Book M, page 247
Bounded on the northwest by Savage and L. Redman, southeast by Archibald Stinson and Loveless Savage.

Reves, Jesse
100 acres, St. Paul Parish
Granted August 2, 1774 Grant Book M, page 246
Bounded on the southeast by Rogers and vacant land, southwest by L. Rodman, and on the northeast by Theophilus Davis.

Richardson, Daniel
150 acres, St. Paul Parish
Granted July 5, 1774 Grant Book M, page 99

Bounded on the northeast by land surveyed for unknown, and partly on the southwest and partly on the northwest by the said Daniel Richardson.

Richardson, Daniel
200 acres, St. Paul Parish
Granted November 1, 1774 Grant Book M, page 723
Bounded on the northeast and southeast by said Daniel Richardson, northwest by John McFarland, and southwest by Loveless Savage.

Ring, Christopher
400 acres, St. Paul Parish
Surveyed May 15, 1767 Plat Book C, page 362
Granted April 5, 1768 Grant Book G, page 84
Tract originally surveyed for Wood Tucker, thence ordered to Christopher Ring on February 2, 1768 (see Plat Book C, page 362.) Granted to Christopher Ring.

Roaten, John Jr.
100 acres, St. Paul Parish
Granted October 4, 1774 Grant Book M, page 594
Bounded on the northeast by George Barnes.

Roaten, John
300 acres, St. Paul Parish
Granted July 5, 1774 Grant Book M, page 95

Robinson, David
150 acres, Wrightsboro Township, St. Paul Parish
Granted September 6, 1774 Grant Book M, page 394
Bounded on all sides by vacant land.

Robison, Israel
100 acres, Wrightsboro Township, St. Paul Parish
Granted September 6, 1774 Grant Book M, page 404
Bounded on the northeast by Isaac Cowper, northwest and southwest by vacant land, southeast by Dobbins.

Robison, John
200 acres, St. Paul Parish

Granted July 5, 1774 Grant Book M, page 101
Bounded on the west by Edward Pennington and Arthur Wall, south by Peter Young.

Robison, William
200 acres, St. Paul Parish
Surveyed December 28, 1772
Granted August 2, 1774
Plat Book M, page 50
Grant Book M, page 244

Rock, John
100 acres, St. Paul Parish
Granted July 2, 1771 Grant Book I, page 372
Bounded on the southeast by William Davis.

Rosebrough, George
100 acres, St. Paul Parish
Granted February 6, 1770 Grant Book G, page 527

Rosebrough, George
100 acres, St. Paul Parish
Granted January 19, 1773 Grant Book I, page 881
Bounded on the northeast by Randall Ramsey and southwest by the said grantee.

Ross, James
150 acres, St. Paul Parish
Granted June 5, 1770 Grant Book I, page 32
Bounded on the south by land granted Wood and Tucker, on all other sides by vacant land.

Ross, James
100 acres, St. Paul Parish
Granted February 7, 1775 Grant Book M, page 1044
Bounded on the north and south by the said James Ross and east by Benjamin Grubbs.

Sail, Henry
Town Lot #8, Wrightsboro, St. Paul Parish; 100 acres,
Wrightsboro Township, St. Paul Parish, bounded on the north

by said Sail, Surveyed August 8, 1769 Plat Book C, page 320
Granted July 3, 1770 Grant Book I, page 357

Sail, Henry
100 acres, St. Paul Parish
Surveyed August 7, 1769 Plat Book C, page 310
No grant recorded.
Bounded on the north by Upton's Creek.

Sail, Jonathan
100 acres, St. Paul Parish
Surveyed October 7, 1769 Plat Book C, page 313
No grant recorded.
Bounded on the north by Jonathan Sail.

Sallins, Peter
100 acres, St. Paul Parish
Surveyed August 22, 1772 Plat Book M, page 25
Granted October 4, 1774 Grant Book M, page 600
Bounded on the southwest by Craft, Haniel, and John Green.

Salter, John
Town Lot #67, Wrightsboro, St. Paul Parish; 400 acres,
Wrightsboro Township, St. Paul Parish, bounded on the east by
John Howard and John Whitsett, northeast by Little River.
Surveyed June 15, 1769 Plat Book C, page 305
Granted July 3, 1770 Grant Book I, page 154
Tract surveyed as Slatter and granted as Salter. See entry for John
Slatter, page 173, this book.

Sanders, Joshua
100 acres, St. Paul Parish
Surveyed June 14, 1769 Plat Book C, page 320
Granted July 7, 1772 Grant Book I, page 657
Bounded on the north by the Little River.

Sanders, Joshua
100 acres, St. Paul Parish
Surveyed December 14, 1757 Plat Book C, page 306
No grant recorded.
Bounded on the southwest by Williams Creek.

Sanson, Samuel
Town Lot #83, Wrightsboro, St. Paul Parish; 100 acres, Wrightsboro Township, St. Paul Parish.
Surveyed September 2, 1769 Plat Book C, page 316
Granted July 3, 1770 Grant Book I, page 358

Satterwhite, William
300 acres, St. Paul Parish
Granted July 5, 1774 Grant Book M, page 113

Savage, Loveless
100 acres, St. Paul Parish
Granted March 7, 1769 Grant Book G, page 291
Bounded on the northeast by the said Loveless Savage.

Savage, Loveless
200 acres, St. Paul Parish
Surveyed March 14, 1758 Plat Book C, page 337
Granted October 2, 1759 Grant Book B, page 258

Savage, Loveless
100 acres, St. Paul Parish
Surveyed July 28, 1768 Plat Book C, page 299
Granted November 1, 1768 Grant Book G, page 219
Bounded on the west by the said Loveless Savage.

Savage, Loveless
50 acres, St. Paul Parish
Surveyed July 9, 1768 Plat Book C, page 300
Granted November 1, 1768 Grant Book H, page 13
Bounded on the northeast by Charles Smith.

Savage, Loveless
150 acres, St. Paul Parish
Surveyed December 11, 1772 Plat Book C, page 349
Granted July 5, 1774 Grant Book M, page 124
Bounded on the northeast and northwest by the said
Loveless Savage, and southwest by Sims.

Savage, Loveless
100 acres, St. Paul Parish

Surveyed December 5, 1766 Plat Book C, page 304
No grant recorded.
Bounded on the southeast by Savage's old line.

Scott, Alexander
150 acres, St. Paul Parish
Granted August 2, 1774 Grant Book M, page 256

Scott, Alexander
200 acres, St. Paul Parish
Granted February 7, 1775 Grant Book M, page 1048
Bounded on the northeast by Richard Meadows; east by John
Marshal, Daniel Coleman, and Kioka Creek; southwest by John
Ford.

Scott, John
300 acres, St. Paul Parish
Surveyed November 25, 1772
Granted May 4, 1773

Scott, John
100 acres, St. Paul Parish
Granted July 5, 1774
Plat Book C, page 355
Grant Book I, page 997
Grant Book M, page 108
Bounded on the east by the Savannah River, south by land said to
be Benjamin Ores.

Scott, John
100 acres, St. Paul Parish
Granted July 5, 1774 Grant Book M, page 109
Bounded on the northeast by the Savannah River, northwest by
Thomas Gray, and on the southeast by Scott.

Scott, Samuel
100 acres, St. Paul Parish
Granted January 19, 1773 Grant Book I, page 884
Bounded on the southwest by vacant land, southeast by Gray,
northeast by the Savannah River, northwest by land supposed to by
Paias.

Scott, Samuel
200 acres, St. Paul Parish
Surveyed November 25, 1772 Plat Book C, page 355
Granted July 5, 1774 Grant Book M, page 110

Screven, James
200 acres, St. Paul Parish
Granted January 19, 1773 Grant Book I, page 891

Seamore, James
500 acres, District of Augusta, St. Paul Parish
Original survey date unknown but resurveyed on July 16, 1785.
Recorded in Plat Book M, page 1.
Granted May 1, 1762 Grant Book D, page 96
Bounded on the northeast and southeast by the Savannah River.
"Robert Walton of said county (Richmond) bought a reserve of
500 acres of land formerly surveyed for and granted to Thomas
Bassett, in the District of Augusta and Parish of St. Paul, which
was confiscated and sold as the property of James Seamore to the
said Robert Walton. . (see Plat Book M, page 1.)" Tract surveyed
for and granted to Thomas Bassett.

Sell, Jonathan
Town Lot #23, Wrightsboro, St. Paul Parish; 300 acres,
Wrightsboro Township, St. Paul Parish, bounded on the southeast
and southwest by William Farmer.
Surveyed April 15, 1769 Plat Book C, page 323
Granted July 3, 1770 Grant Book I, page 156

Sell, Jonathan
Town Lot #24, Wrightsboro, St. Paul Parish; 100 acres,
Wrightsboro Township, St. Paul Parish, bounded on the north by
land granted the said Sell.
Surveyed August 4, 1769 Plat Book C, page 323
Granted July 3, 1770 Grant Book I, page 158
Tract surveyed as Sail and granted as Sell.

Sergison, Patrick
200 acres, Wrightsboro Township, St. Paul Parish
Granted October 6, 1772 Grant Book I, page 774

Shan, John
200 acres, St. Paul Parish
Granted December 3, 1771 Grant Book I, page 483

Shaw, Alexander
500 acres, St. Paul Parish
Surveyed July 10, 1757 Plat Book C, page 336
No grant recorded.
Bounded on the west by the Savannah River, and north by George Galphin.

Shaw, John
200 acres, St. Paul Parish
Surveyed August 4, 1770
No grant recorded.
Plat Book C, page 342

Sheftall, Levi
300 acres, St. Paul Parish
Surveyed August 30, 1769 Plat Book C, page 332
Granted February 6, 1770 Grant Book G, page 528
Bounded on the northeast by William Kilgore, and northwest by Christian Limbacker.

Sheftall, Mordecai
250 acres, St. Paul Parish
Surveyed October 2, 1769 Plat Book C, page 316
Granted January 2, 1770 Grant Book G, page 507

Sheftall, Mordecai
Surveyed January 26, 1762 Plat Book C, page 330
No grant recorded.

Shepherd, Nathaniel
200 acres, St. Paul Parish
Surveyed September 17, 1769 Plat Book C, page 310
Granted January 19, 1773 Grant Book I, page 895
Bounded on the southeast by John Tinkler.

Shick, John
500 acres, St. Paul Parish

Granted November 1, 1774 Grant Book M, page 728
Bounded on the east by Thomas Johnson, and north by Edmund Cartledge and Little Kioka Creek.

Shields, James
100 acres, St. Paul Parish
Granted November 1, 1774 Grant Book M, page 727

Shields, John
150 acres, St. Paul Parish
Granted October 4, 1774 Grant Book M, page 604
Bounded on the southwest by William Shields, and southeast by William McNurram and Nathaniel Coate.

Shields, William
Surveyed September 18, 1766 Plat Book C, page 328
Granted May 5, 1767 Grant Book F, page 232
Bounded on the northeast by the Savannah River, southeast by Darby Kennedy, northwest by land surveyed for Thomas Reed, southwest by vacant land. Tract includes 3 small islands of 31 acres in the Savannah River. Tract originally surveyed for William Shields, thence ordered to LeRoy Hammond on February 3, 1767. Surveyed as 450 acres for William Shields, thence divided and 250 acres granted LeRoy Hammond (see Plat Book C, page 328.) It is not known to whom the remaining 200 acres were granted.

Shirley, William
250 acres, partly in St. Paul and partly in St. George Parishes
Granted November 7, 1769 Grant Book G, page 466

Shields, William
100 acres, St. Paul Parish
Granted August 2, 1774 Grant Book M, page 260

Shruder, Thomas
50 acres, St. Paul Parish
Granted January 19, 1773 Grant Book H, page 93
Bounded on the southeast by Ralph Kilgore, southwest by Lachlan McBean, north by Great Kiokee Creek, and on the northeast by the Savannah River.

Shruder, Thomas
500 acres, St. Paul Parish
Granted December 6, 1774 Grant Book M, page 832

Sidwell, John
Town Lot #56, Wrightsboro, St. Paul Parish; 300 acres, Wrightsboro Township, St. Paul Parish.
Surveyed May 25, 1769 Plat Book C, page 317
Granted July 3, 1770 Grant Book I, page 157

Sidwell, John
100 acres, St. Paul Parish
Granted January 19, 1773 Grant Book I, page 883
Bounded on the north by Jonathan Sail, and west by said grantee.

Sidwell, John
100 acres, Wrightsboro Township, St. Paul Parish
Surveyed May 18, 1772 Plat Book C, page 356
No grant recorded.
Bounded on the north by John Sails, and west by John Sidwell.

Simpson, James
50 acres, St. Paul Parish
Granted February 7, 1775 Grant Book M, page 1047

Sims, William
400 acres, St. Paul Parish
Surveyed April 20, 1773 Plat Book M, page 79
Granted November 1, 1774 Grant Book M, page 738
Bounded on the south by land surveyed for Edward Barnard and land of Campbell, Furkynets, Pointer, and Edmund Bugg; east and west by vacant impassible land supposed to be vacant.

Sims, William
200 acres, St. Paul Parish
Granted December 6, 1774 Grant Book M, page 829
Bounded on the west by James Ross and James Coldridge, southeast by Charles Crawford, northwest by Henry Jones.

Slatter, John
400 acres (Wrightsboro Township), St. Paul Parish

Surveyed June 15, 1769 Plat Book C, page 305
Granted July 3, 1770 Grant Book I, page 154
Bounded on the north by the Little River, east by John Howard and John Whitsett. Tract surveyed as Slatter and granted as Salter. See entry for John Salter, page 163, this book.

Slatter, John (deceased, former husband of Mary Slatter)
200 acres, Wrightsboro Township, St. Paul Parish
Surveyed April 10, 1771 Plat Book M, page 30, and Plat Book C, page 342
Granted June 2, 1772 Grant Book I, page 624
Bounded on all sides by James Morrow. Plats show Germany's Creek running through tract. Tract surveyed as John Slatter in Plat Book C, page 342 and as Mary Slatter in Plat Book M, page 30. Granted to Mary Slatter.

Smith, Charles
200 acres, St. Paul Parish
Surveyed December 6, 1766 Plat Book C, page 315
Granted August 2, 1768 Grant Book G, page 166
Bounded on the northeast by Loveless Savage.

Smith, Charles
100 acres, St. Paul Parish
Original survey date unknown but resurveyed on November 4, 1817.
Recorded in Plat Book M, page 61.
Granted September 6, 1774 Grant Book M, page 413

Smith, Ebenezer
200 acres, St. Paul Parish
Granted July 7, 1772 Grant Book I, page 687

Smith, James
Town Lot #24, Third row, Augusta, St. Paul Parish
Surveyed October 12, 1762 Plat Book C, page 336
Granted October 29, 1765 Grant Book E, page 319

Smith, Job
200 acres, St. Paul Parish
Surveyed June 22, 1769 Plat Book C, page 312

Granted January 2, 1770 Grant Book G, page 508

Smith, Job
150 acres, St. Paul Parish
Surveyed June 20, 1771 Plat Book C, page 354
Granted July 5, 1774 Grant Book M, page 114
Bounded on the north by William Candler, west by Thomas Ayres and Thomas McDonald (plat says Dowel.)

Smith, John
100 acres, St. Paul Parish
Surveyed January 12, 1773 Plat Book C, page 357
Granted August 2, 1774 Grant Book M, page 252
Bounded on the northwest by Benjamin Harris.

Smith, John
100 acres, Wrightsboro Township, St. Paul Parish
Granted March 7, 1775 Grant Book M, page 1091
Bounded on the northeast by land of Holland Middleton, and all other sides by vacant land.

Smith, Richard
Town Lot #33, Wrightsboro, St. Paul Parish; 250 acres, Wrightsboro Township, St. Paul Parish, bounded on the north by land granted William Hixxon, south by land granted John Moore.
Surveyed July 27, 1769 Plat Book C, page 313
Granted July 3, 1770 Grant Book I, page 159

Spencer, John and McGillivray, Lachlan
500 acres, District of Augusta
Granted February 7, 1758 Grant Book A, page 558
Bounded on the south by James Paris, east by the Savannah River, and north by Butler's Creek.

Stallion, Elias
300 acres, St. Paul Parish
Surveyed November 9, 1759 Plat Book C, page 317
Granted January 3, 1775 Grant Book M, page 941
Bounded on the northeast by the Savannah River.

Stanley, John
200 acres, St. Paul Parish
Surveyed July 10, 1770 Plat Book C, page 340
No grant recorded.
Bounded on all sides by vacant land.

Stanley, William
400 acres, St. Paul Parish
Surveyed March 2, 1773 Plat Book C, page 356
Granted November 1, 1774 Grant Book M, page 729
Bounded on the northeast by William Ayres and Ashmore, southeast by Morton.

Stapler, Thomas
300 acres, St. Paul Parish
Surveyed July 20, 1772 Plat Book C, page 359
Granted July 5, 1774 Grant Book M, page 119
Bounded on the northeast by Robert Rae, and northwest by Thomas Stapler.

Stetstill, Thomas
200 acres, St. Paul Parish
Granted January 19, 1773 Grant Book I, page 894
Bounded on the east by Peter Candler.

Stewart, John
350 acres, St. Paul Parish
Surveyed October 29, 1759 Plat Book C, page 330
Granted April 13, 1761 Grant Book C, page 57
Bounded on the east by the Savannah River, south by Nehemiah Wade, and north by Jacob Beall.

Stewart, John
200 acres, St. Paul Parish
Surveyed May 22, 1769 Plat Book C, page 306
Granted November 1, 1774 Grant Book M, page 735
Bounded on the northwest by said John Stewart and vacant land, and southeast by Thomas Lynn. Plat shows tract bounded on the northwest by George Upton.

Stewart, John
100 acres, St. Paul Parish
Surveyed March 13, 1770 Plat Book C, page 323
No grant recorded.
Bounded on the northeast and southeast by John Stewart.

Stewart, John Jr.
Town Lot #4, Wrightsboro, St. Paul Parish; 100 acres, Wrightsboro Township, St. Paul Parish, bounded on the southwest by land of said grantee, southeast by John Stewart, Sr., northeast by Gresson.
Surveyed March 13, 1770 Plat Book C, page 341
Granted April 2, 1771 Grant Book I, page 303

Stincey, Archibald
150 acres, St. Paul Parish
Surveyed April 4, 1770 Plat Book C, page 303
No grant recorded.
Bounded on the northeast by Loveless Savage, and southeast by John Walton.

Stringer, Francis
900 acres, St. Paul Parish
Surveyed May 17, 1767 Plat Book C, page 301
No grant recorded.
Bounded on the northeast by the Savannah River, Stamp
Branch, Peter Turguined, Francis Stringer, Widow Friar,
Thomas Reid, and the Savannah Road; southeast by Widow Friar
and vacant land.

Struthers, William
500 acres, St. Paul Parish
Surveyed November 7, 1759 Plat Book C, page 336
Granted December 7, 1762 Grant Book D, page 245
Bounded on the northeast by the Savannah River, and southeast by Peter Randan.

Stubbs, Ann
Town Lot #54, Wrightsboro, St. Paul Parish; 150 acres, Wrightsboro Township, St. Paul Parish.

Surveyed June 26, 1769 Plat Book C, page 346
Granted January 7, 1772 Grant Book I, page 502

Stubbs, Deborah
Town Lot #69, Wrightsboro, St. Paul Parish; 300 acres,
Wrightsboro Township, St. Paul Parish, bounded on the southeast
by John Hodgins, southwest by Indian land.
Surveyed June 9, 1769 Plat Book C, page 345
Granted January 7, 1772 Grant Book I, page 503

Stubbs, John
Town Lot #2, Wrightsboro, St. Paul Parish; 450 acres,
Wrightsboro Township, St. Paul Parish.
Surveyed June 20, 1769 Plat Book C, page 305
Granted July 3, 1770 Grant Book I, page 155

Stubbs, John
150 acres, Wrightsboro Township, St. Paul Parish
Surveyed February 12, 1772 Plat Book C, page 357
Granted July 7, 1772 Grant Book I, page 695
Bounded on the north by said grantee and James McFarland,
southwest by Richard Moore. In addition, the plat shows tract
bounded on the northwest by James Hart.

Stubbs, Nathaniel
100 acres, Wrightsboro Township, St. Paul Parish
Granted December 6, 1774 Grant Book M, page 830
Bounded on all sides by vacant land.

Sullivan, Owen
400 acres, St. Paul Parish
Surveyed April 18, 1772 Plat Book C, page 354
Granted January 19, 1773 Grant Book I, page 892
Bounded on the northwest by the Little River.

Sullivan, Owen
251 acres, St. Paul Parish
Surveyed October 6, 1766 Plat Book C, page 317
No grant recorded.
Bounded on the southeast by Owen Day and Thomas Bassett,
southwest by Nicholas Murphy, northwest by Jackson.

Sutherton, Richard
Town Lot #38, between Back Street and the Common, Augusta.
Surveyed June 10, 1763 Plat Book C, page 336
Granted December 5, 1769 Grant Book H, page 32
Plat says lot was in the fourth, or back, row, Augusta, St. Paul Parish. Surveyed as Southerton and granted as Sutherton.

Sutherton, Richard
100 acres, St. Paul Parish
Surveyed July 7, 1764 Plat Book C, page 301
No grant recorded.
Bounded on the northwest by John Lamare, and southeast by Henry Bell.

Sutor, Sarah
150 acres, St. Paul Parish
Granted July 5, 1774 Grant Book M, page 125
Bounded on the northeast by Drury Mims, southwest by William Elim, and on the southeast by John Smith.

Swents, John
150 acres, St. Paul Parish
Granted July 5, 1774 Grant Book M, page 120

Tarvin, John
100 acres, St. Paul Parish
Granted January 3, 1775 Grant Book M, page 946
Bounded on the northwest by Rachel Wells, Nathaniel Parsley, and vacant land; southeast by Daniel Reeves and Peter Randon.

Tarvin, William
350 acres, St. Paul Parish
Surveyed May 18, 1772 Plat Book C, page 375
Granted August 2, 1774 Grant Book M, page 263
Bounded on the south by Thomas Pace. Tract surveyed as Tervin and granted as Tarvin.

Tarvin, William
250 acres, St. Paul Parish
Granted January 3, 1775 Grant Book M, page 947
Bounded on the northwest by Edward Barnard,

northeast by Michael Illy, and on the southwest by William Candler.

Taylor, William
100 acres, St. Paul Parish
Surveyed February 13, 1767 Plat Book C, page 364
Granted March 7, 1769 Grant Book G, page 286
Tract originally surveyed for William Taylor, thence ordered to Nathaniel Parsley on February 10, 1769 (see Plat Book C, page 364.) Granted to Nathaniel Parsley.

Telfair, Edward
500 acres, St. Paul Parish
Surveyed March 12, 1770 Plat Book C, page 371
Granted July 3, 1770 Grant Book I, page 62
Bounded on the southeast by John Ordanely (plat says Odanenly), northeast by land granted to Barnard Heard, partly on the northwest by Little River, on all other sides by vacant land.

Tennen, Hugh
200 acres, St. Paul Parish
Surveyed May 9, 1769 Plat Book C, pages 370 and 429
Granted October 4, 1774 Grant Book M, page 561
Tract originally surveyed for Hugh Tennen, thence ordered to Richard Howard on December 3, 1771 (see Plat Book C, page 370.) Granted to Rice Howard (plat shows name to be Richard Howard.) Bounded on the northeast and southeast by Walter Jackson, and northwest by Ralph Kilgore.

Tervin, John
100 acres, St. Paul Parish
Surveyed December 11, 1772 Plat Book C, page 374
Granted July 5, 1774 Grant Book M, page 132
Bounded on the northeast by land surveyed for Nathan Barnett, southwest by William Tarvin.

Thompson, John
100 acres, Wrightsboro Township, St. Paul Parish
Granted September 6, 1774 Grant Book M, page 380
Bounded on all sides by vacant land.

Thompson, Nicodemus
150 acres, St. Paul Parish
Granted December 6, 1774 Grant Book M, page 834
Bounded on the northeast by Nicodemus Thompson and Charles Smith.

Thornton, Abraham
200 acres, St. Paul Parish
Surveyed April 30, 1773 Plat Book C, page 377
Granted September 6, 1774 Grant Book M, page 371
Bounded on the southwest by Randel Ramsey.

Tindall, William
200 acres, St. Paul Parish
Granted July 5, 1774 Grant Book M, page 130
Bounded on the east by Euchee Creek.

Tinkler, John
600 acres, St. Paul Parish
Surveyed February 7, 1769 Plat Book C, page 366
Granted October 3, 1769 Grant Book G, page 444
Bounded on the southeast by John Jordan.

Tinkler, John
250 acres, St. Paul Parish
Surveyed June 1, 1769 Plat Book C, page 369
Granted November 7, 1769 Grant Book G, page 468
Bounded on the northwest by Wood Tucker.

Tinley, William
46 acres, being part of a 50 acre lot in Augusta, St. Paul
Parish, allotted to John Tinley, deceased father of the said William Tinley.
Surveyed March 9, 1762 Plat Book C, page 364
Granted October 4, 1763 Grant Book D, page 351
Bounded on the northeast by the Savannah River, southeast by David Douglas, southwest by James Dean, and northwest by the Common of the Town of Augusta.

Tinley, William
50 acre Town Lot (no number given), Augusta, St. Paul Parish

Surveyed March 9, 1762 Plat Book C, page 363
No grant recorded.
Bounded on the southwest by Patt Clark, northwest by David Douglas, and on the southeast by Edward Barnard.

Tobler, David
250 acres, St. Paul Parish
Surveyed November 24, 1759 Plat Book C, pages 81 and 369
No grant recorded.
Tract located on the Savannah River and Butler's Creek. Bounded on the east by the Savannah River, north by Thomas Bassett. Tract ordered to Arthur Harris and recertified to David Tobler on January 16, 1765 (see Plat Book C, page 369.) Surveyed for Arthur Harris.

Torquintz, Peter
100 acres, St. Paul Parish
Surveyed January 4, 1757 Plat Book C, page 363
No grant recorded.
Bounded on the east by the Savannah River.

Tubear, David
250 acres, St. Paul Parish
Granted February 5, 1765 Grant Book E, page 100
Bounded on the east by the Savannah River and Benjamin Williams, north by Thomas Bassett.

Tucker, Wood
400 acres, St. Paul Parish
Surveyed May 15, 1767 Plat Book C, page 362
Granted April 5, 1768 Grant Book G, page 84
Tract originally surveyed for Wood Tucker thence ordered to Christopher Ring (see Plat Book C, page 362.) Granted to Christopher Ring.

Upton, Edward
100 acres, St. Paul Parish
Granted January 3, 1775 Grant Book M, page 951
Bounded on the northeast, northwest, and southwest by Joseph Hollingsworth; southeast by James Vernon.

Upton, George
150 acres, St. Paul Parish
Granted August 2, 1768

Upton, John
100 acres, St. Paul Parish
Surveyed February 23, 1770
Granted May 5, 1772

Upton, John
100 acres, St. Paul Parish
Granted November 1, 1774
Grant Book G, page 167
Plat Book M, page 36
Grant Book I, page 613
Grant Book M, page 748
Bounded on the northwest by Edmund Bugg, on all other sides by Howard and Few.

Upton, John
100 acres, St. Paul Parish
Granted November 1, 1774 Grant Book M, page 749
Bounded on the southwest by John Donelly and vacant land, south by John Shields, east by John McNeillon, and north by Mr. Brown.

Upton, Richard
100 acres, St. Paul Parish
Granted November 1, 1774 Grant Book M, page 747

Van, John Jr.
100 acres, St. Paul Parish
Surveyed March 6, 1758 Plat Book C, page 429
Granted December 7, 1762 Grant Book D, page 242
Bounded on the south by Broad River. Original warrant says tract located on the north side of Broad River about 1 mile above the mouth thereof and 66 miles above Augusta.

Venning, Mary (widow)
Township Lot (no number given), Township of Augusta, containing 50 acres.
Granted October 7, 1766 Grant Book E, page 383

Bounded on the southeast by William Davis, west by Mr. Macartan and Mr. Campbell, northeast by Bryan Shelly and John Fitch, east by Augusta Commons.

Vernon, Amos
Town Lot #18, Wrightsboro, St. Paul Parish; 200 acres, Wrightsboro Township, St. Paul Parish, bounded on the northwest by Isaac Vernon.
Granted July 3, 1770 Grant Book I, page 160

Vernon, Isaac
Town Lot #10, Wrightsboro, St. Paul Parish; 350 acres, Wrightsboro Township, St. Paul Parish, bounded on the southeast by Amos Vernon.
Granted July 3, 1770 Grant Book I, page 161

Vernon, Isaac and Maddock, Joseph
1100 acres, Wrightsboro Township, St. Paul Parish
Granted February 7, 1775 Grant Book M, page 1018
Bounded on the north by Joseph Maddock, west by John Oliver, south by George Birk and Isaac Vernon and vacant land, east by Robert McClung and vacant land.

Wade, Hezekiah
100 acres, St. Paul Parish
Granted October 6, 1772 Grant Book I, page 776
Bounded on the east by Jacob Beall, and south by Ann Fitch.

Wade, Nehemiah
300 acres, St. Paul Parish
Granted April 13, 1761 Grant Book C, page 55
Bounded on the east by the Savannah River, south by John Lamer, north and west by John Stewart, and on every other side by the Savannah River.

Wade, Nehemiah
300 acres, St. Paul Parish
Surveyed November 10, 1757 Plat Book M, page 4 and Plat Book C, page 441
Granted February 7, 1775 Grant Book M, page 1060
Bounded on the southeast by James McHenry.

Wade, Nehemiah
Town Lot #40, in the fourth row, Augusta, containing 1 acre
Warrant dated October 17, 1755
Survey and grant not recorded. See original warrant on file in Colonial Detached Plat File.

Walden, Robert
Town Lot #12, Wrightsboro, St. Paul Parish; 100 acres, Wrightsboro Township, St. Paul Parish.
Granted November 6, 1770 Grant Book I, page 205

Walker, Joel
400 acres, St. Paul Parish
Granted July 4, 1769 Grant Book G, page 374
Bounded on the north by Henry Beall and Mrs. Southerton, northeast by George Galphin, south by Nechud Ward, southwest by vacant land.

Walker, Saunders
150 acres, St. Paul Parish
Granted August 2, 1774 Grant Book M, page 276
Bounded on the south and west by Claiborn, east by William Candler, and north by Keff.

Wall, Arthur
100 acres, St. Paul Parish
Granted November 1, 1774 Grant Book M, page 754
Bounded on the northwest by William Hickson; northeast by John Stewart, Sr.; southeast by Thomas Lynn.

Wallace, William
200 acres, St. Paul Parish
Granted April 7, 1772 Grant Book I, page 576

Wallacon, Daniel
250 acres, St. Paul Parish
Granted November 1, 1774 Grant Book M, page 759
Bounded on the east by William Jones.

Waller, Samuel
100 acres, St. Paul Parish

Granted July 5, 1774 Grant Book M, page 134
Bounded on the southwest by Perry, and southeast by said Samuel
Waller and John Crawford.

Walraven, Elias
100 acres, St. Paul Parish
Granted June 6, 1769 Grant Book G, page 348
Bounded on the southwest by Christian Limbacker.

Walton, John
250 acres, St. Paul Parish
Granted July 5, 1774 Grant Book M, page 133
Bounded on the south and east by McGilvray.

Walton, John
250 acres, St. Paul Parish
Granted February 7, 1775 Grant Book M, page 1063
Bounded on the north by John Upton, Sherwood Bugg, and vacant
land; east by land supposed to be James Ross; south by Richard
Upton and Lud Williams; west by Few and Howard.

Walton, Robert
500 acres, District of Augusta, St. Paul Parish
Original survey date unknown, but resurveyed on July 16, 1785.
Recorded in Plat Book M, page 1.
Granted May 1, 1762 Grant Book D, page 95
"Robert Walton of said county (Richmond) bought a reserve of
500 acres of land formerly surveyed for and granted to Thomas
Bassett, in the District of Augusta and Parish of St. Paul, which
was confiscated and sold as the property of James Seamore to the
said Robert Walton. . ." (see Plat Book M, page 1.) Tract surveyed
for and granted to Thomas Bassett. Bounded on the northeast and
southeast by the Savannah River and Rocky Creek.

Ward, Bryan
100 acres, St. Paul Parish
Surveyed April 16, 1758 Plat Book C, page 431
Granted December 7, 1762 Grant Book D, page 249
Bounded on the north by the Savannah River, south by Charles
Weatherford, west by Weatherford.

Warren, Frances
Lot #28, Township of Augusta, containing 50 acres
No survey or grant recorded, only the following endorsement, recorded in Plat Book C, pages 174-175. Originally surveyed for Nicholas Murphy on October 2, 1749 and signed over by Nicholas Murphy to William Finley (date not shown) and signed over by William Finley to Richard and Frances Warren on November 30, 1750.

Warren, Richard
Lot #28, Township of Augusta, containing 50 acres
No survey or grant recorded, only the following endorsement, recorded in Plat Book C, pages 174-175. Originally surveyed for Nicholas Murphy on October 2, 1749 and signed over by Nicholas Murphy to William Finley (date not shown) and signed over by William Finley to Richard and Frances Warren on November 30, 1750.

Waters, Thomas
Town Lot #32, Augusta, St. Paul Parish, containing 1 acre
Granted April 7, 1767 Grant Book F, page 214
Bounded on the northeast by Back Street, west by Lot #31, east by Lot #33, and south by the Common of the said town.

Watson, Jacob
Town Lot #63, Wrightsboro, St. Paul Parish; 100 acres, Wrightsboro Township, St. Paul Parish, bounded on the east by John Watson, southeast by Thomas Watson, northwest by Isaac Jackson.
Granted November 6, 1770 Grant Book I, page 203

Watson, Jacob
100 acres, Wrightsboro Township, St. Paul Parish
Granted April 7, 1772 Grant Book I, page 575
Bounded on the southwest by the Indian's land, and southeast by John Watson.

Watson, John
100 acres, Wrightsboro Township, St. Paul Parish
Granted April 7, 1772 Grant Book I, page 574

Bounded on the southwest by the Indian's land, and northwest by Jacob Watson.

Watson, John
Town Lot #87, Wrightsboro, St. Paul Parish; 100 acres, Wrightsboro Township, St. Paul Parish.
Granted November 6, 1770 Grant Book I, page 204

Watson, Thomas
Town Lot #32, Wrightsboro, St. Paul Parish; 500 acres, Wrightsboro Township, St. Paul Parish.
Granted July 3, 1770 Grant Book I, page 164

Weatherford, Charles
150 acres, St. Paul Parish
Surveyed April 16, 1758 Plat Book C, page 431
Granted December 7, 1762 Grant Book D, page 243
Bounded on the north by Bryan Ward and Martin Weatherford; south by Fishing Creek; east by the Savannah River. Tract surveyed as Charles Weatherford.

Weatherford, Martin
200 acres, St. Paul Parish
Granted March 5, 1771 Grant Book I, page 277
Bounded on all sides by vacant land.

Weatherford, Martin
200 acres, St. Paul Parish
Granted November 1, 1774 Grant Book M, page 770
Bounded on the southwest by Peter Turkeynetz and Thomas Bassett, northeast by Owen Day and Anderson, northwest and southwest by land surveyed for Owen Sullivan.

Weatherford, Martin
100 acres, St. Paul Parish
Surveyed April 16, 1758 or 1768 Plat Book C, page 431
No grant recorded.
Bounded on the northeast by the Savannah River, southeast by Bryan Ward, northwest by William Weatherford, and southwest by Charles Weatherford.

Weatherford, William
100 acres, St. Paul Parish
Surveyed April 16, 1758 or 1768 Plat Book C, page 431
No grant recorded.
Bounded on the northeast by the Savannah River, southeast by Martin Weatherford.

Weekley, Thomas
350 acres, St. Paul Parish
Surveyed February 23, 1769 Plat Book M, page 64
Granted July 4, 1769 Grant Book G, page 376
Bounded on the northeast by Leonard Clayborne, and southeast by William Joiner. Tract surveyed as Thomas Weakley and granted as Thomas Weekley.

Welch, Peter
300 acres, St. Paul Parish
Granted May 3, 1768 Grant Book G, page 114
Bounded on all sides by vacant land.

Weldon, Isaac
150 acres, St. Paul Parish
Granted July 5, 1774 Grant Book M, page 136
Bounded on all sides by vacant land.

Weldon, Jacob
500 acres, St. Paul Parish
Granted January 19, 1773 Grant Book I, page 897
Bounded on all sides by vacant land.

Weldon, Jacob
300 acres, St. Paul Parish
Granted March 7, 1775 Grant Book M, page 1093
Bounded on all sides by vacant land.

Wells, Humphry
150 acres, St. Paul Parish
Granted November 1, 1774 Grant Book M, page 752
Bounded on the east by the said Humphry Wells.

Wells, Samuel
200 acres, St. Paul Parish
Granted July 5, 1774 Grant Book M, page 142
Bounded on all sides by vacant land.

Welsh, John
Town Lot #62, Wrightsboro, St. Paul Parish; 100 acres,
Wrightsboro Township, St. Paul Parish, bounded on the south by
the Indian's land.
Granted July 3, 1770 Grant Book I, page 165

Wells, Benjamin
300 acres, St. Paul Parish
Granted February 6, 1770 Grant Book G, page 531
Bounded on all sides by vacant land.

West, John
350 acres, St. Paul Parish
Granted May 5, 1767 Grant Book F, page 259
Bounded on the north by the Little River.

Westcoat, Daniel
100 acres, St. Paul Parish
Granted December 1, 1767 Grant Book F, page 434
Bounded on the northeast by the Savannah River.

Westcoat, Daniel
100 acres, St. Paul Parish
Granted February 7, 1775 Grant Book M, page 1055
Bounded on the southeast by Henry Downs, northwest by said
Daniel Westcoat, and on the northeast by the Savannah River.

Wheat, William
200 acres, Wrightsboro Township, St. Paul Parish
Granted October 1, 1771 Grant Book I, page 445
Bounded on the southwest by land surveyed for Thomas Gillman,
northwest by Little Ogeechee River, on all other sides by vacant
land.

Whigham, Thomas
250 acres, Wrightsboro Township

Granted July 5, 1774 Grant Book M, page 138
Bounded on the northwest by George Donelson and vacant land, on all other sides by vacant land. Grants says tract in Wrightsboro Township, St. George Parish. This is an error, as Wrightsboro was in St. Paul Parish.

Whitefield, George; Rae, Robert; Rae, James; Graham, Thomas
500 acres, St. Paul Parish
Granted January 1, 1771 Grant Book I, page 242

Whitsett, John
Town Lot #73, Wrightsboro, St. Paul Parish; 200 acres, Wrightsboro Township, St. Paul Parish, bounded on the northwest partly by John Howard and partly by John Slatter, northeast by Ralph Kilgore, southwest by John Whitsett, southeast by vacant land.
Granted July 3, 1770

Whitsett, John Jr.
Grant Book I, page 162
Town Lot #35, Wrightsboro, St. Paul Parish; 250 acres, Wrightsboro Township, St. Paul Parish, bounded on the northeast by John Whitsett, Jr.
Surveyed June 8, 1769
Granted July 3, 1770
Plat Book M, page 45
Grant Book M, page 3

Wiggon, William
650 acres, St. Paul Parish
Granted August 2, 1774 Grant Book M, page 270
Bounded on the northeast by (blank) Combes and land said to be Gray's, southeast by Colonel J. Jackson, and southwest by James Iverey.

Williams, Lud
125 acres, St. Paul Parish
Granted February 7, 1775 Grant Book M, page 1053
Bounded on the south by Daniel McCarty and vacant land, east by George Cowen, and west by Richard Upton.

Williams, William
100 acres, St. Paul Parish
Granted August 2, 1774 Grant Book M, page 269
Bounded on the northeast by Eli Fort.

Williamson, Benjamin
203 acres, District of Augusta
Granted February 7, 1758 Grant Book A, page 551
Bounded on the north by the Savannah River, south by Butler's Creek, west by Thomas Bassett, and on the east by Christopher Fulbright.

Williamson, Richard
700 acres, St. Paul Parish
Granted May 1, 1770 Grant Book I, page 11
Bounded partly on the southwest and partly on the northwest by Nathaniel Harris, and southeast by William Felps and Benjamin Wells.

Wilson, Samuel
Town Lot #13, Wrightsboro, St. Paul Parish; 200 acres, Wrightsboro Township, St. Paul Parish, bounded on all sides by vacant land.
Granted July 3, 1770 Grant Book I, page 163

Winslet, Samuel
Town Lot #94, Wrightsboro, St. Paul Parish; 100 acres, Wrightsboro Township, St. Paul Parish, bounded on the northwest by land of said Samuel Winslet, northeast by land of John Carson.
Granted November 6, 1770 Grant Book I, page 206

Winslet, Samuel
100 acres, St. Paul Parish
Granted September 6, 1774 Grant Book M, page 389
Bounded on the southeast by said Samuel Winslet, northeast by John Carson, and on all other sides by vacant land.

Wisely, Sarah
Lot #40, Augusta Township, St. Paul Parish, containing 50 acres
Granted December 4, 1759 Grant Book B, page 334

Bounded on the south by Benjamin Horn, west by Samuel Gandy, east by John Fitch, and on the north by vacant land.

Wood, Isaac
100 acres, St. Paul Parish
Surveyed April 6, 1758 Plat Book C, page 431
Granted December 7, 1762 Grant Book D, page 248
Bounded on the east by the Savannah River, north by Aaron Berreston's improvement on Williams Creek, and on every other side by vacant land.

Wood, Isaac
100 acres, partly in St. George Parish and partly in St. Paul Parish.
Granted November 1, 1768 Grant Book G, page 222
Bounded on all sides by vacant land.

Wood, Isaac
100 acres, St. Paul Parish
Granted August 2, 1774 Grant Book M, page 266
Bounded on the northeast by Ebenezer Smith.

Wood, Nathaniel
200 acres, St. Paul Parish
Granted January 19, 1773 Grant Book I, page 896
Bounded on all sides by vacant land.

Wright, Dionysus
400 acres, St. Paul Parish
Granted July 5, 1774 Grant Book M, page 140
Bounded on the east by William Satterwhite, northwest by Harris, and southwest by William Holliday and said Dionysus Wright.

Wright, James (Gov.)
1519 acres, Wrightsboro Township, St. Paul Parish
Granted September 6, 1774 Grant Book M, page 382
Bounded on the northwest by Joseph Maddock and Thomas Jackson; northeast by John Davis, Page, John Watson, and vacant land; southeast by Job Smith, Samuel Oliver, and vacant land; southwest by Jonathan Sell, John Sidwell, Joseph Maddock, and Isaac Vernon's mill land and vacant land.

Wright, James (Gov.)
1285 acres, Wrightsboro Township, St. Paul Parish
Granted September 6, 1774 Grant Book M, page 383
Bounded on the southeast by John Graham, Hunter, Samuel Oliver, and vacant land; northeast by Joseph Stubbs and vacant land; west by the old Indian line and path; south by Francis Jones.

Wright, James (Gov.)
500 acres, Wrightsboro Township, St. Paul Parish
Granted September 6, 1774 Grant Book M, page 384
Bounded on all sides by vacant land.

Wright, Mesach
150 acres, St. Paul Parish
Granted November 1, 1774 Grant Book M, page 753
Bounded on the north and south by Thomas Young, northwest by Sherwood Bugg and land supposed to be one Bryan's.

Wright, Samuel
Lots #34 and #35, Township of Augusta, St. Paul Parish, containing 50 acres each, for a total of 100 acres.
Granted April 5, 1763 Grant Book D, page 301
Bounded on the south by Joseph Oakes, east by John Francis William, and on other sides by vacant lots #25, #26, and #36.

Wright, Shedrick
150 acres, St. Paul Parish
Granted February 7, 1775 Grant Book M, page 1062
Bounded on all sides by vacant land.

Wylly, Francis
200 acres, St. Paul Parish
Granted July 4, 1758 Grant Book B, page 4
Bounded on the southeast by John Pettygrew.

Yonge, Henry Jr.
200 acres, St. Paul Parish
Granted July 5, 1774 Grant Book M, page 145
Bounded on the northeast by McCartan, Turquenend, and Bassett; southwest by Cashall.

Yonge, Henry Jr.
200 acres, St. Paul Parish
Granted July 5, 1774 Grant Book M, page 146
Bounded on the southwest by Sherwood Bugg, and northeast by Robert Hatcher.

Yorke, Robison
100 acres, St. Paul Parish
Granted February 7, 1775 Grant Book M, page 1064
Bounded on the south by unknown, and on all other sides by vacant land.

Young, Margaret
150 acres, St. Paul Parish
Granted January 19, 1773 Grant Book I, page 899
Bounded on the east by Brewer.

Young, Thomas
1000 acres, Wrightsboro Township, St. Paul Parish
Surveyed July 15, 1774 Plat Book M, page 8
Granted October 4, 1774 Grant Book M, page 612
Bounded on the southwest by the old Indian line and path; southeast by vacant land; northeast by Francis Green, John Dover, and vacant land; northwest by vacant land.

Young, Thomas
500 acres, St. Paul Parish
Granted October 4, 1774 Grant Book M, page 613
Bounded on the northwest by John Bacon and vacant land, southeast by David Cossy and land surveyed for Hozah, northeast by David Boyd and vacant land.

Young, Thomas
500 acres, St. Paul Parish
Granted October 4, 1774 Grant Book M, page 614
Bounded on the northwest by Richard Castleberry and McLelebum, southwest by Doctor Welch or Sherwood Bugg and said Thomas Young, northeast by John Newman and vacant land, southeast by vacant land.

Young, Thomas
300 acres, St. Paul Parish
Granted October 4, 1774 Grant Book M, page 615
Bounded on all sides by vacant land.

Youngblood, John
200 acres, St. Paul Parish
Granted November 1, 1774 Grant Book M, page 766
Bounded on all sides by vacant land.

Youngblood, John Jr.
300 acres, St. Paul Parish
Granted July 5, 1774 Grant Book M, page 143
Bounded on the southeast by an old survey, northwest and southwest by William Satterwhite, and east by Fuller.

Youngblood, Peter
100 acres, St. Paul Parish
Granted January 19, 1773 Grant Book I, page 898
Bounded on all sides by vacant land.

Youngblood, Peter; Youngblood, John; Fuller, John
500 acres, St. Paul Parish
Granted January 3, 1775 Grant Book M, page 971
Bounded on the northeast by Benjamin Youngblood and David Threats; northwest by Jacob Horn, Joel Crawford, and Benjamin Youngblood; southwest by Jacob Horn and vacant land.

# THE FIRST MINUTE BOOK,
# WARREN INFERIOR COURT

The Inferior Court handled or had jurisdiction of all estates in Georgia until 1852 when the office of Ordinary in each county was created and estates, guardianships, wills, marriage licenses, and such matters were transferred to that office where they have been since. The Inferior Court in its original jurisdiction, had in addition to the just mentioned matters, jurisdiction over all county affairs including the levying of taxes, opening and closing and maintenance of public roads, and other duties now performed by the Boards of County Commissioners. The Court also had the jurisdiction over suits on notes, accounts, and other civil cases similar to the jurisdiction now exercised by County Courts. The following is an abstract of the first Minute Book dealing with estates, dating from 1794 and extending until 1807. The pages were unnumbered.

September 20, 1794: The will of Thomas Drake was proved by the oath of James Robison, and admitted to probate. October 3, 1794: Letters of administration with the will annexed were granted Habukkuk Wright on the estate of Adam Hill, deceased.

May 10, 1795: The will of Hardy Wester was admitted to probate, and Fannie Wester and Sampson Ivey qualified as executors of same.

May 10, 1795: Phoebe Hill applied for letters of dismission as Administratrix on the estate of Thomas Hill, deceased.

June 9, 1795: Samuel Slocum, Administrator of estate of Seth Slocum, applied for letters dismissory.

August 12, 1795: Anna Terrell Johnston applies for letters of administration on estate of Malcolm Johnston. Application was granted September 12, 1795.

October (blank), 1795: Pearson Young applies for administration on the estate of Robert Bur (torn off and lost.) Same was granted December 15, 1795. Jacob Young, surety on administrator's bond.

November 9, 1795: The will of Gahazi Davis, alias Shockley, was proved by the testimony of Peter Hodo, Esquire, one of the subscribing witnesses, and admitted to probate. Reubin McGee qualified as executor.

September 7, 1795: Samuel Moore's will was duly proven and admitted to probate. Olive Moore and Jody Newsom qualified as executors, December 18, 1795.

February 1, 1796: The will of Nathaniel Hood was probated on the oaths of the subscribing witnesses, William Hardin and Sampson Ivy.

February 16, 1796: Sarah Hill applies for letters of administration on the estate of Joshua Hill, deceased. Adam Jones and Wyatt Bonner to be securities of the administratrix bond.

January 2, 1797: The will of George Medlock was proved by the testimony of James Taylor and George Taylor, subscribing witnesses, and letters testamentary ordered to issue to George Medlock Jr.

February 16, 1797: James Vaughn applied for letters of administration on the estate of Alexander Vaughn. Same was later granted, and Samuel Alexander accepted as surety on her bond.

May 27, 1797: Michael Burkhalter applies for letters of administration on estate of David Newsom. Same was duly granted and Basil Wright and Sterling Gardner accepted as securities on the administrator's bond.

July 18, 1797: William Cocks and Sally Threewitts apply for administration on estate of Joel Threewitts. Duly granted and Thomas Cocks and Turner Persons accepted as sureties on bond.

July 28, 1797: Sarah Nibb Wynne and Benjamin Wynne apply for letters of administration on John Wynne's estate. Duly granted; William Roberson surety on their bond.

November 17, 1797: Dixon Perryman and James Douglas apply for administration on estate of Rev. Jeptha Vining. James Douglas only was appointed, and Harmon Perryman and Joshua Vining were accepted as securities on his bond.

December 26, 1797: Cassandra Montray applied for letters testamentary on the will of her deceased father, John Montray.

December 29, 1797: John Travis applied for letters testamentary on the will of Thomas Smith, deceased, and offered the same for probate. It was proved on the oath of Jones Kendrick and admitted to probate.

March 4, 1798: John Matthews was granted letters testamentary as executor on the will of Burrell Brown, the will being proven by the oath of Leroy Minis, a subscribing witness, and admitted to probate.

April 13, 1798: Mary Cooper applies for administration on the estate of James Cooper, deceased, and same was granted. Harmon Wilkinson and Peter Castleberry, sureties on her bond.

April 26, 1798: Elizabeth Goodwin applies for letters of administration on estate of Peter Goodwin, deceased. Duly granted.

June 4, 1798: Jesse Kitchen applies for letters testamentary on will of Robert Hinton, and offered the will for probate. It was proven on oaths of Elisha Hert and Ambrose Edmondson, subscribing witnesses. The latter was accepted as surety on the administrator's bond.

October 20, 1798: Thomas Jones applies for letters of administration of the will annexed on estate of Winney Pinson. A caveat was filed December 4, 1798 by John Kelly, and he was appointed with Benjamin Mitchell and Solomon Newsom, sureties.

December 6, 1798: John Vance applies for letters of administration on the estate of James Vance, deceased. Same was granted, with Milby McGree, surety on bond. Inventory and Appraisement in this matter was filed April 10, 1799.

December 14, 1798: Letters testamentary were ordered granted to Debera Chapman as executrix of the will of John Chapman, and the will admitted to probate, it being proven by oath of Benjamin Chapman, a subscribing witness.

January 10, 1799: Shaderick Fluwellin, Executor of the will of Ephriam King, deceased, applied for letters dismissory. Same was granted March 2, 1799.

April 20, 1799: Frederick Daniel applies for administration on estate of John Thomas, and same was duly granted July 18, 1799, with William Mims, surety.

April 24, 1799: Pheriby Cook and Jonathan Hagerty apply for administration on estate of Isaac Cook, deceased.

April 29, 1799: William Stith Jr., applies for administration on estate of William Stith Sr., and was duly appointed.

May 16, 1799: Fergus Linn applies for administration on estate of John Linn. Same was granted July 8, 1799, and Daniel McCowan and Thomas Jones accepted as sureties on bond.

May 16, 1799: Sophia Trent applies for administration on estate of John Trent, deceased, and was appointed July 18, 1799.

May 27, 1799: Susannah Butler applied for administration on estate of Noble Butler, deceased, and she was appointed July 18, 1799, with (blank) Beall and Enos Butler, sureties on her bond.

June 3, 1799: Richard Beasley and William Earnest, the duly nominated executors of the will of James Beasley, Sr., offered the will for probate, and it was proven by oaths of William Howard and James Beasley, and ordered recorded; and they were appointed executors of the will.

July 1, 1799: The will of Henry McNiece, deceased, was proven by the oath of Edmond Hays, a subscribing witness, and admitted to record. No executor was mentioned in the minutes.

July 18, 1799: Jonathan Hagerty applied for guardianship of Pheriby and Celethy Cook, orphans of Isaac Cook, Edward Hill security on bond, and was duly appointed.

November 29, 1799: Lydia Hall and Richard B. Fletcher, Esq., apply for letters testamentary on the will of Lieut. Thomas Hall, deceased. The will was proven by the testimony of Daniel Saunders and MaryAnn Wilkins, subscribing witnesses, and ordered recorded.

December 24, 1799: David Neal and Samuel Neal apply for administration on estate of Thomas Neal, deceased. They were appointed February 11, 1800; James McCaran and Joseph Duckworth, sureties on their bond.

February 10, 1800: Lydia Napper applied for letters of administration with the will annexed on will of James Napper.

February 10, 1800: Isaac Burson applies for letters of administration on estate of David Davis, and was duly appointed.

February 11, 1800: A. Persons and Littleberry Walker apply for administration on estate of Joel Walker, and were duly appointed, with Nicholas Williams, Richard Heath and Amos Persons, securities on bond.

February 11, 1800: Jonathan Hagerty was appointed Administrator of estate of Isaac Cook, deceased, with Edward Hill, surety on his bond.

March 18, 1800: Lydia Heartfield applies for administration on estate of George Heartfield. She was appointed August 11, 1800; Benjamin Hopward, surety on bond.

April 7, 1800: Joshua Butt Sr. applies for administration on estate of Joshua Butt Jr.

April 7, 1800: Frances Hill, Administratrix of Richard Hill, deceased, applies for letters dismissory.

July 10, 1800: John Horn, executor of will of Jacob Horn, was granted letters of dismission.

August 11, 1800: John Travis, Executor of will of Thomas Smith, was granted letters of dismission.

August 11, 1800: Reubin McGee, Executor of will of Gahazi Davis, applied for letters dismissory.

August 11, 1800: Alexander Fluwellin, Administrator of Betty Fluwellin estate, applies for letters dismissory.

August 25, 1800: Radford and John Butts apply for administration on the estate of Joshua Butts, deceased. They were appointed October 6, 1800, with Solomon Slatter and George Parum as sureties on their bond.

September 24, 1800: William Berry and James Mitchell were appointed temporary administrators on estate of Abner Mitchell, deceased. Permanent letters of administration were granted Robert Rutherford, April 28, 1801. Inventory of estate filed April 28, 1801. Robert Abercrombie and Henry Shelton, sureties on bond.

October 17, 1800: Richard Castleberry and William Newman were granted letters of dismission from their administration of Samuel Newman estate.

November 9, 1800: Asa Wright applied for administration of Samuel Wright, deceased. He was appointed June 8, 1801, with Johnston Wright and Blake Pearcy, sureties on his bond.

November 19, 1800: Rebecca Kemp applied for administration on estate of Hipple Kemp, deceased. She was appointed February 9, 1801, with Seth Wolsey surety on her bond as Administratrix.

December 4, 1800: Sarah Rose and Edmond Rose apply for administration of estate of William Rose, deceased. They were appointed February 9, 1801, with Shadrick Fluwellin, surety on their bond.

January 10, 1801: The will of Thomas Dove was proven by the oaths of David Dove and Thomas Dove, and admitted to probate.

February 9, 1801: The will of Thomas Hilson, deceased, was proven by the oath of Thomas Phillips, a subscribing witness, and admitted to record.

February 9, 1801: The will of George Medlock, deceased, was proved by the oath of George Taylor, a subscribing witness, and admitted to record.

February 9, 1801: Reubin Barrow applies for administration on estate of James Barrow, deceased. He was appointed June 8, 1801; David Newsom, surety on bond.

February 10, 1801: Col. Robert Abercrombie and Joseph Howell apply for administration on estate of Archibald Kinsey, and were duly appointed; Matthew Hubert and James Jones, sureties on bond.

February 11, 1801: Lydia Hartfield, Administratrix of estate of George Hartfield, was granted letters dismissory.

March 1, 1801: David Hubert applies for administration on estate of John Cook, deceased. He was appointed June 8, 1801, with Joseph Bower and Abner Fluwellin, sureties on bond.

March 10, 1801: Patty Neal applies for administration on estate of Samuel Neal, deceased, and was appointed August 10, 1801; James McCormack, surety on her bond.

April 14, 1801: Nancy Burson and Isaac Burson apply for administration on estate of Jonathan Burson, deceased. They were appointed August 11, 1801; sureties on their bond, John English, Michael Cody.

August 2, 1801: Jacky Davenport was granted letters dismissory from the administration of the Malcolm Johnston estate.

August 10, 1801: Frances Hill, Executrix of Henry Hill estate, was granted letters dismissory.

November 2, 1801: Robert Abercrombie applies for administration on estate of William C. Abercrombie, and was appointed February 10, 1802; William Flournoy and M. Hubert, sureties on bond.

December 1, 1801: Hardy Smith applies for administration on estate of James Napper. On February 7, 1802, Lydia Napper and Samuel Ridgewell were appointed administrators with the will annexed. Solomon Newsom Sr., and Elisha Brown were accepted as sureties on their bond.

December 1, 1801: Jacob Ball applies for administration on estate of Eli Bull, and was appointed February 9, 1802; M. Hardin, Jesse Bull, sureties.

January 1, 1802: Zilphia Hogins and James Hogins apply for administration on estate of Robert Hogins, deceased.

January 20, 1802: Samuel Winslet and John Williams apply for administration on estate of John Carson, and were appointed May 3, 1802; sureties on bond, Solomon Lockett, Josiah Beall, Mark Hardin, and Howell Hight.

January 23, 1802: William Flournoy applies for letters of administration on estate of Jacob Flournoy, and was appointed

February 9, 1802: Mary Burson and Joseph Burson offered the will of Joseph Burson for probate, and it was duly proven, and they qualified as executors.

February 10, 1802: Polly McKinney offered the will of Moses McKinney for probate, and it was admitted to record; she qualified as Executrix of same.

February 19, 1802: Elizabeth Todd and Job Todd apply for Administration of estate of Hardy Todd with the will annexed, and offered the will for probate which was proved.

February 24, 1802: Elizabeth Murphy applied for administration on estate of Edward Murphy, deceased. She was appointed June 1, 1802; John Rushing and John Wilson, securities on her bond.

March 1, 1802: Letters testamentary were granted on the will of William Kendall, deceased, to Jeremiah Kendall and Henry Kendall and Phillip Brantley, as executors, and they were qualified, and the will as admitted to probate.

March 2, 1802: Henry Graybill was granted letters dismissory from his administration of the James Hilton estate.

March 2, 1802: Letters dismissory were ordered to issue to Matthew Hubert and David Hubert and John Rutherford on their administration of the estate of Benjamin Hubert, deceased.

March 9, 1802: Presley Spinks applies for administration on estate of Benjamin Dicken, deceased, with the will annexed. A caveat was filed by Richard Snipes on behalf of himself and Lewis Dicken.

March 29, 1802: Margaret Holladay applied for letters of administration on estate of Ambrose Holladay. On May 3, 1802, she with Elijah Worthen were appointed Administrators with James Harvill, William Harvill and Joseph Harvill, sureties on bond.

May 3, 1802: The will of David Davis, deceased, was duly proven by the oath of Robert Moses, a subscribing witness, and it was ordered recorded.

May 3, 1802: Elizabeth Myrick applies for letters of administration on estate of Owen Myrick, deceased. She was appointed February 15, 1804; Thomas Edmonds and Septimus Weatherby, sureties on her bond.

June 10, 1802: John Matthews, Esq., applies for letters of administration on estate of Stephen Fluwellin, deceased. Henry Kendall, Jesse Matthews, sureties.

August 5, 1802: Thomas Hutchins applies for administration on estate of John Hutchins, and was appointed February 15, 1803; Solomon Thompson and Joel Heath, sureties on his bond.

November 25, 1802: John Bishop and Samuel Cooper apply for administration on estate of James Bishop, and were appointed February 15, 1803; Joel Heath and Thomas Hutchins, sureties on bond.

January 13, 1803: Frederick Newsom applies for administration on estate of David Newsom, deceased.

January 13, 1803: Mary Parker and Solomon Thompson apply for administration on estate of James Parker, deceased. John Matthews and Amos Parsons, sureties on bond.

January 25, 1803: Robert Parker applies for administration on estate of William Parker, deceased.

February 15, 1803: William White applies for administration on estate of William White Sr., and was duly appointed; Jacob Burkhalter and William Matthews, sureties on bond. On July 6, 1807, letters dismissory were duly granted to William White, Administrator on said William White Sr., estate.

February 16, 1803: The will of Peter Perkins, deceased, was proven by the oath of Solomon Thompson, and letters testamentary ordered to issue to John Baker and John Torrence as executors.

February 16, 1803: Elizabeth Newsom, Frederick Newsom, Solomon Newsom and David Newsom apply for letters of administration on estate of Solomon Newsom, deceased; and were duly appointed, August 1803. Pending granting of same, Jody Newsom was appointed temporary Administrator, October 17, 1803; David Newsom was appointed Administrator, Thomas Dent,

Robert Moses Sr., William Ussery, Jody Newsom, sureties on bond.

February 23, 1803: Stephen Lawrence applies for administration on estate of Nathan Wootten, and was appointed with Joseph Carter, surety on bond.

May 2, 1803: James Bond applies for administration on estate of Peter Bond, deceased.

June 21, 1803: Alcy Lee applies for letters of administration on the estate of Richard Lee, deceased. She was appointed with Thomas Rogers and William Pilcher, sureties on her bond.

August 9, 1803: Tulley Briggs applies for administration on estate of Wiggins Killebrew, deceased. John Rushing, surety on bond.

August 9, 1803: Martha Sells applies for administration on estate of Thomas Sells. Isaac Davis and Jeremiah Burkhalter, sureties on bond.

August 9, 1803: Elizabeth Rockmore applies for administration, with the will of James Rockmore, testate. The will was probated and she was appointed with David Robertson and William Ussery, sureties on her bond.

August 10, 1803: John Neaves applies for letters of administration on estate of Daniel Neaves. Shedrick Fluwellin, surety on bond.

September 19, 1803: Samuel Barksdale and Pinkethman Harvey apply for administration on estate of John Barksdale, deceased. On October 22, 1803, the above applicants with Stephen Burnley were appointed Administrators, Michael Harvey, Josiah Beall, sureties.

October 17, 1803: John Rushing and Enoch Renfroe Jr., were granted letters testamentary on the will of Enoch Renfroe Sr., and the will was probated.

October 17, 1803: The will of William Bardin, deceased, was proved, and Mary Bardin qualified as executrix of same.

October 22, 1803: Aaron Lipham, James Waggoner and George Waggoner apply for temporary administration on estate of Henry Waggoner, deceased, and were appointed, William Waggoner and Solomon Slatter, securities on bond.

December 5, 1803: John Martin applies for administration on estate of William McKinley, deceased. He was appointed, with Joseph McKinley, surety on bond.

December 5, 1803: Frederick and Sarah Newsom apply for administration on estate of John Newsom, and were appointed; Michael Burkhalter, surety on bond.

December 29, 1803: Nathaniel Ward applied for administration on estate of William Morrison, deceased, and was appointed; Michael Burkhalter, surety on bond.

January 2, 1804: Hannah Chapman applies for administration on estate of Laban Chapman, and was appointed with William Chapman, Robert Parker, sureties.

January 11, 1804: Rhoda Battle and Samuel Alexander apply for administration on estate of John Battle, and were appointed; Robert Abercrombie and Micajah Little, sureties on bond.

January 22, 1804: Sally Geesland and Benjamin Geesland were appointed temporary administrators on estate of William Geesland, deceased. John Moses, James Gray, sureties.

January 23, 1804: Richard Fletcher applies for administration on estate of Thomas Lent Hall, and was appointed in 1806.

January 23, 1804: The will of John Myrick was admitted to probate, and John Myrick Jr., and Nathaniel Myrick qualified as executors.

March 5, 1804: Thomas Jones was appointed temporary administrator of the estate of Henry Jones, deceased. Sureties on bond: John Nunn, William Jones.

September 6, 1804: The will of Joab Brooks was duly probated, and his widow and William Brooks qualified as executors.

September 6, 1804: A warrant of appraisement was issued in re: Moses Butts Sr., estate; Moses and William Butts, Administrators.

September 6, 1804: Michael Harbuck was appointed temporary administration on estate of David Newsom, deceased.

October (blank) 1804: James Davison was appointed temporary administrator of estate of James Jones Sr. Michael Burkhalter, Thomas Dent, sureties on bond.

October 1, 1804: Henry Duberry and Harris McFarling were appointed temporary administrators on estate of Jesse Duberry, deceased. On December 11, 1804, Polly and Henry Duberry apply for permanent letters of administration on estate.

October 24, 1804: James Davison was appointed temporary administrator on estate of Richard Butler, deceased.

December 11, 1804: Mary Stone was appointed temporary administratrix on the estate of Micajah Stone; Robert Jenkins and Jeremiah Beall, sureties on her bond.

December 11, 1804: Margaret and Robert Beasley were appointed temporary Administrators on estate of Richard Beasley, deceased. James Gray, surety on their bond.

January 7, 1805: Elizabeth Pruitt and Byrd Pruitt were appointed temporary Administrators on estate of Levi Pruitt, deceased; Isaiah Tucker, Joel Neal, Harden Pruitt, sureties on bond.

January 8, 1805: Mary Waggoner, David W. Waggoner and George B. Waggoner were appointed temporary Administrators on estate of James Waggoner, deceased; George Waggoner and William Waggoner, sureties on bond.

January 28, 1805: Thomas Hutchins, Administrator of John Hutchins estate, was granted letters of dismission.

March 4, 1805: The will of John Brown was duly probated, and Samuel M. Smith qualified as executor.

March 6, 1805: John Kelly was appointed temporary Administrator of estate of Thomas Rhoden Pinson, deceased.

March 9, 1805: Zachariah Deason was appointed temporary Administrator on estate of Benjamin Deason, deceased.

April 13, 1805: Tully Biggs was granted letters dismissory from his administration of the Wiggins Killebrew estate.

May 24, 1805: Winnifred Benton was appointed temporary administratrix on estate of Aaron Benton, deceased. Leroy Mims and Johnston Wright, sureties.

August 13, 1805: Benjamin Howard was appointed temporary Administrator on estate of William Kitchen Sr., deceased.

August 14, 1805: Alexander Moore was granted letters dismissory from his Administration of the Mordecai Moore estate.

August 14, 1805: The will of William Travis, deceased, was duly probated and Amos Travis qualified as executor of the same.

September 3, 1805: Zachariah Booth as the greatest creditor, was appointed temporary Administrator on estate of John K. Candler, deceased; John Hicks and Richard Curry, sureties on his bond.

October 15, 1805: The will of Henry Harp, deceased, was proven by the oaths of Jesse Ward and Charles Beddingfield, subscribing witnesses; and Susannah Harp and Solomon Beddingfield qualified as executors.

October 15, 1805: The will of Robert Stanford was duly probated.

March 3, 1806: Radford Butts and John Butts, Administrators on estates of Joshua Butts Sr., and Joshua Butts Jr., were granted letters of dismission.

March 3, 1806: The will of Peter Newsom was duly probated.

March 3, 1806: The will of Samuel Heart, deceased, was duly proven by the oaths of Septimus Weatherby and John Myrick, and Isaac Heart qualified as Executor. The will and the proceedings were then returned to Washington County.

March 24, 1806: Jesse White was appointed temporary Administrator on estate of Shimei Drake, deceased; Samuel Alexander, surety on bond.

July Term, 1806: The will of Abraham Johnston was proven on the oath of Ezekiel Alexander, and was duly probated.

July Term, 1806: The will of John Myrick Sr., was offered for probate. The Court heard the testimony of the subscribing witnesses, and a caveat having been filed, appointed Thomas Flinn as temporary Administrator, whereupon the case was appealed to the Superior Court by consent, July 7, 1806.

January 31, 1806: Samuel Jackson was appointed temporary Administrator on estate of Samuel Rutherford; John McGlamery, surety on bond.

January 4, 1806: Daniel Perryman was appointed temporary Administrator on the estate of Montford Perryman, deceased.

January 31, 1806: Letters dismissory were granted to Robert Abercrombie, Administrator on the estate of William C. Abercrombie, deceased.

May 5, 1806: Asa Wright was granted letters of dismission from the administration of the Samuel Wright estate.

May 5, 1806: David Neal was granted letters of dismission from the administration of the Thomas Neal estate.

June 14, 1806: Mary Jarrett was appointed temporary administratrix on estate of Alexander Jarrett, deceased.

September 1, 1806: Benjamin S. Woodard was appointed temporary administrator on estate of Francis Woodard; Harmon Perryman, surety on bond.

October 11, 1806: Thaddeus Beall Jr., and Elias Beall were appointed temporary administrators on estate of Josiah Beall, deceased. Thaddeus Beall Sr., surety on their bond.

November 3, 1806: The will of Barnabas Jones was probated on the oath of Joseph Bonner, a subscribing witness; and Patty Jones qualified as executrix.

January 1, 1807: Winnifred Atchison was appointed temporary administratrix on estate of James Atchison, deceased; George Hargraves, surety on her bond.

January 5, 1807: John Bayn, executor of will of Robert Stanford, was granted letters dismissory.

January 5, 1807: The will of Samuel Parker, deceased, was duly probated; and Mary Parker qualified as executrix.

February 2, 1807: The will of Drury McCullers was probated on the oaths of John Sallis and James Smith, subscribing witnesses.

February 2, 1807: Samuel Alexander as the greatest creditor, applies for letters of administration on the estate of James Heflin as the will of the deceased could not be proven. He was duly appointed March 2, 1807; John Simmons, surety.

March 30, 1807: Nancy Darden was appointed temporary administratrix on estate of Stephen Darden, deceased. She and Jethro Darden were appointed permanent administrators, May 4, 1807. Sureties on bond: Jacob Darden, Jethro Darden and William Darden.

May 4, 1807: Isaiah Tucker, surety on the bond of Byrd Pruitt and Elizabeth Pruitt, Administrators of estate of Levi Pruitt, deceased, having been relieved as bondsman at his request, the administrators were cited to attend the next term of the Court and given new bond, as in default thereof they would be removed.

May 4, 1807: Letters dismissory were ordered issued to Jane Vaughn as Administratrix on estate of Alexander Vaughn, deceased.

May 30, 1807: Martha Jones was appointed temporary administratrix of estate of Thomas Jones, deceased. Permanent administration on said estate was granted to her and John Lamar, July 6, 1807; Benjamin Sandeford and Matthew Hubert, sureties on their bond.

# MINUTES OF INFERIOR COURT – 1807-1814

September 7, 1807 – Justices of the Court present and presiding: John Torrence, Elisha Hurt, Henry Candler, Archelaus Flewellin.

Eleanor Spann applied for administration on Francis Spann's estate and was appointed Administratrix, notice having previously given as required by law. Sureties on bond accepted: John Burton, Wyatt Bonner.

September 7, 1807 – Reubin McGee and Ephriam McGee applied for administration with will annexed on estate of Nathan Davis. Notice having been given they were appointed Administrators with will annexed, and duly qualified. Peter Buckles and Joseph White accepted as sureties on bond.

November 2, 1807 – Septimus Weatherby applied for administration of estate of George Weatherby and was appointed and qualified. Sureties accepted on bond: John Myrick and G. Smith.

January 4, 1808 – Rhoda Battle appeared before the court and made choice of her third of the estate of John Battle, deceased.

January 4, 1808 – Milly Stith petitioned for Letters Testamentary on the will of William Stith, and offered the will for probate. On the testimony of the subscribing witnesses John Stith, Hartwell Jones, John Henery. She duly qualified as executrix.

January 4, 1808 – James Dozier and John Dozier applied for Letters Testamentary on will of James Dozier, deceased, and offered the will for probate. On the testimony on the subscribing witnesses William Berry and Thomas Berry the will was probated and petitioners qualified as executors of the same.

January 4, 1808 – Sterling Gardner and Walter Bell applied for Administration with the will annexed, on estate of Thomas Neal, deceased, and offered the will for probate. On testimony of the subscribing witnesses Shadrach Flewellin and Solomon Slatter it was probated and petitioners were appointed Administrators with the will annexed and duly qualified.

January 4, 1808 – Chapple Heath and Joseph Hill applied for administration with the will annexed, on estate of Richard Heath, deceased. Will was probated on testimony of the subscribing witnesses John Baker, William Baker. Petitioners were appointed Administrators with will annexed and qualified.

January 4, 1808 – William B. Allison petitioned for administration with the non-cupative will attached, on estate of Margaret Allison, and petitioned for the probate of the will. On the testimony of the witnesses Rebecca Walker, Mary Huskey and Elizabeth Huskey as to the spoken will of deceased, the will as probated, and petitioner was appointed. Sureties on his bond: William Berry, John Allison.

January 4, 1808 – George Dykes petitioned for administration with the non-cupative will annexed on estate of Charity Powell, and was appointed.

January 4, 1808 – Lewis Wright and Joseph Wright petitioned for administration on estate of Jesse Wright, deceased. Notice having been given and there being no objections he was appointed. Amos Wright, surety on bond.

January 4, 1808 – Lorany Mitchell petitioned for administration on estate of James Mitchell, deceased intestate. She was appointed and qualified. Sureties accepted on her bond: William Berry, Joseph Bowen.

March 7, 1808 – Joseph Wright and Chloe Wright on their petition were appointed Administrators on estate of Dr. Warriss (?) D. Ryan, deceased and qualified. Surety on their bond: Basil Wright.

March 7, 1808 – Nowell Robertson and George Granberry presented the will of Moses Granberry, deceased, for probate. It was duly probated and they were appointed Executors of the will and qualified.

March 7, 1808 – Charles Logue was appointed Administrator on estate of Nathaniel Williams, deceased. Surety on his bond: Nowell Robertson.

March 7, 1808 – John Slatter was appointed Administrator on estate of James Slatter deceased. Surety accepted on his bond: Joel Slatter.

March 7, 1808 – Nowell Robertson was appointed Administrator on estate of James Willis Sr., deceased. Sureties on his bond: James Willis, George Granberry.

March 7, 1808 – Daniel Culpepper offered for probate the will of William Culpepper, deceased. It was duly probated and he was appointed Executor of same.

March 7, 1808 – Levan McGee presented his petition praying for a deed to be made to him in terms of a Bond for Title made to him by Henry Jones in his lifetime, whereby he agreed to make him title for 270 acres of land lying on both sides of the Georgetown-Augusta Road dated January 17, 1803. Rule Nisi issued directing Elizabeth Jones, Administratrix of deceased, to show cause at next term why same should not be made.

March 7, 1808 – Isaiah Tucker asked to be released as a bondsman on the bond of Elizabeth Pruitt and Bird Pruitt as Administrators of Levi Pruitt. They were directed to show cause at next term why he should not be released as prayed.

March 7, 1808 – Elias Beall and Thaddeus Beall, Administrators of Josiah Beall estate, were granted leave to sell three slaves of the estate in order to pay the debts of the estate.

March 7, 1808 – Michael Burkhalter petitioned to be released as surety on bond of Sarah Newsom, Administratrix of John Newsom. Rule Nisi issued directing said Sarah to show cause at next term, etc.

March 7, 1808 – John Rushing and James Willson petitioned to be released as sureties on bond of Elizabeth Rosser (formerly Elizabeth Murphy) Administratrix on estate of Edward Murphy. Rule Nisi issued, etc.

May 2, 1808 – Benjamin Oliver Jr. applied for administration on estate of Peter Oliver. He was appointed and qualified. John Oliver, surety.

May 2, 1808 – Thomas Carr caveats to appointment of Turner Parsons as Administrator on estate of Reubin Brit__ (illegible) on the ground that Parsons is not next of kin or a creditor of deceased, also on the further ground that he, Carr, is already Administrator by appointment in Columbia County where deceased died and where his property lies. Caveator says Parsons is said to be authorized by persons calling themselves heirs and who reside in Connecticut and are not heirs.

July 4, 1808 – Mary Parker, Solomon Thompson, Administrators of James Parker estate, were dismissed, the estate having been fully administered.

July 4, 1808 – Rhoda Chapman and Temperance Chapman, minors over age of 14 years, choose Millie Chapman to be their Guardian, and she was appointed.

July 4, 1808 – Jeremiah Beall and Thomas Beall were appointed Administrators of estate of Thaddeus Beall, deceased. Thomas Pennington, surety on their bond.

September 5, 1808 – Jane Vaughn, Administratrix of Alexander Vaughn's estate, was dismissed, having administered the estate.

September 5, 1808 – Likewise, Adam Jones and Priscilla his wife, Administratrix of Charles Baker's estate, were dismissed.

September 5, 1808 – John J. Zachry was appointed Administrator of Edmond Wiggins estate, and qualified. George Hargraves and Timothy Matthews, sureties.

September 5, 1808 – Winnifred Verdun and John Verdun presented for probate the will of John Verdun, deceased. It was probated and they qualified as Executors.

November 7, 1808 – The will of Thomas Fontaine was probated on the testimony of the subscribing witnesses Cader Wesley and Sally Fontaine. James Allen qualified as Executor. Elisha Hart Esq., and John Fontaine named executors in the will, relinquished their right to serve, and Sally Fontaine relinquished her rights as a legatee.

November 7, 1808 – Rebecca Posey was appointed and qualified as Administratrix on the estate of Samuel Posey, deceased.

January 2, 1809 – Archelaus Flewellin and Elizabeth Wright were appointed Administrators on William Wright's estate, and duly qualified.

January 2, 1809 – Sally Jones was appointed Administratrix on Tamerlane Jones estate.

January 2, 1809 – James Martin was appointed Administrator on William McKinley's estate.

January 2, 1809 – Littleberry Little was appointed Administrator on Nathaniel Newsom's estate.

January 2, 1809 – Emelia Beall, relict of Thaddeus Beall, came forward and made choice of her third part of estate as dower.

January 2, 1809 – Nicholas Williams was appointed Administrator of Noel Pitts' estate.

March 6, 1809 – Polly Torrence was appointed Administratrix on William Torrence estate.

March 6, 1809 – Rebecca Duckworth and Joseph Duckworth were appointed Administrators on estate of William Duckworth's estate.

March 6, 1809 – The will of Thomas Ansley was duly probated, whereupon Abel Ansley, Samuel Ansley, Thomas Ansley and Joseph Ansley qualified as executors of the will, being named as such in the will.

March 6, 1809 – John Fontaine came forward and qualified as joint executor with James Allen on the will of Thomas Fontaine, deceased.

March 6, 1809 – Severn Rukie was appointed Administrator of estate of William McKinley and qualified as such.

May 1, 1809 – Mary Newsom was appointed Administratrix on David Newsom's estate.

May 1, 1809 – Asa Newsom was appointed Administrator de bonis non on estate of Solomon Newsom, deceased, succeeding David Newsom, deceased Administrator.

July 3, 1809 – Sarah Oliver and Thomas Friend Esq. offered for probate the will of Benjamin Oliver Sr. and it was probated and they qualified as Executors of the same.

July 3, 1809 – Robert Jenkins and Anson Beall were appointed Administrators on estate of Robert Jenkins, and qualified as such.

July 3, 1809 – Lettice McCrary was appointed Administratrix on Matthew McCrary's estate.

July 3, 1809 – James Oliver was appointed Administrator with Benjamin Oliver Jr. on the estate of Peter Oliver, deceased, and qualified as such.

September 4, 1809 – Thomas Hutchins, Administrator of John Hutchins estate was dismissed.

September 4, 1809 – Phillip Brantley was appointed Administrator of David Golden's estate.

September 4, 1809 – John Drake was appointed Administrator of Matthew Drake's estate.

November 6, 1809 – William B. Allison and Clayton Hurkey were appointed Administrators on estate of Frederick Hurkey, deceased.

November 6, 1809 – Joseph Duckworth and Ranella Duckworth were appointed Administrators on estate of Jeremiah Duckworth, deceased.

November 6, 1809 – Henry Kendall, Executor of will of William Kendall, deceased, was granted leave to sell a negro belonging to the estate.

January 1, 1810 – Warren Barrow and Richard Barrow, witnesses to the will of Nicholas Booty, deceased, testified to the execution of the will.

January 1, 1810 – Elizabeth Cody and Nathaniel Hutchinson were appointed Administrators of estate of Richard Cody, and duly qualified as such.

January 1, 1810 – Nathaniel Hutchinson applies for an order authorizing the Administrators of David Golden's estate to make him a deed conveying land on Hart's Creek in this county, in terms of Bond for Title made him by Golden in the latter's lifetime. Citation was ordered to issue thereon, and be published.

March 5, 1810 – The will of John Barrow Sr. was probated, and Stephen W. Burnly qualified as Executor of the same.

March 5, 1810 – Mary Castleberry was appointed Administratrix on Jacob Castleberry estate.

March 5, 1810 – Timothy Matthews was appointed Administrator on estate of William Britt.

May 7, 1810 – The will of Joel Heath was probated in due form, and Hartwell Heath and Robert Bonner qualified as Executors of same.

May 7, 1810 – Mrs. Anna Darden, widow of Stephen Darden, made choice of her third of the estate.

May 7, 1810 – Churchwell Gibson was appointed Guardian of Isabella, William and Margarat Barnett, in place of Isaiah Tucker.

July 3, 1810 – Nancy Bonner was appointed Administratrix on Wyatt Bonner estate.

July 3, 1810 – Robert Thompson Jr. was appointed Administrator on Robert Thompson estate.

July 3, 1810 – George Parham was appointed Administrator on William Hill's estate.

July 3, 1810 – Mrs. Rebecca Duckworth, relict of William Duckworth, deceased, made choice of her third of the estate.

July 3, 1810 – Phillip Brantley, Administrator of David Golden estate was authorized to make deed to Nathaniel Hutchinson in compliance with bond for title made by deceased to Hutchinson, as petitioned for by latter.

November 5, 1810 – The will of David Raglin was probated and admitted to record.

November 7, 1810 – Joseph Wright and Chloe Ryan, Administrators of Laurence D. Ryan's estate were dismissed, having closed out the estate.

January 7, 1811 – The will of Amos Wright was probated in due form.

February 4, 1811 – John Hobson was appointed Administrator of Mrs. Millie Heath, de benesse and qualified as such. He was authorized to sell the negroes of deceased. It is stated she was sole heir of William Stith, deceased.

March 4, 1811 – The will of Jonathan Lock was probated in due form, and Mary Lock and John Lock qualified as Executors of same.

March 4, 1811 – John Lamar, Administrator of Thomas Jones estate was dismissed.

March 4, 1811 – Elizabeth Myrick, widow of Owen Myrick, comes into Court with her minor son, Nathaniel Myrick, and agrees that if he lives with her and be under her direction and in her service until he is 21 years old, she will not make any charge against him in the final settlement of the estate of his said father, Owen Myrick, for any support furnished him until he is 21.

May 6, 1811 – John Torrence qualified as Clerk of the Court of Ordinary.

May 6, 1811 – The will of James Carter was duly probated, and Moore Carter, Jesse Carter, Jacob Carter, qualified as Executors of same. John Bayn also named by the will as an Executor, declined to serve.

July 1, 1811 – John Aikins was appointed Administrator of David Thompson's estate.

July 1, 1811 – Noah Kelsey, Guardian of the orphans of John Battle, was ordered to come into court by next term and give bond.

July 1, 1811 – William B. Allison, Administrator of Frederick Husky, was dismissed.

July 1, 1811 – Moore Carter was appointed guardian of James Carter, a minor son (over 14 years of age) of James Carter, deceased.

September 2, 1811 – Debora Chapman, Administratrix of John Chapman, applied for dismission.

September 2, 1811 – Thomas Chappell, Administrator of Sion Wheless estate, was dismissed.

September 2, 1811 – William Pitts' will was probated and the Executor named in the will was duly qualified.

September 2, 1811 – The will of George Waggoner was duly probated.

September 2, 1811 – Wylie Jiles Brady was appointed Guardian of John Jiles, a minor over 14 years of age, and he qualified as such Guardian.

September 2, 1811 – Elizabeth Parham and Samuel Pitts apply for administration on estate of John Parham, deceased.

October 8, 1811 – The will of Blake Lasseter, deceased, of Halifax County, North Carolina, was presented and was probated here on oath of Henry Cocroft.

October 8, 1811 – Nicholas Williams was appointed Guardian of Nicholas Williams Pitts, an orphan over age of 14 years, by his choice; and was also appointed by the Court as Guardian of Nancy Williams Pitts, Nestor Pitts, Solomon Pitts, Jack Pitts, Elizabeth Pitts, minor children of Noel Pitts, deceased, late of State of North Carolina. Said Guardian qualified, giving bond in sum of $10,000 with Sterling Gardner as surety on his bond.

November 4, 1811 – Elizabeth Parham and Samuel Pitts were appointed Administrators of estate of John Parham, on giving bond in sum of $20,000.

November 4, 1811 – Wiley G. Brady was appointed Administrator of Thomas Phillips estate, together with Joseph and John Phillips, sons of the deceased.

November 4, 1811 – George Washington Ray, a minor bound out to William Ansley until he is 21 years old. Ansley required to give bond for $500, and to give said minor when he is 21 a good horse, bridle and saddle and a decent suit of clothes, also give him two years' schooling.

November 4, 1811 – John E. Little, Administrator of Micajah Little estate, and Robert Abercrombie apply to be released as bondsmen on bond of Samuel Alexander and Rhoda Battle, Administrators of John Battle estate. Citation was ordered to issue for next term, etc.

November 4, 1811 – Lewis Parham petitions for an order directing James Bonner, Administrator in right of his wife, and Nancy Conner, Administratrix of Wyatt Bonner estate to make him title to 100 acres in compliance with Bond for Title made Parham in the lifetime of deceased. Citation ordered to issue for next term, directing Administrators to show cause if any they can why they should not be required to make the deed as prayed.

November 4, 1811 – James Bonner and Nancy Bonner, Administrators of Wyatt Bonner estate were granted leave to sell a negro slave of the estate.

November 4, 1811 – John Blakey was appointed Guardian for Jesse, Sarah and Levi Blakey, minor children of said John Blakey, they being over 14, having chosen him to be their Guardian; and he was also appointed Guardian of Mary, John, Susannah, Mary, John and Nancy Blakey, his minor children under age of 14 years.

December 2, 1811 – James Bonner was appointed Guardian of Sarah Parham Hill, age over 14 years, at her request.

December 2, 1811 – James Neal and Thomas Maddux were appointed Administrators of estate of David Neal, deceased. Their bond was fixed at $10,000.

December 2, 1811 – The will of George Waggoner, deceased, was probated in due form.

December 2, 1811 – John Burkhalter Sr., was appointed Administrator of estate of John Burkhalter Jr., deceased. Bond was fixed at $1000.

December 2, 1811 – Mrs. Elizabeth Parham, widow of John Parham, came into court and made choice of her part of the estate, by taking one-third of the real estate, and a child's part of the personal property.

December 2, 1811 – Matthew and Rebecca Parham, orphans over 14 years of age, of John Parham, chose John C. Turner as their guardian. He was appointed.

December 2, 1811 – Turner Persons, Shadrach Flewellin, Archelaus Flewellin, William Blount, John Myrick were appointed partitioners to divide the estate of John Parham, deceased, between the heirs.

December 2, 1811 – Archelaus Flewellin was appointed Guardian of Hellena, Sally, Winnifred and Nancy Wright, orphans of William Wright, deceased.

December 2, 1811 – Rachel Ruff and Jack Ruff, minor persons of color, were bound out to David Mims. It is stated that Rachel will be 12 years old in February next, and Jack will be 10 next April. Fanny, Judith and Bethena Ruff, minor children of colour, were bound out to Benajah Wynne until they are 18. Fanny will be 18 next March, Judith will be 15 in December, and Bethena two years old in July.

December 2, 1811 – Elisha Hurt, Turner Persons, Radford Butt, Shadrach Flewellin and John C. Turner were appointed partitioners to divide the estate of William Wright deceased, among the heirs.

December 2, 1811 – The will of Robert Wynne was duly probated.

February 3, 1812 – The Administrators of Wyatt Bonner estate were directed to make title to Lewis Parham as per his petition previously filed.

February 3, 1812 – Isaiah Tucker, Daniel Culpepper, Sterling Gardner, Nicholas Flewellin and Henry Hight were appointed partitioners to divide and turn over to Joseph Wright, his part or moiety of two-thirds of the personal property of deceased.

February 3, 1812 – Mrs. Martha Pitts came into court and made choice of a child's part for her share of the estate of her deceased husband Noel Pitts.

February 3, 1812 – Clement Wynne qualified as Executor of will of Robert Wynne, deceased.

February 3, 1812 – Received and approved the report of partitioners appointed to divide the estate of John Parham.

February 3, 1812 – Received and approved the report of partitioners appointed to divide the estate of William Wright.

February 3, 1812 – Peter Clower, Administrator in right of his wife, on estate of James Mitchell, deceased, was dismissed, having wound up the estate.

March 2, 1812 – Inventory of the Howell Gregory estate was received; and F. Beall was appointed permanent Administrator of the estate.

March 2, 1812 – William Taylor, age 11 years next September, son of William and Patsy Taylor, was bound out to Solomon

Thompson until age of 21 years, Thompson was directed to give bond and to give the child schooling and when 21 to give him a good horse, saddle, bridle and a decent suit of Sunday clothes.

March 2, 1812 – Miss Jincy Waggoner, age over 14, orphan of Henry Waggoner, chose William McFarlin as her Guardian and he was appointed.

March 2, 1812 – Anthony Jones was appointed Guardian of Barnabas Jones, Polly Jones, minor children under 14, of Barnabas Jones, deceased.

May 4, 1812 – James Waggoner, orphan of Henry Waggoner, made choice of William McFarland as his Guardian succeeding Wyatt Bonner, his deceased guardian; said orphan being over 14 years old.

May 4, 1812 – Leave to sell 230 acres of land was granted Administrators of David Thompson.

May 4, 1812 – Nancy Abercrombie, William Jones, Aaron Smith, were appointed temporary Administrators of Colonel Robert Abercrombie, deceased.

May 4, 1812 – John Jones and Martha Jones, orphans over 14 of Barnabas Jones, made choice of Henry Jones as their Guardian and he was appointed.

May 4, 1812 – William Hodgins, about 8 years of age, was bound out to Richard Bray until he is 21, to learn the carpenter's trade. Bray was directed to give the boy two years' schooling, and when 21 to give him a decent suit of Sunday clothes and a common set of carpenter tools.

May 4, 1812 – William McFarlin was appointed Guardian of James Waggoner and Jincy Waggoner, orphans of Henry Waggoner, deceased.

May 4, 1812 – Mrs. Nancy Abercrombie, the widow of Robert Abercrombie, William Jones and Aaron Smith were appointed temporary Administrators of estate of deceased. Bond was fixed at

$50,000. Ezekiel Smith of Hancock County and Solomon Lockett were approved as sureties.

July 6, 1812 – John Hobson, Administrator of Colonel William Stith's estate, was granted leave to sell tract of 300 acres in this county and a tract of 250 acres situated in Camden County.

July 6, 1812 – William B. Allison, Administrator of estates of Frederick Husky and of Margaret Allison, was dismissed, having closed out said estates.

July 6, 1812 – Mrs. Nancy Abercrombie, William Jones and Aaron Smith were appointed permanent Administrators of Colonel Robert Abercrombie estate, and bond was fixed at $50,000.

July 6, 1812 – Henry Wilson, John Wilson and James Wilson were cited to show cause at next term in September, why John Rolling should not recover pay from them for keeping William Wilson four months in 1811.

August 12, 1812 – The Court convened in special session this date and appointed a committee from the five Justices of the Court to attend Mrs. Elizabeth Waggoner, the widow of George Waggoner, and administer the oath and qualify her as Executrix on said will, she being infirm and unable to come to court, or leave her residence.

September 7, 1812 – Anthony Jones and Henry Jones were granted Letters of Guardianship for the orphans of Barnabas Jones.

September 7, 1812 – Silas Burkholts was appointed Guardian of Linny Rayse, a minor.

September 7, 1812 – The Court dismissed the case of John Rolling seeking payment for four months keeping of William Wilson, "one of the list of county pensioners."

November 2, 1812 – The will of Rubin Barrow, deceased, was probated on the testimony of Benjamin Bledsoe and William Brannon, subscribing witnesses.

November 2, 1812 – John Baker, temporary Administrator of estate of Miss Olive Harris, deceased, was appointed permanent Administrator.

January 1, 1813 – Archelaus Flewellin, Administrator of William Wright, deceased, was dismissed.

March 1, 1813 – Polly, Rebecca and Samuel Duckworth, minor children of William Duckworth, deceased, being age of over 14, chose Joseph Duckworth as their Guardian, and he was appointed. At the same time the Court appointed him Guardian for Nelly, Joseph and Gazaway Duckworth, minor children of deceased, under the age of 14. "This to apply only to their part of the dividend due from the estate of their grandfather, Jeremiah Duckworth, deceased."

March 1, 1813 – The Executrix of will of Samuel Parker, was granted leave to sell 257 acres of land in this county owned by deceased.

March 1, 1813 – Mrs. Nancy Abercrombie caveats to application for leave to sell lands of Robert Abercrombie, deceased.

March 1, 1813 – Wilson Bird presented the will of William Bird, deceased, for probate and it was duly probated and he qualified as Executor of same.

March 1, 1813 – John Baker, Solomon Lockett, Aaron Greer were appointed partitioners to divide the personal property of estate of Stephen Darden.

March 1, 1813 – Mrs. Joyce Neal, widow of David Neal Esq., chose a child's part of the estate for her part of the estate.

March 1, 1813 – The Administrators of David Neal estate were granted leave to sell a certain lot in town of Warrenton, and 100 acres whereon the grist and saw mills are located, also 150 acres of pine land.

March 1, 1813 – John Torrence qualified as Clerk of Court of Ordinary.

May 3, 1813 – William Ansley was appointed Guardian of his daughter, Epsy Ansley.

May 3, 1813 – Thomas Myhand was appointed Administrator of Francis Benton's estate.

May 3, 1813 – Ann Darden was appointed Guardian of Nicholas Darden and Moses Darden, orphans over 14 of Stephen Darden; and of Matilda Clowers, minor daughter of Jacob Clowers.

July 5, 1813 – The will of Lowe Jackson was probated in due form.

July 5, 1813 – Reubin Rogers was appointed Guardian of John Emerson, a minor over 14, at the latter's request. Bond fixed at $4000.

September 6, 1813 – James Grenade was appointed Administrator of Benjamin Grenade, deceased, and qualified.

September 6, 1813 – Timothy Matthews was appointed Guardian of Jessie Butt and Sallie Butt, orphans over 14 of William Butt, having been chosen by them; and the Court appointed him Guardian of Nancy Butt and William Butt, orphans under the age of 14 of said William Butt, deceased.

September 6, 1813 – Leave to sell 50 acres was granted the Executrix of Samuel Rutherford.

September 6, 1813 – A Rule was issued against Elizabeth Green, formerly Jones, and Hardy Green, her present husband, Administrators of Henry Jones, deceased, requiring them to appear at next term and show cause why they have not made their returns as required by law.

September 6, 1813 – James Rogers, a minor, was bound out to Joshua Stanford until he is 21, to learn the shoemaker's trade. Said minor will be 11 years old next February.

November 1, 1813 – Solomon Lockett Esq., Solomon Thompson, Archibald Flewellin, William Latimer and Robert A. Beall were named as partitioners to divide the personal property of William Butt estate, so far as respects the widow's part.

November 1, 1813 – The will of John Drake was duly probated.

November 1, 1813 – James Bailey was appointed Administrator of Pierce Bailey estate.

November 1, 1813 – Mahala Story, orphan of Asa Story, was bound to Levi Stanford until she is 16 years old, she now being 7 years old the 7$^{th}$ of this month.

November 1, 1813 – G. B. Waggoner was appointed Administrator with will annexed on estate of George Waggoner, deceased.

November 1, 1813 – The Clerk of the Court of Ordinary of Hancock County, received and reco4rded the estate preceedings in the matter of the George Medlock estate which had been transferred there.

January 7, 1814 – William Drake of North Carolina qualified as Executor of will of John Drake, deceased, was received and approved.

February 7, 1814 – The surviving Administrators of James Waggoner estate were cited to show cause why William Waggoner should not be released on surety on their bond at next term.

February 7, 1814 – The report of partitioners to divide the personal estate of Stephen Darden, deceased, was received and approved.

February 7, 1814 – Mary Marks was appointed Administratrix on Joseph Marks estate.

February 7, 1814 – The will of Mrs. Lucy Thompson was probated, and Alexander Thompson qualified as Executor of same.

February 7, 1814 – Mrs. Catherine Bird, widow of Colonel William Bird, gave notice that would file claim to her dowry in the lands of the estate and take a child's part in the personal estate.

March 7, 1814 – The report of partitioners to divide the William Butt estate among the heirs, was received and adopted.

May 2, 1814 – The will of John Akins was probated in due form.

May 2, 1814 – Caswell Wright, orphan of Isaiah Wright, was bound out to Daniel Hutchinson for a term of four years, to learn the blacksmith trade.

May 2, 1814 – Melton Wright, orphan of said Isaiah Wright, was bound out to William A. Fuller for a term of 3 years to learn blacksmithing.

May 2, 1814 – William Byrom Esq., and William Aikens qualified as Executors of the will of John Akins, deceased.

June 6, 1814 – Charles Brooks applied for Administrator on estate of Henry Brooks' estate.

June 6, 1814 – Harden Pruitt applied for Administrator on Samuel Jones estate.

June 6, 1814 – Thomas Maddux applied for Administrator on John Neal's estate.

July 4, 1814 – The will of James Thompson was duly probated.

July 4, 1814 – The will of William Heath was duly probated.

July 4, 1814 – Leave to sell the realty of William Butt, deceased, consisting of 450 acres was granted.

July 4, 1814 – Harris Pruitt was appointed Guardian of his own minor children who are entitled to legacy left them by their grandfather, James McCormick Esq., deceased.

September 6, 1814 – Charles Brooks, Administrator of Henry Brooks estate was dismissed.

September 6, 1814 – Hardin Pruitt was appointed Guardian of his own minor children who are entitled to legacy left them by their grandfather, James McCormick, deceased.

October 3, 1814 – The will of Sarah Neal was duly probated.

October 3, 1814 – H. B. Thompson was appointed Administrator of James B. Thompson with will annexed.

November 7, 1814 – Mrs. Martha Hardaway, widow of John Hardaway, came into court and made choice of a child's part of her share of the estate.

November 7, 1814 – William Harbuck qualified as Administrator of John Harbuck estate.

November 7, 1814 – Rebecca Neal, widow of John Neal, chose a child's part for her share.

November 7, 1814 – The will of Nathan Castleberry was duly probated.

November 7, 1814 – Thomas Maddux was appointed Guardian of Stith and Thomas Hardaway, orphans of John Hardaway.

November 15, 1814 – Amicable settlement was made between Elizabeth Myrick, widow and Administratrix of Owen Myrick, deceased, and Nathaniel Myrick, son and legatee of deceased.

# ADMINISTRATOR'S BOND BOOK A

Administrations are granted on estates where the deceased died without a will. In cases where there is a will probated and the executor named in the will dies, resigns, or fails to qualify, the Court will appoint an Administrator "with the will annexed." Where there is a previous administration and a new administrator is appointed, he is referred to as the Administrator "de bonis non."

Page 1 – Millie Stith, deceased. Bond of John Hobson, Administrator, with the will annexed, dated February 4, 1811, that is, "with the will of William Stith, deceased, annexed." Sureties: Solomon Lockett, Timothy Matthews.

Page 2 – David Thompson, deceased. Bond of John Aikens, Administrator, dated July 1, 1811. Sureties: John Byrom and William Byrom.

Page 3 – Thomas Phillips, deceased. Bond dated November 4, 1811, of Willy Giles Brady, Joseph Phillips, John Phillips, Administrators. Surety: Cullen Lewis Brady.

Page 4 – John Parham, deceased. Bond of Elizabeth Parham and Samuel Pitts, Administrators, dated November 4, 1811. Sureties: John Turner, Hardy Pitts.

Page 5 – John Burkhalter Jr., deceased. Bond dated December 2, 1811, of John Burkhalter, Administrator. Surety: Hardy Pitts.

Page 6 – David Neal Esq., deceased. Bond of James Maddox and Thomas Maddox, Administrators. Sureties: Thomas Neal, John Hardaway, Reubin Jones.

Page 7 – Noble Orr, deceased. Bond dated May 4, 1812, of Hamilton Goss as Administrator. Surety: George Hargraves.

Page 8 – Robert Abercrombie, deceased, Administrator's Bond dated May 4, 1812, of Nancy Abercrombie, William Jones and Aaron Smith, Administrators.

Page 10 – Howell Gregory, deceased. Bond dated March 2, 1812, of Francis Beall, Administrator. Surety: Samuel Beall.

Page 11 – Miss Olive Harris, deceased. Bond dated September 12, 1812, of John Baker, Administrator. Sureties: Nicholas Williams, Thomas Battle.

Page 13 – Francis Benton, deceased. Bond of Thomas Myhand, Administrator dated May 3, 1813; William Myhand, surety.

Page 14 – Benjamin Grenade, deceased. Bond dated September 6, 1813, of James Grenade, Administrator. Surety: Jeremiah Burkhalter.

Page 15 – Pierce Bailey, deceased. Bond of Jennie Bailey, Administratrix dated November 1, 1813; Elisha Allen, Joseph Johnston and Benjamin Crenshaw, sureties.

Page 16 – George Waggoner, deceased. Bond of George B. Waggoner, Administrator, with the will annexed, dated November 1, 1813. Sureties: George Mitchell, Henry Dewberry, David W. Waggoner.

Page 17 – Joseph Marks, deceased. Bond dated February 7, 1814, of Mary Marks as Administratrix. Sureties: Edwin Baker, Solomon Ogden, William Teddlie, Ansel McKinney.

Page 18 – Jehu Neal, deceased. Bond of Thomas Maddox, Temporary Administrator, dated March 15, 1814. Surety: James Neal. Bond of Thomas Maddox and Rebecca Neal, permanent Administrators, dated June 6, 1814.

Page 19 – Henry Brooks, deceased. Bond of Charles Brooks, Administrator dated June 6, 1814; Thomas Maddux, surety.

Page 20 – Samuel Jones, deceased. Bond dated June 6, 1814, of Hardin Pruitt, Administrator. Surety: Thomas Maddux.

Page 21 – John Hardaway Esq., deceased. Bond dated July 4, 1814, of Washington Hardaway, Administrator. Surety: John Burkhalter.

Page 22 – John Harbuck, deceased. Bond dated November 7, 1814, of William Harbuck, Administrator. Surety: James Neal.

Page 23 – Benjamin B. Beall, deceased. Bond of Robert A. Beall, Administrator dated December 5, 1814; A. Moncrief and Chappel Heath, securities.

Page 24 – James B. Thompson, deceased. Bond of Henry B. Thompson, Administrator, with the will annexed, dated October 3, 1814. Sureties: Chappell Heath, Joseph M. Semmes.

Page 25 – Amos Wright, deceased. Bond of Rachel Wright, Joseph Wright and Amos Wright Jr., Administrators with the will annexed, dated April 3, 1815. Sureties: Reddick Bass, Chappell Heath.

Page 26 – Lewis Wright Esq., deceased. Bond of Solomon Lockett and Nancy Wright, Administrators, dated April 3, 1815. Sureties: Chappell Heath, Jacob Darden.

Page 27 – Asaph Wright Esq., deceased. Bond of John Butt, Administrator, dated March 6, 1815. Surety: Chappell Heath.

Page 29 – Joshua Hopkins, deceased. Bond of Susannah Hopkins, Administratrix, dated July 3, 1815. Sureties: Chappell Heath, Joseph Roberts.

Page 30 - John Curry, Administrator of Jane Burns estate, dated April 17, 1797. Surety: Barrett Brewer.

Page 30 – Wyatt Bonner, deceased. Bond of James Bonner, Administrator, dated September 4, 1815; William Brown and David Sallis, securities.

Page 31 – Lydia Hartfield, Administratrix of George Hartfield estate, dated August 11, 1800. Benjamin Howard, security.

Page 32 – Fergus Linn, Administrator of John Linn estate, dated July 18, 1799. Thomas Jones and Daniel McCowan, sureties.

Page 32 – John Sallis, deceased. Will of David Sallis and John Sallis, Administrators, dated November 6, 1815. Sureties: James Neal, Isaac Burson, Washington Hardaway.

Page 33 – Daniel Frederick, Administrator of John Thomas estate, dated July 18, 1799. William Mims surety.

Page 33 – Susannah Butler, Administratrix of Noble Butler estate, dated July 18, 1799. Beall Butler and Enos Butler, sureties.

Page 33 – John Morris, deceased. Bond of Benjamin Rees, Administrator, dated November 6, 1825; sureties: Jeremiah Burkhalter and David Sallis.

Page 34 – Jonathan Hagerty, Administrator of Isaac Cook estate, dated (blank) 1799. Edward Hill, security.

Page 34 – Elisha Brothers, deceased. Bond of Andrew C. Horn, temporary Administrator, dated November 21, 1815; Josias Vincent, surety.

Page 34 – Stephen Rose, deceased. Bond of Hardy Pitts, Administrator, dated December 4, 1815. Surety: James Neal.

Page 35 – Jonathan Hagerty, Guardian of Pheriby Cook and Seletha Cook, minor daughters of Isaac Cook, deceased. Dated July 18, 1799. Edward Hill, surety.

Page 35 – Daniel Sturdivant, deceased. Bond of George Hargraves, Administrator, dated February 5, 1816. Surety: Chappell Heath.

Page 35 – Joseph Sallis, deceased. Bond of Galby Matthews, Administrator, dated May 5, 1817. Surety: David Sallis.

Page 36 – Holly Walker and Amos Persons, Administratrix and Administrator of Joel Walker estate. Dated April 20, 1800. Richard Heath and Nicholas Williams, sureties.

Page 36 - David Neal and Samuel Neal, Administrators of Thomas Neal estate. Dated February 18, 1800. James McCormick and Joseph Duckworth, sureties.

Page 37 – John Vance, Administrator of James Vance estate. Dated January 14, 1799. Milby McGee, surety.

Page 37 – Daniel Kinsey, deceased. Bond of May 6, 1816, of Edward Kinsey, Administrator. Sureties: Jeremiah Burkhalter, William Ussery.

Page 38 – Adam Heath, deceased. Bond of Richard Heath and Peter Clower as Administrators, dated May 6, 1816. Sureties: Hardy Pitts, Benjamin Sandiford.

Page 39 – Michael Burkhalter, Administrator of David Newsom estate. Dated July 3, 1797. Sterling Gardner and Basil Wright, sureties.

Page 39 – Joseph White, deceased. Bond of Robert White, Administrator, dated May 6, 1815. Sureties: Aaron Denton, John Hamilton.

Page 40 – Thomas Jones, Administrator of Winnie Pinson estate. Dated February 3, 1799. Benjamin Mitchell, Solomon Newsom sureties.

Page 41 – Sarah Rose and Edmond Rose, Administrators of William Rose estate. Dated February 9, 1801. Sureties: Wormsley Rose, Shadrach Fluwellin.

Page 41 – Matthew McCrery, deceased. Bond of John McCrery and Samuel Hall, Administrators, dated July 1, 1816. Sureties: Henry Kendall Sr., Thomas Williams.

Page 42 – Nancy Burson and Isaac Burson, Administrators of Jonathan Burson estate. Dated August 11, 1801. John English and Michael Cody, sureties.

Page 42 – Samuel Neal, deceased. Bond dated August 19, 1816, of James Neal Jr., Temporary Administrator. Surety: James Neal.

Page 43 – Robert Rutherford, Administrator of Abner Mitchell estate. Dated February 10, 1801. R. Abercrombie and Henry Shelton, securities.

Page 43 – Reubin Barrow, Administrator of James Barrow estate. Dated June 8, 1801. Hugh Reese and David Newsom, Sureties.

Page 43 – John Thompson, deceased. Bond of Nathaniel Thompson as Administrator, dated January 6, 1817. Sureties: James Neal Sr., Peyton Baker.

Page 44 – Asa Wright, Administrator of Samuel Wright estate. Dated June 8, 1801. Johnston Wright and Blake Pearcy, securities.

Page 45 – Robert Abercrombie and Joseph Howell, Administrators of Archibald Kinsey estate. Dated August 10, 1801. Matthew Hubert, James Jones, sureties.

Page 45 – James Parham, deceased. Bond of Edmond Parham, Administrator, dated April 5, 1817. Surety: Robert Bonner.

Page 46 – William Crowman, deceased. Bond dated September 1, 1817, of Mary Crowman, Administrator. Sureties: Hezekiah Jones, Thomas Waggoner.

Page 46 – Lydia Nepper and Samuel Ridgewell, Administrators of James Nepper estate with the will annexed. Dated February 8, 1802. Elisha Brown, Solomon Newsom, sureties.

Page 46 – Shadrack Stroddar, deceased. Bond of Letitia Stroddar, Administrator, dated September 14, 1816. Surety: William Goyne.

Page 47 – Robert Abercrombie, Administrator of William C. Abercrombie estate. Dated February 8, 1802. William Flournoy and M. Hubert, sureties.

Page 47 – Jacob Darden, deceased. Bond dated November 3, 1817, of Abner Darden and David Darden, Administrators. Surcties: Robert Hill, William Darden. On September 4, 1826 the administrators of this estate were required to give a new bond which they did with John Harris and James Claxton as sureties.

Page 48 – Jacob Bull, Administrator of Eli Bull estate. Dated February 9, 1802. Mark Hardin and Jesse Bull, sureties.

Page 48 – Elijah Warthen and Margaret Holliday, Administrator and Administratrix of Ambrose Holliday estate. Dated May 4, 1802. Joseph Howell and William Warthen, sureties.

Page 48 – John Travis, deceased. Bond of Amos Travis, Administrator, dated December 1, 1817. Sureties: Simeon Travis, Lawrence Kitchens.

Page 49 – William Flournoy, Administrator of Jacob Flournoy estate. Dated May 3, 1802. Robert Abercrombie and John B. Flournoy, sureties.

Page 49 – Elizabeth Parham, deceased. Bond of John C. Turner and Samuel Pitts, Administrators, dated December 22, 1817. Sureties: William H. Blount, Henry Dewberry.

Page 50 – Samuel Winslet and John Williams, Administrators of John Carson estate. Dated May 3, 1802. Josiah Bell, Solomon Lockett, Howell Hight, Mark Hardin, sureties.

Page 50 – Francis Woodward, deceased. Bond of Benjamin T. Woodward, Administrator, dated March 23, 1818. Sureties: Isham Woodward, William Jackson.

Page 50 – William White, deceased. Bond of Jethro Darden Sr., Administrator, dated March 23, 1818. Surety: James Vaughn.

Page 51 – Elizabeth Murphy and John Murphy, Administrators of Edward Murphy estate. Dated June 1, 1802, John Rushing and John Wilson, sureties.

Page 51 – Warren Andrews, deceased. Bond dated March 23, 1818, of Peyton Baker, administrator. Jeremiah Beall and James Pace, securities.

Page 52 – Mary Parker and Solomon Thompson, Administrators of James Parker estate. Dated February 15, 1803. John Matthews, Amos Persons, sureties.

Page 52 – Robert Barton Jr., deceased. Bond of William Barton, Administrator, dated September 7, 1818; Robert Barton, Nathan Marsh, sureties.

Page 53 – Sarah Cooper, Administratrix of James Bishop's estate. Dated February 15, 1803. Joel Heath, Thomas Hutchinson, sureties.

Page 53 – David Neal, Administrator of Samuel Neal's estate. Dated April 11, 1803. Reubin Jones, John McCormick, sureties.

Page 53 – George H. Davidson, deceased. Bond dated October 5, 1818, of Arthur Moncrief as Administrator, with John Butt, security.

Page 53 – John Wright, deceased. Bond of Joseph Wright and Amos Wright as Administrators, dated September 21, 1818. Surety: John Fontaine.

Page 54 – Henry Williams Sr., deceased. Bond of Henry Williams, Administrator, dated October 24, 1818. Surety: George W. Hardaway.

Page 54 – Stephen Laurence, Administrator of Nathan Wootten estate. Dated April 11, 1803. Joseph Carter surety.

Page 55 – Alsey Lee, Administratrix of Richard Lee estate. Dated August 9, 1803. Thomas Rogers and William Pilcher, sureties.

Page 55 – Joab Brooks, deceased. Bond of Martin Kinsey, Administrator, dated November 2, 1818; John Kitchens, surety.

Page 56 – David Newsom, Administrator of estate of Solomon Newsom Jr., deceased. Dated October 17, 1803. Sureties: Thomas Dent, William Ussery, Jody Newsom.

Page 57 – Tully Biggs, Administrator of Wiggins Killebrew estate. Dated October 17, 1803. Sureties: John Rushing, William Simmons.

Page 57 – Mary Waggoner, deceased. Bond of Zacheus Waggoner, Administrator, dated January 4, 1819. Sureties: David W. Waggoner and George B. Waggoner.

Page 58 – Samuel Barksdale, Pinkittiam Harvey, Stephen Burnley, Administrators of John Barksdale estate. Dated October 22, 1803. Sureties: Michael Harvey, Josiah Beall.

Page 58 – Batson Bass, deceased. Bond of Zadock Bass, Administrator, dated March 9, 1819; John Fontaine, Jeremiah Butt, Nathan Boddie, sureties.

Page 59 – John Beckwith, deceased. Bond dated July 2, 1819, of Willis Beckwith, Administrator. Surety: Benjamin Crenshaw.

Page 59 – Mary James and George Waggoner, and Aaron Lipham, Administrators of Henry Waggoner estate. Dated December 4, 1805. William Lipham, Solomon Slatter, sureties.

Page 60 – Rhoda Battle and Colonel Samuel Alexander, Administrators of John Battle estate. Dated February 13, 1804. Robert Abercrombie and Micajah Little, sureties.

Page 60 – Joseph Sallis, a minor, deceased. Bond dated July 5, 1819, of Galby Matthews, Administrator. Surety: John Sallis.

Page 61 – Joseph Ford, deceased. Bond dated July 5, 1819, of William W. Ford, Administrator. Sureties: Jeremiah Butt, Kendall McTyeire, James Neal Sr.

Page 61 – Elizabeth Roquemore, Administratrix of James Roquemore estate. Dated February 14, 1804. Sureties: David Robertson and William Ussery.

Page 62 - Hannah Chapman, Administratratrix of Labourn Chapman estate. Dated February 15, 1804. William Chapman, Robert Parker, sureties.

Page 62 – Alexander Littleton, deceased. Bond of James Loyless, Administrator, dated September 13, 1819. Surety: James Cody Jr.

Page 63 – Elizabeth Myrick, Administratrix of Owen Myrick estate. Dated February 15, 1804. Thomas Edmondson and Septimus Weatherby, sureties.

Page 63 – John Neves, Administrator of Daniel Neves estate. Dated February 15, 1804. Shadrach Flewellin, surety.

Page 63 – Isaac Ball, deceased. Bond dated September 17, 1819, of Hardy Pitts and Archalaus Butt, Administrators. Surety: James Loyless.

Page 64 – John Martin, Administrator of William McKinley estate. Dated December 15, 1804. Joseph McKinley, security.

Page 65 – Robert Parker, Administrator of William Parker estate. Dated February 15, 1804. James Matthews, Solomon Thompson, sureties.

Page 66 – Elizabeth Jones, Administratrix of Henry Jones estate. Dated December 15, 1804. John Nunn and William Jones, sureties.

Page 66 – John Newsom, deceased. Bond of Gideon Newsom, Administrator, dated February 7, 1820. Sureties: Joshua Newsom, Henry Newsom.

Page 67 – Sallie and Benjamin Geesland, Administrators of William Geesland estate. Dated August 15, 1804. John Moses, James Gray, sureties.

Page 67 – Nathaniel Ward, Administrator of William Morrison estate. Dated August 15, 1804. Michael Burkhalter, security.

Page 67 – Mark Heath, deceased. Bond of Henry Heath, Administrator, dated August 7, 1820. Sureties: Joseph Hill, Chappell Heath.

Page 68 – Mary and Henry Duberry, Administrators of Jesse Duberry estate. Dated December 10, 1804, Jacob Darden, surety.

Page 68 – William Mayes, deceased. Bond dated September 4, 1820, of Mercy Mayes as Administratrix. Sureties: Joshua Draper, Jeremiah Butt, Henry Williams.

Page 69 – Robert Edwards, deceased. Bond of William Edwards and Thomas Avera, Administrators, dated November 6, 1820. Sureties: Henry Hight, Richard Bray.

Page 69 – William Jones and James Jones, Administrators of James Jones estate. Dated December 10, 1804. Michael Burkhalter, Thomas Dent, securities.

Page 69 – Sarah Perkins, deceased. Bond of Jethro Darden Sr., Administrator, dated November 1, 1819. Surety: Sampson Wilder.

Page 70 – Margaret Beasley and Robert Beasley, Administrators of Richard Beasley estate. Dated January 26, 1805. James Gray, surety.

Page 70 – Sarah Newsom, Administratrix of John Newsom estate. Dated February 14, 1805. Michael Burkhalter, surety.

Page 71 – Mary Stone, Administratrix of Micajah Stone estate. Dated February 14, 1805. Robert Jenkins, Jeremiah Bell, sureties.

Page 71 – James Brady, deceased. Bond dated November 6, 1820, of William Shivers, Administrator. Sureties: Jonas Shivers and Vinson Johnson.

Page 72 – Elizabeth Pruitt and Bird Pruitt, Administrators of Levi Pruitt estate. Dated March 4, 1805. Isaiah Tucker, Hardin Pruitt, sureties.

Page 73 – Mary Waggoner, David W. Waggoner and George B. Waggoner, Administrators of James Waggoner estate. Dated August 14, 1805. George and William Waggoner, sureties.

Page 73 – Winnifred Benton, Administratrix of John Benton estate. Dated August 14, 1805. Leroy Mims, Johnston Wright, sureties.

Page 73 – Nathaniel Thompson, deceased. Bond of Nancy Thompson, Administratrix, dated January 29, 1821. Sureties: Michael Cody Sr., Stephen Thompson.

Page 74 – Zachariah Booth, Administrator of John K. Candler estate. Dated December 14, 1805. Security: Richard Curry.

Page 74 - Dinwiddie R. Harrison, deceased. Bond dated January 29, 1821, of Adam Jones, Administrator. Sureties: Daniel Owens, John Moore, Asa Chapman.

Page 75 – Louisa Rosser, Administratrix of James Rosser estate. Dated March 3, 1806. John Rosser and Faddy Whittington, sureties.

Page 75 – John Williams, deceased. Bond of Wingfield Cosby, Administrator, dated January 29, 1821. Surety: Frederick B. Heath and Richard Dozier.

Page 76 – Samuel Jackson, Administrator of Samuel Rutherford estate. Dated May 5, 1806. John McGlamery, surety.

Page 76 – Jesse White, Administrator of Sherrod Drake estate. Dated May 5, 1806. Samuel Alexander, surety.

Page 76 – Benjamin Chapman, deceased. Bond dated March 5, 1821, of Robert and Abner Chapman, Administrators. Sureties: Asa Chapman, Benjamin Hill.

Page 77 – Hannah Jones, Administratrix of Aquilla Jones estate. Dated July 7, 1806. Henry Williams, Isaac Davis, sureties.

Page 77 – Rhoda Battle, deceased. Bond dated May 7, 1821, of Hartwell Battle and James Langdon, Administrators. Sureties: Elisha Allen, William Darden.

Page 78 – Hannah Jarnett, Administratrix of Alexander Jarnett estate. Dated September 1, 1806. James Edge and Nehemiah Edge, suretics.

Page 79 – Benjamin S. Woodward, Administrator of Francis Woodward estate. Dated November 3, 1806. Harmon Perryman, surety.

Page 79 – Thaddeus Beall, and Thaddeus Beall Jr., Administrators of Joseph Beall estate. Dated December 2, 1806. Elias Beall also an Administrator.

Page 79 – Owen B. Stevens, deceased. Bond of Ross Stevens, Administrator, dated September 10, 1821. Sureties: Benjamin Wynne, Benjamin Hurt.

Page 80 – Aquilla Stevens, deceased. Bond of Ross Stevens, Administrator, dated September 10, 1821. Sureties: Benjamin Wynne, Benjamin Hurt.

Page 80 – Absalem Napper and John Burkhalter, Administrators of Drury Napper estate. Dated January 5, 1807. Henry Harbuck and Jeremiah Burkhalter, sureties.

Page 81 – Samuel Alexander, Administrator of James Hefflin estate. Dated March 2, 1807. John Simmons surety.

Page 81 – Robert Johnson, deceased. Bond dated September 10, 1821, of Littleton Johnson, Administrator. Sureties: Edmond Johnson, John P. Carr.

Page 82 – Wingfield Atchinson and Charles Atchinson, Administrators of James Atchinson estate. Dated March 2, 1807. George Hargraves, surety.

Page 82 – Nancy Darden and Jethro Darden, Administrators of Stephen Darden estate. Dated May 4, 1807. Sureties: Jacob Darden, Jethro Darden, William Darden.

Page 83 – Thomas Persons and Rachel Persons, Administrators of Josiah Persons estate. Dated May 4, 1807. Turner Persons, Wormsley Rose, sureties.

Page 83 – Nathaniel S. Messer, deceased. Bond of Philander O. Paris, Administrator, dated December 3, 1821. Surety: John W. A. Pettit.

Page 84 – Isaiah Tucker, deceased. Bond of Churchill Gibson, Administrator, with the will annexed, dated December 13, 1821. Sureties: Asa Chapman, John Fontaine.

Page 85 – Germain Tucker, deceased. Bond of Frances H. Tucker and William B. Hundley, Administrators, dated December 22, 1821. Sureties: Philander Parris, Henry Gibson of Columbia County.

Page 86 – Samuel Duckworth, deceased. Bond dated February 4, 1822, of Joseph Culpepper, Administrator. Sureties: Edward Kinney and William Terry.

Page 88 – William Barksdale, deceased. Bond dated July 2, 1821, of Mary Barksdale, Administratrix. Sureties: Ebenezer Bird, Zachariah Darden

Page 88 - James Gray Sr., deceased. Bond dated May 6, 1822, of James Gray, Administrator. Sureties: Thomas Lockett, Micajah Rogers, David Sallis.

Page 89 – Peter Wiggins, deceased. Bond of Rebecca Wiggins and Reubin May, Administrators dated May 6, 1822. Sureties: Joel Neal, Peter May.

Page 90 – Mary Wade, deceased. Bond of James English as Administrator, dated May 6, 1822: Surety: John Usry.

Page 91 – John Gibson, deceased. Bond dated September 16, 1822, of Persons Bass, Administrator. Sureties: Samuel Fuller, Thomas Gibon.

Page 92 – Samuel Alexander, deceased. Bond dated September 10m 1822, of Moses Alexander, Administrator. Surety: Joseph Hill.

Page 93 – William Wilder, deceased, "formerly of Wilkes County." Bond of Sampson Wilder, Administrator de bonis non, dated September 24, 1822. Surety: Moses Alexander.

Page 94 – Micajah Stone, deceased. Bond of William Stone, Administrator de bonis non, dated November 18, 1822. Sureties: Joseph Hill, Henry Heath.

Page 95 – Mary Stone, widow, deceased. Bond of William Stone, Administrator, dated November 18, 1822. Sureties: Joseph Hill, Henry Heath.

Page 96 – Henry Persons, deceased. Bond of Grigsby E. Thomas, Administrator, dated January 6, 1823. Sureties: Jeremiah Butt, Arthur Moncrief.

Page 97 – Samuel Allen, deceased. Bond of Sherwood Allen, Administrator, dated March 3, 1823; securities, Gideon Allen, Benjamin Allen.

Page 98 – Wilie Grizzle, deceased. Bond dated May 5, 1823, of Thomas Gibson, Administrator. Sureties: Arthur Moncrief, Gerrard Camp.

Page 99 – Charles Brooks, deceased. Bond dated May 5, 1823, of Henry Lockhart and John Fontaine, Administrators. Sureties: Samuel Hall and Joel Neal.

Page 100 – Mannan Beall, deceased. Bond of Elijah Jones and John McCrary, Administrators. Sureties: Samuel Hall and Henley Jones. Dated May 5, 1823.

Page 101 – Blake Baker, deceased. Bond dated May 5, 1823, of Daniel Hutchinson and Idey Baker. Sureties: William Harbuck and Benjamin Sandiford.

Page 102 – John Bailey, deceased. Bond dated May 5, 1823, of James Baker as Administrator. Sureties: Benjamin Crenshaw and Hartwell Battle.

Page 104 – Nathan Fowler, deceased, formerly a citizen of this part of Wilkes now Warren County. Administrator's bond dated June 30, 1823, of Zephaniah Fowler, temporary Administrator, de bonis non of a certain undivided part of said estate. Surety: Elijah Jones.

Page 104 – John Parrish, deceased. Bond dated September 1, 1823, of Gerard Camp as Administrator with the will annexed. Sureties: Benjamin Sandeford, Benjamin Hurt.

Page 105 – John Wilson, deceased. Bond of Joseph Leonard, Administrator, dated September 1, 1823. Surety: Henry Wilson, David Cody.

Page 106 – Ichabod Finch, deceased. Bond of Levi May, Administrator, dated September 1, 1820. Sureties: James Rowland, Thomas Rowland.

Page 107 – William Darden, deceased. Bond dated November 17, 1823, of Jethro Darden, Administrator. Surety: Solomon Lockett.

Page 109 – David Cody, deceased. Lucretia Cody, Administratrix. Administrator's Bond dated November 17, 1823; sureties, Churchill Gibson, William B. Hundley, Peter Cody.

Page 112 – Warren Lockett, deceased. Bond of Solomon Lockett, Administrator, dated December 2, 1823. Sureties: James Ellet, Asa Chapman.

Page 114 – William Akins, deceased. Bond of Joseph D. McFarland and James Bailey, Administrators, dated January 5, 1824. Sureties: Nelson Gunn, Benjamin Crenshaw.

Page 114 – John Akins, deceased. Bond dated January 5, 1824 of John Akins as Administrator de bonis non with will annexed. Surety: Benjamin Hurt.

Page 115 – Richard Bray, deceased. Bond dated January 5, 1824, of Lucy Bray and Amos Wright, Administrators. Sureties: Hartwell Heath and Joseph Wright.

Page 116 – Archelaus Flewellin, deceased. Bond dated January 5, 1824, of Thomas Flewellin, temporary Administrator. Sureties: William H. Blount, James Shivers, Thomas Berry.

Page 118 – William Kinsey, deceased. Bond dated February 2, 1824, of John Kinsey, Administrator. Sureties: Abner McCormick and William Castleberry.

Page 119 – Elizabeth Kelly, Administratrix of John Kelly estate. Dated April 19, 1804. John Carson, John Gibson, sureties.

Page 119 – John Myrdon, deceased. Bond dated March 1, 1824, of Willis Rhymes, Administrator. Surety: Micajah Rogers.

Page 120 – Phoebe Hill, Administratrix of Thomas Hill estate. Dated May 1, 1794. Richard Hill, surety.

Page 120 – Kinchen McKinney, deceased. Bond of John Burkhalter, Administrator, dated March 1, 1824. Surety: Moses McKinney.

Page 120 – William Wood, deceased. Bond of Joseph Wood, Administrator, dated March 1, 1824. Sureties: Harris Wood, Mary Wood, Thomas Jones.

Page 121 – Joseph Boon and James Boon, Administrators of Thomas Boon estate. Dated May 19, 1794. Elisha Pruitt and John Hill, sureties.

Page 121 – Hugh Armstrong, deceased. Administrator's Bond dated March 1, 1824, of Sherman Armstrong, Administrator. Sureties: Jesse Armstrong, Edward Kinney, Samuel S. Hillman.

Page 122 – Priscilla Baker, Administratrix of Charles Baker estate. Dated October 15, 1794. Willis Perry, James Thomas, sureties.

Page 122 – Julius C. Jones, deceased. Bond dated March 1, 1824, of John Jones, Administrator. Surety: Henry Gibson.

Page 123 – Henry Graybill, Administrator of Samuel Helton estate. Dated November 19, 1794. Aaron Benton, surety.

Page 123 – John Battle, deceased. Bond dated March 1, 1824, of John L. Martin as Administrator. Surety: Hartwell Battle.

Page 124 – Adam Jones, Administrator of Jesse Gamble estate. Dated December 18, 1794. Nathaniel Myrick, surety.

Page 124 – Joseph Chambless, deceased. Adam Jones Jr., Administrator. Administrator's bond dated April 7, 1824; sureties, Elijah Jones, Christopher Chambless.

Page 125 – Ambrose Edmondson, deceased. Bond of William G. Edmondson, Administrator, dated September 6, 1824. Sureties: Hackakiah McMath, Henry Hinton.

Page 125 – Alexander Moore, Administrator of Mordecai Moore estate. Dated January 5, 1795. James and Henry Raley, sureties.

Page 126 – Samuel Slocum, Administrator of Seth Slocum estate. Dated February 2, 1795. Orondatus Watson, surety.

Page 126 – Dr. Richard Bray, deceased. Bond dated September 6, 1824, of Henry B. Thompson, Administrator. Sureties: Solomon Lockett and John Fontaine.

Page 127 – Henry Mitchell, Administrator of Thomas Hardin estate. Dated March 5, 1795. No name of surety signed to bond.

Page 127 – Richard Castleberry, William Newman, Administrators of Samuel Newman estate. Dated April 11, 1795. Mark Littleton, surety.

Page 127 – William Thomas, deceased. Bond of Hardy Pitts, Administrator, dated September 6, 1824. Sureties: Elijah Jones, Robert Palmer.

Page 128 – Susannah Strother, Administratrix of William Strother estate. Dated April 20, 1795. David Kelly, surety.

Page 128 – Elisha Allen, deceased, Administrator's Bond dated November 8, 1824, of George T. Allen. Sureties: Abel Funderburk, George Kellum, Benjamin Allen.

Page 129 – Thomas W. Grizzle, deceased. Bond dated January 24, 1825, of Lettice Grizzle, Administratrix. Sureties: William H. Blount, Lewis Jackson.

Page 130 – Martin Kinsey, deceased. Bond dated January 24, 1825, of Delilah Kinsey, Administratrix. Sureties: John W. Kinsey and Robert Black.

Page 132 – Thomas Smith, deceased, late of Richmond now Warren County. Bond of Spivey Fuller, Temporary Administrator, dated February 25, 1825. Sureties: Curtis Lowe and Nathan Beall.

Page 135 – Charles McCoy, deceased. Bond of Reubin Jones, Administrator, dated April 4, 1825. Sureties: Spivey Fuller, Royster Heeth.

Page 136 – Edward Kinsey, deceased. Bond of James Gray, temporary Administrator dated May 2, 1825. Sureties: John Fontaine, John Littleton.

Page 137 – Thomas Terry, deceased. Bond of James McC. Cason, Administrator, dated July 4, 1825. Sureties: William Cason, Hugh Montgomery.

Page 138 – Bond of James Gray, permanent Administrator, dated January 24, 1825. Sureties: John W. Kinsey, Robert Black.

Page 139 – David Cody, deceased. Churchill Gibson and Peter Cody, sureties on the bond of Lucretia Cody, Administratrix, now Lucretia Sherman, released from the bond at their request, and new bond given October 4, 1825, with Eli G. Sherman, John G. Winter and Joseph Denson as sureties.

Page 140 – Lewis Todd, deceased. Bond of Aaron English as Administrator, dated December 5, 1825. Sureties: Matthew English, John English.

Page 141 – Samuel McDowell, deceased. Bond of John G. Winter, Administrator, dated December 5, 1825. Surety: Jeremiah Butt.

Page 144 – David McCullers, deceased. Bond of William Ball, Administrator, dated December 4, 1826. Bondsman: John W. Kinsey.

Page 145 – Amy Gray, deceased. Bond dated October 7, 1826, of James Gray as Administrator. Surety: John Davidson.

Page 145 – Abner Huff, deceased. Bond of Jonathan Huff, Administrator, dated December 4, 1822. Sureties: Middleton Huff and William Stanford.

Page 146 – William Duckworth, deceased. Bond of Joseph Leonard, Administrator, dated January 2, 1827. Sureties: David Cody, Samuel Story.

Page 148 – Jonas Shivers, deceased. Bond of James Shivers, Administrator, dated January 2, 1827. Sureties: Edwin Baker, James Lewellin, Samuel Pitts, Joe. Roberts.

Page 149 – Mountain Hill, deceased. Bond of Ambrose Heath, Administrator, dated January 14, 1827. Sureties: Abner Rogers, John Wright.

Page 150 – Jacob Johnson, deceased. Bond of Jacob Smith, Administrator, dated February 14, 1827. Sureties: John Smith, James Grenade.

Page 151 – John M. Wilson, deceased. Bond of Henry Wilson, Administrator, dated February 14, 1827. Sureties: Henry Williams, Joseph Leonard.

Page 152 – Nancy Flewellin, deceased. Bond dated March 5, 1827, of James Flewellin, Administrator. Sureties: James Shivers, Henry Hight, William Hurt.

Page 153 – Nathan May, deceased. Bond of Reubin May, Administrator, dated May 7, 1827. Sureties: William Castleberry and Elijah Jones.

Page 154 – John Turner, deceased. Bond of James Turner, Administrator, dated October 6, 1827. Sureties: Kendall McTyaire, Abram Grierson.

Page 155 – Drury Pate, deceased. Bond of Joseph Leonard, Administrator, dated September 3, 1827. Sureties: Stith Hardaway and Benjamin Thompson.

Page 156 – William Holder, deceased. Bond of Lydia Holder, Administratrix, dated September 3, 1827. Sureties: John Mays, Joshua Lazenby.

Page 158 – Christopher Hinton, deceased. Bond of Henry Hinton, Administrator, dated September 3, 1827. John Mays, surety.

Page 159 – Moses Thompson, deceased. Bond of Hannah Thompson and Moses Thompson Jr., Administrators, dated December 1, 1827. Sureties: Giles Smith and Jonathan Huff.

Page 160 – Turner Persons, deceased. Bond of Amos J. Persons, Administrator dated December 1, 1827. Sureties: Henry Lockhart, G. W. Persons, Samuel Pitts, Nicholas W. Persons and James Flewellen.

Page 161 – Samuel Camp, deceased. Bond dated October 2, 1827, of Garrard Camp, Administrator. Sureties: Thaddeus Camp, Samuel Hall.

Page 164 – Nancy Cosby, deceased. Bond of Mordecai Johnson, Administrator, dated January 7, 1828. Sureties: Howell Hight, Seaborn Dozier.

Page 165 – Archelaus Butt, deceased. Bond dated December 28, 1827, of John Butt, Administrator. Surety: John Moore.

Page 167 – William Jones, deceased. Bond dated January 7, 1828, of Richard H. Jones, Administrator. Bondsmen: Hartwell Heath, Lewis Parham.

Page 168 – Elizabeth Glover, deceased. Bond dated March 3, 1828, of Frederick Glover, Administrator. Sureties: Isham Glover, Larkin Glover.

Page 171 – William Culpepper, deceased. Bond dated March 21, 1828, of Richard Heath, Administrator. Sureties: Lewis Jackson, Thomas Seals.

Page 173 – William Byrom, deceased. Bond dated September 1, 1828, of Elijah Jones, Administrator. Sureties: John Veazey and John McCrary.

Page 174 – Jesse Stanford, deceased. Bond of Reubin Stanford, Administrator with the will annexed, dated July 11, 1828. Sureties: William B. Harris, Richard S. Lazenby.

Page 177 – Arthur Matthews, deceased. Bond dated December 2, 1828, of Edward Matthews, Administrator. Sureties: William Castleberry, Francis Hardaway.

Page 178 – Jeremiah Wilson, deceased. Bond of Henry Wilson, Administrator, dated January 5, 1829. Sureties: Elias Wilson, Joseph Leonard.

Page 180 – Ann Darden, deceased. Bond of Jethro Darden, Administrator, dated March 2, 1829. Sureties: Septimus Torrence and James Bailey.

Page 181 – Abram Grierson, deceased. Bond dated April 25, 1829, of Susannah Grierson, Administratrix. Sureties: Howell Hight, Ambrose Heath.

Page 182 – Reubin Rogers Sr., deceased. Bond of John Rogers, Administrator, dated May 4, 1829. Sureties: Henry Hight, Willis Darden.

Page 186 – Lewis Parham, deceased. Bond of Fanny Parham and Nathaniel Parham, Administrators, dated November 2, 1829. Sureties: David Mims, Hartwell Heath.

# DEED BOOK A

(Transcribed from the original books A, B, C, D, and E.)

Page 1 – Thompson Bird of Wilkes County to John Peak of Burke County (now Warren County.) Bill of sale dated October 1, 1795, for slave named "Sal" age 15. Witnesses: Peter B. Terrell and John Hinton.

Page 1 – Allen Dorman to Wiley Dorman. Bill of Sale for one negro man Simon and one negro woman Sook for 100 pounds, dated December 10, 1794. Witnesses: John Castleberry and Asa Castleberry.

Page 2 – Francis Doyle and Bennis, merchants of Savannah to William Anglin of Warren County. Deed dated March 8, 1797, for 100 acres in former St. Paul's Parish on Williams Creek adjoining Absalom Jackson at time of survey. Witnesses: Francis Mallory, John Cunningham and William Jones.

Page 2 – Mark Hardin of Warren County to Martin Hardin of same, for 50 pounds, a negro man slave Brister, February 28, 1795. Witness: J. Hardin.

Page 2-3 – William Dryden Administrator of estate of Jno. Dryden, deceased, and James Blount are held and firmly bound unto Septimus Weatherby, Judge of Probate of Warren County, August 24, 1796.

Page 4 – Joseph Carson of Wilkes County to John Gibson of Warren County. Bill of Sale dated January 2, 1796, for a negro girl "Celie" for 182 dollars. Witness: Isaiah Tucker.

Page 5 – John Fox to Benjamin Hill. Bill of Sale dated at Augusta, November 17, 1795, conveying a slave. Witness: James S. Walker.

Page 5 – William Slatter of Warren County to Mary Few of same, a negro woman "Charity", a young negro woman "Peggs" for 430 silver dollars, February 22, 1796. Witnesses: Edmond Walsh, Elizabeth Dysart, John Dysart.

Page 5-6 – Received at Augusta November 17, 1795 of John Fox, $200 for a negro boy slave "Kinchen." Witnesses: James F. Walker

Page 6 – State of Georgia, Wilkes County, now Warren, September 29, 1791. Sarah Mims bound to John Ball for 100 pounds, a certain tract of land joining to said Ball's land and Zadock Rodan's land, where Mary Mims now lives, lying on Rocky Comfort. Witness: John Mims.

Page 7 – Warren County, Georgia, Pierson Young, Administrator and Jacob Young bound unto Septimus Weatherby, 300 pounds, January 18, 1796, estate of (blank) Burton, late of this county, deceased.

Page 7-8 – Warren County, Georgia, by virtue of a Writ of Fiere facias directed to me, taken unto Execution, four negroes: Mill and her child, Phillis, Sarah and Daniel, of the property of Benjamin Dickson, deceased, and thereon a Sale in Market when Vinson Johnson became the purchaser, and paid 150 pounds, June 12, 1795. Witness: Henry Mitchell.

Page 8 – Peter Goodwin of Warren County, 250 pounds paid by Wyche Goodwin of same county, one negro man Mark, negro woman Phillis, negro girl Chancy, negro child boy Anthony, one Sorrel Mare, one horse, June 12, 1795. Witnesses: Cornelius Cardion, James Crisup.

Page 9 – Randolph Revill of Warren County to Martin Hardin, sold a Mulatto boy slave, Austin, August 23, 1796. Witnesses: Mark Hardin, Lemuel Pruitt J.P.

Page 9 – Richmond County, Georgia, Joseph May sold to Richard Whatley, one negro boy, Jim, for 40 pounds, November 8, 1782. Witnesses: James Bowie, Sallie Bowie.

Page 10 – State of Georgia, Warren County, Francis Hill, Administrator, Solomon Slatter, and Richard Fletcher Esq. bound to Septimus Weatherby, October 3, 1796, estate of Richard Hill, deceased. Witness: William Mims.

Page 11 – Warren County, Barbara Lucas and James Caldwell, Administrator and Samuel Yarbrough and Joseph Peary bound unto Septimus Weatherby, May 13, 1796, estate of William Lucas, deceased.

Page 11-12 – Warren County, Elizabeth Goodwin, Administratrix, Wyche Goodwin, William Dean bound unto Septimus Weatherby, July 19, 1796, estate of Peter Goodwin, deceased.

Page 12-13 – Warren County, Reubin, Administrator and George Weatherby bound to Septimus Weatherby, October 18, 1796, estate of Lazarus Gurley, deceased.

Page 13-14 – Warren County, Richard Curry and Benjamin Warner, Administrators, Cary Curry and Norvell Robertson bound to Septimus Weatherby, October 3, 1796, estate of John Curry, deceased. Witness: Etheldred Thomas.

Page 14 – Received of Mr. Joel Threewitts one thousand weight of Tobacco being his part in paying a note off, which he and his mother-in-law (the Widow Cox) gave for rent. I say received by me in 1790. December 31, 1791. Sworn to by James Boon December 16, 1796.

Page 14-15 – Warren County, Georgia, Richard Cocks, Administrator and Thomas Cocks bound unto Septimus Weatherby, January 8, 1796, estate of Thomas Hardin, deceased.

Page 15-16 – Joseph May, Washington County, Georgia, to Solomon Newsom of Warren County, Georgia, six negroes, 33 head of cattle, 4 horses, two bay mares, two colts, four feather beds, September 1, 1796, $1288.57 paid on or before the January 1, 1799. Witness: Thomas Shields J.P.

Page 16 – James Barrow, of Franklin County, North Carolina, to Etheldred Thomas of Warren County, Georgia. Receipt dated January 23, 1797, for his part of several slaves, having given said Thomas power of attorney to sell same, on May 13, 1790. Witnesses: Byrd Jarrell and John Robinson.

Page 16 – Franklin County, North Carolina, received of Etheldred Thomas of Warren County, $250 for negroes May 13, 1790, January 25, 1797. Witnesses: Byrd Jarrell, John Robinson.

Page 17 – John Whitworth of King William County, Virginia, and Samuel Whitworth of Warren County, Georgia, for 20 pounds from James Jones of Warren County, sold to him a negro fellow, February 16, 1795. Witnesses: Sterling Jones and William Jones.

Page 17 – Warren County, Georgia, received of James Jones, November 15, 1797, $400 for negro man slave. Witness: Amose Wright.

Page 17-18 – Wilkes County, Georgia, Know all men by these presents that whereas Eliander, Elizabeth and Catherine Kilgore, and James and Mary Alison, Robert Kilgore Jr. and Robert Kilgore Sr., as Guardian for John Kilgore, we being, the wife and heirs of Ralph Kilgore, deceased of the county and state aforesaid, tract of land in Columbia County, in the possession of one Joel Handby, Joseph Evans, and Richard Buffington, we appoint William Stark or his attorney of Columbia County to recover said land, February 3, 1791. Witnesses: John Owens, David Hedgepeth, Elizabeth Wells.

Page 19 – Richard Smith have sold to Joseph White a certain negro girl for $200, March 17, 1798. Witnesses: T. Harmon, A. Grier J.P.

Page 19-20 – Warren County, Georgia, Jane Vaughn, Administratrix and Samuel Alexander, bound to Septimus Weatherby, this 27th day 1797, estate of Alexander Vaughn, deceased. Witness: A. Grier.

Page 20 – Warren County, Georgia, Lovinah Wheeler, Administratrix, Ichabod Cox, and Edmond Dismukes bound to Septimus Weatherby, January 24, 1798, estate of Sion Wheeler, deceased.

Page 21 – Warren County, Georgia, Mary Cooper, Administratrix, Harmon Wilkerson, and Peter Castleberry bound to Septimus Weatherby, May 16, 1798, estate of James Cooper, deceased.

Page 21-22 – Warren County, Georgia, David Neal, Administrator, John Hobson bound to Septimus Weatherby, March 7, 1797, estate of Zachariah Herold, deceased.

Page 22-23 – Warren County, Georgia, James Scott, Administrator and William Byrom Esq. bound to Septimus Weatherby, November 9, 1796, estate of George Hawthorne, deceased.

Page 28 – James Cotton, to Sterling Jones. Bill of Sale for slave named Beck, dated March 8, 1798.

Page 40 – Buckner Darden of Pickering County, Mississippi Territory, to Henry Peeples of Warren County. Deed dated June 7, 1801, for land in Warren County on Middle Creek. Witnesses: Wormsley Rose, Sterling Jones.

Page 46 – John Dunaway Sr. to John Dunaway Jr. both of Warren County. Deed of Sale dated January 1, 1799, for 70 acres on Brier Creek. Witnesses: P. Hodo and George Dunaway.

Page 90 – Mary Fullar to Allen Whatley of Hancock County. Deed dated September 22, 1795, for 350 acres on Rocky Comfort Creek. Acknowledged by the maker in Richmond County, August 8, 1796.

Page 92 – Wilie Dorman to Allen Dorman. Bill of Sale for slaves dated June 9, 1795. Witnesses: David Neal, James McCormick.

Page 95 – James Davis and wife Lydia, to Phillip Logan, all of Warren County. Deed dated July 10, 1795, for 200 acres on Rocky Comfort Creek, bounded on all sides by vacant land when surveyed in 1784. Witnesses: Joseph Beavy and Jonathan Thompson.

Page 98 – William Bush and wife Mourning, of Montgomery County, Georgia, to John Bruton of Warren County. Deed dated March 27, 1795, for 100 acres in Warren formerly Richmond County on the west side of Beachtree Creek, granted grantor 1788. Witnesses: Isaac Tison and Thomas Lancaster.

Page 100 – Thomas Elliott and wife Elizabeth to Zachariah Gray, all of Warren County. Deed dated November 6, 1794, conveying 5 acres on Duhart's Creek, being part of 100 acres granted Ann Prior and part of 125 acres granted Solomon Gray. Witnesses: Richard Gray, Josiah Carpenter.

Page 107 – John Dryden to Henry Batey, both of Warren County. Deed dated August 14, 1794, for 57 acres on Lambeth's Creek. Witnesses: David Terry, John Peel, John McCoy.

Page 112 – John Course, of Augusta, Richmond County to Solomon Newsom of Warren County. Deed dated May 10, 1794, for two tracts of land of 250 acres each, one granted to Thomas Scott, the other to William Oats, both purchased at Sheriff's sale by William Greenwood Jr., sold as the property of Andrew McClean, deceased; and deeded by Greenwood to grantor. Witnesses: Phillip Clayton, John Garrett.

Page 117 – William Campbell, to Samuel Campbell, both of Greene County. Deed dated May 5, 1795, conveying 322 acres on both sides of Long Creek, being part of two tracts of land originally granted in 1785 to James Thomas. Witnesses: James Campbell and Peter Burns.

Page 118 – Samuel Campbell, of Greene County, to James Boon of Warren County. Deed dated March 21, 1795, conveying the same property as in last deed above. Witnesses: P. Burns and T. H. Baynes.

Page 133 – Thomas Doles and wife Susannah of Warren County, to John Lamar of Hancock County. Deed dated August 8, 1802, for tract of land in Warren County lying on the Ogeechee River and the Augusta Road leading from Burch's Mill. Witnesses: John Marshall and M. Hubert J.P.

Page 137 – James Boon, and Lazarus Gurley, to Thomas Neal. Deed dated December 28, 1795, for 75 acres on Golding's fork, being part of 300 acres granted John Grantham. Witnesses: Turner Persons, Sterling Gardner.

Page 138 – Michael Burkhalter and wife Margaret, to Sterling Gardner. Deed dated February 22, 1796, for 300 acres on east side of Little Rocky Comfort whereon said Gardner now lives. Witnesses: Turner Persons, Thomas Neal.

Page 139 – John Dysart of Hancock County to Patrick Shannon of Wilkes County. Deed dated January 5, 1801, for 200 acres lying in old Wilkes County, granted to Ignatius Few. Witnesses: Aquilla Scott, James Bond, Solomon Ellis.

Page 140 – John Burkhalter, Jacob, Joshua, Jeremiah, Isaac and Jesse, and Michael Harbuck, Nicholas Harbuck and Daniel Hutcherson, to Michael Burkhalter. Deed dated February 29, 1796, to 300 acres on Golding's Creek whereon said Gardner now lives. Witnesses: Turner Persons, Etheldred Thomas, Clark Blandford.

Page 141 – Michael Burkhalter, John, Jacob, Joshua, Isaac, Jesse and Jeremiah of the Counties of Warren and Hancock to Nicholas Harbuck of Warren County. Deed dated February 29, 1796, for 250 acres on Golding's Creek whereon said Harbuck lives. Same witnesses as last above.

Page 147 – Isaac DuBose and wife Sary of Burke County, to Robert Ward also of Burke. Deed dated December 12, 1789, for 100 acres on Rocky Comfort Creek granted in 1785 to grantor. Witness: Charles Harvey J.P.

Page 149 – Henry Champion to Elisha Brown, both of Warren County. Deed dated October 23, 1795 for 200 acres on Brier Creek. Witnesses: Robert Isaacs, John Kent.

Page 150 – David Blackshear of Washington County, to Benjamin Chapman of Warren County. Deed dated February 17, 1795, for 200 acres in said county granted in 1785. Witnesses: Joseph King, Susannah Bush, John Bush J.P.

Page 151 – Michael Buckwalter, John, Jacob, Joshua, Isaac and Jesse, all of Warren and Hancock Counties, to Jeremiah Buckwalter of Warren County. Deed dated February 27, 1796, conveying 147 acres on Golden's Creek whereon said grantee resides. Witnesses: Clark Blandford, Daniel Hutchinson, Henry Harbuck.

Page 154 – Mastin Cox to Samuel Powell, both of Warren County. Deed dated November 25, 1795, for 200 acres on Jumping Gully, granted in 1784 to said Cox. Witnesses: Norrell and Sallie Robertson.

Page 163 – Ambrose Edmundson and Christopher Hinton to Hugh Reese and his family. Deed dated December 9, 1802, conveying a certain parcel of land 60 feet square on the north side of Brier Creek, for a graveyard. Witnesses: Benjamin Reese, John Burkhalter.

Page 165 – John Barton, late of Warren County, to John Torrence of Columbia County. Deed dated November 12, 1794, for 150 acres on Beachtree Creek in former Wilkes now Warren County, granted grantor in 1786. Witnesses: Anthony Carroll, David Neal.

Page 168 – William Bass, to Asa Tindall. Deed dated January 1, 1796, for 25 acres adjoining Ezekiel Williams and other lands of grantor. Witnesses: Alexander Bass Sr., Alexander Bass Jr.

Page 169 – John Barton of Wilkes County, to Robert Barton. Deed dated April 22, 1793, for 150 acres on the northwest end of a tract of 300 acres in former Wilkes now Warren County granted grantor in 1786. Witnesses: Thomas Neal, James McCormick J.P.

Page 170 – Benjamin Braswell of Hancock County, to Henry Hardin of Warren County. Deed dated January 2, 1796, for 150 acres on east side of Middle branch of Upton's Creek, being part of 300 acre tract granted John Dover in 1770 and deeded by him to Joseph Maddock. Witnesses: Isaiah Tucker, Mark Hardin J.P.

Page 174 – Ezekiel Cobb of Columbia County, to James Cobb of Warren County. Deed dated April 15, 1796, conveying 66 2/3 acres of a tract of 200 acres granted in 1788 to Rachel Cobb which is her dower. Witnesses: Francis Grubbs, Elizabeth Jones.

Page 175 – William Cocks and wife Hannah, to Joel Threewitts, all of Warren County. Deed dated January 18, 1794, conveying 100 acres on Whetstone Creek and Drury Mims' branch, granted grantor, lands in Wilkes County at time of grant. Witnesses: Thomas Cocks, James Cocks.

Page 182 – Elizabeth Cromley Sr., Elizabeth Cromley Jr., John Cromley, and William Essery and wife Katherine, heirs of Valentine Cromley, late of Washington County, deceased. Deed dated December 1, 1795, made to John Myrick Jr., of Warren County. Conveys 200 acres adjoining grantee, "which land was located by a duplicate in 1794." Witnesses: Arthur Cromley, George Weatherby J.P. and Solomon Gross.

Page 186 – Joseph Boon to Isaac Ball. Deed dated May 12, 1794, for 200 acres adjoining other lands of grantor. Witnesses: John Talliferro, John Myrick.

Page 198 – Reubin Allen to George Granberry. Deed dated May 14, 1794, for 100 acres in Burke County, lying on south side of Joe's Creek, granted in 1785 to grantor. Witnesses: Moses Granberry, Richard Curry.

Page 199 – Elisha Biggot of South Carolina to William D. Fowns of the Province of Georgia, Wrightsborough Township. Deed dated May 5, 1775, conveying 100 acres in St. Paul's Parish, granted grantor in 1774. Witnesses: Alexander Miller and James Bowers. Probated before John Oliver J.P., July 10, 1775.

Page 200 – William Downs to William Berry "both of the State of Georgia." Deed dated February (blank), 1794, conveying 100 acres in Warren County, formerly Wrightsborough Township, St. Paul's Parish, adjoining John Slatter, granted 1774 to Elisha Biggot, conveyed by him in 1775 to said Downs. Witnesses: William and Stephen Hoge, Abram Johnson J.P.

Page 201 – Richard Bonner of Greene County, to William Berry of Richmond County. Deed dated February 19, 1791, for 200 acres in Richmond County granted grantor in 1791. Witnesses: Abner Mitchell, John Parham.

Page 204 – Benjamin Few of Columbia County to William Bird and Benjamin Hamp of Warren County. Deed dated November 13, 1794, for 200 acres on Ogeechee River, granted 1787 to Isaac Dennis; and 100 acres on same river, and granted grantor 1786. Witnesses: John Wallace, Zachariah Cox.

Page 206 – Howell Featherstone and wife Pamela, to William Bird and Benjamin Augustus Hamp for 5 pounds. Deed dated December 24, 1794 for one acre adjoining "the shoals." Witnesses: Benjamin Upton and John Hammill J.P.

Page 207 – John Dysart of Hancock County to James Threewitts of Warren County. Deed dated February 10, 1803, to 195 acres adjoining Ignatius Few and others. Witnesses: David Thorn, Joel McClendon and John Miles.

Page 207-208 – January 22, 1795, Benjamin Upton and Judith his wife of Warren County, to William Bird and Benjamin Augustus Hamp of same, for 5 shillings, on Ogeechee, a tract of land. Witnesses: Duncan McLean, John Hamill J.P.

Page 208 – Neal Daugherty and Thomas Cowan, of Columbia County, to Mountain Hill and Jesse Armstrong of Warren County. Deed dated February 17, 1794, for 450 acres adjoining Reddick Bass, John Whatley and John Giborn. Witness: John Talliferro.

Page 209-210 – Wilkes County, Georgia, October 22, 1787, Ezekiel Millar and Sarah his wife to John Nixon for 30 pounds, 100 acres bounding John Wells and Ezekiel Millar. Witnesses: L. Pruitt J.P., Joseph Millar, Joseph Battson.

Page 210-211 – February 16, 1796, Jonathan McCrary of Hancock County to Wormssley Rose of Warren County for 280 silver dollars, a tract of land in Warren County on Whetstone Creek, 280 acres more or less. Witnesses: Chappel Heath, Turner Persons.

Page 211-213 – October 5, 1795, heirs, representatives and distributors of Ralph Kilgore, deceased, to wit: Elizabeth Kilgore, Katherine Kilgore, James and Mary Allison, and Robert Kilgore Jr. to William Stark of Columbia County for 200 pounds, 350 acres in Columbia County bounded by Little River, Evans' land, Howard's, Whittock's and Douglas's. Witnesses: William Sally, Thomas J. Moore.

Page 213 – John Barton, of Laurens County, South Carolina, to William Johnson of Warren County. Deed dated November 18, 1795, conveying 230 acres on north side of Stamp branch of

Rocky Comfort, in former Wilkes now Warren County, on Johnson's old line. Witnesses: Joseph Walker, Reubin Walker, Vincent A. Tharp J.P.

Page 214-215 – December 5, 1796, Joseph Richardson of Warren County to Archibald Lacy for 100 dollars, 100 acres, being part of a tract granted to John Cox, recorded in Secretarie's Office, Book OOO, Page 380, bounded by Jack Comer and Stephen Bishop. Witnesses: L. Pruitt J.P., Harmon Perryman.

Page 215-216 – Jordan Lacey swears that he bought a tract of 200 acres on Rocky Creek from Joseph Richardson, December 3, 1796. Jordan Lacey swears that he did sell on March 15, 1792 to John Hampton, then of Washington, who since that date by report removed to the southward and a certain bay mare four feet eight inches high for which the said John Hampton did give and deliver to Jordan Lacey a note of hand payable October 1, wherein John Finney was signed as Security for 3500 of August Inspected tobacco payable to the said Jordan Lacey on order, September 14, 1796.

Page 216 – John Cox of Richmond County, to Joseph Richardson of Wilkes County. Deed dated October 10, 1790, for 200 acres on the Rocky branch of Ogeechee River in Wilkes County granted grantor in 1787. Witnesses: James Bishop and Zechariah Landrum.

Page 217-218 – December 5, 1790, Joseph Richardson of Warren County to Edmond Walsh of Hancock County, for 25 pounds, land on Rocky Creek bounded by Stephen Bishop and Abraham Helton Heath, 100 acres, more or less, part of 200 acres bought from Archibald Lacey.

Page 218 – Joseph Davies (signed "Joseph Davidson") to Jesse Matthews, both of Wilkes County. Deed dated February 15, 1793, conveying 100 acres on Rocky Comfort Creek granted in 1786 to James Cockerman. Witnesses: John Myrick, Elisha Wright.

Page 219 – John Dunaway and Jonathan, to John English, all of Warren County. Deed dated June 4, 1803, for 50 acres on Brier Creek being part of tract granted said John Dunaway in 1785. Witnesses: Moore Carter, James Carter.

Page 219-220 – January 26, 1796, Joel King and Mary King to Ambrose Hadley all of Warren County for 400 silver dollars, land on Whetstone Creek, originally granted to said King. Witnesses: John Hawthorne, Solomon Slatter.

Page 220-221 – December 4, 1794, Peter Mahone of Warren County to John Snelling for 50 pounds, land on Ogeechee, 175 acres, part of 500 acres granted to John Kelly, July 3, 1787. Witnesses: Jacob Flourney, James Elliott.

Page 221-222 – September 22, 1795, Eleazer Mobley of Warren County to Francis Beck of same for 50 pounds, land near Going's mill, originally granted to George Brewer October 29, 1789. Witnesses: Lewis Harvie, Samuel Fields.

Page 222-223 – January 3, 1788, Thomas Gambill and wife Susannah of Green County to John Parrish of Wilkes County for 35 pounds paid by Parrish, 200 acres adjoining B. Few, George Cooper, Widow Coullars, John Edmondson and Henry Parrish. Witnesses: George Brewer, Henry Parrish.

Page 223-224 – May 4, 1789, John Ledbetter of Wilkes County to Frederick Ledbetter of same for 25 pounds, land on Ogeechee, granted to John Ledbetter, May 15, 1785. Witnesses: Solomon Newsom, Arthur Fort J.P.

Page 224-225 – February 25, 1796, Isaac Ledbetter of Washington County to William Jordan of Warren County for 25 pounds, 130 acres, part of 200 acres granted to Isaac Ledbetter, May 13, 1790. Witnesses: John Curry, John Hamill J.P.

Page 225-226 – March 2, 1795, William Franklin and wife Mary to Aleck Smith, all of Warren County for 20 pounds, land on Brier Creek bounding William White, David Robison, 100 acres, part of a tract of 200 granted William Franklin. Witnesses: Robert Isaacs, Benjamin Smith.

Page 226-227 – March 7, 1794, Thomas Stark Sr. of Wilkes County to John Whitlock of Columbia County, Thomas Stark and Elizabeth his wife, for 120 pounds, 150 acres originally granted to

Abraham Dennis, July 3, 1770. Witnesses: Joseph Whitlock and Stephen Staple.

Page 228 – Joseph Brown and wife Ann, to Abraham Johnson, Jr., all of Wrightsborough Township, St. Paul's Parish. Deed dated October 5, 1775, conveying 300 acres on Carson's Creek in said township granted said Brown in 1770. Witnesses: John Stubbs, William Whaley, Joseph Maddock J.P.

Page 232 – Michael Burkhalter, John, Jacob, Joshua, Isaac and Jesse, to Daniel Hutchinson. Deed dated February 29, 1796, conveying 200 acres on Golden's fork adjoining Sterling Gardner, Joseph Richardson, Jeremiah, Michael and Jesse Burkalter, and being part of 800 acre tract granted the heirs of John Burkhalter, deceased. Witnesses: P. Hodo and William Coram.

Page 233-234 – November 15, 1796, William Mims and Naiomi his wife of Warren County, to Henry Kendall of Columbia County for $300, land on Rocky Comfort, 100 acres, half of a 200 acre grant to William Mims. Witnesses: T. Persons, George Weatherby.

Page 234 – William Barnett, Administrator of William Barnett estate of Columbia County, deceased, to John Mattox. Deed dated December 8, 1796, conveying 184 acres in Warren County adjoining Thomas Whatley, William Brewer, Richard Lovett and Richard Castleberry, which land was sold at public outcry by said Administrator at Columbia Courthouse November 1, 1796. Witnesses: Mary A. Crawford, Peter Crawford J.P., Columbia County.

Page 235-236 – December 17, 1795, Robert Jenkins of Warren County to Micajah Stone of same for $1500, land on Williams Creek in Warren County, 320 acres granted to Robert Jenkins, October 7, 1785, recorded in Book JJJ, folio 49. Witnesses: John Jenkins, William Jenkins, Robert Jenkins.

Page 236 – Thomas Bethany, of Wilkes County, to John Jones of same. Deed dated March 28, 1786, conveying 200 acres in Wilkes (now Warren County) granted the grantor in 1784. Witnesses: Susannah Davies, Robert Rutherford and John Rutherford.

Page 236-237 – March 28, 1786, Thomas Bethany of Wilkes County to John Jones of same for 10 pounds, land in Wilkes County 200 acres granted September 29, 1784. Witnesses: Susannah Davies, Robert Rutherford.

Page 237-238 – August 21, 1792, John Jones of Wilkes County to William Cox of same, for 200 pounds, 2 tracts of land in Wilkes County, conveyed to John Jones from Thomas Bethany March 28, 1786, located to Bethany August 12, 1784, registered in Book EEE, folio 64, the second 200 acres conveyed to John Jones by John Rutherford January 10, 1792, who located it April 4, 1785, registered in Book JJJ, folio 869. Witnesses: John Myrick, George Weatherby.

Page 239 – April 1, 1793, Samuel Newman of Wilkes County to William Cocks of same, for 7 pounds for 10 acres in Wilkes County by Joel King, Drury Mims. Witnesses: Thomas Cocks and Walter Newman.

Page 239-240 – May 24, 1796, John J. Wells to Elisha Wright of Warren County for 10 pounds land on Rocky Comfort in Warren County, 20 acres bound by Joseph Millar. Witnesses: Joseph Wright, Joseph Millar.

Page 240-241 – September 14, 1795, Nicholas Jones and Jean his wife to Mathew Parham of Warren County for 50 pounds, 230 acres, Elisha Roberts land, Gray's land. Witnesses: G. Franklin, John Williams.

Page 241-242 – January 2, 1797, Wilkins Smith of Warren County to Mathew Parham of same, for $201.37, 200 acres granted to Thomas Smith Sr. Witnesses: Zeph. Franklin, Wyatt Bonner.

Page 242-243 – January 25, 1791, John Fuller of Washington County to Drewry Mims of Wilkes County for 100 pounds, 200 acres in Wilkes County granted August 2, 1786. Witness: William Mims.

Page 243-244 – 1793, John Fuller of Washington County to Drewry Mims of Wilkes County for 25 pounds, 50 acres in Wilkes

County granted March 2, 1791. Witnesses: Rachel Tennille, Benjamin Tenille J.P.

Page 244-245 – September 3, 1796, Drewry Mims and Elizabeth his wife to Turner Persons for $118, land on Whetstone Creek bound by Thomas Fuller, John Fuller, 50 acres granted to John Fuller March 2, 1791. Witnesses: James Darnell, John Lowe.

Page 245-246 – September 3, 1796, Drewery Mims and Elizabeth to Turner Persons for $460, 200 acres more or less granted to John Fuller August 2, 1796.

Page 246-247 – December 31, 1795, William Johnson and Rosannah his wife of Warren County to Asa Tindall of same for 75 pounds land bounded by Ezekiel Williams, William Bass, David Crockett, 200 acres more or less, the north part of a grant of 500 acres to David Felps December 4, 1790. Witness: William Byrom J.P.

Page 247 – John Dunaway to William Dunaway, both of Wilkes County. Deed dated June 13, 1792, conveying 41 acres adjoining Jacob Duckworth and Moses Hill, being part of 400 acres granted the grantor in 1785. Witness: Peter Hodo.

Page 248 – William Dunaway to Joseph Duckworth, both of Warren County. Deed dated March 15, 1797, conveying the above 41 acre tract. Witnesses: Sallie Hodo and P. Hodo J.P.

Page 249 – Willie Dorman and Allen, to Amos Travis all of Warren County. Bill of Sale for 3 slaves dated November 16, 1801. Witnesses: William McDowell, John Smith.

Page 249-250 – March 1, 1792, Richard Smith of Washington County to Needham Smith of Wilkes County, 100 acres more or less, for 25 pounds. Witnesses: Jody Newsom, Carter Newsom.

Page 250-251 – May 20, 1795, Septimus Weatherby of Warren County to Ambrose Edmondson of Halifax County, North Carolina for 90 silver dollars, land in Warren County bound by J. Myrick, James Miller, granted April 19, 1790. Witnesses: Turner Persons, Thomas Neal.

Page 251-252 – July 7, 1795 Benjamin Jackson of Hancock County to James Roquemore of Warren County for 40 pounds, 200 acres on Little Brier Creek, adjoining Mercer. Witnesses: Drewry Murphey, Willis Whatley.

Page 253-254 – James Roquemore Sr. for love, good will and affection to son, Peter Roquemore, my eldest son, land on Little Brier Creek, my next eldest son James Roquemore Jr., one half of profit and increase of my wench Dinah, 250 acres in Lincoln County adjoining James Green and Benjamin Bentley, and one horse, saddle and 6 head of cattle, my next eldest son Thomas Roquemore, same as to James, my eldest daughter Polly Roquemore, half of profit of negro wench Luce, 6 head of cattle, half of my household furniture, to my son John Roquemore half of profit of above Luce, 287 ½ acres in Montgomery County adjoining James York and John Garrett my wagon and gear, to my daughter Elizabeth Roquemore, negro wench Rose, saddle and 6 head of cattle, half of my household furniture, March 31, 1797. Witnesses: William B. Murphy, Drury Mitchell.

Page 254 – Richard Duns to Richard Barrow. Bill of Sale for slave dated February 20, 1797. Witness: David Blackshear J.P.

Page 254-255 – Town of Warrenton, Georgia April 8, 1797, Sterling Gardner of Warren County and Polley his wife to Judges of Inferior Court and their successors in office, land on Goldwin's Creek on road to Augusta, for laying off into lots, for erecting Public Building.

Page 255 –Jacob Darden to John Bustin, both of Warren County. Deed dated September 17, 1796, for 100 acres on north side of Williams Creek, being part of 900 acres granted to Mr. Murray, whereon John Baker, Esquire, now lives. Witnesses: Robert Hill, N. Williams, T. Persons.

Page 256 – Robert Barnett of Wilkes County, to John McMurrin of Wilkes County. Deed dated December 29, 1791, conveying 200 acres on Long Creek in said county, adjoining lands where grantor lives. Witnesses: Jilson Berry, Andrew Berry J.P.

Page 257 – September 27, 1796, James Sanders to James Lowe all of Warren County for $550, 200 acres. Witnesses: D. Perryman, Thomas Bankston, M. Hubbert J.P.

Page 258 – December 23, 1796, Mark Hardin of Warren County to John Gibson of same for $1250, 140 acres on Middle Creek adjoining Levi Pruitt, Lemuel Pruitt, Tuck and McLinvale. Witnesses: Lewis Wright, Isaiah Tucker.

Page 258-259 – William Sanders to son, Henry Sanders for natural love and good will, all my household furniture, April 10, 1797.

Page 259-260 – April 15, 1795, William Stark of Columbia County to Samuel Cooper of Warren County, for 20 pounds, 100 acres bounded by Carson & Bishop, Jamison's old survey. Witnesses: Noble Butler, William Johnson.

Page 260-261 – April 15, 1795, William Stark to John Bishop- of Warren County, for 20 pounds, 100 acres adjoining J. Hill, Stark, Carson, Gray's old line, part of old survey granted to James Gray conveyed February 26 last, to Stark. Witnesses: Noble Butler, William Johnson.

Page 261 – Littleberry Crews of Hanover County, Virginia, to James Jones of Warren County. Deed dated February 2, 1797, for $500, for 400 acres on Brier Creek adjoining lands of Amy McCullers, granted Isaac Ball in 1788. Witnesses: Turner Persons, Sterling Jones and Matthew Hubert J.P.

Page 262-263 – November 9, 1796, Mary Mims of Warren County to John Ball of same, for $30, land on Rocky Comfort Creek. Witnesses: Lewis. Brantley, William Johnson.

Page 263 – Nathaniel Coats, late Tax Collector of Wilkes County, to David Hillhouse of Washington, Wilkes County. Deed dated March 26, 1796, conveying 950 acres on Williams Creek in what was then Wilkes now Warren County, sold as property of George Murray "to whom it was granted for accumulated taxes in 1788." Witnesses: Francis Gordon, David Terrell.

Page 264 – William Brewer and wife Elizabeth, to Jesse Doles, all of Wilkes County. Deed dated January 14, 1793, conveying 120 acres in said county adjoining lands of James Bishop and Daniel Reynolds, granted grantor January 14, 1793. Witnesses: Francis Calloway and Matthew Brewer.

Page 265 – Samuel Camp to Enoch Renfroe, both of Wilkes County. Deed dated September 2, 1791, conveying 200 acres on Joe's Creek adjoining grantee's lands. Witnesses: Andrew Burns and Jonathan Miller.

Page 266 – John Dixon of Wilkes County to Nathaniel Myrick of Warren County. Deed dated January 8, 1802, for 300 acres on Williams Creek. Witnesses: John Peavy and Septimus Weatherby.

Page 266-267 – May 8, 1794, Philip Gibbs of Warren County to Larkin Chivers of same, for 45 pounds, Philip Gibbs and Phebe his wife, land on waters of Fort's Creek, 250 acres. Witnesses: John Wilson, Nathan Renfroe.

Page 267-268 – March 25, 1797, Rachel Powell of Richmond County to Colonel Charles Pole of McLinburg County, North Carolina for 85 pounds, 250 acres in Warren County on Brier Creek, granted to Rachel Powell. Witnesses: A. Hobson, Samuel Kennedy.

Page 268-269 – February 4, 1797, Robert Stanford to Jesse Stanford for $25, on both sides of Little Sweetwater, 100 acres. Witnesses: Peter Hodo, John Wilson J.P.

Page 269-270 – March 23, 1790, Stephen Mitchell of Richmond County to Enoch Renfroe of Wilkes County, Celia, wife of Stephen Mitchell, for 100 pounds, land on Joe's Creek in Wilkes County, 150 acres vacant on all sides when surveyed July 3, 1787. Witnesses: Adam Jones, Thomas Rogers and Thomas Farmer.

Page 270-271 – November 19, 1796, James Rogers of Warren County to Josiah Carter of same, for 17 pounds 2 shillings and six pence, land on Ogeechee, 10 acres. Witnesses: James Henderson, Thomas Poore, William Byrom J.P.

Page 271-272 – April 16, 1794, Robert Wynne of Warren County to Thomas Poore, of same, for 100 pounds 222 acres on a branch of Ogeechee. Witnesses: James Lucas, Augustus Cotten and William Byrom J.P.

Page 272 - George Dykes of Warren County to Isaac Blount of Washington County. Deed dated March 7, 1797, for 300 acres on west side of Rocky Comfort Creek, being the lower part of the 900 acre tract granted grantor in 1797, for $50. Witnesses: Moses Granberry and John Lawson J.P.

Page 273-274 – 1790, Stephen Mitchell of Richmond County to Thomas Jones of Wilkes County, for 50 pounds, land on west side of Long Creek, originally granted to Stephen Mitchell adjoining Nathan Fowler, March 17, 1785. Witnesses: Adam Jones, Thomas Rogers.

Page 275-276 – March 29, 1796, Nathan Fowler of Warren County to Adam Jones for 25 pounds, land on Long Creek, Brady Branch, originally granted to said Nathan Fowler, 1788. Witnesses: Anderson Berry, Zephaniah Fowler.

Page 276-277 – May 17, 1797, James Thomas of Hancock County to Adam Jones of Warren County for $65, on Long Creek of Ogeechee, P. Adam Jones Jr. Witness: Samuel Camp.

Page 277 – Edward Black, to John Rushing. Deed dated July 8, 1796. Conveys 100 acres on Fort's Creek granted grantor in 1785. Witnesses: Nathan Renfroe and Levi Matthews.

Page 277-278 – July 8, 1796, Edward Black of Warren County to John Rushing of same for 30 pounds, land in Warren County, 100 acres originally granted to Edward Black October 12, 1785. Witnesses: Nathan Renfroe, Levi Matthews.

Page 278 – Matthew English Sr. "in declining health with a daughter, Jenny in like condition," gives to Matthew English Jr. his plantation and personal property, on condition that he take care of both of them for the remainder of their lives. Deed of Gift dated April 17, 1804. Witnesses: Charles Medlock and James McCormick.

Page 278 – May 18, 1797, John Hill of Warren County to Howell Hight $500, 200 acres surveyed for John Hill and recorded in Book T July 4, 1775, adjoining P. Brantley, Adam Jonson. Witness: Levi Pruitt J.P.

Page 278-279 – January 1, 1795, Joseph Pevay of Warren County to Abraham Heath of same, for 30 pounds, 50 acres on Long Creek adjoining Joseph Pevay, John Acres. Witnesses: John Chappell and William Heath.

Page 279-280 – November 7, 1795, William Thomson to John Rushing all of Warren County for 50 pounds, land on Fort's Creek in Warren County granted to Samuel Camp January 22, 1789. Witnesses: Nathan Renfroe, Larkin Chivers.

Page 280-281 – Richard Castleberry and wife Ann, to John Hix, all of Warren County. Deed dated April 20, 1797, for $500, conveying 250 acres adjoining Flournoy and Horton, granted to John Fulsom. Witnesses: Jeremiah Saley, John Castleberry, Henry Hardin J.P.

Page 281-282 – January 14, 1797, John Whitlock and Tabitha his wife of Oglethorpe County to Thomas Buttrill of Columbia County, for 82 pounds, 100 acres part of a tract granted to John and Abraham Dennis July 3, 1770 in Warren County on Little River adjoining Ralph Kilgore, sold by John and Abraham Dennis to Thomas Stark, then to John Whitlock. Witnesses: James McFarland, William Dozer, John Dozer and William Claiborne.

Page 282-283 – October 27, 1795, David Charles Carter 1792 sold for payment of taxes of Benjamin Porter, 200 acres in Warren County originally granted to Abraham Dennis. Witness: R. Worsham J.P.

Page 282-283 – October 27, 1795, David Meriwether Esq. receiver of tax returns for the county of Wilkes to Charles Carter, 1792 sold for payment of taxes of Benjamin Porter, 200 acres in Warren County originally granted to Abraham Dennis. Witness: R. Worsham J.P.

Page 283 – Charles R. Carter and wife Jane, to Benjamin Porter, all of Wilkes County. Deed dated December 1, 1795, conveying 200 acres on Little River and Kilgore's Creek, adjoining Joseph Evans, Benjamin Hardin and grantee, granted to Abraham Dennis, land in Warren County. Witnesses: Lt. Harris, B. Smith J.P.

Page 284-285 – February 21, 1791, John D. Young of State of South Carolina to John Hull of Richmond County, Georgia for 50 pounds, 200 acres on Rocky Comfort, granted to Absolem Jackson February 25,, 1786 adjoining William Landrum, Shadrach Smith. Test: Philip Gibbs, John Lawson.

Page 285 – December 28, 1796, John Hull of Camden County to Byrd Pruitt of Warren County, for 50 pounds, 200 acres on Rocky Comfort, part of 400 acres granted to Absolem Jackson, February 25, 1786, adjoining Shadrach Smith, William Landrum. Witnesses: John Lawson J.P., Charles M. Lawson.

Page 286 – February 4, 1797, Robert Stanford to Spencer Owen of Warren County for 50 dollars, 200 acres on both sides of Little Sweetwater, part of 300 acres granted to Robert Stanford October 29, 1795. Witnesses: P. Hodo, John Wilson.

Page 287 – Frederick Daniel to Ansel McKinney both of Warren County. Deed dated January 7, 1803, for land on Middle Creek. Witnesses: L. Wright and John Matthews.

Page 287 – June 6, 1797, John Henry Pickard of Warren County to Jeremiah Spurlin of same for $70, 80 acres in Warren County part of 200 acres granted to Patrick Brady, November 28, 1796, recorded in Book YYYY, folio 488. Witnesses: John Curry, Claiborne Crawford.

Page 288 – Patrick Brady Sr., to John Henry Pickard. Deed dated March 26, 1796, for $100, for 100 acres on north side of Joe's Creek adjoining grantor and granted to him in 1786. Witnesses: John Hatcher, John Spurlin.

Page 289 – Patrick Brady of Hancock County, to Henry Pickard of Warren County. Deed dated December 21, 1796, $200, for 200 acres on Joe's Creek in former Richmond now Warren County. Witnesses: Francis Dannielly and Jeremiah Spurlin.

Page 289 – Jacob Daushe to his son Daniel Daushe. Deed of Gift dated October 31, 1803, for two tracts of land on one which grantor lives. Witnesses: Levina Morris, John Baker.

Page 290 – July 4, 1796, George Grandberry of Jefferson County to George Dykes of Warren County for 30 pounds, 300 acres on Joe's Creek, being part of two tracts, one granted to George Grandberry May 24, 1796, the other granted to Reubin Allen, October 1, 1785, adjoining Eliakim Tison, Buckelow, Richard Curry. Witnesses: John Lawson J.P., Moses Grandberry.

Page 290-291 – April 21, 1797, John Rutherford of Washington County to Nicholas William of Warren County for $700, land on both sides of Rocky Comfort Creek, all of 400 acres except for one acre sold to a certain Mr. Davies with a further reserve of ten square feet including a grave adjoining at time of survey Clark, Joseph Mims. Witnesses: Frederick Morris and Mortan Minter.

Page 291-292 – June 3, 1797, Henry Kindall and Elizabeth his wife of Warren County to Nicholas William of same, for $345, for land on Rocky Comfort adjoining John Ball, Kid's land, William Mims, 100 acres half of a 200 acre tract granted to William Mims, conveyed by Mims to Kindall. Witnesses: Turner Persons, Richard B. Fletcher J.P.

Page 292-293 – February 20, 1797, John Torrence, farmer, to James Bray, planter, for $85, land on Rocky Comfort adjoining Nathaniel Fulsom, Sterling Jones, Amos Wright, and part of a survey this day conveyed to David Cox, part of a tract granted to John Torrence April 7, 1789, recorded Book GGG, Folio 72 this conveyance for 60 acres. Witnesses: Solomon Slatter, Elisha Hurt J.P.

Page 293-294 – May 1, 1791, Britain McCullers of Washington County to John Nunn of Wilkes County for 100 pounds, 143 acres on both sides of Little Brier Creek adjoining William Smith.

Page 294 – James Bailey, to William Shurley. Deed dated February 6, 1796, for 50 pounds, for 150 acres being half of a tract granted grantor in 1787. Witnesses: J. Grizard and William Kitchens.

Page 295 – Joseph Dunn of Warren County to Little Bryan of Wilkes County. Deed dated April 15, 1804, for land on Ogeechee River, being part of a survey made to Josiah Carter. Witnesses: Edward Crowell and Drury Goyen.

Page 295 – Jonathan Anderson of Hancock County to James W. Green of Warren County. Deed dated July 12, 1795, for 100 acres on Long Creek, near Ogeechee River, being the upper half of 200 acres granted William Anderson and the grantor 1784. Witnesses: Dixon Perryman, William Anderson.

Page 296-297 – September 21, 1792, William Smith and Patty his wife of Washington County to Daniel Atkins of Wilkes County for 60 pounds, 70 acres on Little Brier Creek adjoining John Maynor, Jackson, William Smith. Witnesses: Robert Isaacs, Joseph Adkins.

Page 297-298 – May 22, 1797, Claiborn Newsom to James Mecum for $2, 120 acres on Big Brier Creek. Witness: Moses McKinney.

Page 298 – Jeremiah Duckworth of Warren County to Jacob Duckworth of Hancock County. Deed dated July 24, 1794, conveying lands on Little Brier Creek, being a part of two grants of 200 acres each to grantor and Margaret Davison on headrights, part of which grantor sold to James Carter whereon he now lives, adjoining William Nichols and James May. Witnesses: Joseph Duckworth, James Draper and Jesse Burgen.

Page 300-301 – Jacob Duckworth of Hancock County, to Joseph Duckworth of Warren County. Deed dated June 15, 1797, for 374 acres on Briar Creek, being part of the above mentioned tract. Witnesses: Arthur Fort, Randall Duckworth.

Page 301 – Jesse Embree and wife Anna of Montgomery County to Henry Harp of Warren County. Deed dated May 3, 1796, for 100 acres on Rocky Comfort Creek granted in 1774 to Reubin Barrow. Witnesses: John Howard, James Hardin J.P.

Page 301 – November 26, 1796, James Thweatt of Hancock County to Dixon Perryman of Warren County for $130, 147 acres on Ogeechee. Witnesses: Abner Banckston, Frank Lawson J.P.

Page 302 – John Dunaway to Edmund Dunaway. Deed dated (blank) 1st, 1799 for 50 acres adjoining grantor's home place. Witnesses: George Dunaway, Peter Hodo.

Page 302 – June 19, 1797, Eleazer Mobley to John McMurrin, both of Warren County, for $550, 180 acres on Ogeechee on Georgetown Road, formerly a line of Kelly's, Thomas Friend's line, formerly Few's, part of a grant to George Brewer Jr., November 25, 1788. Witnesses: Robert Barney, Jilson Berry.

Page 302-303 – March 3, 1797, Christopher Pritchell of Halifax County, North Carolina, to William Heath of same, land in Warren County, Georgia on Ogeechee, 200 acres. Witnesses: James Davison, Nancy Heath.

Page 304 – Edmund Dunaway to Joshua Stanford Jr. Deed dated January 19, 1803, for 50 acres above. Witnesses: John Bayn, James Carter.

Page 304-305 – April 23, 1796, Savage Littleton of Warren County to Timothy Landrum of same, for 30 guineas, 116 acres in Warren County adjoining Shelton, Howard, Solomon Newsom, granted April 20, 1796, recorded in Book XXXX, folio 140. Witnesses: John Burkhalter, James McCormick.

Page 305 – Jesse Connell and wife Penelope, to James Rogers, all of Greene County. Deed dated September 3, 1791, conveying 200 acres on Red Lick Creek, branch of Ogeechee River, in Wilkes County, adjoining land granted Moses Powell Sr., and Jeremiah Oates, and granted to grantor Connell in 1786. Witnesses: William Wynne, R. Middleton and James Harvey J.P.

Page 306 – Francis Danielly and wife Elizabeth of Hancock County, to Jeremiah Spurling of Warren County. Deed dated December 24, 1796, to 200 acres on Joe's Creek, being part of 400 acres granted John Tabor. Witnesses: Samuel Brady, Henry Pickard.

Page 307 – Josiah Carter, to his daughter Elizabeth, wife of James Henderson, all of Wilkes County. Deed of Gift dated July 23, 1793, conveying 200 acres on which said Henderson's now live, lying on Walker's branch and adjoining David Lockett, being part of 612 acres granted grantor in 1784. Witnesses: John Veazey and John Wynne J.P.

Page 308-309 – May 27, 1797, William West of Warren County to Richard Terrell of same, for $10, land adjoining Thomas's, Thomas Smith, Castleberry, 300 acres more or less. Witnesses: Mathew McCrary, Willis Rowland.

Page 309-310 – May 27, 1797, William West of Warren County to Richard Terrell for $1200, 500 acres adjoining Gradner's and Fowler's, Baker's, Linsicum's, Berry's, Nugent's. Witnesses: Mathew McCrary, Willis Rowland.

Page 310 – Samuel Camp to William Rushing, both of Wilkes County. Deed dated May 10, 1789, for 250 acres on Fort's Creek in said county, being part of 750 acres granted grantor in 1789. Witnesses: John Rushing, William Thompson.

Page 311-312 – August 13, 1796, John Moutrey of Warren to John Duberry of same, for 40 pounds, part of a survey for William Spikes October 16, 1784, granted to Spikes September 27, 1797. Witnesses: Robert Wynne, William Robertson, William Byrom J.P.

Page 312 – William Anglin to Joseph Matthews both of Warren County. Deed dated January 14, 1797, for 100 acres wherein grantee lives, being part of 300 acres granted Jacob Mercer in 1785. Witnesses: Charles Mayberry, James McCormick J.P.

Page 312-313 – January 14, 1797, Joseph Matthews from William Anglin all of Warren County, for 15 pounds, 100 acres where Joseph Matthews now lives, part of a 300 acre grant to Jacob Mercer July 29, 1785, adjoining widow Powell's land, Brier Creek, adjoining grant conveyed from Jacob Mercer and Jeaby his wife to Henry Champion September 1, 1797. Witnesses: Charles Mayberry, James McCormick J.P.

Page 313-314 – October 6, 1795, Stephen Nobles of Warren County to Ephraim Dicken of same for 100 pounds, 200 acres in Warren County adjoining James Bishop, Runnels, William Nobles, William Lucas, grant to Stephen Noblesd. Witnesses: Jesse Doles, William Northern.

Page 314 – William Byrom, tax collector of Warren County, to Charles Mayberry of Columbia County. Tax deed dated July 18, 1797, conveying 150 acres in Jefferson County formerly Warren County, being part of 240 acre tract, levied on and sold as property of Abraham Pennington for taxes. Witnesses: Henry Kendall and John Wilson J.P.

Page 315-316 – October 7, 1796, Moses Hill to Jesse Ricketson, both of Warren County, for $100, 200 acres adjoining Isaac Simons and vacant land at time of survey, granted to Moses Hill August 19, 1790. Witnesses: John Grenade, Peter Hodo J.P.

Page 316-317 – April 13, 1793, Dixon Hall and Nancy his wife of Greene County to James Rogers of Wilkes County, for 50 pounds, 200 acres in Wilkes County on Long Creek, originally granted to James Wadsworth October 1, 1784, later says Dixon Hall and Anna his wife. Witnesses: Daniel Mitchell, Henry Mitchell.

Page 317-318 – 1797, Rhesa Howard of Columbia County to Henry Hight of Warren County, for $192, land on Hart's Creek adjoining old Richmond County line, 192 acres, part of a 777 acre grant to Rhesa Howard June 4, 1796. Witnesses: Isaiah Tucker, Lemuel Pruitt J.P.

Page 318 – Lewis Brantley, to Ambrose Hadley. Deed dated September 5, 1797, conveying 200 acres on Rocky Comfort Creek granted to John Davies by Governor George Handley. Witnesses: T. Persons, David Broom, L. Pruitt J.P.

Page 318-319 – September 25, 1797, Lewis Brantley of Warren County to Ambrose Hadley of same, for $500, land on Rocky Comfort Creek, 200 acres granted to John Davies. Witnesses: T. Persons and David Broom, L. Pruitt J.P.

Page 319 – George Brewer, of Hancock County, to Joseph Hill of Warren County. Deed dated January 30, 1798, conveying land on Rocky branch of Williams Creek, being part of 400 acre tract granted Benjamin Scott in 1784. Witnesses: Lewis Wright, John Torrence and John Baker J.P.

Page 319-320 – January 30, 1798, George Brewer of Hancock County to Joseph Hill of Warren County for $400, land on Rocky Branch of Williams Creek, land surveyed for Robert Jenkins, now the property of John Rudisell, William White's line, 160 acres originally granted to Benjamin Scott, December 17, 1784. Recorded in Book FFF, Folio 16. Witnesses: Lucs. Wright, Jno. Torrence.

Page 320-321 – October 27, 1796, Solomon Barfield of Hancock County to William Barfield of Warren County for 150 pounds, land on Hart's Creek, 300 acres. Witnesses: Loyd Kelly J.P., Mark Gonder.

Page 321-322 – December 20, 1786, Benjamin Thompson and Ann his wife, of Green County, to John Jones of Wilkes County for 50 pounds, 287 ½ acres, land in Washington County on Cowpen Creek of Little Ogeechee granted to Benjamin Thompson June 27, 1786. Witnesses: James Thompson, Jacob Jackson.

Page 322-323 – Lazarus Gurley of Warren County, 300 acres on fork of Rocky Comfort to William Sullivan adjoining lands of Thomas Neal, Isaac McCrary and James Jones, the same land that William Sullivan sold to Lazarus Gurley until such time as a note of 6000 weight of Inspected Tobacco, due November 1, 1796, December 21, 1795. Witnesses: William Brooks, Thomas Neal Giobson.

Page 323-324 – January 19, 1797, Reubin Jones of Warren County to Sterling Jones of same, mentions Rebecca Jones, wife of Reuben, 148 acres on Rocky Comfort, adjoining Sarah Golding's, Hawthorne, Wright, granted to Reuben Jones, January 9, 1797, recorded Book ZZZZ, Folio 115. Witnesses: William Jones, James Jones.

Page 324 – Henry Champion Sr., and wife Mary, to John Kent, all of Warren County. Deed dated November 25, 1795, conveying 100 acres in the forks of Big and Little Brier Creeks, with the improvements, whereon said Henry Champion Sr., and John Champion now live. Witnesses: John Torrence, Jesse Matthews.

Page 324-325 – November 25, 1795, Henry Champion Sr., farmer to John Kent, farmer of Warren County for 60 pounds, land on west side of Main Bryer Creek, bounded by the new road leading from Providence Ironworks on Sweet Water to Waynesborough, land formerly that of widow Powell, now Jesse Matthews, granted to Jacob Mercer July 29, 1785, conveyed to Champion September 1, 1791, 100 acres more or less. Witnesses: John Torrence, Jesse Matthews, relinquishment of dower by Mary Champion.

Page 326 – John Champion to John Kent, both of Warren County. Deed dated November 30, 1795, conveying the above land "whereon myself and Henry Champion Sr., in his lifetime dwelt." Witnesses: John Torrence, William White, Joseph White.

Page 327 – William Corum to Joseph Armstrong both of Warren County. Deed dated May 18, 1797, conveying 50 acres on Brushy fork of Brier Creek, being part of 420 acres granted grantor in 1797. Witnesses: Evan Thomas, Benjamin Geesling, Robert Willis.

Page 327 – May 18, 1797, Joseph Armstrong from William Corum for $30, 50 acres, part of 420 granted to William Corum May 16, 1797 on Brushy Fork of Cold Brier Creek. Witnesses: Evan Thomas, Benjamin Geesling, Robert Willis.

Page 328 – Ezekiel Alexander to William Crenshaw both of Warren County. Deed dated March 19, 1796, for $80 land on Williams and Caison Creeks, 80 acres more or less. Witnesses: William Smith, Peter Helton.

Page 328-329 – May 2, 1797, Solomon Newsom of Warren to Edward Kinsey of same for $707, 230 acres granted April 26, 1797, registered in Book ZZZZ Folio 575. Witnesses: James McCormick J.P., A. Tharp J.P.

Page 329-330 – November 14, 1792, Jesse Sanford of Green County to Thomas Heath for 50 pounds, 255 acres on Rocky Branch in Wilkes County, originally granted to Jesse Sanford. Witnesses: Cadwall Raines, Wyatt Collier.

Page 331 – John Dismukes Sr., to Ephriam Dismukes, both of Warren County. Deed dated September 18, 1797, for $200, conveying 200 acres on Hardin's Creek, granted grantor 1787. Witnesses: Septimus Weatherby and William Dismukes.

Page 332-333 – October 17, 1797, Samuel Ozborn of Warren County to William Ozborn his son, for $100, land in Wilkes County on Long Creek, part of a 300 acre grant to said Ozborn, February 19, 1790. Witnesses: Fanney Friend, William Flake.

Page 332 – February 17, 1796, Mountain Hill and Elizabeth his wife, Jesse Armstrong and Amivil his wife, all of Warren County to Richard Summons of same for $162, 152 acres in Warren County.

Page 333-334 – March 22, 1796, Ignatius Few of Columbia County to James Scott of Warren County for 206 pounds, 10 shillings, 300 acres in Warren County. Witnesses: W. Wiley, David Mahu, William H. Lee.

Page 334 – John Dismukes Sr. to John Dismukes Jr., both of Warren County. Deed dated September 18, 1797, for $200, for 100 acres on Hardin's Creek adjoining Ephriam Dismukes. Same witnesses as last above.

Page 335 – John Dismukes to Peter Dismukes. Deed dated September 18, 1797, for 100 acres on Ogeechee River adjoining John and Edmond Dismukes. Same witnesses.

Page 336-337 – August 16, 1797, Dial Peary and Hannah his wife of Warren County to Thomas Heath of same, for $750, 300 acres on Long Creek adjoining John F. Flournoy. Witnesses: Henry Mitchell J.P., Fanny Mitchell, relinquish of dower by Hannah Peary.

Page 337 – John Deyampert and wife Mary, to Henry Hardin, all of Warren County. Deed dated August 25, 1797, for $400 for 100 acres on Middle Creek. Witnesses: Gad Harrison and Thomas White J.P.

Page 338-339 – August 5, 1797, Benjamin Few and Rachel his wife of Columbia County, to Henry Hardin of Warren County, for $200, 100 acres in Warren County, land formerly of John Deyampert, adjoining Few's land. Witnesses: William Few, Thomas White J.P,

Page 339 – Anthony Crumley to Lewis Brantley both of Warren County. Deed September 29, 1795, for 30 pounds, for 200 acres on Whetstone Creek. Witnesses: Thomas Low, Thomas Cocks, Young Nelms.

Page 339 – Jethro Darden to James Matthews both of Warren County. Deed dated January 11, 1805, for land on Williams Creek. Witnesses: Thomas Fontaine, Timothy Matthews.

Page 340 – George Brewer, of Warren County, to Abraham Perkins. Deed dated February 2, 1795, conveying part of tract of land granted Benjamin Scott in 1784, and willed by said Scott to Shadrach Kinnebrew who deeded same to grantor in 1792. Witnesses: Joseph White, Thomas Hill.

Page 341-342 – December 26, 1790, Samuel Osburn of Wilkes County to James White of same, for 20 pounds, land on Long Creek of Ogeechee, adjoining John Hutchin's, Torrence's line, Mathew Grant, 100 acres, part of 300 granted to Samuel Osborn April 9, 1790. Witnesses: S. Camp, Mary Camp.

Page 342 – Stephen Mitchell for love, etc. towards my loving son, Stephen Mitchell do give, 5 negroes, November 4, 1797. Witnesses: Moses Fort, Arthur Fort J..P.

Page 342 – Stephen Mitchell to daughter, Lieucresia Neel, lawfully begotten in wedlock, one negroe Cleo in the county of Washington, November 4, 1797. Witnesses: Moses Fort, Arthur Fort J.P.

Page 343 – Stephen Mitchell of Warren County to daughter, Susannah Harvell, lawfully begotten in wedlock of county of Washington, one Negro woman.

Page 343 – Stephen Mitchell of Warren County to Sally Coatman, alias Mitchell, of Washington, one negro girl.

Page 344 – October 13, 1797, Stephen Mitchell of Warren County and his wife to Thomas Farmer of same, for 40 pounds, land in Warren County on Fort's Creek adjoining John Dill, 250 acres, Seiah, wife of Stephen Mitchell. Witnesses: Susannah Fort, Arthur Fort J.P.

Page 344-345 – Warren County, Georgia, October 23, 1797, Clement Forbes of Pitts. County, North Carolina, planter, to Philip Gibbs of Warren County, planter, for 500 silver dollars, 350 acres on Rocky Comfort Creek, patent by Richard Barrow Sr., the grants bearing date August 2, 1774. Witnesses: Arthur Drue, Absalom Barrow, Mebry Barrow, Milbrey Barrow.

Page 345-346 – January 15, 1796, William Davis of Warren County to Lewis Brantley of same, for 80 pounds, 200 acres on Rocky Comfort Creek adjoining Joel King, Drewry Thomson. Witnesses: John Slatter, Robert Moses.

Page 346-347 – March 13, 1797, Nathaniel Williams of Warren County to John Williams of same, for $150, land on cat tail fork of Rocky Comfort, 100 acres, part of a 200 acre tract granted to John Augton, August 10, 1785 adjoining James Parker, A. F. Ellen. Witnesses: Peter Rain, Abraham Perkins.

Page 347-348 – March 26, 1796, Brian McClendon of Warren County to Joseph Grizard, for 30 pounds, 390 acres on Rocky Comfort. Witnesses: William Earnest, Sarah Raley.

Page 348-349 – State of South Carolina, John Hunter of Greenville County for 100 pounds, to Mathew McCrary of the county of Laurens, land in town of Wrightsborough in State of Georgia, No, 15, also a tract of land in parish of St. Paul's, being part of the reserved for the people called Quakers containing 200 acres, at time of original survey bounded by vacant lands on all sides,

November 6, 1770, registered in Secretary's office, Book I, page 198, November 24 (blank).

Page 349-350 – December 13, 1796, John Whitlock of Oglethorpe County, Georgia to John Claiborne Sr. of Warren County for $225, 50 acres, originally granted to John Dennis, 1770, adjoining Doyle, Kilgore's Creek, Thomas Porter. Witnesses: Perry G. Young, John W. Claiborne.

Page 350-351 – December 27, 1796, John Harmon of Warren County to Pleasant Walker of same, 100 acres on Williams Creek. Witnesses: Robert Hill, Benjamin Chapman.

Page 351-352 – February 22, 1796, Pleasant Walker of Warren County from Mathew Jones of Hancock County for 40 pounds, 100 acres in Warren County. Witnesses: John Peyampert, Edmond Crowden J.P.

Page 352-353 – November 21, 1797, John Harmon of Warren County to John Bustin of same, for $40, land on Williams Creek, 20 acres. Witnesses: Robert Hill, A. Grier J.P.

Page 353-354 – November 20, 1797, J. Harmon of Warren County to John Bustin of same, $200 for 100 acres on Williams Creek. Witnesses: Robert Hill, Hans Petagrew.

Page 355 – Pierce Bailey, to Pleasant Walker. Deed dated January 9, 1797, for twenty acres on waters of Williams Creek, being part of the land whereon said Bailey resides. Witnesses: J. Harman and Richard Smith.

Page 356 – Thomas Childrey to Aquilla Jones, both of Warren County. Deed dated December 26, 1797, for 120 acres on Brier Creek adjoining Nicholas White, Joseph Maddock and Joseph Beasley, granted grantor in 1788. Witness: Henry Williams.

Page 357 – September 7, 1797, James McCormick to Michael Coda for $200, 300 acres, granted July 22, 1795 adjoining Isaac Ball, Smith, Hugh Reise. Witnesses: John Sallis, P. Hodo J.P.

Page 358 – December 26, 1797, John Watson of Warren County to Robert Stanford of same, for 520 silver dollars, 100 acres on

White's Creek, originally granted to said John Watson, 1772, Book I, Folio 572. Witnesses: Jonathan Burson, Aquila Jones.

Page 359-360 – December 13, 1791, Moses Hill to Jonathan Burson, Moses Hill and Hannah his wife, for 50 pounds, land in Wilkes County adjoining John Dunaway and Duck's, J. Few, McCarde's, granted October 14, 1788. Witnesses: Alexander McDougal, John Smith.

Page 360-361 – January 24, 1795, Ezekiah Verdin and Jane his wife of Warren County to James Osborn of same, for 40 pounds, 100 acres adjoining William Duprese, William Nichols, Peter Castleberry. Witnesses: Samuel Tedders, William Lem Sr.

Page 361 – William Cocks of Washington County, to Christopher Bustin of Warren County. Deed dated November 25, 1797, for 200 acres on Rocky Comfort Creek granted Thomas Bethany, being the place where Richard Cocks lives. Witnesses: Turner Persons and George Turner.

Page 362 – Jonathan Burson, to Robert Stanford. Deed dated December 29, 1797, for 12 acres on White's Creek, being part of grant made to grantor in 1785. Witnesses: Phillip Gibbs and John Bayn J.P.

Page 363 – Warren County, Georgia, William Sanders to Zelson Berry, land where I now live, for $60. Witnesses: Garret Berry, John A. Johnson, Burl. Jones.

Page 363-364 – February 27, 1796, Amos Stewart and Patsey his wife of Wilkes County to Debera Chapman of Warren County for 370 silver dollars adjoining Williams Creek, Captain Murray's 200 acres, more or less, originally granted to Richard Cureton. Witnesses: Jones Bonner, William Taylor.

Page 364 – Solomon Barfield of Hancock County, to Jesse Barfield of Warren County. Deed dated January 20, 1797, for 100 pounds, conveying 200 acres on Hart's Creek in said Warren County. Witnesses: Matthew Wood, John Runnels J.P.

Page 365-366 – October 7, 1795, Moses Going and Aggy his wife, to William Stith Jr. for $2000, land on north side of Ogeechee, 465 acres, part of 780 acres granted to Ignatius Few, March 2, 1791. Witnesses: Robert Abercrombie, William Friend, William Stith.

Page 366-367 – December 26, 1792, John Mims of Washington County, Georgia to Richard Hill of Wilkes County for 200 pounds, land adjoining Jesse Harper, Charles Williams, 200 acres located by said John Mims, March 15, 1788, recorded book UUU, folio 436. Witnesses: John Ball, Thomas Cavinah.

Page 368 – October 5, 1796, Lewis Powell and Catherine his wife of Warren County to Henry Burnley of Hancock County, for 150 pounds, 231 ½ acres, originally granted to Moses Powels Sr., September 5, 1783 adjoining James Rogers, Bunkley. Witnesses: Benjamin Vinhown, Henry Williams, John Bayn J.P.

Page 368-369 – September 1, 1797, Lightfoot Williams of Lincoln County, North Carolina to Henry Williams Jr. of Warren County, Georgia, for 32 pounds, 100 acres, part of 200, on Briar Creek granted to Cornelius McCarden October 3, 1787. Witnesses: Benjamin Vinhown, Henry Williams, John Bayn J.P.

Page 369 – John Burkhalter and wife Sarah, to Sterling Williamson. Deed dated January 17, 1797, for 150 acres being the southeast part of 300 acre tract granted in 1796. Witnesses: John Williams, James McCormick J.P.

Page 370-371 – November 25, 1797, William Hickson of Columbia County to William Berry of Warren County for $300, 100 acres originally granted to James Habersham February 2, 1773. Witness: James Willis J.P.

Page 371-372 – October 4, 1797, Frances Hill, Administratrix of estate of Richard Hill, deceased, to Sterling Gardner of Warren County for $100, land on Whetstone Creek adjoining Jesse White, Henry Peebles, 100 acres. Witnesses: T. Persons, H. Peebles, R. B. Fletcher J.P.

Page 372 – October 4, 1797, Frances Hill, Administratrix of estate of Richard Hill, deceased, to Sterling Gardner for 700 Spanish Mill

Dollars, 200 acres on Whetstone Creek originally granted to John Mims, October 17, 1785. Witnesses: T. Persons, H. Peebles, R. B. Fletcher J.P.

Page 373-374 – November 10, 1796, John Landrum to Ignatius Few for 100 pounds, land in Warren County on Rocky Comfort adjoining John Hill, originally granted to John Landrum, August 17, 1786. Witnesses: Thomas Hunt, John Hudnell.

Page 374-375 – February 11, 1797, Ignatius Few to Thomas Burk, land on Rocky Comfort, for 100 pounds. Witnesses: John Lee, James Bond.

Page 375 – Jethro Darden to Timothy Matthews both of Warren County. Deed dated January 11, 1805, for 18 acres on Williams Creek. Witnesses: Thomas Fontaine, John Brooks.

Page 375-376 – May 17, 1794, James Gilmore of Warren County to Peter Cox of same, for 80 pounds, 194 acres on Middle Creek adjoining Richmond County line, Ansley's, granted to James Gilmore, December 30, 1788, recorded Book RRR, folio 90. Witnesses: John Gilmore, Joseph Stubbs, Mark Hardin J.P.

Page 377 – May 17, 1794, James Gilmore to Peter Cox for 20 pounds, land on Upton's Creek surveyed March 6, 1787, recorded Book VVV, folio 199. Witnesses: John Gilmore, Joseph Stubbs, Mark Hardin J.P.

Page 378-379 – August 6, 1794, John Maynor of Warren County to Isaac Marchant of same, for 15 pounds, land on Little Briar Creek, 173 acres. Witnesses: Isaac H. and Samuel Ridgewell.

Page 379 – Joseph Armstrong to Jesse Ricketson both of Warren County. Deed dated September 27, 1797, for $45, for 50 acres being part of 420 acres granted William Corum in 1797. Witnesses: Reubin Jones, Peter Hodo J.P.

Page 380 – Joseph Davidson to Jesse Ricketson, both of Warren County. Deed dated November 18, 1797, for 100 acres lying on south fork of Brier Creek, being half of grant made in 1785 to Isaac Simonson. Witness: James Carter.

Page 380 – March 4, 1795, John Peary of Warren County to Joseph Davidson, blacksmith, for 50 pounds, 100 acres on south fork of Briar Creek, half of a 200 acre tract granted to John Peary. Witnesses: William Pleasant, M. Hubert J.P.

Page 380-381 – November 18, 1797, Joseph Davidson of Warren County to Jesse Ricketson for $30, 100 acres on south fork of Briar Creek, half of a tract granted to Isaac Simonson, September 6, 1785. Recorded Book HHH, folio 480. Witnesses: James Carter, John Bayn J.P.

Page 381-382 – October 17, 1797, Joseph Smith of Columbia County to John Grenaid of Warren County for $100, 200 acres granted to Joseph Smith April 29, 1797, adjoining Rose McCormick, Hill Ball. Witness: P. Hodo J.P. Recorded May 1, 1798.

Page 382-383 – May 17, 1794, James Gilmore to Mary Morris for 4 shillings per acre, 4 acres and a half on Middle Creek adjoining Gilmore, granted to James Gilmore December 3, 1788, Book RRR Folio 80. Signed: James Gilmore, Ann Gilmore. Witnesses: Jack Stubbs, Mark Hardin J.P. Recorded May 2, 1798.

Page 383 – Thomas Cocks to John Parham. Deed dated March 16, 1798, for 130 acres on Rocky Comfort Creek. Witnesses: John Matthews, R. B. Fletcher J.P.

Page 383-384 – March 16, 1798, Thomas Cocks of Warren County to John Parham of same, for $200, land on Rocky Comfort Creek, 130 acres. Witness: Jno. Matthews. Recorded May 2, 1798.

Page 384-385 – October 24, 1797, Sterling Gardner of Warren County to Robert Jenkins for $1500, land on Little Rocky Comfort, adjoining Daniel Hutcherson, 300 acres, reserving 7 acres for public utility. Witnesses: Turner Persons, Shadrach F. Ellen. Recorded May 2, 1798.

Page 385-386 – February 16, 1798, Robert Jenkins to Richard Heath, $1714, and 25 cents, land on Williams Creek adjoining Micajah Stone, Burrell Perry, 400 acres. Witnesses: Turner Persons J.P., Sterling Gardner. Recorded May 2, 1798.

Page 386 – February 11, 1798, Robert Jenkins of Warren County to Burrell Perry for $400, 100 acres on Williams Creek. Witnesses: T. Persons, J. Bettle. Recorded May 2, 1798.

Page 387 – October 1, 1790, James Rowland of Richmond County to Peter Cocks of same but now Warren County for 60 pounds, 200 acres originally granted to James Rowland, September 1787. Registered Book II Page 104, No. 221, on Sweet Water Creek. Witnesses: Joseph Stubbs, Richard Smith. Recorded May 4, 1798.

Page 388 – William Cocks Sr. of Washington County to Thomas Cocks of Warren County. Deed dated October 7, 1797, consideration $3.00, conveying 130 acres on Rocky Comfort Creek, being part of two surveys to Thomas Bethany and John Rutherford. Witness: Richard Cocks.

Page 388 – November 2, 1793, John Smith Sr. of Wilkes County to Reuben Magee of Columbia County for 100 pounds, 180 acres, part of a 200 acre tract granted to Nicholas White, September 24, 1784, on both sides of Beaver Dam Creek, fork of Bear Creek, part in Wilkes and part in Columbia. Witnesses: John Bayn J.P., John Smith Jr. Recorded May 4, 1798.

Page 388-389 – October 7, 1797, William Cox of Washington County to Thomas Cocks of Warren County for $3.00, land on Rocky Comfort Creek, adjoining King, being part of 2 surveys, 130 acres, one granted to Thomas Bethany the other to John Rutherford. Witnesses: Richard Cocks, R. Persons. Recorded May 4, 1798.

Page 390 – George Dykes to Redden Ratliff, both of Warren County for $60, 300 acres. Deed dated March 3, 1798, for 300 acres of a 900 acre tract owned by grantor, to be taken from the side that joins James Folks. Witness: Rebekah Bishop.

Page 390-391 – August 30, 1797, Gibson Flournoy of Warren County to Benjamin Wheeler of same for $400, 200 acres, half of grant to John Grantham August 4, 1789. Witnesses: William Sims, M. Hubert J.P. Recorded May 9, 1798.

Page 391-392 – November 10, 1794, Joseph Miller of Warren County to Lemuel Pruitt of same, for 30 pounds, land on Middle Creek adjoining Levi Pruitt, Samuel Pruitt, Mark Hardin, Thomas Weekley, 90 acres. Witnesses: L. Pruitt J.P., Reuben Meadows. Recorded May 9, 1798.

Page 392-394 – January 24, 1798, Thomas Ansley and Rebecca his wife to Abel Ansley of Warren County for $200, land on Still Creek, formerly known as Upton's Creek, part of 2 surveys granted to Thomas Ansley, one 150 acre January 19, 1785, the other May 24, 1787 of John Landrum's original survey, Thomas Ansley Jr., Joseph Hodgins' line, 330 acres. Witnesses: Joseph Landrum, Joseph Ansley, John Wilson J.P. Recorded May 9, 1798.

Page 394-395 – June 1796, Ann Stewart of Warren County to Cabal Stephens of same, for 10 pounds, land on Rocky Comfort, surveyed for Ann Stewart, adjoining John Lawson's line, 100 acres whereon she now lives. Witnesses: Samuel Powell, Robert Thompson.

Page 395-396 – April 15, 1797, Proper Horton and Sarah his wife, to Jacob Flournoy, for $500, 225 acres more or less. Witnesses: Allen Dorman, James Cozart, Edward Kelly. Recorded May 10, 1798.

Page 396-397 – March 17, 1798, Elisha Pruitt to Amos Persons for $25, land on Middle Creek adjoining McInvale, Tucker, Ezekiel Miller, 38 acres. Witness: Lemuel Pruitt J.P. Recorded May 10, 1798.

Page 397-398 – March 15, 1798, Hugh Reese of Warren County to Joseph McMath of same, for $100, all that land granted August 17, 1785, 100 acres on Brier Creek in Wilkes County, now Warren, adjoining William Whair, Newsom. Recorded Book JJJJ, Relinquish of dower Elizabeth Rees. Witnesses: Benjamin Rees, James McCormick J.P. Recorded June 20, 1798.

Page 398-399 – October 18, 1790, Stephen Mitchell and Celia his wife of Richmond County to Reuben Winfrey of Wilkes Cunty, for 50 pounds, land on Long Creek,150 acres adjoining Nathan

Fowler, Thomas Jones. Witnesses: Adam Jones, Kinchen Newsom.

Page 399-400 – Rebeckah Parham of Warren County to son George Parham, one negro man Tom, April 2, 1798. Witnesses: John Matthews, Polly Matthews.

Page 400-401 – May 15, 1798, Caleb Stephens of Warren County to Bethiar Stewart for 10 pounds, land on Rocky Comfort, surveyed for Ann Stewart, 100 acres. Witnesses: Moses Grandberry, Nowell Robertson J.P.

Page 401-402 – January 24, 1797, Walter Newman of Wilkes County to John Slatter of Warren County for 200 pounds, land on Rocky Comfort, adjoining Jones Persons, Harman Perryman, William Cocks, McDonald, Darnal, 90 acres and 43 acres (2 tracts). Witnesses: George Weatherby, Solomon Slatter, R. D. Fletcher J.P.

Page 402-403 – April 5, 1796, David Neal Esq., Sheriff of Warren County to James White and David Robertson Sr. of Columbia County for $12,000 against William Franklin as Executor of Last Will and Testament of Ebenezer Sterns, sale of 100 acres including the conference of Main Brier Creek and Sweetwater, 100 acres originally granted to said Sterns, October 26, 1784, recorded in Book EEE, Folio 279, recorded in Book B Surveyor's Office, Richmond County. Witnesses: Robert White, John Torrence.

Page 403 – John Campbell of Greene County, to Peter Buckhalt of Warren County. Deed dated March 26, 1798, conveying 134 acres on Williams Creek adjoining Reubin Rogers. Witnesses: Micajah Perry and Richard Butler.

Page 404 – Thomas Bohannon, and wife Selah, to Edmond Johnson. Deed dated April 6, 1798, for 100 acres on waters of Long Creek granted in 1798 to Phillip Logan. Witnesses: John Wright and Robert Johnson.

Page 404 – Jethro Darden to John Fontaine both of Warren County. Deed dated January 11, 1805, for 107 acres on headwaters of Williams Creek, being part of a survey formerly belonging to Peter Perkins, deceased.  Witnesses: John Brooks, Timothy Matthews.

Page 404-405 – April 6, 1798, Thomas Bohannon and Selah his wife, to Edmund Johnson, land on Long Creek adjoining Waller, 100 acres.  Witnesses: Johnson Wright, Robert Johnson.

Page 405 – Jethro Darden and wife Ellender to Thomas Fontaine, all of Warren County.  Deed dated January 11, 1805, for 87 acres on Hart's Creek.  Same witnesses.

Page 405 – John Campbell to Richard Butler.  Deed dated September 3, 1795, conveying 100 acres on Williams Creek adjoining Jones Kendrick and other lands of grantor.  Witnesses: John Rudicil, Ignatius Simms.

Page 406-407 – May 9, 1798, John Landrum Sr. to Joseph Landrum Jr. for $100, land on Upton's Creek, part of 550 acre grant to John Landrum August 17, 1785, Book HHH, folio 262, adjoining Thomas Ansley's.  Witnesses: John Cox, John Wilson J.P.

Page 407 – William Coram to Robert Willis, both of Warren County.  Deed dated March 5, 1798, conveying 142 acres on the head of Brier Creek in said county.  Witnesses: John Lowe, P. Hodo J.P.

Page 408-409 – October 11, 1797, John Kent to Joseph Burson for $200, 150 acres, adjoining James Napier, Samuel Ridgwell, William Jones, granted November 11, 1788 registered in Book QQQ, folio 546.  Witnesses: William B. Murphey, Vincent A. Thorp J.P.

Page 409 – February 20, 1797, John Torrence to David Cocks, for 25 pounds, land on Rocky Comfort, bounded by Fulsom, Mims, Amos Wright, James Bray, part of a grant to John Torrence April 7, 1789, Book SSS, folio 72.  Witnesses: Hugh Reese, John Baker J.P.

Page 410 – May 17, 1798, John Rushing to William Simmons for $130 land on Fort's Creek, adjoining Jonathan Miller, Long, 150 acres, part of a grant to Samuel Camp, January 22, 1789, Book JJ, Folio 319. Witnesses: John Curry, Thomas Friend J.P.

Page 411 – Peter Castleberry and wife Catherine, to Matthew McCreeree both of Warren County. Deed dated May 14, 1796, for 130 acres on Long Creek. Witnesses: David Castleberry and Claiborne Castleberry.

Page 412 – January 6, 1798, William Neal of Wilkes County to John Brantley of Warren County for $210, 100 acres adjoining Old Indian path and Hart's Creek, originally granted to John Welch, July 3, 1770 by deed, confirmed to Robert Walden by John Welch, December 3, 1773. Witnesses: Henry Hight, Larkin Brantley.

Page 413 – November 16, 1797, Owen Myrick of Warren County to Ezekiel Miller of same for $170, adjoining Vining, Michael Thomas, 170 acres. Witnesses: Turner Persons, William Rose.

Page 413-414 – May 1, 1790, Newday Onsley of Greene County to Robert Flournoy, of Wilkes, for 500 pounds, 200 acres on Ogeechee, adjoining John Wynne, Jesse Connel, Abraham Reddix. Witnesses: Adam Bowdree, Stephen Burley.

Page 414-415 – June 9, 1798, Robert Flournoy of Jefferson County, to Robert Wynne of Warren County for one dollar, but more for a deed of conveyance made some time in year 1797, 200 acres more or less on Ogeechee bound by Wynne, Connel, Reddix. Witnesses: John Mitchell J.P., Charles Abercrombie, July 14, 1798.

Page 415-416 - August 18, 1797, Solomon Newsom Sr. of Warren County to Arthur Matthews of same, for one dollar, for use and benefit of the Methodist Society one acre to be laid out where the said Matthews shall think best. Witnesses: Joseph Walker, Benjamin Burton J.P.

Page 416-417 – January 6, 1798, Vincent Allen Tharp of Warren County to Arthur Matthews of same for $60, 200 acres adjoining Cobb, Thorp, Trant, Solomon Newsom, Abbot, granted September 15, 1797. Witnesses: Edward Matthews, Benjamin Burton J.P.

Page 417-418 – March 13, 1797, Robert Jenkins of Warren County to Jonathan Locke of same for $500, 200 acres in Wilkes County adjoining Cook's line. Witnesses: Elisha Hurt J.P., William Layne.

Page 418 – Lewis Brantley and wife Susannah, of Hancock County, to Shadrach Fluwellin of Warren County. Deed dated October 22, 1795, conveying 150 acres on Whetstone Creek, being part of 200 acre grant made in 1785. Witnesses: Turner Persons and John Lowe.

Page 419 – March 7, 1797, John Seybold of Wilkes County to Septimus Weatherby of Warren County for $200, land on head branches of Hart's Creek, 280 acres. Witnesses: Silas Grigg, George Weatherby.

Page 420 – March 9, 1797, Mary Mann of Warren County to Arthur Fort of same, for $150, land on Ogeechee River, 100 acres. Witnesses: Barret Brewer, Richard Whitehead.

Page 421-422 – November 2, 1791, John Jones of Wilkes County to Arthur Fort of same for 50 pounds, land in Washington County originally granted to Benjamin Thompson, June 27, 1786, recorded in Book KKK, folio 174, from Benjamin Thompson and wife Ann to John Jones. Witnesses: W. Stith, Peyton T. Stith.

Page 422-423 – May 26, 1798, Solomon Newsom Sr. of Warren County to William Gaza of same, for $300, 108 acres, the southwest corner of a 687 ½ acre tract granted April 15, 1797. Witnesses: Benjamin Burton J.P., James McCormick J.P.

Page 423-424 – August 15, 1797, Milley Grimsley of Hancock County to Parks King of Warren County for 60 pounds, 200 acres. Witnesses: Z. Booth J.P., James Works.

Page 424-425 – September 3, 1796, John McDaniel of Warren County to John Myrick for $600, land on Rocky Comfort adjoining Joseph May, heirs of Joseph, deceased, 600 acres surveyed for John May, deceased, and conveyed to Isaac Ball. Witnesses: Nathaniel Myrick, George Weatherby.

Page 426 – November 3, 1797, Joshua Jones of Warren County to John Myrick for $400, 179 acres adjoining Charles Darnell, Thomas Neal, Henry Shelton, Joseph Boon, Thomas West, Thomas and John Myrick, granted to Joseph May, September 14, 1789, Book SSS, Folio 505. Witnesses: E. Thomas, Richard Cox.

Page 427 – January 3, 1798, John Myrick Sr. to John Myrick Jr. for $300, 180 acres on Rocky Comfort. Witnesses: Thomas Flinn, George Tweatherby.

Page 428 – Joseph Boon of Washington County, to John Myrick Jr., of Warren County. Deed dated March 5, 1798, for 200 acres on Rocky Comfort Creek granted in 1788 to James Brewer. Witnesses: Septimus Weatherby and Thomas Davis.

Page 429 – James Alford to Henry Cooper both of Wilkes County. Deed dated October 18, 1788, for lands on Long Creek of Ogeechee River, in said county, adjoining the widow Linsacum according to grant 1787 to grantor. Witnesses: S. Camp, Mary Camp.

Page 430-431 – July 2, 1798, Lemuel Pruitt and Caty Pruitt his wife of Warren County to Churchill Gibson of same, for $1000, land on Middle Fork of Upton's Creek adjoining Bishop's survey, Thomas Weakley, Levi Pruitt, James McInvale, Joseph Breed. Witnesses: Isaiah Tucker, Levi Pruitt J.P.

Page 431-432 – November 16, 1789, William Wilcher of Richmond County to Jeremiah Wilcher for 100 pounds, land granted to said Wilsher, July 20, 1787. Witnesses: Phillip Gibbs, Allen Brown.

Page 432-433 – April 22, 1791, John Ledbetter of Wilkes County to John Curry of Burke County for 40 pounds, 100 acres on Big Creek of Ogeechee. Witnesses: P. Boyle, Benjamin Jenkins J.P.

Page 433-434 – January 28, 1792, William Keener of Columbia County to Jeremiah Wilcher of same, for 30 pounds, 100 acres in Columbia County on a branch of Big Creek, whereon William Lyons formerly lived, adjoining Joseph Painter, Warlock, William

Wilcher, William Keener, granted 1788 and 1789. Witnesses: Joseph Burson, Jacob Keener, William Lyons.

Page 434 – October 28, 1797, Daniel Kingrey of Warren County to the heirs of John Curry, deceased of Jefferson County for 50 pounds, land in Warren County on Ogeechee River. Witnesses: Carey Curry, Nowell Robertson J.P.

Page 435-436 – December 30, 1797, Jeremiah Wilsher of Warren County to William Williams for $100, tract bought from William Keener. Witnesses: Abraham Yerta, John Williams, Norvell Robertson J.P.

Page 436-437 – December 30, 1797, Jeremiah Wilsher of Jefferson County to Nathaniel Williams Sr. for $100, land whereon said Williams now lives, on Little Creek of Big Creek in Warren County granted to William Wilsher, July 20, 1787. Witnesses: Abraham Yerta, John Williams, Norvell Robertson J.P.

Page 437-438 – Honour Anderson, widow, of Wilkes County to James Williams Green. Deed dated December 13, 1792, for 100 acres of a grant made grantor, part of which land has been sold to Joshua Roe. Witnesses: Ezekiel Miller, Anne Vining.

Page 438-439 – September 22, 1796, John Moses of Warren County to William Howard for 40 pounds, 200 acres in Warren County adjoining Samuel Neal, John Moses Jr., Michael Burkhalter. Witnesses: John Moses Jr., David Thomas.

Page 439-440 – July 24 1797, John Moses of Warren County to William Howard, $10, a tract of land taken up by Kiah Bussey, sold to Robert Moses which John Moses bought of his father, 15 acres. Witnesses: Evan Thomas, Nathan Castleberry.

Page 440-441 – October 24, 1796, Edmond Nugent of Washington County to Henry Cooper of Warren County, Edmond Nugent and Mary his wife for $50, 21 ½ acres, Cooper's Spring Branch. Witnesses: Benjamin Perry, Arthur Jenkins.

Page 441-442 – January 29, 1796, Henry Green Sr. and Elizabeth his wife of Warren County, to Benton Spier of Hancock County for $184, land on Rocky Comfort adjoining Parkins, John Cook, Thomas Seal, 123 ½ acres. Witnesses: Elisha Hunt, James Green.

Page 442-443 – October 22, 1798, Elisha Wright to Henry and William Sanders Jr. all of Warren County for $50, 60 acres on Rocky Comfort, Golding's line. Witnesses: John J. Wells, Richard B. Fletcher J.P.

Page 443-444 – September 7, 1798, Edmund Hayes of Warren County for $75, to Peter Cox, 50 acres adjoining Sanders, Peter Davis. Witnesses: Michael Cody, P. Hodo J.P.

Page 444 – Solomon Barfield of Hancock County, to John Harman of Warren County. Deed dated September 1, 1797, for 157 acres on Williams Creek. Witnesses: Solomon Barfield Jr. and Lloyd Kelly J.P.

Page 445 – Robert Dickins to Thomas Jackson both of Warren County. Deed dated November 20, 1803, for 150 acres on Ogeechee River, being an original grant made in 1786 to John Watkins, except what is reserved for William Bird Sr. and Benjamin A. Hamp. Witnesses: N. Robertson, John Hatcher.

Page 445-446 – October 24, 1795, Stephen Mitchell of Warren County to William Dean of same, for 80 pounds, 100 acres on Rocky Comfort, granted November 5, 1788. Witnesses: S. Harville, James McDade.

Page 446-447 – October 7, 1790, John Pitman of Richmond to John Moutrey of same for 100 pounds, 200 acres in Wilkes County. Witnesses: James Simms J.P., Joel Moutrey.

Page 447 – October 26, 1796, Nathaniel Ward of Warren County to Samuel Barfield of Hancock County for 50 pounds, 150 acres on Williams Creek. Witnesses: Lloyd Kelly J.P., John Waggoner.

Page 447-448 – October 17, 1797, Samuel Osborne of Warren County to William Flake of same, for $150, 100 acres on Long Creek. Witnesses: William Osborn, Fanney Friend.

Page 448 – Isaac Ball to John Myrick. Deed dated September 18, 1798, for 100 acres on north side of Rocky Comfort Creek granted in 1786 to the heirs of John May. Witnesses: Nancy Thomas, E. Thomas.

Page 449-451 – August 7, 1797, David Neal Esq., Sheriff of Warren County, James W. Green of Hancock County did in the Inferior Court of Warren County obtain a judgment against George Weatherby for the sum of (blank) said Sheriff was commanded to levy on the goods and chattels, etc., 122 aces on Rocky Comfort for $53. Witnesses: John Lowe, Francis Stainback.

Page 452 – William Brewer of Wilkes County, to Daniel Runnals. Deed dated April 5, 1790. Conveys 60 acres in Wilkes County on the waters of Ogeechee River adjoining Nathan Brewer. Witnesses: Parks King, George Brewer.

Page 453-454 – January 26, 1796, Christopher William of Hancock County to Daniel Sanders and Arden Sanders of Warren County for 30 pounds, 160 acres, part of a tract of 200 acres granted to said Williams, 1796. Witnesses: Thomas Heath, John Henkins, Matthew Brewer.

Page 455 – William Davidson to Arden Sanders, both of Warren County. Deed dated November 30, 1797, for 100 acres granted 1791 to John Parkins. Witnesses: John Williams, Daniel Sanders.

Page 456 – March 17, 1798, Ardin Sanders of Warren County to Daniel Sanders for $100, half of a tract of 160 acres bought jointly of Christopher Williams, January 26, 1796. Witnesses: Jones Persons, R. B. Fletcher J.P.

Page 457 – October 4, 1791, John Weaver and Elizabeth his wife of Wilkes County to Elisha Pruitt for 40 pounds, 100 acres originally granted to said Weaver, January 22, 1789. Witnesses: Josiah Cocks J.P., L. Pruitt J.P.

Page 457-458 – July 7, 1790, James Jones and Elizabeth his wife to Elisha Pruitt for 30 pounds, land on Middle Creek, 52 acres. Witnesses: M. Hardin, Jesse Armstrong.

Page 460-461 – March 15, 1798, Elisha Pruitt Esq. Collector of Taxes to Moses Darden, non payment of Benjamin Few, 200 acres adjoining Hight, Darling McDonald, James Cobb, Brantley. Witnesses: Mountain Hill, Joel Cloud.

Page 461 – Moses Darden, to Elisha Pruitt, both of Warren County. Deed dated March 15, 1798, for 400 acres on Hart's Creek granted to James Cobbs. Witnesses: Mountain Hill and Joel Cloud.

Page 461 – March 15, 1798, Moses Darden to Elisha Pruitt for $21, land bought of said Pruitt, 400 acres on Hart's Creek. Witnesses: Mountain Hill, Joel Cloud.

Page 462 – March 15, 1798, Moses Darden to Elisha Pruitt, 200 acres. Witnesses: Joel Cloud, Mountain Hill.

Page 462 – 463 – Articles of agreement between Elisha Pruitt and Moses Darden in a certain tract of land on Hart's Creek adjoining lands of Phillip Brantley, Howell Hight, Cox and others, 600 acres which was sold for tax due. Witnessed our hands, March 15, 1798, if land is lost, deed is not considered to be warranted. Witnesses: Joel Cloud, Mountain Hill.

Page 463-464 – March 15, 1798, Elisha Pruitt to Phillip Brantley for $325, land on Hart's Creek, 368 acres. Witness: Lemuel Pruitt J.P.

Page 464 – March 20, 1798, Elisha Pruitt to Lemuel Pruitt for $10, 20 acres on Middle Creek adjoining Lemuel Pruitt, Mark Hardin. Witness: Henry Hardin J.P.

Page 464-465 – March 17, 1798, Elisha Pruitt to Josiah Darden for $350, 200 acres on Hart's Creek. Witnesses: Henry Hardin J.P., Lemuel Pruitt J.P.

Page 465-466 – 1798, Elisha Pruitt to Lemuel Pruitt for $500, 195 acres on Hart's Creek. Witnesses: Henry Hardin J.P.

Page 466-467 – March 24, 1798, Willis Perry to Deacons of Williams Creek Church, both of Warren County for $10, 2 acres. Witnesses: John Baker J.P., Lemuel Pruitt J.P.

Page 467-468 – November 9, 1798, John Harman of Warren County to Josiah N. Kennedy, 157 acres granted to Silas Mercer, August 8, 1792, adjoining Pierce Bailey, Williams, Zechariah Sheffield. Witnesses: Ephraim Smith and Tilman Niblet. Renunciation of dower by Mary Harman.

Page 468-469 – November 5, 1798, Hugh Reese of Warren County to Hardy Newsom of same, for $200, 100 acres on Big Brier Creek granted to Bazil Lamar, from Bazil Lamar to Charlotte Nichols, who became the wife of Henry Glover. Bray Warren, James Carter, James May, deceased. Witnesses: James McMath, James McCormick J.P.

Page 469 – Samuel Alexander, to his relative, Phereby Wootten, both of Wilkes County, Georgia. Deed of Gift dated October 28, 1791, conveying all grantor's interest in the estate of James Wootten, deceased. Witnesses: Duncan Campbell, Arthur Bell.

Page 470 – Asa Alexander, of Greene County, Georgia, to Aseneth Wootten of Wilkes County, "my loving friend and relation." Deed of Gift dated December 21, 1791, to all his interest and claim in the estate of James Wootten, deceased. Witnesses: John and Abner Wilkinson.

Page 470-471 – December 8, 1797, John Nixon and Frances his wife to Joseph Carson of Wilkes County for $500, 100 acres on Middle Creek in Warren County adjoining John Wells, Ezekiel Miller. Witnesses: Richard Carter, Willis Perry, Henry Hardin J.P.

Page 471-472 – April 6, 1796, Joseph Miller and Ann his wife to William Dennis, 100 acres on Middle Creek for 23 pounds. Witnesses: Thomas Weakley, Elizabeth Pruitt, L. Pruitt, J.P.

Page 472 – William Coram to Jesse Ricketson both of Warren County. Deed dated December 19, 1798, for 34 ½ acres on the head branch of Big Brier Creek in said county. Witness: Nathaniel Thomson.

Page 473-474 – December 1, 1797, John Gibson to Reddick Bass both of Warren County for $400, 200 acres on Middle Creek, granted February 28, 1788. Witnesses: A. Persons, L. Pruitt J.P.

Page 474-475 – May 18, 1798, Reubin Winfrey of Columbia County to Walter Slaughter of Warren County for $700, adjoining Nathan Fowler, Mitchell, S. Camp, Adam Jones, 200 acres granted March to Stephen Mitchell and also part of 275 acres granted August 13, 1788 to said Mitchell, conveyed October 18, 1790 to Reuben Winfrey. Witnesses: Adam Jones Sr., Thomas Jones.

Page 475-476 – July 27, 1798, James Stapler of Columbia to Henry Peebles of Warren for $2000, 300 acres on Middle Creek granted to said James Stapler, heir of Amos Stapler, March 4, 1785, adjoining Jesse Harper, J. Castleberry.

Page 476 – Robert Ford of Warren County to relation John Ford Jr., a mare, December 20, 1798. Witnesses: Isaiah Tucker, Henry Hill.

Page 476-477 – December 20, 1794, John Walton of Columbia County to Thomas Young of Bryan County, for 5 shillings, 1000 acres on Middle Ford of Upton's Creek, formerly in Richmond County, originally granted to said Thomas Young. Witnesses: John Carter Walton, Benjamin Skeine.

Page 477-478 – I, John Walton of Columbia County, held unto Thomas Young of Bryan County for 1000 sterling, concerning relinquish of dower on above deed. Recorded January 18, 1799.

Page 478-479 – September 22, 1796, Richard Whatley and Frances his wife of Warren County to John Thomas of same, for 50 pounds, 125 acres on Middle Creek. Witnesses: Gideon George, Richard Carter.

Page 479 – Wyatt Bonner to Thomas Fontaine. Deed dated January 2, 1798, conveying 200 acres granted to Mary, Aley and Darling McDonald in Wilkes County at the time of survey in 1784. Witnesses: Jones Bonner, Z. Franklin.

Page 480 – Jeffrey Barksdale and wife Phoebe, of Hancock County, to James George of Warren County. Deed dated February 5, 1799, conveying 100 acres on Middle Creek surveyed by James McFarland in 1772. Witnesses: Gideon George, Joseph Brantley.

Page 481-482 – March 30, 1798, Thomas Young of City of Savannah, Gentleman, to Henry Hardin of Warren County, planter, for $1500, land granted to said Thomas Young, October 4, 1774, 1000 acres, Wrightsborough Township, Parish of St. Paul, by old Indian line and path, Francis Green, and John Dover. Witnesses: Matthew McAllister, Mayor of Savannah, Thomas Young Jr.

Page 482-483 – January 27, 1787, Sarah Taylor of Wilkes County to James Bishop of same, for 5 shillings, land on Middle Creek adjoining William Anderson, now Miller's land, 100 acres granted March 3, 1784.

Page 484 – James Bishop to Joseph Breed, both of Wilkes County. Deed dated July 10, 1793, conveying 100 acres on Middle Creek being the south half of a grant of land made to Sarah Taylor in 1784, adjoining said Sarah Taylor and William Anderson. Witnesses: E. Pruitt, L. Pruitt J.P.

Page 484 – Francis Doyle and Dennis, merchants of Savannah, to Jacob Bull. Deed dated May 9, 1803, for 250 acres in old St. Paul's Parish, now Warren County, adjoining Isaac and John Dennis and Ralph Kilgore and on Little River. Witnesses: Robert Fisher, John S. Zachary, Willie Jones.

Page 485 – Joseph Beasley and wife Mary, to Joseph Breed. Deed dated October 25, 1795, for 100 acres on a branch of Childress' Creek, being part of 675 acres granted grantor. Witnesses: Joshua Miller, Thomas Weekley.

Page 486 – William Cocks and wife Hannah, to Dial Pearney, all of Wilkes County. Deed dated October 24, 1793, for 200 acres on west side of Rocky Comfort Creek adjoining Jones Persons; two acres reserved "adjoining the mill." Witnesses: Daniel Cocks, Joseph Davidson.

Page 487-488 – June 14, 1798, Dial Peavey of Warren County to John Parham of same, for $450, land on west side of Rocky Comfort adjoining Bohannon, Christopher Bustin, 130 acres. Witnesses: T. Persons, Shadrach Fellin.

Page 488 – Christopher Bustin to John Parham. Deed dated November 7, 1798, for 118 acres on Rocky Comfort Creek. Witnesses: John Matthews, Ambrose Hadley and R. B. Hatcher J.P.

Page 488-489 – December 25, 1798, Joseph Millar of State of South Carolina, Vinton County, to Henry Peebles of Warren County for $20, land on Middle Creek adjoining Augusta Road, Frederick Dennis, 5 acres. Witnesses: Frederick Daniel, Thomas Ford.

Page 489-490 – October 10, 1791, Benjamin Jenkins of Washington County to Arthur Jenkins of same, for 100 pounds, land on Ogeechee River, 200 acres, part of 340 granted to John Ledbetter, April 19, and conveyed to Isaac Ledbetter, May 13, 1790. Witnesses: Isaac Hill, Henry Gardner, James Stubbs J.P.

Page 490-491 – July 1, 1797, Arthur Jenkins of Warren County to Benjamin Upton of same for $430, land on Ogeechee River, Littleton Chambless, Glascok's line, part of 340 acres granted to John Ledbetter. Witnesses: Richard Whitehead, William Jenkins.

Page 492 – George Dykes to Benjamin Upton, both of Warren County. Deed dated November 20, 1794, for 200 acres on Rocky Comfort Creek adjoining Mrs. Johnson and William Bush, having been granted to Robert Wilkins in 1788. Witnesses: Susannah Hammonill and John Hammonill J.P.

Page 492-493 – January 5, 1793, George Upton of Columbia County to Benjamin Upton of Wilkes County for 100 pounds, land on Rocky Comfort in Burke and Columbia, originally granted to Richard Barrow, conveyed to John Grieson, sold by John Dennis, Sheriff to George Upton, 1785, 320 acres. Witnesses: George Walker, Seaborn Jones.

Page 494 – Robert Abercrombie, to Charles Abercrombie. Receipt dated March 3, 1794, for a bond (or promise to pay) in his favor given by William and Joseph Dupins and George Nichols for his proportionate part of lands "in the Kentucky country" mentioned in an award dated December 11, 1789, made and signed by John Mitchell, Henry Graybill, Matthew Rabun, Andrew Baxter,

Samuel Alexander, Andrew Burns, Thomas Harris, William Thedford and Jeremiah Bonner. Witnesses: Samuel and John Saxon.

Page 494-495 – January 23, 1798, Edmond Walsh of Hancock County to Joel McLendon for $150, on Rocky Branch of Ogeechee, adjoining Stephen Bishop, Abraham Helton, Heath, 100 acres, part of a tract of 200 laid off that Joseph Richardson formerly lived on. Witnesses: Thomas Martin, Samuel McGeehee.

Page 495-496 – August 6, 1798, David Felps of Hancock County and Falby Felps his wife to William Dismukes of same for $430, 160 acres on Ogeechee adjoining William and Stephen Lawrence, Esther Jeffreys, Kings, and Perrys, originally granted to David Felps, recorded in Book ZZZZ, folio 288. Witnesses: Sarah Hill, John Wilson J.P.

Page 497 – March 10, 1795, Britton McCullers of Burke County to John Nunn of Warren County, Britton and Patty his wife for 50 pounds, land surveyed for Britton McCullers, December 9, 1789, Book ZZZ, folio 262. Witnesses: Charnick Tharp, Aaron Benton.

Page 498-499 – April 2, 1797, Benjamin A. Hamp of Warren County to William Bird of same for $3000, 100 acres on Ogeechee River, granted to Benjamin Few, January 20, 1786, conveyed to Bird and Hamp, November 13, 1794, one other tract 200 acres, granted to Isaac Dennis, April 26, 1787, one other acre conveyed by Howell Fetherstone and Permela his wife, to Bird and Hamp, December 4, 1794. Witnesses: William Stith, William Bird.

Page 499-500 – April 29, 1797, Peter Mahone of Hancock County to Stephen Marshall of Warren County for $260, land on Rocky Comfort, 200 acres adjoining Hill's. Witnesses: D. Perryman, Andrew King J.P.

Page 500 – David Cocks to Henry Hadley, both of Warren County. Deed dated March 21, 1799, for $195, 100 acres on Whetstone Creek. Witnesses: T. Persons, Shadrack Fluwellin, Elisha Hurt J.P.

Page 501 – January 20, 1799, Solomon Newsom Sr. to Sampson Ivy for $387, 129 acres adjoining McKinnie, Solomon Newsom and Elizabeth his wife. Witnesses: H. Tharp J.P., Benjamin Bruton J.P.

Page 501-502 – May 20, 1797, Jacob Farr to John Farr both of Warren County for $10, 100 acres, part of a 200 grant to Jacob Farr, March 24, 1797, adjoining William Duckworth, E. Leonard, N. Thompson and James Smith. Witnesses: Salley Hodo, Peter Hodo J.P.

Page 502-503 – February 7, 1799, John Farr to Nathaniel Thomson, for $200, land conveyed above. Witnesses: Dorcas Chandler, John Bayn J.P

Page 503 – George Cooper and wife Elizabeth to Benjamin Cooper, all of Warren County. Deed dated May 3, 1797, for 75 acres on Long Creek, being part of a grant to said grantor. Witnesses: Thomas Vining and M. Hubert J.P.

Page 503-504 – May 23, 1797, George Cooper of Warren County to Benjamin Cooper of same for $200, George Cooper and Elizabeth his wife, 75 acres on Long Creek. Witnesses: Thomas Vining, M. Hubert J.P.

Page 504-505 – November 19, 1796, M. Jeremiah Matthews of Warren County to Jesse Matthews for 200 Spanish milled dollars, land adjoining Rutherford, 130 acres, part of a grant to James Cockrum 1786. Witnesses: Elisha Wright, H. Hill.

Page 505 – Samuel Creswell to William Poe, both of Wilkes County. Deed dated August 6, 1788, for 375 acres in Wilkes County, on a branch of Hart's Creek on the Richmond County line, adjoining land granted Aaron Cinquefield and Solomon Barfield. Witnesses: Joseph Cook, M. Williamson J.P.

Page 506 – January 12, 1799, Charles McDonald of Hancock County to Mathew McCrary of Warren County for $220, 195 acres on Rocky Comfort, granted to said McDonald in 1786. Witnesses: Joseph Howard, Isaac Hearn.

Page 507 – I, Seaborn Jones, of City of Augusta, attorney at law, relinquish all claim to land sold by Charles McDonald, January 14, 1799. Witnesses: John Powell, W. Stith J.P.

Page 507-508 – April 23, 1798, Nathan Fowler and Nancy his wife to Matthew McCrary on Ogeechee, 19 ½ acres granted to Nathan Fowler, March 7, 1797. Witnesses: Willis Rowland, Zephaniah Fowler.

Page 508 – Martha Castleberry, Peter and Claiborne, to Matthew McCrary, all of Warren County. Deed dated February 20, 1799, conveying 100 acres on Long Creek, granted to the said Martha in 1791. Witnesses: Arthur Jenkins, Collinson Waters.

Page 509-510 – August 11, 1798, Andrew King of Warren County to Stephen Marshall of same for $450, land on Rocky Comfort, 39 acres. Witnesses: John Matthews, Elisha Hurt J.P.

Page 510-511 – Wilkins Smith of Edgefield County, South Carolina to Robert Moore of Warren County for $70, 50 acres on Little River, Mulkey's land. Witnesses: William Stark, John Dozer, Leonard Dozer.

Page 512 – Joseph Carson of Wilkes County to William Hill of Warren County. Deed dated February 23, 1799, for 100 acres on Middle Creek. Witnesses: John Tindall, Sallie Morrow and Ewing Morrow J.P.

Page 512 – June 26, 1797, Edmond Walsh to Cornelius O'Keefe of Carruk on Suir and Kingdom Tulon, for love and affection of said Edmond doth bear to his sister, Mary Walsh, alias O'Keefe, wife of said Cornelius, 100 acres on Rocky Branch of Ogeechee. Witnesses: William Kinchen, William Felps.

Page 513-514 – January 21, 1794, Garland Morgan and Delila his wife and Jean Morgan, Mary Morgan and Sarah Morgan to John Kelly for 100 pounds, 300 acres on Ogeechee River, granted 1787. Witnesses: Lewis Brady, James Youngblood.

Page 514 – William Bush and wife Mourning, of Wilkes County to Joel Tapley of Richmond County. Deed dated May 10, 1790, conveying 200 acres on east side of Beachtree Creek in Richmond County as per original grant issued in 1788. Witnesses: Joseph Hemphill and Evan Tapley.

Page 516-517 – October 21, 1798, Job Springer and Lydia his wife, administrator and administratrix of estate of James May, deceased, to Edmond Fears, 487 ½ acres in Franklin County granted to John Jarrett, conveyed to William Clark, then to Nicholas Bower. Witnesses: H. G. Caldwell, Joseph Wright.

Page 517-518 – April 25, 1790, Peleg Rogers of Wilkes County to John Mannon of same, for 50 pounds, 100 acres on Little Brier Creek, bounded by Walter Jackson. Witnesses: Benjamin Jackson, Isaac Newton.

Page 518-519 – April 25, 1790, Peleg Rogers to John Mannon for 50 pounds, 100 acres on Little Brier Creek, half of a 200 acre grant to John Mannon, February 22, 1786, adjoining Walter Jackson. Witnesses: Benjamin Jackson, Isaac Newton.

Page 519-520 – April 4, 1794, William Greenwood Jr. of City of Charleston, South Carolina to John Course of Augusta, land 800 acres for 60 pounds, granted to James Jackson, Robert Crooke and Alexander McIntosh, purchased as property of Andrew McLean at Sheriff's sale. Witnesses: John Wilson J.P., John Wilson Jr.

Page 520-521 – August 6, 1794, John Maynor of Warren County to John Mannon for 15 pounds, 100 acres, part of a 200 acre grant on Little Brier Creek. Witnesses: Isaac Hill, Samuel Ridgewell.

Page 521-522 – March 4, 1794, Solomon Lockett of Warren County to Stephen Darden for 100 pounds, land on Williams Creek adjoining Jacob Darden, John Campbell, Robert Carey, Robert Hill. Witnesses: T. Lockett, Jacob Darden.

Page 522-523 – July 15, 1793, Robert Moses Sr. of Wilkes County to Peter Foodwin of Columbia County for 130 pounds, 160 acres adjoining Evan Thomas, Ephraim Pool, John Moses, part of 400 acres granted to said Moses, May 29, 1785. Witnesses: Peter Hodo, Robert Moses Jr.

Page 523-524 – May 17, 1799, Lewis Wright, Sheriff of Warren, to Samuel Yarborough, since Samuel Yarborough did obtain a Judgment for $222 against the administrator of William Lucas, 400 acres on Ogeechee, adjoining John Cox, Bishop, Ryley, Camp and Sanford, granted to William Lucas, November 25, 1797, by public sale, for $135. Witnesses: T. Persons, Samuel Alexander J.P.

Page 524-525 - March 10, 1797, Prosser Horton to Allen Dorman, later Proper Horton for $800, land on Ogeechee, 200 acres. Witnesses: W. Stith Jr., John Hobson.

Page 525-526 – May 3, 1797, James Henderson and Elizabeth his wife to Ichabod Cox for 25 pounds, 100 acres on Ogeechee, Lipman's line, Frazer's line. Witnesses: William Byrom Jr., John Harris, William Byrom J.P.

Page 526 – William Cox and wife Hannah of Washington County, to John Turner of Warren County. Deed dated May 20, 1797, for 250 acres on Whetstone Creek. Witnesses: Turner Persons, Wormsley Rose.

Page 527-528 – May 16, 1799, Levi Pruitt to Thomas Parham for $130, 52 acres on Cannon's Creek, originally granted to Levi Pruitt, December 21, 1791. Witnesses: Lemuel Pruitt J.P., Peter Parham.

Page 528-529 – January 21, 1799, David Runnels of Jackson County to Obadiah Flournoy of Warren County for $200, 60 acres on Ogeechee adjoining Nathan Brewer, Bishop, granted to William Brewer, June, 1789. Witness: Samuel Johnson.

Page 529-530 – February 9, 1799, William Tyler of Columbia to Samuel Johnston for 100 pounds, land on Redlick Creek, granted to Andrew Frazer, February 2, 1785 from said Frazer to Thomas Carr, thence to Tyler. Witnesses: Mary Lovell, William Lovell.

Page 530-531 – February 28, 1799, Samuel Johnson and Elizabeth his wife for $400, to Flemen Hodges, land originally granted to Andrew Frazer, 300 acres. Witness: J. Kennedy.

Page 531 – Samuel Allen Sr., of Greenville County, South Carolina, to Jesse Dykes of Jefferson County, Georgia. Deed dated October 16, 1798, for 200 acres on Joe's Creek in Warren County originally granted 1787 to said Allen, except 15 acres off the lower end deeded to William Allen by said Samuel. Witnesses: Joseph Howell, Norrell Robertson.

Page 532 – Jacob Burkhalter to Hugh Armstrong, both of Warren County. Deed dated May 18, 1799, conveying 100 acres adjoining Thomas Childres. Witnesses: P. Hodo J.P., John Wilson J.P.

Page 532-533 – Warren County, Georgia, John Gaza, Nathan Bouten and Joshua Gaza have received of Benjamin and Jemima Bruton, Administrator of estate of Francis Fontaine Jr., deceased, $75, 10 ½ acres. Witnesses: Sarah Fontaine, Edmond Matthews.

Page 533-534 – July 7, 1797, Nathan Harris of Columbia County to Frederick Little of Burke County for $220, 200 acres originally granted to Elizabeth Cooms adjoining River Ogeechee, Sims. Witnesses: Peter Zualls, John Zualls.

Page 535 – May 14, 1796, Joseph Miller to John J. Wells for 50 pounds, 150 acres on Rocky Comfort, Weatherby, Elisha Wright. Witnesses: L. Pruitt, Thomas Weekley.

Page 535-536 – June 28, 1785, Wilkes County, I William Kelly of aforesaid give unto John Kelly 100 acres whereon John Kelly now lives. Witnesses: Isham Gardner, John Jones. This is to certify that I have relinquished and forever quit claim under my father, William Kelly Sr. all my right, title and interest in the within mentioned tract of 100 acres, August 9, 1786. Witness: John Ledbetter.

Page 537 – January 28, 1797, Richard Whatley of Warren County and Benjamin Few of Columbia County to Richard Carter of Warren County for 50 pounds, 100 acres. Witnesses: Francis Woodward, R. Howard J.P.

Page 538 – March 28, 1797, Moses Going and Agness his wife to Samuel Howell, for 100 pounds, land on Long Creek adjoining

Bankson, Reily, Parish, granted to Edmond Newgent, September 5, 1784. Witnesses: Isaac Banckston, Robert Johnson.

Page 539-540 – January 19, 1799, Jones Persons to Ambrose Hadley for $30, land on Rocky Comfort adjoining William Davies, John Myrick, 12 ½ acres. Witnesses: Elisha Hurt J.P., R. B. Fletcher J.P.

Page 540-541 – November 4, 1798, James Simmons and Mary his wife to Jacks Davenport, all of Warren County for $60, 200 acres adjoining James Hogg. Witnesses: Richard Debenport, William Byrop, William Bunkley.

Page 541 – Reubin Banks of Garrard County, Kentucky, to his friend Samuel Camp of Warren County. Power of Attorney dated September 12, 1799, empowering him to sell his land consisting of 230 acres in Jackson County, Georgia on Rae's Creek. Instrument executed in Garrard County, Kentucky in the presence of William G. Bryant and William Jennings, Benjamin Letcher, Clerk of Court.

Page 542 – Hancock County, Georgia, December 18, 1797, James Golightly to John Caswell of Warren County for $100, adjoining Thomas Jones. Witnesses: Henry Mitchell J.P., William Chandler, John Zachry.

Page 542-543 – November 19, 1791, Alexander Steel of Washington County to Littleton Chambless of Wilkes County for 10 pounds, 50 acres on Ogeechee River, purchased by Steel from John Ledbetter, May 28 last. Witnesses: Duncan McLean, Benjamin Jenkins.

Page 543-544 – September 14, 1795, Richard Story of Warren County to John Hambleton for 15 pounds, 50 acres on north side of Brier Creek, part of 200 acres granted to Needham Smith, January 7, 1787, Book LLL, folio 349. Witness: Vincent A. Tharp.

Page 544-545 – August 19, 1799, John (blank) Sr. to Barton Atchinson, 140 acres adjoining Edward Hill, Thomas Bush, John Hill for $240. Witnesses: Thomas Hill, Edward Hill.

Page 546-547 – John McGaw of Baltimore, Maryland, make John Travis of Warren County, Georgia my attorney. Witnesses: James Bond, John Rockhold, November 13, 1798.

Page 547 – John Bustin, planter, to James Smith, blacksmith, both of Warren County. Deed dated December 8, 1798, for 100 acres on waters of Williams Creek, being part of tract granted to George Murry and sold for taxes to David Hillhouse and by him sold to John Baker and by Baker deeded Jacob Darden and by him to grantor. Witnesses: John Torrence, A. Grier J.P., John Baker J.P.

Page 547-548 – October 23, 1797, John Kelly to John Hillson for 100 pounds, 300 acres, granted May 21, 1787. Witnesses: Thomas Philips, Benjamin Arrandell.

Page 548-549 – July 13, 1799, Solomon Newsom and Elizabeth his wife to Moses McKinney for $600, 500 acres on both sides of Big Brier Creek, granted to said Newsom, July 29, 1795, Book JJJ, folio 92. Witnesses: Benjamin Bruton J.P., William Cason J.P.

Page 549 – Sarah Childree, widow of William Childree, deceased, William Hodgen, William Davidson, and Hannah and Francis Childree, children and heirs of the aforesaid William Childree, deceased, "all of the State of Georgia," to Thomas and William Childree of Warren County "for divers good causes" grantors quit-claim their rights and title and interest in 200 acres on Long Creek in Wilkes now Warren County," being the land surveyed and laid out to William Childree in his lifetime." Deed dated April 11, 1799. Witnesses: Joseph Hodgen, Evans Phelan.

Page 551 – January 20, 1798, Jacob Burkhalter of Warren County to Thomas Childrey for $200, 110 acres adjoining Joseph Davison. Witnesses: Robert Hodgin, P. Hodo, J.P.

Page 551-552 – December 27, 1789, William Glover and Lucy his wife to Robert Thompson for 100 pounds, land on Indian Creek, granted to William Glover, August 26, 1788 adjoining Francis Grubbs, Joel Tapley. Witnesses: John Venson, Allen Glover and John Lawson.

Page 553 – May 14, 1790, Joel Tapley and Mary his wife of Richmond County to Robert Thompson for 60 pounds, land on Deep Creek granted to said Tapley, January 3, 1786. Witnesses: Ezekiel Smith, John Ragland.

Page 554-555 – February 25, 1799, Benjamin Reese and Sarah his wife of Columbia County for $200, 236 acres granted to Sir James Wright and confiscated. Witnesses: Reuben Rees, P. Hodo J.P.

Page 555-556 – September 9, 1799, Hardy Newsom to Jacob Burkhalter, for $300, 100 acres on Big Bryer Creek, granted to Basel Lamar October 11, 1785, adjoining James Carter, Bray Warren, Hardy Newsom. Witnesses: P. Hodo, Hugh Rees.

Page 556-557 – May 29, 1792, Jesse Millar of Wilkes County to James George of Columbia County, land on Middle Creek adjoining James Bishop, 100 acres. Witnesses: Isaiah Tucker, Joshua Millar, Henry Hardin.

Page 557-558 – June 7, 1787, Richard Whatley of Warren County and Benjamin Few of Columbia County, for $200, 92 2/10 acres to James George. Witnesses: Richard Carter, James George Jr.

Page 558-559 – February 2, 1799, John Thomas and Phebe his wife, to James George for 150 silver dollars, land on Middle Creek, 120 acres. Witnesses: L. Gideon George, Joseph George.

Page 559-560 – April 21, 1795, Richard Whatley and Frances his wife to James George for 50 pounds, 125 acres on Middle Creek. Witnesses: Richard Carter, M. Hardin.

Pages 560-561 – November 29, 1799, Judith George, Drury Banks, Lewis Garner, Jesse George, James George, Richard George, Joseph George and Isaiah Tucker of Warren County to Gideon George, 125 acres on Middle Creek for 150 silver dollars. Witnesses: Richard Carter, Lemuel Pruitt Jr.

Page 561-562 – November 29, 1799, Jesse George, Gideon George, Richard George, Joseph George, Drury Banks, Lewis Garner, Judith George & Isaiah Tucker, guardian for John Morris, to James George all of Warren County except for Lewis Garner, who is a resident of Moore County, North Carolina, for $200, 73 acres on Middle Creek, surveyed December 8, 1772, to James Bishop. Witnesses: Richard Carter, Lemuel Pruitt Jr.

Page 562-563 – November 29, 1799, same as above except to Richard George, for $400, 100 acres on Middle Creek.

Page 563-564 – November 26, 1799, Richard Carter of Warren County to Gideon George and Tempe, wife of Richard Carter for $560, 112 acres on Middle Creek. Witnesses: Joseph Rucker, Whitefield Tucker.

Page 564-565 – November 29, 1799, Judith George, Drury Banks, Lewis Garner, James George, Gideon George, Richard George, Joseph George and Isaiah Tucker for $450, to Jesse George, 90 acres on Middle Creek.

Page 565-566 – November 29, 1799, same as above except to Joseph George for 125 silver dollars, 125 acres on Middle Creek.

Page 566-567 – November 20, 1799, Jesse George, James George, Gideon George, Richard George, Joseph George, Drury Banks, Lewis Garner and Isaiah Tucker, to Henry Hardin for $30, land originally granted to James Bishop, 27 acres.

Page 567-568 – November 20, 1799, same as above to Phillip Brantley, for $2000, land granted to James Bishop. Witnesses: William Breed, Lemuel Pruitt J.P.

Page 568-569 – November 22, 1799, William Johnston to Thomas Buckhannon, land on Rocky Comfort, adjoining Torrence, James Davies, Dial Persons, 171 acres for $500. Witnesses: Isaiah Tucker, T. Persons.

Page 569-570 – January 6, 1797, Hugh Rees to Jacob Burkhalter, for 50 pounds, 210 acres, adjoining William Davies, Benjamin Rees, granted to Governor James Wright, deed to John Garrett, Hugh Rees. Witnesses: Benjamin Rees, P. Hodo J.P.

Page 570-571 – March 24, 1799, William Richardson to Michael Peavy, for $500, 121 acres on Long Creek of Ogeechee, survey belonging to William Richardson and Hannah Richardson, orphans of James Richardson, deceased.   Witnesses: J. Peavy, William Mims.

Page 571-572 – February 15, 1798, Wilkins Smith of Columbia County to John Travis, for $500, land granted to William Downs Esq., July 23, 1784, 134 acres. Witnesses: Nancy Dozer, William Dozer.

Page 572 – Jeremiah Duckworth to his son and daughter James and Nellie Carter, both of Warren County.  Deed of Gift for 33 acres whereon grantor now lives; said James and Nellie to have no more of his estate at his death, until the other children are made equal. Dated September 27, 1799. Witnesses: Mary Wilson, John Wilson J.P.

Page 572-573 – September 27, 1799, Jeremiah Duckworth to son and daughter James and Nelly Carter, land on White's Creek, adjoining Thomas Ansley's, Jesse Carter and John Wilson, 133 acres. Witnesses: Jno. Wilson J.P., Mary Wilson.

Page 574 – Samuel Allen of Greenville County, South Carolina, to James Allen of Warren County.  Deed dated October 12, 1799, conveying 50 acres on Joe's Creek in Warren County, being part of 200 acre tract deeded grantor by Samuel and Robert Irwin. Witness: Samuel Powell.

Page 574-575 – October 12, 1798, Samuel Allen of Greenville County, South Carolina, to James Allen of Warren County, Georgia, land on Poe's Creek, 200 acres.  Witnesses: Samuel Powell, Norvell Robertson J.P.

Page 575 – James Allen to James Johnson, both of Warren County. Deed dated October 3, 1799, conveying 68 acres on Jumping Gulley in said county, being part of grant made in 1799 to the grantor. Witnesses: Sally and Norrell Robertson.

Page 575-576 – October 3, 1799, James Allen to James Johnson for $50, 60 acres granted to James Allen February 27, 1799. Witnesses: Sally Robertson, Norvell Robertson J.P.

Page 576 – James Allen, to James Johnson, both of said county. Deed dated October 3, 1799, for 50 acres on Joe's Creek, said county, being part of 200 acres deeded by Samuel and Robert Irwin to Samuel Allen Sr., and by him divided into two parts equal in size, the upper part conveyed to William Allen and the lower half to said James Allen in 1798. Same witnesses as last above.

Page 577 – January 21, 1797, Joseph Hodgin of Warren County to Thomas Childers of same, for 30 pounds, land on northwest side of my Spring Branch to the line of James Bilmore's, 100 acres. Witness: John Wilson J.P.

Page 577-578 – June 1, 1797, Abraham Heath and Winney his wife of Warren County to William Grizzle of same, for $500, 387 acres on Rocky Comfort. Witnesses: Elisha Hurt J.P., Thomas Fontaine.

Page 578-579 – December 8, 1798, John Bustin to James Smith, blacksmith, for $400, land on Williams Creek, John Baker's land, Saxon's land, 100 acres granted to George Murry, sold for taxes to David Hillhouse. Witnesses: John Torrence, A. Grier J.P., John Baker J.P.

Page 579-580 – November 24, 1798, William Johnson to John Ball for $500, land on Rocky Comfort. Witnesses: John Matthews, R. B. Fletcher J.P.

Page 580-581 – July 20, 1799, William Mims to John Ball for $200, 23 acres on Rocky Comfort. Witnesses: John Matthews, R. B. Fletcher J.P.

Page 581 – George Brewer of Hancock County to Joseph White of Warren County. Deed dated June 25, 1798, conveying 100 acres on waters of Williams Creek, being a part of 400 acres granted Benjamin Scott in 1784. Witness: John Baker J.P.

Page 581 – Charles Darnell to Henry Kendall both of Warren County. Deed dated December 16, 1803, for 160 acres on Rocky Comfort Creek, "as the grant made in 1784 will show." Witnesses: Hannah Harrison, J. Perryman.

Page 581-582 – June 21, 1798, George Brewer of Hancock County to Joseph White of Warren County, for $200, land on Williams Creek, adjoining Agn. Few, Burrell Perry, Joseph Hill, originally granted to Benjamin Scott, 400 acres, December 17, 1784. Witnesses: Rolen Brewer, Matthew Brewer.

Page 582-583 – Thomas Lt. Hall of Warren County to daughter Rebeckah Dowdy of Lancaster County, South Carolina, a Negro wench Phillis, a boy named Cezr, boy, girl, and others. Witnesses: T. Persons, Abraham Flewellin.

Page 583 – Hugh Armstrong, to Hardy Newsom both of Warren County. Deed dated September 20, 1799, conveying 100 acres in said county adjoining Hugh Rees. Witnesses: Z. Landrum and Hugh Rees.

Page 583 – Richard Carter and wife Tempey, to Gideon George, all of Warren County. Deed dated November 26, 1799, for 112 acres on Middle Creek. Witnesses: Joseph Tucker, Whitefield Tucker.

Page 584 – November 20, 1799, Henry Hardin to John Gibson, for $30, land originally granted to James Bishop on Middle Creek. Witnesses: William Breed, Lemuel Pruitt J.P.

Page 584-585 – November 20, 1799, John Gibson to Phillip Brantley, for $1000, 10 acres on Middle Creek. Witnesses: William Breed, Lemuel Pruitt J.P.

Page 585-586 – February 21, 1793, Robert Flournoy of Green County to John Cobbs of Columbia County, for 1000 pounds, land on Clower's Branch in Wilkes County adjoining Benjamin Simmons, John Wynne, Leonard Fretwell, Robert Wynne, Thomas Pate, Smith, Perkins, Jesse Warren, 250 acres lying around the tract of John Austin, and 400 acres of cleared ground. Witnesses: W. Williamson, Rowd. Stone.

Page 586 – John Cobbs and wife Mary, of Columbia County, to Nathaniel Coke of Richmond County. Deed dated July 6, 1793, conveying 1000 acres in Wilkes County on the waters of the Ogeechee River and Clowers branch, adjoining Benjamin

Simmons, John and Robert Wynne, Thomas Pate, including 250 acres where John Austin now lives and including the house where Robert Fournoy lately lived. Witnesses: Charles F. Randolph and William Longstreet J.P.

Page 586-587 – July 6, 1793, John Cobbs Sr. of Columbia County to Nathaniel Coke of Richmond County, for 500 pounds, land on Ogeechee, 1000 acres. Witnesses: Charles F. Randolph, William Longstreet J.P.

Page 587 – Robert B. Daniel, Agent for L. and Willie Daniel, to Stephen Jones, Bill of Sale dated May 13, 1807, for several slaves. Witnesses: David Neal and George Hargraves.

Page 587-588 – November 20, 1799, Henry Hardin, Sarah his wife to John Gibson for $700, 640 acres on Upton Creek, originally granted to Thomas Young, October 4, 1774.

Page 588-589 – October 3, 1799, John Gibson to Jacob Turknett, for $300, 140 acres adjoining Isaiah Tucker, Churchill Gibson, James McInvale. Witnesses: J. Tucker, Henry Hardin.

Page 589-590 – December 29, 1797, John Rudisell for $2000, to Abner Chapman, bought of Thomas Davis and others by deed, March 10, 1795. Witnesses: David Chapman, A. Grier J.P., Richard Smith.

Page 590-591 – February 4, 1797, Benjamin Few of Columbia County and Richard Whatley of Warren County for $700, to Willis Perry of Warren, land on Middle Creek, granted to Richard Whatley, August 7, 1795. Witnesses: I. Few, James George.

Page 591 – Isaac Blount of Washington County to Moses Grandberry of Warren County. Deed dated January 20, 1799, conveying 300 acres on west side of Rocky Comfort Creek, being part of 900 acre tract granted George Dykes in 1797. Witnesses: George Grandberry and Phillip Dillard J.P.

Page 591-592 – January 26, 1799, Isaac Blount of Washington County to Moses Grandberry, land granted to George Dykes, 900 acres for $50, 300 acres of said grant.     Witnesses: George Grandberry, Philip Dillard, J.P.

Page 592-593 – January 9, 1798, John Myrick Sr. of Warren County to Nathaniel Myrick for $300, 72 ½ acres.  Witnesses: Septimus Weatherby, Owen Myrick.

Page 593 – Lewis Brantley to Nathaniel Myrick, both of Warren County.  Deed dated November 17, 1798, conveying 50 acres on east side of Whetstone Creek, being part of original tract whereon Shadrach F. Ellin now lives.  Witnesses: Elisha Hurt and T. Persons.

Page 594 – December 29, 1797, Moses Grier to Abner Chapman for $50, land on Williams Creek, originally granted to John O'Neal, October 13, 1785, to Moses Grier by deed May 13, 1787, 11 acres. Witnesses: Asa Scott, Aaron Grier.

Page 595-596 – December 28, 1797, Job Springer and Lydia his wife now the wife of said Springer but late the wife of James May, deceased, Joseph Davidson and Winney, one of the heirs of May deceased, and Darcus Masse and Lydia May, heirs of said James May, to Jacob Burkhalter for $300, land on Briar Creek. Witnesses: Richard Hutchinson, R. P. Hodo J.P.

Page 596 – William Depuis and Joseph, and George Nichols of Warren County, to Robert Abercrombie of Warren County.  Power of Attorney dated July 17, 1794, to recover bond for lands in Kentucky from Charles Abercrombie of Hancock County. Witnesses: Robert Jenkins, Simeon Vanwinkle.

Page 596 – Enoch Ward Ellington of Warren County to John McKinzie "now residing in said county." Deed dated April 17, 1802, for 200 acres on Hart's and Joe's Creeks.  Witnesses: Norvell Robertson, John Hatcher J.P.

Page 596-597 – September 17, 1798, Byrd Pruitt to Levi Pruitt for 5 shillings, land on Rocky Comfort, part of a tract where Byrd Pruitt now lives. Witnesses: George Hargraves, J. B. Hardin.

Page 597-598 – April 1, 1798, John Myrick Sr. to Owen Myrick, son of said John, for $300, 377 acres on Rocky Comfort. Witnesses: Nathaniel Myrick, William Finch.

Page 598-599 – January 21, 1800, Willis Pevey to Richard Carter for 100 silver dollars, land on Middle Creek adjoining Joseph Breed, 200 acres. Witnesses: Gideon George, Hugh Armstrong.

Page 599-600 – December 3, 1798, Levi Pruitt and Elizabeth his wife to Isaiah Tucker for $1350, 2 tracts on Middle Creek, adjoining Wight, Anderson, originally granted to Absolam Islands, 260 acres. Witnesses: John Gibson, Henry Hill, Richard B. Fletcher J.P.

Page 601-602 – July 25, 1797, John Gibson to Isaiah Tucker, marriage contract between said Tucker and my beloved daughter, Salley Gibson, now Salley Tucker, land on Middle Creek, adjoining James McInvale, Amos Pearson, Thees Howard, Churchill Gibson, 161 acres. Witnesses: Barey Barrett, Whitefield Tucker.

Page 602 – William Davidson to Peter Parham, both of Warren County. Deed dated December 28, 1799, for 115 acres adjoining Nathaniel Smith "lying on the old line path." Witness: Martin Hayes.

Page 602-603 – December 28, 1799, William Davidson to Peter Parham for $260, adjoining Nathaniel Smith, 115 acres. Witnesses: Phelan, Martin Hayes.

Page 603 – Robert Abercrombie, to Warren Andrews, both of Warren County. Deed dated August 31, 1797, conveying 227 acres in said county being a part of two tracts granted Benjamin and Ignatius Few. Witnesses: Joseph McGinty, M. Hubert J.P.

Page 603-604 – August 31, 1797, Robert Abercrombie to Warren Andrews for $480, 227 acres, Ryal's Branch. Witnesses: Joseph McGinty, M. Hubert J.P.

Page 604-605 – January 2, 1800, William Noble to Warren Andrews, for $1000, land on Ryal's Branch of Ogeechee River,

200 acres, part of a tract granted to William Noble, January 3, 1785. Witnesses: Robert Abercrombie, W. C. Abercrombie.

Page 605-606 – October 21, 1793, Moses Going of Wilkes County to Warren Andrews, for 100 pounds, 100 acres, part of 780 granted to Ignatius Few, 1791. Witnesses: Robert Abercrombie, John Oliver.

Page 606 – November 14, 1796, Nathan Stubbs of Columbia County to Wyatt Bonner for $107, for 100 acres granted to Nathan Stubbs. Witnesses: Z. Franklin, Jno. Williams.

Page 608 – February 11, 1800, Michael Cody and Mary his wife, to John Freeman for $500, 300 acres granted to James McCormick, 1795, Book PPPP, folio 747, adjoining Isaiah Ball, Smith, Hugh Rees. Witnesses: Moses Neal, Peter Hodo.

Page 608 – Henry Cox and Mary and Alcy, and Darling McDaniel, of Columbia County, to Wyatt Bonner. Deed dated August 10, 1791, conveying 200 acres in Wilkes County, granted to said Alcy, Mary and Darling McDaniel in 1784. Witnesses: John Oliver, James Wheeler.

Page 608 – Michael Cody and wife Mary, to John Freeman, all of Warren County. Deed dated February 11, 1800, for 300 acres adjoining Isaac Ball, Hugh Rees; and granted in 1795 to James McCormick. Witnesses: Moses Neal, Peter Hodo J.P.

Page 608 – Arthur David, farmer, to Peregrine Young, blacksmith, both of Warren County. Deed dated June 8, 1805, for 100 acres on Williams Creek. Witnesses: Timothy Matthews, Solomon Lockett.

Page 609-610 – August 10, 1791, Henry Cox and Mary his wife of Columbia County, to Wyatt Bonner for 50 pounds, 200 acres adjoining Wilder, originally granted to Alex McDaniel, Mary McDaniel and Darling McDaniel, September 9, 1784. Witnesses: John Oliver, James Wheeler.

Page 610-611 – May 8, 1799, John Moses to George Clifton for $200, 228 acres on Watson's Mill on Sweet Water adjoining Moses. Witnesses: Joel Neal, Peter Hodo J.P.

Page 611 – Samuel Allen, of Greenville County, South Carolina, to Martin Cox of Warren County, Georgia. Deed dated October 16, 1798, for 200 acres on Joe's Creek adjoining Jesse Dykes and Isham Peacock, originally granted in 1786 to said grantor. Witness: Nancy Powell.

Page 611-612 – October 16, 1798, Samuel Allen of Greenville County, South Carolina to Masten Cox of Warren County, Georgia for $100, 200 acres adjoining Jesse Dykes, Isham Peacock, granted to said Allen, March 31, 1796. Witnesses: Nancy Powell, Norvell Robertson J.P.

Page 612 – William Allen of Buncombe County, North Carolina, to Martin Cox of Warren County, Georgia. Deed dated January 22, 1798, to 115 acres on Joe's Creek, part of which was granted Joseph Irwin 1786, afterwards deeded by Samuel and Robert Irwin, Executors of said Joseph Irwin, to Samuel Allen in 1787. Witnesses: Sally Robertson and Norrell Robertson J.P.

Page 612-613 – January 22, 1798, William Allen of Dunkham County, North Carolina to Martin Cox of Warren County, Georgia for 20 pounds, 5 shillings, 115 acres on Joe's Creek, granted to Samuel Allen, July 12, 1787. Witnesses: Salley Robertson, Norvell Robertson J.P.

Page 613-614 – January 18, 1800, Moses Grier to Abner Chapman for $100, 90 acres on Williams Creek adjoining Aaron Grier, McLaughlin, Hammac, Fleming. Witnesses: A. Grier J.P., Debera Chapman.

Page 615-616 – December 2, 1796, John Perkins of Hancock County to Isham Boman of Warren County for 50 pounds, 100 acres on Rocky Comfort adjoining Nathaniel Williams, Perkins, Aaron Benton, Benjamin Dees, Jonathan Lock. Witnesses: William Gilleland, Robert Boman.

Page 616-617 – December 18, 1799, Benjamin Smith of Warren County to John Smith for $43, 100 acres, part of a 200 acre tract in Wilkes County when surveyed, now Warren County, on Brier Creek. Witnesses: David Wheeler, Isham Wheeler.

Page 617-618 – Ebenezer Starnes for 20 pounds, to Benjamin Smith, land on north side of Brier Creek adjoining William Wammack, 200 acres, November 20, 1787. Witnesses: William Wammack, B. McCullers.

Page 619 – August 19, 1799, James W. Green of Hancock County to Ambrose Hadley of Warren County for $280, land on south side of Rocky Comfort, 112 acres adjoining John Ball, Valentine Cromley, John Davis. Witnesses: John Neves, Francis Stanback.

Page 620 – John Ball to John Matthews, both of Warren County. Deed dated March 15, 1800, to 228 acres on north side of Rocky Comfort Creek. Witnesses: F. Matthews, H. Candler J.P.

Page 620-621 – November 3, 1798, William Newman of Warren County to Jones Persons, for $100, land on Rocky Comfort adjoining Rutherford, 100 acres. Witnesses: T. Persons, William Gusling.

Page 621 – Justices of Inferior Court, Warren County, viz., Arthur Fort, John Lawson, Levi Pruitt, Samuel Alexander and William Stith, Esquires, to Solomon Statler, Turner Persons, Shadrack F. Ellin and Amos Persons. Deed dated August 12, 1799, for town lots 2 and 3 in the town of Warrenton, on Union Street. Witnesses: Septimus Weatherly and Henry Hardin J.P.

Page 623 – Solomon Barfield of Hancock County to John Rudisell of Warren County. Deed dated August 24, 1798, conveying the remaining part of 375 acres granted in 1785 to Samuel Criswell and grantor Barfield. Witnesses: A. Scott, Duncan McCowan.

Page 624 – John Davis to Nicholas Williams, both of Warren County. Deed dated October 12, 1797, for 76 acres on Rocky Comfort Creek, granted grantor in 1796. Witnesses: John Matthews, Abraham Roe.

Page 625 – June 20, 1799, William Mims and Neoma his wife to Nicholas Williams for $500, 100 acres on Rocky Comfort. Witnesses: John Matthews, Solomon Slatter.

Page 626-627 – December 23, 1799, Benjamin Smith to William McCowles if Richmond County for $257, 200 acres originally in Wilkes County granted January 25, 1787. Witnesses: James Roquemore, Joseph White.

Page 627-628 – Robert Christmas of Greene County, to Simon Salter of Richmond County. Deed dated September 25, 1786, for 200 acres on Hart's Creek in Wilkes County. Witnesses: Lewis Jones, Charles Linn.

Page 629-630 – September 25, 1786, Robert Christmas to Simon Salter for 5 shillings, land on Hart's Creek, granted 1786, adjoining Askinus' land. Witnesses: Lew Jones, Charles Linn.

Page 630 – Joseph Evans of Columbia County to William Berry of Warren County. Deed dated February 13, 1805, for 250 acres in Warren County granted John Howard in 1770. Witnesses: William B. Allison and Andrew B. Stephens.

Page 630-631 – October 3, 1786, Simon Salter to John Pinkston for 100 pounds a year's lease, land on Hart's Creek. Witnesses: Lew Jones, Charles Linn.

Page 631-632 – December 12, 1798, John Pinkston of Washington County to Josias Randall for $400, 200 acres in Warren County. Witnesses: Josias Wright, Archibald Smith.

Page 632-633 – March 7,1799, Lewis Wright, sheriff of Warren County to Moses Going, whereas Henry Candler and Moses Going each obtained a judgment in Inferior Court against William Sanders, 352 acres, the greater part of a grant to Ignatius Few, June 18, 1793, adjoining Wooten, Williams, Alexander. Witnesses: Anderson Berry, John McMurrain.

Page 634-635 – May 11, 1799, Haddon Parham and Joel Heath to Josias Wright, for $300, land adjoining Bowman, Christmas, Andrew Kingnow in hands of Josias Wright. Witnesses: Rayston Heath, Richard B. Fletcher J.P.

Page 635 – May 27, 1797, John Moutrey to Burrell Broom for 300 silver dollars, 200 acres adjoining Kings, Bohannons, Marshalls, John Moutrar. Witnesses: Ambrose Edmondson, John Myrick.

Page 636 – James Davies to John Ball, both of Warren County. Deed dated April 7, 1800, for 100 acres on Rocky Comfort Creek originally surveyed for the widow Perret, adjoining the widow Mims, Stephen Wright and John Torrence. Witnesses: Wood Moreland, David Broom.

# DEED BOOK B

(Transcribed from the original books F and G.)

Page 2 – Francis Doyle and Bennis, merchants of Savannah, to William Anglin of Warren County. Deed dated March 8, 1797 for 100 acres in former St. Paul's Parish on Williams Creek adjoining Absalom Jackson at time of survey. Witnesses: Francis Mallory, John Cunningham and William Jones.

Page 7 – William Franklin and wife Mary of Warren County, to William Cowles of Columbia County. Deed dated April 25, 1801, for 135 acres in Warren County, adjoining Alex Smith. Witnesses: William White Sr., George Hendon J.P.

Page 7 – John Watson of Columbia County to Thomas Childress of Warren. Deed dated May 16, 1801, for 25 acres on White's Creek, being part of 100 acres granted to Jacob Watson. Witnesses: Edward Stills, John Wilson.

Page 8 – George Granberry of Jefferson County to Reubin Barrow of Warren County. Deed dated September 5, 1798, for 100 acres on Joe's Creek and Rocky Comfort Creek. Witnesses: Benjamin Warner and Moses Granberry.

Page 12 – James Boon of Warren County, to Prior Gardner now of Halifax County, North Carolina. Deed dated October 24, 1796, for lands on Long Creek in Warren County, originally granted James Thomas in 1785 or 1787. Witnesses: T. Persons, Wormsley Rose.

Page 13 – Moses Going and wife Agnes to Prior Gardner. Deed dated June 23, 1797 for 92 acres on Long Creek. Witnesses: Reubin Winfrey, Samuel Harvell.

Page 14 – Moses Going and wife Agnes to Samuel Alexander all of Warren County. Deed dated October 16, 1800, for 352 acres lying partly in Wilkes and part in Warren County on Ogeechee River. Witnesses: M. Alexander, J. Bankston.

Page 17 – William Howard to Jacob Tomlin, both of Warren County. Deed dated October 25, 1798, for 100 acres on the road from Warren Courthouse to Augusta. Witnesses: James Tomlin and Benjamin Howard.

Page 18 – David Castleberry of Hancock County, to Edward Castleberry of Warren County. Deed dated December 27, 1799, for 112 acres on Ogeechee River granted to Hill Barnes in 1787. Witnesses: Joseph Howell, Calingston Waters.

Page 18 – Jacob Tomlin to Michael Flinn both of Warren County. Deed dated January 29, 1799, conveying 100 acres adjoining Samuel Neal and John Moses Jr., on the road from Warren Courthouse to Augusta. Witnesses: James Tomlin and James McCormick J.P.

Page 19 – Etheldred Thomas to Peter Newsom both of Warren County. Deed dated February 9, 1801, for 110 acres on south sides of Watery Branch. Witnesses: L. Pruitt and William Byrom.

Page 23 – Henry Cooper to Arthur Jenkins. Deed dated November 25, 1800, for 132 acres on Long Creek granted to Edward Nugent in 1794. Witnesses: S. Camp and Richard Terrell.

Page 23 – Deposition or affidavit of Nathan Bridges, dated December 1, 1801, to the effect that he bit off a part of the left ear of Benjamin Gates on February 21st, last, in a dispute over a case pending between James Durham and Edward Murphy. Sworn to before Norvell Robertson J.P.

Page 26 – David Castleberry of Jackson County, to Mark Littleton of Warren County. Deed dated December 23, 1797, for land in Warren County adjoining Richard Castleberry. Witnesses: Jacob Littleton and Alexander Mason J.P.

Page 31 – Peter Hodo Esq., to Drury McCullers both of Warren County. Deed dated January 6, 1801, for 100 acres the home place of grantor. Deed signed: Peter Hodo Jr. Witnesses: Richard Hodo, James McCormick, James Carter.

Page 37 – David Golding to Sterling Jones both of Warren County. Deed dated May 8, 1801, for land on Golding's Creek. Witnesses: Samuel Beall, John Matthews.

Page 39 – Peter Hodo and wife Sallie, to Drury McCullers, all of Warren County. Deed dated June 25, 1801, for 200 acres being part of a 1000 acre grant to grantor. Witnesses: James Coda and William Coram.

Page 39 – Polly Hokett, a single woman, to Sampson Wilder, both of Warren County. Deed dated December 23, 1800, for 50 acres on Hart's Creek bounded on three sides by grantee, and being part of 200 acre grant to Martha Burleston, and being a part of the land where said Martha now lives. Witnesses: D. McDaniel, A. Persons.

Page 39 – John Torrence, planter, to Ansel Parrish, farmer, both of Warren County. Deed dated April 2, 1801, for 104 acres on Long Creek where the public road from Smith's Mills on Ogeechee River to Augusta crosses said creek; same having been granted Whelias McCullers, deceased. Witnesses: Joel Neal, James McCormick J.P.

Page 40 – Buckner Darden of Pickering County, Mississippi Territory, to Henry Peeples of Warren County. Deed dated June 7, 1801 for land in Warren County on Middle Creek. Witnesses: Wormsley Rose, Sterling Jones.

Page 41 – Solomon Barfield of Washington County, deed of gift dated February 14, 1792, to his son-in-law Sampson Wilder and wife Mary of Wilkes County, conveying land on Hart's Creek in Wilkes County, adjoining said Wilder and Charles Webb. Witness: Levi Pruitt J.P.

Page 46 – John Dunaway Sr. to John Dunaway Jr., both of Warren County. Deed of Sale dated January 1, 1799, for 70 acres on Brier Creek. Witnesses: P. Hodo and George Dunaway.

Page 47 – Septimus Weatherby to Thomas Fontaine, both of Warren. Deed dated December 31, 1801, for 280 acres on Hart's Creek adjoining Josiah Randall and Wormsley Rose. Witnesses: David Cox, J. Matthews J.P.

Page 49 – John Clower to Peter Clower, both of Warren County. Deed dated November 9, 1799, for 200 acres in former Wilkes now Warren County. Witnesses: Jacob Clower and Ransom Howell J.P.

Page 50 – Hammond Wilkerson of Montgomery County to Jones Persons of Warren County. Deed dated December 1, 1801, for 150 acres on south side of Rocky Comfort. Witnesses: T. Persons and A. Persons.

Page 52 – Thomas Cureton of Warren County to Robert Pugh of Wilkes County. Deed dated October 13, 1795, for 353 ½ acres on Beaver Dam and Williams Creeks. Witnesses: Job Pugh and R. Christmas J.P.

Page 54 – Lewis Wright, Sheriff Warren County to Manoah Hubert of said county. Deed dated February 9, 1801, for 191 acres on Long Creek. Witnesses: Benjamin Wells, M. Hubert J.P.

Page 55 – John Torrence, planter, to Hugh Armstrong both of Warren County. Deed dated October 13, 1799, for 309 acres on Middle or Town Creek, lying on the Richmond County line. Witnesses: Thomas Sell, R. Hutchinson, Henry Hardin J.P.

Page 57 – Thomas Childre to James Wilson both of Warren County. Deed dated January 12, 1802, for 25 acres on 'White's Creek. Witnesses: Jesse Carter, John Wilson J.P.

Page 59 – Thomas Childre to Edward Sills both of Warren County. Deed dated January 9, 1800, for land on White's Creek. Same witnesses as last above.

Page 59 – Thomas White of Columbia County to John A. Torrence of Warren. Deed dated October 23, 1799, for tract of land, acreage not stated, lying on Childre's fork of Middle Creek granted grantor in 1785. Witnesses: W. Short and Jesse Butt.

Page 60 – George Clifton to James Gray both of Warren County. Deed dated November 13, 1800, for 440 acres being a part of two surveys on which grantor now lives, and lying on both sides of the road from Warrenton to Watson's Mills, granted Robert Moses in 1785. Witnesses: Thomas Dent and G. W. Cotton.

Page 61 – David Hubert and wife Delphy, of Warren County, to Nathan Jones of Columbia County. Deed dated July 5, 1800, for 100 acres on Rocky Comfort Creek. Witnesses: John Anglin and M. Hubert.

Page 65 – Henry Candler to Henry Waggoner, both of Warren county. Deed dated November 2, 1795, for 126 acres. Witnesses: J. K. Candler, Benjamin Oliver Jr., William Stith J.P.

Page 66 – I. Few to John Dunaway, Power of Attorney dated December 10, 1798, to sell 66 acres to John English.

Page 66 – John Hutson to Jacob Beall. Bill of Sale for slaves dated May 11, 1799. Witnesses: Mary Bond and Jesse Butt.

Page 67 – Isaac Ball, to Harmon Ferryman. Deed dated September 9, 1800, for 200 acres adjoining lands of James Cooper, deceased. Witnesses: S. Flournoy, Jacob Castleberry.

Page 68 – Adam Hardin of Washington County, to William Porter of Warren County. Deed dated March 5, 1802, for 200 acres in former Wilkes now Warren County. Witnesses: Zared Irwin J.P., John Bruton.

Page 69 – Theophilus Howell to Samuel Allen. Deed dated December 25, 1801, for 250 acres on Jumping Gully. Witnesses: Sallie Robertson, Norvell Robertson.

Page 70 – Sarah Golding, Relinquishment of Dower rights or otherwise in 515 acres on Golding's Creek "formerly owned by my deceased husband." Made in favor of Daniel Golden, Reubin Jones and Henry Golding. Witnesses: George Hargraves and John Torrence.

Page 70 – Sarah Golding to her daughter Rebecca Jones. Gift of slave named James, age 6 years, dated July 26, 1799. Witnesses: Elisha Wright, Clark Blandford.

Page 71 – Richard Hutchinson, David Golding and Richard Green, to Reubin Jones, all of Warren County. Deed dated July 26, 1799, conveying all their interest and rights in 500 acres on Golding's

Creek granted the heirs of Henry Golding in 1791. Witnesses: Elisha Wright and Clark Blandford.

Page 72 – Thomas Wooten Esq., to James McCormick both of Wilkes County. Deed dated May 20, 1788, for 280 acres in Wilkes, now Warren, granted grantor in 1785. Witnesses: Nathaniel Coats and David Neal.

Page 73 – George Upton to James McCormick both of Warren County. Deed dated August 11, 1794, conveying 150 acres on Rocky Comfort Creek, located in Richmond County, when surveyed in 1787, now in Warren. Witnesses: Hugh Reese, David Neal.

Page 74 – Sarah Hill to Asa Tindall, both of Warren County. Deed dated February 7, 1799, for 30 acres where grantor lives. Witnesses: John Hill, Stephen Lawrence.

Page 75 – John Hobson, Sheriff Warren County, to Lewis Wright of Warren. Sheriff's Deed dated October 17, 1801, conveying 191 acres on Long Creek, sold as property of William Reeley. Witnesses: Henry Hardin, E. Thomas.

Page 76 – Sampson Wilder to John Rudicille both of Warren County. Deed dated February 1, 1800, for 300 acres on Hart's Creek. Witnesses: Robert Perryman and Henry Hardin J.P.

Page 78 – John Clark, Sheriff of Wilkes County, to Samuel Northington. Tax Deed dated September 2, 1793, for 600 acres sold for taxes as property of John Freeman. Witness: H. Mounger J.P.

Page 79 – Sarah Golding to her son, Henry Golding. Gift of slave named Phoeby age about 25 years, dated July 26, 1799. Witnesses: Elisha Wright, Clark Blandford.

Page 79 – Etheldred Thomas and wife Nancy to Neville Ward all of Warren County. Deed dated February 6, 1798, for 500 acres on Rocky Comfort, granted to grantor. Witness: John Lowe.

Page 80 – Richard Beasley to Robert Perryman. Deed dated February 17, 1799, for fifty acres of land.

Page 80 – Nathan Fowler of Wilkes County, planter, to Adam Jones and Edmond Nugent, "elders and managers for a Baptist Church now embodied on or near Long Creek." Deed dated October 1, 1788, for two acres "where the meeting house now stands." Witnesses: David Neal, James McCormick J.P. Recorded March 22, 1802.

Page 83 – Ichabod Cox to Cary Cox, both of Warren County. Deed dated March 17, 1801, for 25 acres on north fork of Williams Creek called Beaverdam. Witnesses: John Travis, John Smith.

Page 83 – Harris Branham to Sampson Wilder. Deed dated January 2, 1793, for land on Hart's Creek in Wilkes County, being part of a grant made 1788 to the heirs of Patty Burleston. Witnesses: Mountain Hill and Elisha Pruitt.

Page 85 – John Hobson to Henry Harris. Deed dated February 12, 1801, for 200 acres on Ogeechee River granted 1790 to Joseph Raeley. Witnesses: Andrew King, R. B. Fletcher.

Page 86 – Amos Wright Sr., to Sterling Jones both of Warren County. Deed dated December 14, 1801, for 308 acres. Witness: Elisha Wright.

Page 87 – William Wilder to Sampson Wilder both of Warren County. Deed dated November 15, 1798, for 58 acres on Hart's Creek adjoining grantee's land and lands of Giles Dewberry. Witnesses: Q. Tucker and Whitefield Tucker.

Page 87 – John Caswell to Simon Harrell both of Warren County. Deed dated August 13, 1800, for 100 acres adjoining Thomas Jones. Witnesses: Samuel and Gray Harrell.

Page 93 – William Hamilton and Theophilus Hargraves of Charles County, Maryland, and George Hargraves of Warren County, Georgia, to Hugh Reese. Bill of Sale for slaves, dated February 11, 1802. Witnesses: P. Sturdivant and Richard Hill.

Page 95 – Absolem Beardon, and wife Hannah, to John McCormick, planter, all of Wilkes County. Deed dated September 9, 1790, for 200 acres on Rocky Comfort Creek surveyed for grantor November 15, 1785. Witnesses: Bird Pruitt, David Neal, James McCormick J.P.

Page 96 – James George and wife Polly to James Gerard. Deed dated July 11, 1801, for 120 acres on Middle Creek. Witnesses: Richard and Nathaniel Hutchinson.

Page 100 – Richard Beasley, planter, to Thomas Maddux. Deed dated October 14, 1799, for 100 acres originally granted to George Newman, May 24, 1785. Witnesses: David Neal and James McCormick, J.P.

Page 100 – Joseph Williamson to Thomas Maddox both of Warren County. Deed dated November 2, 1801, for 172 acres granted 1801 to grantor. Witness: James Neal.

Page 102 – Lewis Wright to Richard Heath. Deed dated June 1, 1802, for 200 acres on Rocky Comfort granted 1796 to William Boman. Witness: Timothy Matthews J.P.

Page 103 – Martin Hardin to Mark Hardin, both of Warren County. Deed dated October 18, 1796, for 400 acres on Rocky Comfort Creek granted Nicholas Long. Witnesses: Randolph Revill and James Hardin.

Page 105 –Thomas Hawthorn to John Zachary, both of Warren County. Deed dated June, 1794, on 250 acres of land on Ogeechee River adjoining said Zachary. Witnesses: Henry Mitchell, Thomas Jones.

Page 107 – Isaac Burson, to Jonathan Burson. Deed dated January 11, 1802, for 100 acres on Brushy form of Brier Creek. Witnesses: Isaac Burson, P. Hodo J.P.

Page 108 – Sterling Gardner to Martin Hardin both of Warren County. Deed dated April 19, 1802, for lot #1 on Union Street, in the town of Warrenton. Witness: Lewis Wright.

Page 113 – Asa Cox and wife Mariah, to John Gilpin, all of Warren County. Deed dated May 9, 1801, for grantor's home place land on Williams Creek. Witnesses: Cary Cox and Martha Cox.

Page 113 – Joseph George and wife Susannah to Ezekiel Miller, both of Warren County. Deed dated November 21, 1800, for 100 acres on Childre's Creek. Witnesses: Gideon George, Henry Hardin, Jesse Miller.

Page 114 – John Fletcher and wife Martha to Wiley Harris, all of Warren County. Deed dated October 7, 1800, for 100 acres near Benjamin Wells' spring branch and Golden's Creek. Witnesses: Wormsley Rose, Ambrose Edmondson, Sterling Gardner.

Page 116 – Solomon Newsom to Etheldred Thomas. Bill of Sale dated October 18, 1802, for six slaves which he says were transferred by said Thomas to him in 1790 "in a fictitious manner." Witnesses: James McCormick J.P., Jody Newsom J.P.

Page 117 – Isaac Burson, and wife Elizabeth, to Esther Beverly. Deed dated September 14, 1802, for 100 acres originally granted grantor. Witnesses: W. D. Bundley, E. Beall, D. Sturdivant.

Page 117 – Edmund Green to his son William B. Green. Deed of Gift dated September 28, 1802, for all his livestock, household goods, etc. Witness: Bryant Marchant.

Page 118 – Jesse Barfield, to Elisha Hurt, Esq. Deed dated May 16, 1800, for two tracts of land on Hart's Creek being part of a 500 acre tract granted to Solomon Barfield by Governor John Houstoun. Witnesses: H. Grier, R. B. Fletcher J.P.

Page 120 – Stephen Mitchell of Liberty County to Ambrose Holliday of Warren County. Deed dated October 15, 1801, conveying 750 acres in Warren County where the grantor formerly lived and whereon the grantee now lives, and composed of the following tracts: (1) 100 acres granted Richard Crutchfield October 28, 1783; (2) 100 acres granted John Coleman October 11, 1785; (3) 200 acres granted Roger Qualls, surveyed November 4, 1786; (4) 100 acres granted Thomas Yarbrough, surveyed October 27, 1783; (5) 100 acres granted the grantor Mitchell, surveyed for him October 21, 1784; (6) 15 acres surveyed February 15, 1788; (7) 100 acres granted grantor October 21, 1784. Witnesses: Hugh Taylor, Solomon Beckcom. In separate instrument recorded with deed, grantor's wife Mrs. Selah Mitchell, waives all dower rights in said lands; witness to her signature, William Warthen J.P.

Page 120 – David Roberson of Richmond County to John Matthews of Warren County. Deed dated July 3, 1802, for 50 acres on Big Brier Creek being part of a tract granted Absolem Jackson and surveyed for him April 1787. Witnesses: John Smith and Thomas Westberry. Probated by Westberry before H. Cason J.P. October 29, 1802.

Page 120 – Peter Perkins to William White both of Warren County. Bill of Sale for slave girl "Rachel" dated February 2, 1801. Witness: T. Matthews J.P.

Page 122 – Joshua Roe and wife Sarah to William Heath and Thomas Doles, all of Warren County. Deed dated December 31, 1801, for one acre on Long Creek on the Augusta Road. Witnesses: Joseph Deloach, Samuel Yarbrough.

Page 122 – Joshua Roe and wife Sarah, to Thomas Doles, all of Warren County. Deed dated December 31, 1801, for 35 acres on Long Creek, granted Abraham Hilton. Witnesses: Joseph Deloach and Samuel Yarbrough.

Page 123 – Thomas Bohannon and wife Celie to Thomas Doles. Deed dated June 18, 1801, for 107 acres. Witnesses: Samuel Johnston, Archibald Lay.

Page 124 – William Hutchinson and wife Martha, formerly Martha Burkhalter, to Joseph Fickling of South Carolina. Deed dated November 6, 1802, for 189 acres on Golding's Creek. Witness: Sterling Jones.

Page 124 – Francis Beck, to John Rushing. Deed dated February 14, 1801, for 125 acres on Rocky Comfort Creek adjoining Verden. Witnesses: H. Candler, Thomas Friend J.P.

Page 125 – Richard Brooks Fletcher to William Culpepper Sr. Bill of Sale for slave dated July 28, 1794. Witness: Daniel Culpepper.

Page 126 – James Parker to Robert Parker, Joseph White and James Matthews all of Warren County. Deed dated November 24,

1801, for 120 acres granted James Green and Abner Flewellin and by them deeded to grantor. Witnesses: Orren Parker and T. Matthews J.P.

Page 126 – Nathaniel Folsom and wife Esther to Solomon Slatter all of Warren County. Deed dated October 5, 1799, for 100 acres lying on Whetstone Creek. Witnesses: John Matthews, Shadrack F. Ellin.

Page 129 – Joseph May of Washington County, to his daughter, Elizabeth Newsom. Gift instrument dated October 28, 1802, conveying two negro boys now in the possession of her husband Frederick Newsom. Witnesses: Isaac Hunt, Jody Newsom J.P.

Page 129 – Robert Walton and Abraham Jones, Executors of will of William Glascock, deceased, holders of judgment against estate of Adam Hiles, deceased, in the part due the estate of John Beddingfield, deceased, disclaim all "pretensions" to the said judgment in favor of Mary and John Beddingfield, heirs of said John Beddingfield, deceased, and authorize them and their guardians to collect it and retain proceeds. Witnesses: James Morse, C. Louderman.

Page 131 – Collin Wootten and Faitha to John Rhymes, all of Warren County. Deed dated February 16, 1802, for 300 acres on Ogeechee River, being part of grant to Drury Rogers August 31, 1785. Witnesses: Willie Jones, Daniel Morris.

Page 132 – John Hill of Jackson County to John Rhymes of Warren County. Deed dated March 8, 1801, for 250 acres on north side of Ogeechee River granted grantor in 1788. Witnesses: Wootten O'Neal and John Pottle.

Page 133 – Jonathan Hagerty to John Rhymes, both of Warren County. Deed dated January 8, 1802, for 170 acres on Ogeechee River granted Ignatius Few in 1784. Witnesses: John Bush Sr., and John Bush Jr.

Page 134 – Benjamin Cooper to William Cooper. Deed dated January 23, 1804, for 15 acres on Long Creek. Witnesses: James and Robert Fillingim.

Page 135 – John Gibson to Noah Butts. Deed dated November 6, 1801, for 129 acres on Middle Creek. Witnesses: Isaiah Tucker and Hiram Perry.

Page 136 – John Caldwell of Columbia County, to Robert Johnson. Deed dated January 16, 1801, for land, acreage not stated. Witnesses: D. Hubert and Thomas Vining.

Page 136 – Asa Cox and Mariah to John Gilpin, all of Warren County. Deed dated May 9, 1801, for 14 acres. Witnesses: Cary and Martha Cox and John Battle J.P.

Page 137 – John Rushing to Samuel Skelly both of Warren County. Deed dated January 31, 1802, for 125 acres on Rocky Comfort Creek. Witnesses: Ephriam Renfroe, Norvell Robertson J.P., John Hatcher J.P.

Page 138 – Andrew McClary, James and Samuel, of Mecklenburg County, North Carolina, to Elijah Warthen of Washington County, Georgia. Deed dated January 20, 1800, for 150 acres lying on Ogeechee River. Witnesses: Phillip Rawls, Richard Warthen, William Warthen J.P.

Page 139 – Henry Graybill of Hancock County to William Heath of Warren County. Deed dated January 1, 1799, for 100 acres on Long Creek. Witness: T. Dugger.

Page 140 – Solomon Matthews to Robert Parker, both of Warren County. Deed dated January 23, 1802, for 120 acres on Williams Creek. Witnesses: Archelaus Flewellin and John Matthews J.P.

Page 140 – Amos Wright to Reubin Jones both of Warren County. Deed dated November 13, 1802, for 169 acres on Golding's Creek. Witnesses: Jesse Matthews and John Matthews J.P.

Page 142 – John Slatter of Pendleton County, South Carolina, to John Bates of Warren County. Deed dated January 14, 1795, for 422 acres granted John Slatter Sr., same lying on Little River. Witnesses: Wilkins Smith, Abraham Johnston J.P.

Page 144 – John Mims Jr., William Mims Jr., and Matthew Mims, to Wood Moreland of Hancock County. Deed dated November 16,

1802, for 124 acres on Rocky Comfort Creek. Deed executed in Washington County. Witnesses: Ishmael Brook, David Mims.

Page 145 – John Torrence to James Williams both of Warren County. Deed dated June 16, 1801, for 125 acres on Long Creek granted grantor. Witness: Jesse James.

Page 146 – Margaret Green to Jesse Carter both of Warren County. Deed dated November 24, 1802, for 150 acres on White's Creek, being part of grant made 1786 to Jeremiah Duckworth. Witnesses: John Bayn, Jeremiah Burkhalter.

Page 147 – Patrick Shannon of Wilkes County to Daniel Vaughn of Warren County. Deed dated September 19, 1801, for 200 acres granted Ignatius Few January 1785. Witnesses: Thomas Porter, James Vaughn.

Page 148 – Robert Wynne Sr. of Warren County to Daniel Mitchell of Hancock County. Deed dated March 2, 1802, for 93 acres on Lick Creek of Ogeechee River "where I now live except three acres for my spring" and except six acres owned by Thomas Pate. Witnesses: Daniel Zachary and Stephen W. Burnley.

Page 149 – Norvell Robertson to Richard Curry both of Warren County. Deed dated April 16, 1801, for 135 acres on Rocky Comfort being part of 454 acre tract surveyed for grantor February 15, 1799 and granted him September 10, 1800, adjoining grantee's land. Witnesses: John C. Turner and Lucy Turner.

Page 150 – Joseph Harvell to Richard Curry, both of Warren County. Deed dated February 1, 1801, for 300 acres on Joe's Creek, granted grantor in 1790. Witnesses: Norvell Robertson, John Hatcher.

Page 150 – Ignatius Few of Columbia County to Claiborne Castleberry of Warren County. Deed dated November 9, 1800, for land on Long Creek being part of grant made in 1784 to grantor. Witnesses: Collenson Waters, William Rousseau.

Page 151 – Arthur Fort and wife Susannah of Ogeechee, Warren County, to John Hammill, merchant, of Georgetown, Warren

County. Deed dated May 4, 1799, for seven acres on Fort's Creek being a part of grant made in 1785 to said Fort. Witness: Richard Whitehead.

Page 155 – Benjamin Upton and wife Judith of Rocky Comfort, Warren County, to John Hammill of Georgetown, Warren County. Deed dated March 29, 1800, for 12 acres in the town of Georgetown, lying on the Augusta road, said county of Warren. Witnesses: Benjamin Bruton J.P., Norvell Robertson J.P.

Page 157 – Jesse Connell of Hancock County to William Ansley of Warren County. Deed dated February 27, 1801, for 163 acres on Rocky Creek in former Wilkes now Warren County. Witnesses: R. Middleton, Joel Dickinson and R. Flournoy.

Page 158 – Michael Whatley of Greene County to Frederick Daniel of Warren County. Deed dated September 1, 1802, for 48 ½ acres on Middle Creek granted 1788. Deed made to replace lost deed made in 1796 between the parties. Witnesses: William Daniel, John J. Wells, Nathan Culpepper.

Page 159 – Joseph Cook to Benjamin Howard Jr., both of Wilkes County. Mortgage dated June 8, 1788. Witness: Thomas Richardson.

Page 159 – Jacob Turknett to Churchill Gibson both of Warren County. Deed dated November 17, 1802, for lands adjoining grantee and Isaiah Tucker. Witnesses: Isaiah Tucker, Clerk Superior Court and Whitfield Tucker.

Page 161 – Solomon Newsom Sr., of Wilkes County, planter, to Frederick Newsom, Asa Newsom, Jody Newsom and William Newsom Jr., and David Newsom, planters, of same county. Deed dated June 1, 1791, conveying 750 acres in Washington County granted grantor February 2, 1786, and lying on the Oconee River. Consideration L50. Witnesses: James McCormick J.P., Wyche Goodwin J.P.

Page 162 – James Bishop of Hancock County, to Vinson Johnston of Warren County Deed dated February 5, 1801, for 226 ½ acres on Long Creek, granted to Childree and afterwards deeded by the

Childree heirs to said Bishop. Witnesses: Francis Stanback and M. Hubert J.P.

Page 163 – Robert Moore to Jacob Butt, both of Warren County. Deed dated February 24, 1800. Conveys 50 acres granted Thomas Smith, deceased. Witnesses: Jones Kendrick, Robert Benton, Eli Ball.

Page 164 – David McCoy of Wilkes County to Asa Cox of Warren County. Deed dated July 16, 1790, for 14 acres. Witnesses: Thomas Luckett, John Hammock and James Patterson J.P.

Page 165 – Cary Cox and wife Martha to Asa Cox, all of Warren County. Deed dated December 29, 1799, for land on north fork of Williams Creek called Beaverdam, being part of grantor's home place land. Witnesses: Moses Crawford, Ichabod Cox.

Page 165 – John Parham to his son Thomas Parham. Gift of slave dated August 9, 1802. Grantor reserves use of slave for the remainder of his lifetime and that of his wife Elizabeth. Witnesses: Z. Franklin, Hartwell Jones.

Page 166 – Same parties as in last instrument above; same date and witnesses. Deed of Gift and sale (consideration $100) for 334 acres where said John Parham now lives, being part of 600 acre tract granted John Jamieson and sold by the Commissioners of Confiscated Estates as his property, to John Barnett, same lying on the Augusta road. Life estate reserved in grantor and his wife Elizabeth.

Page 167 – Benjamin Bruton and wife Jemima of Montgomery County, Georgia to William Simpler of Warren County. Deed dated March 3, 1803, conveying 514 acres on Rocky Comfort Creek, composed of two or three different tracts. Witnesses: Benjamin Upton and John Smith.

Page 168 – Benjamin Upton and wife Judith of Rocky Comfort, Warren County, to William Bird of the Shoals of the Ogeechee in Warren County. Deed dated October 20, 1801; consideration $600. Conveys one acre adjoining the shoals of the Ogeechee where is located the Bird & Hamp Mills and Iron Works. Witnesses: William Simpler and Matthew Grantham.

Page 170 – Thomas Boman, to John Greeson. Deed dated February 7, 1803, for 127 ½ acres on Hart's Creek. Witnesses: Lemuel Pruitt and Thomas Jones.

Page 170 – William Simpler to Samuel Allen. Deed dated March 3, 1803, conveying 250 acres on Hart's Creek, of which 125 acres was granted to James Blount and by him deeded to Larkin Chivers and by him to grantor; and the other 125 acres granted John Hollenshead and by him deeded to John Embree and by him to John Harrell and by him to John Brooks and by him to grantor. Witnesses: Benjamin Upton, N. Robertson J.P.

Page 172 – Elisha Pruitt to Thomas Boman both of Warren County. Deed dated March 15, 1798, for 127 ½ acres lying on Hart's Creek, 100 acres of which was granted to James Cobbs and balance to grantor. Witnesses: Joel Cloud, Mountain Hill.

Page 173 - John McCormack to Abraham Salls, both of Warren County. Deed dated March 5, 1803, for 400 acres on Deep Creek, granted grantor September 1, 1797. Witnesses: Thomas Edmondson, Charles Stewart.

Page 173 – John Mulkey "of Georgia" to Jacob Bull of Warren County. Deed dated January 24, 1803, for 100 acres on Little River granted Walter Jackson July 3, 1770, and deeded John Mulkey, May 3, 1780. Witnesses: David Mercer, William Berry J.P.

Page 175 – John Williams to John Niday both of Warren County. Deed dated December 31, 1802, for 124 acres on Caison's Creek, being part of the property of John Caison, deceased. Witnesses: Z. Franklin and Amos Johnston.

Page 177 – Abner Flewellen to Timothy Matthews. Deed dated November 10, 1802, for 60 acres on Rocky Comfort Creek. Witnesses: John Matthews, E. Hurt.

Page 177 – Christopher Williams of Wilkes County to Abner Flewellin. Deed dated March 19, 1793, conveying land on west side of Whetstone Creek in Wilkes, now Warren County whereon Miss Mary Few lives, granted to John Mims in 1787. Witnesses: Elisha Hurt and Jeremiah Matthews.

Page 179 – Nathan Marsh and Elizabeth his wife, to John Champion, all of Warren County. Deed dated October 9, 1802, for 350 acres granted Joseph May, May 28, 1788, and by him deeded to John Marsh, and by John Marsh to William Dean who deeded same to grantor. Land lying in former Richmond County, now Warren, on Deep Creek. Witnesses: Daniel Butler, John Gage.

Page 181 – John Saxon to Samuel Fleming both of Warren County. Deed dated February 7, 1801, for 168 acres on Williams Creek. Witnesses: Henry Bonner and Elisha Darden.

Page 183 – Henry Golding to William Bardin Jr. Deed dated February 26, 1803, for 176 acres on Rocky Comfort Creek. Witnesses: Sterling and Rebecca Jones.

Page 186 – Sarah Golding to Richard Green and wife Sarah, all of Warren County. Deed of Gift dated November 5, 1802, for slave. Witnesses: Amos Green, Thomas Sells.

Page 187 – John Wilson to Margaret Green. Deed dated July 12, 1802, 150 acres on White's Creek. Witnesses: Fitz M. Hunt and Mary Hunt.

Page 188 – Thomas Fontaine, Francis F. Risher and James Threewitts to Turner Persons, all of Warren County. Deed dated October 6, 1801, for land on Whetstone Creek. Witnesses: Solomon Slatter, Elisha Hurt.

Page 189 – Wormsley Rose and wife Susanna to Turner Persons, all of Warren County. Deed dated December 26, 1801, for 300 acres on Whetstone Creek granted July 22, 1785. Witnesses: John C. Turner and Lucy Turner.

Page 190 – Abner Fluwellin to James Parker both of Warren County.  Deed dated November 24, 1801, for 123 acres on headwaters of Whetstone Creek. Witness: Robert Parker.

Page 190 – Richard Slaughter to Samuel Newman, both of Warren County.  Deed dated March 20, 1803, for 100 acres on Long Creek, being part of 400 acres granted September 23, 1784, to Ignatius Few. Witnesses: Jones Persons, H. Candler J.I.C.

Page 191 - Claiborne Castleberry of Jackson County to Richard Slaughter of Warren County.  Deed dated September 14, 1801, for land on Long Creek. Witness: Zephariah Fowler.

Page 192 – Abraham Perkins to Timothy Matthews both of Warren County.  Deed dated January 20, 1802, for 94 acres on Williams Creek, being part of tract granted Benjamin Scott December 17, 1784 and by his will devised to Shadrack Kennebrew and by the latter deeded to George Brewer and by him deeded to grantor February 2, 1794. Witnesses: William Butt, William White.

Page 193 – Joseph Watson of Columbia County to Jacob Watson of Warren County.  Deed dated February 10, 1803, for 170 acres lying partly on main fork of Big Brier Creek and partly on the prong of Beaverdam, except one acre at the mouth end of the mill dam. Witnesses: William Smith, Joseph Carter J.P.

Page 194 – James Thweatt of Hancock County to Barbara Lucas of Warren County.  Deed dated February 7, 1800, for 50 acres on Ogeechee River granted Jacob Carter, and being the place where said Barbara now lives. Witnesses: Thomas Bohannon, Joseph Peevy.

Page 196 – Moses McKenny of Warren County to Joseph Watson of Columbia County.  Deed dated May 14, 1801, for 170 acres on north side of main prong of Big Brier Creek and in fork of the Beaverdam, except one acre at the south end of mill dam. Witnesses: Jacob Watson, P. Hodo J.P.

Page 197 – John Watson of Columbia County to Robert Stanford of Warren County.  Deed dated February 12, 1800, for 75 acres on

White's Creek, being part of 100 acres granted Jacob Watson in 1772. Witness: Jesse Burgen.

Page 198 – Jonathan Burson, to Robert Stanford. Deed dated June 6, 1800, for six acres laid out of a 200 acre tract granted grantor in 1785. Witnesses: Charles Bayn, John Bayn, John Wilson J.P.

Page 199 – Robert Stanford of Warren County to Stephen Stanford of Columbia County. Deed dated June 6, 1800, for 200 acres adjoining grantee and granted to Jonathan Stanford November 28, 1795. Witnesses: Charles Bayn, John Bayn, John Wilson J.P.

Page 200 – Jacob Watson to Michael Cody both of Warren County. Deed dated January 8, 1803, for 72 acres on both sides of Big Brier Creek. Witnesses: P. Hodo J.P. and Richard Hodo.

Page 201 – John Gibson to Phillip Brantley. Deed dated February 15, 1800, for 100 acres on Middle Creek. Witnesses: Isaiah Tucker and Willis Perry.

Page 202 – Ann Stuart to Polly Stuart and Jerusha Stuart, all of Warren County. Deed dated April 10, 1803, for 200 acres whereon said Ann Stuart lives, on Deep Creek. 100 acres of the upper part is conveyed to Jerusha, and the lower 100 acres to both Polly and Jerusha. Witnesses: Jesse Pittman, William Allen and Jody Newsom J.P.

Page 205 – Joseph Willis to Jerusha Stuart both of Warren County. Deed dated April 27, 1803, for 20 acres on Rocky Comfort granted to Alexander Caswell and now owned by grantor known by name of the Benson tract. Witness: Moses Granberry.

Page 206 – Richard Curry of Hancock County to Cary Curry of Warren County. Deed dated May 21, 1803, for 482 acres on Joe's Creek. Witnesses: Amos Travis, N. Robertson J.P.

Page 206 – John Matthews, Executor of will of Burrell Brooner to Andrew King. Executor's deed dated December 1, 1801, for 200 acres on Long Creek. Witnesses: W. Stith J.P., N. Williams, J.P.

Page 208 – Edward Pleasant Morgan to Lewis Hilson and Aaron Hilson "and others." Deed dated October 21, 1802. Conveys 300 acres on Ogeechee River granted May 21, 1787. Witnesses: J. Giles, Willy G. Braddy, James Johnston.

Page 209 – Benjamin Moore, planter, to James Taylor, planter, both of Warren County, son-in-law of said Moore. Deed of Gift dated September 12, 1803, for all of his slaves except one girl named Sarah whom he had already given to his daughter, Nancy Taylor, wife of said James Taylor. Also conveys his horses, cows, 18 head of hogs, household goods, farming tools, etc. Witnesses: Thomas Edmondson and Benjamin Howard Jr.

Page 210 – Radford Butt, Henry Walker, William Jones, George Parham, Elizabeth Parham and Hartwell Heath, all of Warren County, "legal heirs" of Thomas Parham, late of Halifax County, North Carolina, deceased, to John Parham. Bill of Sale for slave "Rose" and her 6 month old son; dated September 3, 1803. Witness: L. Pruitt J.I.C.

Page 210 – Margaret McAllister to William Bole, both of Warren County. Deed dated September 24, 1801, for 50 acres on Rocky Comfort Creek, being part of land granted John Darden August 17, 1786. Witnesses: Edward Sherley, L. Pruitt J.I.C.

Page 210 – Heirs of Thomas Parham, deceased, of Halifax County, North Carolina, viz: Raiford Butt, Henry Walker, William Jones, George Parham, Elizabeth Parham, all of Warren County, and Hartwell Heath, also of Warren, to John Parham of Warren. Bill of Sale for two slaves, conveying their interest, slaves owned by said Thomas Parham at his death. Dated September 3, 1803. Witness: Levi Pruitt J.I.C., Warren County.

Page 211 – David Golding of Warren County to Samuel Fickling of St. Paul's Parish, Charleston district, South Carolina. Deed dated October 28, 1803, for 108 acres on Golden's Creek. Witnesses: Francis Fickling, Reubin Jones.

Page 212 – Alexander Perryman, Esq., Harmon Perryman, Benjamin Howard Jr., Etheldred Thomas, Esq. Bond payable to the Governor dated November 1, 1803, for Alexander Perryman as Sheriff of Warren County.

Page 213 – John McCormack to John Dark, both of Warren County. Deed dated October 25, 1802, for 120 acres deeded grantor by John Burkhalter January 16, 1797. Witnesses: Randall Duckworth, James McCormick J.P.

Page 214 – John Baker and John Torrence, Executors of will of Peter Perkins, late of Warren County, deceased, to Jethro Darden. Deed dated April 10, 1803, conveying the home place of deceased on Williams Creek, containing 196 acres. Witnesses: Robert Hill, Debora Chapman, Solomon Lockett J.P.

Page 215 – John Sallis and James Gray of Warren County to Drury Mims of Washington County. Deed dated April 6, 1802, for 400 acres on Long Creek granted to Drury and David McCullers September 23, 1784. Witnesses: Hugh Reese, James McCormick J.P. Consideration $1400.00.

Page 215 – Dread Wilder of Wilkes County to Peter Perkins. Deed dated May 14, 1787, for 196 acres in then Wilkes adjoining Benjamin Scott, and lands of grantee and of Mary McDaniel and her children; being part of 350 acres granted grantor in 1784. Witnesses: Charles Linn, James Christmas, Sampson Wilder.

Page 217 – Benjamin Moore of Warren County to James Taylor of Hancock County. Deed dated July 20, 1802, for 150 acres on Rocky Comfort, granted grantor May 24, 1786. Witnesses: Thomas Edmondson, Edmond E. Taylor.

Page 218 – Christopher Bustin, to Benjamin Wright, both of Warren County. Deed dated November 23, 1803, for 175 acres on south side of Rocky Comfort Creek. Witnesses: David Brown, John Matthews J.P.

Page 221 – John Matthews to Christopher Bustin both of Warren County. Deed dated October 18, 1803, conveying 71 acres on Rocky Comfort Creek. Witnesses: David Broom, Ishmael Broom.

Page 221 – William Rigbee to Thomas Rigbee both of Warren County. Deed dated August 6, 1802, for his undivided interest in 122 acres on Ogeechee River being part of survey granted Joseph

Carter and deeded by James Thweatt to said William and Thomas Rigbee. Witnesses: John Blackney and Fisher Gaskin.

Page 221 – Nicholas Williams to Christopher Bustin both of Warren. Deed dated July 14, 1803, for 75 acres on Rocky Comfort Creek. Witnesses: Brittain Pearman and John Matthews.

Page 222 – Stephen Wright to Christopher Bustin both of Warren County. Bill of Sale for slave "Sucky" dated December 3, 1803. Witness: David Broom.

Page 222 – Samuel Camp to Richard Slaughter, both of Warren County. Deed dated June 15, 1800, to 138 acres on Long Creek. Witnesses: Samuel Newsom, Arthur Fort J.I.C.

Page 224 – David Mims to Shadrach F. Allen both of Warren County. Deed dated December 9, 1803. Conveys 100 acres on Rocky Comfort Creek. Witnesses: David Brown and Archelaus Flewellin J.P.

Page 225 – Moses Butt, late of Halifax County, North Carolina, now of Warren County, to his son William Butt. Power of Attorney dated December 6, 1802, authorizing him to attend to all business for him, etc. Witnesses: Polly and John Matthews, E. Hert J.I.C.

Page 226 – Harden Sanders of Tattnall County to James Myhand of Warren. Deed dated December 26, 1803, for 223 acres on Rocky Comfort adjoining Jonathan Lock, Andrew Bush, Leroy Mims and William Butts. Witnesses: Stephen Mitchell and John Matthews J.P., Warren County.

Page 227 – Joseph Fickling and wife Elizabeth of St. Paul's Parish, Colleton District, South Carolina to Barnard Woods of the same place. Deed dated November 12, 1803.

Page 227 – William Pilcher to John Hinton both of Warren County. Deed dated January 21, 1802, conveying 25 acres of 200 acre tract on Big Ogeechee River granted William Pilcher, deceased. Witnesses: Thomas Jackson, Benjamin Gates.

Page 227 – Lewis Pilcher and Rease, to Richard Lee, all of Warren County. Deed dated October 26, 1801, conveying their undivided interest in 200 acres on the Ogeechee River granted William Pilcher, deceased. Witnesses: Thomas Jackson, Benjamin Gates, B. Robinson.

Page 230 – Walter Slaughter to John Rushing both of Warren County. Deed dated March 10, 1803, for 300 acres on Long Creek, deeded grantor 1798-1800 by Reubin Winfree, Adam Jones and Samuel Camp. Witness: John Ledbetter Sr.

Page 231 – John Michael and Samuel Laurence and Ann Michael to Vinson Johnson all of Warren County. Deed dated January 13, 1803, for 600 acres on Ogeechee River. Witnesses: R. Abercrombie and James Harvey.

Page 232 – Joseph White to Lewis Wright both of Warren County. Deed dated September 18, 1801, for 100 acres on Williams Creek adjoining heirs of John Chapman, deceased, Joseph Hill and Burrell Perry. Witnesses: Solomon Thompson, Robert Parker, Timothy Matthews J.P.

Page 233 – Richard Slaughter to John Rushing, both of Warren County. Deed dated March 10, 1803, for 63 acres on Long Creek. Witness: John Ledbetter Sr.

Page 236 – Anderson Crawford of Columbia County to John Rushing of Warren County. Deed dated July 5, 1800, for 65 acres on north side of Ogeechee River. Witnesses: Thomas W. Murrell and J. Appling J.I.C.

Page 237 – Samuel Camp to Walter Slaughter both of Warren County. Deed dated December 24, 1800, for 65 acres on Long Creek. Witnesses: Thomas Friend, Prior Gardner J.P.

Page 238 – Samuel Camp to Cader Harrell. Deed dated June 15, 1800, for land on Fort's Creek. Witnesses: Samuel Newman and Arthur Fort J.I.C.

Page 239 – William Nance of Warren County to John Moreland of Jefferson County. Deed to secure debt dated January 17, 1804, securing debt of $2000, conveying all his household goods, three barrels Jamaica rum, one barrel Madiera wine, one barrel of Cognac brandy, two cases of gin, one travelling case and all fixtures in Nance's barroom, also stud horse, 37 head of cattle, 200 bushels corn, fodder and one barrel of gin. Witnesses: William Clark, William Hardwick J.P.

Page 241 – Richard Beasley to his son David Beasley, both of Warren County. Deed of gift dated January 6, 1804, for 233 ½ acres on Rocky Comfort Creek. Witnesses: Thomas Edmondson, L Pruitt J.I.C.

Page 241 – Richard Beasley, to his son Robert Beasley, both of Warren County. Deed of Gift dated January 6, 1804, for adjoining tract to that above.

Page 242 – James Roquemore, planter, to Shadrick Potts both of Warren County. Deed dated April 25, 1803, for 20 acres on Little Brier Creek, being the south part of a survey for Benjamin Jackson in 1787, adjoining grantee's lands. Witnesses: Baines Carter, Ithamer Ward.

Page 243 – Joseph Matthews to Shadrick Potts both of Warren County. Deed dated October 28, 1802, for 82 acres being a part of 300 acre tract on Big Brier Creek owned by grantor. Witnesses: Thomas Westberry and James Roquemore.

Page 244 – Thomas O'Steen, late of Burke County, to William Marlow of same. Deed dated July 23, 1793, for 100 acres granted March 17, 1786. Witnesses: John Davis, Robert Marlow. Probated by latter in Effingham County, July 24, 1793 before John London J.P., Effingham County.

Page 246 – Phillip Gibbs to Reubin Barrow both of Warren County. Deed dated March 20, 1802, for 100 acres known as the Samuel Powell improvement about six miles below Georgetown. Witnesses: John and James Barrow.

Page 246 – Hugh Reese to Reubin Jones both of Warren County. Deed dated August 16, 1803, conveying negro woman slave and her four children. Witnesses: George Hargraves and Hill Chapman.

Page 247 – John Matthews to Shadrick Potts both of Warren County. Deed dated January 15, 1803, for 50 acres on Big Brier Creek, being part of grant made to Absalom Jackson, surveyed in April 1787, and devised to grantor. Witnesses: Peter Rockmore and Thomas Westberry.

Page 248 – John Wilson and wife Margaret, to Peter Qualls, all of Warren County. Deed dated October 29, 1798, for 300 acres on Joe's Creek of Ogeechee River granted 1790 to Samuel Johnston. Witnesses: Lewis Brady, John Qualls.

Page 250 – Isaac Ball and wife Sarah, to Etheldred Thomas. Deed dated August 20, 1803, for 540 acres on both sides of Rocky Comfort Creek granted to the heirs of John May in 1785. Witnesses: Royal Nelms and Caswell Ball.

Page 253 – Malachi Culpepper of Elbert County to Reubin Barrow. Bill of Sale for slave, dated February 11, 1803. Witnesses: Alexander Avera, James Barrow.

Page 253 – John Parham Sr. to Thomas Parham both of Warren County. Deed dated February 19, 1804, for 350 acres on Caison's Creek. Witnesses: Shadrick Flewellin, John Matthews, E. Hunt J.I.C.

Page 253 – William Stark of Columbia County to James Dozier of Warren. Deed dated July 1, 1803, for 350 acres on Little River surveyed for Ralph Kilgore. Witnesses: James Willis, Jeney G. Willis.

Page 255 – Robert Stanford to Jesse Stanford both of Warren County. Deed dated October 2, 1803, for 98 acres on south side of Little Sweetwater Creek. Witnesses: Lewis Stanford, P. Hodo J.P.

Page 256 – Lewis Brady to John Keaton both of Warren County. Deed dated January 10, 1799, for 200 acres on Pilcher's Creek. Witnesses: Jacob Giles, Peter Qualls, Nowell Robertson J.P.

Page 259 – Jacob Burkhalter and wife Mary, to Benjamin Reese, both of Warren County. Deed dated February 11, 1804 for 100 acres on Big Brier Creek. Witnesses: P. Hodo, Jody Newsom J.P.

Page 260 – Thomas Childre to John Williams. Deed dated January 8, 1798, for 50 acres on White's Creek where grantee lives. Witnesses: John Watson, Robert Stanford, Henry Williams.

Page 261 – John Watson Sr. of Columbia County to Robert Stanford of Warren. Deed dated January 13, 1803, for 450 acres to include a mill seat on both sides of Sweetwater Creek in Columbia and Warren Counties, being part of grant to Joseph Maddock and to John Watson. Witnesses: John Stanford and Blitha Ruke.

Page 262 – John Bayn to William Brown. Deed dated December 9, 1803, for 86 acres being part of 200 acres granted Priscilla Mays. Witnesses: Robert Stanford, George Dunaway.

Page 264 - William Byrom, Tax Collector of Warren County, to Elizabeth Dove of Richmond County. Deed dated July 18, 1798, conveying land on Brier Creek, sold for taxes due for year 1797, as property of John Jamieson, to whom it was granted. Witnesses: J. Wilson J.P., James McCormick J.P.

Page 265 – Robert Stanford to Reubin McGee both of Warren County. Deed dated October 21, 1803, for 80 acres on White's Creek. Witness: Jesse Stanford.

Page 268 – James Farless of Warren County to Joseph Williams of Jefferson County. Deed dated November 3, 1797, for land lying on both sides of Deep Creek, Warren County. Witnesses: John Lawson, James Williams.

Page 269 – David Cook to B. Burkshire both of Richmond County. Bond for Title for land on Carson's Creek, dated September 11, 1786. Witnesses: Ezekiel and Albenia Standley.

Page 269 – Jacob Martin Sr. to James Farless both of Warren County. Deed dated December 2, 1795, conveying 300 acres on south side of Deep Creek, being in two surveys, one of 100 acres granted Joel Tapley April 19, 1790, and one of 200 acres granted

August 7, 1795 to grantor. Witnesses: W. Dawson, John Lawson J.P.

Page 271 – Austin Pruitt to Levi Pruitt both of Warren County. Deed dated January 8, 1802. Conveys 150 acres being part of 350 acre tract granted John Torrence March 21, 1769 and lying on Rocky Comfort, and by him deeded to Bird Pruitt and by him to grantor. Also, 200 acres granted Absalom Jackson October 12, 1785, and deeded by him to John D. Young and by him to John Hull and by him to Bird Pruitt and by him to grantor; said tract known as Pruitt's Mills. Witnesses: James McCormick Jr. and James McCormick J.P.

Page 272 – William Coram to Jesse Ricketson both of Warren County. Deed dated March 1, 1804, for land on Brier Creek where grantor lives, granted him. Witnesses: George Hargraves and D. Bush.

Page 272 – William Ward to Newt Ward both of Warren County. Deed dated February 7, 1804, for 150 acres granted James Raley in 1787. Witnesses: John O'Neal, Hannah O'Neal, N. Robertson, John Hutchinson J.P.

Page 274 – John Manion of Richmond County and wife Elizabeth to John Wilson of same county. Deed dated October 16, 1788, for 200 acres on Brier Creek adjoining Jeremiah Duckworth. Witnesses: Fitzmaurice Hunt, Sarah Hunt.

Page 275 – Gideon George and wife Tabitha to Hugh Armstrong all of Warren County. Deed dated February 26, 1804, for 113 acres on Middle Creek. Witnesses: Drury Banks and John Bayn.

Page 278 – Levi Pruitt to John Torrence of Warren County. Release dated March 8, 1803, whereby he released Torrence from all demands, suits, etc., on account of interference with the lines of tract of land on Rocky Comfort deeded by Torrence to his father, Bird Pruitt. Witnesses: W. Rose, H. Peebles, H. Candler J.I.C.

Page 282 – Richard Story to Peter Williams both of Warren County. Deed dated January 10, 1799 for 200 acres on both sides of White's Creek, surveyed in 1787. Witness: Thomas Smith.

Page 283 – Joseph Guy to Peter Williams. Deed dated December 31, 1802, for ten acres on White's Creek. Witnesses: John Bayn and James Carter.

Page 285 – Edward Story to Peter Williams both of Warren County. Deed dated September 21, 1803, for 100 acres on Brier Creek granted 1787 to Rachel Wells and by her deeded to John Watson 1792. Witnesses: Sally Roberts, John Bayn J.P.

Page 286 – John Wood to Peter Williams both of Warren. Deed dated December 22, 1800, for 75 acres being part of grant in 1787 to John Jamerson, and lying on Big Brier Creek. Witnesses: Isham Wheeler and John Bayn J.P.

Page 287 – Reubin Magee to Peter Williams both of Warren County. Deed dated January 25, 1804, conveying 10 acres on Whetstone Creek, being part of 904 acres granted J. Jamerson March 10, 1798. Witnesses: John Watson Jr., John Payne J.P.

Page 288 – William Wood and wife Mary to Edward Story, all of Warren County. Deed dated November 18, 1798, for 100 acres on Brier Creek granted 1789 to Richard Wells. Witness: John Wood.

Page 290 – John Zachry to James Zachry. Bill of Sale dated December 10, 1803 for slave boy named Brooks. Witnesses: Simon Harrell and M. Hubert J.P.

Page 291 – John Zachry of Warren County to Abner Zachry. Bill of Sale dated December 10, 1803, for slave "Ned." Same witnesses as last above.

Page 292 – William Thomas to Abel James both of Warren County. Deed dated February 13, 1804, for 90 acres being part of 100 acre tract in former Wilkes County on Long Creek, granted to Mary Thomas, wife of Jeptha Vining in 1786, and which land she later sold the grantor. Witnesses: Jesse James, Manoah Hubert.

Page 293 – Dixon Perryman of Columbia County to John Sexton of Warren County. Deed dated July 30, 1801, for 147 acres on Ogeechee River granted Josiah Carter. Witnesses: Hiram Hubert, D. H. Zachry.

Page 294 – John Saxon of Wilkes County to Joseph Dunn of Warren County. Deed dated July 6, 1802, for 147 acres on waters of Ogeechee River, granted to Josiah Carter. Witness: Henry Thompson.

Page 296 – Hugh Reese Sr. of Warren County to his daughter Polly Burkhalter. Gift of negro girl "Nan" dated May 4, 1804. Witnesses: Solomon Newsom and Jody Newsom J.P.

Page 296 – Joseph White and Robert Parker to James Matthews all of Warren County. Deed dated November 15, 1802, conveying 120 acres on Whetstone Creek granted to James Green and Abner Flewellin. Witnesses: Solomon Thompson, James Parker.

Page 298 – John Cratin and wife MaryAnn to James Elliott, all of Warren County. Deed dated February 18, 1802, for 170 acres bought by grantor from Willis Perry, reserving however 1 ½ acres "where the meeting house is." Witnesses: Thomas and Solomon Lockett.

Page 299 – Micajah Stone to James Elliott both of Warren County. Deed dated September 30, 1800, for six acres on Williams Creek, being part of 320 acres surveyed for Robert Jenkins in 1785. Witnesses: John Rogers, Robert Grier, Solomon Lockett J.P.

Page 300 – Harmon Perryman of Warren County to Mary Perryman. Bill of Sale for slave dated February 1, 1797. Witnesses: D. Perryman, Alsy Harris.

Page 301 – Levi Pruitt of Warren County to his sister, Nancy Williams. Gift of slave wench "Dinah" and her children, dated March 5, 1804. Witness: John Torrence.

Page 302 – Abraham Perkins to John Benton and Eli Benton, all of Warren County. Deed dated September 10, 1800, for 100 acres on Rocky Comfort. Witnesses: Timothy Matthews, Aaron Benton.

Page 303 – William Rushing of Washington County to John Rushing of Warren County. Deed dated September 13, 1803, for 250 acres on Fort's Creek granted Samuel Camp January 22, 1789, and by him deeded grantor May 10, 1789. Witnesses: Samuel Camp and William J. Crawford.

Page 307 – George Clifton to Jesse Carter, planter, both of Warren County. Deed dated September 21, 1803, for 225 acres on Brier Creek. Witnesses: James Mecum and Randall Duckworth.

Page 307 – Ansel Parrish of Warren County to his daughter Dicy Acreage and her children; Gift of bay mare, two colts, sorrel mare and colt. Dated August 13, 1804. Witnesses: William Lovett J.P., L. Pruitt J.P.

Page 308 – Claiborn Newsom of Columbia County to Jesse Carter of Warren. Deed dated October 19, 1803, for 300 acres on north side of Big Brier Creek. Witnesses: James Cody, Peter Hodo, Daniel Starnes. Wife, Hester Newsom, also signs deed.

Page 309 – Joseph McMath, planter, and wife Elizabeth, to Jesse Carter, all of Warren County. Deed dated September 21, 1803, for 200 acres granted Hugh Reese in a larger tract. Witnesses: James Mecum and Randall Duckworth.

Page 310 – Phillip Pool and Mary Pool, Executors, and New Tapley, Elizabeth Tapley, Judith Wilder, William Tapley, the heirs of Joel Tapley of Warren County, deceased, to Henry Harp, planter, of same county. Deed dated August 6, 1793, conveying 50 acres on Rocky Comfort Creek in Columbia County, it being a part of 287 ½ acre tract granted to the heirs of Mark Tapley August 15, 1788, "to be held and supported by the heirs of Mark Tapley before mentioned." Witnesses: John Wilder, William Gray. Probated by Wilder before Benjamin Bruton J.P., October 10, 1797.

Page 310 – John Williams to Levin Stanford both of Warren County. Deed dated September 17, 1800, for 50 acres on White's Creek and on Robert Stanford's gin branch to the road that leads to Burson's Mill, granted Thomas Childree Sr., and deeded by him to said grantor. Witness: Robert Stanford.

Page 312 – Richard Slaughter to Enoch Ellington both of Warren County. Deed dated September 20, 1802, for 76 acres near Long

Creek, being part of grant made in 1792 to Samuel Camp. Witnesses: Walter Slaughter, Barton Atchinson, Josiah Ellington.

Page 313 – Richard Ship of Hancock County to Vincent Johnston of Warren. Deed dated April 10, 1804, for 200 acres bounded by Ogeechee River, William Stith, John Hobson and grantee, granted to Matthew Hubert. Witnesses: John J. Davidson, Drewry Jackson.

Page 319 – James Bray to George Parham, both of Warren County, to Jonathan Smith of Columbia County. Deed dated December 14, 1803, conveying their one-third interest in 550 acres on creek formerly called Green's Creek now Childres Creek, formerly the property of Nathaniel and Alexander Smith who died 1789 intestate in that part of Wilkes now Warren County, leaving heirs viz: Mary Smith, the widow, and son James Smith, and the said Nancy since intermarried with said Barbarie. Witnesses: D. Neal J.P., John Torrence J.I.C.

Page 320 – Isaac Barbarie and wife Nancy of Warren County, to Jonathan Smith of Columbia County. Deed dated December 14, 1803, conveying their one-third interest in 550 acres on creek formerly called Green's Creek now Childres Creek, formerly the property of Nathaniel and Alexander Smith who died 1789 intestate in that part of Wilkes now Warren County, leaving heirs viz: Mary Smith, the widow, and son James Smith and the said Nancy since intermarried with said Barbarie. Witnesses: D. Neal J.P., John Torrence J.I.C.

Page 321 – Abraham Perkins to William Butt both of Warren County. Deed dated January 12, 1802. Conveys 100 acres on Rocky Comfort, being part of grant made to John Perkins July 13, 1791, and by him deeded grantor February 7, 1796. Witnesses: William White, T. Matthews J.P.

Page 322 – Peter Cox and wife Deborah (formerly Stubbs) to John Cox. Deed dated March 15, 1791, for 168 acres on line between Wilkes and Columbia Counties, in former St. Paul's Parish, being part of 300 acre tract originally granted the said Deborah Stubbs (now Cox.)  Witnesses: Benjamin Watson, Benjamin Harrison, William Thomas J.P.

Page 326 – Margaret McAllister, widow, to Charles McAllister, her son, of Warren County.  Deed of sale dated April 18, 1803, for 50 acres being part of 100 acre tract on northwest side of Rocky Comfort granted John Darden August 17, 1786, and deeded by Darden to Noel Thornton and by him and wife deeded grantor September 6, 1791.  Witnesses: William Bole and Boaz Kitching.

Page 327 – George Franklin of Washington County to Daniel Atkins of Warren County.  Deed dated January 2, 1802, for 100 acres on Big Brier Creek, being part of grant made by Governor George Handley of Georgia, to William Franklin of Warren County, deceased.  Witnesses: David Harris, George Herndon.

Page 328 – Lewis Wright, Sheriff Warren County to William Bird.  Sheriff's deed dated October 27, 1803, conveying 100 acres on River Ogeechee, levied on and sold as property of John Wallace to satisfy judgment in favor of Amos Wright, land being the place where said Wallace lives, and having been granted Pamella Horn in 1789.  Witness: Josiah Beall.

Page 331 – Newt Wood to John Brooks both of Warren County.  Deed dated July 19, 1804, for 150 acres being part of grant to James Railey in 1789.  Witnesses: William Earnest and William Shurley.

Page 331 – William Wood to Daniel Akins both of Warren County.  Deed dated November 20, 1800, for 13 acres being part of 143 acre tract granted 1790 to Britain McCullers, and lying on Little Brier Creek.  Witnesses: V. T. A. Tharp, William Cason J.P.

Page 332 – William Maddox of Richmond County to Thomas Ferry of same.  Deed dated January 4, 1796, for 362 acres granted John Barnett, lying in formerly Wilkes now Warren County, on Brier Creek, granted July 17, 1794.  Witnesses: John Burnett, A. Crawford J.P.  Wife Ann Maddox signs the deed also.

Page 335 – Peter Qualls and wife Nance, to Henrietta Nance, all of Warren County.  Deed dated October 12, 1801, for 300 acres on

Joe's Creek a branch of the Ogeechee River, granted Samuel Johnston April 19, 1790. Witnesses: John Bridges and Britain Bridges.

Page 336 – James Semmes to Henry Kendall. Bill of Sale dated January 19, 1805, for slave named Bob.

Page 337 – John Moses Jr., planter, to John Burkhalter, both of Warren County. Deed dated December 20, 1802, conveying 500 acres being part of two tracts on Brier Creek, 400 acres of which was granted Hezekiah Bussey, and remainder being part of tract granted P. Hodo, September 1784, and by him deeded grantor, and the other tract deeded by Bussey to Robert Moses Sr. Witnesses: James Mecom, Samuel Moses.

Page 340 – David Beasley to Robert Beasley. Deed dated January 3, 1805, for 233 acres on Rocky Comfort Creek. Witnesses: George Hargraves J.I.C., C. D. Stuart.

Page 340 – Benjamin Upton to Moses Granberry both of Warren County, planter. Deed dated October 20, 1801, for 171 acres on Rocky Comfort Creek adjoining grantee's lands, and granted grantor in 1801. Witnesses: Mick. Castleberry, Norvell Robertson.

Page 341 – Wood Moreland to Soldom Matthews of Warren County. Deed dated December 12, 1803, for 120 acres on Rocky Comfort Creek. Witnesses: Ishmael Broom and Houseman Passmore.

Page 343 – Moses Granberry to his son George Granberry both of Warren County. Deed of Gift dated May 19, 1804, for 200 acres on Rocky Comfort Creek "except one acre where the mill stands." Witnesses: Francis Wise, Daniel Simpson.

Page 344 – John Smith to Moses Granberry, both of Warren County. Deed dated January 20, 1801, for 292 acres on Rocky Comfort granted 1790 to Arthur Fail. Witness: William McDowell.

Page 345 – Charles McAllister to James Eastwood both of Warren County. Deed dated December 22, 1804, for 60 acres on Rocky

Comfort being part of 100 acre survey to John Darden and deeded grantor by Margaret McAllister, "being the tract whereon grantor has resided for many years." Witnesses: Turner Persons and John Stallings.

Page 347 – James Moore of Halifax County (name of state not shown) to Jeremiah Butt of Warren. Deed dated December 30, 1800, conveying a slave. Witness: Noel Potts.

Page 348 – John Simmons to Jesse Bunkley both of Warren County. Deed dated August 17, 1798, for 186 acres on Ogeechee River adjoining Lewis Bunkley and Lewis Powell, being part of grant in 1785 to Moses Powell. Witnesses: William Byron, William Lovett, Henry Mitchell.

Page 349 – Jesse Bunkley and Keziah Lucas, widow of Hancock County. Agreement made between them dated June 3, 1804, agreeing to divide the slaves of Joshua Bunkley, deceased, of Charles County, Virginia, which he, the deceased, bequeathed in his will to his wife Mildred Bunkley (now the late Mildred Rutland.) The said Mildred having died, the slaves were inherited by said Jesse and Keziah. Witnesses: John Lucas Jr., Samuel Barksdale and Terrell Barksdale.

Page 352 – John P. Parker and wife Rachel, to Thomas Kelly, all of Warren County. Deed dated October 15, 1803, conveying 41 acres it being said Rachel's share of 373 ½ acres formerly belonging to her deceased father John Kelley. Witnesses: James Waggoner and David W. Waggoner.

Page 354 – Jesse Brooks to Jezekiah Williams, both of Warren County. Deed dated October 21, 1799, for 100 acres on Rocky Comfort. Witnesses: James Gizzard, John McClung.

Page 355 – Phillip Gibbs to William Kener Jr. and wife Vashti, all of Warren. Deed dated May 24, 1803, for tract of land where the grantees live. Witnesses: Elhannon Gibbs, Zacheus Gibbs.

Page 356 – William Berry Sr., to Jilson Berry, both planters of Warren County. Deed dated July 10, 1795, for 100 acres on Long Creek being part of grantor's headright granted him in 1785.

Witnesses: Francis Beck, Presley Berry, Mary Berry, Anderson Berry, Jarrott Berry.

Page 356 – Enoch Rentfro to John Rushing both of Warren County. Deed dated December 27, 1804 for 350 acres on Joe's Creek granted Stephen Mitchell August 13, 1788, and by him deeded March 20, 1790, to Enoch Rentfro now deceased. Also part of 775 acres granted Samuel Camp January 22, 1789, and by him to said deceased September 2, 1791; and both said tracts devised by said Enoch Rentfro's will to his son the said Enoch Rentfro. Witnesses: William Sherley and Larkin Chivers.

Page 357 – Baxter Pool, mechanic, and wife Ann, of Richmond County, to Noah Kelsey of same. Deed dated October 30, 1790, for 450 acres in Wilkes County granted Edmond Bugg Hicks October 24, 1787, and by him deeded grantor December 7, 1789. Witness: Edward Randolph; acknowledged before Thomas Watkins J.P.

Page 359 – John Wilkins of Winston County, South Carolina and William Williams of Burke County, Georgia, to Noah Kelcy of Burke County. Deed dated March 15, 1802, for 350 acres on Evans Creek of Ogeechee River, in Warren County, originally granted October 17, 1785, to Ezekiel Williams, deceased. Also 150 acres adjoining also granted said Ezekiel Williams, deceased. Said lands willed by said Ezekiel to his said son, John Williams with a proviso that if he, John, died without issue the lands were to go to John's brother, the said William Williams. Witness: Robert Iverson J.P.

Page 361 – Joseph Bryan to Noah Kelsey of Richmond County. Deed dated January 9, 1792, for 450 acres in Wilkes County. Witness: Thomas Watkins J.P.

Page 362 – William Goza, blacksmith, to Solomon Newsom Jr., both of Warren. Deed dated November 20, 1804 for part of two tracts granted Solomon Newsom Sr., deceased. Witnesses: Aaron Goza and Jody Newsom.

Page 363 – Henry Mandell of Jefferson County, Mississippi, to William Collins of same. Power of Attorney dated October 1,

1804, to recover all lands and accounts due him in Georgia. Witnesses: Jesse Withers J.P., who is certified to by John Henderson J.P., Natchez, Mississippi.

Page 364 – Anderson Berry to Jilson Berry, both planters, of Warren County. Deed dated December 3, 1802, for 60 acres. Witnesses: William Killibrew, Arthur Jenkins, William Ellis.

Page 365 – Samuel Skelly to John Rushing both of Warren County. Deed dated December 29, 1804, for 125 acres on Rocky Comfort adjoining lands of Virden. Witness: John Hatcher J.P.

Page 369 – John Myrick Jr., to Henry Kendall, both of Warren County. Deed dated October 11, 1803, for 292 acres lying on Whetstone Creek. Witnesses: Alexander Flewellin and John Matthews J.P.

Page 370 – John Talliferro and wife Mary to Charles Darnalls all of Wilkes County. Deed dated (blank) 1793, for 125 acres granted in 1787. Witnesses: Jones Persons, Jonathan McCrary.

Page 371 – Joseph Grizard to Silas Todd, both of Warren County. Deed dated March 27, 1804, for land where grantee lives, granted Brian McClendon on February 1st, last. Witnesses: John Brooks, William Earnest.

Page 374 – Jeremiah Beall to George Cotton, both of Warren County. Deed dated November 24, 1803, for lands on Golding's Creek. It is stipulated that the springs on said land may be used by the public. Witnesses: James Mecune, Jeremiah Butt.

Page 375 – Jeremiah Beall to George Cotton. Deed dated February 13, 1805, for a parcel of land 25 feet square whereon said Cotton's store now stands, it being part of grantor's home place. Witness: James McCormick J.P.

Page 376 – Richard Sammons to Reddick Bass. Deed dated January 21, 1805 for 152 acres on Middle Creek adjoining grantee. Witnesses: L. D. Bryan, Henry Hill.

Page 377 – Levi Pruitt Esq. to Thomas Maddux, both of Warren County. Deed dated June 22, 1804, conveying 30 acres in northeast corner of 200 acre tract granted in 1785 to John Young and since by divers deeds, now vested in grantor. Same adjoins other lands of grantee. Witnesses: Thomas Edmundson, James McCormack J.P.

Page 378 – Phillip Gibbs and wife Phoebe, to Richard White Nance, all of Warren County. Deed dated May 26, 1803, for land on Big Creek granted Jeremiah Wilcher. Witnesses: Thomas Miles, Sarah Eiland.

Page 379 – Schedule of personal property dated January 14, 1805, owned by Hugh McGee, deceased, and inherited by his daughter, Julia McGee and delivered her by William and Catherine Nance.

Page 381 – Stephen Marshall to Elisha Hurt both of Warren County. Deed dated April 13, 1805, conveying 50 acres on Rocky Comfort. Witnesses: Jesse Matthews and Sterling Gardner J.P.

Page 383 – William Tarver and wife Mary to Jacob Darden all of Warren County. Deed dated February 13, 1804, conveying the said Mary's one-third undivided part of 550 acres on Childress Creek owned by Nathaniel Alexander Smith at his death in 1789, intestate, a citizen of Wilkes County, leaving a widow Mary Smith, daughter Nancy Smith, and a son James Smith, the said widow Mary having intermarried with said William Tarver. Witnesses: William Torrence, John Baker, John Torrence J.P.

Page 385 – Samuel Fickling to his son Barnard W. Fickling both of Warren County. Deed of Gift dated December 17, 1804, conveying all his estate at his death, on condition said son shall pay Samuel's daughters, Ann Jones and Elizabeth Fickling, a certain sum of money. Witnesses: Archibald and Shadrack Flewellin.

Page 386 – James Mossman, Executor of will of James McKay, late of Chatham County, Georgia, to Thomas Young, Esq., all of Chatham County. Deed dated April 23, 1801, conveying 500 acres in former St. Paul's Parish now Columbia County, granted said James McKay December 6, 1774. Sale made under order granted by Court of Ordinary of Chatham County. Public Sale. Witnesses: George U. Nichols and Thomas Young Jr.

Page 388 – Jeremiah Beall and wife Elizabeth, to Solomon Slatter, John C. Turner, Wormsley Rose, Willie Harris and Nicholas Williams as Trustees. Deed dated June 4, 1805, for one acre near Warrenton "for the sole purpose of building thereon a meeting house for the utility of the public, to be used on certain days by the Methodists, at other times by the Baptists, Presbyterians, or any other sect who believes in and preaches the Gospel." Consideration 25 cents. Witnesses: Stephen Marshall and Andrew King J.P.

Page 389 – Joshua Reynolds to John Verdin both of Warren County. Deed dated April 15, 1801, for 50 acres on Rocky Comfort where grantee now lives. Witnesses: Samuel Beall and L. Pruitt J.I.C.

Page 390 – Jeremiah Beall and Josiah Beall, to John Matthews. Deed for one acre of land dated March 8, 1825. Witness: James Bynum, George Hargraves J.I.C.

Page 391 - Samuel Story to Moses Hill both of Warren County. Deed dated October 30, 1804, for 50 acres on north side of Big Brier Creek granted 1787 to Needham Smith. Witnesses: Samuel Story and William Cason J.P.

Page 392 – Thomas Ansley and wife Rebecca to Abel Ansley all of Warren County. Deed dated January 24, 1798, for 330 acres on Still Creek granted grantor in 1785. Witnesses: Joseph Landrum, Joseph Ansley, John Wilson J.P.

Page 393 – Samuel Fickling, to his granddaughter, Elizabeth F. Jones (daughter of Sterling Jones.) Deed of Gift dated December 17, 1804, for a slave woman Rachel, possession to pass to said Elizabeth at her marriage. Witnesses: Archibald and Shadrack Flewellin.

Page 393 – Lewis Wright to Milly Chapman, widow, both of Warren County. Deed dated April 17, 1804. Conveys four acres on Williams Creek adjoining her lands, and being in northeast corner of grantor's land granted 1784 to Benjamin Scott. Witnesses: William Chapman and Stephen Butt.

Page 394 – Harbert Sims to William Wade both of Warren County. Deed dated August 12, 1803, for 90 acres adjoining Bartlett Sims Jr., Lou Snellings and lying on the river road, willed to grantor by his father, Bartlett Sims Sr. Witnesses: William Brook, Bartlett Sims.

Page 395 – William Wilkins and wife Sarah of Clarke County to James Matthews of Warren County. Deed dated March 20, 1805, for 50 acres on Hart's Creek granted to Peter Perkins. Witnesses: Elizabeth Kellem, Joshua Browning J.P.

Page 396 – Peter Perkins of Warren County to "my dear grandson John Wilkins", minor son of William and Sarah Wilkins. Deed of Gift dated October 18, 1802, conveying 50 acres of grantor's home plantation of 200 acres on Hart's Creek granted grantor December 30, 1788. Said William and Sarah Wilkins to hold said property for their said son until he is 21, with power to sell and re-invest if they think best for his benefit. Witnesses: Solomon Thompson, Timothy Matthews J.P., John Torrence J.I.C.

Page 397 – Elizabeth Westmoreland, Administratrix of Isham Westmoreland estate of Hancock County, to Mary Parker, Administratrix and Solomon Thompson, Administrator of James Parker estate, of Warren County. Deed dated December 15, 1804, for 200 acres on Williams Creek granted Peter Perkins 1788, and adjoining Jethro Darden and said Parker estate lands. Witnesses: Jacob Lockett and George Clower.

Page 398 – James Wheeler and wife Susannah, to Thomas Fontaine, all of Warren County. Deed dated February 18, 1804, for 50 acres on Williams Creek being the southeast corner of 200 acre tract granted 1784 to Susannah Wall, widow, now vested in said Wheeler by reason of his intermarriage with said Susannah Wall. Witnesses: David Cox, Solomon Lockett J.P.

Page 400 – John Greeson Sr. to Lucy Thompson Sr., and Lucy Thompson Jr. and Alexander Thompson. Deed dated February 6, 1804, for land on Williams Creek granted in 1785 to George Palmore. Witnesses: Thomas Fontaine, Josias Wright.

Page 401 – John Fontaine to James Allen, both planters of Warren County. Deed dated February 1, 1805 for 50 acres on Williams Creek granted Susannah Wall, widow, in 1784. Witnesses: Thomas Fontaine and David Cox.

Page 402 – Sampson Wilder to Francis Risher both of Warren County. Deed dated April 13, 1805, for 50 acres adjoining other lands of the parties, and James Waggoner. Witnesses: Hiram Perry, A. Persons, John Torrence J.P.

Page 403 – George Palmer and wife Mary of Burke County, to John Greeson of Wilkes County. Deed dated May 4, 1787 for 500 acres in what was then Wilkes County, lying on Williams Creek. Witnesses: Hall Hudson, William Jones J.P., Mary Jones.

Page 408 – Wilkerson Bailey and wife Jincy of Columbia County, to Charles Linn of same. Deed dated December 28, 1801, for 70 acres being 1/5$^{th}$ part of 350 acres granted 1788 to Charles Linn Sr., and devised by his will to his son, John Linn since deceased, and now the property of said Wilkerson by reason of his intermarriage with Jane Linn, widow of said John Linn. Witnesses: Aquilla Howard, Thomas White, J.P.

Page 412 – John Neyland and wife Elizabeth of Columbia County, to Charles Linn of same. Deed dated February 21, 1803, for 70 acres in former Richmond now Warren County, being one-fifth part of 350 acre tract granted Charles Linn, deceased, December 30, 1788, and by his will devised to his son John Linn, since deceased, and by marriage to John's sister Elizabeth by said Neyland is now vested in latter. Witnesses: Bailey Wilkenson, Thomas Beall.

Page 413 - William Smith of Columbia County to Henry Cox of Warren. Deed dated January 28, 1805 for 50 acres on Caison's Creek granted to Charles Linn Sr., and by him left to his son, John Linn, and by the latter's heirs deeded to Charles Linn Jr. Witnesses: Walter Dent and Thomas White.

Page 415 – Stephen Stanford of Columbia County to Joseph Harrell and his wife Patsy of Warren County. Deed dated March 5, 1803, for 100 acres lying in Warren and Columbia Counties on

White's Creek, being part of 300 acres granted Joseph Maddock and by him deeded grantor. Witnesses: Jesse Carter and John Bayn J.P.

Page 416 – Hardy Newsom to Isaac Brooks both of Warren County. Deed dated August 13, 1805, for 100 acres adjoining Hugh Ross and Thomas Childers. Witnesses: Nathaniel Thompson and John Bayn J.P.

Page 417 – Alexander Perryman, Sheriff Warren County, to William Earnest. Sheriff's deed dated June 1805, for 60 acres on Rocky Comfort to include the mill-seat, being part of 100 acres granted John Darden; levied on and sold as the property of James Eastwood to satisfy Inferior Court execution issued in favor of William Pitts. Witnesses: Thomas Dent, D. Neal J.P.

Page 418 – Alexander Perryman, Sheriff Warren County to David Neal as Agent for William Brooks of Warren County. Sheriff's deed dated May 13, 1805, conveying 50 acres on Rocky Comfort bounded by home place lands of the relict of William Kitchens where she now resides. Levied on and sold as property of William Todd to satisfy J. P. Court execution in favor of Abraham Yearty. Witnesses: N. Robertson, William Goza, H. Candler J.I.C.

Page 423 – Alexander Perryman, Sheriff Warren County to William Pitts of Warren County. Sheriff's deed dated June 5, 1802, for 150 acres on Rocky Comfort granted William Kitchings April 22, 1803, and deeded by him to James Eastwood April 25, 1803, and levied on and sold as Eastwood's property to satisfy an Inferior Court fifa in favor of John Parham, Guardian of William Pitts. Witnesses: T. Persons, John Stallings.

Page 424 – Ignatius Few of Columbia County to Timothy Lee of Warren County. Deed dated May 16, 1799, for 100 acres on Long Creek, being part of a grant made grantor in 1784. Witnesses: John Robertson and Samuel Buffington.

Page 426 – Clourdsley Camp to Samuel Camp. Bill of Sale dated December 31, 1804, conveying "all I am possessed of, cattle, household goods, etc. and all my crops of tobacco, cotton, etc, until he is paid what I owe him." Witnesses: Manoah Hubbard, Thaddeus Camp, Henry Candler.

Page 432 – Benjamin Porter of Wilkes County to William Woodruff of the State of South Carolina. Deed dated October 17, 1803, for 203 acres in former Richmond now Warren County, being part of 264 acres granted Abraham Dennis, lying on Little River. Witnesses: William Poe and James Course J.I.C.

Page 433 – John Niday to Jesse Stubbs both of Warren County. Deed dated March 31, 1804, for 124 ½ acres being part of a larger survey late the property of John Cason Sr., deceased, and sold by John Williams to grantor; land lying on Caison's Creek. Witnesses: Charles Porter J.P., James McFarland J.P.

Page 434 – James Weeks to Samuel Johnston both of Warren County. Deed dated May 17, 1805, for 24 acres on Red Lick Creek, waters of Ogeechee River, granted to Isaac Bush. Witnesses: William Byrom Jr., William Byrom J.P.

Page 435 – Asa Cox to Moses Darden, both of Warren County. Deed dated January 17, 1805, for 950 acres on Williams Creek, granted George Murray in 1784. Witness: Robert Hill.

Page 436 - William Mays to Beverly Hester both of Warren County. Deed dated September 27, 1805, conveying 100 acres on Brier Creek, part of survey made August 12, 1784, for Isaac Burson and adjoining Edward Kinsey, John Burkhalter, Thomas Walker. Witnesses: Charles D. Stuart, M. Hubert J.P.

Page 439 – James Smith, blacksmith, to Asa Cox, planter, both of Warren County. Deed dated May 5, 1804, for 100 acres on Williams Creek being part of grant made 1784 to Joe Murray. Witnesses: Ebenezer Smith, Ebenezer Torrence.

Page 439 – Cornelius Whittington of Hancock County to Samuel Camp of Warren County. Deed dated October 19, 1802, for 200 acres granted 1794 to grantor. Witnesses: Alexander Montgomery and Jesse Talbott J.P.

Page 440 – Matthew Parham to Edward Parham both of Warren County. Quit claim deed dated March 10, 1805, conveying his interest in 200 acres where grantor lives. Witnesses: Z. Franklin J.P., Henry Walker, James Parham.

Page 441 – William Burkhalter and wife Rebekah, of Edgefield County, South Carolina, to Clark Blandford of Warren County. Deed dated December 27, 1804, for 200 acres on Rocky Comfort Creek. Witnesses: Peter Ryan and John Lyon.

Page 442 – Robert Marlow, planter, Joseph Marlow, planter, Priscilla Marlow and Charity Marlow, of Hancock County, to Thomas Jackson, planter, of Warren County. Deed dated August 13, 1794, for 100 acres on Ogeechee River, granted March 20, 1786. Witnesses: Robert Dickens, Susannah Jackson.

Page 444 – Samuel Stubbs to Wyatt Bonner both of Warren County. Deed dated January 10, 1801, for 20 acres adjoining Adam Jones and George Parham. Witnesses: Z. Franklin and Ann A. O'Brien.

Page 446 – William Chambers to Thomas Jackson, both of Warren County. Deed dated September 14, 1804, for eight acres on the Georgetown Road. Witnesses: N. Robertson J.P., and John Hatcher J.P.

Page 448 – John Williams to George Parham both of Warren County. Deed dated November 10, 1800, for 53 acres adjoining land granted John Carson and Holland Middleton, and adjoining Robert Bonner. Witnesses: James Bonner, Wyatt Bonner.

Page 449 – John Carson to George Parham both of Warren County. Deed dated February 20, 1800, for 228 acres on Carson's Creek, surveyed by James McFarland and granted said Carson. Witnesses: Z. Franklin and W. Hill.

Page 450 – Jones Persons to Joseph Howard both of Warren County. Deed dated December 31, 1805, conveying 150 acres on Rocky Comfort and 50 acres adjoining the 50 acres granted by John Verdin December 3, 1804, and the 150 acres granted Joseph Higginbotham. Witnesses: T. Persons, Joseph Duckworth J.P.

Page 452 – Henry Crittenden of Washington County to John Spurlin of Warren County. Power of Attorney dated December 1, 1803, authorizing Spurlin to receive of John Speed of Richmond County, North Carolina, the said Henry's part of the money due him and Spurlin for the purchase of tract of land there sold by them to Speed. Witness: Barnett Brown.

Page 454 – Jesse Sanford of Hancock County to Thomas Moody of Warren. Deed dated September 7, 1805, for 290 acres on Rocky Comfort being part of 790 acres granted grantor. Witnesses: John Pinkston and William Sanford.

Page 455 – Jeremiah Beall and wife Elizabeth, of Warren County, to David Bush of Warrenton. Deed dated December 6, 1803, for parcel of land adjoining the courthouse square on the south. Witnesses: D. Neal J.P., L. Pruitt J.I.C.

Page 460 – Benjamin Reese of Columbia County to Thomas Sell of same. Deed dated September 10, 1799, for 57 acres in Warren County. Witnesses: Catherine White and Thomas J. White J.P.

Page 462 – Wyatt Bonner to Samuel Stubbs both of Warren County. Deed dated January 10, 1801, for 28 acres adjoining Stubbs, Joel Cloud. Witnesses: Ann O'Brien, L. Franklin J.P.

Page 463 – Samuel Stubbs and wife Mary to Thomas Haynes, all of Warren. Deed dated March 14, 1805, for 300 acres on Upton's Creek now known as Hart's Creek, part of which was granted Peter Hart in 1770. Witness: Joel Rives.

Page 464 – Nathan Stubbs of Columbia County to Samuel Stubbs of Warren County. Deed dated June 24, 1797, for 100 acres in former St. Paul's Parish now Warren County, being part of grant in 1770 to Peter Hart. Witnesses: Z. Franklin, Thomas White.

Page 466 – Henry Bonner to Asa Chapman both of Warren County. Deed dated July 12, 1805, for 100 acres granted grantor. Witnesses: Timothy Matthews and Archelaus Flewellin J.P.

Page 466 – Peter Cox Sr. to Peter Dandoon both of Warren County. Deed dated March 16, 1805, for 229 acres on Maddox's

Creek bought by grantor from James Gilmore. Witnesses: Robert Lazenby, Thomas Howard, Sampson S. Steele.

Page 467 – Thomas Bazemore to John Smith. Deed dated February 7, 1806, for slave "Jenny" age 17 years. Witnesses: Joseph White and Isham Wheeler.

Page 469 – John Torrence to William Scott. Deed dated November 25, 1803, for 100 acres on Childress Creek granted grantor. Witnesses: William Harris, G. George.

Page 470 – David Robinson, John Wilson, Fitz. M. Hunt, Administrators of David Robertson, deceased, of Richmond County, to William M. Cowles of Richmond County. Administrator's deed dated January 11, 1806, for 145 acres in Warren County being part of grant to Absalom Jackson in April 1787, adjoining Daniel Atkins, Shadrick Pitts and Roquemore. Sale made under order of Court of Ordinary, Richmond County. Witnesses: J. Kennon and Thomas Westberry.

Page 471 – William Scott of Columbia County to Mary Sell, Administrator of the estate of Thomas Sell, deceased, of Warren County. Deed dated October 22, 1805, for 170 acres on Childress Creek. Witnesses: John Quinn, John Scott.

Page 472 – Henry Peebles of Warren County to his daughter, Betsy Peebles. Gift of eight slaves February 5, 1806. Witnesses: A. Persons, Sterling Gardner J.P.

Page 472 – Henry Peebles of Warren County to his son, William H. Peebles. Gift of eight slaves February 5, 1806. Same witnesses as last above.

Page 473 – Samuel Skelly to John Rushing. Bill of Sale for four slaves dated February 1, 1806. Witness: R. Whitehead.

Page 474 – Ignatius Few of Columbia County to Joseph Hill of Warren County. Deed dated April 27, 1803, for 200 acres on Williams Creek granted Isham Wheelas in 1793. Witnesses: Moses Granberry, Norvell Robertson.

Page 474 – John Guthrie of Buncombe County, North Carolina to Nathan Davis of Warren County. Bond for Title dated March 20, 1805, to make titles to Davis for 80 acres on Brier Creek granted to Richard Smith. Witnesses: Williamson Rowland, William Cason J.P.

Page 475 – George Brewer of Baldwin County, to Joseph Hill of Warren County. Deed dated January 20, 1806, for land on Williams Creek. Witnesses: Mack Heath, Wood Moreland.

Page 476 - Jerusha Stewart to Joel Willis both of Warren County. Deed dated April 27, 1803, for 20 acres on Rocky Comfort being part of grant in 1793 to Ann Stewart. Witness: Moses Granberry.

Page 477 – Benjamin Oliver of Virginia, to Job Wilder of Warren County. Deed dated February 27, 1806, for 200 acres on Hart's Creek. Witnesses: Benjamin Oliver Jr., and Sampson Wilder.

Page 478 – Henry Castleberry of Clarke County to John Hardaway both of Warren County. Deed dated July 4, 1805, for 84 acres in Warren County. Witnesses: Charles Harvell and David Neal J.P.

Page 479 – Henry Castleberry and wife Sarah, to John Hardaway, both of Warren County. Deed dated November 1, 1802 for 200 acres granted 1787 to said grantor, land then in Wilkes County. Witnesses: Robert Moses and James McCormick J.P.

Page 480 – Jeremiah Beall, merchant of Warrenton, to Henry Kendall. Deed dated February 25, 1806, for 50 acres on north side of Broad Street adjoining town of Warrenton, together with one lot in Warrenton where grantor lives. Witnesses: T. Persons, John C. Turner, William D. Bunkley.

Page 482 – Wyatt Bonner and wife Ann, to Thomas Haynes, all of Warren County. Deed dated February 17, 1806, for 100 acres where grantee lives, granted Nathan Stubbs and by him deeded grantor, 1796. Witnesses: J. Stith, Z. Franklin J.P.

Page 485 – Alexander Caswell and wife Mary of Burke County, to John Lawson of Columbia County. Deed dated October 8, 1792, for 150 acres on Rocky Comfort Creek in Columbia County. Witnesses: John Benson, Thompson Lawson.

Page 488 – Jeremiah Beall to George Cole, both of Warren County. Deed dated January 4, 1805, for parcel of land adjoining the public square and Dr. Bush. Witnesses: David Bush and George Hargraves J.I.C.

Page 489 – Benjamin Upton to Tobias Upton both of Warren County, planter. Deed dated January 11, 1802, for 200 acres on Rocky branch and Ogeechee River, adjoining Isaac Ledbetter. Witness: William Hancock.

Page 491 – James Thweatt to Thomas Bohannon both of Wilkes County. Deed dated February 7, 1800, for 107 acres on Ogeechee River, granted Josiah Carter. Witnesses: Peter Peavy and Joseph Peavy.

Page 493 – Jeremiah Beall to Thomas Dent, both of Warren County. Deed dated August 4, 1800, for town lot in Warrenton on the public square. Witnesses: Richard Dent and James McCormick J.P.

Page 494 – David Newsom, Administrator of estate of Solomon Newsom, deceased, of Warren County to Thomas Dent of same. Administrators deed dated May 6, 1806, for 149 ½ acres on Rocky Comfort, being part of the realty of the deceased, sold under order of Court of Ordinary of Warren County, granted February Term 1806. Public Sale. Witnesses: Gresham Smith and Thomas Friend J.P.

Page 495 – John Claiborne Sr. to Jacob Bull both of Warren County. Deed dated January 4, 1805, for 50 acres originally granted 1770 to John Dennis "and taken from a tract on which Thomas Buttril now lives near the mouth of Kilgore's Creek." Witnesses: Joseph Evans, Stanton Porter and Charles Porter J.P.

Page 496 – Joel Willis of Warren County to Benjamin Bledsoe of Columbia County. Deed dated December 5, 1805, for 200 acres in forks of Rocky Comfort and Deep Creeks being parts of grants to

Roger and John Lawson and Alexander Caswell, whereon the grantor lives. Witnesses: Norvell Robertson, George Dykes J.P.

Page 498 – Thomas Stapler of Jackson County to William Kenor of Warren County. Deed dated January 13, 1786, for 200 acres on Joe's Creek. Witnesses: Amos Stapler and William Norman J.P.

Page 499 – Ignatius Few of Columbia County to John Dysart of Warren County. Deed dated July 10, 1795, for 200 acres on Williams Creek. Witnesses: John W. Deveraux and Mark Candler.

Page 501 – Jesse Matthews of Baldwin County, to Elisha Hurt of Warren County. Deed dated April 9, 1806, for 42 acres on north side of Rocky Comfort. Witnesses: A. Persons, Sterling Gardner, J.P.

Page 501 – Helton Peevy to William Warren both of Warren County. Deed dated February 9, 1801, for 110 acres on Long Creek. Witnesses: Stephen Marshall, James Zachary.

Page 503 – Zachariah Tucker of Lincoln County, Kentucky to "his trusty friend" Isaiah Tucker of Warren County, Georgia. Power of Attorney dated April 8, 1806, to attend to all his business in Georgia, "especially to collect my distributive share of the estate of John Pierce Jr., deceased, of the City of Augusta, Georgia." Witnesses: T. Persons and A. Persons.

Page 505 – Josiah Beall to Henry Shelton. Bill of Sale for two slaves, no date. Witness: John Matthews.

Page 506 – Henry Moses of Baldwin County, to Sterling Gardner of Warren County. Deed dated April 8, 1806, for 120 acres on Whetstone Creek. Witnesses: Benjamin Hurt and Archelaus Flewellin, J.I.C.

Page 506 – William Wright to Henry Shelton. Bill of Sale for slave named George, 13 years old; dated March 22, 1803. Witnesses: Mark Harden Jr., Thomas Dent.

Page 507 – Thomas Smith to Henry Williams Jr. both of Warren County. Deed dated November 1, 1804, 172 acres on Brier Creek. Witnesses: Rhesa Jones, John Bayn.

Page 509 – James Wheeler and wife Susannah of Warren County to James Allen of Columbia County. Deed dated February 28, 1804, for 150 acres on Williams Creek lying on the Richmond County line at time of survey, being part of a grant made to Susannah Wall, widow, in 1784, and now vested in said Wheeler by reason of his intermarriage with said Susannah Wall, now Wheeler. Witnesses: John Fontaine, Solomon Lockett.

Page 510 – Amos Persons to Robert Beasley both of Warren County. Deed dated July 25, 1806, for 100 acres being part of 200 acres granted Elijah Peters January 4, 1786, and by him deeded Benjamin Moore March 17, 1786, and by Moore deeded to Thomas Edmondson by him to grantor; said land being the place where Joel Lassetter now lives. Witnesses: James Gray, Isaac Ball J.P.

Page 511 – George Brewer of Hancock County, to William White of Warren County. Deed dated May 7, 1797, for 40 acres on Williams Creek. Witnesses: Rolen Brewer and Joseph White.

Page 512 – James Northington to John Zachry. Bill of Sale for slave boy named George, dated August 22, 1806. Witnesses: John Stewart, Ransom Duke and George Owen J.P.

Page 513 – Henry Mitchell of Hancock County, Administrator of Thomas Harton estate, to John Zachry of Warren County. Administrator's deed dated January 30, 1805, conveying 250 acres in Warren County; deed made under order of Court of Ordinary of Hancock County, to comply with the terms of a bond for title or contract to sell made by deceased in his lifetime to said Zachry. Witnesses: H. B. Crowder, John Crowder, J.I.C.

Page 516 – Matthew Parham to James Parham both of Warren County. Deed dated November 8, 1802, for 100 acres on Kilgore's Creek, being part of 230 acres surveyed for Nicholas Jones. Witnesses: Z. Franklin, Rebekah Walker.

Page 516 – Mary Smith to her son Abisha Brewer. Deed of Gift dated January 5, 1798, conveying all her dower rights in 550 acres "taken up" by her late husband, Nathaniel Alexander Smith, deceased. Witness: Clary Simons.

Page 517 – Isham Wheelas of Greene County to Timothy Matthews of Warren County. Deed dated June 3, 1805, for 25 acres on Williams Creek granted grantor in 1793. Witnesses: Ignatius Semmes and Joseph Hill.

Page 518 – William Culpepper to his son Daniel Culpepper both of Warren County. Gift of slave "Sarah" and her four children, dated August 22, 1806. Witnesses: Joseph Evans, Stanton Porter and Charles Porter J.P.

Page 519 – Charles Rayburn to Abraham Sauls both of Warren County. Deed dated January 11, 1806, for 200 acres on the dividing ridge between Brier Creek and Rocky Comfort, granted September 10, 1785. Witnesses: John Matthews, Frances Chandler.

Page 520 – Phillip Gibbs to John Bridges both of Warren County. Deed dated December 16, 1800, for 100 acres on Big Creek known as Eliacom Tyson's improvement. Witnesses: Benjamin Bridges, James Wheeler.

Page 521 - Evan Thomas to Martin Keiner both of Warren County. Deed dated January 31, 1806, for 100 acres "taken out" by Reese Price, and deeded by him to Phillip Gibbs and by the latter to John Bridges and by him to grantor. Witnesses: Joshua Grantham, Larkin Chivers, George Dykes J.P.

Page 522 – Elizabeth Pruitt, widow of Levi Pruitt Esq., to John McCormack. Release of her dower rights July 21, 1806, to undescribed lands. Witness: James McCormack J.P.

Page 524 – Samuel Fickling and Barnard Wood Fickling to Reubin Jones, all of Warren County. Deed dated September 4, 1806, for 285 acres on Golden's Creek granted to the heirs of Henry Golden, deceased, and being all the land formerly owned by Daniel and Henry Golden. Witnesses: George Hargraves, Elisha Hurt.

Page 525 – John Francis Flournoy to Benjamin Carr both of Warren County. Deed dated February 13, 1806, for 291 ½ acres adjoining Matthew Hubert. Witnesses: Alexander Perryman and M. Hubert J.P.

Page 526 – John O'Neal to William Simpler both of Warren County. Deed dated May 3, 1806, for 194 ½ acres adjoining Robert Barton, E. Thomas, William Averitt, James Cash; also 10 acres on Water branch adjoining said 194 ½ acres. Witnesses: Reubin Reese, Nathaniel Duck.

Page 527 – Elijah Williams to William Mays both of Warren County. Deed dated January 7, 1800, for 200 acres on Brier Creek being part of grant in 1794 to Byrd Braswell. Witness: P. Hodo J.P.

Page 528 – McGlammery to John Pierson both of Warren County. Deed dated January 14, 1805, for 100 acres granted Butham May, December 14, 1790. Witnesses: James Pierson and John Bayn J.P.

Page 530 – John Guthrie of Buncombe County, North Carolina, to John Pierson of Warren County, Georgia. Deed dated March 12, 1795, for 300 acres on Big Brier Creek adjoining Jesse Story. Witnesses: Jeremiah Pierson Jr., William Rowland.

Page 531 – Catherine Smith; Sarah Farr; John McCarthy and Mary M. McCarthy; Cassandra Smith; Jacob and Dorcas Johnson, Joseph Smith and Elizabeth Smith; James and Catherine Grenade, Jonathan and Pheriby Smith, of the counties of Columbia and Warren, to Jacob Smith of Warren County. Deed dated November 6, 1803, for land lying in Warren County and Columbia County on Upton's and Middle Creeks. Witnesses: William Duckworth, Gideon George.

Page 535 – John Matthews to Henry Kendall. Deed dated November 4, 1806, for one acre in town of Warrenton. Witnesses: George Hargraves, Archelaus Flewellin J.I.C.

Page 538 – Richard Shirley to Randol Johnson both of Warren County. Deed dated October 18, 1806, for 50 acres on Rocky Comfort being part of a grant to Thomas McClendon. Witnesses: William Simmons, John Hatcher J.P.

Page 539 – John McGlammery to John Pierson, both of Warren County. Deed dated January 14, 1805, for 215 acres granted Jane

Brooks July 22, 1795, and by her deeded to J. Hood, same lying on Big Brier Creek. Witnesses: James Pierson, John Bayn J.P.

Page 540 – Claiborn Newsom of Columbia County to John Adams of Warren County. Deed dated October 19, 1803, for 102 acres on Big Brier Creek. Witnesses: James Cody, P. Hodo.

Page 541 – John Brooks to William Simpler, both of Warren County. Deed of 100 acres dated May 3, 1806. Witnesses: Reubin Reese, Nathan Duck.

Page 542 – Claiborn Newsom of Columbia County to Drewry Bass of Warren. Deed dated September 6, 1802, for 100 acres adjoining grantee and Freeman and Sallie and other lands of grantor. Witnesses: P. Hodo, Ephriam Ivy.

Page 543 – James Williams to Richard Sammons both of Warren County. Deed dated June 10 1806, for 125 acres on Long Creek being the northwest part of 350 acres granted John Torrence and by him deeded grantor. Witnesses: T. Persons, Richard Bray, Isaiah Tucker J.P.

Page 544 – John Chappell of Greene County to Septimus Weatherby of Warren County. Deed dated December 10, 1796, for 130 acres on the head waters of Rocky Comfort and Long Creeks, granted grantor in 1786. Witnesses: Harmon Perryman, Peter Mahone.

Page 546 – John Moses of Washington County to Samuel Moses of Warren County. Deed dated December 15, 1806, for 300 acres on Brier Creek granted Phillip Pool and Hezekiah Bursey. Witnesses: John Moses, Robert Moses. Probated in Washington County, December 17, 1806, before John Achord J.P.

Page 547 – Joseph McMath to Michael Burkhalter both of Warren County. Deed dated November 13, 1806, for lot 309, 2$^{nd}$ District of Baldwin County, lying on Turkey Creek, containing 202 ½ acres. Witnesses: George Hargraves and Thomas Gibson.

Page 548 – Edmund Cody to Thomas Pate. Deed dated December 30, 1806, for 200 acres on Brier Creek granted 1790 to Isaac Ball. Witnesses: John Bayn and Washington Hardaway.

Page 549 – Alexander Moore, Administrator of estate of Mordecai Moore of Columbia County, deceased, to Randolph Johnson of Warren County. Administrator's deed dated December 14, 1805, for 200 acres on south side of Rocky Comfort, surveyed for Jesse Sanford and by him deeded to Abel James and by James to said Mordecai Moore, now deceased. Sale made under order granted by Court of Ordinary of Warren County. Witnesses: James Johnson, Lewis Johnson. Probated September 20, 1806, by James Johnson before William Cason J.P.

Page 550 – Robert Pullin to Edmond Taylor both of Warren County. Deed dated January 4, 1804, for 81 acres on Brier Creek, being part of 550 acres granted grantor June 3, 1803. Witnesses: Benjamin Briant, John M. Neal. Execution of deed acknowledged by the grantor before John Riley J.P., Warren County.

Page 552 – Churchwell Gibson to Margaret Barrett and her two youngest sons, Henry and Charles Barrett "better known as Henry and Churchwell Gibson," all of Warren County. Deed of Gift dated November 13, 1805, in consideration "of the love and good will I have for them and services rendered by them," conveying 450 acres being the grantor's home place deeded to him by Lemuel Pruitt and Jacob Turknett. Witnesses: Isaiah Tucker and Henry Gibson.

Page 553 – Henry Bonner Jr. to Abner Chapman. Deed dated May 12, 1804, for 100 acres on Williams Creek, called the "Cane-brake." Witnesses: Thomas Matthews and William Berry J.P.

Page 554 – Mary Pace to John Pace both of Warren County. Deed dated October 23, 1804, conveying 143 ¾ acres adjoining Reese Green and others. Witnesses: James Tapper, Silas Pace.

Page 557 – Zachariah Sheffield to Joel Matthews both of Warren County. Deed dated December 3, 1800, for 150 acres on Williams Creek sold by the Sheriff under a fifa from Warren Superior Court in favor of Solomon Saxon against the Administrators of Silas

Mercer, deceased, April 1800. Witnesses: Stephen W. Burnley and Benjamin Matthews.

Page 558 – Benjamin Reese of Columbia County to Mary Pace of Wilkes. Deed dated November 25, 1803, for 136 ½ acres adjoining Reese, Green and others. Witnesses: John Pace, Hugh Reese.

Page 559 – Samuel Williams of Richmond County to Moses Hill of Warren County. Deed dated January 5, 1807, for 100 acres on Brier Creek granted 1789 to Rachel Wills. Witnesses: J. Bayn and John Williams.

Page 560 – Zachariah Sheffield to Robert Sheffield both of Warren County. Deed dated May 8, 1805, for 100 acres on Lick Creek, being part of grant of 200 acres to the grantor. Witnesses: Benjamin Crenshaw and Clement Wynne.

Page 563 – John Burkhalter to Edward Kinsey both of Warren County. Deed dated January 3, 1807, for 91 acres on Brier Creek. Witnesses: E. Thomas, Sterling Gardner.

Page 567 – Johnson Wright to William Jones both of Warren County. Deed dated September 2, 1805 for 200 acres on Rocky Comfort and Long Creek in former Wilkes now Warren County. Witnesses: Abner Locke and Royster Heath.

Page 568 – Moses Granberry to Benjamin Upton and John P. Martin, Trustees of the Baptist Church "called and known by the name of Church of Christ at Fellowship." Deed dated June 7, 1806, for land where the church stands on the head branch of Rocky Comfort Creek known as Granberry's Mill branch. Witnesses: William O. Hill, N. Robertson, George Dykes.

Page 569 – David Robertson Sr. of Richmond County, planter, to Isham Wheeler of Warren County, planter. Deed dated February 19, 1802, for 200 acres granted William Womack July 12, 1787 and by him deeded to Fitzhugh Hunt and by him deeded to grantor; land in former Wilkes County. Witnesses: David Wheeler, Thomas Westberry.

Page 572 – William Few to Norvell Robertson. Deed dated November 1, 1803, for 212 acres in former Richmond now Warren County, being part of two grants, one made to Richard Barrow in 1774 and the other in 1787 to George Upton. Witness: Joseph Wheeler.

Page 573 – Phillip Brantley and wife Nancy to Henry Hardin, all of Warren County. Deed dated January 11, 1806, for 114 acres on Middle Creek. Witnesses: Hiram Perry, Jeptha Brantley and Benjamin Brantley.

Page 573 – Alexander Perryman, Sheriff Warren County to Joseph Hutchinson of Augusta. Sheriff's deed dated September 3, 1805, for 520 acres granted to Martin Hardin November 13, 1801, and by him deeded to James Hutchinson October 26, 1802; and levied on and sold as property of said James Hutchinson to satisfy a judgment and execution from Camden Superior Court in re: Joseph Hutchinson vs. James Hutchinson. Witnesses: J. Hamill, Jody Newsom J.I.C.

Page 574 – Jacob Watson to William Smith both of Warren County. Deed dated December 24, 1803, conveying 100 acres known as the old fort tract adjoining the grantee's lands and Michael Coda, lying on Dry fork and Big Brier Creeks. Witnesses: John Saunders, William Cason J.P.

Page 575 – William Smith to Edmond Cody both of Warren County. Deed dated April 2, 1807, for 128 acres adjoining Michael Cody, Henry Harris and Benjamin Adams. Witnesses: William D. Bunkley and E. Hurt J.I.C.

Page 576 – Mary Perryman, released Harmon Perryman of Warren County, from his warranty in a bill of sale for slave wench dated February 1, 1797. Witnesses: A. Perryman and Caswell Ball.

Page 577 – Nathan Brewer to Thomas Bohannon both of Warren County. Deed dated January 9, 1805, for 50 acres on Ogeechee River. Witnesses: William Hardwick, Jesse Doles.

Page 579 – Grant to Roger Lawson dated March 3, 1767, signed by Sir James Wright, Governor of the Province of Georgia, for 200 acres in the Parish of St. George, bounded at the time of survey on all sides by vacant land.

Page 584 – William Crawford to John Rushing, both of Warren County. Deed dated December 5, 1806, for land near Long Creek. Witnesses: J. Rushing, James Ledbetter.

Page 585 – Jacob Castleberry to Turner Persons, both of Warren County. Deed dated January 5, 1807, for 60 acres on Whetstone Creek. Witnesses: Isaac Ball and Septimus Weatherby.

Page 587 – James Matthews of Warren County to Isham Matthews of Halifax County, North Carolina. Power of Attorney dated June 3, 1807, authorizing him to collect from Lewis Daniel of Halifax County a negro man "Bob" and all money due him by Daniel. Witnesses: James Myhand and Elisha Hurt J.I.C.

Page 589 – Robert Carry and wife Katherine to Hezekiah Cooksey. Deed dated February 7, 1807, for 250 acres on Williams Creek granted to Boling Cureton and deeded by him to Ann Carry and by her to grantor. Witnesses: Walter Nally and George Stewart.

Page 590 – Abner Flewellin of Baldwin County to Samuel Posey of Warren County. Deed dated February 7, 1807, for several tracts in Warren County. Witnesses: George Hargraves and Archibald Flewellin.

Page 591 – Ann Carry to Robert Carry, both of Warren County. Deed dated November 23, 1804, for the above land.

Page 593 – William Roberson to Septimus Weatherby both of Warren. Deed dated January 29, 1802, for 50 acres on Ogeechee River, being part of 200 acres granted John Pate July 25, 1786, and deeded to grantor by Thomas Pate, only heir of said John Pate, December 22, 1801. Witnesses: John Hayse, Andrew King J.P.

Page 594 – Stephen Marshall to Elisha Hurt both of Warren County. Deed dated December 26, 1806, conveying 454 acres on Rocky Comfort, being part of tract of land granted Abraham Heeth. Witnesses: David Mims and Jeremiah Davidson.

Page 599 – John Oliver and Sally his wife, Benjamin Oliver and Nancy his wife, to Francis Stainback, all of Warren County. Deed dated July 31, 1807, for 170 acres on Long Creek, being part of two tracts surveyed for John Anglin and granted him August 1, 1787 and August 1, 1798, respectively. Witnesses: Edmond Rose and Matthew Hubert J.P.

Page 600 – James Bishop of Hancock County to Francis Stainback of Warren County. Deed dated February 5, 1807, for 10 acres adjoining grantee's lands on Long Creek. Witnesses: James W. Green, Matthew Hubert J.P.

Page 601 – Benjamin Wright to Archelaus Flewellin both of Warren County. Deed dated December 22, 1806, for 245 acres on south side of Rocky Comfort adjoining John Lock, Elisha Hurt and Nicholas Williams and an old survey on which David Mims now lives, also one acre to include a spring where John Davidson formerly lived and which he sold to Nicholas Williams. Witnesses: Zacheus Burt, James Burt.

Page 602 – George Morris to Nowell Williams both of Warren County. Deed dated December 29, 1801, for 70 acres on Rocky Comfort. Witnesses: Elsey Williams and N. Williams J.P.

Page 603 – John Ball of Washington County to Archelaus Flewellin of Warren County. Deed dated January 5, 1805, for 91 acres on Rocky Comfort Creek. Witnesses: Abram Brinkley and Benjamin Wright.

Page 604 – James Brooks to Joseph Davidson both of Warren County. Deed dated June 12, 1803, for 100 acres on Rocky Comfort Creek granted 1788 to Baxter Jordan. Witnesses: John May and John McKinzie.

Page 605 – Martha Smith, widow, to her son William Smith, both of Warren County. Deed of Gift dated July 13, 1807, for the land where she lives, etc. Witnesses: Parsons Pace and Joseph White.

Page 606 – Charles Collins of Burke County to John Dickens of Columbia County. Deed dated November 17, 1792, for 100 acres on Big Creek "taken up" by William Marlow 1786. Witnesses: Thomas Jackson and Robert Dickens.

Page 607 – Lewis Brady to John Dicken, both of Warren County. Deed dated June 28, 1807, for 450 acres on the Ogeechee River, being part of 900 acre tract granted grantor in 1798. Witnesses: Willoughby Jordan, James Saunders, Thomas Stokes.

Page 609 – James French to William Few both of Warren County. Deed dated September 1, 1806, for 100 acres adjoining Ignatius Few. Witnesses: Mark Heeth and Solomon Lockett.

Page 612 – John McMurrin to Thomas Harris both of Warren County. Deed dated January 20, 1804, for 200 acres on Long Creek granted Robert Barnett Sr., January 4, 1791. Witnesses: Gibson Berry and Pryor Gardner J.P.

Page 613 – William Gardner to Thomas Harris. Deed dated October 11, 1804, for 16 ½ acres adjoining grantee. Witnesses: Pryor Gardner J.P., Fannie Gardner.

Page 613 – Peter Qualls of Warren County to John Moore of Washington County. Deed dated September 17, 1806, for 115 acres on Joe's Creek being part of grant to Samuel Irwin and deeded by the executors of said Irwin's will to Samuel Allen Sr., and also being a part of grant to Samuel Allen; and by William Allen deeded Martin Cox and by him to grantor. Also 93 ½ acres said Cox and by him to the said Qualls, same adjoining the 115 acre tract. Witnesses: Alexander Avera and George Dykes J.P.

Page 614 – Luke Williams to Tilman Niblett both of Warren County. Deed dated December 4, 1804, for 79 acres on the headwaters of Williams Creek, being part of survey made in 1792 for Micajah Stone, adjoining John Baker and Pierce Bailey. Witnesses: Samuel Torrence, Stafford Williams, Austin Baker.

Page 616 – Luke Williams to Stafford Williams both of Warren County. Deed dated same as last above, for 125 acres being south part of tract in last deed above, adjoining Asa Cox and Joel Matthews. Witnesses: Nathan Williams, Samuel Torrence and Austin Baker.

Page 617 – Micajah Stone to Luke Williams both of Warren County. Deed dated April 13, 1798, for 200 acres on Williams Creek granted grantor in 1792. Witnesses: James Smyth, Ebenezer Smyth, John Baker, J.P.

Page 618 – Elender Ridgewell of Warren County, assigns all her rights in the contemplated land lottery for the lately-ceded lands on Oconee River. Witness: Paul McCormick.

Page 619 – John Matthews of Hancock County to James Burt of Warren County. Deed dated February 19, 1805, for 100 acres on Rocky Comfort, adjoining Zacheus Burt. Witnesses: Zacheus Burt and William Banks.

Page 620 – John Matthews of Warren County to Zacheus Burt of same county. Deed dated November 20, 1802, for 130 acres on Rocky Comfort adjoining Nicholas Williams. Witnesses: Shadrach Flewellin and E. Hurt J.I.C.

Page 621 – Michael Swicord of South Carolina to Alexander Perryman of Georgia. Bill of Sale for slave named David dated June 27, 1805. Witness: Graham Smith.

Page 622 – William Chamberg to William Bird both of Warren County. Deed dated January 1, 1804, for 150 acres granted grantor 1797, and adjoining Joseph McKinley and Richard Bulloch. Witnesses: Wilson Bird, Thomas Carroll.

Page 625 – Lewis Wright to Richard Heath both of Warren County. Deed dated May 8, 1806, for 100 acres on Williams Creek adjoining Burrell Perry. Witnesses: Charles Matthews and Sterling Gardner J.P.

Page 626 – Lewis Wright to Richard Heath. Bill of Sale dated January 14, 1806, for slave wench "Sall." Witnesses: James Matthews, Charles Matthews.

Page 627 – Same parties, Bill of Sale for 5 slaves dated May 3, 1806.

Page 629 – John Burkhalter and wife Sarah to John McCormick, all of Warren County, planters. Deed dated January 15, 1797, for

150 acres in said county. Witnesses: John Williams and James McCormick J.P.

Page 631 – Emperor Wheeler and wife Catherine to James Beasley Sr., both of Wilkes County. Deed dated February 24, 1791, for 352 acres granted grantor 1786 except 63 acres "reserved" for Richard Beasley. Witnesses: James Gray, Richard Beasley.

Page 632 – John Bates to William Berry both of Warren County. Deed dated January 20, 1806, for 312 acres on Little River. Witnesses: J. Riviere, Thomas Berry, William Bimes.

Page 634 – John McCormick and wife Sally, to Jacob Landrum all of Warren County. Deed dated January 3, 1808, for 100 acres being the northeast ½ of a 200 acre tract granted Elizabeth Landrum August 10, 1785, and deeded by her to grantor August 22, 1792; also 30 acres being the southwest part of 150 acres deeded to grantor by John Burkhalter January 16, 1797, and previously granted to Burkhalter. Witnesses: Thomas Dark and James McCormick J.P.

Page 635 – Jesse Sanford of Hancock County to William Sanford Sr. and wife Rachel "of the state and county aforesaid." Deed of Gift dated September 7, 1805, for 186 acres on Hart's Creek in Warren County. Life estate only conveyed to grantees and after their deaths land to pass in fee simple to Thornton Stanford of Hancock County. Witnesses: B. Hubert and Hubert Reynolds J.P.

Page 635 – Newt Ward to Arthur Matthews. Deed dated December 28, 1807, for 15 acres. Witnesses: Solomon Slatter and Sterling Gardner J.P.

Page 636 – Lewis Brady to his son, Cullen Lewis Brady, both of Warren County. Deed of Gift dated February 25, 1807, for 250 acres where the grantor now lives, adjoining Wilie Giles Brady. Witnesses: James Grizzard and Willie Giles Brady.

Page 636 – Etheldred Thomas to Arthur Matthews both of Warren County. Deed dated December 28, 1807, for 200 acres on Stamp Branch, granted grantor in 1790. Witnesses: Solomon Slatter and Sterling Gardner.

Page 637 – Noah Butt to Robert Culpepper, both of Warren County. Deed dated January 28, 1808, for 37 acres on Hart's Creek. Witnesses: Daniel and William Culpepper.

Page 638 – Absalom Cobb of Hancock County to Charles McAllister of Warren County. Deed dated August 2, 1804, for 93 acres on Rocky Comfort Creek granted Baxter Jordan in 1786. Witnesses: H. Nicholson and Joab Brooks.

# WILL BOOK A

Page 1 – Benjamin Hubert, Last Will and Testament, dated May 1, 1793, probated July 6, 1794. Gives to his wife Mary all estate, real and personal, for her support; at her death their youngest son, David Hubert, to have 100 acres to include the plantation where testator then lived, also a slave Bob, son David to pay testator's three daughters, Fannie Runnels, Polly Rutherford and Hester Runnels a specified sum of money. Grandson, Hubert Runnels, at the death of wife Mary, to have a cow and calf, a small shotgun and 100 acres known as the Brewer tract. At death of said wife Mary, all property other than the above, to be divided into eight lots and drawn for; son, William Hubert to have first draw; son Matthew Hubert to have two draws; then Polly Rutherford, Hester Runnels, sons Gabriel Hubert, David Hubert, and Jacob Williams to draw in the order named. If daughter Fannie dies before her mother, her part to fall to my said grandson Hubert Runnels. Executors: John Rutherford, Matthew Hubert and David Hubert. Witnesses: Matthew Hubert, Elijah Runnels, Gibson Flournoy.

Page 2 – Administrator's Bond dated August 24, 1796, of John Dryden, Administrator of Estate of William Dryden; James Blount, security. Witness: Thomas Doster.

Page 3 – James Young. Last Will and Testament dated June 4, 1794; no date of probate. Gives to wife, 5 shillings; to his beloved son, John Fewocks, 300 acres on Ready Creek, waters of Brier Creek, two slaves, horses, household furniture, for his lifetime. Final division of estate to go to Jacob, James, William and John Pearson Young, and William Bowland. William Young Jr. to receive certain cattle. Witnesses: Samuel Slocum, William Young Sr., Louisa Corbitt.

Page 5 – Jacob Horn, planter, of Richmond County, Georgia. Last Will and Testament dated May 1, 1793; probated July 6, 1794. Gives to wife Margaret for her lifetime, a slave "Jennie", cattle and other personal property. Gives to son John Horn a ewe and lamb; to son, Jesse Horn, 200 acres, being the western part of the tract on which testator lives, together with slave Ann; to son, Isaac Horn, 200 being the Eastern part of the said home place tract, together with horse. To daughter Elizabeth Henderson, a ewe and lamb; and the same to daughter, Mary Powell; to daughter, Martha Horn, a mare called "Gin", and to daughter Ellinor Horn the increase of said mare; to daughter, Sarah Horn, a cow named "Cherry". Executors: Sons, John and Jesse Horn. Witnesses: Robert Patterson, John Barberer, Abel Lennard.

Page 8 – Betty Fluwellin. Last Will and Testament dated March 28, 1794; no date of probate. Bequeaths to sons, Howell, William, Abner and Shaderick Fluwellin five shillings each; to son, Alexander Fluwellin, two slaves for his lifetime; to Elizabeth, daughter of Solomon Slatter, at his death, but if she dies without heirs, then to be divided among all testatrix's own children; given to son, the said Alexander, "all my right to the land I now live on, or any other land I have a right to, together with all my pewter, household goods. Gives to daughter, Nancy Slatter, a saddle, flax-wheel and wearing apparel. Witnesses: Septimus Weatherby, Daniel Grantham, Nancy Slatter.

Page 9 – Benjamin Simmons, planter. Last Will and Testament dated March 16, 1795; probated April 11, 1795. Gives to son James Simmons, 200 acres originally granted Moses Powell Sr., and deeded by him to testator, adjoining the land where testator lives; to daughter, Rebeckah Simmons, a slave named "Beck", a bed, to be hers upon her reaching her majority or marriage. Residue of estate is devised to son, John Simmons, he to pay son, Henry Simmons, L150 upon him reaching his majority, and also pay to daughters Pollie and Jincey Simmons $300.00 each upon each of them becoming of age or marriage; also to provide testator's wife Lucy Simmons with a "genteel maintenance for her widowhood on the place where I now live." Executors: James Simmons and John Simmons. Witnesses: Malcolm Johnson, John Simmons, John Wynne J.P.

Page 11 – Hardy Wester, of Warren County. Last Will and Testament, dated May 18, 1795; probated July 8, 1795. Gives to his wife Fanny, his horses, household goods including his pewter, three shotguns, punch-bowl, cotton and linen wheels, and $29.00 in money. No land mentioned. To daughters, Nancy and

Elizabeth Wester, five shillings each. Executors: Wife, Fanny Wester, and Sampson Ivy.

Page 14 – Gahazi Davis "known by this name, alias Gahazi Shockley." Last Will and Testament dated November 9, 1795; probated December 18, 1795. Devises to Barsheba Granard, a sorrel mare "Nell"; to brother, Nathan Shockley, "known by the name of Nathan Davis," all of testator's land. Executor: Reubin McGee of said county. Witnesses: P. Hodo, Thomas Ansley, James Smith.

Page 15 – Richard Cocks, principal, Thomas Cocks surety, Administrator's Bond on estate of Thomas Hardin, deceased, dated January 18, 1796.

Page 16 – Nathaniel Hood. Last Will and Testament dated November 17, 1795; probated February 1, 1796. Gives his entire estate to his brother, John Hood, who is also named Executor. Witness: William Hardin.

Page 17 – Thomas Drake, blacksmith. Last Will and Testament dated March 1, 1794; no date of probate shown. He gives or directs that a tract of 300 acres on Rocky Comfort Creek and a tract of land on the Ohoopee be sold and the proceeds used to educate testator's four children. He directs that his son, Francis Drake, be apprenticed to a blacksmith to learn that trade. His son, Lemuel Braxton Drake, to be apprenticed to a bricklayer to learn that trade; and son, Early Drake, be apprenticed to his brother Francis. He directs that his property be divided into five parts, one each to his wife Sarah and the sons above named and daughter Theney Drake. Executors: Friends, Tandy Clark Key, Daniel Evans, and wife Sarah Drake. Witnesses: James Robinson, John Fove, Priscilla Fove.

Page 19 – David Lockett. Last Will and Testament dated June 7, 1796; probated March 12, 1796. He directs that his estate be kept together for use of his wife and the children under age; that a still be bought, and that the money received from sale of his tobacco be put out at interest. Provides for youngest children Winfrey, Reubin, Doctor and Sally Lockett, giving them L30 each. The land bought of Daniel Phelps to be sold except 50 acres whereon "my sister Gipson lives." "My bounty land warranty" to go to two youngest sons Reubin and Doctor Lockett. He directs that all his estate be kept together until son Doctor comes of age. Son David to have a bed and other items. Certain lands with three slaves are given to his wife. Residue to be divided between my children, Solomon, Thomas, Abner, Davis, Winfrey, Reubin, Doctor and Sally Lockett; and son Thomas to have the land where he now lives. Executors: Sons, Solomon and Thomas Lockett. Witnesses: Alexander Bass and Henry Peek.

Page 21 – Administrator's Bond, Mary Cooper, Administratrix of estate of James Cooper, deceased. Sureties: Harmon Wilkerson, Peter Castleberry. Dated May 16, 1798.

Page 21 – Samuel Moore of Warren County. Non-cupative will, sworn to September 7, 1795, by Captain Solomon Newsom, who says that on the evening of the 1$^{st}$ inst., Samuel Moore, now deceased, sent for him, deponent, and deponent arrived at Moore's home the next day and found him in his perfect senses but very ill; that Moore told him he was desirous of making his will as soon as he could get Jody Newsom. He said that Moore wished nothing sold of his estate but that his wife and children have all the income until they the children were of age; that all the estate should be in the hands of his wife and Jody Newsom and "to be dealt out to the children as they become of age, and they in their discretion should sell his land and the proceeds with what is due him from Colonel Lewis, be invested in two young negroes." Sworn to before Wyche Goodwin J.P. and L. Pruitt J.P.

Page 24 – Administrator's Bond, William Cox and Sally Threewitts, Administrators, estate of Thomas Cox, deceased, dated October 5, 1797. Sureties: Thomas Cocks, T. Persons.

Page 25 – Administrator's Bond, dated April 12, 1798, of James Douglas, Administrator of Rev. Jepthah Vining estate. Securities: Harmon Perryman and Joshua Vining.

Page 26 – George Franklin, Administrator of William Franklin, deceased. Administrator's Bond dated February 9, 1797; surety, Alexander Smith. Witness: Andrew King.

Page 1 – Amos Wright. Last Will and Testament dated April 18, 1810; probated January 7, 1811. To his wife Rachel he gives all his estate in Warren County for her lifetime or widowhood. If she re-marries then all the estate except the land to be divided among his children viz: Elisha, Basil, Lewis, Joseph, Amos, James, Lucy, Chloe and Drusilla Wright. To his grandson Joseph Ryan he gives money for "a good education." He directs his land in Wayne County be sold. To his son John he gives one French crown. No executor named. Witnesses: Daniel Sturdivant, Jeremiah Butt, John Butt.

Page 2 – Jonathan Lock "very sick in body." Last Will and Testament dated December 24, 1810, probated March 4, 1811. Gives to his wife Mary the home plantation for her lifetime or widowhood. If she marries, she is to take her third of the estate, instead of under the will. At her death or re-marriage the land where he lives and a lot of land he drew in the $7^{th}$ district of Wilkinson County to be sold and divided among his four children, Abner, Mancey, John and Jesse Lock. Executors: Wife, Mary, and son John Lock. Witnesses: Elisha Hurt, Andrew Bush and James Bush.

Page 5 – William Pitts. Last Will and Testament dated August 2, 1811; probated September 2, 1811. To "my dearly beloved mother" he gives one-third of his estate, and one-third each to his brothers Samuel and Hardy Pitts, except minor bequests to his sister Patience Oliver, sister Nancy Parham "now Nancy Turner", brother Matthew Parham, sister Rebecca Parham, each to have $1.00. Executors: Samuel and Hardy Pitts. Witnesses: Radford Butt, John Lewis, Selah Hadley.

Page 6 – George Waggoner. Last Will and Testament dated February 6, 1797; probated September 2, 1811. Gives to his wife Elizabeth his entire estate except five shillings each to his children William, Sarah Webb, James, Henry, Mary Shaw, John George, and Becky Ward. Executors: Wife Elizabeth and William Smith. Witnesses: William Luckett, Charles Webb, John McCray.

Page 9 – Blake Lassiter of Halifax County, North Carolina. Last Will and Testament dated August 21, 1809, probated in Warren County, October 8, 1811. Gives to Willis Lassiter of Warren County, Georgia, certain slaves and a right to others in possession of William G. Grimes in Greene County, Georgia. Witnesses: Septimus Weatherby, Henry Cocroft.

Page 10 – Robert Wynne. Last Will and Testament dated April 22, 1811; probated December 2, 1811. Gives to his daughter Lucy Mullins, son Clement Wynne, daughter Elizabeth Walker, son Peter Wynne, daughter Mary Walker, son Robert Wynne, son Dudley Wynne, daughter Nancy Wynne, daughter Susannah Edwards, daughter Lydia Hunter, five shillings each. To daughters Patsy and Cynthia Wynne, a feather bed and other small items, each. The residue of his estate to be equally divided among "my six last children", viz, William Wynne, Frances Culpepper, Thomas Wynne, Patsy Wynne and Cynthia Wynne. Executors: Clement Wynne and Jack S. Davenport. Witnesses: Hardy Hobson, James Peavy, Francis Benton.

Page 21 – Lowe Jackson "very sick in body." Last Will and Testament dated May 6, 1813, probated July 5, 1813. Gives his entire estate to wife Ailey Jackson in fee simple. Executor: John Rushing Sr. Witnesses: Vincent Davis, Joseph Murray.

Page 23 – Lucy Thompson. Last Will and Testament dated July 6, 1813; probated February 7, 1814. Gives to her daughter Lucy Kerr a slave for her lifetime, then to be the property of Augustus Thompson Kerr, son said Lucy Kerr. Gives the residue of her estate to her son Alexander Thompson, he to be the executor. Witnesses: James Allen, Zitha Allen, Mariah Allen.

Page 26 – James B. Thompson. Last Will and Testament dated December 3, 1813; probated July Term, 1814. Gives to his wife Priscilla all his estate for her lifetime or widowhood. Upon her death or re-marriage, one-half of the estate shall go to nephew, James Thompson Jr., except land lots 231 and 238 in Wilkinson County, to nephew William Thompson Jr., with my gun and powder horn "which was his father's in his lifetime." To godson Joseph W. Luckett, a horse, saddle and bridle. To his cousin

Joseph Brocks of Jasper County, testator's clothes. Executors: William R. Luckett and brother Henry B. Thompson. Witnesses: Henry B. Thompson, William R. Puckett and George Lewis.

Page 28 – Sarah Neal, "low in health." Last Will and Testament dated October 27, 1814, probated October 3, 1814. She gives certain slaves to her daughters Elizabeth Bray, Dianna Persons, Rebecca Beall, Patsy Gibson, Sarah Gardner and Drusilla Pitts, and son Elisha Neal. To granddaughter Frances Gardner a slave named Caty. Executor: Hardy Pitts. Witnesses: Frederick W. Masters, John C. Turner.

Page 30 – William Heath. Last Will and Testament dated December 12, 1813; probated July 4, 1814. Gives to his son John, a "bay filly" and other items. Residue of estate to his wife Sary for her lifetime or widowhood, then to wife (if in life) and "my children." Executor: Brother, John Heath. Witnesses: William Barrow and John Kellum.

Page 31 – Irby Dewberry Sr. Last Will and Testament dated January 8, 1816; probated February 5, 1816. Gives all his estate to his wife Mary for her lifetime or widowhood, then to be divided between children, Elizabeth, wife of Benjamin Wynne, Frances, wife of Clement Wynne, the three daughters of Sarah Wynne, deceased, former wife of Peter Pynne, viz: Nancy, Elizabeth and Frances Wynne; Pollie Darden, Thomas Dewberry, John Dewberry and James Dewberry. Says he gives no legacy to his three grandsons, the sons of Sarah Wynne, deceased, "as they are able to make their own way." Executors: Son-in-law Benjamin Wynne, and son-in-law William Darden. Witnesses: Benjamin Chapman, Zachariah Darden, Henry B. Thompson.

Page 33 – Sampson Ivey. Last Will and Testament dated February 28, 1814; probated February 5, 1816. Gives to his wife Millie his home plantation for her lifetime, then to go to his five children Thomas Ivy, Polly Williams (nee Ivy), Jincy McKenney (nee Ivy), Elizabeth and Charlotte Ivy. Executor: Son, Thomas Ivy. Witnesses: Barnard W. Fickling, Moses McKenney, John Lewis.

Page 37 – William Lowe of Halifax County, North Carolina. Last Will and Testament dated September 12, 1814; probated in Warren County May 6, 1816. Gives to Nancy Yarborough the plantation whereon he then lives, with all his livestock, etc., also $400.00 of his money in the hands of Kinchen Wheeles. Witnesses: William Anderson, Sarah Anderson, Mary Anderson.

Page 38 – Abram Sanders. Last Will and Testament dated July 17, 1817; probated September 1, 1817. Gives all his estate to his wife Mary for her lifetime or widowhood, then to be divided between his "beloved" children, James Sanders, Abram Sanders, Rebecca Sanders, Mary Thompson, Sarah Grenade, Charley Sanders and Anna Sanders. Executors: Wife Mary, and son James Sanders. Witnesses: John Howard, Abel Ansley, Thomas Coram.

Page 40 – William Goynne. Last Will and Testament dated January 4, 1816, probated September 1, 1817. He gives certain sums of money to his grandchildren, John and Mount Herman Goynne, sons of his son Hiram. He directs that his home, lands, etc. be kept as a home for his wife and after her death to go to his son Hiram. Son, Tyra Goynne, he gives a bed and other items. To his daughters Rebecca Dick and Alice King, and sons John, Drury, William and Hardy Goynne, he gives $1.50 each. No executor named. Witnesses: Joseph Johnston, Obedience Ray, Hartwell Battle.

Page 43 – Joseph Peavy Sr. Last Will and Testament dated August 25, 1810, probated November 3, 1817. Gives to his wife Ann all his estate for her lifetime, then to be divided between "all my children"; except a horse and saddle to grandson Wade Hampton Peavy, and bed and mattress to daughter Mary Peavy. Executors: Wife Ann, son Abraham Peavy. Witnesses: Stephen W. Burnley, Parthena Burnley.

Page 43 – Mark Harden. Last Will and Testament dated April 13, 1813, probated November Term, 1817. He gives to his sons, Henry, Mark, Martin, James and John Harden, and daughters Polly George, Judith Willis and Sallie Hardin $2.00 each. All the residue of his estate he gives to his wife Frances and their two daughters Patsy and Nancy Harden and son William Harden, "to be used by them in common" and after wife's death to be divided between said Patsy, Nancy and William. Executors: Isaiah Tucker, Richard Flesher and wife Frances Harden.

Page 44 – William White. Non-cupative Will made the day of his death, February 2, 1818; probated February 7, 1818. Gives to his sons Green and Austin White, a horse each; to sons Timothy, Matthew and William White, $100.00 each; to daughters Nancy, Peggy, Unity and Betsy White, a feather bed each. Remainder of estate to be equally divided between all of said children. Jethro Darden, witness, swore to the above as being said White's spoken will, sworn to before D. Dennis J.P.

Page 46 – Francis Stainback, planter. Last Will and Testament dated September 5, 1817; probated March 23, 1818. Gives to his "beloved spouse" Nancy Stainback the use of the land where he lives for her lifetime, and half of all his personal property in fee simple. To his nephew David Stainback he gives one-third of the other half of the personal property; and the remaining two-thirds of one-half to his nephew George Stainback and nieces Nancy Robinson and Elizabeth Chisholm (children of his brother Thomas Stainback.) To Mary Radcliffe and her heirs, certain slaves and the land whereon he lives at wife's death; and to Elizabeth Pace and Dolly Oxford and the heirs of their bodies, he gives certain slaves. Executors: Warren Andrews and George Turner. Witnesses: William Anderson, Ephriam Ivy, Harbert Pate.

Page 47 – Job Swain. Last Will and Testament; probated March 1, 1819. Gives to his wife Susannah his home plantation with its appurtenances for her widowhood or until his son John is of legal age. Also wife Susannah he gives 14 slaves for her widowhood, then to pass to his sons Richard, James and William Swain when of age. To daughter Nancy Rogers he gives a slave "Sherman." To son Thomas Swain one "square" of land in Telfair County which he, testator, bought of Underwood. To son, Josiah Swain, certain slaves. To son Richard Swain one "square" of land in Pulaski County, being lot 344, drawn by Barton Atchinson, together with slaves. To his daughter Margaret Peek he gives two slaves. To his son John Swain he gives certain land and slaves. Mentions his four youngest children as being Richard, James,

William and John.  Executors: Wife and son Richard Swain. Witnesses: Noah Kelcey, Charles Atchison, Thomas Doster.

Page 49 – Elisha Roberts.  Last Will and Testament dated May 10, 1818; probated March 6, 1819.  He directs that his wife May possess and enjoy his whole estate for her lifetime as a support for herself and his three younger children.  At her death his son Josias Randol Roberts to have the slave "Lewis", and residue of the estate to be divided equally among all his children.  Executor: Friend, Zephaniah Franklin.  Witnesses: Sarah Cloud, May Ryan, Dennis L. Ryan.

Page 57 – Howell Hight Sr.  Last Will and Testament dated February 2, 1821; probated February 13, 1821.  To his wife Anne Hight, his home place of 580 acres, with the livestock and slaves, for her lifetime.  To sons, Howell, Wiley, Gilbert Hight and daughters Sally Johnson, Polly Crenshaw, Sukey Grierson and Anne Sheffield, one-eighth of his estate each.  To son, Julius Hight, $30.00 in cash.  To his grandchildren (children of his son Julius), viz., Lucinda, Alfred, Sukey, Henry, Howell, Nancy, Elizabeth, Edna, Cornelius and William, the land on Hart's Creek where he said Julius now lives, together with land lot 74, 7th district of Wilkinson County drawn by testator in the land lottery, together with one-eighth of testator's estate, when the youngest of said children is of age; said son, Julius, to be trustee for his said children.  To testator's grandchildren Pascal Crenshaw, Elizabeth Grierson (late Elizabeth Crenshaw), and Sallie Johnson (children of testator's daughter Sallie Johnson,) one-eighth part of testator's estate.  To his grandchildren Lucy, Sally and Zilla Ann Sheffield, Delilah, Peyton, Frances Caroline and Wyatt Oliver Grierson (children of testator's daughter, Suky Grierson) one-eighth part of his estate.  Executors: Churchill Gibson.  Witnesses: Henry Hill, Robert Bonner, Dennis L. Ryan.

Page 62 – George Harris.  Last Will and Testament dated October 20, 1817; probated September 3, 1821.  Gives to his sons Ezekiel, Thomas, Benjamin and John Harris, certain items of furniture and feather bed each.  He directs his lands all be sold (including home place tract) and proceeds divided between the following legates, Sally Elliott one share; the children of Samuel Harris, deceased son, one share; Rebecca Sims one share; children of daughter Ann Moodie that may be living at his decease, one share; Malinda Myrick, one share; and sons, Ezekiel, Thomas, Benjamin and John Harris, one share each. "All ready money at my decease to be divided between my wife Catherine and the above named legatees." He gives the home place to his wife Catherine for her use for her life time. Executors: Sons, Thomas and John Harris. Witnesses: Robert Hill Sr., Moses Darden, Jesse Darden.

Page 66 – Isaiah Tucker. Last Will and Testament dated August 9, 1821; probated November 5, 1821. Says he is in business with his son Germain Tucker to whom he gives $5.00 "in addition to former gifts made him." To his granddaughter Elizabeth Tucker (daughter of son John, deceased), to Walter Lucas who married testator's daughter Betsy Tucker, and to daughter Lucretia Cody, and to daughter Nancy Holcombe he gives $5.00 "in addition to former gifts made to them." To his son Edmond Tucker, daughters Louisa and Julia Tucker, sons Matthew and Mark Tucker and daughter Miriam Tucker, he gives each $1400.00 in cash and a feather bed. Said sons Edmond, Matthew and Mark being under age. Testator directs that his son Edmond be sent to Augusta Academy to be educated. He requests that Miriam be placed with her uncle and aunt, Henry and Mary Gibson and that they educate her. Executor: Son, Germain Tucker. Witnesses: John Breed, Churchill Gibson, D. Dennis.

Page 69 – Benjamin Upton. Last Will and Testament dated January 28, 1813; probated November Term 1821. He directs that his wife Judith may use all his estate as she pleases for her life time, and at her death the home place to be divided between his two daughters Rebecca Chalker and Obedience Brannon. Residue to his other children Sarah Highnott, Nancy Murray, Tobias Upton, Polly Conner. Executors: Neville Robertson, Simeon Travis and Samuel Allen. Witnesses: Selina Murray, Charlotte Murray, Alexander Avera.

Page 77 – Harbert Pate. Last Will and Testament dated March 12, 1822; probated May 6, 1822. Gives to his wife Charlotte the land where he lives with appurtenances for her lifetime, then with all other land he owns to go to his three sons, David, Edmund and

Cordy N. Pate. To daughters Polly Ray and Elizabeth Broom, beds already in their possession; to said sons and daughter Nancy Pate, bed etc. To son-in-law, John Ray, $1.00. Executors: David Pate, Ezekiel F. Broom and Thomas Gibson. Witnesses: Thomas Lewis and John W. Jackson.

Page 80 – John Parrish. Last Will and Testament dated August 23, 1819, probated May 5, 1823. Gives a slave to his wife Elizabeth; to sons Hampton, William and Allen Parrish, daughters Linney Cooper, Sally Rowe, Polly James and Dicy Smith $5.00 each; to his son Anselm, a horse; to grandchildren John and Thomas Parrish (sons of said Hampton Parrish), Wilson and Epsey Parrish (son and daughter of William), to John and Elizabeth Cooper (children of said Linney), to Lucinda and John Floyd Rowe (children of said Sally), to James and Wiley James (sons of said Polly) $50.00 each. Residue of estate to be divided between his sons Allen and Anselm and daughters Elizabeth and Patsy. Executor: Thomas Friend. Witnesses: Benjamin Sandiford, Benjamin F. Friend, John O. Friend, Moses Gatlin.

Page 81 – Benjamin Wheeler. Last Will and Testament dated March 21, 1817; probated November 14, 1822. Gives to his wife Mary one-fourth of the lands where he lives, to include the residence, for her lifetime or widowhood. The other three-fourths he gives to his three sons Merritt, Vinson and James, jointly. He gives two feather beds now in possession of Mary Signor Broom to her two daughters, Sarah and Tempy Broom. Residue of his estate to be equally divided between his three daughters Sarah Bell, Susannah Anglin and Mary Signor Broom. Executors: Isaac Ball, James Wheeler. Witnesses: John Hubert, Hannon Hubert.

Page 83 – Archibald Lacy. Last Will and Testament dated September 21, 1822, probated November 4, 1822. Gives all his estate to his wife Sarah for her lifetime, and after her death to their daughter Pollie to have certain property and residue to his six children Elizabeth, John, Martha, Nancy, Pleasant, Sarah, and grandson Randolph Lacy. Executors: Pleasant M. Lacy and Gerrard Camp. Witnesses: Hiram Hubert, Vinson Johnson and James T. Dickens.

Page 84 – Andrew Danielly. Last Will and Testament dated December 27, 1822; probated January 22, 1823. Gives to his wife Rhoda for her lifetime or widowhood, the 200 acre tract where he lives adjoining Peter Castleberry and Pollie Parker, together with certain slaves, household goods, etc. To daughters, Rachel and Jane Chambless, certain sums of money. Remainder of slaves to go to his children, Mac D., John, Arthur, Francis and Ann Danielly. Unto each of his 2nd wife's children certain items of personal property. Executors: Wife Rhoda and son, Mac D. Danielly. Witnesses: Samuel Hall, John Parker, Enoch Farmer.

Page 85 – Rev. Winder Hillman. Last Will and Testament dated October 25, 1823; probated March 3, 1823. Gives to Elizabeth Hillman (not yet 16), daughter of Joshua Hillman, a slave. Gives to son Joshua Hillman all money owing to testator. To son Samuel Hillman, testator's watch and half of his library (wife having first choice of same) and the land testator drew in the lottery lying in Early County, Samuel to pay the grant fees for said land. Residue of his estate to his wife Gracy in fee simple. Executors: Wife Gracy and Samuel Hillman. Witnesses: Drury Banks, Sarah Walker, Robert Walker.

Page 89 - William Fagalie. Last Will and Testament dated June 24, 1822; probated July 7, 1823. Gives to his wife Lucy for her lifetime or widowhood the land whereon he lives, being 772 acres, then to go to his five sons John, William, James, Robert and Franklin Fagalie. To daughter, Mary Fagalie, feather bed, etc. To daughter, Casea Williams, cows, etc. To daughters Barbara and Fannie Fagalie when of age, a feather bed and other items, each. He directs that the six youngest children, viz., Barbara, William, James, Robertson, Franklin and Fannie be educated. Executors: James Williams and Gray Cummings. Witnesses: Joseph Williams Jr., John Fagalie and John W. Vanze.

Page 90 – Thomas Haynes. Last Will and Testament, dated June 25, 1823; probated November 3, 1823. Gives to sons Charles Eaton Haynes and Thomas Haynes, certain slaves; and to said sons in trust for his daughter Catherin Bonner and her children, $300.00, and slaves to daughter Frances Bonner, and slaves to daughter Elizabeth Robinson. He gives slaves to his daughters

Mary Ryan and Susannah Livingston. To son, William Peyton Haynes, testator's home place. To daughter, Martha M. Dozier, certain slaves. Executors to sell and dispose of testator's land in Wayne County at their discretion. Executors: Charles Eaton Haynes and Thomas Haynes (sons), and son-in-law Dennis L. Ryan. Witnesses: Zephaniah Franklin, G. D. Franklin and H. A. Franklin.

Page 97 – Archulaus Flewellen. Last Will and Testament dated June 13, 1821. Caveat filed when it was offered for probate January Term, 1824, of court, caveat filed by Thomas Persons on account of erasures and interlineations. Will ordered probated April Term, 1824, and admitted to record. To son James Flewellen testator gives the slaves and money he has already given him. To son, Thomas Flewellen, certain slaves, etc., "above the other gifts already made him." To grandson Thomas Flewellen Persons, six slaves and other items, now in possession of his father Thomas Persons, same having been given by testator to Cibell Persons, the mother of Thomas after her marriage. To his daughter, Martha Flewellen, seven slaves, etc. To wife and "my three youngest children, Enos Russell Flewellen, Lawrence Augustus Flewellen and MaryAnn Flewellen, minors," 25 head of slaves, livestock, etc., and the use of the home place of testator of 600 acres. Executors: Sons, James and Thomas Flewellen and Dennis L. Ryan. Witnesses: John S. Heatts, George B. Waggoner and John Torrence.

Page 104 – Thomas Posey. Last Will and Testament dated April 24, 1824. No date of probate shown. Gives all his estate to his mother Rebecca Lewis and brothers Samuel Marcus Posey (a minor) and Lemuel Posey. Executors: Sion Hill and Samuel Marcus Posey. Witnesses: James Smith, Nancy Smith, Rebecca Smith.

Page 107 – Aaron Grier. Last Will and Testament dated September 16, 1824; probated October 20, 1824. To his daughter Elizabeth he gives a slave, household goods, etc. To his son Robert Grier he gives lot of land #140, 13th district of old Wilkinson County, and $50 in cash. To his grandchildren, Aaron G. and Alexander Stephens, each $400.00 when the younger is 18 years of age. To his daughter, Katherine Findley, he gives slaves named Clary and Ailey. To his son, Aaron W. Grier, he gives one-half of his home place lands with certain slaves; and to his son Thomas Grier, he gives the other half. To his sons and daughters he gives his library of books. Executors: Sons, Robert and Aaron W. Grier. Witnesses: Moses Alexander, William Wright and Washington Darden.

Page 109 – Thomas Tarry. Last Will and Testament dated November 10, 1824; probated January 24, 1825. To "his relatives" Samuel Tarry and Gideon Flewornan he gives $1 each. Remainder of his estate including 100 acres of land, he gives to his wife Hannah in fee simple. Executors: Wife, Hannah, and James McCason. Witnesses: William McCason, James McCason.

Page 111 – Elpthinston Cary. Last Will and Testament dated January 9, 1821, probated March 7, 1825. Gives to his wife Elizabeth his home place plantation purchased of Samuel Heming, for her lifetime, together with certain slaves in fee simple. At her death the property to be divided between James Cary's wife Nancy and her heirs, Elisha Cary's children, and the children of Henry B. Thompson viz: Joseph, Benjamin Lancaster Thompson, George H. Thompson, and Nancy Ann Thompson. Executors: Wife Elizabeth, and Henry B. Thompson. Witnesses: M. Alexander, Adam Miller and Robert Grier.

Page 114 – Joseph McMath. Last Will and Testament dated August 24, 1824, probated September 5, 1825. To his wife Elizabeth he gives 100 acres where he lives, with all his personal property, for her lifetime, then to be divided "amongst my heirs." He gives a "special bequest" of $500.00 to his granddaughter Sally Barbarie. Executors: Wife Elizabeth and son, William McMath. Witnesses: Hachaliah McMath, Elijah McMath, Claiborne Wall.

Page 116 – Barnett Snider. Last Will and Testament dated September 26, 1820; probated November 2, 1825. Gives to his wife Elizabeth the plantation where he lives, for her lifetime, then to be equally divided between sons Jacob and Barnett and daughter Elizabeth Joanne. He gives a cow to Fanny Thigpen. He gives his perishable property to his daughter, Elizabeth. Executor: John McCoy. Witnesses: James Barfield, Joseph Phillips, John McCoy.

Page 120 – Stephen Mitchell of Liberty County, to Ambrose Holliday of Warren County. Deed dated October 15, 1801, conveying 750 acres in Warren County where grantor formerly lived and whereon the grantee now lives, and composed of the following tracts: (1) 100 acres granted Richard Crutchfield October 28, 1783; (2) 100 acres granted John Coleman October 11, 1785; (3) 200 acres granted Roger Qualls, surveyed November 4, 1786; (4) 100 acres granted Thomas Yarbrough, surveyed October 27, 1783; (5) 100 acres granted the grantor Mitchell, surveyed for him October 21, 1784; (6) 15 acres surveyed February 15, 1788; (7) 100 acres granted grantor October 21, 1784. Witnesses: Hugh Taylor, Solomon Beckcom. In separate instrument recorded with deed, grantor's wife Mrs. Selah Mitchell, waives all dowry rights in said lands; witness to her signature, William Warthen J.P.

Page 121 – Robert Hill Sr. Last Will and Testament dated May 16, 1825; probated October 7, 1825. Gives to daughters Sarah Hill and Temperance Darden and son Benjamin Hill, two slaves each; to sons Sion and Abner Hill, two slaves and bed each; to son, Seaborn Hill, two slaves, bed and testator's home place; to sons Benjamin, Robert Jr., and Abner, lot of land #63 in Gwinnett County containing 250 acres. Executors: Sion Hill, Robert Hill Jr. Witnesses: Elbert Darden, Henry W. Darden, and John Harris.

Page 124 – James Cody. Last Will and Testament dated November 2, 1825. Probated December 5, 1825. Directs that all his property be kept together in possession of his wife Elizabeth for her lifetime, for her support, then to be divided between their children Edmond, Benjamin, Robert, Celia, Elias, Christopher C., Catherine, Annalizar, Lucretia and James Cody, minors at the time. Executors: Barnett Cody and George W. Hardaway. Witnesses: Michael Cody, Peter Cody, Daniel Dennis.

Page 126 – John Lock. Last Will and Testament dated May 19, 1823; probated March 6, 1826. Gives to his son James Lock and daughter Sarah Booty $1.00 each; to daughter, Rebecca Lock, a cow and calf; to daughters Rebecca, Elizabeth and Liddy Lock all the remainder of his real and personal property. Executors: Daughters, Elizabeth and Lydia Lock. Witnesses: William Langham, Benjamin B. Langham and Lewis Jackson.

Page 128 – Joshua Stanford Sr. Last Will and Testament dated May 4, 1825; probated May 1, 1826. He gives to son Joseph Stanford the home place; to granddaughter Harriet Deshield a cow and calf. Residue of his estate to his eight children viz: Levi, John and Joshua Stanford, Sophia Draper, Levin Stanford, Mary Wilson, Ellender Lazenby and Sarah Ansley. Executor: Son, Joseph Stanford. Witnesses: John Willson, Benjamin Harrison, William Harrison.

Page 129 – Nicholas Harbuck. Last Will and Testament dated October 5, 1822; probated July 3, 1826. Gives to wife Barbara the land whereon he lives, for her lifetime, then to be divided between daughters, C. E. Golding, Rebecca Brantley, Mary Hutchinson and her children, Barbara and Nicholas Hutchinson; Susan Geesling and her children Redian Green and Anna Barbara Teesling and their brothers and sisters; Anna Harbuck and her son Greenberry Lee Harbuck; and to daughter Lavinia Armstrong and daughter Anna Harbuck, daughter Lavinia to have a certain sum above equal share "because she is infirm." Executors: Wife, Barbara, Henry Shelton, Jeremiah Butt, William Harbuck Jr., and Thomas Gibson. Witnesses: Michael Harbuck, William Harbuck and Thomas Gibson.

Page 129 – Joseph May of Washington County, to his daughter Elizabeth Newsom. Gift instrument dated October 28, 1802, conveying two negro boys now in the possession of her husband Frederick Newsom. Witnesses: Isaac Hunt, Jody Newsom J.P.

Page 136 – John Hamilton Sr. Last Will and Testament dated June 14, 1826; probated September 4, 1826. Gives to wife Mary the land on Big Brier Creek where he lives, together with all perishable property, for her lifetime or widowhood, except $200 to daughter Mary. After wife's death or re-marriage estate remaining to be divided to "my children", except that son Daniel Hamilton is to receive the 40 acres he owns on Big Brier Creek. Executors: E.

Perryman Sr., and Aaron Adkins. Witnesses: E. Perryman, Jesse Story, Aaron Adkins.

Page 138 – Rebecca Latimer (wife of William Latimer of Warren County.) Last Will and Testament dated August 27, 1823, probated November 16, 1826. Says that by virtue of her marriage contract made with husband when they married, she makes this her last will and testament. Gives to her son, Charles Latimer, 400 acres of the land on which she lives, for which land he is her Trustee; such portion to include any houses he may choose, also his choice of her slaves, given in consideration of his "particular attention to me and the care of the family." To daughter, Maria Furlow, a slave named Cato. Residue of her estate to be divided between her five sons William Marshall Latimer, Charles Latimer, Samuel Marcus Latimer, James Latimer and Horace Augustus Latimer. Executors: Son, Charles Latimer. Witnesses: Robert A. Beall, Jeremiah Perry, Walker Perry.

Page 138 – Andrew McClary, James and Samuel, of Mecklenburg County, North Carolina, to Elijah Warthen of Washington County, Georgia. Deed dated January 20, 1800, for 150 acres lying on Ogeechee River. Witnesses: Phillip Rawls, Richard Warthen, William Warthen J.P.

Page 140 – Jesse Durden. Last Will and Testament dated November 21, 1826, probated January 2, 1827. He gives life estate in his land, cattle, etc., to his wife Christian, and after her death to Priscilla, Pollie and Calvin, children of Arcada Hearn. Executor: Henry Gibson of Columbia County. Witnesses: William B. Hundley, Joab Spivey, Thomas W. Battle.

Page 140 – Solomon Matthews to Robert Parker, both of Warren County. Deed dated January 23, 1802, for 120 acres on Williams Creek. Witnesses: Archelaus Flewellin and John Matthews J.P.

Page 143 – Jonas Shivers. Last Will and Testament dated September 6, 1825; probated December 4, 1826. He gives to his son Barnaby, son Willis, son William, son Thomas, and grandson Jonas Shivers (son of Barnaby) certain sums of money; to his granddaughter Martha Hibler (daughter of William Shivers), a certain slave; to granddaughter Lilly Ann Shivers, a certain slave; to granddaughter Nancy Shivers (daughter of Willis Shivers) a slave; to grandson George W. C. Shivers (son of Willis) the sum of $500 in cash, and a like amount to grandson Obediah Shivers (son of Willis), to his son James Shivers, forty head of slaves, and the tract of land where he lives, and his land in Hancock County. Residue of estate to his son James Shivers. Executor: Son, James Shivers. Witnesses: C. E. Haynes, Gideon Hagood, Joseph Roberts, Littleberry Luckie.

Page 144 – John Mims Jr., William Jr., and Matthew, to Wood Moreland of Hancock County. Deed dated November 16, 1802, for 124 acres on Rocky Comfort Creek. Deed executed in Washington County. Witnesses: Ishmael Brook, David Mims.

Page 147 – Joseph Stanford. Last Will and Testament dated March 26, 1827; no date of probate shown. Gives to his wife Margaret for her lifetime or widowhood the land where he resides, and his other lands on Little Sweetwater Creek and on the Greensborough road, and all his perishable property. To his son Christopher Stanford, the tract of land known as the Mitchell tract, with cattle. To his son-in-law Henry Hand, $5.00. To his son Isaiah Stanford he gives his personal property and home place at the death of his said wife Margaret. Executor: Wife, Margaret. Witnesses: Thomas W. Battle, James Watson, Hillery Langford.

Page 150 – John Torrence. Last Will and Testament dated May 13, 1825. Codicil dated June 8, 1827. Recorded September 6, 1827. To his wife Jemima he gives his large family Bible and all other divinity books; also life estate in his home and farm property; and he directs that if his son Septimus Torrence and family continue to live there, he shall share it. To his son Samuel Torrence, 350 acres and the improvements where he (Samuel) lives. To son John Winston Torrence, 110 acres where he now lives. To granddaughter Caroline W. Torrence (daughter of son William Torrence, deceased) 284 acres where said William lived at his death, her mother Mary Semmes, widow of James M. Semmes, "to equally enjoy it." To his son Ebenezer Torrence he gives 537 acres, he to pay Caroline W. and said John W., a certain sum each to equalize legacies. To daughter Mary White and Abigail Watson

600 acres he owns in Washington County, they to release all claim to lot #30, 22$^{nd}$ district of Early County drawn in the name of their deceased brother Benajah Torrence. Mention made of claim to 1000 acres in Jackson County drawn in name of George Weatherby, and land lot #177, 2$^{nd}$ district Early County, drawn in testator's own name. Executors: Son, Ebenezer, Samuel and Septimus Torrence. Codicil provisions: Because of deficiency in eyesight of son John Winston Torrence he gives him land lot #88 in Carroll County, drawn by testator in 1827 land lottery, also lot 146 in 18$^{th}$ district of Lee County. He appoints son Ebenezer Torrence of Greene County, as executor. Witnesses: Benjamin Bledsoe, John Fontaine, Thomas Gibson.

Page 163 – Robert Moore to Jacob Butt, both of Warren County. Deed dated February 24, 1800. Conveys 50 acres granted Thomas Smith, deceased. Witnesses: Jones Kendrick, Robert Benton, Eli Ball.

Page 164 – David McCoy of Wilkes County to Asa Cox of Warren County. Deed dated July 16, 1790, for 14 acres. Witnesses: Thomas Luckett, John Hammock and James Patterson J.P.

Page 167 – David Willson. Last Will and Testament dated October 15, 1827, probated January 7, 1828. He directs that all his estate be kept together until his youngest child becomes of age, and to be in charge of his wife Ann for her lifetime or widowhood; if she should re-marry, then she to receive only a child's part. He directs that his daughter Harriet Lazenby having already received property from him, that his other children be made equal to that which she has received. Executors: Wife Anne, brother Joel Willson and John M. Lazenby. Witnesses: William Drake Jr., Richard E. Lazenby, John R. Stanford.

Page 169 – John McCormick. Last Will and Testament dated January 22, 1828; probated March 3, 1828. Gives to his wife Sarah the land where he lives "provided she will not convey any part or the whole of it to any person except my own children or grandchildren." He gives to his son James McCormick land lot #82 in the 13$^{th}$ district of Irwin County, and $300.00 in cash. To his daughter, Susannah Duckworth $50.00 in cash. To son Paul

McCormick a certain part of testator's home place in fee simple. To daughter, Scena Cody, another part of his home place. To his grandchildren (children of Polly Cody) viz., SarahAnn, Abner, Green, Mary, Scena and Michael, a slave. To sons Paul and Abner H., and daughter Scena Cody, land lots 106 and 237 in 13th district and lot #92 in 10th district of Early County. To George McCormick "alias, George Kitchen, son of Sarah," lot #87, 30th district Lee County. Executors: Wife, Sarah, son Paul and Barnett Cody. Witnesses: Thomas Gibson, William P. Butt, John Reynolds.

Page 172 – John C. Smith. Last Will and Testament dated November 13, 1827; probated March 3, 1828. Gives a slave each to his daughters Frances, Sarah and Martha and sons William, Benjamin and John Smith. Residue of estate to his wife Nancy to be hers until the children arrive at their majority or marries. Executor: John B. Anderson. Witnesses: William Shivers Jr., William W. Anderson, Jesse E. Smith.

Page 173 – John McCormack to Abraham Salls, both of Warren County. Deed dated March 5, 1803, for 400 acres on Deep Creek, granted grantor September 1, 1797. Witnesses: Thomas Edmondson, Charles Stewart.

Page 173 – John Mulkey "of Georgia" to Jacob Bull of Warren County. Deed dated January 24, 1803, for 100 acres on Little River granted Walter Jackson July 3, 1770, and deeded John Mulkey, May 3, 1780. Witnesses: David Mercer, William Berry J.P.

Page 174 – Jesse Stanford. Last Will and Testament dated September 20, 1819; probated February 4, 1828. Gives to his wife Parthena, his home place property to son Reubin, the remainder of his real estate, and the home place after his wife's death. To his grandson Jesse Ruark, lot of land #174 in 11th district of Wilkinson County containing 202 ½ acres; to his daughter, Ebbe Ruark, an equal share in all his undevised property at his death. Gives to Emily Mash a featherbed formerly belonging to her grandmother Bethany Mash now my beloved wife Bethany Stanford. No executor.   Witnesses: Esther McDonald, William McDonald, Andrew McDonald.

Page 175 – Elizabeth King.  Last Will and Testament; probated November 5, 1827.  Gives all her slaves to the heirs of her daughters Mary Poythress and Sarah Zachry.  Witnesses: John B. Harrell, James T. Dickin.

Page 176 – Robert Palmer.  Last Will and Testament dated November 5, 1826; probated July 7, 1828.  Gives to his wife Winnifred all the land where he lives, being 1028 acres, with his slaves and other personal property, also lot 376, 12$^{th}$ district of Irwin County (when drawn) to be hers for her lifetime or widowhood, "provided she supports and educates all my children and sets off to each of my sons at his majority a suitable portion of the land", and the daughters to have certain other types of property.  Children not named in will.  Executors: Hardy Pitts and Absalom T. Dawkins.  Witnesses: Mary Ennis, Ira Neal, Thomas Gibson.

Page 181 – Clement Wynne.  Last Will and Testament dated November 5, 1825; probated January 16, 1829.  Gives to his wife Frances all his estate for her lifetime or widowhood except $500.00 in cash to daughter Sally Wynne.  He says he confirms gifts of land heretofore made to his sons James and Irby Wynne, and daughter May Johnson (nee May Wynne.)  Executors: Sons, James and Irby Wynne.  Witnesses: Benjamin Allen, William Wynne, Benjamin Hart.

Page 188 – Reubin Magee.  Last Will and Testament dated April 11, 1818; probated May 4, 1829.  Gives to his son Ephriam Magee 423 acres where he now resides.  Residue of his estate to his wife Elizabeth for her lifetime or widowhood, then to be divided as follows: To daughter, Mary E. Stanford, certain slaves, she to pay daughter Sarah M. Magee a certain amount to equalize legacy; to daughter, Elizabeth L. Edmondson, the land he bought of Moses Hill; to grandson, James Magee the son of Leah, $250.00 if and when of age; $50.00 to Sweetwater Church.  Residue to be divided between his five daughters Elender and Mary E. Stanford, Leah N. Pearson, Elizabeth L. Edmondson and Sarah M. Magee.

Executors: Wife Elizabeth and son-in-law Thomas Edmondson. Witnesses: Robert Lazenby, John Mitchell and William Stanford.

Page 191 – Elisha Hurt, planter. Last Will and Testament dated March 24, 1829; probated April 6, 1829. He gives to son Benjamin Hurt all the land purchased from Joseph J. Battle; and to son William Hurt the land testator purchased from Richmond Terrell, and one-third each of his slaves and other personalty, in possession of his son William and Elisha Worthen. The remaining third to go to the heirs of deceased daughter Polly Baker, viz., Leonora Akins (formerly Baker), Eliza Worthen (nee Baker), Priscilla, Cidney M., Elisha H. and Benjamin H. Baker. He gives to his son-in-law Austin Baker $5. Executors: Benjamin and William Hurt. Witnesses: Bennet Yeats, James Pilcher, Larkin Glover.

## About the Author
Lois Helmers

Lois Helmers, author of *"Meigs County, Ohio and her Soldiers in the Civil War"* and co-author of *"The Ghosts of Kennesaw Mountain"*, is a true lover of History and Genealogy. She has begun a quest for local history and this book, *"Early Records of Warren County, Georgia"* is her third book in this project. Local histories and genealogical records are fascinating and are a valuable tool for anyone tracing their roots. These records are not all readily available, even on the internet, and so Lois's quest is to research, gather information, preserve it and put it all in one book so researchers and the average reader with an interest in history and genealogy will be able to enjoy the fruits of her labor and learn about their local history.

Her works are available in all formats. Please visit our website for purchasing options.

www.Badgley Publishing Company.com

# INDEX

Aaron, Peggy, 18
Aarons, Vevinah, 17
Abbett, Abner, 34
Abbett, Ezekiel, 2
Abbett, Henry, 2
Abbett, Nancy, 14
Abbett, William, 35
Abercrombie, Bathsheba, 17
Abercrombie, Charles, 275,
    285, 300
Abercrombie, Col. Robert, 181
Abercrombie, Colonel Robert,
    205, 206
Abercrombie, Elizabeth, 17
Abercrombie, Ketrina, 18
Abercrombie, Nancy, 205, 206,
    207, 213
Abercrombie, R., 217, 329
Abercrombie, Robert, 180, 182,
    186, 189, 202, 205, 207, 213,
    218, 219, 221, 268, 285, 300,
    301, 302
Abercrombie, W. C., 302
Abercrombie, William C., 182,
    189, 218
Abley, Ambrose, 25
Achord, John J.P., 358
Acreage, Dicy, 336
Acres, John, 254
Adams, Benjamin, 361
Adams, David, 29
Adams, Elizabeth, 23
Adams, Henry, 31
Adams, John, 358
Adams, Nancy, 32
Adkins, Aaron, 388
Adkins, Joseph, 257
Aikens, John, 213
Aikens, William, 210
Aikins, John, 201
Ailey

slave, 385
Akins, Daniel, 338
Akins, Isabella, 32
Akins, John, 210, 228
Akins, Leonora, 393
Akins, William, 228
Alexander, Apsilla, 19
Alexander, Asa, 282
Alexander, Colonel Samuel,
    221
Alexander, Ezekiel, 13, 189,
    262
Alexander, M., 307, 385
Alexander, Moses, 226, 385
Alexander, Polly, 15
Alexander, Samuel, 114, 176,
    186, 189, 190, 202, 224, 225,
    226, 282, 286, 304, 307
Alexander, Samuel J.P., 290
Alexander, William, 2, 37
Alford, Cullen, 19
Alford, James, 277
Allen, Benjamin, 227, 230, 392
Allen, David, 2
Allen, Dicy, 31
Allen, Elisha, 214, 224, 230
Allen, George T., 230
Allen, Gideon, 2, 227
Allen, James, 196, 197, 296,
    297, 346, 355, 376
Allen, Jean, 26
Allen, John, 2, 37
Allen, Mariah, 376
Allen, Matthew, 58
Allen, Reubin, 243, 256
Allen, Samuel, 2, 227, 296, 303,
    311, 322, 364, 381
Allen, Samuel Sr., 291, 297,
    364
Allen, Shadrach F., 328
Allen, Sherwood, 227

Allen, William, 291, 297, 303, 325, 364
Allen, Zitha, 376
Alleson, William, 37
Allison, James, 244
Allison, John, 194
Allison, Margaret, 194, 206
Allison, Mary, 244
Allison, William B., 24, 194, 198, 201, 206, 305
Alston, Philip, 37, 73
Amos, Polly, 34
Anderson, Charles, 37, 64
Anderson, David, 37, 91
Anderson, Honour, 278
Anderson, James, 2, 37
Anderson, John, 2, 38
Anderson, John B., 391
Anderson, Jonathan, 257
Anderson, Mary, 378
Anderson, Nancy, 35
Anderson, Sarah, 378
Anderson, William, 93, 257, 284, 378, 379
Anderson, William W., 391
Andrews, Allen, 31
Andrews, Cleveras, 26
Andrews, Hannah, 28
Andrews, Micajah, 2, 38, 81
Andrews, Nicholas, 35
Andrews, Nicolas, 2
Andrews, Thomas, 77
Andrews, Warren, 219, 301, 302, 379
Andsley, Thomas, 46
Anglin, Elijah, 18
Anglin, John, 23, 311, 363
Anglin, Susannah, 14, 382
Anglin, William, 235, 259, 307
Ann
    slave, 369
Ansley, Abel, 197, 272, 344, 378

Ansley, Benjamin, 38
Ansley, Epsy, 208
Ansley, James, 23
Ansley, Joseph, 197, 272, 344
Ansley, Rebecca, 272, 344
Ansley, Samuel, 32, 197
Ansley, Sarah. *See* Stanford
Ansley, Thomas, 38, 130, 197, 272, 274, 296, 344, 371
Ansley, Thomas Jr., 272
Ansley, William, 22, 202, 208, 320
Anthony
    slave, 236
Anthony, Elizabeth, 6
Anthony, Henry T., 25
Anthony, Joseph, 6
Appling, J. J.I.C., 329
Appling, John, 2
Archer, James, 2
Armstrong, Amivil, 263
Armstrong, Hugh, 229, 291, 298, 301, 310, 333
Armstrong, James, 20, 32, 35
Armstrong, Jesse, 229, 244, 263, 280
Armstrong, Joseph, 262, 269
Armstrong, Lavinia. *See* Harbuck
Armstrong, Robert, 35
Armstrong, Sherman, 229
Arrandell, Benjamin, 293
Ashfield, Henry, 38, 67, 112
Ashmon, F., 2
Ashmore, Frederick, 39, 64, 114
Ashmore, James, 39, 128
Ashton, Ed, 2
Ashton, Edward, 39
Atchinson, Arnold, 22
Atchinson, Barton, 292, 337, 379
Atchinson, Charles, 225
Atchinson, James, 225

Atchinson, Wingfield, 225
Atchison, Barton, 13
Atchison, Charles, 380
Atchison, Henry, 22
Atchison, James, 190
Atchison, John, 23
Atchison, Winnifred, 190
Atkins, Daniel, 257, 338, 351
Atkinson, Joshua, 2, 39
Atwood, Isaac, 2, 37, 39, 98, 111
Augton, John, 265
Augusta Academy, 381
Augusta, Georgia, 42, 83, 116, 121, 165, 235, 288, 289, 354
Austin
  slave, 236
Austin, John, 298, 299
Austin, Rich, 2
Austin, Richard, 39, 82
Avant, Henry, 16
Avent, Hixy, 29
Avera, Alexander, 19, 331, 364, 381
Avera, Thomas, 34, 223
Averett, Susannah, 34
Averil, Cynthia, 30
Averitt, William, 357
Ayres, Abraham, 40, 49, 78
Ayres, Abram, 2
Ayres, Thomas, 2, 40, 55, 57, 117, 153
Ayres, William, 40, 154
Bacon, John, 40, 84, 139, 173
Bagwell, Littleberry, 25
Bailey, Abner, 29
Bailey, David, 27
Bailey, George, 40, 128
Bailey, James, 22, 209, 228, 234, 257
Bailey, Jennie, 214
Bailey, Jincy, 346
Bailey, John, 227

Bailey, Peggy, 33
Bailey, Pierce, 209, 214, 266, 282, 364
Bailey, Wilkerson, 346
Baker, 393
Baker, Austin, 18, 364, 393
Baker, Benjamin H., 393
Baker, Betsy, 13
Baker, Blake, 227
Baker, Catherine, 16
Baker, Charles, 196, 229
Baker, Cidney M., 393
Baker, Edwin, 33, 214, 232
Baker, Elisha H., 393
Baker, Eliza, 393
Baker, Idey, 227
Baker, James, 227
Baker, John, 184, 194, 207, 214, 256, 293, 297, 327, 343, 364
Baker, John Esquire, 250
Baker, John J.P., 261, 274, 281, 293, 297, 365
Baker, Joseph, 28
Baker, Nancy, 33
Baker, Peyton, 218, 219
Baker, Polly, 30, 393
Baker, Priscilla, 229, 393
Baker, William, 194
Baldwin County, Georgia, 352, 354, 358, 362
Baldwin, David, 41, 82
Ball, Anderson, 19
Ball, Caswell, 34, 331, 361
Ball, Eli, 321, 390
Ball, Henrietta, 30
Ball, Hill, 270
Ball, Isaac, 16, 222, 243, 251, 266, 276, 279, 302, 311, 331, 359, 362, 382
Ball, Isaac J.P., 355
Ball, Isaiah, 302
Ball, Jacob, 182

Ball, John, 236, 251, 256, 268, 297, 304, 306, 363
Ball, Sarah, 331
Ball, William, 30, 231
Baltimore, Maryland, 293
Banckston, Abner, 258
Banckston, Isaac, 292
Banks, Drury, 294, 295, 333, 383
Banks, Polly, 24
Banks, Reubin, 292
Banks, Sarah, 28, 35
Banks, William, 365
Bankston, Isaac, 13
Bankston, J., 307
Bankston, Thomas, 251
Barbarie, Isaac, 22, 337
Barbarie, Nancy, 337
Barbarie, Sally, 385
Barber, Nancy, 26
Barberer, John, 370
Barden, Ephathan, 22
Barden, Sherod, 18
Bardin, Mary, 186
Bardin, William, 186
Bardin, William Jr., 323
Barfield, James, 386
Barfield, Jesse, 267, 315
Barfield, Samuel, 279
Barfield, Solomon, 41, 261, 267, 279, 287, 304, 309, 315
Barfield, Solomon Jr., 279
Barfield, William, 261
Barksdale, Isaac, 140
Barksdale, Jeffrey, 283
Barksdale, John, 185, 221
Barksdale, Mariah, 29
Barksdale, Mary, 226
Barksdale, Phoebe, 283
Barksdale, Samuel, 24, 185, 221, 340
Barksdale, Terrell, 340
Barksdale, William, 226

Barnard, Edward, 41, 42, 45, 57, 74, 83, 92, 93, 98, 110, 114, 119, 130, 131, 136, 137, 151, 157, 160
Barnard, Timothy, 42, 88
Barnes, George, 43
Barnes, Hill, 308
Barnet, William, 138
Barnett, Isabella, 199
Barnett, John, 321, 338
Barnett, Margarat, 199
Barnett, Nathan, 43, 158
Barnett, Robert, 250
Barnett, Robert Sr., 364
Barnett, William, 43, 92, 199, 247
Barney, Robert, 258
Barrett, Barey, 301
Barrett, Charles, 359
Barrett, Henry, 359
Barrett, Margaret, 359
Barrow, Absalom, 265
Barrow, Edy, 25
Barrow, James, 181, 218, 237, 330, 331
Barrow, John, 330
Barrow, John Sr., 199
Barrow, Mebry, 265
Barrow, Milbrey, 265
Barrow, Milly, 35
Barrow, Reubin, 181, 218, 257, 307, 330, 331
Barrow, Richard, 31, 199, 250, 285, 361
Barrow, Richard Sr., 265
Barrow, Rubin, 206
Barrow, Sarah, 32
Barrow, Warren, 34, 199
Barrow, William, 28, 377
Barry, George, 43
Barton, John, 242, 244
Barton, Robert, 219, 242, 357
Barton, Robert Jr., 219

Barton, William, 219
Basemore, Kissy, 25
Bass, Alexander, 372
Bass, Alexander Jr., 242
Bass, Alexander Sr., 242
Bass, Batson, 221
Bass, Betsy, 15
Bass, Drewry, 358
Bass, Elizabeth, 15
Bass, Mary, 13
Bass, Persons, 226
Bass, Reddick, 244, 282, 342
Bass, William, 242, 249
Bass, Zadock, 221
Bassett, Nathaniel, 41, 53
Bassett, Thomas, 41, 43, 44, 53, 66, 85, 87, 96, 116, 130, 148, 156, 160, 164, 170
Bassett, Thomas Sr., 44
Bates, James M., 35
Bates, John, 318, 366
Batey, Henry, 240
Battle, Hartwell, 224, 227, 229, 378
Battle, John, 186, 193, 201, 202, 221, 229
Battle, John J.P., 318
Battle, Joseph J., 393
Battle, Rhoda, 186, 193, 202, 221, 224
Battle, Thomas, 30, 214
Battle, Thomas W., 389
Battson, Joseph, 244
Baxter, Andrew, 285
Bayn, Charles, 325
Bayn, J., 360
Bayn, John, 190, 201, 258, 319, 325, 332, 333, 334, 354, 359
Bayn, John J.P., 267, 268, 270, 271, 334, 347, 357, 358
Baynes, T. H., 240
Bazemore, Kizzy, 25
Bazemore, Thomas, 351

Beall Springs, 9
Beall, Amelia, 15, 29
Beall, Anson, 198
Beall, Benjamin B., 215
Beall, E., 315
Beall, Elias, 23, 190, 195, 225
Beall, Elizabeth, 344, 350
Beall, Emelia, 197
Beall, F., 204
Beall, Francis, 214
Beall, Henry, 163
Beall, Jacob, 44, 162, 311
Beall, Jeremiah, 187, 196, 219, 342, 344, 350, 352, 353
Beall, Jinney, 29
Beall, Joseph, 225
Beall, Josiah, 182, 185, 190, 195, 221, 338, 344, 354
Beall, Mannan, 227
Beall, Margaret, 29
Beall, Nancy, 19
Beall, Nathan, 231
Beall, Rebecca, 377
Beall, Robert A., 208, 215, 388
Beall, Sally, 32
Beall, Samuel, 214, 308, 344
Beall, Thaddeus, 195, 196, 197, 225
Beall, Thaddeus Jr., 190, 225
Beall, Thaddeus Sr., 190
Beall, Thomas, 196, 346
Beall, Walter, 27
Bearden, Sarah, 17
Beardon, Absolem, 313
Beardon, Hannah, 313
Beasley, David, 330, 339
Beasley, James, 178
Beasley, James Sr., 178, 366
Beasley, Joseph, 266, 284
Beasley, Margaret, 187, 223
Beasley, Mary, 24, 284
Beasley, Richard, 178, 187, 223, 312, 314, 330, 366

Beasley, Robert, 187, 223, 330, 339, 355
Beavin, Benjamin, 44
Beavy, Joseph, 239
Beck
  slave, 239, 370
Beck, Francis, 246, 316, 341
Beck, George, 44, 65
Beckcom, Solomon, 315, 386
Beckwith, John, 221
Beckwith, Willis, 221
Beddingfield, Charles, 188
Beddingfield, Gideon, 30, 32
Beddingfield, John, 317
Beddingfield, Mary, 317
Beddingfield, Solomon, 188
Begbie, Francis, 44, 45
Beidell, Absolem, 45, 93
Bell, Arthur, 282
Bell, Henry, 45, 157
Bell, Jacob, 45, 138
Bell, Jeremiah, 223
Bell, Josiah, 219
Bell, Sarah, 382
Bell, Walter, 193
Bellto, Henry, 57
Benagin, David, 25
Bennett, John, 45, 61, 68
Bennett, Robert, 16
Bennett, William, 138
Benson, John, 353
Bentley, Benjamin, 250
Benton, Aaron, 188, 229, 286, 303, 335
Benton, Eli, 335
Benton, Elizabeth, 19
Benton, Francis, 33, 208, 214, 376
Benton, John, 24, 223, 335
Benton, Robert, 321, 390
Benton, Susannah, 35
Benton, Winnifred, 35, 188, 223
Bentz, Charles, 45

Bereston, Aaron, 46
Berry, Anderson, 253, 305, 341, 342
Berry, Andrew J.P., 250
Berry, Garret, 267
Berry, Gibson, 364
Berry, Jarrott, 341
Berry, Jennie, 21
Berry, Jilson, 250, 258, 340, 342
Berry, Mary, 341
Berry, Presley, 341
Berry, Thomas, 193, 228, 366
Berry, William, 180, 193, 194, 243, 268, 305, 366
Berry, William J.P., 322, 359
Berry, William Sr., 340
Berry, Zelson, 267
Bethany, Thomas, 247, 267, 271
Bettle, J., 271
Beverly, Esther, 315
Beville, John, 27
Bevins, B., 125
Bevins, Benjamin, 78, 79, 81
Biggot, Elisha, 46, 243
Biggs, Tully, 188, 220
Bill, Jacob, 128
Bilmore, James, 297
Bimes, William, 366
Bird, Caroline, 31
Bird, Catherine, 5, 209
Bird, Colonel William, 1, 5, 209
Bird, Ebenezer, 25, 26, 226
Bird, Eliza, 29
Bird, Elizabeth, 22
Bird, Emily M., 27
Bird, Fitzgerald, 5
Bird, John, 5
Bird, Richard, 46, 126
Bird, Thompson, 235
Bird, William, 5, 22, 207, 243, 244, 286, 321, 338, 365
Bird, William Sr., 279

Bird, Wilson, 5, 207, 365
Birk, George, 113, 162
Bishop, Amy, 17
Bishop, Elbert, 32
Bishop, Ephriam, 16
Bishop, James, 46, 124, 184, 220, 245, 252, 284, 294, 295, 298, 320, 363
Bishop, John, 184, 251
Bishop, Nancy, 16
Bishop, Rebekah, 271
Bishop, Sally, 31
Bishop, Stephen, 245, 286
Black, Edward, 253
Black, Robert, 14, 230, 231
Blackney, John, 328
Blackshear, David, 241
Blackshear, David J.P., 250
Blair, Hugh, 24
Blake, William, 46
Blakey, Jesse, 203
Blakey, John, 203
Blakey, Levi, 203
Blakey, Mary, 203
Blakey, Nancy, 203
Blakey, Sarah, 203
Blakey, Susannah, 203
Blanchard, Rheuben, 46
Blandford, Clark, 241, 311, 312, 349
Bledsoe, Benjamin, 206, 353, 390
Bledsoe, Polly, 34
Blount, Elias, 14
Blount, Elizabeth, 35
Blount, Isaac, 253, 299
Blount, James, 322, 369
Blount, John, 25
Blount, William, 33, 203
Blount, William H., 219, 228, 230
Bob
    slave, 339, 362, 369

Boddie, Nathan, 221
Boggs, Joseph, 46, 51, 60
Bohannon, Celie, 316
Bohannon, Selah, 273, 274
Bohannon, Thomas, 273, 274, 316, 324, 353, 361
Bole, William, 326, 338
Bolton, Robert, 47
Boman, Isham, 20, 303
Boman, Robert, 303
Boman, Thomas, 322
Boman, William, 314
Bond, Clara, 19
Bond, James, 185, 241, 269, 293
Bond, Mary, 311
Bond, Peter, 185
Bonner, Ann, 352
Bonner, E., 383
Bonner, Elizabeth, 383
Bonner, Frances, 383
Bonner, Henry, 13, 323, 350
Bonner, Henry Jr., 359
Bonner, James, 15, 34, 202, 203, 215, 349
Bonner, Jeremiah, 286
Bonner, John, 29
Bonner, Jones, 267, 283
Bonner, Joseph, 190
Bonner, Martha M., 384
Bonner, Mary, 384
Bonner, Mildred, 28
Bonner, Nancy, 34, 199, 202
Bonner, Richard, 243
Bonner, Robert, 16, 199, 218, 349, 380
Bonner, Sallie, 15
Bonner, Susannah, 384
Bonner, Wyatt, 176, 193, 199, 202, 204, 205, 215, 248, 283, 302, 349, 350, 352
Boon Joseph,, 243

Boon, James, 229, 237, 240, 307
Boon, Joseph, 229, 277
Boon, Thomas, 229
Booth, Abraham, 47
Booth, Polly, 15
Booth, William, 47
Booth, Z. J.P., 276
Booth, Zachariah, 188, 224
Booty, Nicholas, 24, 199
Booty, Sarah, 386
Bostick, Chesley, 47
Bostick, John, 48
Bostick, William, 130
Bourquin, Henry, 48
Bourquin, Henry Lewis, 48
Bouten, Nathan, 291
Bowdree, Adam, 275
Bowen, Joseph, 194
Bower, Joseph, 181
Bower, Nicholas, 289
Bowers, James, 243
Bowie, James, 48, 236
Bowie, Sallie, 236
Bowland, William, 369
Bowman, Robert, 17
Bowman, Thomas, 19
Boyd, David, 173
Boyd, John, 48, 93
Boyle, P., 277
Boynton, Elijah, 35
Boynton, Franky, 27
Boynton, Lucy, 27
Boynton, Moses, 18
Braddy, Willy G., 326
Bradley, John, 72
Bradley, Joshua, 40, 48, 78, 128
Brady, Cullen Lewis, 213, 366
Brady, James, 223
Brady, Lewis, 288, 331, 364, 366
Brady, Mary, 18
Brady, Patrick, 255

Brady, Patrick Sr., 255
Brady, Peggy, 21
Brady, Peggy W., 21
Brady, Samuel, 258
Brady, Wiley G., 202
Brady, Wilie Giles, 366
Brady, Willy Giles, 213
Brady, Wylie Jiles, 201
Branham, Harris, 313
Branham, James, 14
Brannon, Obedience, 381
Brannon, William, 206
Brantley, Benjamin, 361
Brantley, Frances, 13
Brantley, Jeptha, 32, 361
Brantley, John, 14, 275
Brantley, Joseph, 283
Brantley, Larkin, 275
Brantley, Lewis, 251, 260, 264, 265, 276, 300
Brantley, Mary, 25
Brantley, Nancy, 34, 361
Brantley, P., 254
Brantley, Phillip, 25, 183, 198, 281, 295, 298, 325, 361
Brantley, Rebecca. *See* Harbuck
Brantley, Susannah, 276
Braswell, Benjamin, 242
Braswell, Byrd, 357
Bray, Dr. Richard, 230
Bray, Elizabeth, 377
Bray, James, 14, 256, 274, 337
Bray, Lucy, 228
Bray, Richard, 205, 223, 228, 358
Brazil, Polly, 30
Breed,, 26
Breed, John, 20, 381
Breed, Joseph, 277, 284, 301
Breed, Nancy, 29
Breed, Sallie, 24
Breed, William, 13, 295, 298
Brewer, Abisha, 355

Brewer, Barret, 276
Brewer, Barrett, 215
Brewer, Elizabeth, 252
Brewer, George, 246, 264, 280, 297, 298, 324, 352, 355
Brewer, George Jr., 258
Brewer, Henry, 20
Brewer, James, 49, 277
Brewer, Lavinah, 30
Brewer, Matthew, 252, 280, 298
Brewer, Nathan, 280, 290, 361
Brewer, Phoebe, 14
Brewer, Rolen, 298, 355
Brewer, Sally, 16
Brewer, William, 247, 252, 280, 290
Brewtib, Nathan, 13
Briant, Benjamin, 359
Bricon, John, 49
Bridges, Benjamin, 356
Bridges, Britain, 339
Bridges, John, 339, 356
Bridges, Nathan, 308
Briggs, Tulley, 185
Brinkley, Abram, 363
Brister
    slave, 235
Britt, Clarissa, 35
Britt, Polly, 19
Britt, William, 199
Brocks, Joseph, 377
Bromley, Stephen W., 33
Brook, Ishmael, 319, 389
Brook, Jonah, 24
Brook, William, 345
Brooks
    slave, 334
Brooks, Baalam, 20
Brooks, Charles, 210, 214, 227
Brooks, Dennis, 23
Brooks, Elizabeth, 31
Brooks, Henry, 210, 214
Brooks, Isaac, 347

Brooks, James, 363
Brooks, Jane, 358
Brooks, Jesse, 340
Brooks, Joab, 23, 187, 220, 367
Brooks, John, 29, 269, 274, 322, 338, 342, 358
Brooks, Mary, 26
Brooks, Nathaniel, 27
Brooks, Phillip, 25
Brooks, William, 20, 187, 261, 347
Broom, Adam, 24
Broom, David, 260, 306, 327, 328
Broom, Elizabeth, 382
Broom, Ezekiel F., 382
Broom, Ishmael, 23, 327, 339
Broom, Mary Signor, 382
Broom, Sarah, 382
Broom, Tempy, 382
Brooner, Burrell, 325
Brothers, Elisha, 216
Brown, Allen, 277
Brown, Ann, 247
Brown, Barnett, 350
Brown, Betsy, 15
Brown, Burrell, 177
Brown, Coleman, 49
Brown, David, 327, 328
Brown, Elisha, 182, 218, 241
Brown, Eliza, 27
Brown, Francis, 110
Brown, Henry, 30
Brown, James, 49, 61, 137
Brown, John, 49, 188
Brown, Joseph, 50, 117, 247
Brown, Rae, and Company, 119, 140
Brown, Solomon, 16
Brown, William, 26, 215, 332
Browning, Joshua J.P., 345
Bruton, Benjamin, 291, 321

Bruton, Benjamin J.P., 287, 293, 320, 336
Bruton, Jemima, 291, 321
Bruton, John, 239, 311
Bruton, Lavina, 14
Bruton, Polly, 21
Bryan County, Georgia, 283
Bryan, John, 50, 52, 71
Bryan, Joseph, 341
Bryan, L. D., 342
Bryan, Little, 257
Bryan, William, 50
Bryant, Benjamin, 30
Bryant, William G., 292
Bryson, Betsy, 25
Buckelaw, James, 25
Buckhalt, Peter, 273
Buckhannon, Thomas, 295
Buckholts, Henrietta, 27
Buckholts, Silas, 27
Buckles, Peter, 193
Buckwalter, Isaac, 241
Buckwalter, Jacob, 241
Buckwalter, Jeremiah, 241
Buckwalter, Jesse, 241
Buckwalter, John, 241
Buckwalter, Joshua, 241
Buckwalter, Michael, 241
Buffin, Caroline Matilda, 20
Buffington, Samuel, 347
Buffington, Sarah, 14
Bugg, Edmund, 42, 45, 50, 54, 73, 94, 133, 151, 161
Bugg, John, 50
Bugg, Sherwood, 42, 50, 51, 60, 73, 94, 104, 135, 164, 172, 173
Bugg, William, 56
Bull, Eli, 182, 218
Bull, Henrietta, 32
Bull, Jacob, 218, 284, 322, 353, 391
Bull, Jesse, 182, 218

Bulloch, Archibald, 51
Bulloch, Richard, 365
Buncombe County, North Carolina, 303, 352, 357
Bundley, W. D., 315
Bunkley, Jesse, 340
Bunkley, John, 29
Bunkley, Joshua, 340
Bunkley, Lewis, 340
Bunkley, Lucy, 24
Bunkley, Mildred, 340
Bunkley, Polly, 28
Bunkley, William, 24, 292
Bunkley, William D., 352, 361
Bureston, Aaron, 124
Burgamy, William, 42, 52, 60
Burge, John, 23
Burgen, Jesse, 257, 325
Burgholder, Harriet, 34
Burgin, Daniel, 31
Burk, Thomas, 269
Burke County, Georgia, 241, 277, 285, 286, 291, 330, 341, 346, 352, 363
Burkes, John, 52
Burkhalter, Epsy, 35
Burkhalter, Isaac, 241, 247
Burkhalter, Jacob, 184, 241, 247, 291, 293, 294, 295, 300, 332
Burkhalter, Jeremiah, 185, 214, 216, 217, 225, 241, 247, 319
Burkhalter, Jesse, 241, 247
Burkhalter, John, 213, 214, 225, 229, 241, 242, 247, 258, 268, 327, 339, 348, 360, 365, 366
Burkhalter, John Jr., 203, 213
Burkhalter, John Sr., 203
Burkhalter, Jones, 25
Burkhalter, Joshua, 241, 247
Burkhalter, Margaret, 240
Burkhalter, Martha, 316
Burkhalter, Mary, 332

Burkhalter, Michael, 176, 186, 187, 195, 217, 222, 223, 240, 247, 278, 358
Burkhalter, Nancy, 14
Burkhalter, Patsy, 19
Burkhalter, Polly. *See* Reese
Burkhalter, Rebekah, 349
Burkhalter, Sally, 24
Burkhalter, Sarah, 268, 365
Burkhalter, William, 349
Burkholts, Silas, 206
Burkshire, B., 332
Burleston, Martha, 309
Burleston, Patty, 313
Burley, Stephen, 275
Burner, John, 73
Burnes, John, 52
Burnet, Daniel, 52
Burnet, John, 52, 94
Burnett, John, 78, 338
Burnley, Aley, 30
Burnley, Elizabeth, 25
Burnley, Hannah, 29
Burnley, Henry, 268
Burnley, Parthena, 378
Burnley, Stephen, 185, 221
Burnley, Stephen W., 319, 360, 378
Burnley, Tabitha, 13
Burnly, Stephen W., 199
Burns, Andrew, 52, 252, 286
Burns, Jane, 215
Burns, P., 240
Burns, Peter, 240
Bursey, Hezekiah, 358
Burson, Elizabeth, 315
Burson, Isaac, 179, 181, 216, 217, 314, 315, 348
Burson, Jonathan, 181, 217, 267, 314, 325
Burson, Joseph, 182, 274, 278
Burson, Mary, 182
Burson, Nancy, 181, 217

Burson, Tabitha, 23
Burt, James, 22, 363, 365
Burt, Moody, 137
Burt, Rebecca, 22
Burt, Zacheus, 363, 365
Burton, Benjamin J.P., 276
Burton, Benjamin J.P., 275
Burton, John, 193
Burton, Joseph, 52
Bush, Andrew, 328, 375
Bush, D., 333
Bush, David, 350, 353
Bush, Isaac, 348
Bush, James, 375
Bush, John J.P., 241
Bush, John Jr., 317
Bush, John Sr., 317
Bush, Mourning, 288
Bush, Susannah, 241
Bush, Thomas, 292
Bush, William, 239, 285, 288
Bushm, Mourning, 239
Bushnel, David, 5
Bussey, Hezekiah, 339
Bussey, Kiah, 278
Bustin, Christopher, 267, 284, 285, 327, 328
Bustin, John, 250, 266, 293, 297
Butler, Beall, 216
Butler, Daniel, 323
Butler, Enos, 178, 216
Butler, Mary, 17
Butler, Noble, 178, 216, 251
Butler, Patrick, 53
Butler, Patsy, 23
Butler, Richard, 187, 273, 274
Butler, Susannah, 178, 216
Butler, William, 20
Butrel, Mary, 27
Butt, Archalaus, 222
Butt, Archelaus, 233
Butt, Jacob, 321, 390
Butt, James, 31

Butt, Jeremiah, 221, 222, 227, 231, 340, 342, 375, 387
Butt, Jesse, 310, 311
Butt, Jessie, 208
Butt, John, 215, 220, 233, 375
Butt, Joshua Jr., 179
Butt, Joshua Sr., 179
Butt, Keziah, 15
Butt, Moses, 27, 328
Butt, Nancy, 208
Butt, Noah, 367
Butt, Radford, 204, 326, 375
Butt, Raiford, 326
Butt, Sallie, 208
Butt, Stephen, 344
Butt, William, 208, 209, 210, 324, 328, 337
Butt, William P., 391
Buttril, Thomas, 353
Buttrill, Thomas, 254
Butts, Azariah, 18
Butts, John, 30, 180, 189
Butts, Joshua, 180
Butts, Joshua Jr., 189
Butts, Joshua Sr., 189
Butts, Moses Sr., 187
Butts, Noah, 318
Butts, Radford, 180, 189
Butts, William, 187, 328
Bynum, James, 344
Byrom, John, 213
Byrom, Patsey, 26
Byrom, William, 213, 233, 260, 308, 332
Byrom, William Esq., 210
Byrom, William II, 32
Byrom, William J.P., 249, 253, 259, 290, 348
Byrom, William Jr., 290, 348
Byron, William, 340
Byrop, William, 292
Cadagan, George, 74, 136
Cafter, Pollie, 15

Cahoon, Rebecca, 21
Caison, John, 322
Caldwell, Alexander, 53
Caldwell, H. G., 289
Caldwell, James, 2, 237
Caldwell, John, 318
Callihan, David, 53
Calloway, Francis, 252
Camden County, Georgia, 206, 255
Camp, Clody, 31
Camp, Clourdsley, 347
Camp, Elizabeth, 32
Camp, Garrard, 233
Camp, Gerard, 227
Camp, Gerrard, 227, 382
Camp, Mary, 264, 277
Camp, Nancy, 18
Camp, S., 277, 308
Camp, S. l., 264
Camp, Sally, 31
Camp, Samuel, 233, 252, 253, 254, 259, 275, 292, 328, 329, 335, 336, 337, 341, 347, 348
Camp, Thaddeus, 233, 348
Campbell, Duncan, 282
Campbell, James, 240
Campbell, John, 53, 273, 274, 289
Campbell, Martin, 53, 66, 111, 115, 116
Campbell, Samuel, 240
Campbell, William, 240
Candler, Captain William, 141
Candler, Daniel, 6
Candler, H., 316
Candler, H. J.I.C., 324, 333, 347
Candler, H. J.P., 304
Candler, Henry, 193, 305, 311, 348
Candler, J. K., 311
Candler, John K., 188, 224
Candler, Mark, 354

Candler, Peter, 117, 154
Candler, William, 6, 42, 53, 54,
    68, 73, 75, 90, 94, 95, 100,
    103, 108, 111, 153, 158, 163
Captain Murray, 267
Cardal, Sarah, 31
Cardion, Cornelius, 236
Carey, Robert, 289
Carlton, Henry, 30
Carpenter, Benjamin, 23
Carpenter, Josiah, 240
Carr, Benjamin, 356
Carr, John P., 225
Carr, Thomas, 196, 290
Carroll County, Georgia, 390
Carroll, Anthony, 242
Carroll, Britton, 35
Carroll, Thomas, 365
Carry, Ann, 362
Carry, Katherine, 362
Carry, Robert, 362
Carson, John, 48, 50, 54, 170,
    182, 219, 228, 349
Carson, Joseph, 235, 282, 288
Carter, Allen, 28
Carter, Baines, 330
Carter, Charles, 254
Carter, Charles R., 255
Carter, Concord, 23
Carter, David Charles, 254
Carter, Elizabeth, 15, 259
Carter, Jacob, 201, 324
Carter, James, 201, 245, 257,
    258, 269, 270, 282, 294, 296,
    308, 334
Carter, Jane, 255
Carter, Jesse, 201, 296, 310,
    319, 336, 347
Carter, Joseph, 13, 185, 220,
    328
Carter, Joseph J.P., 324
Carter, Josiah, 252, 257, 259,
    334, 335, 353

Carter, Lavinah, 28
Carter, Moore, 201, 245
Carter, Nellie, 296
Carter, Nelly, 296
Carter, Rachel, 35
Carter, Richard, 282, 283, 291,
    294, 295, 298, 301
Carter, Sally, 28
Carter, Tempe, 295
Carter, Tempey, 298
Cartledge, Edmund, 54, 55, 113,
    125, 150
Cartledge, Edward, 38
Cartridge, Edmund, 81
Cary, Elisha, 385
Cary, Elizabeth, 385
Cary, Elpthinston, 385
Cary, James, 385
Cary, Nancy, 385
Cary, Sallie, 15
Cary, Thomas, 14
Cash, James, 357
Caskell, Nicholas, 42
Cason, H. J.P., 316
Cason, James McC., 231
Cason, John Sr., 348
Cason, William, 231
Cason, William J.P., 293, 338,
    344, 352, 359, 361
Cassel, Jacob, 51
Castell, Jacob, 55
Casten, Jacob, 60
Castle, Jacob, 55, 120
Castleberry, Ann, 254
Castleberry, Asa, 235
Castleberry, Catherine, 275
Castleberry, Claiborne, 275,
    288, 319, 324
Castleberry, David, 21, 275, 308
Castleberry, Edward, 16, 308
Castleberry, Henry, 352
Castleberry, Jacob, 50, 199,
    311, 362

Castleberry, John, 235, 254
Castleberry, Martha, 288
Castleberry, Mary, 199
Castleberry, Mick., 339
Castleberry, Nathan, 211, 278
Castleberry, Paul, 55
Castleberry, Peter, 177, 267,
  275, 288, 383
Castleberry, Richard, 40, 55, 57,
  173, 180, 230, 247, 254, 308
Castleberry, Sarah, 352
Castleberry, Solomon, 26
Castleberry, Susannah, 27
Castleberry, William, 40, 55,
  56, 57, 101, 228, 232, 234
Castleberry, Winnie, 25
Caswell, Alexander, 325, 352,
  354
Caswell, John, 292, 313
Caswell, Mary, 352
Cato
  Slave, 388
Caty
  slave, 377
Cavinah, Thomas, 268
Cezr
  slave, 298
Chadwick, Thomas, 56
Chaffing, John, 27
Chalker, Rebecca, 381
Chamberg, William, 365
Chambers, Harden, 26
Chambers, John, 32
Chambers, Mary, 23
Chambers, William, 349
Chambless, Christopher, 229
Chambless, Henry, 32
Chambless, Jane, 383
Chambless, Joseph, 229
Chambless, Littleton, 285, 292
Chambless, Rachel, 383
Chambliss, William, 22

Champion, Henry, 241, 259
Champion, Henry Sr., 262
Champion, John, 262, 323
Champion, Mary, 262
Champion, Murphy, 26
Champion, Rhoda, 24
Chancy
  slave, 236
Chandler, Dorcas, 287
Chandler, Frances, 356
Chandler, Polly, 13
Chandler, William, 50, 56, 292
Chapman, Abner, 224, 299,
  300, 303, 359
Chapman, Ambrose, 26
Chapman, Asa, 28, 224, 225,
  228, 350
Chapman, Benjamin, 27, 178,
  224, 241, 266, 377
Chapman, David, 24, 299
Chapman, Debera, 178, 267,
  303
Chapman, Debora, 201, 327
Chapman, Eliza, 31
Chapman, Hannah, 186, 221
Chapman, Hill, 331
Chapman, John, 178, 201, 329
Chapman, Laban, 18, 186
Chapman, Labourn, 221
Chapman, Millie, 196
Chapman, Milly, 24, 344
Chapman, Rhoda, 196
Chapman, Robert, 32, 224
Chapman, Tabitha, 18, 24
Chapman, Temperance, 196
Chapman, William, 186, 221,
  344
Chappell, John, 254, 358
Chappell, Thomas, 201
Charity
  slave, 235
Charles County, Maryland, 313
Charles County, Virginia, 340

Charleston, South Carolina, 289
Chastain, James, 14
Chatham County, Georgia, 343
Cheely, Thomas, 1
Chevalier, Charles Francis, 56
Chevers, Gideon, 86
Chew, Samuel, 56
Childers, Thomas, 297, 347
Childre, Thomas, 310, 332
Childree, Francis, 293
Childree, Hannah, 293
Childree, Sarah, 293
Childree, Thomas, 293
Childree, Thomas Sr., 336
Childree, William, 293
Childres, Thomas, 291
Childress, Thomas, 307
Childrey, Thomas, 266, 293
Chisholm, Elizabeth, 379
Chitwin, Joseph, 56
Chivers, Larkin, 252, 254, 322, 341, 356
Christian, John, 57
Christmas, James, 327
Christmas, R. J.P., 310
Christmas, Robert, 305
Church of Christ at Fellowship, 360
Cinquefield, Aaron, 287
Claiborne, John Sr., 266, 353
Claiborne, John W., 266
Claiborne, Leonard, 40, 42, 55, 56, 57, 60
Claiborne, Leonard Jr., 57
Claiborne, William, 254
Clark, Barbara, 57
Clark, Christopher, 132
Clark, Daniel, 57, 119
Clark, John, 58, 106, 312
Clark, Nancy, 13
Clark, Patrick, 57, 76, 136
Clark, Patt, 160
Clark, Sarah, 48

Clark, William, 58, 92, 289, 330
Clarke County, Georgia, 345, 352
Clarke, John, 69
Clarke, Patrick, 58
Clary
    slave, 385
Claxton, James, 218
Clayborne, Leonard, 167
Clayton, Phillip, 240
Cleckler, John, 49
Clement, William, 59
Clemm, William, 59, 70
Cleo
    slave, 264
Clickler, John, 59
Clifton, George, 302, 310, 336
Clinton County, New York, 9
Closman, Frederick, 59
Cloud, Hannah, 32
Cloud, Joel, 59, 82, 88, 281, 322, 350
Cloud, Sarah, 380
Clower, George, 345
Clower, Jacob, 310
Clower, John, 309
Clower, Peter, 29, 204, 217, 309
Clower, Polly, 15
Clowers, Jacob, 18, 208
Clowers, Matilda, 208
Cluckler, John, 108
Coalman, Daniel, 81
Coan, James, 54, 60, 129
Coate, Nathaniel, 150
Coatman, Sally. See Mitchell
Coats, Henry, 60, 120
Coats, James, 51, 60, 120
Coats, Nathaniel, 60, 251, 312
Cobb Dicy, 33
Cobb, Absalom, 367
Cobb, Ezekiel, 242
Cobb, James, 29, 104, 242, 281
Cobb, James Jr., 60

Cobb, John, 14, 73, 94
Cobb, Joseph, 60
Cobb, Rachel, 242
Cobbs, James, 60, 281, 322
Cobbs, John, 61, 298
Cobbs, John Sr., 299
Cobbs, Mary, 298
Cochran, Cornelius, 78
Cochrane, Cornelius, 61, 67, 136
Cochrum, Mary, 35
Cockerman, James, 245
Cockrum, James, 287
Cocks, Daniel, 284
Cocks, David, 274, 286
Cocks, Hannah, 242, 284
Cocks, James, 242
Cocks, Josiah J.P., 280
Cocks, Peter, 271
Cocks, Richard, 237, 267, 271, 371
Cocks, Thomas, 14, 176, 237, 242, 248, 264, 270, 271, 371, 372
Cocks, William, 176, 242, 248, 267, 273, 284
Cocks, William Sr., 271
Cocroff, Henry, 22
Cocroft, Henry, 201, 376
Coda, James, 309
Coda, Michael, 266, 361
Cody, Abner, 391
Cody, Annalizar, 386
Cody, Barnett, 386, 391
Cody, Benjamin, 386
Cody, Catherine, 386
Cody, Celia, 386
Cody, Christopher C., 386
Cody, David, 228, 231, 232
Cody, Edmond, 361, 386
Cody, Edmund, 359
Cody, Elias, 386
Cody, Elizabeth, 199, 386

Cody, Green, 391
Cody, James, 23, 336, 358, 386
Cody, James Jr., 221
Cody, Lucretia, 228, 231, 381, 386
Cody, Mary, 302, 391
Cody, Michael, 181, 217, 279, 302, 325, 361, 386, 391
Cody, Michael Sr., 223
Cody, Peter, 228, 231, 386
Cody, Polly, 391
Cody, Richard, 199
Cody, Robert, 386
Cody, Sally, 23
Cody, Sarah, 18
Cody, SarahAnn, 391
Cody, Scena, 391
Cody, Susannah, 34
Coffield, John, 34
Cohoon, Teletha, 29
Coke, Nathaniel, 298, 299
Colbreath, Peter, 63
Coldridge, James, 151
Coldwell, Alexander, 95, 129
Cole, George, 353
Coleman, Daniel, 61, 103, 125, 147
Coleman, John, 315, 386
Coleman, Nancy, 29
Coleman, Rachel, 32
Coling, Pollie, 15
Collier, Wyatt, 263
Collins, Andrew, 61
Collins, Charles, 363
Collins, William, 341
Colman, Daniel, 62, 68, 114
Columbia County, Georgia, 121, 196, 226, 242, 243, 244, 246, 247, 251, 254, 260, 263, 264, 268, 270, 273, 277, 283, 285, 289, 291, 294, 296, 298, 299, 302, 305, 307, 310, 311, 318, 319, 324, 325, 329, 332,

334, 336, 337, 346, 347, 350, 351, 352, 353, 354, 357, 358, 359, 363, 388
Combes, William, 62
Comer, Jack, 245
Conaway, Henry, 27
Cone, James, 38
Connecticut, 196
Connell, Daniel, 20
Connell, Jesse, 258, 320
Connell, Penelope, 258
Conner, Elijah, 17
Conner, Nancy, 202
Conner, Polly, 381
Cook, Celethy, 179
Cook, David, 332
Cook, Fairiby, 17
Cook, Isaac, 178, 179, 216
Cook, John, 181
Cook, Joseph, 287, 320
Cook, Pheriby, 178, 179, 216
Cook, Seletha, 216
Cook, Selethe, 17
Cooke, James, 25
Cooke, Robert, 62, 98, 120
Cooksey, Hezekiah, 362
Cooksey, Sophia, 33
Cooms, Elizabeth, 291
Cooper, Benjamin, 287, 317
Cooper, Charity, 21
Cooper, Elizabeth, 287, 382
Cooper, George, 20, 246, 287
Cooper, Henry, 277, 278, 308
Cooper, Isaac, 62
Cooper, James, 177, 311, 372
Cooper, John, 382
Cooper, Linney, 382
Cooper, Mary, 177, 372
Cooper, Samuel, 184, 251
Cooper, Sarah, 220
Cooper, William, 27, 317
Coosey, David, 72
Coppe, Jonathan, 62

Coram, Thomas, 378
Coram, William, 247, 274, 282, 309, 333
Corbitt, Louisa, 369
Cordery, Thomas, 114
Cornberger, John, 63
Cornell, George, 62
Corum, William, 262, 269
Cosby, Nancy, 233
Cosby, Wingfield, 224
Cosey, David, 63
Cossy, David, 173
Costly, Elizabeth, 17
Cotten, Augustus, 253
Cotton, G. W., 310
Cotton, George, 15, 29, 342
Cotton, James, 16, 239
Coughsan, Mary Ann, 15
Course, James J.I.C., 348
Course, John, 240, 289
Cowan, Thomas, 244
Cowen, George, 63, 169
Cowen, Robert, 108
Cowles, William, 307
Cowles, William M., 351
Cowper, Isaac, 143
Cox, Asa, 314, 318, 321, 348, 364, 390
Cox, Betsy, 30
Cox, Cary, 313, 314, 318, 321
Cox, David, 256, 309, 345, 346
Cox, Deborah. *See* Stubbs
Cox, Elizabeth, 18
Cox, Hannah, 290
Cox, Henry, 302, 346
Cox, Ichabod, 290, 313, 321
Cox, John, 20, 245, 274, 290, 337
Cox, Mariah, 314, 318
Cox, Martha, 314, 318, 321
Cox, Martin, 303, 364
Cox, Mary, 302
Cox, Masten, 303

Cox, Mastin, 242
Cox, Patsy, 30
Cox, Peter, 269, 279, 337
Cox, Peter Sr., 350
Cox, Richard, 277
Cox, Thomas, 372
Cox, Tolliver, 21
Cox, William, 248, 271, 290, 372
Cox, Zachariah, 243
Cozart, James, 272
Crane, Jeremiah, 19
Cratin, John, 335
Cratin, Louisa Sophia, 35
Cratin, MaryAnn, 335
Craus, Leonard, 63
Crawford, A. J.P., 338
Crawford, Anderson, 329
Crawford, Charles, 63, 82, 85, 109, 151
Crawford, Claiborne, 255
Crawford, Frances, 25
Crawford, John, 40, 50, 63, 72, 94, 129, 164
Crawford, Mary, 21
Crawford, Mary A., 247
Crawford, Moses, 321
Crawford, Peter J.P., 247
Crawford, William, 362
Crawford, William J., 336
Crenshaw, Benjamin, 15, 214, 221, 227, 228, 360
Crenshaw, Daniel, 17
Crenshaw, Elizabeth, 380
Crenshaw, Pascal, 380
Crenshaw, Polly, 380
Crenshaw, Sally, 33
Crenshaw, William, 262
Creswell, Samuel, 287
Crews, Littleberry, 251
Crissap, James, 22
Crisup, James, 236
Criswell, Samuel, 304

Crittenden, Elizabeth, 64
Crittenden, Henry, 350
Crittenden, Martha, 16
Crittenden, William, 64
Crockett, David, 249
Crokett, John, 24
Cromley, Arthur, 243
Cromley, Elizabeth Jr., 243
Cromley, Elizabeth Sr., 243
Cromley, John, 243
Cromley, Valentine, 243, 304
Crook, Elizabeth, 16
Crook, Robert, 64, 121
Crooke, Robert, 69, 289
Crossly, Pierce, 18
Crosswell, Mary, 64
Crowden Edmond, J.P., 266
Crowder, H. B., 355
Crowder, James, 29
Crowder, John J.I.C., 355
Crowell, Edward, 257
Crowman, Mary, 218
Crowman, William, 218
Crumley, Anthony, 264
Crutchfield, Richard, 315, 386
Culbreath, Peter, 129
Culpepper, Argent, 13
Culpepper, Daniel, 25, 195, 204, 316, 356, 367
Culpepper, Frances, 376
Culpepper, Joseph, 226
Culpepper, Malachi, 331
Culpepper, Nathan, 26, 320
Culpepper, Patsy, 30
Culpepper, Robert, 27, 367
Culpepper, William, 195, 233, 356, 367
Culpepper, William Sr., 316
Cummings, Gray, 383
Cunningham, John, 235, 307
Cunningham, Robert M., 27
Cureton, Boling, 362
Cureton, Richard, 64, 267

Cureton, Thomas, 310
Curry, Carey, 278
Curry, Cary, 237, 325
Curry, Jane, 19
Curry, John, 215, 237, 246, 255,
    275, 277, 278
Curry, Richard, 188, 224, 237,
    243, 256, 319, 325
Cutbreath, Peter, 94, 141
Cutbreth, Peter, 64
Dale, James J., 31
Dandoon, Peter, 350
Daniel
    slave, 236
Daniel, Frederick, 178, 255,
    285, 320
Daniel, Isaac, 18
Daniel, Jeremiah, 19
Daniel, John, 33
Daniel, L., 299
Daniel, Lewis, 362
Daniel, Nancy, 30, 32
Daniel, Robert, 22
Daniel, Robert B., 299
Daniel, William, 65, 320
Daniel, Willie, 299
Danielly, Andrew, 383
Danielly, Ann, 383
Danielly, Arthur, 383
Danielly, Elizabeth, 258
Danielly, Francis, 258, 383
Danielly, Jane, 383
Danielly, John, 65, 129, 383
Danielly, Mac D., 383
Danielly, Rachel, 383
Danielly, Rhoda, 383
Dannelly, Rachel, 32
Dannielly, Francis, 256
Dansby, Catherine, 34
Dansby, Jacob, 16
Darden, Abner, 218
Darden, Ann, 208, 234
Darden, Anna, 199

Darden, Buckner, 239, 309
Darden, Clotilda, 27
Darden, David, 218
Darden, Dicy, 18
Darden, Elbert, 386
Darden, Elisha, 323
Darden, Eliza, 23
Darden, Elizabeth, 26, 29
Darden, Ellender, 274
Darden, Henry W., 386
Darden, Jacob, 190, 215, 218,
    222, 225, 250, 289, 293, 343
Darden, Jennie, 27
Darden, Jesse, 381
Darden, Jethro, 190, 225, 228,
    234, 264, 269, 273, 327, 345,
    379
Darden, Jethro Sr., 219, 223
Darden, John, 326, 338, 340,
    347
Darden, Josiah, 281
Darden, Micajah, 18
Darden, Moses, 208, 280, 281,
    348, 381
Darden, Nancy, 190, 225
Darden, Nicholas, 208
Darden, Pollie, 377
Darden, Polly, 32
Darden, Sally, 18, 34
Darden, Stephen, 190, 199, 207,
    208, 209, 225, 289
Darden, Temperance. *See* Hill
Darden, Washington, 385
Darden, William, 26, 190, 218,
    224, 225, 228, 377
Darden, Willis, 234
Darden, Zachariah, 226, 377
Dark, John, 327
Dark, Thomas, 366
Darnall, James, 17
Darnalls, Charles, 342
Darnell, Charles, 277, 297
Darnell, James, 249

Dasher, Martin, 65
Dashiels, George, 26
Daugherty, Neal, 244
Daushe, Daniel, 256
Daushe, Jacob, 256
Davenport, Jack S., 376
Davenport, Jacks, 292
Davenport, Jacky, 182
David
    slave, 365
David, Arthur, 302
Davidson, George H., 220
Davidson, Jeremiah, 362
Davidson, Jesse, 31
Davidson, John, 28, 35, 231,
    363
Davidson, John J., 337
Davidson, Joseph, 269, 270,
    284, 300, 363
Davidson, Levicy, 32
Davidson, William, 26, 280,
    293, 301
Davidson, Winney, 300
Davies, James, 295, 306
Davies, John, 260
Davies, Joseph. *See* Joseph
    Davidson
Davies, Susannah, 247
Davies, William, 292, 295
Davis, Allen, 21
Davis, David, 179, 183
Davis, Dolphin, 35
Davis, Elizabeth, 24
Davis, Gahazi, 180, 371, *See*
    Shockley
Davis, Isaac, 185, 224
Davis, James, 239
Davis, John, 65, 82, 171, 304,
    330
Davis, Lydia, 239
Davis, Matthew, 16
Davis, Nancy, 28

Davis, Nathan, 23, 193, 352,
    371
Davis, Orian, 35
Davis, Patience, 27
Davis, Peggy, 33
Davis, Polly, 17
Davis, Samuel, 21
Davis, Tabitha, 34
Davis, Theophilus, 65, 72, 142
Davis, Thomas, 20, 65, 277, 299
Davis, Vincent, 376
Davis, Watkins, 31
Davis, William, 16, 75, 116,
    144, 162, 265
Davison, Frances, 21
Davison, James, 17, 187, 258
Davison, Joseph, 293
Davison, Margaret, 257
Dawkins, Absalom T., 392
Dawkins, Elinor, 14
Dawkins, George, 14
Dawson, W., 333
Day, Joseph, 44
Day, Josiah, 65, 66
Day, Mary, 65, 66
Day, Owen, 37, 66, 131, 156
Day, Sarah, 44
Day, Stephen, 43, 66, 75, 138
Dean, Charles, 20
Dean, James, 159
Dean, Samuel, 69
Dean, William, 237, 279, 323
DeArey, Joseph, 66
Deaser, Moses, 63
Deason, Benjamin, 188
Deason, Michael, 33
Deason, Polly, 33
Deason, Thomas, 30
Deason, Zachariah, 188
Debenport, Richard, 292
Dees, Benjamin, 303
Deloach, Joseph, 316
Denison, Patrick, 66

Denmark, William, 35
Dennis, Abraham, 67, 247, 254, 255, 348
Dennis, Betsy, 14
Dennis, D., 381
Dennis, Daniel, 29, 386
Dennis, Elizabeth, 25
Dennis, Frederick, 285
Dennis, Isaac, 46, 67, 243, 284, 286
Dennis, Jacob, 67, 71, 117
Dennis, Jesse, 19
Dennis, John, 46, 67, 121, 254, 266, 284, 285, 353
Dennis, Lucy, 20, 30
Dennis, M., 23
Dennis, Patsy, 22
Dennis, Priscilla, 35
Dennis, Richmond, 32
Dennis, William, 282
Denson, Joseph, 231
Dent, Richard, 353
Dent, Thomas, 184, 187, 220, 223, 310, 347, 353, 354
Dent, Walter, 346
Denton, Aaron, 217
Depuis, William, 300
Deruzeau, Daniel, 59
Deshield, Harriet, 387
Desieur, Leonard, 17
Deveraux, Charles H., 21
Deveraux, John W., 354
Devereux, Daniel, 114
Dewberry, Giles, 313
Dewberry, Henry, 214, 219
Dewberry, Irby, 33
Dewberry, Irby Sr., 377
Dewberry, James, 377
Dewberry, John, 377
Dewberry, Mary, 377
Dewberry, Pollie, 26
Dewberry, Thomas, 377
Deyampert, John, 264

Deyampert, Mary, 264
Dias, Moses, 101
Dick, Rebecca, 378
Dicken, Benjamin, 183
Dicken, Ephraim, 260
Dicken, Jean, 14
Dicken, John, 364
Dicken, Lewis, 183
Dicken, Mary, 35
Dickens, Elijah, 34
Dickens, Elizabeth, 33
Dickens, James T., 382
Dickens, John, 363
Dickens, Robert, 349, 364
Dickens, Sally, 21
Dickey, George, 72
Dickie, George, 68
Dickin, James T., 392
Dickins, Robert, 279
Dickinson Culpepper, 29
Dickinson, Joel, 320
Dickson, Benjamin, 236
Dicott, Elizabeth, 42
Didcott, Elizabeth, 68
Digby, John, 27
Digby, Margaret, 19
Dill, John, 265
Dillard, Philip J.P., 300
Dillard, Phillip J.P., 299
Dinah
    slave, 250, 335
Dismukes, Edmond, 263
Dismukes, Ephriam, 263
Dismukes, John, 263
Dismukes, John Jr., 263
Dismukes, John Sr., 263
Dismukes, Martha, 24
Dismukes, Peter, 263
Dismukes, Sarah, 17
Dismukes, William, 263, 286
Dixon, John, 252
Dixon, Rowland, 16
Dobbins, John, 68

Dodds, John, 68
Dodson, John, 107
Doherty, Cornelius, 39, 74
Doles, Elizabeth, 18
Doles, Jesse, 252, 260, 361
Doles, Nancy, 20
Doles, Susannah, 240
Doles, Thomas, 16, 240, 316
Dolittle, Joseph, 68
Donelly, John, 69, 161
Donelson, George, 169
Donnolly, Catherine, 69
Donnolly, James, 69
Dorman, Allen, 235, 239, 249,
    272, 290
Dorman, Wiley, 235
Dorman, Wilie, 239
Dorman, Willie, 25, 249
Doster, Thomas, 369, 380
Doster, William, 33
Douglas, David, 58, 69, 98, 159,
    160
Douglas, James, 177, 372
Douglas, John, 58, 69
Dove, David, 22, 181
Dove, Elizabeth, 332
Dove, Peggy, 17
Dove, Thomas, 181
Dove, Zilpha, 19
Dover, John, 69, 82, 84, 173,
    242, 284
Dowdy, Rebeckah, 298
Downs, Henry, 69, 107
Downs, William, 243
Downs, William Esq., 296
Doyle, Dennis, 284
Doyle, Francis, 235, 284, 307
Dozer, John, 254, 288
Dozer, Leonard, 288
Dozer, Nancy, 296
Dozer, William, 254, 296
Dozier, Dunwoodie, 31
Dozier, Elizabeth, 31

Dozier, James, 193, 331
Dozier, John, 193
Dozier, Martha M., 384
Dozier, Richard, 224
Dr. Bush, 353
Drake, Early, 371
Drake, Francis, 371
Drake, John, 198, 209
Drake, Lemuel Braxton, 371
Drake, Matthew, 198
Drake, Nancy, 30
Drake, Sarah, 14, 371
Drake, Shemei, 21
Drake, Sherrod, 224
Drake, Shimei, 189
Drake, Theney, 371
Drake, Thomas, 371
Drake, William, 209
Drake, William Jr., 390
Draper, James, 257
Draper, Joshua, 222
Draper, Josiah, 23
Draper, Josua, 27
Draper, Solomon, 30
Draper, Sophia. See Stanford
Draper, Thomas, 28
Drue, Arthur, 265
Dryden, John, 240, 369
Dryden, William, 369
Duberry, Henry, 187, 222
Duberry, Jesse, 15, 187, 222
Duberry, John, 259
Duberry, Mary, 222
Duberry, Pollie, 15
Duberry, Polly, 187
DuBose, Isaac, 241
DuBose, Sary, 241
Duck, Nathan, 358
Duck, Nathaniel, 357
Ducks, Jeremiah, 81
Duckworth, Allen, 34
Duckworth, Gazaway, 207
Duckworth, Hester, 31

Duckworth, Jacob, 249, 257
Duckworth, Jeremiah, 69, 198, 207, 257, 296, 319, 333
Duckworth, Joseph, 179, 197, 198, 207, 216, 249, 257
Duckworth, Joseph J.P., 349
Duckworth, Nelly, 207
Duckworth, Patsy, 23
Duckworth, Polly, 28, 207
Duckworth, Randall, 257, 327, 336
Duckworth, Ranella, 198
Duckworth, Rebecca, 197, 200, 207
Duckworth, Samuel, 207, 226
Duckworth, Susannah, 390
Duckworth, William, 197, 200, 207, 232, 287, 357
Duff, Dennis, 70, 81
Dugger, T., 318
Duke, Ransom, 355
Dunaway, Edmund, 258
Dunaway, George, 239, 258, 309, 332
Dunaway, James, 18
Dunaway, John, 245, 249, 258, 267, 311
Dunaway, John Jr., 239, 309
Dunaway, John Sr., 239, 309
Dunaway, Jonathan, 25, 245
Dunaway, Rebecca, 20
Dunaway, William, 30, 249
Dunbar, Priscilla, 10
Dunkham County, North Carolina, 303
Dunkin, John, 70, 120
Dunn, Benjamin, 70
Dunn, John, 70
Dunn, Joseph, 257, 335
Dunn, Mary, 21
Dunn, Robert, 70
Duns, Richard, 250
Dupins, Joseph, 285

Dupins, William, 285
Duprese, William, 267
Durden, Christian, 388
Durden, Jesse, 388
Durham, James, 308
Durozeaux, Daniel, 70, 114
Dykes, Allen, 34
Dykes, George, 194, 253, 256, 271, 285, 299, 360
Dykes, George J.P., 354, 356, 364
Dykes, Jesse, 291, 303
Dysart, Elizabeth, 235
Dysart, John, 235, 241, 244, 354
Eades, Daniel, 24
Eades, Mary, 18
Eades, Renay, 31
Early County, Georgia, 383, 390, 391
Earnest, William, 178, 265, 338, 342, 347
Eastwood, James, 339, 347
Eatton, Mary, 70
Eckles, Edward, 70
Edge, James, 224
Edge, Margaret, 33
Edge, Nehemiah, 224
Edgefield County, South Carolina, 288, 349
Edmonds, Sally, 28
Edmonds, Thomas, 183
Edmondson, Ambrose, 177, 230, 249, 315
Edmondson, Elizabeth L., 392
Edmondson, John, 246
Edmondson, Nancy, 23
Edmondson, Patsy, 19
Edmondson, Penny, 22
Edmondson, Thomas, 221, 322, 326, 327, 330, 355, 391, 393
Edmondson, William G., 230
Edmundson, Ambrose, 242
Edmundson, Thomas, 343

Edwards, Jinsy, 33
Edwards, Robert, 223
Edwards, Susannah, 376
Edwards, William, 223
Eerherd, Gabriel, 71
Effingham County, Georgia, 330
Eiland, Sarah, 343
Elam, William, 71
Elbert County, Georgia, 331
Elim, William, 157
Ellen, A. F., 265
Ellen, Shadrach F., 270
Ellet, James, 228
Ellin, Shadrach F., 300
Ellin, Shadrack F., 304, 317
Ellington, Elizabeth, 35
Ellington, Enoch, 336
Ellington, Enoch Ward, 300
Ellington, Josiah, 337
Ellington, Obedience, 17
Elliott, Elizabeth, 239
Elliott, James, 14, 246, 335
Elliott, Peter, 71
Elliott, Sally, 380
Elliott, Thomas, 239
Ellis, Elizabeth, 14
Ellis, Robert, 31
Ellis, Solomon, 241
Ellis, William, 342
Elly, Jacob, 71
Elly, Michael, 71
Emanuel, John, 71
Embree, Anna, 257
Embree, Jesse, 257
Embree, John, 322
Emerson, John, 208
Emet, James, 72
Emett, James, 49, 82
Emitt, James, 72
English, Aaron, 231
English, James, 226
English, Jenny, 253

English, John, 181, 217, 231, 245, 311
English, Matthew, 231
English, Matthew Jr., 253
English, Matthew Sr., 253
Ennis, Mary, 392
Essery, Katherine, 243
Essery, William, 243
Evans, Daniel, 371
Evans, Joseph, 255, 305, 353, 356
Ewell, William, 22
Fagalie, Barbara, 383
Fagalie, Casea, 383
Fagalie, Fannie, 383
Fagalie, Franklin, 383
Fagalie, James, 383
Fagalie, John, 383
Fagalie, Lucy, 383
Fagalie, Mary, 383
Fagalie, Robert, 383
Fagalie, Robertson, 383
Fagalie, William, 383
Fail, Arthur, 339
Fair, Jacob, 21
Faming, Joachim Noel, 72
Fanner, William, 72
Fannier, William, 38
Farless, James, 332
Farley, Joseph, 72
Farlin, James, 14
Farmer, Enoch, 383
Farmer, Thomas, 252, 265
Farmer, William, 72, 148
Farr, Crisa, 31
Farr, Ensil, 30
Farr, Jacob, 287
Farr, John, 287
Farr, Sarah, 357
Farrel, John, 72
Faulks, Polly, 24
Fears, Edmond, 289
Featherstone, Howell, 244

Featherstone, Pamela, 244
Fellin, Shadrach, 284
Felps, David, 249, 286
Felps, Falby, 286
Felps, William, 170, 288
Fenn, Zachariah, 73, 140
Ferguson, Neil, 24
Ferry, Thomas, 338
Ferryman, Harmon, 311
Fetherstone, Howell, 286
Fetherstone, Permela, 286
Few, Agn., 298
Few, Benjamin, 51, 73, 94, 138,
    243, 264, 280, 286, 291, 294,
    299, 301
Few, I., 299, 311
Few, Ignatius, 73, 138, 241,
    244, 263, 268, 269, 301, 302,
    305, 317, 319, 324, 347, 351,
    354, 364
Few, Mary, 235, 323
Few, Rachel, 264
Few, William, 28, 73, 264, 361,
    364
Fewocks, John, 369
Fickling, Barnard, 24
Fickling, Barnard W., 343, 377
Fickling, Barnard Wood, 356
Fickling, Elizabeth, 18, 328,
    343
Fickling, Francis, 326
Fickling, George, 22
Fickling, Joseph, 316, 328
Fickling, Samuel, 16, 326, 343,
    344, 356
Fields, Polly, 25
Fields, Samuel, 246
Filligin, Peggy, 25
Fillingim, James, 317
Fillingim, Robert, 317
Fillingin, Moses, 22
Fillingin, Nancy, 22
Finch, Celia, 19

Finch, Elizabeth, 22
Finch, Ichabod, 228
Finch, Nancy, 23
Finch, Patsy, 26
Finch, William, 301
Findley, Katherine. *See* Grier
Finlay, John, 69
Finley, William, 73, 130, 165
Finney, John, 245
Fisher, Nicholas, 77
Fisher, Robert, 284
Fisher, Thomas, 35
Fitch John, 58
Fitch, Ann, 73, 74, 162
Fitch, John, 45, 48, 53, 73, 74,
    92, 116, 136, 138, 162, 171
Fitzsimmons, Walter, 15
Flake, Nancy, 21
Flake, Sally, 28
Flake, Thomas, 21
Flake, William, 263, 279
Flemen, David, 74
Fleming, Elizabeth, 34
Fleming, Robert, 31
Fleming, Samuel, 323
Flesher, Richard, 379
Fletcher, John, 315
Fletcher, Martha, 315
Fletcher, R. B., 313
Fletcher, R. B. J.P., 268, 270,
    280, 292, 297
Fletcher, R. D. J.P., 273
Fletcher, Richard, 22, 186
Fletcher, Richard B. J.P., 256,
    279, 301
Fletcher, Richard B. Esq., 179
Fletcher, Richard Brooks, 316
Fletcher, Richard Esq., 236
Flewellen, Abner, 322
Flewellen, Archulaus, 384
Flewellen, Enos Russell, 384
Flewellen, James, 233, 384

Flewellen, Lawrence Augustus, 384

Flewellen, Martha, 384

Flewellen, MaryAnn, 384

Flewellen, Thomas, 384

Flewellin, Archibald, 362

Flewellin, Abner, 317, 323, 335, 362

Flewellin, Abraham, 298

Flewellin, Alexander, 15, 342

Flewellin, Archelaus, 193, 197, 203, 207, 228, 318, 363, 388

Flewellin, Archelaus J.I.C., 354, 357

Flewellin, Archelaus J.P., 328, 350

Flewellin, Archibald, 208, 343, 344

Flewellin, Fanny, 17

Flewellin, James, 232

Flewellin, Nancy, 232

Flewellin, Nicholas, 204

Flewellin, Patsy, 19

Flewellin, Shadrach, 193, 203, 204, 222, 365

Flewellin, Shadrack, 343, 344

Flewellin, Shadrick, 331

Flewellin, Thomas, 228

Flewornan, Gideon, 385

Flinn, Lavina, 32

Flinn, Michael, 308

Flinn, Thomas, 189, 277

Flourney, Jacob, 246

Flournoy, Gibson, 271, 369

Flournoy, Jacob, 182, 219, 272

Flournoy, John B., 219

Flournoy, John F., 263

Flournoy, John Francis, 356

Flournoy, Obadiah, 290

Flournoy, R., 320

Flournoy, Robert, 275, 298

Flournoy, S., 311

Flournoy, William, 18, 182, 218, 219

Fluellin, Elizabeth, 32

Fluwellen, Sally, 29

Fluwellin, Abner, 181, 324, 370

Fluwellin, Alexander, 180, 370

Fluwellin, Betty, 180, 370

Fluwellin, Howell, 370

Fluwellin, Shaderick, 178, 370

Fluwellin, Shadrach, 217, 276

Fluwellin, Shadrack, 286

Fluwellin, Shadrick, 181

Fluwellin, Shedrick, 185

Fluwellin, Stephen, 184

Fluwellin, William, 370

Folks, James, 271

Folsom, Esther, 317

Folsom, Nathaniel, 317

Fontaine, Francis Jr., 291

Fontaine, John, 197, 220, 221, 225, 227, 230, 231, 273, 346, 355, 390

Fontaine, Mary, 16, 33

Fontaine, Nancy, 13

Fontaine, Sally, 22, 196, 197

Fontaine, Sarah, 291

Fontaine, Thomas, 15, 196, 197, 264, 269, 274, 283, 297, 309, 323, 345, 346

Foodwin, Peter, 289

Forbes, Clement, 265

Ford, John, 147

Ford, John Jr., 283

Ford, Joseph, 221

Ford, Rebecca, 15

Ford, Robert, 283

Ford, Thomas, 74, 114, 118, 285

Ford, William W., 221

Forrest, John, 15

Forrester, Stephen, 75

Fort, Arthur, 7, 257, 276, 304, 319

Fort, Arthur J..P., 264
Fort, Arthur J.I.C., 328, 329
Fort, Arthur J.P., 246, 265
Fort, Eli, 75
Fort, Eliza, 31
Fort, Moses, 264
Fort, Susannah, 265, 319
Fort, Tomlinson, 7
Fournoy, Robert, 299
Fove, John, 371
Fove, Priscilla, 371
Fowl, George, 63
Fowler, Hillery, 14
Fowler, John, 20
Fowler, Nancy, 288
Fowler, Nathan, 227, 253, 273,
    283, 288, 313
Fowler, Zephaniah, 227, 253,
    288
Fowler, Zephariah, 324
Fowns, William D., 243
Fox, James, 75
Fox, John, 235, 236
Frances. *See*
Francis, Frederick, 73, 75, 94
Franklin County, Georgia, 289
Franklin County, North
    Carolina, 237, 238
Franklin, G., 248
Franklin, G. D., 384
Franklin, George, 338, 373
Franklin, H. A., 383, 384
Franklin, L. J.P., 350
Franklin, Mary, 246, 307
Franklin, Patsy, 14
Franklin, William, 246, 273,
    307, 338, 373
Franklin, Z., 283, 302, 321, 322,
    349, 350, 355
Franklin, Z. J.P., 349, 352
Franklin, Zeph., 248
Franklin, Zephaniah, 380, 384
Frazer, Andrew, 290

Frazer, James, 41
Frederick, Daniel, 216
Freeman, Jessie, 31
Freeman, John, 302, 312
French, James, 364
Fretwell, Leonard, 298
Fretwell, Lucy, 30
Friend, Benjamin F., 382
Friend, Fanney, 263, 279
Friend, John O., 382
Friend, Thomas, 258, 329, 382
Friend, Thomas Esq., 198
Friend, Thomas J.P., 275, 316,
    353
Friend, William, 268
Frierson, James, 48
Fugett, Charity, 15
Fulbright, Christian, 75
Fulbright, Christopher, 62, 170
Fullar, Mary, 239
Fuller, John, 75, 248, 249
Fuller, Jonathan, 22
Fuller, Joshua, 75
Fuller, Samuel, 226
Fuller, Spivey, 231
Fuller, Thomas, 56, 76, 249
Fuller, William A., 210
Fulsom, John, 254
Fulsom, Nathaniel, 256
Funderburk, Abel, 230
Furlow, Maria, 388
Fyffe, Gilbert, 58
Fyffe, John, 76
Gafford, James, 33
Gage, John, 323
Galphin, Barbara, 76, 119
Galphin, George, 47, 51, 76, 77,
    78, 81, 98, 108, 111, 118,
    119, 139, 140, 163
Galphin, Thomas, 78
Gambill, Susannah, 246
Gambill, Thomas, 246
Gamble, Jesse, 229

Gancy, Benjamin G., 31
Gandy, Samuel, 171
Gardiner, Fannie, 26
Gardner, Elisha, 33
Gardner, Fannie, 364
Gardner, Frances, 377
Gardner, Henry, 285
Gardner, Isham, 291
Gardner, Mary Rose, 8
Gardner, Patsy, 26
Gardner, Polley, 250
Gardner, Prior, 307
Gardner, Prior J.P., 329
Gardner, Pryor J.P., 364
Gardner, Sally, 20
Gardner, Sarah, 377
Gardner, Sterling, 8, 176, 193,
    202, 204, 217, 240, 247, 250,
    268, 270, 314, 315, 354, 360,
    366
Gardner, Sterling J.P., 343, 351,
    365, 366
Gardner, Sterling, J.P., 354
Gardner, Suckey, 31
Gardner, William, 20, 364
Garner, Lewis, 294, 295
Garner, Thomas, 81
Garnet, Thomas, 38, 79
Garrard County, Kentucky, 292
Garrett, John, 240, 250, 295
Garrett, Petheny, 33
Gaskin, Fisher, 328
Gaskins, Fisher, 17, 34
Gates, Benjamin, 308, 328, 329
Gatlin, Moses, 21, 382
Gatling, Moses, 16
Gaza, John, 291
Gaza, Joshua, 291
Gaza, William, 276
Geaslin, Sarah, 26
Geesland, Benjamin, 186, 222
Geesland, Sallie, 222
Geesland, Sally, 186

Geesland, William, 186, 222
Geesling, Benjamin, 262
Geesling, Samuel, 29
Geesling, Susan, 387
Gelphin, William, 79
George
    slave, 354, 355
George, Elizabeth, 27
George, G., 351
George, Gideon, 13, 283, 294,
    295, 298, 301, 315, 333, 357
George, James, 13, 283, 294,
    295, 299, 314
George, James Jr., 294
George, Jesse, 294, 295
George, Joseph, 294, 295, 315
George, Judith, 294, 295
George, L. Gideon, 294
George, Polly, 28, 314, 378
George, Richard, 294, 295
George, Susannah, 315
George, Tabitha, 333
Georgetown, 319, 320, 330
Gerard, James, 314
Germany, John, 45, 79, 121
Germany, Robert, 48, 79
Germany, Samuel, 80, 85, 95,
    126
Gerrard, Devereaux, 80
Gerrard, Deviux, 87
Getson, Samuel, 68, 80
Ghesling, Drusilla, 35
Ghesling, Elizabeth, 35
Gibbs, Elhannon, 340
Gibbs, Phebe, 252
Gibbs, Philip, 252, 255, 265
Gibbs, Phillip, 267, 277, 330,
    340, 343, 356
Gibbs, Phoebe, 343
Gibbs, Vashti, 20, 340
Gibbs, Zacheus, 340
Gibon, Thomas, 226
Giborn, John, 244

Gibson Thomas, 391
Gibson, Betsy, 21
Gibson, Catherine, 28
Gibson, Caty, 26
Gibson, Churchill, 225, 228,
231, 277, 299, 301, 320, 380,
381
Gibson, Churchwell, 25, 199,
359
Gibson, Elizabeth, 22
Gibson, George Micajah, 8
Gibson, Henry, 226, 229, 359,
381, 388
Gibson, Isabella, 35
Gibson, James, 18
Gibson, John, 17, 31, 35, 226,
228, 235, 251, 282, 298, 299,
301, 318, 325
Gibson, Martha Amanda, 8
Gibson, Mary, 381
Gibson, Mary D., 8
Gibson, Mary Rose, 8
Gibson, Patsy, 22, 26, 377
Gibson, Peggy, 34
Gibson, Rachel, 28
Gibson, Rebeccah, 27
Gibson, Salley, 301
Gibson, Thomas, 8, 28, 227,
358, 382, 387, 390, 392
Gibson, Thomas H., 8
Gibson, William, 8, 28
Gigg, Thomas, 116
Giggs, Thomas, 83
Gilbert, Bird, 32
Giles, J., 326
Giles, Jacob, 331
Gillans, Thomas, 81
Gillard, Thomas, 102
Gilleland, William, 303
Gilliland, Thomas, 80, 139
Gillman, Thomas, 168
Gilmore, Ann, 270
Gilmore, James, 269, 270, 351

Gilmore, John, 269
Gilpin, John, 19, 314, 318
Giobson, Thomas Neal, 261
Glascock, William, 317
Glasgow, Polly, 16
Glover, Allen, 293
Glover, Charlotte, 282
Glover, Elizabeth, 233
Glover, Frederick, 17, 233
Glover, Henry, 282
Glover, Isham, 233
Glover, John, 81
Glover, Larkin, 233, 393
Glover, Lucy, 293
Glover, William, 293
Going, Aggy, 268
Going, Agnes, 307
Going, Agness, 291
Going, Moses, 268, 291, 302,
305, 307
Goings, Polly, 13
Golden, Charity, 14
Golden, Daniel, 311, 356
Golden, David, 15, 198, 199,
200
Golden, Henry, 81, 356
Golding, C. E.. See Harbuck
Golding, David, 308, 311, 326
Golding, Henry, 311, 312, 323
Golding, Sarah, 261, 311, 312,
323
Golightly, James, 292
Gonder, Mark, 261
Goodale, Thomas, 142
Goodgame, John, 81
Goodgeon, Captain, 129
Goodgion, William, 81
Goodwin, Elizabeth, 16, 177,
237
Goodwin, Peter, 177, 236, 237
Goodwin, Wyche, 236, 237
Goodwin, Wyche J.P., 320, 372
Gordon, Francis, 251

Gosea, Elijah, 29
Goss, Hamilton, 213
Goyen, Drury, 257
Goyne, William, 218
Goynne, Drury, 378
Goynne, Hardy, 378
Goynne, Hiram, 378
Goynne, John, 378
Goynne, Mount Herman, 378
Goynne, Tyra, 378
Goynne, William, 378
Goza, Aaron, 341
Goza, William, 341, 347
Graham, James, 81
Graham, John, 81, 100, 121, 172
Graham, Thomas, 139, 140, 169
Granade, James, 357
Granard, Barsheba, 371
Granberry, George, 194, 195, 243, 307, 339
Granberry, Moses, 194, 243, 253, 307, 325, 339, 351, 352, 360
Granberry, Stephen, 31
Grandberry Moses, 256
Grandberry, George, 256, 299, 300
Grandberry, Moses, 273, 299
Grant Mathew, 264
Grantham,, 370
Grantham, Daniel, 370
Grantham, John, 240, 271
Grantham, Joshua, 356
Grantham, Matthew, 322
Graves, James, 82, 141
Graves, Robert, 54, 82
Gray, Amy, 231
Gray, Elizabeth, 30
Gray, Isaac, 82
Gray, James, 34, 76, 83, 118, 119, 134, 137, 186, 187, 222, 223, 226, 231, 251, 310, 327, 355, 366
Gray, James Jr., 34
Gray, James Sr., 226
Gray, John, 115
Gray, Richard, 240
Gray, Solomon, 240
Gray, Thomas, 147
Gray, William, 135, 336
Gray, Zachariah, 239
Graybill, Henry, 183, 229, 285, 318
Greathouse, Jacob, 83, 93
Green County, Georgia, 246, 261, 263, 298
Green, Amos, 323
Green, Edmund, 315
Green, Elizabeth, 208, 278
Green, Francis, 173, 284
Green, Hardy, 30, 208
Green, Henry Sr., 278
Green, Isaac, 84
Green, James, 250, 279, 317, 335
Green, James W., 257, 280, 304, 363
Green, James Williams, 278
Green, John, 30, 32, 86, 122, 145
Green, John Jr., 84
Green, Margaret, 319, 323
Green, Redian, 387
Green, Reese, 359
Green, Richard, 311, 323
Grcen, Rowland, 15
Green, Sarah, 323
Green, Sibbia, 13
Green, Tempy, 30
Green, Thomas, 63
Green, William, 26
Green, William B., 315

Greene County, Georgia, 240, 243, 258, 260, 273, 282, 305, 320, 356, 358, 376, 390
Greenville County, South Carolina, 291, 296, 303
Greenwood, William Jr., 289
Greenwood, William Jr.,, 240
Greer, Aaron, 207
Greer, Thomas, 84
Greesom, Peggy, 20
Greeson, Hester, 30
Greeson, John, 15, 322, 346
Greeson, John Sr., 345
Greeson, William, 33
Gregory, Howell, 204, 214
Greirson, James, 84
Grenade, Benjamin, 208, 214
Grenade, Catherine, 357
Grenade, Elijah, 19
Grenade, James, 208, 214, 232
Grenade, John, 260
Grenade, Joseph, 26
Grenade, Leamander, 25
Grenade, Martha, 31
Grenade, Rebekah, 28
Grenade, Sarah, 378
Grenaid, John, 270
Grier, A. J.P., 266, 293, 297, 299, 303
Grier, Aaron, 300, 303, 384
Grier, Aaron Jr., 23
Grier, Aaron W., 385
Grier, Elizabeth, 384
Grier, H., 315
Grier, Margaret, 26
Grier, Moses, 300, 303
Grier, Polly, 23
Grier, Robert, 335, 384, 385
Grier, Thomas, 129, 385
Grierson, Abraham, 35
Grierson, Abram, 232, 234
Grierson, Colonel James, 82
Grierson, Delilah, 380

Grierson, Elizabeth, 380
Grierson, Frances Caroline, 380
Grierson, James, 48, 108, 137
Grierson, Peyton, 380
Grierson, Sukey, 380
Grierson, Suky, 380
Grierson, Susannah, 234
Grierson, William, 102
Grierson, Wyatt Oliver, 380
Grieson, John, 285
Griffin, Furney, 18
Griffin, John, 17
Griffin, Michael, 85, 126
Grigg, Silas, 276
Grimes, Thomas, 28
Grimes, William G., 376
Grimsley, Milley, 276
Grimsley, Nancy, 14
Grissle, Willie, 16
Grizard, J., 257
Grizard, Joseph, 265, 342
Grizzard, James, 340, 366
Grizzle, Lettice, 230
Grizzle, Stephen, 33
Grizzle, Thomas W., 230
Grizzle, Wilie, 227
Grizzle, William, 297
Gross, Solomon, 243
Grove, Thomas, 72
Groves, James, 85
Grubbs, Benjamin, 144
Grubbs, Francis, 242, 293
Grubbs, Jacob, 139
Grubbs, John, 85
Grubs, Benjamin, 85
Gunn, Jenny, 24
Gunn, Nelson, 29, 228
Gunn, Radford, 2
Gunn, William, 34
Gurley, Lazarus, 237, 240, 261
Gusling, William, 304
Guthrie, John, 352, 357
Guy, Joseph, 334

Guyland, Phoebe, 19
Gwinnett County, Georgia, 386
Habersham, James, 268
Hackett, Polly, 18
Hadley, Ambrose, 260, 285, 292, 304
Hadley, Betsey, 34
Hadley, Henry, 19, 286
Hadley, Sarah, 16
Hadley, Selah, 375
Hagathy, Jonathan, 17
Hagens, Thomas, 85
Hagerty, Jonathan, 178, 179, 216, 317
Hagin, John, 55
Hagood, Gideon, 389
Hains, Gregory, 58
Halifax County, North Carolina, 201, 249, 258, 307, 326, 328, 362, 376, 378
Hall, Anna, 260
Hall, Dixon, 260
Hall, Lieut. Thomas, 179
Hall, Lydia, 179
Hall, Nancy, 260
Hall, Nathaniel, 85, 96
Hall, Samuel, 217, 227, 233, 383
Hall, Thomas, 26
Hall, Thomas Lent, 186
Hall, Thomas Lt., 298
Hambleton, Concord, 22
Hambleton, John, 292
Hamill, John J.P., 244, 246
Hamilton, Daniel, 387
Hamilton, J. F., 9
Hamilton, John, 217
Hamilton, John Sr., 387
Hamilton, Mary, 387
Hamilton, William, 313
Hammill, John, 319, 320
Hammill, John J.P., 244
Hammock, John, 321, 390

Hammond, LeKay, 75
Hammond, LeRoy, 85, 134, 150
Hammonill, John J.P., 285
Hammonill, Susannah, 285
Hamp, Benjamin, 243
Hamp, Benjamin A., 1, 279, 286
Hamp, Benjamin Augustus, 244
Hampton, John, 245
Hampton, Nathan, 86, 126
Hancock County, Georgia, 239, 240, 241, 242, 244, 255, 257, 258, 267, 276, 279, 283, 297, 300, 304, 318, 319, 320, 324, 325, 327, 337, 340, 345, 348, 349, 350, 355, 363, 365, 366, 367, 389
Hancock, Joseph, 18
Hancock, Milly, 30
Hancock, William, 353
Hand, Henry, 389
Handley, Governor George, 260, 338
Handley, James, 24
Haniel, Craft, 86
Hanover County, Virginia, 251
Harbuck, Anna, 387
Harbuck, Barbara, 387
Harbuck, Elizabeth, 15
Harbuck, Greenberry Lee, 387
Harbuck, Henry, 30, 225, 241
Harbuck, Jacob, 28
Harbuck, James, 35
Harbuck, John, 211, 215
Harbuck, Lavina, 35
Harbuck, Michael, 187, 241, 387
Harbuck, Nancy, 28
Harbuck, Nicholas, 241, 387
Harbuck, Rebecca, 19, 25
Harbuck, William, 30, 211, 215, 227, 387
Harbuck, William Jr., 387
Hardaway, Fannie, 34

Hardaway, Frances, 33
Hardaway, Francis, 234
Hardaway, George W., 220, 386
Hardaway, John, 23, 211, 213, 352
Hardaway, John Esq., 214
Hardaway, Martha, 211
Hardaway, Stith, 211, 232
Hardaway, Thomas, 211
Hardaway, Washington, 23, 214, 216, 359
Harden, Elizabeth, 31
Harden, Frances, 378
Harden, James, 378
Harden, John, 378
Harden, Mark, 378
Harden, Mark Jr., 354
Harden, Martin, 378
Harden, Nancy, 378
Harden, Patsy, 378
Harden, William, 378
Hardin, Adam, 311
Hardin, Bala, 30
Hardin, Benjamin, 30, 255
Hardin, Cathy, 22
Hardin, Henry, 242, 264, 284, 294, 295, 298, 299, 312, 315, 361
Hardin, Henry J.P., 254, 281, 282, 304, 310, 312
Hardin, J., 235
Hardin, J. B., 300
Hardin, James, 19, 314
Hardin, James J.P., 257
Hardin, M., 182, 280, 294
Hardin, Mark, 13, 182, 218, 219, 235, 236, 251, 272, 281, 314
Hardin, Mark J.P., 242, 269, 270
Hardin, Martin, 235, 236, 314
Hardin, Mary, 13
Hardin, Sallie, 378

Hardin, Sarah, 299
Hardin, Thomas, 230, 237, 371
Hardin, William, 176, 371
Harding, Benjamin, 14
Hardwick, George W., 33
Hardwick, William, 361
Hardwick, William J.P., 330
Hardy, John, 22
Hardy, Mary, 22
Hargraves, George, 190, 196, 213, 216, 225, 299, 300, 311, 313, 331, 333, 356, 357, 358, 362
Hargraves, George J.I.C., 339, 344, 353
Hargraves, Henrietta, 27
Hargraves, Theophilus, 313
Hargrove, Mary, 14
Harlan, Ezekiel, 86
Harman, J., 266
Harman, John, 279, 282
Harman, Mary, 282
Harmon, J., 266
Harmon, John, 266
Harold, Patsy, 31
Harp, Henry, 188, 257, 336
Harp, Susannah, 188
Harper, Edward, 22
Harper, Jesse, 268, 283
Harrall, Susannah, 22
Harrell, Cader, 329
Harrell, Gray, 313
Harrell, John, 322
Harrell, John B., 392
Harrell, Joseph, 346
Harrell, Lewis, 31
Harrell, Patsy, 346
Harrell, Samuel, 313
Harrell, Simon, 313, 334
Harrell, William, 35
Harris, Abegail, 14
Harris, Alsy, 335
Harris, Anne, 32

Harris, Arthur, 86, 160
Harris, Benjamin, 87, 128, 153, 380
Harris, Catherine, 381
Harris, David, 338
Harris, Elizabeth, 21, 34
Harris, Ezekiel, 380, 381
Harris, George, 380
Harris, Henry, 19, 23, 313, 361
Harris, James, 87
Harris, John, 218, 290, 380, 386
Harris, Lt., 255
Harris, Lucy, 29
Harris, Martha, 35
Harris, Matthew, 24
Harris, Nathan, 24, 87, 291
Harris, Nathaniel, 170
Harris, Olive, 207, 214
Harris, Rebecca, 16
Harris, Sally, 27
Harris, Samuel, 21, 380
Harris, Susannah, 14
Harris, Thomas, 286, 364, 380
Harris, Verlinda, 29
Harris, Wiley, 315
Harris, William, 351
Harris, William B., 234
Harris, Willie, 344
Harrison, Benjamin, 338, 387
Harrison, Dinwiddie R., 224
Harrison, Elizabeth, 33
Harrison, Gad, 264
Harrison, Hannah, 297
Harrison, John, 18, 32
Harrison, William, 387
Harriss, Thomas, 23
Harrold, Samuel, 22
Hart, Benjamin, 392
Hart, Elisha Esq., 196
Hart, Isaac, 14
Hart, James, 87, 156
Hart, Peter, 82, 87, 350
Hart, Samuel, 60, 88

Hart, Thomas, 105
Hart, William, 13
Hartfield, George, 181, 215
Hartfield, Lydia, 181, 215
Harton, Thomas, 355
Hartsfield, Lydia, 20
Hartshorne, John, 88
Harvell, Charles, 352
Harvell, Joseph, 319
Harvell, Samuel, 307
Harvey, Charles J.P., 241
Harvey, James, 329
Harvey, James J.P., 258
Harvey, John, 115
Harvey, Michael, 15, 185, 221
Harvey, Pinkethman, 185
Harvey, Pinkittiam, 221
Harvie, Lewis, 246
Harvill, James, 183
Harvill, Joseph, 183
Harvill, Polly, 21
Harvill, Sallie, 35
Harvill, William, 183
Harville, Eliza, 32
Harville, S., 279
Harville, Ursie, 17
Harwell, Ann, 88
Harwell, Mary, 31
Hatch, Albert, 9
Hatch, Albert S., 9
Hatch, Sarah Elizabeth, 9
Hatcher, Elizabeth, 31
Hatcher, John, 255, 279, 319
Hatcher, John J.P., 300, 318, 342, 349, 357
Hatcher, Pollie, 25
Hatcher, R. B. J.P., 285
Hatcher, Robert, 42, 51, 68, 80, 86, 88, 173
Hathorne, Susannah, 21
Hawthorn, Thomas, 314
Hayes, Edmund, 279
Hayes, Martin, 301

Haynes, C. E., 389
Haynes, Catherin, 383
Haynes, Catherine, 29
Haynes, Charles Eaton, 383, 384
Haynes, Mary, 30
Haynes, Thomas, 350, 352, 383, 384
Haynes, William Peyton, 384
Hays, Bailey, 21
Hays, Edmond, 179
Hays, John, 13
Hays, Sally, 21
Hayse, John, 362
Heard, Barnard, 89, 158
Heard, John, 89
Hearn, Arcada, 388
Hearn, Calvin, 388
Hearn, Isaac, 287
Hearn, Pollie, 388
Hearn, Priscilla, 388
Heart, Isaac, 189
Heart, Samuel, 189
Heartfield, George, 179
Heartfield, Lydia, 179
Heath, Abraham, 254, 297
Heath, Abraham Helton, 245
Heath, Adam, 217
Heath, Ambrose, 232, 234
Heath, Chappel, 215, 244
Heath, Chappell, 215, 216, 222
Heath, Chapple, 194
Heath, Elizabeth, 16, 22, 24
Heath, Fanny Burge, 26
Heath, Frederick B., 224
Heath, Hartwell, 21, 199, 228, 233, 234, 326
Heath, Henry, 222, 226
Heath, James, 22
Heath, Joel, 184, 199, 220
Heath, John, 377
Heath, Lucena, 13
Heath, Mack, 352

Heath, Mark, 222
Heath, Millie, 200
Heath, Nancy, 22, 258
Heath, Patsy, 16, 17
Heath, Polly, 34
Heath, Rebeckah, 28
Heath, Richard, 179, 194, 216, 217, 233, 270, 314, 365
Heath, Royster, 360
Heath, Sally, 15
Heath, Sary, 377
Heath, Temperance, 33
Heath, Thomas, 263, 280
Heath, William, 15, 210, 254, 258, 316, 318, 377
Heath, Winney, 297
Heatts, John S., 384
Heeth, Abraham, 362
Heeth, Mark, 364
Heeth, Royster, 231
Hefflin, James, 225
Heflin, James, 190
Helton, Abraham, 286
Helton, Peter, 262
Helton, Samuel, 229
Heming, Samuel, 385
Hemphill, Joseph, 289
Hencott, Craft, 60
Hencrick, John, 128
Henderson, Elizabeth, 259, 290, 370
Henderson, James, 252, 259, 290
Henderson, John, 35
Henderson, John J.P., 342
Hendon, George J.P., 307
Hendon, Peter, 109
Henery, John, 193
Henkins, John, 280
Henry, John, 17
Henry, Sally, 24
Henry, William, 30
Herd, John, 81, 89

Herd, Stephen, 51, 88, 89
Herds, Brevard, 40
Hern, Maret, 18
Herndon, George, 338
Heron, James, 89
Herrington, David, 30, 32
Herrold, Simon, 26
Hert, E. J.I.C., 328
Hert, Elisha, 177
Hester, Beverly, 348
Hibler, Martha, 388
Hichee, John, 92
Hickimbottom, Joseph, 131
Hickinbottom, Joseph, 89
Hickinbottom, Thomas, 89
Hicks, Edmond Bugg, 341
Hicks, James, 33
Hicks, John, 188
Hickson, William, 163, 268
Higginbotham, Joseph, 349
Higginbotham, Judith, 22
Higginbotham, Judity, 90
Higginbotham, Thomas, 90
Higginbottom, Thomas, 90
Highfield, Anson, 26
Highland, Nicholas, 20
Highnott, Sarah, 381
Hight, Alfred, 380
Hight, Anne, 28, 380
Hight, Cornelius, 380
Hight, Edna, 380
Hight, Elizabeth, 380
Hight, Gilbert, 380
Hight, Henry, 204, 223, 232,
    234, 260, 275, 380
Hight, Howell, 22, 182, 219,
    233, 234, 254, 281, 380
Hight, Howell Sr., 380
Hight, Julius, 380
Hight, Lucinda, 380
Hight, Nancy, 380
Hight, Pollie, 15
Hight, Sukey, 380

Hight, Susannah, 23
Hight, Wiley, 34, 380
Hight, William, 380
Highwood, Craft, 120
Hilburn, James, 17
Hiles, Adam, 317
Hill Robert, 266
Hill, Abner, 386
Hill, Abram, 28
Hill, Adam, 175
Hill, Benjamin, 224, 235, 386
Hill, Betsy, 21
Hill, Charity, 13
Hill, Edward, 179, 216, 292
Hill, Elizabeth, 263
Hill, Elizabeth M., 25
Hill, Fielding, 35
Hill, Frances, 180, 182, 268
Hill, Francis, 236
Hill, H., 287
Hill, Hannah, 267
Hill, Henry, 21, 182, 283, 301,
    342, 380
Hill, Isaac, 285, 289
Hill, J., 251
Hill, James, 65, 90, 106, 120
Hill, John, 20, 90, 229, 254,
    269, 292, 312, 317
Hill, Joseph, 23, 24, 194, 222,
    226, 261, 298, 329, 351, 352,
    356
Hill, Joshua, 176
Hill, Mary, 21
Hill, Moses, 249, 260, 267, 344,
    360, 392
Hill, Mountain, 232, 244, 263,
    281, 313, 322
Hill, Nancy, 14, 29
Hill, Phoebe, 175, 229
Hill, Polly, 26
Hill, Prudence, 13
Hill, Rebecca, 14

Hill, Richard, 180, 229, 236, 268, 313
Hill, Robert, 34, 218, 250, 266, 289, 327, 348
Hill, Robert Jr., 386
Hill, Robert Sr., 381, 386
Hill, Sally, 15
Hill, Sarah, 18, 34, 176, 286, 312, 386
Hill, Sarah Parham, 203
Hill, Seaborn, 386
Hill, Sion, 384, 386
Hill, Sucky, 33
Hill, Theophilus, 27
Hill, Thomas, 175, 229, 264, 292
Hill, W., 349
Hill, William, 200, 288
Hill, William O., 360
Hill, Willoughby S., 32
Hill, Winnie, 22
Hillhouse, David, 251, 293, 297
Hilliday, William, 115
Hillman, Elizabeth, 383
Hillman, Gracy, 383
Hillman, Joshua, 383
Hillman, Rev. Winder, 383
Hillman, Samuel, 383
Hillman, Samuel S., 229
Hillman, Windor, 30
Hillson, John, 293
Hilson, Aaron, 325
Hilson, Lewis, 325
Hilson, Thomas, 181
Hilton, Abraham, 316
Hilton, Elizabeth, 15
Hilton, James, 183
Hinton, Christopher, 233, 242
Hinton, Henry, 230, 233
Hinton, John, 235, 328
Hinton, Robert, 177
Hinton, Thomas, 23
Hix, John, 254

Hixson, William, 90
Hixxon, William, 41, 153
Hobbs, Willis, 31, 33
Hobson, A., 252
Hobson, Hardy, 376
Hobson, John, 200, 206, 213, 290, 312, 313, 337
Hobson, Sallie, 20
Hobson, Zachary, 25
Hodgen, Joseph, 293
Hodgen, William, 293
Hodgerson, Hannah, 27
Hodges, Andrew, 20
Hodges, Flemen, 290
Hodges, Jincy, 22
Hodgin, John, 91
Hodgin, Joseph, 297
Hodgin, Robert, 293
Hodgins, John, 156
Hodgins, Joseph, 272
Hodgins, William, 205
Hodo, P., 239, 247, 255, 294, 309, 332, 339, 358, 371
Hodo, P. J.P., 249, 266, 270, 274, 279, 291, 293, 295, 314, 324, 325, 331, 357
Hodo, Peter, 249, 252, 258, 289, 302, 309, 336
Hodo, Peter Esq., 308
Hodo, Peter Esquire, 176
Hodo, Peter J.P., 260, 269, 287, 302
Hodo, Peter Jr., 308
Hodo, R. P. J.P., 300
Hodo, Richard, 308, 325
Hodo, Salley, 287
Hodo, Sallie, 249, 309
Hogan, Daniel, 91
Hogans, Lydia, 20
Hogans, Sarah, 23
Hoge, Stephen, 243
Hoge, William, 243
Hogg, James, 292

Hogins, James, 182
Hogins, Robert, 182
Hogins, Zilphia, 182
Hogwood, James, 21
Hokett, Polly, 309
Holaday, Elizabeth, 30, 32
Holcombe, Nancy, 381
Holden, Jeremiah, 24
Holder, Lydia, 233
Holder, William, 233
Holeman, David, 26
Holiday, William, 91
Holingsworth, Joseph, 115
Holladay, Ambrose, 183
Holladay, Margaret, 183
Holland, Susannah, 33
Holland, William, 32
Hollayan, Patrick, 53
Hollenshead, John, 322
Holliday, Ambrose, 91, 113,
    219, 315, 386
Holliday, Margaret, 219
Holliday, William, 91, 171
Hollingsworth, Joseph, 45, 91,
    160
Hollis, John, 19
Holloway, John, 91
Holmes, David, 92
Hood, Abraham, 92
Hood, Dempsey, 13
Hood, J., 358
Hood, John, 371
Hood, Nathaniel, 176, 371
Hoof, William, 23, 24
Hopkins, Joshua, 215
Hopkins, Richard, 24
Hopkins, Susannah, 215
Hopson, Hardy, 34
Hopward, Benjamin, 179
Horn, Absolem, 92
Horn, Andrew C., 216
Horn, Benjamin, 83, 92, 171
Horn, Elijah, 15, 27

Horn, Ellinor, 370
Horn, Isaac, 369
Horn, Jacob, 92, 94, 138, 180,
    369
Horn, Jesse, 92, 94, 138, 369
Horn, John, 180, 369
Horn, Margaret, 369
Horn, Martha, 370
Horn, Michael, 15
Horn, Pamella, 338
Horn, Sarah, 24, 370
Horton, Proper, 272, 290
Horton, Prosser, 290
Horton, Sarah, 272
Hosaick, Alexander, 93
Hosiach, Alexander, 92
Hotnel, Elizabeth, 15
Houstoun, Governor John, 315
Houstoun, James, 93
Houstoun, John, 10, 93
Houstoun, Sir Patrick, 11, 93
Howard, Aquilla, 346
Howard, Benjamin, 13, 93, 188,
    215, 308
Howard, Benjamin Jr., 320, 326
Howard, Brown, 129
Howard, John, 28, 41, 51, 73,
    76, 93, 94, 129, 138, 145,
    152, 169, 257, 305, 378
Howard, Joseph, 287, 349
Howard, R. J.P., 291
Howard, Rhesa, 260
Howard, Rice, 94
Howard, Richard, 94, 158
Howard, Sallie, 20
Howard, Sarah, 21
Howard, Thees, 301
Howard, Thomas, 351
Howard, William, 178, 278, 307
Howell, Celia, 20
Howell, James, 20, 95
Howell, Joseph, 181, 218, 219,
    291, 308

Howell, Joshua, 27
Howell, Millie, 24
Howell, Mourning, 19
Howell, Ransom J.P., 310
Howell, Samuel, 19, 291
Howell, Theophilus, 311
Howell, Zilpha, 20
Hubbard, Manoah, 348
Hubbard, Richard, 95
Hubbert, M. J.P., 251
Hubert, B., 366
Hubert, Benjamin, 183, 369
Hubert, D., 318
Hubert, David, 181, 183, 311, 369
Hubert, Delphy, 311
Hubert, Gabriel, 369
Hubert, Hannon, 382
Hubert, Hiram, 334, 382
Hubert, Jacob Williams, 369
Hubert, John, 382
Hubert, M., 182, 218, 311
Hubert, M. J.P., 240, 270, 271, 287, 301, 310, 321, 334, 348, 356
Hubert, Manoah, 310, 334
Hubert, Mary, 369
Hubert, Matthew, 181, 183, 191, 218, 337, 356, 369
Hubert, Matthew J.P., 251, 363
Hubert, Polly, 31
Hubert, William, 369
Hudnell, John, 269
Hudson, Hall, 346
Huff, Abner, 232
Huff, Jonathan, 232, 233
Huff, Middleton, 232
Hull, John, 255, 333
Hume, James, 95
Hume, John, 95
Humphreys, Benjamin, 21
Humphreys, Lanier, 17

Hundley, William B., 226, 228, 388
Hunneycutt, Myrick, 28
Hunt, E. J.I.C., 331
Hunt, Elisha, 279
Hunt, Fitz M., 323
Hunt, Fitz. M., 351
Hunt, Fitzhugh, 360
Hunt, Fitzmaurice, 333
Hunt, Isaac, 317, 387
Hunt, Mary, 323
Hunt, Sarah, 333
Hunt, Thomas, 269
Hunt, William, 15
Hunter, Alexander, 16
Hunter, John, 96, 265
Hunter, Lydia, 376
Hurkey, Clayton, 198
Hurkey, Frederick, 198
Hurt, Benjamin, 225, 227, 228, 354, 393
Hurt, E., 322
Hurt, E. J.I.C., 361, 365
Hurt, Elisha, 193, 204, 300, 323, 343, 354, 356, 362, 363, 375, 393
Hurt, Elisha Esq., 315
Hurt, Elisha J.I.C., 362
Hurt, Elisha J.P., 256, 276, 286, 288, 292, 297
Hurt, William, 232, 393
Huskey, Elizabeth, 194
Huskey, Mary, 194
Husky, Frederick, 201, 206
Hustice, Mary, 27
Huston, Thomas, 27
Hutchens, James, 27
Hutcherson, Daniel, 241, 270
Hutcheson, John, 29
Hutchin, John, 264
Hutchins, Alla, 24
Hutchins, Elizabeth, 33
Hutchins, Hannah, 22

Hutchins, John, 33, 184, 188, 198
Hutchins, Nancy, 24
Hutchins, Polly, 33
Hutchins, Thomas, 184, 188, 198
Hutchinson, Barbara, 387
Hutchinson, Daniel, 14, 210, 227, 241, 247
Hutchinson, John J.P., 333
Hutchinson, Martha, 316
Hutchinson, Mary. *See* Harbuck
Hutchinson, Nathaniel, 19, 199, 200, 314
Hutchinson, Nicholas, 387
Hutchinson, R., 310
Hutchinson, Richard, 14, 300, 311, 314
Hutchinson, Thomas, 220
Hutchinson, William, 19, 316
Hutchison, Elizabeth, 18
Hutchison, Sally, 17
Hutson, John, 311
Hyde, Samuel, 26
Hygh, John, 34
Illy, Michael, 96, 158
Inglis, Alexander, 85, 96
Irby, Sally, 33
Irwin County, Georgia, 390, 392
Irwin, Jared, 106, 109
Irwin, Joseph, 303
Irwin, Robert, 296, 297, 303
Irwin, Samuel, 296, 297, 303, 364
Irwin, Zared J.P., 311
Isaacs, Robert, 241, 246, 257
Islands, Absolam, 301
Iverey, James, 169
Iverson, Robert J.P., 341
Ivey, Dinkins, 20
Ivey, Jincy, 33
Ivey, Millie, 377

Ivey, Moses, 27
Ivey, Sampson, 175, 377
Ivey, Terrence, 28
Ivy, Charlotte, 377
Ivy, Elizabeth, 377
Ivy, Ephriam, 19, 358, 379
Ivy, Jiney, 377
Ivy, Lavina, 25
Ivy, Moses, 35
Ivy, Polly, 24, 377
Ivy, Rebeckah, 33
Ivy, Sampson, 176, 287, 371
Ivy, Thomas, 34, 377
Jack, James, 97
Jackson County, Georgia, 290, 292, 317, 324, 354, 390
Jackson, Aaron, 34
Jackson, Absalom, 96, 125, 235, 307, 331, 333, 351
Jackson, Absolem, 255, 316
Jackson, Ailey, 376
Jackson, Benjamin, 67, 97, 250, 289, 330
Jackson, Colonel J., 169
Jackson, Colonel James, 50, 114, 139
Jackson, Drewry, 337
Jackson, Elizabeth, 35
Jackson, Harriet, 34
Jackson, Isaac, 51, 78, 97
Jackson, James, 32, 39, 52, 62, 64, 97, 98, 111, 120, 121, 289
Jackson, John W., 382
Jackson, Lewis, 230, 233, 387
Jackson, Lowe, 208, 376
Jackson, Mary, 31
Jackson, Moses, 30
Jackson, Nancy, 17
Jackson, Nathan, 17
Jackson, Nathaniel, 99
Jackson, Polly, 23
Jackson, Samuel, 189, 224
Jackson, Susannah, 34, 349

Jackson, Thomas, 78, 99, 171, 279, 328, 329, 349, 364
Jackson, Walter, 94, 99, 158, 289, 322, 391
Jackson, William, 26, 45, 52, 60, 73, 94, 99, 219
Jacobs, Sarah, 13
Jamerson, J., 334
Jamerson, John, 334
James
  Slave, 311
James, Abel, 21, 334, 359
James, Daniel, 22
James, Elizabeth, 25
James, James, 382
James, Jesse, 319, 334
James, Jessee, 14
James, John, 33
James, Mary, 221
James, Polly, 382
James, Sarah, 16
James, Wiley, 382
Jamieson, John, 48, 99, 321, 332
Janson, Samuel, 42
Jarers, James, 39
Jarnett, Alexander, 224
Jarnett, Hannah, 224
Jarratt, Deverix, 99
Jarrell, Byrd, 237, 238
Jarrett, Alexander, 190
Jarrett, John, 289
Jarrett, Mary, 190
Jarrett, Polly, 28
Jarvis, James, 100
Jarvis, Peter, 75
Jasper County, Georgia, 377
Jefferson County, Georgia, 256, 260, 275, 278, 291, 307, 329, 332
Jefferson County, Mississippi, 341
Jeffreys, Esther, 286

Jenkins, Arthur, 278, 285, 288, 308, 342
Jenkins, Benjamin, 285, 292
Jenkins, Benjamin J.P., 277
Jenkins, Edward, 22
Jenkins, James, 28
Jenkins, John, 247
Jenkins, Phoebe, 19
Jenkins, Rebecca, 23
Jenkins, Robert, 187, 198, 223, 247, 261, 270, 271, 276, 300, 335
Jenkins, William, 247, 285
Jennie
  slave, 369
Jennings, William, 292
Jenny
  slave, 351
Jervice, James, 72
Jessup Brothers, 2
Jiles, John, 201
Jim
  slave, 236
Johnson, Abraham Jr., 247
Johnson, Abram J.P., 243
Johnson, Catherine, 26
Johnson, Dorcas, 357
Johnson, Edmond, 225, 273
Johnson, Edmund, 274
Johnson, Elizabeth, 290
Johnson, Jacob, 232, 357
Johnson, James, 296, 297, 359
Johnson, John A., 267
Johnson, Lewis, 100, 359
Johnson, Littleton, 225
Johnson, Malcolm, 370
Johnson, May, 392
Johnson, Mordecai, 233
Johnson, Randol, 357
Johnson, Randolph, 359
Johnson, Richard, 100

Johnson, Robert, 225, 273, 274, 292, 318
Johnson, Rosannah, 249
Johnson, Sallie, 380
Johnson, Sally, 380
Johnson, Samuel, 290
Johnson, Sarah, 22
Johnson, Thomas, 72, 150
Johnson, Vinson, 223, 236, 329, 382
— Johnson, William, 100, 244, 249, 251, 297
Johnston, Aaron, 31
Johnston, Abraham, 189
Johnston, Abraham J.P., 318
Johnston, Amos, 31, 322
Johnston, Anna Terrell, 175
Johnston, Edmond, 33
Johnston, Elizabeth, 19
Johnston, Jacob, 33
Johnston, James, 28, 326
Johnston, John, 25
Johnston, John Addison, 13
Johnston, Joseph, 32, 214, 378
Johnston, Malcolm, 175, 182
Johnston, Milly, 27
Johnston, Phillip, 19
Johnston, Polly, 18, 29
Johnston, Sally, 24
Johnston, Samuel, 27, 290, 316, 331, 339, 348
Johnston, Sarah, 32
Johnston, Tabitha, 27
Johnston, Vincent, 337
Johnston, Vinson, 320
Johnston, William, 66, 295
Joiner, William, 56, 167
Jones William, 187
Jones, Aaron, 17
Jones, Abraham, 317
Jones, Adam, 176, 196, 224, 229, 252, 253, 273, 283, 313, 329, 349

Jones, Adam Jr., 229
Jones, Adam Sr., 283
Jones, Andrew, 93, 100, 129
Jones, Ann, 29, 343
Jones, Anthony, 32, 205, 206
Jones, Aquila, 267
Jones, Aquilla, 224, 266
Jones, Barnabas, 190, 205, 206
Jones, Benjamin, 47, 101, 120
Jones, Betsey, 31
Jones, Burl., 267
Jones, David, 23, 26, 28
Jones, Elijah, 29, 227, 229, 230, 232, 233
Jones, Elizabeth, 23, 26, 27, 30, 195, 208, 222, 242, 280
Jones, Elizabeth F., 344
Jones, Frances, 32
Jones, Francis, 101, 172
Jones, Hannah, 224
Jones, Hartwell, 193, 321
Jones, Henley, 227
Jones, Henry, 82, 101, 151, 187, 195, 205, 206, 208, 222
Jones, Hezekiah, 218
Jones, Jacob, 101
Jones, James, 181, 218, 223, 238, 251, 261, 280
Jones, James Sr., 187
Jones, Jean, 14, 248
Jones, John, 101, 106, 117, 121, 205, 229, 247, 261, 276, 291
Jones, John P., 19
Jones, Joshua, 277
Jones, Julius C., 229
Jones, Lew, 305
Jones, Lewis, 305
Jones, Martha, 34, 191, 205
Jones, Mary, 346
Jones, Mathew, 266
Jones, Mrs. Susannah, 24
Jones, Nancy, 17, 26
Jones, Nathan, 311

Jones, Nicholas, 248, 355
Jones, P. Adam Jr., 253
Jones, Patience, 30
Jones, Patsy, 31
Jones, Patty, 190
Jones, Polly, 25, 205
Jones, Priscilla, 196
Jones, Rebecca, 261, 311, 323
Jones, Reubin, 213, 220, 231,
    261, 269, 311, 318, 326, 330,
    356
Jones, Rhesa, 354
Jones, Rhoda, 21
Jones, Richard, 101, 102
Jones, Richard H., 233
Jones, Robert, 102, 128
Jones, Sally, 197
Jones, Samuel, 28, 210, 214
Jones, Sarah, 28
Jones, Seaborn, 285, 288
Jones, Stephen, 299
Jones, Sterling, 238, 239, 251,
    256, 261, 308, 309, 313, 316,
    323, 344
Jones, Susannah, 16
Jones, Tamerlane, 197
Jones, Thomas, 24, 25, 26, 92,
    102, 104, 177, 178, 187, 191,
    200, 215, 217, 229, 253, 273,
    283, 292, 313, 314, 322
Jones, William, 17, 18, 19, 27,
    56, 103, 163, 205, 206, 213,
    222, 223, 233, 235, 238, 261,
    274, 307, 326, 360
Jones, William J.P., 346
Jones, Willie, 284, 317
Jonson, Adam, 254
Joques, Father Isaac, 2
Jordan, Baxter, 363, 367
Jordan, Charles, 42, 103
Jordan, John, 159
Jordan, William, 246
Jordan, Willoughby, 364

Keaton, John, 331
Keener, Jacob, 278
Keener, John, 16, 20
Keener, William, 20, 277, 278
Keff, James, 60, 103
Keiffer, Theobald, 140
Keiner, Martin, 356
Kelcey, Noah, 380
Kelcy, Noah, 341
Kellem, Elizabeth, 345
Kelley, John, 340
Kellum, George, 230
Kellum, John, 377
Kellum, William, 18
Kelly, David, 230
Kelly, Edward, 272
Kelly, Elizabeth, 30, 228
Kelly, John, 177, 188, 228, 246,
    288, 291, 293
Kelly, Lloyd J.P., 279
Kelly, Loyd J.P., 261
Kelly, Rachel, 16
Kelly, Sims, 30
Kelly, Spencer, 103
Kelly, Thomas, 340
Kelly, William, 291
Kelly, William Sr., 291
Kelsey, Noah, 201, 341
Kemp, Hipple, 180
Kemp, Polly, 30
Kemp, Rebecca, 20, 180
Kendall, Eliza, 30
Kendall, Henry, 183, 184, 199,
    247, 260, 297, 339, 342, 352,
    357
Kendall, Henry Sr., 217
Kendall, Jemima, 35
Kendall, Jeremiah, 183
Kendall, William, 183, 199
Kender, Peter, 103
Kendrick, Jones, 17, 177, 274,
    321, 390
Kener, William Jr., 340

Kennebrew, Shadrack, 324
Kennedy, Darby, 86, 150
Kennedy, J., 290
Kennedy, John, 59, 104
Kennedy, Josiah N., 282
Kennedy, Samuel, 252
Kennon, J., 351
Kenor, William, 354
Kenshaw, Thomas, 104
Kent, John, 241, 262, 274
Kentucky, 300
Kerr Lucy, 376
Kerr, Augustus Thompson, 376
Kershaw, Thomas, 51
Key, Tandy Clark, 371
Kiefer, Theobald, 63
Kilgore, Elizabeth, 244
Kilgore, John, 16
Kilgore, Katherine, 244
Kilgore, Ralph, 46, 67, 94, 104, 150, 158, 169, 244, 254, 284, 331
Kilgore, Robert Jr., 244
Kilgore, William, 105, 108, 149
Killabrew, John, 29
Killebrew, Wiggins, 185, 188, 220
Killibrew, William, 342
Kinchen
    slave, 236
Kinchen, William, 288
Kindall, Elizabeth, 256
Kindall, Henry, 256
King William County, Virginia, 238
King, Alice, 378
King, Andrew, 288, 313, 325, 373
King, Andrew J.P., 286, 344, 362
King, Elizabeth, 392
King, Ephriam, 178
King, Joel, 248, 265

King, John, 31, 105
King, Joseph, 241
King, Parks, 276, 280
King, Peggy, 31
King, Polly, 30, 35
Kingrey, Daniel, 278
Kinnebrew, Shadrach, 264
Kinney, Edward, 226, 229
Kinney, Vicy, 26
Kinsey, Archibald, 181, 218
Kinsey, Cassy, 24
Kinsey, Daniel, 32, 217
Kinsey, Delilah, 230
Kinsey, Edward, 217, 231, 262, 348, 360
Kinsey, Elizabeth, 27
Kinsey, Joel, 27
Kinsey, John, 228
Kinsey, John W., 230, 231
Kinsey, Lucy, 29
Kinsey, Martin, 220, 230
Kinsey, William, 228
Kitchen, George, 391
Kitchen, Jesse, 177
Kitchen, William Sr., 188
Kitchens, John, 220
Kitchens, Lawrence, 219
Kitchens, William, 257, 347
Kitching, Boaz, 338
Kitchings, William, 347
Krinze, Lewis, 33
Lacey, Archibald, 245
Lacey, Jordan, 245
Lacy, Archibald, 245, 382
Lacy, Bolland, 35
Lacy, Elizabeth, 382
Lacy, John, 382
Lacy, Martha, 382
Lacy, Nancy, 382
Lacy, Pleasant, 382
Lacy, Pleasant M., 382
Lacy, Pollie, 382
Lacy, Polly, 34

Lacy, Randolph, 382
Lacy, Sarah, 382
Laimonet, James, 72
Lamar, Basel, 294
Lamar, Bazil, 282
Lamar, John, 57, 191, 200, 240
Lamar, William, 61
Lamar, Zachariah, 105
Lamare, John, 157
LaMarr, William, 105
Lamer, John, 105, 162
Lancaster County, South
    Carolina, 298
Lancaster, Thomas, 239
Landrum, Elizabeth, 366
Landrum, Jacob, 366
Landrum, John, 269, 272
Landrum, John Sr., 274
Landrum, Joseph, 272, 344
Landrum, Joseph Jr., 274
Landrum, Timothy, 258
Landrum, William, 19, 255
Landrum, Z., 298
Landrum, Zechariah, 245
Lane, John, 65
Langdon, James, 224
Langford, Delilah, 23
Langford, Hillery, 389
Langham, Benjamin B., 387
Langham, William, 387
Lantor, Jacob, 106
Lantor, Thomas, 134
Larimore, Isaac, 106
Larrimore, James, 106
Lary, Winfrey, 25
Lasple, James G., 104
Lasseter, Blake, 201
Lasseter, Joel, 24
Lassetter, Joel, 355
Lassiter, Blake, 376
Lassiter, Willis, 376
Latimer, Charles, 388
Latimer, Horace Augustus, 388

Latimer, James, 388
Latimer, Rebecca, 388
Latimer, Samuel Marcus, 388
Latimer, William, 208, 388
Latimer, William Marshall, 388
Laurence, Samuel, 329
Laurence, Stephen, 220
Laurens County, South
    Carolina, 244
Lawrence, Stephen, 185, 286,
    312
Lawrence, William, 286
Lawson, Charles M., 255
Lawson, Frank J.P., 258
Lawson, John, 255, 272, 293,
    304, 332, 352, 354
Lawson, John J.P., 253, 255,
    256, 333
Lawson, Roger, 354, 361
Lawson, Thompson, 353
Lawton, Nancy, 13
Layne, William, 276
Lazenby, Ellender, 387
Lazenby, Harriet, 390
Lazenby, John M., 390
Lazenby, Joshua, 233
Lazenby, Richard E., 390
Lazenby, Richard S., 234
Lazenby, Robert, 351, 393
Ledbetter, Frederick, 246
Ledbetter, Isaac, 246, 285, 353
Ledbetter, James, 31, 362
Ledbetter, John, 246, 277, 285,
    291, 292
Ledbetter, John Sr., 329
Ledbetter, Obedience, 32
Ledbetter, Samuel, 16
Lee County, Georgia, 390, 391
Lee, Alcy, 185
Lee, Alsey, 220
Lee, John, 106, 113, 269
Lee, Polly, 24
Lee, Richard, 185, 220, 329

Lee, Sarah, 18
Lee, Thomas, 106
Lee, Timothy, 347
Lee, William H., 263
Lem, William Sr., 267
Lemar, John, 77
Lennard, Abel, 370
Leonard, Joseph, 24, 228, 232,
    234
Lesly, James, 29
Lesslie, Joseph, 107
Letcher, Benjamin, 292
Lewellin, James, 232
Lewis
    slave, 380
Lewis, Colonel, 372
Lewis, David, 107
Lewis, Francis, 81
Lewis, George, 377
Lewis, Isaac, 43, 48, 107
Lewis, John, 29, 108, 375, 377
Lewis, Rebecca, 384
Lewis, Sarah, 25
Lewis, Thomas, 382
Liberty County, Georgia, 315,
    386
Lightenstone, John, 108
Limbacker, Christian, 92, 108,
    149, 164
Limbacker, Christopher, 108
Limbacker, George, 55, 108,
    109
Linch, Polly, 28
Lincoln County, Georgia, 250
Lincoln County, Kentucky, 354
Lincoln County, North
    Carolina, 268
Lindsey, Patsy, 29
Lindsey, Pollie, 20
Linn, Charles, 305, 327, 346
Linn, Charles Jr., 346
Linn, Charles Sr., 346
Linn, Elizabeth, 346

Linn, Fergus, 178, 215
Linn, John, 178, 215, 346
Linn, William, 81, 108, 129
Lipham, Aaron, 186, 221
Lipham, William, 221
Little, Archibald, 27
Little, Frederick, 291
Little, John E., 202
Little, Littleberry, 30, 197
Little, Micajah, 186, 202, 221
Littleton, Alexander, 221
Littleton, Jacob, 308
Littleton, James, 33
Littleton, John, 27, 231
Littleton, Leah, 13
Littleton, Mark, 230, 308
Littleton, Savage, 258
Livingston, Aaron, 26
Livingston, Adam, 26
Livingston, Highland, 31
Livingston, Susannah, 384
Lloyd, Thomas, 80, 109, 134
Lloyd, William, 15
Lock, Abner, 375
Lock, Elizabeth, 386
Lock, James, 386
Lock, Jesse, 375
Lock, John, 34, 200, 363, 375,
    386
Lock, Jonathan, 200, 303, 328,
    375
Lock, Liddy, 386
Lock, Mancey, 375
Lock, Mary, 200, 375
Lock, Nancy, 29
Lock, Rebecca, 386
Locke, Abner, 360
Locke, Jonathan, 276
Locke, Sallie, 24
Lockett, Abner, 372
Lockett, David, 259, 371, 372
Lockett, Davis, 372
Lockett, Doctor, 21, 371

Lockett, Jacob, 345
Lockett, James, 34
Lockett, Reubin, 18, 371
Lockett, Sally, 21, 371
Lockett, Solomon, 182, 206,
    207, 213, 215, 219, 228, 230,
    289, 302, 335, 355, 364, 372
Lockett, Solomon Esq., 208
Lockett, Solomon J.P., 327,
    335, 345
Lockett, Synthia, 28
Lockett, T., 289
Lockett, Thomas, 226, 335, 372
Lockett, Warren, 228
Lockett, Winfrey, 371
Lockhart, Henry, 227, 233
Lockhart, Thomas, 33
Lockridge, Robert, 71, 83, 109
Logan, Hugh, 19
Logan, Phillip, 13, 239, 273
Logan, Sarah, 16
Logue, Charles, 194
Lokey, Wrigley, 29
London, John J.P., 330
Long, Nicholas, 314
Longstreet, William J.P., 299
Louderman, C., 317
Loughlin, Samuel, 15
Loumore, Isaac, 109
Loumore, John, 109
Lovell, Mary, 290
Lovell, Pollie, 25
Lovell, William, 290
Lovett, Anna, 14, 17
Lovett, Carrie, 27
Lovett, Rebeckah, 26
Lovett, Richard, 24, 247
Lovett, Thomas, 19
Lovett, William, 340
Lovett, William J.P., 336
Low, Isaac, 47, 50, 101, 110,
    117, 126
Low, Thomas, 264

Lowe, Betsy, 17
Lowe, Beverly, 110
Lowe, Curtis, 231
Lowe, James, 251
Lowe, John, 249, 274, 276, 280,
    312
Lowe, Sarah, 16
Lowe, Thomas, 23
Lowe, William, 378
Lowrance, Peter, 110
Loyless, Henry, 28
Loyless, James, 221, 222
Lucas, Barbara, 237, 324
Lucas, Charles, 71, 110
Lucas, James, 253
Lucas, John Jr., 340
Lucas, Keziah, 340
Lucas, Walter, 381
Lucas, William, 290
Luce
    slave, 250
Luckett, Joseph W., 376
Luckett, Thomas, 13, 321, 390
Luckett, William, 31, 375
Luckett, William R., 377
Luckie, Littleberry, 389
Lunsford, Polly, 16
Lyford, William, 111
Lynn, James, 28
Lynn, John, 25
Lynn, Nancy, 29
Lynn, Thomas, 54, 111, 154,
    163
Lynn, William, 38, 111
Lyon, John, 349
Lyon, Nancy, 33
Lyon, Samuel, 80, 111
Lyons, William, 277, 278
Macartan, Francis, 98, 111, 114
Macbran, Lachlan, 104
Macgillivray, Lachlan, 112
Mackay, William, 112

Maddock, Joseph, 38, 106, 112, 113, 132, 134, 162, 171, 242, 266, 332, 347
Maddock, Joseph J.P., 247
Maddox, Ann, 338
Maddox, James, 213
Maddox, Thomas, 17, 213, 214, 314
Maddox, William, 338
Maddux, Thomas, 203, 210, 211, 214, 314, 342
Maffett, Nathan, 35
Magee, Elender, 392
Magee, Elizabeth, 392, 393
Magee, Elizabeth L., 392
Magee, Ephriam, 392
Magee, James, 392
Magee, Leah, 392
Magee, Leah N., 392
Magee, Mary E., 392
Magee, Reuben, 271
Magee, Reubin, 334, 392
Magee, Sarah M., 392
Mahone, Peter, 246, 286, 358
Mahu, David, 263
Mallory, Francis, 235, 307
Malone, Lucinda, 29
Malone, Mordecai, 22
Malone, Polly, 17
Mandell, Henry, 341
Maner, Mary, 113
Maneren, Robert, 113
Manion, Elizabeth, 333
Manion, John, 333
Mann, Mary, 276
Manning, Mrs. Nancy, 34
Manning, Peggy, 16
Mannon, John, 289
Marchant, Bryant, 315
Marchant, Isaac, 269
Mark
    slave, 236
Marks, Joseph, 209, 214

Marks, Mary, 209, 214
Marlow, Charity, 349
Marlow, Joseph, 349
Marlow, Priscilla, 349
Marlow, Robert, 330, 349
Marlow, William, 330, 364
Marsh, Betsy, 13
Marsh, Elizabeth, 323
Marsh, John, 323
Marsh, Nathan, 219, 323
Marshal, John, 147
Marshall, John, 114, 240
Marshall, Mathew, 114
Marshall, Patsy, 19
Marshall, Stephen, 286, 288, 343, 344, 354, 362
Martin, Clement Sr., 114
Martin, Jacob Sr., 332
Martin, James, 197
Martin, John, 186, 222
Martin, John L., 229
Martin, John P., 360
Martin, Thomas, 286
Mash, Bethany, 391
Mash, Emily, 391
Mash, Mary, 32
Mason, Alexander J.P., 308
Mason, Ann, 114
Mason, Michael, 114
Masse, Darcus, 300
Masters, Frederick W., 377
Mathis, Oliver, 43
Matthews, Arthur, 234, 275, 366
Matthews, Benjamin, 25, 27, 32, 360
Matthews, Charles, 365
Matthews, Edmond, 291
Matthews, Edward, 234, 275
Matthews, Elizabeth, 19
Matthews, F., 304
Matthews, Galby, 216, 221
Matthews, Isham, 362

Matthews, J. J.P., 309
Matthews, James, 115, 222, 264, 316, 335, 345, 362, 365
Matthews, Jeremiah, 323
Matthews, Jesse, 15, 184, 245, 262, 287, 318, 343, 354
Matthews, Jno., 270
Matthews, Joel, 359, 364
Matthews, John, 25, 30, 32, 34, 115, 177, 184, 219, 255, 270, 273, 285, 288, 297, 304, 308, 316, 317, 322, 325, 327, 328, 331, 344, 354, 356, 357, 365
Matthews, John Esq., 184
Matthews, John J.P., 318, 327, 328, 342, 388
Matthews, Joseph, 259, 330
Matthews, Levi, 253
Matthews, M. Jeremiah, 287
Matthews, Mary, 22
Matthews, Oliver, 110, 115
Matthews, Pollie, 26
Matthews, Polly, 26, 27, 273, 328
Matthews, Sarah, 31
Matthews, Soldom, 339
Matthews, Solomon, 318, 388
Matthews, T. J.P., 316, 317, 337
Matthews, Thomas, 115, 359
Matthews, Timothy, 19, 196, 199, 208, 213, 264, 269, 274, 302, 322, 324, 335, 350, 356
Matthews, Timothy J.P., 314, 329, 345
Matthews, William, 13, 184
Mattox, John, 247
Maxwell, William, 115, 137
May, Butham, 357
May, Elizabeth, 35
May, James, 257, 282, 289, 300
May, John, 276, 280, 331, 363
May, Joseph, 236, 237, 276, 317, 323, 387

May, Levi, 228
May, Lydia, 300
May, Nathan, 232
May, Peter, 226
May, Reubin, 226, 232
Mayberry, Charles, 259, 260
Maybrunk, Burrell, 26
Mayes, Mercy, 222
Mayes, William, 222
Maynor, John, 257, 269, 289
Mays, Drusilla, 35
Mays, John, 233
Mays, Priscilla, 332
Mays, William, 348, 357
McAllister, Charles, 338, 339, 367
McAllister, Margaret, 326, 338, 340
McAllister, Matthew, 284
McBean, Lachlan, 83, 150
McCaran, James, 179
McCarden, Cornelius, 268
McCartan, Francis, 53, 115, 116
McCarthy, John, 357
McCarthy, Mary M., 357
McCarty, Alexander, 14
McCarty, Daniel, 73, 94, 108, 116, 169
McCarty, Jacob, 110, 116
McCarty, James, 35
McCarty, Joseph, 89
McCason, James, 385
McClary, Andrew, 318, 388
McClary, James, 318, 388
McClary, Samuel, 318, 388
McClean, Andrew, 240
McClen, Robert, 117
McClendon, Brian, 265, 342
McClendon, Joel, 244
McClendon, Thomas, 357
McCling, Robert, 115
McClung, George M., 15
McClung, John, 340

McClung, Robert, 45, 113, 117, 162
McCluny, Robert, 93
McCormack, James, 181
McCormack, James J.P., 343, 356
McCormack, John, 322, 327, 356, 391
McCormick, Abner, 228
McCormick, Abner H., 391
McCormick, George, 391
McCormick, James, 28, 210, 216, 253, 258, 266, 302, 308, 312, 390
McCormick, James Esq., 210
McCormick, James J.P., 242, 259, 268, 272, 276, 282, 308, 309, 313, 315, 320, 327, 332, 333, 342, 352, 353, 366
McCormick, James Jr., 333
McCormick, John, 220, 313, 365, 366, 390
McCormick, Paul, 365, 391
McCormick, Rose, 270
McCormick, Sally, 366
McCormick, Sarah, 390
McCowan, Daniel, 178, 215
McCowan, Duncan, 304
McCowan, Susannah, 18
McCowles, William, 305
McCoy,, 231
McCoy, Charles, 231
McCoy, David, 321, 390
McCoy, John, 16, 240, 386
McCoy, Sarah, 22
McCrary, Isaac, 261
McCrary, John, 29, 227, 233
McCrary, Jonathan, 244, 342
McCrary, Lettice, 198
McCrary, Mathew, 259, 265, 287
McCrary, Matthew, 198, 288
McCrary, Patsy, 19

McCrary, Robert, 21
McCray, John, 15, 375
McCreeree, Matthew, 275
McCrery, John, 217
McCrery, Lettice, 32
McCrery, Matthew, 217
McCrery, Samuel, 29
McCullers, Amy, 251
McCullers, B., 304
McCullers, Britain, 256, 338
McCullers, Britton, 286
McCullers, David, 231, 327
McCullers, Drury, 190, 308, 309, 327
McCullers, Patty, 286
McCullers, Whelias, 309
McDade, James, 279
McDaniel, Alcy, 302
McDaniel, Alex, 302
McDaniel, D., 309
McDaniel, Darling, 302
McDaniel, Ishmael, 35
McDaniel, John, 25, 276
McDaniel, Mary, 302, 327
McDonald, Aley, 283
McDonald, Andrew, 392
McDonald, Charles, 287, 288
McDonald, Darling, 281, 283
McDonald, Esther, 392
McDonald, John, 63, 117
McDonald, Mary, 283
McDonald, Thomas, 153
McDonald, William, 392
McDougal, Alexander, 267
McDowell, Samucl, 231
McDowell, Thomas, 40, 117
McDowell, William, 249, 339
McDuffie County, Georgia, 11
McDuffie, Effie, 25
McEwen, John, 35
McFarland William, 129

McFarland, James, 48, 67, 68, 71, 114, 117, 121, 141, 156, 254, 283, 349
McFarland, James J.P., 348
McFarland, John, 143
McFarland, Joseph D., 228
McFarland, William, 54, 118, 205
McFarlin, Elender, 30
McFarlin, William, 205
McFarling, Harris, 187
McGaw, John, 293
McGee, Ephriam, 23, 193
McGee, Hugh, 343
McGee, Julia, 343
McGee, Leaven, 21
McGee, Levan, 195
McGee, Milby, 217
McGee, Nelly, 22
McGee, Polly, 31, 33
McGee, Reubin, 176, 180, 193, 332, 371
McGeehee, Samuel, 286
McGillivray, Lachlan, 57, 78, 118, 119, 140, 153
McGillivray, Laughlin, 76
McGinty, Joseph, 301
McGlamery, Elizabeth, 23
McGlamery, John, 189, 224
McGlamery, Mary, 20
McGlammery, John, 357
McGraw, Nancy, 19
McGree, Milby, 178
McHenry, James, 120, 162
McIntosh, Alexander, 62, 98, 120, 289
McIntosh, William, 120
McInvale, James, 277, 299, 301
McKay, James, 120, 121, 343
McKay, Patrick, 121
McKay, William, 121
McKenney, Jincy, 377
McKenney, Moses, 377

McKenny, Moses, 324
McKindley, Mary, 16, 20
McKinley, Joseph, 186, 222, 365
McKinley, William, 186, 197, 198, 222
McKinnen, Charles William, 121
McKinney, Ansel, 214, 255
McKinney, Harris, 33
McKinney, Kinchen, 229
McKinney, Moses, 34, 182, 229, 257, 293
McKinney, Polly, 182
McKintosh, Alexander, 64, 121
McKinzie, John, 300, 363
McLean, Andrew, 98, 122, 289
McLean, Duncan, 244, 292
McLendon, Joel, 286
McLinburg County, North Carolina, 252
McMath, Elijah, 385
McMath, Elizabeth, 336, 385
McMath, Gracy, 30
McMath, Hachaliah, 385
McMath, Hackakiah, 230
McMath, James, 282
McMath, Joseph, 272, 336, 358, 385
McMath, William, 34, 385
McMunan, William, 60
McMurrain, John, 305
McMurran, William, 84, 86, 122
McMurrin, John, 250, 258, 364
McNabb, Elizabeth, 25
McNash, William, 25
McNease, Henry, 34
McNease, Polly, 34
McNeil, John, 109
McNeill, William, 33
McNeillon, John, 161
McNeuir, Daniel, 122

McNiear, Daniel, 48
McNiece, Henry, 179
McNiece, Nelly, 35
McNish, John, 122
McNurram, William, 150
McQueen, James, 123, 125
McTier, Robert, 13
McTyaire, Kendall, 232
McTyeire, Kendall, 221
Meadoweys, Richard, 45
Meadows, Reuben, 272
Meadows, Richard, 81, 123, 147
Mecklenburg County, North
    Carolina, 318, 388
Mecum, James, 257, 336
Mecune, James, 342
Medlock, Charles, 253
Medlock, George, 176, 181, 209
Medlock, George Jr., 176
Medlock, Phoebe, 21
Memy, Joseph, 124
Mendenhall, Mary, 26
Mercer, David, 322, 391
Mercer, Jacob, 259, 262
Mercer, Jeaby, 259
Mercer, Silas, 282, 360
Meriwether, David Esq., 254
Merritt, Hannah, 30
Messer, Nathaniel S., 225
Methodist Society, 275
Michael, Ann, 329
Michael, John, 329
Middlebrooks, Pollie, 15
Middleton, Hatton, 95
Middleton, Holland, 52, 54, 93,
    123, 153, 349
Middleton, Holland Jr., 123
Middleton, Holt, 123
Middleton, Hugh, 46, 51, 111,
    121, 123
Middleton, R., 258, 320
Middleton, Robert, 42, 51, 124
Milbank, William, 81

Miles, Daniel, 46, 124
Miles, John, 244
Miles, Thomas, 343
Miles, William, 124
Mill
    slave, 236
Millar, Ezekiel, 244
Millar, Jesse, 294
Millar, Joseph, 244, 248, 285
Millar, Joshua, 294
Millar, Sarah, 244
Millbank, William, 125
Millen, David, 125
Miller, Adam, 385
Miller, Alexander, 243
Miller, Ann, 282
Miller, Ezekiel, 275, 278, 282,
    315
Miller, Honor, 18
Miller, James, 249
Miller, Jesse, 22, 315
Miller, John, 125
Miller, Jonathan, 252, 274
Miller, Joseph, 18, 272, 282,
    291
Miller, Joshua, 284
Miller, Sarah, 21
Miller, Thomas, 125
Miller, William, 120
Millirons, Betsy, 26
Millirons, Elizabeth, 28
Mims, Betsy, 16
Mims, David, 15, 203, 234, 319,
    328, 362, 363, 389
Mims, Drewery, 249
Mims, Drewry, 248
Mims, Drury, 157, 248, 327
Mims, Elizabeth, 249
Mims, John, 236, 268, 269, 323
Mims, John Jr., 318, 389
Mims, Joseph, 256
Mims, Leroy, 19, 188, 223, 328
Mims, Mary, 236, 251

Mims, Matthew, 17, 318, 389
Mims, Naiomi, 247
Mims, Neoma, 304
Mims, Sarah, 14, 236
Mims, William, 15, 178, 216, 236, 247, 248, 256, 296, 297, 304
Mims, William Jr., 318, 389
Mims, Wright, 30
Minis, Leroy, 177
Minter, Mortan, 256
Minton, James, 22
Mitchel, John, 103
Mitchell Loveny, 29
Mitchell, Abner, 180, 217, 243
Mitchell, Benjamin, 177, 217
Mitchell, Celia, 252, 272
Mitchell, Daniel, 260, 319
Mitchell, Drury, 250
Mitchell, Fanny, 263
Mitchell, George, 214
Mitchell, Goodwin, 18
Mitchell, Henry, 230, 236, 260, 314, 340, 355
Mitchell, Henry J.P., 263, 292
Mitchell, Hetty, 22
Mitchell, James, 13, 180, 194, 204
Mitchell, John, 104, 125, 285, 393
Mitchell, John J.P., 275
Mitchell, Joshua, 21
Mitchell, Lorany, 194
Mitchell, Merrit, 17
Mitchell, Sarah, 24
Mitchell, Seiah, 265
Mitchell, Selah, 316, 386
Mitchell, Stephen, 252, 253, 264, 265, 272, 279, 283, 315, 328, 341, 386
Mitchell, Thomas, 16
Mitchell, William, 31, 96, 125
Mobley, Eleazer, 246, 258

Moncrief, A., 215
Moncrief, Arthur, 220, 227
Moneyham, John, 28
Montgomery County, Georgia, 239, 250, 257, 310, 321
Montgomery, Alexander, 348
Montgomery, Hugh, 231
Montray, Cassandra, 15, 177
Montray, John, 177
Moodie, Ann, 381
Moodie, Thomas, 125
Moody, Granville, 32
Moody, Thomas, 350
Mooney, Joseph, 78, 126
Mooney, Thomas, 58
Moore County, North Carolina, 295
Moore, Alexander, 188, 230, 359
Moore, Ann, 15
Moore, Benjamin, 326, 327, 355
Moore, Betsy, 16
Moore, Charles, 35
Moore, Elizabeth, 19, 20
Moore, James, 340
Moore, John, 15, 19, 24, 126, 136, 153, 224, 233, 364
Moore, Michael Esq., 34
Moore, Millie, 31
Moore, Mordecai, 71, 82, 126, 136, 188, 230, 359
Moore, Nancy, 13, 16, 30
Moore, Naomi, 18
Moore, Olive, 176
Moore, Polly, 29
Moore, Rebecca, 24
Moore, Richard, 14, 101, 126, 156
Moore, Richard Jr., 101
Moore, Robert, 288, 321, 390
Moore, Sally, 34
Moore, Samuel, 176, 372
Moore, Thomas, 127, 136

Moore, Thomas J., 244
Moorman, Pleasant, 19
More, John, 120
Moreland, John, 329
Moreland, Wood, 15, 306, 318, 339, 352, 389
Morgan, David, 21
Morgan, Delila, 288
Morgan, Edward Pleasant, 325
Morgan, Elizabeth, 27
Morgan, Garland, 288
Morgan, Jean, 288
Morgan, Mary, 288
Morgan, Nancy, 19
Morgan, Sarah, 14, 288
Morris, Daniel, 317
Morris, Drusilla, 27
Morris, Elizabeth, 24
Morris, Frederick, 256
Morris, George, 363
Morris, John, 28, 216, 294
Morris, Lavina, 24
Morris, Levina, 256
Morris, Lucy, 35
Morris, Mary, 270
Morris, Rosy, 34
Morris, Thomas, 65, 127, 142
Morrison, William, 186, 222
Morrow, Ewing J.P., 288
Morrow, George, 127
Morrow, James, 54, 127, 152
Morrow, Robert, 42
Morrow, Sallie, 288
Morse, James, 317
Morse, John, 74, 127, 128
Morton, Samuel, 128
Moser, Adam, 128
Moses, Henry, 354
Moses, John, 186, 222, 278, 289, 302, 358
Moses, John Jr., 278, 308, 339
Moses, Joshua, 14

Moses, Robert, 183, 265, 278, 310, 352, 358
Moses, Robert Jr., 289
Moses, Robert Sr., 185, 289, 339
Moses, Samuel, 23, 358
Moss, Henry, 20
Mossman, James, 129, 343
Mounger, H. J.P., 312
Moutrey, Joel, 279
Moutrey, John, 259, 279
Mulkey, John, 322, 391
Mullens, William, 28
Mullins, Lucy, 376
Mullins, Peter, 18
Mullins, Sucky, 22
Mullryne, John, 129
Murphey, Drewry, 250
Murphey, Edward, 129
Murphey, William B., 274
Murphy, Ambrose, 24
Murphy, Edward, 106, 183, 195, 219, 308
Murphy, Elizabeth, 23, 183, 195, 219
Murphy, John, 219
Murphy, Nicholas, 73, 129, 156, 165
Murphy, Richard, 25
Murphy, William B., 250
Murray, Charlotte, 381
Murray, George, 251, 348
Murray, Joe, 348
Murray, John, 38
Murray, Joseph, 376
Murray, Nancy, 381
Murray, Selina, 381
Murray, William, 22
Murrell, Thomas W., 329
Murry, George, 293, 297
Murry, John, 130
Myhand, James, 328, 362
Myhand, Nancy, 23

Myhand, Thomas, 35, 208, 214
Myhand, William, 29, 214
Myrdon, John, 229
Myrick, Elizabeth, 183, 200,
    211, 221
Myrick, J., 249
Myrick, John, 29, 186, 189,
    193, 203, 243, 245, 248, 276,
    279, 292
Myrick, John Jr., 186, 243, 277,
    342
Myrick, John Sr., 189, 277, 301
Myrick, Malinda, 381
Myrick, Nathaniel, 186, 200,
    211, 229, 252, 276, 300, 301
Myrick, Owen, 183, 200, 211,
    221, 275, 301
Myrick, Thomas, 277
Nally, Walter, 362
Nan
    slave, 335
Nance, Catherine, 343
Nance, Henrietta, 338
Nance, Richard White, 343
Nance, William, 329, 343
Nantz, Reubin, 25
Napier, Benjamin, 25
Napier, James, 274
Napper, Absalem, 225
Napper, Drury, 225
Napper, James, 179, 182
Napper, Lydia, 179, 182
Narris, Nathan, 141
Natchez, Mississippi, 342
Neal J, D..P., 337
Neal, Betsy, 14
Neal, D. J.P., 337, 347, 350
Neal, David, 179, 189, 203,
    207, 216, 220, 242, 299, 312,
    313, 314, 347
Neal, David Esq., 207, 213,
    273, 280
Neal, David J.P., 352

Neal, Drusilla, 28
Neal, Elisha, 17, 377
Neal, Elizabeth, 28
Neal, Ira, 392
Neal, James, 92, 130, 203, 214,
    215, 216, 217, 314
Neal, James Jr., 217
Neal, James Sr., 218, 221
Neal, Jehu, 214
Neal, Joel, 187, 226, 227, 302,
    309
Neal, John, 210, 211
Neal, John M., 359
Neal, Jonathan, 130
Neal, Joyce, 207
Neal, Moses, 302
Neal, Patsy, 28, 33
Neal, Patty, 181
Neal, Polly, 17, 23
Neal, Rebecca, 27, 211, 214
Neal, Sallie, 20
Neal, Samuel, 179, 181, 216,
    217, 220, 278, 308
Neal, Sarah, 211, 377
Neal, Thomas, 179, 189, 193,
    213, 216, 240, 241, 242, 249,
    261, 277
Neal, William, 275
Neaves, Daniel, 185
Neaves, John, 185
Ned
    slave, 334
Neel, Lieucresia. *See* Mitchell
Nelms, Royal, 331
Nelms, Young, 264
Nelson, James, 130
Nepper, James, 218
Nepper, Lydia, 218
Neves, Daniel, 222
Neves, James, 22
Neves, John, 222, 304
Newberry, William, 131
Newgent, Edmond, 292

Newman, Elizabeth, 18
Newman, George, 314
Newman, John, 173
Newman, Jonathan, 27
Newman, Samuel, 14, 17, 180,
  230, 248, 324, 329
Newman, Walter, 13, 248, 273
Newman, William, 14, 180,
  230, 304
Newsom, Amos, 32
Newsom, Asa, 18, 198, 320
Newsom, Captain Solomon, 372
Newsom, Carter, 249
Newsom, Claiborn, 257, 336,
  358
Newsom, Crawford, 32
Newsom, David, 176, 181, 184,
  187, 198, 217, 218, 220, 320,
  353
Newsom, Dicy, 28
Newsom, Elizabeth, 32, 184,
  287, 293, 317, *See* Elizabeth
  May
Newsom, Frances, 13
Newsom, Frederick, 184, 186,
  317, 320, 387
Newsom, Gideon, 222
Newsom, Hardy, 20, 282, 294,
  298, 347
Newsom, Henry, 222
Newsom, Hester, 336
Newsom, Jody, 176, 184, 220,
  249, 320, 341, 372
Newsom, Jody J.P., 315, 317,
  325, 332, 335, 387
Newsom, John, 186, 195, 222,
  223
Newsom, Joshua, 222
Newsom, Kinchen, 273
Newsom, Kinsy, 26
Newsom, Marion, 26
Newsom, Mary, 198
Newsom, Nancy, 18

Newsom, Nathaniel, 197
Newsom, Penelope, 35
Newsom, Peter, 189, 308
Newsom, Polly, 32
Newsom, Rebecca, 30, 31
Newsom, Rie, 28
Newsom, Samuel, 328
Newsom, Sarah, 186, 195, 223
Newsom, Solomon, 177, 184,
  198, 217, 218, 237, 240, 246,
  258, 262, 293, 315, 335, 353
Newsom, Solomon Jr., 220, 341
Newsom, Solomon Sr., 182,
  275, 276, 287, 320, 341
Newsom, William, 33
Newsom, William Jr., 320
Newton, Isaac, 289
Newton, James, 131
Newton, Samuel, 131, 138
Neyland, Elizabeth, 346
Neyland, John, 346
Niblet, Tilman, 282
Niblett, Tilman, 364
Nichols, Charlotte, 25, 282
Nichols, George, 285, 300
Nichols, George U., 343
Nichols, Joseph, 300
Nichols, Letty, 22
Nichols, William, 257, 267
Nicholson, H., 367
Nicholson, Thomas, 131
Niday, John, 322, 348
Night, Robert, 22
Nixon, Frances, 282
Nixon, John, 244, 282
Nixon, Nelly, 24
Nixon, Peggy, 21
Noble, William, 301
Nobles, Anna, 16
Nobles, Jonathan, 14
Nobles, Rebecca, 19
Nobles, Stephen, 260
Norden, Thomas, 137

Nordon, Thomas, 131
Norman, William J.P., 354
Norris, Abner, 33
North Carolina, 202, 209, 265
Northen, William, 33
Northern, William, 260
Northington, James, 355
Northington, Samuel, 312
Norton, Elizabeth, 18
Nugent, Edmond, 278, 313
Nugent, Edward, 308
Nugent, Margaret, 27
Nugent, Mary, 278
Nunn, John, 187, 222, 256, 286
Nunn, Nancy, 29
O'Briant, Ann, 20
O'Brien, Ann, 350
O'Brien, Ann A., 349
O'Keefe, Cornelius, 288
O'Neal, Hannah, 333
O'Neal, John, 300, 333, 357
O'Neal, Mary, 14
O'Neal, Wootten, 317
O'Steen, Thomas, 330
Oakes, Joseph, 131, 172
Oaks, Joseph, 66
Oates, Jeremiah, 258
Oats, William, 240
O'Brian, Patrick, 96
O'Brien, Patrick, 120
O'Bryan, Patrick, 131
Odam, Isaac, 132
Odanenly, John, 158
Ogden, Solomon, 214
Ogeechee, 319
Oglethorpe County, Georgia,
  254, 266
Oglethorpe, James Edward, 3
Ogletree, Claiborne, 21
Ogletree, Temperance, 31
Oliver, Alexander, 102, 106,
  132
Oliver, Benjamin, 20, 352, 363

Oliver, Benjamin Jr., 196, 198,
  311, 352
Oliver, Benjamin Sr., 198
Oliver, Catherine, 28
Oliver, Charles, 18
Oliver, James, 49, 132, 198
Oliver, John, 16, 112, 113, 132,
  162, 196, 302, 363
Oliver, John J.P., 243
Oliver, Nancy, 363
Oliver, Patience, 375
Oliver, Peter, 196, 198
Oliver, Robert, 25
Oliver, Sally, 28, 363
Oliver, Samuel, 171, 172
Oliver, Sarah, 198
Onsley, Newday, 275
Ordanely, John, 158
Ores, Benjamin, 147
Orick, James, 133
Orr, Noble, 213
Orrick, James, 100
Osborn, James, 267
Osborn, William, 279
Osborne, Samuel, 279
Osburn, Samuel, 264
Owen, Ephraim, 82, 133
Owen, George J.P., 355
Owen, Polly, 26
Owen, Spencer, 255
Owens, Daniel, 224
Owensbee, Arthur, 64
Owin, Ephraim, 93
Oxford, Dolly, 379
Ozborn, Samuel, 263
Ozborn, William, 263
Pace, Barnabas, 133
Pace, Elizabeth, 379
Pace, Hardy, 32
Pace, James, 219
Pace, John, 359, 360
Pace, Knowls, 133
Pace, Mary, 359, 360

Pace, Parsons, 363
Pace, Polly, 20
Pace, Richard, 133
Pace, Silas, 31, 106, 113, 134, 359
Pace, Thomas, 134, 157
Page, John Watson, 171
Paine, Samuel, 122, 134
Painter, Joseph, 277
Palmer, George, 346
Palmer, Mary, 346
Palmer, Robert, 230, 392
Palmer, Winnifred, 392
Palmore, George, 345
Parey, Dial, 68
Parham, Betsy, 34
Parham, Edmond, 218
Parham, Edward, 349
Parham, Elizabeth, 25, 201, 202, 203, 213, 219, 321, 326
Parham, Fanny, 20, 234
Parham, George, 21, 200, 273, 326, 337, 349
Parham, James, 218, 349, 355
Parham, John, 34, 201, 202, 203, 204, 213, 243, 270, 284, 285, 321, 326, 347
Parham, John Sr., 331
Parham, Lewis, 202, 204, 233, 234
Parham, Mathew, 248
Parham, Matthew, 203, 349, 355, 375
Parham, Nancy, 21, 34, 375
Parham, Nathaniel, 234
Parham, Peter, 290, 301
Parham, Rebecca, 203, 375
Parham, Rebeckah, 273
Parham, Susannah, 19
Parham, Thomas, 290, 321, 326, 331
Paris, James, 70, 83, 85, 137
Paris, Peter, 133, 134

Paris, Philander O., 225
Parish, Hampton, 34
Parish, Polly, 33
Parker, Elizabeth, 29
Parker, Frances, 18
Parker, James, 184, 196, 219, 265, 316, 324, 345
Parker, John, 16, 48, 134, 383
Parker, John P., 340
Parker, Mary, 184, 190, 196, 219, 345
Parker, Orren, 24, 317
Parker, Pollie, 383
Parker, Polly, 35
Parker, Rachel, 340
Parker, Robert, 22, 184, 186, 221, 222, 316, 318, 324, 329, 335, 388
Parker, Samuel, 190, 207
Parker, William, 184, 222
Parkins, John, 280
Parks, Charles, 64, 93, 134
Parris, James, 134, 137
Parris, Peter, 54, 135
Parris, Philander, 226
Parrish, Allen, 382
Parrish, Ansel, 309, 336
Parrish, Anselm, 382
Parrish, Elizabeth, 382
Parrish, Epsey, 382
Parrish, Hampton, 382
Parrish, Henry, 246
Parrish, John, 227, 246, 382
Parrish, Linnie, 20
Parrish, Patsy, 382
Parrish, Sally, 35
Parrish, Thomas, 382
Parrish, William, 382
Parrish, Wilson, 382
Parrot, Peter, 101
Parsley, Nathaniel, 135, 157, 158
Parsley, Richard, 135

Parsons, Amos, 26, 184
Parsons, Turner, 196
Parum, George, 180
Parvey, Dial, 135
Passmore, Houseman, 339
Pate, Charlotte, 381
Pate, Cordy N., 382
Pate, David, 381, 382
Pate, Drury, 32, 232
Pate, Edmund, 381
Pate, Harbert, 379, 381
Pate, Isaac, 28
Pate, John, 362
Pate, Nancy, 382
Pate, Thomas, 298, 299, 319, 359, 362
Patillo, Littleberry, 16
Patrick, Luke, 16
Patterson, James J.P., 321, 390
Patterson, John, 21
Patterson, Robert, 370
Paulk, Micajah, 135
Paulk, William, 27
Pavey, Daniel, 54
Pavey, Dial, 135
Payne, John, 135
Payne, John J.P., 334
Payne, Pheriba, 24
Payne, Samuel, 136
Peacock, Isham, 303
Peacy, David, 42
Peak, John, 235
Pearcy, Blake, 180, 218
Pearman, Brittain, 328
Pearney, Dial, 284
Pearson, Amos, 301
Pearson, Leah N., 392
Pearson, Samuel, 30
Peary, Dial, 263
Peary, Hannah, 263
Peary, John, 270
Peary, Joseph, 237
Peavey, Dial, 284

Peavy, Abraham, 378
Peavy, Ambrose, 13
Peavy, Ann, 378
Peavy, Hilton, 16
Peavy, J., 296
Peavy, James, 376
Peavy, John, 252
Peavy, Joseph, 353
Peavy, Joseph Sr., 378
Peavy, Mary, 378
Peavy, Michael, 295
Peavy, Nellie, 16
Peavy, Peter, 17, 353
Peavy, Susannah, 14
Peavy, Wade Hampton, 378
Peebles, Betsy, 351
Peebles, Dudley, 24
Peebles, Ephriam, 14
Peebles, H., 333
Peebles, Henry, 283, 285, 351
Peebles, Pollie, 15
Peebles, Susannah, 24
Peebles, Theresa, 15
Peebles, William H., 351
Peek, Henry, 372
Peek, James, 35
Peek, Margaret, 379
Peel, John, 240
Peeples, Henry, 239, 309
Peevy, Elizabeth, 35
Peevy, Helton, 354
Peevy, Joseph, 324
Peevy, Phalby, 35
Peggs
    slave, 235
Pembleton, Frances, 19
Pencen, Thomas Roden, 136
Pendleton County, South Carolina, 318
Pennington, Abraham, 260
Pennington, Edward, 144
Pennington, Rebeccah, 29
Pennington, Thomas, 196

Perkins John, 68
Perkins, Abraham, 264, 265, 324, 335, 337
Perkins, Jennie, 17
Perkins, John, 45, 60, 120, 136, 303, 337
Perkins, Peter, 61, 78, 99, 136, 184, 274, 316, 327, 345
Perkins, Polly, 18
Perkins, Sarah, 223
Perrett, John, 136
Perritt, Nathaniel, 14
Perry Rawls, 129
Perry, Benjamin, 278
Perry, Burrell, 270, 271, 298, 329, 365
Perry, Hiram, 318, 346, 361
Perry, Hyram, 21
Perry, Jeremiah, 22, 388
Perry, Micajah, 24, 273
Perry, Philip, 129
Perry, Polly, 32
Perry, Rawls, 136
Perry, Walker, 388
Perry, William, 14
Perry, Willis, 229, 281, 282, 299, 325, 335
Perryman, A., 361
Perryman, Alexander, 26, 347, 356, 365
Perryman, Alexander Esq., 326
Perryman, D., 251, 286, 335
Perryman, Daniel, 189
Perryman, Dixon, 14, 177, 257, 258, 334
Perryman, E., 388
Perryman, E. Sr., 388
Perryman, Harman, 273
Perryman, Harmon, 177, 190, 224, 245, 326, 335, 358, 361, 372
Perryman, J., 297
Perryman, Martha, 16

Perryman, Mary, 335, 361
Perryman, Montford, 189
Perryman, Robert, 312
Persons, A., 179, 282, 309, 310, 346, 351, 354
Persons, Amos, 179, 216, 219, 304, 355
Persons, Amos J., 233
Persons, Cibell, 384
Persons, Dial, 295
Persons, Dianna, 377
Persons, G. W., 233
Persons, Henry, 227
Persons, Jones, 273, 280, 284, 292, 304, 310, 324, 342, 349
Persons, Josiah, 225
Persons, Lucy, 32
Persons, Nicholas W., 233
Persons, R., 271
Persons, Rachel, 225
Persons, Rebeckah, 298
Persons, T., 247, 250, 260, 268, 271, 284, 286, 290, 295, 300, 304, 307, 310, 347, 349, 352, 354, 358, 372
Persons, Thomas, 225, 384
Persons, Thomas Flewellen, 384
Persons, Turner, 14, 176, 203, 204, 225, 233, 240, 241, 244, 249, 251, 256, 267, 270, 275, 276, 290, 304, 323, 340, 362
Persons, Turner J.P., 270
Petagrew, Hans, 266
Peters, Elijah, 355
Pettegrew, John, 139
Petticrew, John, 137
Pettit, John W. A., 225
Pettygrew, Jane, 84, 137
Pettygrew, John, 41, 53, 116, 134, 137, 172
Pevay, Joseph, 254
Pevey, Willis, 301
Peyampert, John, 266

Phelan, Evans, 293
Phelps, Abenton, 70
Phelps, Avington, 137
Phelps, Daniel, 372
Phelps, William, 64, 110, 137
Philips, Thomas, 293
Phillip, John, 48
Phillips, James, 115, 137
Phillips, John, 44, 74, 80, 138,
202, 213
Phillips, Joseph, 202, 213, 386
Phillips, Peter, 138
Phillips, Thomas, 181, 202, 213
Phillips, Zachariah, 69, 138
Phillis
slave, 236, 298
Phoeby
Slave, 312
Pickard, Elizabeth, 26
Pickard, Henry, 255, 258
Pickard, John Henry, 255
Pickering County, Mississippi,
239, 309
Picket, James, 138
Pierce, John Jr., 354
Pierce, Sallie, 20
Pierson, James, 357, 358
Pierson, Jeremiah Jr., 357
Pierson, John, 357
Pierson, Rebekah, 27
Pilcher, James, 393
Pilcher, Lewis, 329
Pilcher, William, 185, 220, 328,
329
Pile, William, 32
Pinkston, John, 305, 350
Pinson, Thomas Rhoden, 188
Pinson, Winney, 177
Pinson, Winnie, 217
Pitman, John, 45, 279
Pittman, Jesse, 325
Pitts, Drusilla, 377
Pitts, Elizabeth, 202

Pitts, Hardy, 28, 213, 216, 217,
222, 230, 375, 377, 392
Pitts, Jack, 202
Pitts, Martha, 204
Pitts, Nancy Williams, 202
Pitts, Nestor, 202
Pitts, Nicholas Williams, 202
Pitts, Noel, 197, 202, 204
Pitts, Patience, 25
Pitts, Samuel, 201, 202, 213,
219, 232, 233, 375
Pitts, Shadrick, 351
Pitts, Solomon, 202
Pitts, William, 201, 347, 375
Pleasant, William, 270
Plummer, Micajah, 65
Poe, William, 287, 348
Pole, Colonel Charles, 252
Pool, Ann, 341
Pool, Baxter, 341
Pool, Ephraim, 289
Pool, Jeremiah, 30
Pool, Mary, 336
Pool, Phillip, 336, 358
Pool, Polly, 31, 33
Pool, Sarah, 22
Pooler, Quinton, 78, 138
Poor, Frances, 20
Poor, John, 20
Poore, Elisha, 16
Poore, Thomas, 252, 253
Porter, Benjamin, 254, 255, 348
Porter, Charles J.P., 348, 353,
356
Porter, Stanton, 353, 356
Porter, Thomas, 266, 319
Porter, William, 311
Posey, Lemuel, 384
Posey, Rebecca, 197
Posey, Samuel, 197, 362
Posey, Samuel Marcus, 384
Posey, Thomas, 384
Potter, Elizabeth, 20

Pottle, John, 317
Potts, Noel, 340
Potts, Rebecca, 25
Potts, Shadrick, 330, 331
Powell, Catherine, 268
Powell, Charity, 194
Powell, James Edward, 138
Powell, John, 288
Powell, Lewis, 268, 340
Powell, Mary, 370
Powell, Moses, 340
Powell, Moses Sr., 258, 268,
  370
Powell, Nancy, 303
Powell, Perry, 33
Powell, Rachel, 252
Powell, Samuel, 242, 272, 296,
  330
Poythress, Mary, 392
Pratt, Leonard, 31
Preston, Christopher, 14
Price, Reese, 356
Prince, Henry, 20
Prior, Ann, 240
Pritchell, Christopher, 258
Proctor, William, 21
Pruitt, Austin, 17, 333
Pruitt, Bird, 195, 223, 314, 333
Pruitt, Byrd, 25, 187, 191, 255,
  300
Pruitt, Caty, 277
Pruitt, E., 284
Pruitt, Elisha, 229, 280, 281,
  313, 322
Pruitt, Elisha Esq., 280
Pruitt, Elizabeth, 187, 191, 195,
  223, 282, 301, 356
Pruitt, Harden, 187, 210
Pruitt, Hardin, 210, 214, 223
Pruitt, Harris, 210
Pruitt, L., 291, 308
Pruitt, L. J.I.C., 326, 330, 344,
  350

Pruitt, L. J.P., 244, 245, 260,
  272, 280, 282, 284, 336, 372
Pruitt, L., J.P., 282
Pruitt, Lemuel, 251, 272, 277,
  281, 322, 359
Pruitt, Lemuel J.P., 236, 260,
  281, 290, 295, 298
Pruitt, Lemuel Jr., 294, 295
Pruitt, Levi, 187, 191, 195, 223,
  251, 272, 277, 290, 300, 301,
  304, 333, 335
Pruitt, Levi Esq., 342, 356
Pruitt, Levi J.I.C., 326
Pruitt, Levi J.P., 254, 277
Pruitt, Nathaniel, 18
Pruitt, Sally, 25
Pruitt, Samuel, 272
Puckett, William R., 377
Pugh, Job, 310
Pugh, Robert, 310
Pulaski County, Georgia, 379
Pullin, Robert, 359
Punkett, Mary, 19
Pynne, Peter, 377
Quakers, 96, 113, 265
Qualls, John, 331
Qualls, Nance, 338
Qualls, Peter, 331, 338, 364
Qualls, Roger, 139, 315, 386
Quinn, John, 25, 351
Rabun, Matthew, 285
Rachel
  slave, 316, 344
Radcliffe, Mary, 379
Rae, James, 139, 140, 169
Rae, John, 47, 73, 76, 78, 83,
  92, 119, 139, 140
Rae, John Jr., 80
Rae, Robert, 130, 139, 140, 154,
  169
Raeley, Joseph, 313
Ragland, John, 294
Raglin, David, 200

Rahn, Jasper, 140
Railey, James, 338
Rain, Peter, 265
Raines, Cadwall, 263
Rains, William, 140
Raley, Henry, 230
Raley, James, 230, 333
Raley, Sarah, 265
Ramsey, Isaac, 141
Ramsey, John, 140, 141
Ramsey, Randall, 141, 144
Ramsey, Randel, 159
Ramsey, William, 129, 141
Randall, Josiah, 309
Randall, Josias, 305
Randan, Peter, 155
Randle, Willis, 31
Randolph, Charles F., 299
Randolph, Edward, 341
Randon, Peter, 141, 157
Ransom, Marcella, 35
Rany, Benjamin, 134
Raskin, Francis F., 19
Ratliff, Redden, 271
Rawls, Phillip, 318, 388
Ray, Ann, 22
Ray, George Washington, 202
Ray, John, 382
Ray, Jonas, 17
Ray, Obedience, 378
Ray, Polly, 382
Rayburn, Charles, 17, 356
Rayburn, Mary, 22
Rayse, Linny, 206
Read, Thomas, 86, 131, 138
Reading, Timothy, 34
Red, John, 141
Red, Thomas, 59, 108, 142
Redless, Thomas, 23
Redman, William, 142
Reed, John, 17
Reed, Thomas, 150
Reeley, William, 312

Rees, Benjamin, 216, 272, 295
Rees, Daniel, 142
Rees, Elizabeth, 272
Rees, Hugh, 294, 295, 298, 302
Rees, Reuben, 294
Rees, Theresa, 34
Reese, Benjamin, 242, 294, 332,
    350, 360
Reese, Hugh, 218, 242, 272,
    274, 282, 312, 313, 327, 330,
    336, 360
Reese, Hugh Sr., 335
Reese, Isham, 24
Reese, Reubin, 357, 358
Reese, Sarah, 294
Reese, William, 32
Reeves, Daniel, 157
Reid, James, 81
Reid, Thomas, 155
Reise, Hugh, 266
Renfroe, Enoch, 252
Renfroe, Enoch Jr., 185
Renfroe, Enoch Sr., 185
Renfroe, Ephriam, 318
Renfroe, Nathan, 252, 253, 254
Renn, Presley, 142
Rentfro, Enoch, 341
Revers, John K., 24
Reves, Jesse, 142
Revill, Randolph, 236, 314
Revison, Isaac, 18
Reynolds, Daniel, 252
Reynolds, Hubert J.P., 366
Reynolds, Jane, 29
Reynolds, John, 391
Reynolds, Joshua, 344
Rhodes, David, 27
Rhodes, John, 14
Rhodes, Joseph, 34
Rhodes, Sally, 34
Rhymes, John, 317
Rhymes, Willis, 229
Richards, Phoebe, 25

Richardson, Daniel, 48, 142
Richardson, Hannah, 18, 295
Richardson, James, 296
Richardson, Joseph, 245, 247, 286
Richardson, Thomas, 320
Richardson, William, 18, 295
Richmond County, Georgia, 8, 148, 164, 239, 240, 243, 245, 271, 288, 298, 305, 332, 341, 369
Richmond County, North Carolina, 350
Rickerson, Sally, 28
Ricketson, James, 28
Ricketson, Jesse, 260, 269, 270, 282, 333
Ridgewell, Elender, 365
Ridgewell, Isaac H., 269
Ridgewell, Samuel, 182, 218, 269, 274, 289
Riece, Daniel, 141
Rigbee, Thomas, 327
Rigbee, William, 327
Rigby, Elizabeth, 31
Rigby, Nancy, 29
Riley, John J.P., 359
Ring, Christopher, 143, 160
Risher, Francis, 346
Risher, Francis F., 323
Rives, Joel, 350
Riviere, J., 366
Roaten, John, 143
Roaten, John Jr., 143
Roats, Lemuel, 32
Roberson, David, 316
Roberson, John, 27
Roberson, William, 177, 362
Roberts, Elisha, 248, 380
Roberts, Joe., 232
Roberts, Joseph, 215, 389
Roberts, Josias Randol, 380
Roberts, May, 380

Roberts, Sally, 334
Roberts, Sarah, 27
Roberts, Willis, 19
Robertson, David, 185, 221, 351
Robertson, David Sr., 273, 360
Robertson, John, 21, 347
Robertson, Martha, 22
Robertson, N., 279, 333, 347, 360
Robertson, N. J.P., 322, 325, 349
Robertson, Neville, 381
Robertson, Norrell, 242, 291, 296
Robertson, Norrell J.P., 303
Robertson, Norvell, 237, 300, 311, 319, 339, 351, 354, 361
Robertson, Norvell J.P., 296, 303, 318, 320
Robertson, Nowell, 194, 195
Robertson, Nowell J.P., 273, 278, 331
Robertson, Salley, 303
Robertson, Sallie, 242, 311
Robertson, Sally, 296, 303
Robertson, William, 259
Robinson, B., 329
Robinson, David, 143, 351
Robinson, Elizabeth, 383
Robinson, James, 371
Robinson, John, 88, 237, 238
Robinson, Nancy, 379
Robison, David, 246
Robison, Israel, 143
Robison, John, 143
Robison, William, 144
Rock, John, 75, 144
Rockhold, John, 293
Rockmore, Elizabeth, 185
Rockmore, James, 185
Rockmore, Peter, 331
Rodan, Zadock, 236
Roe, Abraham, 304

Roe, Joshua, 278, 316
Roe, Sarah, 316
Rogers, Abner, 232
Rogers, Catherine, 23
Rogers, Drury, 317
Rogers, James, 33, 208, 252, 258, 260, 268
Rogers, John, 234, 335
Rogers, Martha Mitchell, 8
Rogers, Micajah, 8, 226, 229
Rogers, Michael, 30
Rogers, Nancy, 15, 379
Rogers, Peleg, 289
Rogers, Polly, 24, 30, 32
Rogers, Reubin, 208, 273
Rogers, Reubin Sr., 234
Rogers, Sally, 32
Rogers, Tempy, 33
Rogers, Thomas, 185, 220, 252, 253
Rogers, Treacy, 21
Rolling, John, 206
Roney, Henry C., 11
Roney, Jane V., 11
Roney, Thomas, 11
Roquemore, Elizabeth, 221, 250
Roquemore, James, 221, 250, 305, 330
Roquemore, James Jr., 250
Roquemore, James Sr., 250
Roquemore, John, 250
Roquemore, Peter, 250
Roquemore, Polly, 250
Roquemore, Thomas, 250
Rose
    slave, 250, 326
Rose, Avy, 16
Rose, Edmond, 180, 217, 363
Rose, Sally, 30
Rose, Sarah, 180, 217
Rose, Stephen, 216
Rose, Susanna, 323
Rose, W., 333

Rose, William, 180, 217, 275
Rose, Wormsley, 217, 225, 239, 244, 290, 307, 309, 315, 323, 344
Rosebergh, George, 141
Rosebrough, George, 144
Ross, Hixon, 120
Ross, Hugh, 347
Ross, James, 85, 144, 151, 164
Ross, John, 27
Ross, Nancy, 16, 20
Ross, Thomas, 104
Rosser, Elizabeth, 195
Rosser, James, 224
Rosser, John, 224
Rosser, Louisa, 224
Rosy, Churchwell, 35
Rouse, Parot, 32
Rousseau, William, 319
Rowe, Chloe, 21
Rowe, Elizabeth, 23
Rowe, Holland, 22
Rowe, John Floyd, 382
Rowe, Joshua, 31
Rowe, Lucinda, 382
Rowe, Lydia, 23
Rowe, Michael, 21
Rowe, Patsy, 23
Rowe, Rhoda, 17
Rowe, Sally, 382
Rowland, Daniel, 32
Rowland, James, 228, 271
Rowland, John, 23
Rowland, Lavina, 13
Rowland, Thomas, 228
Rowland, William, 357
Rowland, Williamson, 352
Rowland, Willis, 259, 288
Ruark, Ebbe, 391
Ruark, Jesse, 391
Rucker, Joseph, 295
Rudicil, John, 274
Rudicille, John, 312

Rudisell, John, 261, 299, 304
Ruff, Bethena, 203
Ruff, Fanny, 203
Ruff, Jack, 203
Ruff, Judith, 203
Ruff, Rachel, 203
Ruke, Blitha, 332
Rukie, Severn, 198
Runnals, Daniel, 280
Runnels, David, 290
Runnels, Elijah, 369
Runnels, Fannie, 369
Runnels, Hester, 369
Runnels, Hubert, 369
Runnels, John J.P., 267
Runnolds, John, 31
Runnolds, Johnston, 16
Runnolds, Joshua, 16
Rushin, Elizabeth, 33
Rushing, J., 362
Rushing, Jenny, 26
Rushing, John, 31, 183, 185,
    195, 219, 220, 253, 254, 259,
    274, 316, 318, 329, 335, 341,
    342, 351, 362
Rushing, John Sr., 376
Rushing, William, 259, 335
Russell, David, 37, 112
Russell, John, 23
Rutherford, John, 183, 247, 248,
    256, 271, 369
Rutherford, Polly, 369
Rutherford, Robert, 180, 217,
    247
Rutherford, Samuel, 189, 208,
    224
Rutland, Mildred, 340
Ryan, Chloe, 200
Ryan, Dennis L., 30, 380, 383,
    384
Ryan, Joseph, 375
Ryan, Laurence D., 200
Ryan, Mary, 384

Ryan, May, 380
Ryan, Peter, 14, 349
Sail, Henry, 144
Sail, Jonathan, 93, 145, 151
Sails, John, 151
Sal
    slave, 235
Sale, Henry, 93
Saley, Jeremiah, 254
Sall
    slave, 365
Sallet, Jonathan, 102
Sallins, Peter, 145
Sallins, Peter, 129
Sallis, David, 22, 215, 216, 226
Sallis, James, 33
Sallis, John, 190, 216, 221, 266,
    327
Sallis, Joseph, 216, 221
Sallis, Josiah, 30
Salls, Abraham, 322, 391
Sally, William, 244
Salter, John, 145, 152
Salter, Simon, 305
Sammons, Richard, 342, 358
Sandeford, Benjamin, 191, 227
Sanders, Abram, 378
Sanders, Anna, 378
Sanders, Arden, 280
Sanders, Charley, 378
Sanders, Daniel, 280
Sanders, Harden, 328
Sanders, Henry, 251, 279
Sanders, James, 251, 378
Sanders, John, 29
Sanders, Joshua, 40, 121, 145
Sanders, Mary, 378
Sanders, Priscilla, 17
Sanders, Rebecca, 31, 378
Sanders, Rosanna, 25
Sanders, William, 14, 251, 267,
    305
Sanders, William Jr., 279

Sandford, Peggy, 22
Sandiford, Benjamin, 217, 227, 382
Sanford, Jesse, 263, 350, 359, 366
Sanford, Presley, 13
Sanford, Rachel, 366
Sanford, William, 350
Sanford, William Sr., 366
Sanson, Samuel, 146
Sarah
    slave, **236, 326, 356**
Satterwhite, William, 64, 137, 141, 146, 171, 174
Sauls, Abraham, 356
Saunders, Daniel, 179
Saunders, James, 364
Saunders, John, 361
Saunders, Joshua, 82
Savage, Loveless, 134, 142, 146, 152, 155
Savannah, Georgia, 3, 235, 284, 307
Saxon, John, 15, 286, 323, 335
Saxon, Samuel, 286
Saxon, Solomon, 359
Sayager, Stephen, 15
Scot, Alexander, 38, 51
Scott, A., 304
Scott, Alexander, 93, 147
Scott, Aquilla, 241
Scott, Asa, 300
Scott, Benjamin, 261, 264, 297, 298, 324, 327, 344
Scott, James, 263
Scott, John, 78, 86, 93, 147, 351
Scott, Mary, 28
Scott, Samuel, 147
Scott, Thomas, 240
Scott, William, 351
Screven, James, 148
Seals, Spencer, 25
Seals, Thomas, 233

Seamore, James, 44, 148, 164
Sell, Jonathan, 72, 88, 113, 148, 171
Sell, Mary, 351
Sell, Thomas, 310, 350, 351
Sells, Martha, 185
Sells, Thomas, 185, 323
Semmes, Ignatius, 356
Semmes, James, 339
Semmes, James M., 389
Semmes, Joseph M., 215
Semmes, Joseph Mil'n., 34
Semmes, Mary, 389
Seventz, John, 46
Sexton, John, 334
Seybold, John, 276
Seymore, Young, 29
Shambless, Thomas, 35
Shamling, Elizabeth, 28
Shan, John, 149
Shannon, Patrick, 241, 319
Shaw, Alexander, 76, 77, 119, 149
Shaw, John, 45, 149
Shaw, Mary, 375
Shaw, Patsy, 27
Shaw, Phoebe, 14
Shaw, William, 27
Sheffield, Anne, 380
Sheffield, Eliza, 22
Sheffield, John, 23
Sheffield, Lucy, 380
Sheffield, Robert, 28, 360
Sheffield, Sally, 380
Sheffield, Susannah, 35
Sheffield, Zachariah, 359, 360
Sheffield, Zechariah, 282
Sheffield, Zilla Ann, 380
Sheftall, Levi, 81, 149
Sheftall, Mordecai, 149
Shelly, Bryan, 162
Shelton, Henry, 180, 217, 277, 354, 387

Shepard, Benjamin, 15
Shepherd, John Tinkler, 96
Shepherd, Nathaniel, 149
Sherley, Edward, 326
Sherley, Nancy, 25
Sherley, Nathan, 26
Sherley, William, 341
Sherman
  slave, 379
Sherman, Eli G., 231
Sherman, Lucretia, 231
Shick, John, 149
Shields, James, 150
Shields, John, 150, 161
Shields, Thomas J.P., 237
Shields, William, 54, 86, 150
Shillings, Ambrose, 25
Ship, Richard, 337
Shirley, Richard, 357
Shirley, William, 150
Shivers, Barnaby, 388
Shivers, George W. C., 389
Shivers, James, 228, 232, 389
Shivers, Jonas, 223, 232, 388
Shivers, Lilly Ann, 389
Shivers, Nancy, 389
Shivers, Obediah, 389
Shivers, Thomas, 388
Shivers, William, 223, 388
Shivers, William Jr., 391
Shivers, Willis, 388
Shockley, Gahazi, 371
Shockley, Nathan, 371
Shoder, William, 30
Short, Edward, 15
Short, Nancy, 20
Short, W., 310
Shruder, Thomas, 150, 151
Shurley, William, 257, 338
Sidwell, John, 93, 151, 171
Sill, Margaret, 31
Sills, Edward, 310

Simmons, Benjamin, 298, 299, 370
Simmons, Hannah, 14
Simmons, Henry, 370
Simmons, James, 15, 292, 370
Simmons, Jincey, 370
Simmons, John, 190, 225, 340, 370
Simmons, Lucy, 370
Simmons, Mary, 292
Simmons, Phoebe, 20
Simmons, Pollie, 370
Simmons, Rebecca, 19
Simmons, Rebeckah, 370
Simmons, Thomas, 19
Simmons, William, 18, 220, 274, 357
Simms, Ignatius, 274
Simms, James J.P., 279
Simms, Mary, 20
Simon
  slave, 235
Simons, Isaac, 260
Simons, Sally, 19
Simonson, Isaac, 269, 270
Simpler, William, 321, 322, 357, 358
Simpson, Daniel, 339
Simpson, James, 151
Simpson, Jane, 28
Simpson, Mary Ann, 16
Sims, Bartlett, 345
Sims, Bartlett Jr., 345
Sims, Bartlett Sr., 345
Sims, Betsy, 13
Sims, Catherine, 15
Sims, Dr. Ignatius, 16
Sims, Harbert, 345
Sims, Jane, 31
Sims, John, 16
Sims, Rebecca, 381
Sims, William, 101, 151, 271
Singefield, Aaron, 41

Skeine, Benjamin, 283
Skelly, Samuel, 318, 342, 351
Slade, Belinda, 27
Slatter, Betty, 24
Slatter, Elizabeth, 27, 370
Slatter, James, 195
Slatter, Joel, 195
Slatter, John, 46, 68, 94, 145,
    151, 169, 195, 243, 265, 273,
    318
Slatter, John Sr., 318
Slatter, Mary, 152
Slatter, Nancy, 370
Slatter, Peggy, 17
Slatter, Solomon, 180, 186, 193,
    221, 236, 256, 273, 304, 317,
    323, 344, 366, 370
Slatter, William, 21, 235
Slaughter, Richard, 324, 328,
    329, 336
Slaughter, Walter, 283, 329, 337
Slocum, Samuel, 175, 230, 369
Slocum, Seth, 175, 230
Smallwood, Elisha, 28
Smith, Aaron, 17, 205, 206, 213
Smith, Agnes, 19
Smith, Aleck, 246
Smith, Alex, 307
Smith, Alexander, 337, 373
Smith, Archibald, 305
Smith, B. J.P., 255
Smith, Benjamin, 246, 303, 304,
    305, 391
Smith, Cassandra, 357
Smith, Catherine, 30, 357
Smith, Charles, 146, 152, 159
Smith, Dicy, 382
Smith, Ebenezer, 49, 128, 137,
    152, 171, 348
Smith, Eddea, 30
Smith, Elizabeth, 32, 357
Smith, Ephraim, 282
Smith, Ezekiel, 206, 294

Smith, Fanny, 29
Smith, Frances, 391
Smith, G., 193
Smith, Gardner, 19
Smith, Giles, 233
Smith, Graham, 365
Smith, Gresham, 353
Smith, Hannah, 24
Smith, Hardy, 182
Smith, Jacob, 232, 357
Smith, James, 21, 152, 190,
    293, 297, 337, 343, 348, 371,
    384
Smith, Jesse E., 391
Smith, Job, 51, 152, 171
Smith, Joel, 28
Smith, John, 21, 32, 35, 46, 153,
    157, 232, 249, 267, 303, 313,
    316, 321, 339, 351, 391
Smith, John C., 391
Smith, John Jr., 271
Smith, John Sr., 271
Smith, Jonathan, 337, 357
Smith, Joseph, 270, 357
Smith, Lavinah, 30
Smith, Linsey, 28
Smith, Lovett, 31
Smith, Martha, 363, 391
Smith, Mary, 25, 29, 337, 343,
    355
Smith, Mourning, 14
Smith, Nancy, 22, 23, 34, 343,
    384, 391
Smith, Nathaniel, 301, 337
Smith, Nathaniel Alexander,
    343, 355
Smith, Needham, 249, 292, 344
Smith, Patsy, 33
Smith, Patty, 257
Smith, Pheriby, 357
Smith, Pollie, 20
Smith, Rebecca, 384

Smith, Richard, 120, 126, 153, 249, 266, 271, 299, 352
Smith, Sally, 34
Smith, Samuel M., 25, 188
Smith, Sarah, 391
Smith, Shadrach, 255
Smith, Thomas, 41, 177, 180, 231, 321, 333, 354, 390
Smith, Thomas Sr., 248
Smith, Wilkins, 248, 288, 296, 318
Smith, William, 256, 257, 262, 324, 346, 361, 363, 375, 391
Smyth, Ebenezer, 365
Smyth, James, 365
Smythe, John, 35
Snelling, John, 246
Snelling, William, 26
Snellings, Lou, 345
Snider, Barnett, 385
Snider, Elizabeth, 385
Snider, Elizabeth Joanne, 385
Snider, Jacob, 385
Snipes, Richard, 183
Sook
    slave, 235
South Carolina, 243, 255, 265, 285, 316, 326, 328, 348, 365
Southerton, Richard, 57
Spann, Eleanor, 193
Spann, Francis, 193
Speed, John, 350
Spencer, John, 119, 153
Spencer, Richard, 41
Spier, Benton, 278
Spikes, William, 259
Spinks, Presley, 34, 183
Spinks, Rosamond, 27
Spinks, Sally, 32
Spinks, Susannah, 17
Spivey, Joab, 388
Springer, Job, 289, 300
Springer, Lydia, 289, 300

Spurlin, Jeremiah, 255, 256
Spurlin, John, 255, 350
Spurling, Eliza, 31
Spurling, Jeremiah, 258
Stainback, David, 379
Stainback, Francis, 280, 363, 379
Stainback, George, 379
Stainback, Nancy, 379
Stainback, Thomas, 379
Stallings, John, 340, 347
Stallion, Elias, 153
Stanback, Francis, 304, 321
Standford, James, 33
Standley, Albenia, 332
Standley, Ezekiel, 332
Standley, William, 128
Stanford, Bethany, 391
Stanford, Christopher, 389
Stanford, Eleanor, 32
Stanford, Elender, 392
Stanford, Elvy, 23
Stanford, Isaiah, 389
Stanford, Jane V., 11
Stanford, Jesse, 234, 252, 331, 332, 391
Stanford, John, 332, 387
Stanford, John R., 390
Stanford, Jonathan, 325
Stanford, Joseph, 387, 389
Stanford, Joshua, 208, 387
Stanford, Joshua Jr., 258
Stanford, Joshua Sr., 387
Stanford, Levi, 209, 387
Stanford, Levin, 22, 336, 387
Stanford, Lewis, 331
Stanford, Margaret, 389
Stanford, Mary, 27
Stanford, Mary E., 392
Stanford, Nellie, 26
Stanford, Parthena, 391
Stanford, Reubin, 234, 391

Stanford, Robert, 188, 190, 252, 255, 266, 267, 324, 325, 331, 332, 336
Stanford, Sophia, 23
Stanford, Stephen, 325, 346
Stanford, Thornton, 366
Stanford, William, 232, 393
Stanley, John, 154
Stanley, William, 128, 154
Staple, Stephen, 247
Stapler, Amos, 81, 283, 354
Stapler, James, 283
Stapler, Thomas, 81, 95, 129, 154, 354
Stark, Elizabeth, 246
Stark, Thomas, 246, 254
Stark, Thomas Sr., 246
Stark, William, 244, 251, 288, 331
Starnes, Daniel, 336
Starnes, Ebenezer, 304
Statler, Solomon, 304
Staton, Patsy, 21
Steel, Alexander, 292
Steele, Sampson S., 351
Stephens, Aaron G., 384
Stephens, Alexander, 384
Stephens, Andrew B., 305
Stephens, Andrew R., 26
Stephens, Cabal, 272
Stephens, Caleb, 273
Stephens, Joshua, 19
Stephens, Pleasant, 34
Stephens, Rachel, 20
Sterns, Ebenezer, 273
Stetstill, Thomas, 154
Stevens, Aquilla, 225
Stevens, Owen B., 225
Stevens, Ross, 225
Stewart, Amos, 267
Stewart, Ann, 272, 273, 352
Stewart, Bethiar, 273

Stewart, Charles, 19, 27, 322, 391
Stewart, George, 362
Stewart, Jerusha, 352
Stewart, John, 44, 45, 80, 90, 154, 162, 355
Stewart, John Jr., 41, 155
Stewart, John Sr., 155, 163
Stewart, Patsey, 267
Stills, Edward, 307
Stincey, Archibald, 155
Stinson, Archibald, 142
Stith, Colonel William, 206
Stith, J., 352
Stith, John, 193
Stith, Millie, 213
Stith, Milly, 193
Stith, Peyton T., 276
Stith, W., 276
Stith, W. J.P., 288, 325
Stith, W. Jr., 290
Stith, William, 193, 200, 213, 268, 286, 304, 337
Stith, William J.P., 311
Stith, William Jr., 178, 268
Stith, William Sr., 178
Stokes, Thomas, 364
Stone, Elizabeth, 26
Stone, Mary, 187, 223, 227
Stone, Micajah, 187, 223, 226, 247, 270, 335, 364, 365
Stone, Polly, 32
Stone, Rowd., 298
Stone, William, 226, 227
Stonestreet, Richard, 35
Story, Asa, 209
Story, Edward, 334
Story, James, 96
Story, Jesse, 357, 388
Story, Mahala, 209
Story, Richard, 292, 333
Story, Robert, 61, 104, 125
Story, Samuel, 232, 344

~ 467 ~

Strange, Littleberry, 13
Stringer, Francis, 155
Stroddar, Letitia, 218
Stroddar, Shadrack, 218
Strother, Rebeckah, 30
Strother, Susannah, 230
Strother, William, 230
Struthers, William, 155
Stuart, Ann, 325
Stuart, C. D., 339
Stuart, Charles D., 348
Stuart, Jerusha, 325
Stuart, John Jr., 82
Stuart, Polly, 325
Stubbs, Ann, 155
Stubbs, Deborah, 18, 91, 156
Stubbs, Jack, 270
Stubbs, James J.P., 285
Stubbs, Jesse, 348
Stubbs, John, 101, 102, 117,
    156, 247
Stubbs, Joseph, 172, 269, 271
Stubbs, Mary, 21, 350
Stubbs, Nathan, 302, 350, 352
Stubbs, Nathaniel, 156
Stubbs, Samuel, 349, 350
Sturdivant, D., 315
Sturdivant, Daniel, 216, 375
Sturdivant, P., 313
Sucky
    slave, 328
Sullivan, Owen, 37, 130, 156
Sullivan, William, 261
Sullivant, John, 20
Summons, Richard, 263
Sutherton, Richard, 157
Sutor, Sarah, 157
Swain, James, 379
Swain, Job, 379
Swain, John, 379
Swain, Josiah, 379
Swain, Peggy, 35
Swain, Richard, 379

Swain, Susannah, 379
Swain, Thomas, 379
Swain, William, 379
Sweetwater Church, 392
Swents, John, 157
Swicord, Michael, 365
Tabor, John, 258
Tait, Robert, 28
Tait, William, 20
Talbott, Jesse J.P., 348
Talliferro, John, 243, 244, 342
Talliferro, Mary, 342
Tapley, Elizabeth, 336
Tapley, Evan, 289
Tapley, Joel, 288, 293, 332, 336
Tapley, Mark, 336
Tapley, Mary, 294
Tapley, New, 336
Tapley, William, 336
Tapper, James, 359
Tapper, Mary, 25
Tarry, Hannah, 385
Tarry, Samuel, 385
Tarry, Thomas, 385
Tarver, Mary, 343
Tarver, William, 343
Tarvin, John, 157
Tarvin, William, 157, 158
Tattnall County, Georgia, 328
Tattnall, Josiah, 129
Taylor, Arthur, 20
Taylor, Edmond, 359
Taylor, Edmond E., 327
Taylor, George, 176, 181
Taylor, Hugh, 315, 386
Taylor, James, 16, 176, 326,
    327
Taylor, Jerusha, 23
Taylor, Nancy. See Moore
Taylor, Patsy, 204
Taylor, Robert, 23
Taylor, Sarah, 284

Taylor, William, 18, 30, 49, 59, 96, 131, 135, 158, 204, 267
Tedders, Samuel, 267
Teddley, William, 32
Teddlie, William, 214
Teesling, Anna Barbara, 387
Telfair County, Georgia, 379
Telfair, Edward, 158
Temrin, Hugh, 124
Tenille, Benjamin J.P., 249
Tennen, Hugh, 94, 99, 158
Tennille, Rachel, 249
Terrell, David, 251
Terrell, Peter B., 235
Terrell, Richard, 259, 308
Terrell, Richmond, 393
Terry, David, 240
Terry, Thomas, 24, 231
Terry, William, 226
Terry, Willis, 33
Tervin, John, 158
Tharp, Charnick, 286
Tharp, H. J.P., 287
Tharp, John, 31
Tharp, Nancy A., 32
Tharp, V. T. A., 338
Tharp, Vincent A., 292
Tharp, Vincent A. J.P., 245
Tharp, Vincent Allen, 275
Thedford, William, 286
Thigpen, Fanny, 385
Thomas, Daniel, 30
Thomas, David, 278
Thomas, E., 277, 280, 312, 357, 360
Thomas, Etheldred, 237, 238, 241, 308, 312, 315, 331, 366
Thomas, Etheldred Esq., 326
Thomas, Evan, 262, 278, 289, 356
Thomas, Grigsby E., 227
Thomas, James, 229, 240, 253, 307

Thomas, John, 19, 178, 216, 283, 294
Thomas, Mary, 334
Thomas, Nancy, 280, 312
Thomas, Phebe, 294
Thomas, William, 230, 334
Thomas, William J.P., 338
Thompson, Alexander, 209, 345, 376
Thompson, Ann, 261, 276
Thompson, Benjamin, 232, 261, 276
Thompson, Benjamin Lancaster, 385
Thompson, David, 201, 205, 213
Thompson, Drury, 14
Thompson, George H., 385
Thompson, H. B., 211
Thompson, Hannah, 233
Thompson, Henrietta, 16
Thompson, Henry, 335
Thompson, Henry B., 35, 215, 230, 377, 385
Thompson, James, 210, 261
Thompson, James B., 211, 215, 376
Thompson, James Jr., 376
Thompson, John, 14, 52, 158, 218
Thompson, Jonathan, 239
Thompson, Joseph, 385
Thompson, Lucy, 209, 376
Thompson, Lucy Jr., 345
Thompson, Lucy Sr., 345
Thompson, Mary, 378
Thompson, Moses, 233
Thompson, Moses Jr., 233
Thompson, Nancy, 223
Thompson, Nancy Ann, 385
Thompson, Nathaniel, 218, 223, 347
Thompson, Nicodemus, 159

Thompson, Phoebe, 14
Thompson, Priscilla, 376
Thompson, Robert, 199, 272, 293
Thompson, Robert Jr., 199
Thompson, Solomon, 18, 184, 196, 205, 208, 219, 222, 329, 335, 345
Thompson, Stephen, 223
Thompson, William, 259
Thompson, William Jr., 376
Thomson, Drewry, 265
Thomson, John, 138
Thomson, Nathaniel, 282, 287
Thomson, William, 254
Thorn, David, 244
Thorn, Sallie, 20
Thornton, Abraham, 159
Thornton, Noel, 338
Thorp, Vincent A. J.P., 274
Thrasher, John, 17
Threats, David, 82, 94
Threeas, David, 141
Threewitts, Elizabeth, 19
Threewitts, James, 22, 244, 323
Threewitts, Joel, 176, 237, 242
Threewitts, Sally, 15, 176, 372
Thrower, Silson, 13
Thurman, John, 2
Thurman, Winnie, 23
Thweatt, James, 258, 324, 328, 353
Tieson, Thomas, 35
Tilby, Nathan McG., 13
Tillman, Mary, 32
Tinckler, John, 74
Tindall, Asa, 242, 249, 312
Tindall, Charlotte, 23
Tindall, John, 288
Tindall, William, 159
Tinkler, John, 129, 134, 149, 159
Tinkler, William, 75

Tinley, John, 159
Tinley, William, 159
Tison, Eliakim, 256
Tison, Isaac, 239
Tobler, David, 87, 160
Todd, Elizabeth, 183
Todd, Hardy, 183
Todd, Job, 20, 183
Todd, Lewis, 231
Todd, Silas, 20, 342
Todd, Stephen, 17
Todd, William, 347
Tom
  slave, 273
Tomlin, Jacob, 307, 308
Tomlin, James, 308
Tommy, Sally, 14
Toney, Thomas, 53
Torquintz, Peter, 160
Torrence, Abegail, 15
Torrence, Benajah, 390
Torrence, Caroline W., 389
Torrence, Ebenezer, 348, 389, 390
Torrence, Jemima, 389
Torrence, Jno., 261
Torrence, John, 184, 193, 200, 207, 242, 256, 261, 262, 273, 274, 293, 297, 306, 309, 310, 311, 319, 327, 333, 335, 351, 358, 384, 389
Torrence, John A., 310
Torrence, John J.I.C., 337, 345
Torrence, John J.P., 343, 346
Torrence, John Winston, 389, 390
Torrence, Mary, 34
Torrence, Polly, 197
Torrence, Samuel, 364, 389, 390
Torrence, Septimus, 234, 389, 390

Torrence, William, 28, 197, 343, 389
Travis, Amos, 188, 219, 249, 325
Travis, John, 177, 180, 219, 293, 296, 313
Travis, Simeon, 219, 381
Travis, William, 188
Trent, John, 178
Trent, Sophia, 178
Tubear, David, 160
Tucker, Betsy, 381
Tucker, Edmond, 381
Tucker, Elizabeth, 381
Tucker, Frances H., 226
Tucker, Germain, 226, 381
Tucker, Isaiah, 187, 191, 195, 199, 204, 223, 225, 235, 242, 251, 260, 277, 283, 294, 295, 299, 301, 318, 320, 325, 354, 359, 379, 381
Tucker, Isaiah J.P., 358
Tucker, J., 299
Tucker, John, 381
Tucker, Joseph, 298
Tucker, Josephus, 19
Tucker, Julia, 381
Tucker, Louisa, 381
Tucker, Mark, 381
Tucker, Matthew, 381
Tucker, Miriam, 381
Tucker, Q., 313
Tucker, Salley, 301
Tucker, Susannah, 19
Tucker, Whitefield, 295, 298, 301, 313
Tucker, Whitfield, 23, 320
Tucker, Wood, 75, 159, 160
Tucker, Zachariah, 354
Tuning, Nancy, 19
Turguined, Peter, 155
Turknett, Jacob, 299, 320, 359
Turner, George, 267, 379

Turner, James, 24, 232
Turner, John, 34, 213, 232, 290
Turner, John C., 29, 203, 204, 219, 319, 323, 344, 352, 377
Turner, Lucy, 319, 323
Turner, Nancy, 27, 375
Turner, Patsey, 34
Turner, Rebecca, 25
Turner, Succy, 32
Tweatherby, George, 277
Tydwell, Lydia, 33
Tyler, William, 290
Upton, Benjamin, 61, 244, 285, 320, 321, 322, 339, 353, 360, 381
Upton, Edward, 160
Upton, George, 108, 154, 161, 285, 312, 361
Upton, John, 51, 161, 164
Upton, Judith, 244, 320, 321, 381
Upton, Polly, 17
Upton, Richard, 73, 94, 161, 164, 169
Upton, Tobias, 353, 381
Usry, John, 226
Usry, Middleton, 32
Ussery, William, 185, 217, 220, 221
Valraven, Elias, 55
Van Munch, Richard, 85, 96
Van, John Jr., 161
Vance, James, 178, 217
Vance, John, 178, 217
Vanwinkle, Simeon, 300
Vanze, John W., 383
Vaughn, Alexander, 176, 191, 196
Vaughn, Daniel, 319
Vaughn, James, 29, 176, 219, 319
Vaughn, Jane, 191, 196
Vaughn, Mary, 13

Veazey, John, 233, 259
Venning, Mary, 161
Venson, John, 293
Verdin, Ezekiah, 267
Verdin, Jane, 267
Verdin, John, 344, 349
Verdin, Polly, 21
Verdun, John, 196
Verdun, Winnifred, 196
Vernon, Amos, 162
Vernon, Isaac, 113, 115, 162, 171
Vernon, James, 160
Vincent, Josias, 216
Vinhown, Benjamin, 268
Vining, Ann, 14
Vining, Anne, 278
Vining, Jane W., 26
Vining, Jeptha, 334
Vining, John, 31
Vining, Joshua, 177
Vining, Rev. Jeptha, 177
Vining, Rev. Jepthah, 372
Vining, Samuel, 116
Vining, Sarah, 16
Vining, Thomas, 287, 318
Virginia, 6, 352
Volraven, Elias, 108
Wade, Hezekiah, 44, 162
Wade, James, 21
Wade, John, 23
Wade, Mary, 226
Wade, Nehemiah, 45, 105, 154, 162
Wade, Rachel, 28
Wade, William, 19, 345
Wadley, Millie, 14
Wadsworth, James, 260
Waggoner, Amos, 26
Waggoner, David W., 187, 214, 220, 223, 340
Waggoner, Elizabeth, 206, 375
Waggoner, G. B., 209

Waggoner, George, 186, 188, 201, 203, 206, 209, 214, 221, 223, 375
Waggoner, George B., 187, 214, 220, 223, 384
Waggoner, Henry, 186, 205, 221, 311, 375
Waggoner, James, 186, 188, 205, 209, 223, 340, 346, 375
Waggoner, Jincy, 205
Waggoner, John, 279
Waggoner, John George, 375
Waggoner, Mary, 187, 220, 223
Waggoner, Patsy, 29
Waggoner, Rachel, 18
Waggoner, Thomas, 218
Waggoner, William, 186, 188, 209, 223, 375
Waggoner, Zacheus, 220
Walahom, Daniel, 57
Walden, Robert, 102, 163, 275
Walen, Saunders, 60
Walker, Andrew, 18
Walker, Beady, 21
Walker, Benjamin, 23
Walker, Elizabeth, 22, 376
Walker, Fanny, 14
Walker, Francis, 20
Walker, George, 285
Walker, Henry, 20, 326, 349
Walker, Holly, 216
Walker, James F., 236
Walker, James S., 235
Walker, Joel, 77, 80, 87, 163, 179, 216
Walker, John, 29
Walker, Joseph, 81, 245, 275
Walker, Littleberry, 179
Walker, Mary, 376
Walker, Pleasant, 266
Walker, Polly, 34
Walker, Rebecca, 194
Walker, Rebekah, 355

Walker, Reubin, 245
Walker, Robert, 383
Walker, Sarah, 383
Walker, Saunders, 163
Walker, Thomas, 348
Walker, Thomas T., 21
Wall, Arthur, 144, 163
Wall, Claiborne, 385
Wall, Deborah, 19
Wall, Mary, 16
Wall, Penny, 22
Wall, Sally, 24
Wall, Susannah, 345, 346, 355
Wallace, John, 243, 338
Wallace, Nancy, 18
Wallace, William, 39, 128, 163
Wallacon, Daniel, 163
Waller, Samuel, 82, 129, 163
Wallicon, Daniel, 37
Walraven, Elias, 108, 164
Walsh, Doctor, 57
Walsh, Edmond, 235, 245, 286, 288
Walsh, Mary. *See* O'Keefe
Walton, John, 116, 155, 164, 283
Walton, John Carter, 283
Walton, Robert, 44, 148, 164, 317
Wammack, William, 304
Wammock, Richard, 53
Ward, Becky, 375
Ward, Bryan, 164, 166
Ward, Ithamer, 330
Ward, Jesse, 188
Ward, John, 26
Ward, Nathaniel, 186, 222, 279
Ward, Nechud, 163
Ward, Neville, 312
Ward, Newt, 333, 366
Ward, Robert, 241
Ward, William, 15, 24, 333
Warner, Benjamin, 237, 307

Warner, Solomon, 31
Warner, William, 33
Warren, Bray, 22, 282, 294
Warren, Frances, 73, 130, 165
Warren, Jesse, 298
Warren, Joseph, 1, 11
Warren, Richard, 73, 130, 165
Warren, William, 354
Warrenton, 1, 207
Warrenton Academy, 5
Warrenton, Georgia, 250, 304, 310, 314, 344, 350, 352, 357
Warthen, Elijah, 219, 388
Warthen, Richard, 318, 388
Warthen, William, 219
Warthen, William J.P., 316, 318, 386, 388
Washington County, Georgia, 189, 237, 241, 243, 248, 249, 253, 256, 257, 267, 268, 271, 276, 277, 278, 285, 290, 292, 299, 305, 309, 311, 317, 318, 319, 320, 327, 335, 338, 350, 358, 363, 364, 387, 390
Waters, Calingston, 308
Waters, Collenson, 319
Waters, Collinson, 288
Waters, Thomas, 165
Watkins, John, 279
Watkins, Thomas J.P., 341
Watson, Abigail, 389
Watson, Benjamin, 338
Watson, Charity, 24
Watson, Jacob, 51, 165, 307, 324, 325, 361
Watson, James, 389
Watson, John, 51, 165, 166, 266, 307, 324, 332, 334
Watson, John Jr., 334
Watson, John Sr., 332
Watson, Joseph, 324
Watson, Orondatus, 230
Watson, Polly, 31

Watson, Thomas, 65, 78, 165, 166
Watson, William, 15
Wayne County, Georgia, 375, 384
Weakley, Thomas, 167, 277, 282
Weatherby George J.P., 243
Weatherby, Benjamin, 28
Weatherby, George, 193, 237, 247, 248, 273, 276, 280, 390
Weatherby, Rebecca, 33
Weatherby, Septimus, 183, 189, 193, 221, 236, 237, 249, 252, 263, 276, 277, 309, 358, 362, 370, 376
Weatherford, Charles, 164, 166
Weatherford, Martin, 166, 167
Weatherford, William, 166, 167
Weatherly, Septimus, 304
Weaver, Elizabeth, 280
Weaver, John, 280
Webb, Charles, 18, 309, 375
Webb, Sarah, 375
Weekley, Thomas, 167, 272, 284, 291
Weeks, James, 15, 348
Welch, Doctor, 173
Welch, John, 275
Welch, Peter, 167
Weldon, Isaac, 85, 167
Weldon, Jacob, 167
Weldon, Mary, 19
Wells, B., 61
Wells, Benjamin, 64, 137, 168, 170, 310, 315
Wells, Betsy, 21
Wells, Humphry, 167
Wells, John, 66, 244, 282
Wells, John J., 248, 279, 291, 320
Wells, Rachel, 157, 334
Wells, Richard, 334

Wells, Samuel, 60, 168
Welsh, John, 168
Wenslet, Samuel, 48
Wesley, Cader, 196
West, John, 95, 100, 168
West, Thomas, 277
West, William, 259
Westberry, Thomas, 316, 330, 331, 351, 360
Westcoat, Daniel, 168
Wester, Elizabeth, 371
Wester, Fannie, 175
Wester, Fanny, 370
Wester, Hardy, 175, 370
Wester, Nancy, 370
Westmoreland, Elizabeth, 345
Westmoreland, Isham, 345
Whair, William, 272
Whaley, William, 247
Whatley, Allen, 239
Whatley, Anny, 15
Whatley, David, 20
Whatley, Frances, 283, 294
Whatley, John, 244
Whatley, Michael, 320
Whatley, Richard, 236, 283, 291, 294, 299
Whatley, Thomas, 247
Whatley, Willis, 250
Wheat, William, 70, 81, 102, 168
Wheelas, Isham, 351, 356
Wheeler, Amos, 23
Wheeler, Benjamin, 271, 382
Wheeler, Catherine, 366
Wheeler, David, 303, 360
Wheeler, Emperor, 366
Wheeler, Isham, 303, 334, 351, 360
Wheeler, Isom, 30
Wheeler, James, 24, 302, 345, 355, 356, 382
Wheeler, Joseph, 361

Wheeler, Marritt, 20
Wheeler, Mary, 382
Wheeler, Mary S., 24
Wheeler, Merritt, 382
Wheeler, Sally, 16
Wheeler, Susannah, 18, 345, 355
Wheeler, Vincent, 24
Wheeler, Vinson, 382
Wheeler, Winnie, 29
Wheeles, Kinchen, 378
Wheless, Milberry, 33
Wheless, Sion, 201
Whigham, Thomas, 168
White, Austin, 379
White, Betsy, 379
White, Catherine, 350
White, Green, 379
White, James, 264, 273
White, Jesse, 189, 224, 268
White, John, 35
White, Joseph, 29, 193, 217, 262, 264, 297, 298, 305, 316, 329, 335, 351, 355, 363
White, Mary, 389
White, Matthew, 379
White, Nancy, 21, 379
White, Nicholas, 266, 271
White, Peggy, 379
White, Robert, 217, 273
White, Thomas, 310, 346, 350
White, Thomas J. J.P., 350
White, Thomas J.P., 264, 346
White, Timothy, 379
White, Unity, 379
White, William, 23, 184, 219, 246, 261, 262, 316, 324, 337, 355, 379
White, William Sr., 184, 307
Whitefield, George, 139, 140, 169
Whitehead, R., 351

Whitehead, Richard, 276, 285, 320
Whiting, Milliford, 15
Whitlock, John, 246, 254, 266
Whitlock, Joseph, 247
Whitlock, Tabitha, 254
Whitsett, John, 94, 145, 152, 169
Whitsett, John Jr., 169
Whittington, Cornelius, 348
Whittington, Faddy, 224
Whitworth, John, 238
Whitworth, Samuel, 238
Wiggins, Edmond, 196
Wiggins, Peter, 226
Wiggins, Rebecca, 226
Wiggon, William, 169
Wilcher, Jeremiah, 277, 343
Wilcher, William, 277
Wilder, Dread, 327
Wilder, Job, 352
Wilder, John, 336
Wilder, Judith, 336
Wilder, Mary, 309
Wilder, Sampson, 223, 226, 309, 312, 313, 327, 346, 352
Wilder, William, 15, 226, 313
Wiley, W., 263
Wilkenson, Bailey, 346
Wilkerson, Hammond, 310
Wilkes County, Georgia, 226, 235, 241, 252, 257, 282, 283, 284, 288, 307, 313, 320, 321, 341
Wilkins, John, 341, 345
Wilkins, MaryAnn, 179
Wilkins, Robert, 285
Wilkins, Sarah, 345
Wilkins, Thomas, 15
Wilkins, William, 345
Wilkinson County, Georgia, 375, 376, 380, 384, 391
Wilkinson, Abner, 282

Wilkinson, Harmon, 177
Wilkinson, John, 282
Wilkinson, Nancy, 18
William McCason, 385
William Turin and Company, 139
William, Christopher, 280
William, John Francis, 172
William, Nicholas, 256
Williams Creek Church, 281
Williams, Agnes, 13
Williams, Benjamin, 129, 160
Williams, Captain, 58
Williams, Casea, 383
Williams, Charles, 268
Williams, Christopher, 280, 323
Williams, David, 21
Williams, Elijah, 357
Williams, Elsey, 363
Williams, Ezekiel, 242, 249, 341
Williams, Fanny, 28
Williams, Henry, 16, 220, 222, 224, 232, 266, 268, 332
Williams, Henry Jr., 268, 354
Williams, Henry Sr., 220
Williams, Isaac, 21
Williams, James, 17, 18, 319, 332, 358, 383
Williams, Jesse, 33
Williams, Jezekiah, 340
Williams, Jno., 302
Williams, John, 18, 182, 219, 224, 248, 265, 268, 278, 280, 322, 332, 336, 341, 348, 349, 360, 366
Williams, Joseph, 332
Williams, Joseph Jr., 383
Williams, Joshua, 25
Williams, Lightfoot, 268
Williams, Lud, 164, 169
Williams, Luke, 364, 365
Williams, Moses, 22, 25

Williams, N., 250
Williams, N. J.P., 325, 363
Williams, Nancy, 21, See Pruitt
Williams, Nathan, 364
Williams, Nathaniel, 194, 265, 303
Williams, Nathaniel Sr., 278
Williams, Nicholas, 13, 179, 197, 202, 214, 216, 304, 328, 344, 363, 365
Williams, Nowell, 363
Williams, Patsy, 21
Williams, Peter, 333, 334
Williams, Polly, 377
Williams, Sally, 14
Williams, Samuel, 360
Williams, Sarah, 20
Williams, Sibella, 17
Williams, Stafford, 17, 364
Williams, Thomas, 24, 217
Williams, William, 16, 170, 278, 341
Williamson, Benjamin, 62, 170
Williamson, Joseph, 13, 314
Williamson, M. J.P., 287
Williamson, Richard, 170
Williamson, Sterling, 268
Williamson, W., 298
Williford, Dora, 17
Williford, Gracy, 20
Williford, Pollie, 25
Willis, Jacob, 32
Willis, James, 195, 331
Willis, James J.P., 268
Willis, James Sr., 195
Willis, Jeney G., 331
Willis, Joel, 352, 353
Willis, Joseph, 325
Willis, Judith, 378
Willis, Price, 29
Willis, Robert, 262, 274
Willis, William, 18
Willoughby, Dicy, 17

Wills, Rachel, 360
Willson, Ann, 390
Willson, David, 390
Willson, Harriet, 390
Willson, James, 195
Willson, Joel, 390
Willson, John, 387
Wilmouth, Sally, 32
Wilsher, Jeremiah, 278
Wilsher, William, 278
Wilson, Archelaus, 34
Wilson, Elias, 234
Wilson, Henry, 27, 206, 228,
    232, 234
Wilson, J. J.P., 332
Wilson, James, 206, 310
Wilson, Jeremiah, 234
Wilson, Jno. J.P., 296
Wilson, John, 20, 24, 88, 90,
    106, 183, 206, 219, 228, 252,
    255, 296, 323, 331, 333, 351
Wilson, John J.P., 252, 260,
    272, 274, 286, 289, 291, 296,
    297, 310, 325, 344
Wilson, John Jr., 289
Wilson, John M., 232
Wilson, Margaret, 331
Wilson, Mary, 296, *See*
    Stanford
Wilson, Nancy, 23
Wilson, Samuel, 170
Wilson, Sarah, 34
Wilson, William, 206
Windham, Joshua, 27
Winfree, Reubin, 329
Winfrey, Reuben, 272
Winfrey, Reubin, 283, 307
Wing, Abraham, 2
Wingate, Gatsy M., 33
Winslet, Samuel, 170, 182, 219
Winston County, South
    Carolina, 341
Winter, John G., 231

Wirgley, John, 30
Wise, Francis, 339
Wisely, Sarah, 62, 83, 170
Withers, Jesse J.P, 342
Wolsey, Seth, 180
Womack, John, 25
Womack, Patsy, 26
Womack, William, 360
Wood, Harris, 229
Wood, Isaac, 92, 171
Wood, James, 20
Wood, John, 334
Wood, Joseph, 229
Wood, Mary, 229, 334
Wood, Matthew, 267
Wood, Nathaniel, 171
Wood, Newt, 338
Wood, William, 229, 334, 338
Woodard, Benjamin S., 190
Woodard, Francis, 190
Woodruff, William, 348
Woods, Barnard, 328
Woods, John, 30
Woods, Nathaniel, 48
Woodward, Benjamin S., 224
Woodward, Benjamin T., 219
Woodward, Elizabeth, 20
Woodward, Francis, 219, 224,
    291
Woodward, Isham, 219
Woolsey, Alice, 18
Woolsey, Seth, 18
Wooten, Pheriby, 19
Wooten, Thomas Esq., 312
Wootten, Aseneth, 282
Wootten, Collin, 317
Wootten, Faitha, 317
Wootten, James, 282
Wootten, Nathan, 185, 220
Wootten, Phereby, 282
Works, James, 276
Worsham, R. J.P., 254
Worthen, Elijah, 183

Worthen, Elisha, 393
Worthen, Eliza, 393
Wright, Amos, 194, 200, 220,
  228, 256, 274, 318, 338, 375
Wright, Amos Sr., 313
Wright, Asa, 180, 189, 218
Wright, Asaph Esq., 215
Wright, Basil, 176, 194, 217,
  375
Wright, Benjamin, 327, 363
Wright, Caswell, 210
Wright, Charity, 20
Wright, Chloe, 194, 375
Wright, Dionysus, 87, 137, 141,
  171
Wright, Dionysus, 115
Wright, Drusilla, 375
Wright, Elisha, 245, 248, 279,
  287, 291, 311, 312, 313, 375
Wright, Elizabeth, 197
Wright, Governor, 51
Wright, Governor James, 171,
  295
Wright, Habukkuk, 175
Wright, Hellena, 203
Wright, Isaiah, 210
Wright, James, 375
Wright, Jared, 33
Wright, Jemima, 25
Wright, Jesse, 194
Wright, John, 31, 220, 232, 273,
  375
Wright, Johnson, 274, 360
Wright, Johnston, 180, 188,
  218, 223
Wright, Joseph, 34, 194, 200,
  204, 220, 248, 289, 375
Wright, Josias, 305, 345
Wright, L., 255
Wright, Lewis, 17, 29, 194, 251,
  261, 290, 305, 310, 312, 314,
  329, 338, 344, 365, 375
Wright, Lewis Esq., 215

Wright, Lucs, 261
Wright, Lucy, 375
Wright, Melton, 210
Wright, Mesach, 172
Wright, Mrs. Elizabeth, 33
Wright, Nancy, 203, 215
Wright, Pheriba, 27
Wright, Rachel, 375
Wright, Sally, 203
Wright, Samuel, 172, 180, 189,
  218
Wright, Sarah, 18
Wright, Shedrick, 172
Wright, Sir James, 78, 294, 361
Wright, Stephen, 306, 328
Wright, William, 197, 203, 204,
  207, 354; 385
Wright, William D., 22
Wright, Winnifred, 203
Wrightsboro, 37
Wrightsborough, 265
Wrightsborough, Georgia, 284
Wylly, Francis, 100, 172
Wynne, Benajah, 204
Wynne, Benjamin, 177, 225,
  377
Wynne, Clement, 204, 360, 376,
  377, 392
Wynne, Cynthia, 376
Wynne, Dudley, 376
Wynne, Elizabeth, 377
Wynne, Frances, 13, 377, 392
Wynne, Franky, 29
Wynne, Irby, 392
Wynne, James, 392
Wynne, Jincy, 23
Wynne, John, 21, 177, 298, 299
Wynne, John J.P., 259, 370
Wynne, Lemuel, 30
Wynne, Lydia, 16
Wynne, May, 392
Wynne, Nancy, 376, 377
Wynne, Patsy, 376

Wynne, Peter, 376
Wynne, Polly, 13
Wynne, Robert, 204, 253, 259, 275, 298, 299, 376
Wynne, Robert Jr., 17
Wynne, Robert Sr., 319
Wynne, Sally, 392
Wynne, Sarah, 377
Wynne, Sarah Nibb, 177
Wynne, Susannah, 24
Wynne, Tabitha, 18
Wynne, Thomas, 376
Wynne, William, 29, 258, 376, 392
Yarborough, Nancy, 378
Yarborough, Samuel, 290
Yarbrough, Hannah, 22
Yarbrough, Nancy, 17
Yarbrough, Samuel, 34, 237, 316
Yarbrough, Susannah, 16
Yarbrough, Thomas, 315, 386
Yearty, Abraham, 347
Yeats, Bennet, 393
Yerta, Abraham, 278
Yonge, Henry Jr., 172
York, James, 250
Yorke, Robison, 173
Young, Jacob, 176, 236, 369
Young, James, 369
Young, John, 343
Young, John D., 255, 333
Young, John Pearson, 369

Young, Margaret, 173
Young, Pearson, 176
Young, Peregrine, 302
Young, Perry G., 266
Young, Peter, 144
Young, Pierson, 236
Young, Thomas, 42, 172, 173, 283, 284, 299
Young, Thomas Esq., 343
Young, Thomas Jr., 284, 343
Young, William, 369
Young, William Jr., 369
Young, William Sr., 369
Youngblood, Benjamin, 63, 94
Youngblood, James, 288
Youngblood, John, 75, 174
Youngblood, John Jr., 174
Youngblood, Peter, 63, 65, 94, 174
Zachary, Celia, 15
Zachary, Daniel, 319
Zachary, James, 354
Zachary, John, 314
Zachary, John S., 284
Zachary, Nancy, 25
Zachry, Abner, 334
Zachry, D. H., 334
Zachry, James, 334
Zachry, John, 292, 334, 355
Zachry, John J., 196
Zachry, Sarah, 392
Zualls, John, 291
Zualls, Peter, 291

Made in the USA
San Bernardino, CA
31 May 2014